RESPONDING TO FAMILY VIOLENCE

The comprehensive theory- and research-based guidelines provided in this text help answer the personal and professional questions therapists have as they provide competent clinical treatment to clients who have experienced family violence. It presents academic, scholarly, and statistical terms in an accessible and user-friendly way, with useful take-away points for practitioners such as clarifying contradictory findings, summarizing major research-based implications and guidelines, and addressing the unique clinical challenges faced by mental health professionals. Both professionals and students in graduate-level mental health training programs will find the presentation of information and exercises highly useful, and will appreciate the breadth of topics covered: intimate partner violence, battering, child maltreatment and adult survivors, co-occurring substance abuse, the abuse of vulnerable populations, cultural issues, prevention, and self-care. Professionals and students alike will find that, with this book, they can help their clients overcome the significant traumas and challenges they face to let their strength and resilience shine through.

Christine E. Murray, PhD, is an associate professor in the Department of Counseling and Educational Development at The University of North Carolina at Greensboro (UNCG). She is also the Program Director for the Program to Advance Community Responses to Violence Against Women in the UNCG Center for Women's Health and Wellness.

Kelly N. Graves, PhD, is an associate professor in the Department of Human Development and Services at North Carolina Agricultural and Technical State University (NCAT), and the Executive Director of the NCAT Center for Behavioral Health and Wellness.

RESPONDING TO FAMILY VIOLENCE

A Comprehensive, Research-Based Guide for Therapists

Christine E. Murray and Kelly N. Graves

Routledge
Taylor & Francis Group
NEW YORK AND LONDON

First published 2013
by Routledge
711 Third Avenue, New York, NY 10017

Simultaneously published in the UK
by Routledge
27 Church Road, Hove, East Sussex BN3 2FA

Routledge is an imprint of the Taylor & Francis Group, an informa business

Library of Congress Cataloging in Publication Data
Murray, Christine E.
Responding to family violence : a comprehensive, research-based guide for therapists / by Christine E. Murray & Kelly N. Graves. — 1st ed.
p. cm.
Includes bibliographical references and index.
ISBN 978-0-415-88560-7 (hardback : alk. paper) — ISBN 978-0-415-88561-4 (pbk. : alk. paper)
1. Family violence. I. Graves, Kelly N. II. Title.
HV6626.M87 2013
362.82'92—dc23

2012013390
ISBN: 978-0-415-88560-7 (hbk)
ISBN: 978-0-415-88561-4 (pbk)
ISBN: 978-0-203-09445-7 (ebk)

Typeset in Bembo and Stone Sans
by EvS Communication Networx, Inc.

Printed and bound in the United States of America by Sheridan Books, Inc. (a Sheridan Group Company)

I dedicate this book to Arielle, whose vibrant life and enthusiastic support inspired me to finally write this book.

—C. E. M.

I dedicate this book to Alyssa, who reminds me every day to truly remember what is most important in life, and to Lindy, whose courage and compassion for helping others was the driving force for my contributions to this book.

—K. N. G.

CONTENTS

PART III

FOREWORD

Nadine J. Kaslow, PhD, ABPP

Unfortunately, family violence is the most popular crime in our country today. It is a crime without boundaries, as it impacts children, adults, the elderly, and vulnerable populations from all backgrounds and walks of life. Family violence negatively impacts the health and well-being of survivors and perpetrators alike. Violence is a learned behavior and thus experiencing violence in the home leads to more violence in more homes and in our communities. As mental health professionals and as citizens, we have an ethical responsibility to educate ourselves about family violence, help individuals and families cope with such violence, and influence our culture in ways that puts an end to this terrifying and demoralizing societal problem. *Responding to Family Violence* offers invaluable insights into understanding the devastating nature and impact of family violence, breaking the cycle of family violence, and preventing family violence so that our children and grandchildren and their children can lead violence-free lives.

Throughout my extensive research in areas of intimate partner violence, other forms of family violence, and related negative outcomes (e.g., suicidality, post-traumatic stress disorder [PTSD]), I have often wished for a high quality handbook to introduce trainees and colleagues alike to this often-overlooked topic. The authors are to be commended for filling a gap in the existing resources for clinicians at all stages of professional development, from trainees to experts, who wish to learn from the available clinical research, but who do not know where to start with the overwhelming quantity of existing evidence. There are resources available for those who wish to understand family violence, but none are as comprehensive or effective in relaying the clinical implications of extant knowledge as the current text. Indeed, *Responding to Family Violence* covers the whole landscape, attending to such diverse topics as intimate partner violence, child maltreatment, and elder abuse.

With the exception of a few programs that offer specific training, most graduate programs overlook providing systematic education in the tragically pervasive problem of family violence. Similarly, there is a relative dearth of continuing education programs on this topic of considerable clinical and public health significance. In my role as a trainer for graduate and postgraduate students, as well as a national presenter on this topic, I have had the privilege of introducing or providing continuing professional development sessions on the topic of family violence. In these educational encounters, I have been impressed by people's thirst for knowledge related to understanding, assessing, and treating the various forms of family violence and their desire to do so in a manner that takes development, gender, sexual orientation, ability/disability status, and race/ethnicity, etc., into account. It seems that in many programs, the topic of family violence is addressed only at a cursory level, perhaps in part due to discomfort with the issues and the feelings that arise from working with individuals and families whose lives have been touched by violence. Common reactions include fear, anger, helplessness, hopelessness, and sadness. Lack of specific education leaves many mental health professionals feeling overwhelmed when their clients/patients reveal a history of family violence (even more so if the violence is currently occurring). Although mental health professionals are not expected to be experts on every clinical presentation, family violence is so prevalent and so greatly impacts people's mental and physical well-being that resources such as this handbook are necessary additions to the training and career development of clinicians from multiple disciplines.

Particularly in my role as a trainer, I find that many graduate and post-graduate students feel inadequately trained in family violence and its sequelae (e.g., PTSD), most notably with regard to specific approaches for assessment, intervention, and prevention. The authors of this text are to be congratulated for the thoughtful and thorough job they do in providing specific guidelines for assessment and treatment of the various forms of family violence. This is a welcome addition to the field, as training tends to touch on epidemiology and basic facts about family violence, without addressing the more pressing concerns for therapists (perhaps best captured by the simple question, "so now what do I do?"). Research in this area is not always helpful either—people may consult existing articles and textbooks, but find that clinical implications are rarely articulated, or are incoherently expressed, or are not adequately tied to the relevant evidence-base. This well-written book offers a coherent, thoughtful, and very scholarly yet practical approach to understanding, assessing, treating, and preventing family violence.

Aside from my role as a trainer, I have been involved heavily in the competencies movement in psychology, which parallels competency efforts in other disciplines. Although competency-based training and credentialing places particular emphasis on areas of competence that are less topic-specific, the competency framework indicates that mental health professionals should be familiar with basic knowledge in common clinical presentations, including current research findings and information about the skills and techniques required to address various clinical presentations. In addition, they must be informed about the attitudes and values required for effective and ethical practice targeting various conditions/disorders/problems. Particularly for those clinicians who are not directly involved in research in family violence or who do not specialize in family violence practices, this text provides an invaluable glance at the most current information related to the knowledge, skills, and attitudes required for understanding, assessing, and treating family violence.

In addition to clinicians having a comprehensive and effective assessment and treatment armamentarium, they need to take good care of themselves when they help others whose lives are touched by family violence. Thus, I read with much interest and enthusiasm the chapter that focused on the importance of self-care. This is an extremely significant topic that is generally overlooked in training and professional practice and even more rarely enforced, yet it is essential for competent practice. It can be quite challenging for therapists engaged in helping people whose lives are affected by family violence and the associated traumas to maintain adequate self-care, yet it is imperative that they do so in order to both be effective and to not get burned out. Thus, all clinicians can benefit from a thorough examination of this chapter.

Even as someone with expertise in family violence, I found the current text enormously helpful in directing my attention to specific areas of current research and practice that are beyond my usual scope of professional functioning. Throughout my research career, I have predominantly focused upon interventions for intimate partner violence and related outcomes and on the relationship between abused mothers and their children, but there are other areas of family violence that are necessarily interrelated. Despite being a family psychologist and thinking systemically, the reality is, my own research has not addressed perpetrators. Thus, this all-inclusive book offers me a meaningful perspective on the research related to perpetrators of intimate partner violence and child maltreatment, which can help round out my thinking and approach.

Hopefully, armed with the information offered in this compendium, mental health practitioners and researchers will be able to develop, implement, and disseminate more evidence-based and integrated services to assist those who have experienced or witnessed family violence. In addition, we will be more able to offer programs that ensure greater accessibility of these services for everyone concerned. Further, we will be able to more productively advocate on behalf of policies that ensure greater protection and safety for those who are experiencing violence within the context of their own families and in their own homes. While we still have a long way to go to stopping this epidemic, this book highlights the amazing progress that has been made to date and outlines fruitful avenues for future work.

PREFACE

Christine E. Murray

Most, if not all, therapists can think back to clients with whom they wish they could have worked differently. Here's one of mine: During my second practicum experience in my master's program, a couple was referred to me for counseling after the husband was arrested on domestic violence charges and ordered to attend what he described as "anger management" classes. Both partners came to the first session, and the wife said that she requested that a requirement for them to attend couples therapy be added to the husband's probation agreement. The husband completed his anger management classes, and all the couple needed to do for him to be discharged from probation was complete couples therapy and get a letter from their counselor (me!) stating that they had done so. During our initial session, which was conjoint, both partners reported to me that the violence had ended, the husband was no longer violent, and they wanted to finish the couples therapy and have me send the letter to the probation officer as soon as possible so they could put that ordeal behind them. The couple reported to me that they did not have any major goals to address in counseling, and the wife said that she agreed with her husband that they were just in couples therapy to finish the last probation requirement. I took them at their word, didn't do any further formal assessment, met with them one or two more times to discuss general relationship issues, and terminated with them.

Fast forward a few years later to when I was sitting in the family violence course I took as a doctoral student. One of the first things we were taught in that course was that couple therapy should not be done in cases when domestic violence was present. I will never forget the sinking feeling in my stomach when I remembered back to that couple I had worked with during my practicum. "Oh no!" I thought, "What could I have missed? What if the wife was still being abused, and I totally missed it? And what if I did something that could have potentially put her at risk for getting hurt more?" Of course, we cannot change the past, but that sinking feeling in the pit of my stomach is a major reason that I have spent the years since then (and plan to continue to do so into the foreseeable future) trying to grasp the complexities of family violence and how to address those issues in therapy.

After completing my graduate studies, I first did full-time clinical work, in which I was a therapist at a community mental health agency. Most of my clients were adults with severe, persistent mental health disorders. I was overwhelmed by how many of these clients—I estimate approximately 90%—had experienced some form of family violence, and many faced multiple forms of family violence and other traumas over the course of their lifetimes. Client after client would enter my therapy office and disclose stories of abuse they experienced in some of their closest intimate and/or family relationships. I was overwhelmed, to say the least. As I struggled to determine how best to help each client face their unique challenges, I began to realize more and more the major, and sometimes debilitating impact that family violence could have on those who experience it. But along with these challenges, I also sat in wonder and amazement at the resilience and strength of my clients. Indeed, they faced many struggles, but in light of the significant traumas they faced, their survival, resourcefulness, and openness to new experiences and relationships was incredibly inspiring. Grappling with the major questions that arose through this work led me to further crystallize my curiosity about and passion for work that addresses the topic of family violence, especially the prevention of it.

Fast forward a few more years into the future, and you will find me not the student, but the professor, in a graduate course for advanced master's-level counseling students on the topic of family violence. One of my top priorities when I began teaching the course was to find the "perfect" textbook that would provide my students with information about family violence, but also offer clear, theory- and research-based guidelines for clinical practice. I searched high and low for this book, but I kept coming up empty-handed. One promising text was out-of-print. Others were overly narrow in focus, such as addressing only one form of family violence. Still others provided great background information but lacked detailed implications for clinical practice. As I continued asking every publisher's representative with whom I came into contact if they knew of such a book, the response I began to receive consistently was, "I don't know of any such book. I guess you'll have to write it." Of course, it has taken several years to move from first hearing that message, to deciding that indeed I would have to write that book, to crafting the proposal, to finalizing a contract with the publisher, to writing the book, and ultimately bringing it to press. The contributions of Dr. Kelly Graves to this book cannot be understated. As a clinical psychologist with expertise in trauma-informed care and evidence-based clinical practice strategies, her wealth of knowledge and clinical insights have strengthened this book in ways I could not have envisioned.

My hope for this book is that it will provide therapists at all levels—from beginning students to experienced clinicians—with information to help them work more effectively with clients impacted by family violence. Having now taught the family violence course for several years, and also having interacted in many other venues with therapists and other professionals on the topic of family violence over that time, I believe I understand many of the complex questions that arise—both personally and professionally—when therapists begin to reflect on the dynamics of family violence. This book, unfortunately, does not hold all the answers to those questions—no book could do that. However, I sincerely hope that the information provided in this volume will help therapists move closer to answering those questions as they provide competent clinical treatment to clients who have experienced family violence.

ACKNOWLEDGMENTS

Christine E. Murray:

I have deep appreciation for the opportunity to write this book and for all the people who helped to make it possible. I am extremely grateful for the contributions of Dr. Kelly Graves to this volume. Kelly is a wonderful co-author, collaborator, and friend, and I am confident that this book would have been sorely lacking had it not been for her contributions.

I am thankful for the personnel at Routledge Mental Health for their strong support of this project. In particular, Dr. George Zimmar and Marta Moldvai were extremely responsive, helpful, and enthusiastic during all phases of preparing and writing this book.

I want to extend a special word of thanks to Erin Kelley for her early suggestions on this book. Erin, you are a great friend and colleague!

I have been fortunate to have worked with a number of graduate research assistants at the University of North Carolina at Greensboro (UNCG) who assisted with various aspects of this book—these include Janee' Avent, Dominiquie Boyce, and Molly Johnson.

In addition to my graduate assistants, I am extremely grateful to all of my current and former students in my family violence class. Your questions, reactions, and personal reflections have certainly shaped my thinking about family violence and helped me in so many ways to conceptualize the topics addressed in this book.

I am thankful for my colleagues in the UNCG Department of Counseling and Educational Development. In addition, I appreciate my collaboration with other colleagues at UNCG, especially through the Center for Women's Health and Wellness.

I am fortunate to be surrounded by wonderful, supportive friends and family members. I am so thankful for the support and encouragement they provided throughout the writing of this book. In particular, I want to thank my parents, Leslie Ward and Michael and DiAnn Borasky, and my siblings, Jennifer Mitts and Alan Borasky.

Finally, I extend my deepest gratitude and appreciation to my sons, Evan and Bryce. Although they are likely too young to fully comprehend this now, I want them to know how much I appreciate them. Their silliness was the ultimate stress-reducer when writing this book. Evan and Bryce—I hope that you will both grow up to know peaceful, joy-filled, loving relationships in all areas of your lives.

Kelly N. Graves:

I am extremely honored and humbled to have partnered with my colleague and friend, Dr. Christine E. Murray, on the writing of this book. Christine, you are incredibly knowledgeable and have a special gift of applying your knowledge in a way that truly makes a difference in the lives of so many people. I believe that this book and the way that we came to partner on this was divinely ordered and I am so grateful for you and our friendship.

I am fortunate to have had wonderful mentors that have prepared me to contribute to this book. I particularly want to thank Dr. Nadine Kaslow and Dr. Terri Shelton. Dr. Kaslow and Dr. Shelton, I can only hope that one day I can be the mentor to someone else that you have been to me. I will work hard to pay it forward.

I am thankful for my colleagues in the North Carolina A&T State University Center for Behavioral Health and Wellness and the Department of Human Development and Services. When the right people get together at the right time for the right reason, it is amazing what can be accomplished!

I particularly want to dedicate this book to my friend, my hero, my role model, Mrs. Lindy Beauregard. Lindy, you have inspired me in so many ways, and I am forever grateful for our friendship and sisterhood. I know that we are connected here and beyond.

My thanks also extend to my family, friends and colleagues that have had both a direct, and indirect, role in the writing of this book, including my parents, Timothy Rogers and Luanne Durr, my grandparents, James and Ruth Poland, my stepfather, Anthony Durr, my siblings, Jessica Lindahl, Benjamin Durr, and Jerry Lee Davis, my church and church family, and Jon and Cathy Tabor, Linda Carter, and Marica Weston. You each have taught me so many things and I am thankful for you daily.

To my husband, Arthur Graves, thank you for your ultimate patience on the many late nights of working hard on this book and for your encouragement throughout the process. You are truly an amazing man and a model for how men should treat women. I am blessed to be called your wife.

And, to my dearest Alyssa, you are my greatest gift from God and my best legacy. I am so thankful and proud to be your mother. You inspire me every day to enjoy life to the fullest and I pray that throughout your life you find all the happiness and peace that your heart can hold. I will forever love you.

ABOUT THE AUTHORS

Christine E. Murray, PhD, is an associate professor in the Department of Counseling and Educational Development at The University of North Carolina at Greensboro (UNCG). She is also the Program Director for the Program to Advance Community Responses to Violence Against Women in the UNCG Center for Women's Health and Wellness. In the Counseling department, Dr. Murray is the Coordinator of the Couple and Family Counseling Program and teaches graduate-level courses in family counseling, family violence, sexuality counseling, and counseling research methods.

Dr. Murray received her Bachelor of Arts degree in Psychology and Sociology from Duke University. She earned her Master of Education, Specialist in Education, and Doctor of Philosophy degrees in Marriage and Family Counseling and Counselor Education from the University of Florida, where she was a Presidential Fellow.

Dr. Murray is a Licensed Marriage and Family Therapist and Licensed Professional Counselor in North Carolina, as well as a Nationally Certified Counselor. Dr. Murray has worked as a therapist with couples, families, and individuals facing a wide range of personal and relational challenges. She worked as a therapist in the adult outpatient department in a community mental health agency, where she worked primarily with adults who experienced chronic mental health disorders. She has also worked as a therapist in a variety of other settings, including a school for at-risk adolescents, a children's outpatient mental health treatment department, a juvenile delinquency diversion program, and churches. Across all of these settings, she worked frequently with clients impacted by various forms of family violence, including current and past intimate partner violence, childhood physical and sexual abuse, and emotional and verbal abuse.

Dr. Murray's primary research interest relates to the bridging the gap between research and practice in the area of domestic violence. In addition to the domestic violence research-practice gap, the family violence-related topics she has addressed through her research and scholarship include coping strategies used by women who have been battered, same-sex intimate partner violence, community-based approaches to domestic violence programming, dating violence among college students, applications of family systems theory to family violence, and intimate partner violence prevention research.

Dr. Murray holds memberships in several professional organizations, including the American Association for Marriage and Family Therapy (Clinical Member), the American Counseling Association, the International Association of Marriage and Family Counselors, and the Association for Counselor Education and Supervision.

Kelly N. Graves, PhD, is an Associate Professor in the Department of Human Development and Services at North Carolina Agricultural and Technical State University (NCAT), and the Executive Director of the NCAT Center for Behavioral Health and Wellness. Within the Center for Behavioral Health and Wellness, Dr. Graves directs three units, including a Clinical Services Unit, a Research and Evaluation Unit, and a Training and Technical Assistance Unit. These units work together to provide direct, community-based behavioral health services integrated with the latest research to ensure a strong research to practice link. Within the Human Development and Services Department, Dr. Graves teaches graduate-level courses in family violence, trauma informed care, and applied research, and is assisting in the development of the first doctoral program in Rehabilitation Counseling within a historically black college and university (HBCU).

Dr. Graves received her Bachelors of Arts degree in Psychology from Virginia Polytechnic and State University (Virginia Tech), and her Masters of Science degree in General/Experimental Psychology from Wake Forest University. She continued on to the University of North Carolina at Greensboro, where she received her PhD in Clinical Psychology and completed her clinical internship at Emory University School of Medicine.

Dr. Graves is a licensed Clinical Psychologist in the state of North Carolina, as well as a Health Services Provider throughout the state. Her primary focus area is on university-community engaged programming that bridges the gap between research and practice by developing systems that are data-driven, collaborative, culturally congruent, and individualized to meet the needs of the target population. Dr. Graves has a particular focus on risk and resiliency among children exposed to violence and trauma across services systems (law enforcement, mental health, social services, and juvenile justice), developing trauma-informed systems, and positive youth development through leadership and mentoring. In addition to providing direct services in those areas, Dr. Graves has designed and implemented multiple local, state, and federal research programs that examine and enhance the implementation and delivery of services across multiple service settings.

Dr. Graves holds memberships in several professional organizations, including the American Psychological Association and International Society of Violence, Abuse, and Trauma.

1

OVERVIEW OF A RESEARCH-INFORMED APPROACH TO RESPONDING TO FAMILY VIOLENCE

Family violence is one of the most common, and yet challenging, issues that therapists encounter for two central reasons. First, clients who have experienced past or current family violence are very common in the clinical field and typically have very complicated backgrounds and are in need of multiple forms of support. In a recent survey of 347 marriage and family therapists, for example, nearly all participants—98.6%—indicated that they had worked with clients who were in domestic violence situations (Blasko, Winek, & Bieschke, 2007). Second, the existing research demonstrates that it is an issue for which many practicing therapists are ill-prepared to address (Gauthier & Levendosky, 1996). Many therapists are undertrained in family violence issues (Wingfield & Blocker, 1998), although this area of practice requires specialized training in order for therapists to be competent to address it (Wingfield & Blocker, 1998).

According to Hamberger and Ambuel (1997), therapist training in intimate partner violence (IPV) has lagged far behind the training that physicians in training typically receive in medical school. This historical perspective is notable in light of a more recent survey of medical students in the United States, in which the researchers (Frank et al., 2006) found that over 90% of the students indicated that they had received some training in addressing IPV. However, only about 20% of these students said that the training they had received was extensive. Additional survey research with mental health professionals provides additional support to the notion that many therapists are ill-prepared for addressing family violence issues in their clinical practice. In a recent doctoral dissertation study, Bozorg-Omid (2007) conducted a survey of members of the American Mental Health Counselors Association (AMCHA). Bozorg-Omit demonstrated that although 90% of the survey respondents had received some training in family violence issues, about one-half of these did not receive that training in their formal graduate education. Moreover, nearly 80% of the participants described their graduate school training in family violence issues as inadequate.

In addition to lacking formal training and education in family violence issues, there has been a lack of accessible sources to guide therapists in their clinical practice. Although numerous high quality books on family violence exist, our observations have been that, to date, most of the existing books focus either only on some forms of family violence, primarily on general background information (and not clinical applications) about family violence, and/or are not grounded on the most current research-based information found within the scholarly literature on family violence. As such, therapists seeking information on family violence have lacked the availability of a comprehensive, in-depth clinical consideration of these issues, and especially such a consideration that is grounded in research. Our aim in writing this book was to develop such a resource for practicing therapists and therapists-in-training. This book is designed to familiarize readers with the dynamics of multiple forms of family violence—including IPV, child maltreatment, and abuse in special populations such as elders and individuals with disabilities. Beyond the "basics" of these dynamics, clinical guidelines are presented for assessment and intervention.

Defining Family Violence

In this book, we define *family violence as any form of maltreatment—including physical, sexual, and emotional (inclusive of both verbal and psychological abuse), as well as neglect—perpetrated or witnessed by one or more members of a family and/or intimate relationship upon one or more other members of that family or relationship.*

Clinical Challenges Associated with Family Violence

Multiple clinical challenges may arise for therapists when working with clients impacted by family violence. These include the complexity of family violence cases, clarifying the role of the therapist within the family violence response system, partnering with community resources within the family response system, seeking research-based guidelines for clinical practice, and managing the self-care challenges that arise when addressing family violence.

The Complexity of Family Violence Cases

Family violence can be a challenge to address based on the complex dynamics involved. In addition to basic survival and safety needs of themselves and other family members, clients often experience extensive traumatic stress responses that impact their cognitive and social functioning (e.g., Daignault & Hébert, 2009; Helfrich, Fujiura, & Rutkowsky-Kmitta, 2008; Reinhard, Wolf, & Cozolino, 2010). Very often, clients participating in therapy for family violence reveal additional experiences and histories of other forms of violence, such as childhood trauma. This intergenerational transmission of family violence has been documented in the research literature (Tracy & Johnson, 2006). Beyond familial experiences, clients' cultural backgrounds and other social forces may contribute to the continuation of their violent experiences (Jenkins, 1996; Jenkins, Hampton, & Gullotta, 1996). Complex, poly-victimization experiences may render it more challenging for clients to become removed from circumstances contributing to their victimization or to overcome and stop their perpetration of abuse.

Family Violence Response Systems

Family violence is not just a phenomenon that impacts mental health, and several other systems are involved in preventing, responding to, and treating family violence issues. Thus, therapists must be aware of local resources that clients can seek as additional sources of support to help them achieve safety and make progress toward their treatment goals. In this book, readers will learn about what we describe as the *family violence response systems* that are typically in place in local communities that address various forms of family violence. A *family violence response system* is defined as *a coordinated, multidisciplinary, community response team that provides information, support, crisis and safety planning assistance, and resources to individuals impacted by family violence.* Family violence response systems may include legal and criminal justice systems, healthcare systems, social service agencies, natural support and peer support groups, and a variety of other systems that may include schools, workplaces, and religious institutions. Many clients impacted by family violence already will be involved in various aspects of these response systems, and, in fact, these systems may be the reason that clients find their ways to their therapists' offices, as in cases when abuse perpetrators are court-mandated to attend treatment. Still, it is imperative that the therapist connect with these key community resources to ensure a strong support system is in place for the clients that they are working with throughout the therapeutic process.

Understanding the multiple layers of clients' involvement in family violence response systems presents a unique challenge for therapists. Consider, for example, a family in which a child witnessed his father perpetrating severe IPV against his mother, and this was reported to the local Child Protective Services (CPS) unit. The child's father was arrested and referred to a court diversion batterer intervention program. The child's mother sustained physical injuries in the violent episode that required her to seek medical attention. She also began to seek victim advocacy services from a program for battered women in the community, as well as psychotherapy from a community mental health agency. The child was assigned a caseworker through CPS, personnel from his school were notified of the situation, and he also began to receive outpatient counseling through the same mental health agency as his mother. Certainly, the therapist for this child will interface with many aspects of the family violence response systems with which the family is involved. Knowing when and how to do so appropriately can become quite a challenge for therapists.

When working with clients impacted by family violence, therapists may be challenged to go beyond the functions they typically associate with conducting psychotherapy. For example, consistent with principles of trauma-informed care, attending to basic survival and safety needs take priority over exploring clients' emotional and psychological functioning. Furthermore, therapists also are challenged to help their clients navigate these response systems and assume a "case management" function. Therapists must inform and empower clients to understand the unique role that they play within these systems and how clients' work done with their therapists may be related to other aspects of these systems. For example, batterers who have been court-mandated to attend batterer intervention programs should be fully informed as to how participation and progress in the program will impact any legal sanctions they may face. Likewise, when multiple components of response systems are involved in clients' lives, there may be additional exceptions to confidentiality that could impact the process of therapy.

Seeking Research-Based Guidance for Practice

Although a substantial body of research exists that addresses the study of family violence, the translation of this research to practice often is not achieved. As will be discussed later in this chapter, a series of recent studies aimed at understanding and developing potential solutions to addressing the gap between family violence research and practice was conducted (Murray & Smith, 2009; Murray, Smith, & Avent, 2010; Murray & Welch, 2010). Through these studies, several factors were identified that hinder the application of research to practice in the area. First and foremost, many therapists lack access to useful research. The high cost of academic journals puts research out of reach for many community-based therapists. Second, many busy therapists simply do not have the time or energy needed to locate, read, and interpret individual research studies, particularly given that academic language used in published research studies is often difficult to decipher among non-research professionals. Third, much of the existing research on family violence lacks clearly defined practical relevance. Therapists have observed that many researchers lack a clinical background that would sensitize them to the needs of therapists, and while the findings are helpful, researchers often fail to consider or report the clinical relevance of their studies. Furthermore, research is notorious for producing contradictory findings, which causes confusion for therapists in determining the best course of action to take when working with specific clients. The practical implications of a particular research study can indeed be difficult to identify, and many researchers fail to make these implications clear. Thus, to date, many therapists have been limited in their ability to access and benefit from research-based information to help guide them in their clinical work.

Personal Challenges Associated with Working with Family Violence

Finally, any therapist who has worked with clients impacted by family violence likely can attest to the immense personal challenges that are often brought to the forefront when working with such complex, evocative, and potentially saddening or anger-provoking cases. Despite their extensive clinical training and experience, therapists are first and foremost human, and therefore they are not immune from being challenged emotionally and even spiritually by the dynamics involved in family violence. In recognition of the personally challenging nature of working clinically with family violence issues, this book contains a chapter dedicated to the issue of self-care for therapists. Readers may find it useful to read that chapter first, especially if they anticipate that they will have a difficult time managing their emotional and personal responses to learning more about the various forms of family violence.

The Context of Ethics

All therapists are bound by the professional ethical guidelines associated with their respective credentials and organizational memberships. This book assumes that readers are familiar with basic ethical principles and decision-making guidelines pertinent to their areas of practice. Throughout this book, readers will find case studies in several chapters that illustrate the most pertinent ethical issues they may face when working with clients impacted by family violence. Our discussion of these issues through case studies is grounded in the ethical codes of various related professional organizations, including the American Association for Marriage and Family Therapy (AAMFT; 2001), the American Counseling Association (ACA; 2005), the American Psychological Association (APA; 2002), and the National Association of Social Workers (NASW; 2008). Although each of these codes has its own unique nuances, they are united in their shared foundations in promoting client welfare. Therefore, although the specific standards addressing particular ethical challenges within each code vary, we focus throughout this book on addressing the general themes that can guide therapists in their work with clients impacted by family violence.

The context of safety and lethality issues surrounding the various forms of family violence gives rise to unique ethical challenges for therapists. First, as will be stated throughout this book in many different ways, client safety is *the* primary consideration for therapists when working with clients who have experienced family violence. As Maslow's (1954) hierarchy of needs demonstrates, safety is the foundation upon which all subsequent layers are built, including the therapeutic process. This also is consistent with the principles of trauma-informed care, which highlight that safety also must be addressed as the first order of business in the therapeutic process before trauma healing can begin. When applied to family violence-related ethical dilemmas, safety considerations must be the lens through which all alternative courses of action are evaluated. Therapists must be aware that abusive behaviors can present actual threats to the physical, emotional, and psychological well-being of victims and the family members around them (e.g., children), and, in some cases, lives may be at stake. Thus, therapists may face therapeutic and ethical dilemmas when working with victims and/or perpetrators of family violence. Safety must therefore be at the forefront of ethical decision-making processes as they relate to family violence situations.

Ethical issues associated with family violence also are unique in their intersection with legal issues. As will be addressed throughout this book, many forms of family violence are crimes. Therefore, therapists must be informed as to all relevant local, state, and federal laws (e.g., related to mandatory reporting of child abuse, the filing of protective orders, and standards for batterer intervention programs). As such, therapists must ensure that the outcomes of the ethical decisions they make are in accordance with all relevant laws and regulations.

The Research Basis for This Book

One of our major goals in writing this book was to build upon the existing body of research on family violence and to translate that information into useable clinical guidelines for therapists. A focus of our research has been on what we have termed the "domestic violence research-practice gap" (Murray & Smith, 2009; Murray et al., 2010). We define this term as *a disconnection between existing research findings and common service delivery practices in … domestic violence prevention and intervention* (Murray & Smith, 2009, p. 4). Although the focus of this book is in the area of family violence, gaps between research and practice are quite common in the mental health professions (Murray, 2009). Our observation is that the research-practice gap in this area is somewhat unique given the historical and professional context, in which there is evidence that there has been a history of tension and antagonism between some groups of researchers and service providers (Gondolf, Yllö, & Campbell, 1997; Hamberger, 2001; Murray & Smith, 2009; Riger, 1999; Williams, 2004). As such, building links between research and practice was an important objective of this book.

The Extensive Body of Family Violence Research

To be certain, the body of knowledge about family violence within the scientific literature is extensive. Moments before writing this sentence, we entered the search terms *family violence, child maltreatment, child abuse, child neglect, intimate partner violence, domestic violence,* and *elder abuse* into the PsycINFO database, and this search yielded 33,189 results! This does not include all of the studies on family violence that could be found using different search terms or by searching additional electronic databases, including those directly relevant to the mental health professions (e.g., Social Work Abstracts) and those relevant to other academic disciplines (e.g., sociology, economics, and medicine) in which family violence may be studied. Indeed, even studies that are not related directly to clinical practice may be informative to therapists in helping them to conceptualize and treat their clients.

The vastness of this body of knowledge is likely one of the main reasons that many important advances are slow to be applied to clinical practice. Many practicing therapists are pressed for time as it is. Between spending time with clients, completing paperwork, filing insurance, and managing the business aspects of their practice, there is little time left for doing extensive reading of research studies. Even if practitioners did have the time to read such studies, where would they begin? And, once they read a study, how do they determine the real implications of the study for their actual work? It is not uncommon to read a 20+ page research article in a peer-reviewed journal, only to find a mere one to two paragraphs dedicated to implications for clinical practice. Furthermore, these implications often are couched in highly tentative and technical language and may discourage a practitioner from applying the findings to practice. For example, in a study on different subtypes of batterers, Holtzworth-Munroe, Meehan, Herron, Rehman, and Stuart (2000) wrote, "It is premature to recommend particular interventions for various subtypes of batterers" (p. 1016).

Appropriate Caution in Applying Research to Practice

We believe that it is appropriate that family violence researchers are cautious to encourage the immediate and direct application of their findings to making changes to policies and clinical practices. Every research finding must be appropriately situated and understood within the context of the methodological limitations and other relevant contextual variables, such as local norms and customs, characteristics of the study sample's demographics, and the applicability of the findings to different clinical settings. An example from the body of research on batterers, which will be discussed more extensively in Part 1 of this book, illustrates the importance of caution when making potential changes to clinical practice based on the findings of one particular study. In 1995, John Gottman and his colleagues (1995) published a groundbreaking study in which they found a very fascinating difference between the two main types of male batterers that were distinguished in their research. These researchers found that, among one group of batterers, the men experienced an increase in heart rate during a marital conflict situation with their spouses, as would be expected to happen along with the increase in stress that might occur during such conflict. However, among the other group of batterers, the men actually demonstrated a decreased heart rate while engaged in the marital conflict situation—they actually appeared to calm down when engaged in conflict with their spouse. These findings received widespread attention and were published in a highly publicized book by Jacobson and Gottman (1998), called *When Men*

Batter Women (Meehan, Holtzworth-Munroe, & Herron, 2001). Perhaps much less publicized, however, is the fact that some of the major findings by Gottman et al. (1995) regarding differences between these two groups of batterers have not stood up to replication in at least two different studies (Babcock, Green, Webb, & Graham, 2004; Meehan et al., 2001). As Babcock et al. (2004) state, "In light of two failed replications of the typology based on batterers' HR reactivity, it does not appear that this widely publicized typology withstands scientific scrutiny" (p. 400).

Imagine, then, if all laws about how court-mandated intervention programs for convicted batterers were revised after Gottman et al.'s (1995) initial finding so that batterers were assigned to treatment based on a physiological test of their heart rate reactivity, with differential treatments being assigned for those whose heart rates decrease during conflict and those whose heart rates increase during conflict. Such new laws could result in ineffective treatment strategies and increased costs and administrative burdens for local municipalities who had to oversee this new differential treatment program. As more research is done, differences in batterers' heart rate reactivity still ultimately may prove to be a useful means for distinguishing and assigning differential treatment for batterers, in particular because certain methodological approaches could have contributed to the differential findings (Gottman, 2001). Nonetheless, the replication failure findings (Babcock et al., 2004; Meehan et al., 2001) point to the importance of not making hasty changes to clinical practice and policy in the face of limited, unreplicated research findings (Meehan et al., 2001). So, too, should therapists proceed with informed caution when considering the practical implications of any relevant research findings.

The challenge for therapists, as well as policy- and decision-makers within mental health service organizations, is how best to proceed within the limitations of the available information about family violence. Put simply, therapists cannot sit idly by while they wait for researchers to provide definitive answers about the challenging questions about family violence that arise in their clinical practice. Rather, therapists must make decisions based on the best available information while constantly staying abreast of the advances in research to ensure that new information can be integrated appropriately into practice. Furthermore, therapists should put in place methods to evaluate the clinical effectiveness and utility of the new approaches and information they incorporate into their work.

Translating Research into Practice

All of these issues were at the forefront of our minds in aiming to write a book that is grounded in recent research and relevant to clinical practice. We wrote with a keen awareness that, given the time lag between the writing and publication of the book, some of the information it contains would already be updated within new studies by the time the book reaches its readers. Thus, we used the following strategies in order to cover the most clinically-relevant and recent advances in research on family violence.

Because it would indeed be impossible to review all of the existing research on family violence, we used detailed procedures to hone in on credible recent research that addresses practice-relevant questions. For the most part, we focused on studies published during or after the year 2000, although earlier studies were included if they were seminal publications that continue to influence current scholarship regarding family violence. The focus of this book also is on studies that were published in peer-reviewed journals, such that the peer review process was assumed to provide an additional check on the methodological strength of each included study. In addition, for each topic addressed in this book, we used a variety of strategies to search the existing literature (e.g., through scholarly databases) in order to locate the most clinically relevant research. Once located, we reviewed with a critical eye toward evaluating the relevance and meaning of the studies for clinical practice. Because space limitations preclude extensive discussions of any of the studies we reviewed, therapists may find it useful to seek out the full-text of the cited studies that are most directly relevant to their practice settings, either through local university or public libraries

The research basis for this book is inclusive of studies that were conducted using a wide range of methodological approaches, including both qualitative and quantitative designs. Despite recent pushes for evidence-based practices that are very specific in how those practices are defined (e.g., Flay et al., 2005), we believe strongly that therapists can benefit from the information produced through different methodological approaches. Although qualitative studies may be limited in the extent to which they can be generalized, they can provide valuable insight into the depth of the concerns clients may experience related to family violence. Qualitative studies also can be useful for developing theories about family violence-related phenomena and exploring the nuances of individuals' experiences and perceptions of family violence. Quantitative research may not provide as much in-depth coverage of research topics as qualitative research, but quantitative research can provide valuable information about common trends within populations impacted by family violence. Furthermore, quantitative studies can be useful for testing the effects of intervention approaches and generating statistics about the incidence and prevalence of family violence. By remaining open to the different types of insights that these research methods can provide, therapists can benefit from increasing both the breadth and depth of their understanding of family violence.

Overall, this book was intended to be written in an accessible and user-friendly language that presents academic, scholarly, and statistical terms in an easily understood language geared toward the therapist without an extensive training and experience in research methodology. We set out to find the most relevant and useful information contained within the existing body of research on family violence and present it in a format that is accessible to busy therapists. We drew upon our own clinical, research, and teaching experiences in order to focus in on the most typical clinical questions that arise when working with family violence issues in therapy.

Overview of the Following Chapters

In order to address these questions, this book is laid out in four parts. Part 1 addresses IPV. In addition to describing general background information about IPV, clinical assessment and treatment of the major types of IPV (i.e., intimate terrorism and situational couple violence) will be reviewed. Part 2 addresses the treatment of various forms of childhood maltreatment—including physical abuse, sexual abuse, emotional abuse, and neglect, including a discussion of working with adults who survived childhood maltreatment. Part 3 includes a chapter on addressing the abuse of vulnerable populations, including the elderly and individuals with disabilities. Part 4 provides in-depth coverage of several specific clinical challenges faced by therapists addressing family violence issues such as substance abuse and cultural issues. Other issues explored in Part 4 include prevention, outreach, advocacy, and self-care strategies to help therapists avoid burnout.

Throughout the book, readers will find several features designed to make the information accessible and useful. Several hypothetical case studies are provided to illustrate the content of the chapters. These case studies are fictional, but they are designed to reflect the real-life dynamics of family violence situations. Several chapters contain case studies dedicated primarily to addressing ethical challenges related to this work.

Readers should note that, throughout the book, we use the term *therapist* to represent professionals across the mental health disciplines who conduct psychotherapy. These disciplines may include clinical social workers, marriage and family therapists, mental health counselors, substance abuse counselors, pastoral counselors, psychologists, and psychiatrists. Although members of each of these disciplines may have different professional trainings, the information in this book is intended to be applicable to psychotherapy across professional disciplines. Finally, although the chapters in this book are somewhat arbitrarily divided (e.g., IPV, child maltreatment, and elder abuse), we want to emphasize that the overlap among these types is often extensive. Moreover, overlapping forms of violence and abuse within families certainly hold clinical relevance for practicing therapists. One often cannot separate out neatly the effects of experiencing or witnessing multiple forms of abuse, and the underlying dynamics contributing to these multiple forms warrant considerable clinical attention. As such, we strongly encourage readers to consider the content of this book in its entirety, such that the full context and scope of family violence can be understood.

PART I

2

INTIMATE PARTNER VIOLENCE

Background and Overview of Response Systems

In order to effectively treat clients impacted by intimate partner violence (IPV), therapists must first understand what it is, how it impacts client behavior, how it impacts client-therapist interactions, and how therapy fits within the context of larger IPV-related response systems. This chapter familiarizes therapists with these issues before we discuss treatment considerations in the next three chapters. We begin by defining terms related to IPV and prevalence statistics, followed by a description of different types of IPV, including different types and characteristics of battering perpetrators. Then, we move to a discussion of larger social issues relevant to IPV, including what we call the IPV response system. Finally, the chapter concludes with information about IPV within some specific populations, such as dating couples and same-sex partners.

Definitions: What is Intimate Partner Violence?

Many different terms are used to describe IPV, and people can differ widely in what they mean by the terms they use (Derrington, Johnson, Menard, Ooms, & Stanley, 2010). So, a basic step in understanding IPV is to define it. Basic does not mean easy, however. Readers are probably familiar with many of the terms that have been used to describe IPV: *domestic violence*, *dating violence*, *battering*, *spousal abuse*, *wife abuse*, and *intimate partner abuse*, to name a few. Further complicating these terminology issues are the different terms used to describe people who experience IPV. Are those who commit IPV best referred to as abusers, batterers, perpetrators, or offenders? Are those who are abused most appropriately described as victims or survivors? As we'll discuss, these definitions become even more complicated when we consider that the latest research indicates that there are different types of IPV, and so one overarching label may not fully capture all of the nuances of this phenomenon.

For this book, we define IPV as any form of physical, sexual, emotional, psychological, and/or verbal abuse between partners in an intimate relationship. By intimate relationship, we are referring to individuals in a current or former relationship in which two partners "share an emotional, romantic, and/or sexual connection" (Murray, 2007, p. 57), and we include both heterosexual and same-sex relationships. The term *IPV* should be considered an umbrella term, in that it encompasses a diverse range of violent and abusive relationship dynamics (Derrington et al., 2010; Smith, Thornton, DeVellis, Earp, & Coker, 2002).

Physical Abuse

Tjaden and Thoennes (2000) defined physical abuse as "behaviors that threaten, attempt, or actually inflict physical harm. The definition includes a wide range of behaviors, from slapping, pushing, and shoving to using a gun" (p. 16). Physically abusive behaviors can range widely in severity. Marshall (1992a, b) conducted two studies to differentiate severity levels of male- and female-perpetrated physical abuse. Marshall believed that the severity of physical abuse can be considered in several ways, including the level of seriousness, aggressiveness, abusiveness, threat, violence, degree of physical harm, and degree of psychological/emotional harm. Marshall aimed to introduce some objectivity in identifying levels of severity, so she surveyed college students and community members. For male perpetrators, she identified nine severity categories, with the least severe category being mild threats (e.g., acting like a bully, pulling hair) and the most severe categories being demanding sex and punching. For female perpetrators, eight categories emerged, with the least severe category being mild violence (e.g., shaking one's partner, pulling hair) and the most severe category being choking. Of course, violent behaviors representing different levels of severity may be used simultaneously, but Marshall's distinctions help to provide some framework for beginning to understand how couples may demonstrate differing levels of violence within their relationships.

Sexual Abuse

Within intimate relationships, sexual abuse can refer to a range of behaviors, including rape. Tjaden and Thoennes (2000) defined rape as "an event that occurs without the victim's consent and involves the use of threat or force to penetrate the victim's vagina or anus by penis, tongue, fingers, or object or the victim's mouth by penis. The definition includes both attempted and completed rape" (p. 16). Other behaviors that could be considered sexual abuse within the context of intimate relationships include forcing or coercing one's partner to engage in pornography, exhibitionistic forms of sexual activities, prostitution, sexual activities with animals or other individuals, or other risky sex practices (Mouradian, 2000). It is important to note that although there may be higher rates of rape among females, rape can occur among both men and women.

Emotional/Psychological/Verbal Abuse

Emotional abuse is "the use of verbal and other non-physical forms of aggression to intimidate, subjugate, and control another human being" (Jacobson & Gottman, 1998, p. 148). Psychological abuse involves "acts of recurring criticism and/or verbal aggression toward a partner, and/or acts of isolation and domination of a partner. Generally, such actions cause the partner to be fearful of the other or lead the partner to have a very low self-esteem" (O'Leary, 1999, p. 19). Because these terms are overlapping and multidimensional, we use the terms *emotional abuse, psychological abuse,* and *emotional/psychological abuse* interchangeably.

Sackett and Saunders (1999) identified four types of emotional/psychological abuse: jealous control, ignoring, criticizing behaviors, and ridiculing of traits. Ridiculing traits appears to be the most severe form, in that it was related closely to lower self-esteem and greater fear among one sample of women receiving services from a domestic violence agency. Other examples of emotionally/psychologically abusive behaviors include verbal degradation (e.g., name calling), demonstrating selfishness and punitiveness, treating the partner like a piece of property, jealousy, making a partner account for how and where she or he spends his or her time, and isolation (Jory, Anderson, & Greer, 1997; Tjaden & Thoennes, 2000; Tolman, 1999). Stalking, which also could fall under the category of emotional/psychological abuse, may involve harassment of the victim (Hegarty, Bush, & Sheehan, 2005; Hegarty, Sheehan, & Schonfeld, 1999), as well as "repeated visual or physical proximity; nonconsensual communication; verbal, written, or implied threats; or a combination thereof that would cause fear in a reasonable person, with 'repeated' meaning on two or more occasions" (Tjaden & Thoennes, 2000, p. 16).

For the most part, it is not illegal to use emotional abuse within intimate relationships (Jacobson & Gottman, 1998). Physical abuse almost always occurs within a context of emotional abuse, although emotional abuse may be present in the absence of physical abuse (Jacobson & Gottman, 1998). For example, emotional abuse may serve a control function in a couple's relationship and often continues after physical abuse stops (Jacobson & Gottman, 1998). Battering victims appear to be more likely to leave their relationships when severe emotional abuse is present (Jacobson & Gottman, 1998). Emotional abuse may be as damaging as physical abuse (Kelly, 2004; O'Leary, 1999; Sackett & Saunders, 1999), and it may also predict later physical abuse (Kelly, 2004; O'Leary, 1999; Sackett & Saunders, 1999).

IPV Terminology: Types, Perpetrators, Victims, and Survivors

We refer to two main categories of IPV: situational couple violence and battering, and we describe each type in greater detail later in this chapter. Briefly, when we discuss *situational couple violence*, we are referring to IPV that occurs exclusively in the context of situation-specific couple conflict and does not reflect broader power and control dynamics in the couple's relationship (Johnson, 2006, 2009; Johnson & Ferraro, 2000; Johnson & Leone, 2005). We use the term *battering* to refer to violence that occurs within a "patterned and repeated use of coercive controlling behavior to limit, direct, and shape a partner's thoughts, feelings, and actions" (Almeida & Durkin, 1999, p. 313). In addition to these two types, we want to note that violent or abusive behaviors within intimate relationships may reflect self-defense, which is also referred to as *violent resistance* (Johnson, 2006, 2009; Johnson & Ferraro, 2000).

To describe individuals who perpetrate battering against their intimate partners, we use the term *battering perpetrators.* We use two different terms, *victim* and *survivor* to refer to individuals who are victimized by battering in their intimate relationships. We use the term *battering victims* when referring to individuals who have current or recent experiences of victimization, and the term *battering survivors* when referring to individuals who have become permanently separated from their experiences of battering victimization. Within the broader domestic violence movement, there appears to have been a gradual shift from viewing battered women as victims toward the use of the term *survivor*, as the term *victim* is viewed by some as stigmatizing and disempowering (Dunn, 2005; Merritt-Gray & Wuest, 1995). However, we believed that using the victim-survivor terminology remained appropriate for the following reasons. First, the terms remain useful for distinguishing current/recent and past experiences of victimization in order to make clear to which client population we are referring. Second, helping individuals move from viewing themselves as victims to viewing themselves as survivors may be one part of the therapy process (Dunn, 2005). Third, although the use of the term *survivor* has become more common, the term *victim* is still used widely within criminal justice and social service settings (e.g., victim impact statements, victim advocates), and this terminology can therefore provide a basis for interdisciplinary communications. Fourth, individual clients within this population can vary in terms of how they self-identify with respect to these and other labels (Southworth, Finn, Dawson, Fraser, & Tucker, 2007). Finally, even defining individuals as *survivors* still defines the population in relation to their experiences with the abuse (Wuest & Merritt-Gray, 2001). Therefore, neither the term *victim* nor *survivor* adequately encompasses the complexity of these individuals' experiences (Dunn, 2005), although a more fitting, uncomplicated label has not yet been proposed within the literature. Thus, while we use the terms *victim* and *survivor* to describe this clinical population, we urge therapists to remain vigilant that such terms do not overshadow the individuals behind the labels, nor should these individuals be viewed solely in light of their victimization experiences.

Statistics: How Common is IPV?

We have just made clear the definitions we are using to describe IPV and people who experience. Unfortunately, such definitional clarity is not consistently applied in the existing research on IPV. Two of the biggest problems in the existing research are that different methods have been used to recruit participants and that researchers have used different definitions and measurement strategies. A sample drawn from a general population survey can lead to very different results than one drawn from battered women's shelters or other clinical settings (Holtzworth-Munroe, 2005). Likewise, researchers often include different types of violence or other abusive behaviors, which can lead to differential rates across studies. For example, some studies assess for only physical violence, while others include psychological/emotional and/or sexual as well. Furthermore, many studies examine rates of IPV without attending to the context of the violent behaviors (Smith, Smith, & Earp, 1999), meaning that behaviors used in self-defense could be classified incorrectly as abusive. Even the order in which people are asked the same questions about IPV can influence the extent to which they disclose their experiences of perpetration and victimization (Ramirez & Straus, 2006). Therefore, even relatively minor methodological considerations can have a major impact on the findings.

Despite these methodological limitations, evidence indicates that IPV is a very common phenomenon. One of the most widely cited studies is the National Violence Against Women Survey (NVAWS; Tjaden & Thoennes, 2000), which was sponsored by the US National Institute of Justice (NIJ) and the Centers for Disease Control and Prevention (CDC). This random telephone-based survey was conducted with 8,000 women and 8,000 men in the United States (US). About 25% of women and 8% of men reported a lifetime history of some form of physical and/or sexual assault, and 1.5% of women and .9% of men reported these experiences in the past 12 months. Stalking was a relatively common experience within IPV, occurring for about 5% of women and .6% of men at some point in their lives. The NVAWS data also indicated that women are more likely to experience IPV and are more likely to sustain injuries based on IPV as compared to men. IPV rates appear to be higher among individuals with non-White ethnic backgrounds, with the exception of Asian/Pacific Islanders, who demonstrated the lowest rates. The results also indicated that physical and sexual assault appear to be most likely to occur within the context of ongoing relationships, but stalking is more likely following the termination of the relationship.

Smith et al. (2002) used a population-based sample to study the prevalence and co-occurrence of battering, physical assault, and sexual assault within IPV.

Among 268 women ages 18 to 45 years, IPV experiences within the past year were as follows: any form of IPV (approximately 18%), battering (approximately 14%), physical assault (approximately 9%), sexual assaults (approximately 8%), and having been battered without also having been physically or sexually assaulted (6%), which Smith et al. (2002) referred to as "psychological battering" (p. 1222). There was a high co-occurrence (70%) of physical or sexual assault with battering.

McFarlane and Malecha (2005) provided further evidence that sexual abuse within IPV appears to commonly co-occur with physical victimization. These researchers studied sexual assault among 148 women who had been IPV victims. Sexual assault rates were high, with 68% reporting that their partners had also sexually assaulted them, and about 80% reporting that they had experienced more than one incident of sexual assault by their partners. Compared with the women who had experienced physical but not sexual abuse, those who also had experienced sexual assault experienced more negative mental and physical health consequences.

Of particular interest to therapists are statistics about how common IPV is within clinical populations. Although they did not recruit directly from mental health treatment settings, Coker, Smith, McKeown, and King (2000) demonstrated higher rates of IPV in a clinical setting compared to the general population sampled in the NVAWS. These researchers surveyed a sample of 1,401 women aged 18 to 65 who were recruited from two family practice clinic settings and found that 9.8% of the participants reported experiencing current or recent IPV, and 37.6% reported that they had experienced physical assault at some point in their lives. Further evidence that IPV experiences are likely among clinical populations is that, according to Helfrich, Fujiura, & Rutkowski-Kmitta. (2008), battered women in shelters have extremely high rates of seeking mental health services, even as high are over 30 times the rates of the general US population.

Published IPV rates are likely underestimates of the full extent of the problem. IPV certainly can be considered to be a socially undesirable behavior (Ramirez & Straus, 2006), which may lead people to underreport their experiences (Vega & O'Leary, 2007). As one example of this, NVAWS data suggest that most IPV goes unreported to the criminal justice system (Tjaden & Thoennes, 2000). Some other factors that may lead to underreporting include feelings of shame, fear of retaliation, and minimizing the extent of the abuse (Tjaden & Thoennes, 2000).

Gender and IPV Perpetration and Victimization

It has been typical practice in educational, research, and practice settings to default to using male terms (e.g., him, he) to refer to perpetrators and female terms (e.g., she, her) to refer to victims. However, this default is increasingly called into question by research demonstrating that these distinctions are not always quite so clear, both in heterosexual and same-sex relationships. Perhaps one of the most controversial areas of existing IPV research relates to differential findings about whether males and females perpetrate IPV equally (Graves, Sechrist, White, & Paradise, 2005; Holtzworth-Munroe, 2005; Johnson, 2006; Kelly & Johnson, 2008; Kimmel, 2002; Straus, 2006, 2009; White, Smith, Koss, & Figueredo, 2000). The battered women's movement has largely considered IPV to be violence perpetrated by men against women, and this is consistent with patriarchal theories explaining IPV causes (Dobash & Dobash, 1979). However, evidence also exists that women use violent behaviors at rates similar to men in intimate relationships (Archer, 2000; Graves et al., 2005; Hamel, 2007), although women and men may have different motivations for their use of violence in intimate relationships (Kernsmith, 2005). There also is growing recognition that males can be victims of IPV, and that they may demonstrate unique needs that are unmet by services traditionally set up to support female victims (Tsui, Cheung, & Leung, 2010). Perhaps the best explanation for these conflicting findings can be found in Johnson's (2006, 2009; Johnson & Ferraro, 2000) differentiation between intimate terrorism (i.e., battering) and situational couple violence. Johnson (2006, 2009; Johnson & Ferraro, 2000; Johnson & Leone, 2005) asserted that most existing research fails to account for different forms of violence, and therefore methodological limitations of research produces the conflicting findings. Johnson's (2006, 2009) conclusion based on existing research is that, in heterosexual relationships, battering is more likely to be perpetrated by males, but situational couple violence may be perpetrated at similar rates by males and females. This is consistent with Ehrensaft's (2008) suggestion that females are more likely to perpetrate violence in relationships demonstrating lower levels of violence.

Despite these advances in understanding IPV, there currently is a lack of complete information to allow us to understand fully how perpetration varies based on gender (Graves et al., 2005; Holtzworth-Munroe, 2005). Some basic generalizations regarding the differences between male- and female-perpetrated violence can be drawn, although there is a high potential for exceptions to these. First, male-perpetrated IPV against female victims appears to have more negative and severe consequences, and females may be more likely to fear male-perpetrated IPV than males are to fear female-perpetrated IPV (Ehrensaft, 2008; Holtzworth-Munroe, 2005; Holtzworth-Munroe, Smutlzer, & Bates, 1997; Kernsmith, 2005). This may be due in part to typical physical size differentials between the genders (Holtzworth-Munroe, 2005). In addition, males (as well as law enforcement and service systems) may be less likely to take seriously the IPV perpetrated by females than vice versa (Holtzworth-Munroe, 2005). Thus, IPV should not be considered a "gender-neutral phenomenon" (White et al., 2000, p. 694), and therapists must consider carefully the influence of gender on their clients' experiences with IPV.

IPV In-Depth: New Understandings of Different Types of Violence and Perpetrators

Earlier research tended to treat IPV as though it were a singular phenomenon that was experienced similarly across populations. In fact, the failure to account for different forms of IPV has led to confusion and controversies among researchers and practitioners regarding how best to understand and intervene with individuals affected by it. More recent research findings demonstrate that IPV is not a "one size fits all" phenomenon (Anderson, 2010; Mears & Visher, 2005). Researchers have identified different types of IPV and types of perpetrators (e.g., Jacobson & Gottman, 1998; Johnson, 2006, 2009; Johnson & Ferraro, 2000). This research suggests that distinctions are crucial to effectively matching treatment approaches to client needs. However, although many important trends have emerged from this research, the applicability of the findings to practice remains uncertain (Anderson, 2010). In this section, we provide in-depth coverage of the two main types of IPV (i.e., situational couple violence and battering) and the growing body of research examining different types of perpetrators.

Michael Johnson, a researcher at Penn State University, and his colleagues (e.g., Johnson, 2006, 2009; Johnson & Ferraro, 2000; Johnson & Leone, 2005; Kelly & Johnson, 2008; Leone, Johnson, & Cohan, 2007) proposed one of the most significant distinctions in types of IPV that can help therapists understand the different potential dynamics at play. According to Johnson (2006), there are four primary types of IPV, and the historical and ongoing failure to acknowledge these types has led to problems with research, policy, and interventions (Johnson, 2009; Johnson & Ferraro, 2000). Johnson (2006; Johnson & Leone, 2005; Kelly & Johnson, 2008) believes that these different types of violence likely have different causes, consequences, and implications for intervention. It is important to note that Johnson (2009; Johnson & Leone, 2005; Leone et al., 2007) does not differentiate the forms of violence based on the severity or the frequency with which it occurs, but rather it is the presence of control dynamics that distinguish the types. Although it may be useful to target interventions to each type, there are not yet clear screening strategies to easily and accurately identify the type being experienced (Johnson, 2009). Johnson (2009) takes a cautious stance and advises that professionals should proceed in any IPV case as though it is intimate terrorism until it is clear that it is not. Furthermore, even within the various categories of IPV, several other distinctions may be made to reflect additional levels of complexity regarding the causes and dynamics of IPV (Kelly & Johnson, 2008).

Johnson (2006) argues that the IPV types should be distinguished by determining the extent to which the violence reflects one or both partners' intention to exert power and control over the partner. The four main types of IPV identified by Johnson are as follows: situational couple violence, intimate terrorism (i.e., battering), violent resistance, and mutual violent control. Kelly and Johnson (2008) added a fifth type, separation-instigated violence. Research remains inconclusive about how clear the distinctions can be drawn between the types (Holtzworth-Munroe, 2005). In particular, it remains unknown how to predict whether and when lower levels of violence will escalate to more severe forms, as well as whether the "types" are different phenomena or simply developmental levels of the same phenomenon (Derrington et al., 2010; Holtzworth-Munroe, 2005; Leone et al., 2007). And, despite the significant advances that Johnson's typology has brought to the field, research is still not definitively able to prove that his proposed distinctions are accurate (Anderson, 2010). With this in mind, we discuss in-depth the dynamics of each of the types of IPV proposed by Johnson and his colleagues.

Situational Couple Violence

Situational couple violence refers to the use of violent behaviors without a corresponding context of other controlling behaviors (Johnson, 2006, 2009; Johnson & Leone, 2005; Kelly & Johnson, 2008). Johnson previously referred to this form of violence as *common couple violence,* but he changed to use the term *situational couple violence* to avoid implying that this form of violence is acceptable (Johnson, 2006). Situational couple violence occurs in the context of specific relationship conflicts or stressors (Johnson, 2009; Johnson & Ferraro, 2000; Kelly & Johnson, 2008). Therefore, if the couple is not currently experiencing conflict, there likely is no violence present. This form of violence is thought to occur when conflict-based tensions escalate to the point that one or both partners respond with violence (Johnson, 2009; Johnson & Leone, 2005). Situational couple violence may result from deficits in one or both partners' conflict management skills (Kelly & Johnson, 2008), and the victim typically does not fear the perpetrator (Kelly & Johnson, 2008). Situational couple violence may occur just once or be a chronic pattern (Johnson, 2009; Johnson & Leone, 2005; Kelly & Johnson, 2008), but typically is less frequent than intimate terrorism (i.e., battering; Johnson & Ferraro, 2000; Kelly & Johnson, 2008). Although control tactics may be present, they are limited to the immediate context of the situation (Johnson, 2009), and the partner(s) using them are attempting to control a particular situation rather than the entire relationship (Leone et al., 2007).

Johnson (Johnson & Ferraro, 2000; Johnson & Leone, 2005; Kelly & Johnson, 2008) suggests that situational couple violence is more likely to be identified in general population surveys. Situational couple violence is more common than battering, possibly as much as three to four times more (Derrington et al., 2010), and is the most common form of IPV (Johnson, 2009; Kelly & Johnson, 2008). According to Straus and Gelles (1986, as cited in Olson, 2002), situational couple violence occurs in about one-half of US couples. Typically, this form of violence is more likely to be gender-symmetrical in heterosexual relationships (Johnson, 2006; Kelly & Johnson, 2008) and is more likely to be mutual between partners (Johnson & Ferraro, 2000). However, even in situational couple violence, males are more likely to be violent more frequently, and women are more likely to be injured seriously (Johnson & Ferraro, 2000).

Situational couple violence can be severe (Derrington et al., 2010; Johnson & Leone, 2005) and can lead to injuries and even death (Derrington et al., 2010). However, this form of IPV is usually less severe than intimate terrorism (Johnson & Ferraro, 2000; Kelly & Johnson, 2008) and appears to be less likely to escalate (Johnson, 2006; Johnson & Ferraro, 2000). In terms of relationship outcomes, situational couple violence is less likely to result in lower marital satisfaction or relationship termination (Johnson, 2009) and more likely to stop after the couple ends their relationship (Kelly & Johnson, 2008). Couples demonstrating this form of violence are thought to be more amenable to cognitive-behavioral approaches and interventions targeting conflict and anger management, impulse control, problem-solving, and strengthening relationship skills (Johnson, 2009; Johnson & Leone, 2005; Kelly & Johnson, 2008). However, because even situational couple violence can be quite severe, therapists are encouraged to proceed cautiously and assume that any reported experiences of IPV are battering until it is clear that they are not (Derrington et al., 2010).

Intimate Terrorism/Battering

Intimate terrorism is characterized by generalized power and control dynamics (Johnson, 2006, 2009; Johnson & Ferraro, 2000; Johnson & Leone, 2005). Although we refer to intimate terrorism primarily as battering throughout the rest of this book, we will use the term *intimate terrorism* in this section to reflect Johnson's terminology. This form of violence also may be referred to as *coercive controlling violence* in court-based settings because the term *intimate terrorism* may be less applicable in those settings (Kelly & Johnson, 2008). Previously, Johnson also referred to intimate terrorism as *patriarchal terrorism*, but he changed this term because he came to consider that not all intimate terrorism was rooted in patriarchal values (Johnson, 2006).

Intimate terrorism reflects the use of violent behaviors within a pattern of generally controlling behaviors (Johnson, 2006; Johnson & Ferraro, 2000; Johnson & Leone, 2005; Kelly & Johnson, 2008). Johnson (2006; Johnson & Leone, 2005; Kelly & Johnson, 2008) suggests that this pattern of controlling behaviors is reflected in the widely used "Power and Control Wheel," which was developed within the Domestic Abuse Intervention Programs, commonly referred to as "The Duluth Model" (see http://www.theduluthmodel.org/, and this model will be discussed in greater detail in Chapter 4). The Power and Control Wheel situates the physical and sexual violence within eight "spokes" of emotionally and psychologically controlling power and control dynamics, including economic abuse, threats and intimidation, social isolation, minimization of the abuse, and invoking male privilege. Long-term, pervasive, and generalized power and control dynamics are the defining factors of intimate terrorism (Johnson, 2009).

Intimate terrorism is more likely to be identified in studies using clinical samples (Kelly & Johnson, 2008) as well as within studies using law enforcement and arrest charge databases (Graves, Hunt, Sumner, Varner, Flueggee, & Casterline, under review). Within heterosexual relationships, it is primarily perpetrated by males (Johnson, 2006, 2009; Kelly & Johnson, 2008), although females could perpetrate this form of IPV (Kelly & Johnson, 2008; Migliaccio, 2002). Although intimate terrorism is thought to be less common than situational couple violence, it is much more likely to be severe (Johnson & Leone, 2005; Leone et al., 2007), increase in frequency (Johnson & Ferraro, 2000), escalate to more severe levels of violence over time (Johnson, 2006; Johnson & Ferraro, 2000; Leone et al., 2007), result in injury (Johnson, 2009; Johnson & Ferraro, 2000; Johnson & Leone, 2005), and result in fear, anxiety, and mental health symptoms (e.g., PTSD) for the victim (Johnson & Leone, 2005; Kelly & Johnson, 2008; Leone et al., 2007), as well as a sense of entrapment (Leone et al., 2007). However, intimate terrorism may not necessarily involve frequent or severe violence if the emotional control is very strong (Johnson, 2009; Johnson & Leone, 2005). Compared with situational violence, perpetrators of intimate terrorism are likely less responsive to interventions (Johnson, 2009), although in treatment they may be best suited to feminist-informed intervention approaches (Kelly & Johnson, 2008). With this form of violence, conjoint couple counseling likely poses an increased risk (Johnson, 2009; Johnson & Leone, 2005; Kelly & Johnson, 2008). In terms of relationship outcomes, intimate terrorism victims are more likely to leave their relationships and seek help (Johnson & Leone, 2005).

The study of intimate terrorism/battering has a much more extensive history than that of situational couple violence, so more is known about common dynamics experienced within this form of violence. Early warning signs of a potential batterer may include quick courtships, extreme charm, jealousy, early attempts to control and isolate (which may be misinterpreted as signs of love), mistreatment of others, blaming others, and abusing substances (Short et al., 2000). Battering is widely thought to follow a three-phase cycle of violence in which tension builds gradually (i.e., the tension-building phase), then a period of severe violence occurs (i.e., the explosion phase), followed by a period of attempted reconciliation that often includes efforts to charm the partner and expressions of remorse for the violence (i.e., the "honeymoon" phase), with the cycle repeating until violence is firmly entrenched in the relationship (Walker, 1984). In the tension-building and honeymoon phases, either no violence or low-level violence may be present. Thus, violence may be episodic, although the frequency of these episodes can vary widely and other abusive dynamics (e.g., emotional abuse) may be more consistent (Jacobson & Gottman, 1998).

For example, physical violence may not be present for extended periods of time because emotional abuse may be all that a perpetrator needs to control his or her partner during those times (Jacobson & Gottman, 1998).

As new technologies emerge, therapists must remain vigilant in understanding how they can potentially be used by perpetrators as methods of controlling victims (Finn & Banach, 2000; Southworth et al., 2007). For example, perpetrators may send threats via e-mails or track victims' behaviors on-line as further extensions of in-person controlling behaviors (Finn & Banach, 2000). Other technologies, such as GPS devices and cell phones, can be used by perpetrators to harass and stalk their victims, which is referred to as *cyberstalking* (Southworth et al., 2007).

Before exploring battering in greater depth by examining experiences of perpetrators and victims, we provide an additional context about the other forms of IPV identified by Johnson.

Violent Resistance

Johnson (2006, 2009; Johnson & Ferraro, 2000) refers to *violent resistance* as the use of violent behaviors to protect oneself when being victimized by a controlling perpetrator. Violent resistance involves violence that is not done to exert control over one's partner, but rather in response to a partner who is violent toward them (Johnson, 2006, 2009; Kelly & Johnson, 2008). Indeed, many individuals who are being abused do not respond passively but resist actively the violence through physical force (Downs, Rindels, & Atkinson, 2007; Johnson, 2009). This is often referred to as fighting back or self-defense (Johnson, 2009), but the term *violent resistance* is used instead of self-defense due to possible complications from the legal definitions of self-defense (Johnson & Ferraro, 2000; Kelly & Johnson, 2008). Therapists who fail to assess context and intention could mistakenly label self-defensive behaviors as abuse perpetration.

Mutual Violent Control

The term *mutual violent control* describes a relationship in which both partners perpetrate intimate terrorism (Johnson, 2006; Johnson & Ferraro, 2000). Here, both partners vie for control of the other (Johnson & Ferraro, 2000). Mutual violent control is typically gender-symmetrical in heterosexual relationships (Johnson, 2006), but it also is very rare (Johnson & Ferraro, 2000).

Separation-Instigated Violence

Johnson has written the least extensively about *separation-instigated violence,* and this form of violence occurs within the context of a relationship termination (Kelly & Johnson, 2008). Separation-instigated violence typically occurs in couples who have not demonstrated prior violence (Kelly & Johnson, 2008), but rather the violence is set off by the stress of the separation and/or feeling humiliated by the separation (Kelly & Johnson, 2008). The partner who has been left is more likely the perpetrator (Kelly & Johnson, 2008), and violence may occur only one or two times at the initial outset of the separation (Kelly & Johnson, 2008). Violence severity can range from minor to severe (Kelly & Johnson, 2008), and the perpetrator may experience feeling out of control and is acting in an atypical manner (Kelly & Johnson, 2008).

Understanding Battering Perpetrators

Batterer Typologies. Johnson (2009) proposes that intimate terrorism can be perpetrated by different types of batterers. The existing research demonstrates that battering perpetrators may be differentiated based on the extent to which they differ on key characteristics. To provide additional context for treatment considerations when working with perpetrators, we begin this section with an in-depth discussion of the two most extensively-studied batterer typologies.

"Cobras" versus "Pit Bulls" (Gottman et al., 1995; Jacobson & Gottman, 1998). In 1995, Gottman and colleagues distinguished between two types of male battering perpetrators based on heart rate reactivity during marital conflict, and expanded their findings in a popular book, When Men Batter Women (Jacobson & Gottman, 1998). The differences found between the two types were intriguing. Among one group of perpetrators, labeled Cobras or Type 1 batterers, the men's heart rates decreased while engaged in conflict with their wives. The other group, labeled Pit Bulls or Type 2 batterers, demonstrated a more expected pattern of increased heart rate during conflict. In other words, the Cobras appeared to experience physiological calming in what would ordinarily be thought to be an experience that would lead to physiological arousal. Although these researchers did not find differences between Cobras and Pit Bulls in the severity of physical violence in their marriages, the two groups differed in other significant ways. Compared with Pit Bulls, Cobras demonstrated (a) more emotional aggression, (b) higher levels of anger and sadness among their wives, (c) more generalized violence perpetration outside of the marital relationship, (d) greater childhood experiences of witnessing IPV, (e) more characteristics of antisocial personality disorder and aggressive-sadistic personality disorder, and (f) more substance dependence. The Cobras, however, demonstrated higher levels of dependent personality disorder. Interestingly, at a two-year follow-up assessment, the Cobras were significantly more likely to be divorced. Gottman et al. (1995) caution that methodological considerations must be made in understanding the findings of their research (e.g., the way the sample was recruited and potential relationship dynamics that may contribute to victims' willingness to participate in research). However, their results indicate that it may one day be possible to differentiate battering perpetrators based on physiological indicators.

Gottman et al. (1995) discussed the need for further replication of their findings before they could be meaningfully applied to clinical practice. To date, two groups of researchers (Babcock et al., 2004; Meehan et al., 2001) conducted replication studies of Gottman et al.'s (1995) work, and neither found support for the original findings. These findings led Babcock et al. (2004) to state, "In light of two failed replications of the typology based on batterers' HR reactivity, it does not appear that this widely publicized typology withstands scientific scrutiny" (p. 400).

Generally Violent/Antisocial, Borderline/Dysphoric, and Family-only (Holtzworth-Munroe & Stuart, 1994). Holtzworth-Munroe and Stuart (1994) synthesized existing research on battering perpetrator typologies and conceptualized three subtypes based on three dimensions: (a) violence severity, (b) violence generality, and (c) the presence of psychopathology and/or personality disorders. Furthermore, they proposed a developmental model that encompassed two sets of developmental risk factors: distal (e.g., family-of-origin experiences and peer relationships) and proximal (e.g., attachment and social skills). Based on these factors, these researchers proposed that there are three major subtypes of battering perpetrators: Family Only (FO), Dysphoric/Borderline (DB), and Generally Violent/Antisocial (GVA). FO perpetrators are the least severe, with their violence limited primarily to family members, and having minimal psychopathology or personality disorders. FO perpetrators were estimated to comprise approximately 50% of the population of perpetrators. In applying the distal and proximal risk factors to this type, they were hypothesized to have the lowest levels of family-of-origin violence, be generally well-functioning and able to empathize, but demonstrate impaired communication skills with their spouses, such that escalating conflicts may lead to violence.

DB perpetrators demonstrate moderate severity, including sexual and psychological abuse, with most violence occurring in their families (although some violence outside of the family may be present), and high levels of psychological distress. Comprising about 25% of the population, DB perpetrators may have Borderline Personality Disorder, problems with substance abuse, and dependence on their partners and fear of losing them (Holtzworth-Munroe, 2000).

GVA perpetrators are the most violent, show the highest levels of aggression outside of their families, and have the most extensive criminal histories and substance abuse patterns. Comprising 25% of the batterer population, they also may demonstrate psychopathy and/or Antisocial Personality Disorder (Holtzworth-Munroe, 2000).

In general, research conducted since the original Holtzworth-Munroe and Stuart (1994) article supports their conceptualization (Holtzworth-Munroe, Meehan, Herron, Rehman, & Stuart, 2000, 2003; Waltz, Babcock, Jacobson, & Gottman, 2000). Despite these advances, a major question remains unanswered as to whether differences represent distinct groups, or whether they simply represent stages of a developmental course of IPV perpetration (Holtzworth-Munroe, 2000). It remains impossible to predict which perpetrators will, and which will not, escalate to higher levels of violence (Holtzworth-Munroe, 2000). However, research suggests that individuals who demonstrate relatively lower levels of violence, but have risk factors typically associated with GVA perpetrators may be more likely to demonstrate escalations, and those who demonstrate lower levels of violence but are more similar in terms of risk factors to FO perpetrators may be less likely to escalate in their use of violence (Holtzworth-Munroe et al., 2003).

Integration Models. There is no clear agreement as to whether and how to use battering perpetrator typologies to guide treatment (Carlson & Jones, 2010). In light of the various, and at times inconsistent, findings regarding typologies of battering perpetrators (Chiffriller, Hennessy, & Zappone, 2006), Gottman (2001) suggested that research ultimately may demonstrate that the most clinically-useful approach to differentiating batterers will combine some aspects of Gottman et al.'s (1995) and Holtzworth-Munroe and Stuart's (1994) classification approaches.

The Continuum of Conflict and Control model (Carlson & Jones, 2010) offers a useful framework for therapists interested in integrating the various battering perpetrator typologies that exist currently in the research literature. It suggests that the most relevant characteristics of the perpetrator include the presence of *substance abuse, anger, and psychopathology.* Generally, therapists also must aim to understand the perpetration of violence within the function it serves—from responding to conflict to achieving or maintaining control over one's partner. Although future research must be done to develop more clear guidelines for using this model in clinical practice, it impresses upon therapists the importance of considering the various background characteristics of the perpetrator and the violence when working with this population.

Common Characteristics among Battering Perpetrators and Victims

Although certain characteristics may be common among battering perpetrators and victims, they are heterogeneous populations (Holtzworth-Munroe, 2000; Holtzworth-Munroe et al., 1997; Holtzworth-Munroe & Stuart, 1994). Although individual clients will vary in the extent to which they display these characteristics, familiarity with them will help therapists be more comprehensive in their clinical assessment and treatment planning.

Understanding Battering Perpetrators

The mean age of batterers in many published studies is about 35 years old (McCloskey, Sitaker, Grigsby, & Malloy, 2003). Research has produced mixed findings regarding the employment statuses of battering perpetrators, although some evidence suggests that perpetrators demonstrate an imbalance of resources (e.g., income) in comparison to their wives (Holtzworth-Munroe et al., 1997). Mixed findings also exist related to whether certain ethnic minority backgrounds are overrepresented in battering perpetrator populations (McCloskey et al., 2003). Based on a survey of 150 representatives of batterer intervention programs (BIPs) from 35 states, Dalton (2007) estimated that 58% of BIP clients in the United States are Caucasian, 21% African American, 17% Latino American, 2% Asian American, 1% Native American, and 1% represent other ethnic backgrounds.

Battering perpetrators may demonstrate aggressiveness and impulsivity (Holtzworth-Munroe et al., 1997). One reflection of this is that a high proportion—perhaps up to 75%—of battering perpetrators had a previously criminal offense (McCloskey et al., 2003). Perpetrators may use substance use or abuse as an excuse for violence (Field, Caetano, & Nelson, 2004; Jacobson & Gottman, 1998), and substance use and abuse are common among battering perpetrators (Holtzworth-Munroe et al., 1997; McCloskey et al., 2003; Rynerson & Fishel, 1993; Tilley & Brackley, 2005). In addition, whether a perpetrator accepts responsibility for using violence can influence treatment effectiveness (Holtzworth-Munroe et al., 1997; Wallach & Sela, 2008). Perpetrators may use a variety of cognitive attributions to avoid accepting responsibility, especially minimizing and justifying their use of violence (Tilley & Brackley, 2005). For example, they may acknowledge that they are violent but claim that it is justified or excusable (e.g., due to stress), they may deny that the violence occurred, or they may claim that their violent behaviors are culturally acceptable (Wallach & Sela, 2008). Finally, the intergenerational transmission of violence may be applied to understanding the background of battering perpetrators. Holtzworth-Munroe et al. (1997) suggest that experiencing violence in one's family-of-origin, and especially witnessing parental IPV, is a risk factor for becoming a battering perpetrator.

Understanding Battering Victims

As will be discussed in-depth in Chapter 4, working with battering victims can be very challenging for therapists, who may feel pulled to rescue their clients from their abusive situations, and who also may grapple with understanding victims' reasons for remaining in their abusive relationships. Experiencing battering victimization can be understood as a traumatic experience. Within the *DSM-IV-TR* (American Psychiatric Association, 2000), a trauma is defined as an event that involves "actual or threatened death or serious injury, or a threat to the physical integrity of self or others" and a response involving "intense fear, helplessness, or horror" (p. 467). Two defining features of the trauma of battering victimization are that it occurs within the context of a close, intimate relationship and that it is typically a chronic pattern. Battering-related trauma may have unique consequences because the victimization occurs at the hands of a partner who should love and care for the victim. Some evidence suggests that victims may become traumatically bonded to their abusers (D'Ardenne & Balakrishna, 2001), with research confirming high rates of mental health disorders among victims (Helfrich et al., 2008). However, "It is imperative that IPV not be equated with mental illness but rather considered as a risk factor that, when identified, serves to initiate a series of informed responses and further exploration of each individual woman's presentation and service needs" (Helfrich et al., 2008, p. 450). Further complicating the connections between IPV victimization and mental health consequences is the fact that although mental health disorders may be considered a consequence of IPV victimization, there is also evidence that mental health disorders may precede experiences of IPV and can therefore be considered risk factors for victimization (Berg, 2004; Ehrensaft, 2008).

Physical Health Symptoms. According to the US CDC (2003), the cost of medical and mental health services related directly to IPV in the US exceeds $4 billion every year. IPV victimization can have a very negative impact on victims' health (Gerlock, 1999). Plichta (2004) reviewed research published between 1993 and 2003 that examined the impact of IPV on women's health. The primary direct health outcomes studied during this time included mortality, injuries, traumatic brain injury, strangulation, disability, chronic pain, and pregnancy complications. Additional indirect health outcomes include impaired general physical health, sexually transmitted diseases, sexual dysfunction, and unhealthy behaviors. Plichta also examined research on the impact of IPV on women's use of healthcare. Abused women may be more likely to have needs for healthcare for which they do not seek medical attention. Other physical health-related consequences of IPV victimization may include weight gain (Sato-DiLorenzo & Sharps, 2007) and chronic pain (Kendall-Tackett, Marshall, & Ness, 2003).

Another health-related concern is abuse during pregnancy. Pregnant women are in frequent contact with their doctors during pregnancy (Escriba-Aguir, Ruiz-Perez, & Saurel-Cubizolles, 2007), and therefore this may be a time when female victims are likely to come to the attention of healthcare providers. In a survey of 200 women who had recently given birth, 10% of the women reported that they experienced abuse during pregnancy, with nearly 70% reporting their significant others as the perpetrators (Jeanjot, Barlow, & Rozenberg, 2008). IPV during pregnancy can lead to negative consequences for both the woman and the unborn child (Escriba-Aguir et al., 2007; Kaye,

Mirembe, Bantebya, Johansoon, & Ekstrom, 2006; Martin, Macy, Sullivan, & Magee, 2007; Melhado, 2005).

Career Issues. Victims' work performance may be impacted adversely by abuse-related symptoms (Helfrich et al., 2008), costing the US nearly $1 billion each year in lost work productivity (CDC, 2003). Battering victims may be more likely than situational couple violence victims to miss work as a consequence of their victimization (Johnson & Leone, 2005). Nearly 45% of the battered women in one study (Helfrich et al., 2008) reported that their symptoms interfered with their ability to work, and approximately 25% indicated that they were unable to work entirely. IPV victimization can impact victims' careers in several ways, including becoming uncomfortable in groups, fearing judgment from others, being afraid to leave their children in the care of others, and experiencing negative effects from trauma (e.g., exhaustion and guilt) (Chronister, Linville, & Kaag, 2008).

The Social Context Surrounding IPV

IPV does not occur in a vacuum. As Johan Galtun, a peace scholar cited in Kaethe Weingarten's (2003) book, *Common Shock,* said, "If one husband beats his wife, that is obviously an instance of personal violence ... but when one million husbands keep one million wives in ignorance there is structural violence" (p. 5). Although recognition of IPV has grown within the general population over the past several decades, common societal myths continue to surround and perpetuate IPV (Peters, 2008). There also is growing recognition that demographic characteristics such as gender, sexual orientation, and ethnicity can shape IPV victimization experiences (Anderson, 2010). In this section, we consider both how larger social forces—such as intergenerational familial patterns and sociodemographic patterns—are related to the development of IPV, as well as the broader social systems that are in place to respond to IPV.

Intergenerational Influences on IPV

Intergenerational patterns of family violence are well-documented in existing research (e.g., Kernsmith, 2005; Kwong, Bartholomew, Henderson, & Trinke, 2003; O'Leary, Malone, & Tyree, 1994; Whiting, Simmons, Havens, Smith, & Oka, 2009). Although there have been some mixed findings as to whether experiencing family-of-origin violence is a risk factor for IPV victimization (Anderson, 2010; Holtzworth-Munroe et al., 1997), it is widely thought that a family history of violence (including childhood abuse and witnessing interparental IPV) is a risk factor for experiencing violence as an adult (Berg, 2004; Coker et al. 2002; Coker et al., 2000; Ehrensaft, 2008; Tjaden & Thoennes, 2000).

Ehrensaft (2008) put forth a longitudinal, research-based theory on the development of IPV. According to this theory, experiences at all stages of life (including early childhood and adolescence) can contribute to the development of IPV. In particular, Ehrensaft suggests that early exposure to abusive family dynamics can lead children into a developmental course characterized by impaired relationship functioning across peer relationships, including eventual intimate relationships. Problematic peer associations can interplay with individuals' impaired relationship skills to contribute to increased risks of IPV. A major contribution of Ehrensaft's work is that it addresses the developmental nature of IPV. It appears that an intergenerational transmission of IPV may be a stronger pattern for battering than for situational violence (Anderson, 2010). Certainly, not all individuals who experience or witness childhood abuse go on to become perpetrators or victims, but these experiences can impact clients' current experiences with IPV. For example, past experiences with violence can normalize violence, and therefore violence may seem less significant or risky. As will be addressed further in Chapter 6, children who witness IPV may show aggressive and delinquency behaviors, emotional difficulties (e.g., anger, depression, anxiety, lower self-esteem), and impaired functioning (e.g., in school or social relationships) (Holtzworth-Munroe et al., 1997; Kelly & Johnson, 2008).

A new area of research is the manner in which battering perpetrators use children as a means of controlling their children (Beeble, Bybee, & Sullivan, 2007), with 88% of battered women reporting that their assailants had used children to control them. Of the assailants, 41% were the biological fathers of the victims' children, 22% were stepfathers, 20% were termed *father figures* (i.e., men who were not in an official father role but did play a major role in parenting), and 17% were not in any sort of father figure role. The tactics the assailants used included using their children to keep tabs on their whereabouts, attempting to turn the children against them, and coaxing children to convince the mothers to get back into relationships with the abusers. Perpetrators were especially likely to use children to control their victims when the women were ending the relationships and when there was court-ordered visitation for the fathers. Biological fathers appeared to be most likely to use the children in abuse tactics, which the researchers speculated may result from greater access to and closer relationships with the children. The authors suggest that women's decisions to remain in relationships with their abusers may be influenced by their abusers' use of children to control them.

Sociodemographic Patterns and IPV

Currently, IPV is better able to be predicted at a population level rather than an individual level (Begun, 1999). That is, research can demonstrate that certain groups of people are more likely to experience IPV, but these findings are not accurate at identifying which individuals are likely to become perpetrators and victims. Some characteristics that existing research suggests make it more likely that people will experience IPV include the following: (a) being younger (Berg, 2004; Holtzworth-Munroe et al., 1997); (b) being separated, divorced (Berg, 2004), or cohabitating (Holtzworth-Munroe et al., 1997); (c) abusing substances or having a partner who does so (Berg, 2004; Coker et al., 2002; Coker et al., 2000; (d) demonstrating poor communication patterns and lower marital satisfaction (Holtzworth-Munroe et al., 1997); (d) demonstrating aggressive and defensive personality characteristics (O'Leary et al., 1994); and (e) having a history of behavioral problems as an adolescent (Ehrensaft, 2008). Having a lower income level/socioeconomic status (including lower income and education levels) also can be considered a risk factor for experiencing IPV (Berg, 2004; Holtzworth-Munroe et al., 1997; Smith et al. 2002), but it is important to note that IPV occurs across all socioeconomic groups.

Individuals who experience IPV, especially battering, may be more likely to be socially isolated and lack integration into their communities. Victims may perceive that they have limited support available from friends and family members (McLeod, Hays, & Chang, 2010). Some may even view their family members and friends as being on the side of their abusers (McLeod et al., 2010). Indeed, friends and family members may blame victims for their roles in abusive relationships (West & Wandrei, 2002).

Understanding the IPV Response System

According to Busby (1996), "There are few problems in society that attract as many people to 'help out' as does family violence ... If the therapist acts in isolation, solely concerned with the process within the therapy room, it is likely that clients will be receiving inadequate care" (p. viii). Therapists are but one component of the larger systems in place to respond to IPV. We refer to the combined role of these components as the *IPV response system*, and this includes legal, healthcare, social service, victim advocacy, child protection, and other systems (e.g., workplaces, religious institutions, and schools) that play a role in identifying and addressing IPV. Four broad areas of the IPV response system include prevention programs, mental health and educational interventions, social services, and legal systems (O'Leary, 2001). Each of these should be drawn upon in meeting the needs of any given client (O'Leary, 2001), and multidisciplinary approaches are often needed to best support battering victims (Smith & Randall, 2007).

Therapists may need to step outside of traditional counseling roles into case management roles from time to time, in order to ensure that clients are connected with appropriate resources that can help them. Therapists should develop referral sheets with information about local and national resources and services relevant to IPV (Derrington et al., 2010), and it may be useful to include these with standard intake paperwork for therapy clients. Whenever possible, therapists should learn about their clients' involvement with other systems. When such involvements are identified, therapists should get client consent to communicate with representatives from as many of these other systems as is appropriate and possible. Therapists must become familiar with the people and organizations doing work related to IPV in their geographic areas. The availability of resources for services for victims can vary widely, especially between rural and urban areas (Eastman & Bunch, 2007). The remainder of this section addresses the major components of the IPV response system, including legal, healthcare, and social service systems, and the role of researchers who study IPV. Finally, integrated systems, often referred to as *coordinated community response systems,* are discussed.

Legal Systems. In considering therapy addressing IPV, we must not lose sight of the fact that many forms of IPV are, in fact, against the law and therefore may be subject to criminal proceedings. Legal definitions surrounding IPV vary from state to state (Derrington et al., 2010). As such, therapists must become familiar with the relevant legal statutes in their areas. A useful source for this information is the website WomensLaw.org (http://www.womenslaw.org/). Two aspects of the legal system that interface with IPV cases are police officers and the court system.

Police Officers. Police officers often are the first responders to incidents of IPV, although describing them as first responders does not necessarily mean that the incidents they respond to are the first ones experienced by the couple. Some police agencies involve mental health counselors as part of response teams sent on domestic violence calls. At other times, however, police officers may be the only professionals on site at the time and place of the incident. The response of police officers can have a profound impact on what happens next for the couple. Some communities have implemented mandatory arrest policies for domestic violence cases, which stipulate that police officers are required to make an arrest when it is evident that domestic violence occurred. In other cases, police officers may use discretion as to whether they will arrest a perpetrator. The level and type of details that police officers record in their reports of the IPV calls to which they respond can influence the likelihood of successful prosecution of those cases. Police officers may be asked to testify in court proceedings when perpetrators are prosecuted.

Another way that police officers may be involved in IPV cases is in serving orders of protection (i.e., restraining orders or protective orders). These orders are handled within state court systems and typically stipulate the types of protection that a person can be granted from another person, including restricting an alleged perpetrator from having contact with an alleged victim (WomensLaw.org, 2010). Other stipulations may include requiring the perpetrator to relinquish weapons, provide child support, and make temporary custody arrangements (National Network to End Domestic Violence, 2008). These orders usually are not in effect until the perpetrator has been served the document by a representative of the court system. Police officers also are called upon to enforce the terms of the protective order, such as by making an arrest if the perpetrator violates the terms (WomensLaw.org, 2010). Some states have different types and levels (e.g., temporary vs. permanent) of orders that may apply to domestic violence and that require different process to obtain. As such, it is imperative that therapists learn about the types of orders available in their jurisdictions, as well as the process for getting them so that they will be able to refer clients to the correct resources for doing so. Clearly, police officers must be familiar with IPV-related laws in order to enforce them. Although it is likely that all police officers will have a basic level of understanding of most domestic violence-related statutes, some may hold misperceptions related to nuances in laws, such as how they apply to same-sex couples. Police officers also may experience stress in responding to IPV situations because they require the police officers to play both a criminal justice (i.e., to the perpetrator) and social service (i.e., to the victim) role (Balenovich, Grossi, & Hughes, 2008).

The Court System. Once an arrest has been made, a decision must be made as to whether to prosecute the case, and this decision is typically made within the office of the district or state attorney. The general goals of prosecuting battering perpetrators include retribution, deterrence, rehabilitation, incapacitation, and retribution (Hare, 2006). Therapists who learn many of the intricacies of the laws surrounding IPV may become frustrated by limitations of the legal system's response to IPV. NVAWS data suggest that IPV is not very likely to be prosecuted (Tjaden & Thoennes, 2000). Depending on the jurisdiction, cases may be able to be prosecuted even if the victim chooses not to cooperate and/or testify in the case. Therapists should learn how cases are handled in their areas so that they can help their clients understand these processes. For example, it may be important for a client to know whether a case is being prosecuted as "The State vs. The Perpetrator" as opposed to "The Victim vs. The Perpetrator." However, because of the large amount of evidence needed, a lack of participation on the part of the victim may seriously impair the ability to successfully prosecute the perpetrator. If the case is prosecuted, the perpetrator most likely will have a defense attorney, which may be either a public defender or a private attorney. Because the defense attorney's role is to defend the perpetrator, this person may contribute to an adversarial process for the victim in that they are trying to discredit the victim's story. This can be a frustrating process for victims, even more so because juries may be less likely to convict IPV perpetrators if they believe that the victim did something to provoke the violence (Kern, Libkuman, & Temple, 2007).

Much controversy surrounds so-called *no-drop* policies, in which IPV victims are not allowed to drop charges once they are filed, with some viewing these policies as benefitting the judicial system more than victims (Hare, 2006). Victims may have many reasons that they oppose the prosecution of their perpetrators, including fear of their perpetrator, lack of faith in the judicial system, previous negative experiences with the judicial system, and emotional and financial dependence upon the perpetrator (Hare, 2006). On the other hand, victims may want to see their perpetrators prosecuted in order to convey punishment upon them (Hare, 2006). Many victims, however, do not believe that even a jail sentence would be an effective way to change their partners (Hare, 2006). In addition, victims may feel frustrated with the judicial system due to the slow pace and time demands that accompany prosecution (Hare, 2006).

IPV perpetrators appear to be treated differently within the criminal justice system. Compared to a group of other violent offenders, IPV perpetrators' probations were shorter (15 vs. 22 months), had more conditions on their probation (e.g., paying fines, being mandated to treatment, and to received specialized probation), were less likely to be serving community service, and required more close supervision and contact between the probation officers and the victims (Olson & Stalans, 2001). Domestic violence offenders were three times more likely than the other offenders to revictimize the same victim. Domestic violence offenders who abused substances were more likely than those who did not to violate their probation conditions.

Healthcare Systems. Due to physical health consequences of IPV, it is a salient issue for healthcare settings (Phelan, 2007), and therapists should be familiar with the healthcare settings in their area that are available to individuals who have experienced IPV-related physical health consequences. The question of whether and how physicians and healthcare professionals should screen patients for IPV has been debated (Phelan, 2007; Rhodes & Levinson, 2003). Although some evidence supports the use of universal IPV screening (Glowa, Frasier, & Newton, 2002; Phelan, 2007), many physicians feel uncomfortable asking patients about their experiences, although there is some evidence that training physicians in how to assess for IPV can increase their levels of comfort (Glowa et al., 2002). Most physicians appear to screen for IPV only after the patient self-reports victimization, although waiting for such disclosures means that cases that are not disclosed may be missed (Phelan, 2007). Additional questions regarding IPV screening in healthcare settings include the type of screening that is most appropriate and what responsibility the healthcare provider has after IPV is detected (Phelan, 2007).

Social Service Systems. Formal efforts to address IPV at a societal level generally can be credited to the battered women's movement, which grew out of feminist activism to establish criminal justice responses, shelters and services, and public awareness of the needs of victims of domestic violence (Derrington et al., 2010). Advocates in the battered women's movement put forth feminist-based theories of understanding IPV that focused primarily on patriarchy as a cause of IPV (Ehrensaft, 2008). Typically, domestic violence service agencies are funded through the Violence Against Women Act (VAWA) (Derrington et al., 2010).

The types of services often included in domestic violence agencies include crisis intervention (including hotlines), shelters, legal aid, counseling and support groups, batterer intervention programs, economic self-sufficiency programs, and victim advocacy (Derrington et al., 2010; Gorde, Helfrich, & Finlayson, 2004). Many domestic violence service organizations also have an Internet presence to provide education about abusive relationships and inform the community about their services (Finn, 2000). Safety planning is a standard intervention for battering victims in social service agencies (Derrington et al., 2010), and this process will be discussed in-depth in Chapter 4. Staff members in domestic violence agencies may vary in their levels of education and training (Murray & Welch, 2010). Within a given community, these services may be found in a single agency or spread across multiple agencies. Therefore, therapists should be familiar with the range and source of services in their geographic areas. It is important to add that many agencies are set up primarily to serve female victims and may not be equipped to address the unique needs of male victims (Tsui et al., 2010).

Shelters are an important resource for battering victims. Battered women's shelters began to emerge in the 1960s and 1970s as a result of the battered women's movement (O'Leary, 2001). Most shelters are not run by mental health professionals (O'Leary, 2001). Shelters are often located in discreet, undisclosed locations. However, in some communities, the location of the shelter is known widely in the community. Battered women's shelters typically provide short-term support to women, although the length of time women may stay can vary. Shelters may need to move victims from one shelter to another if remaining there would pose a dangerous situation (Shavers, Levendosky, Dubay, Basu, & Jenei, 2005). Staff of battered women's shelters may be hesitant to address parenting issues for fear of appearing to blame behavioral problems on anything other than the IPV (Ehrensaft, 2008). The extent to which shelters are able and equipped to assist male victims and lesbian victims varies from community to community.

Another IPV-related social service is batterer intervention programs (BIPs), which are discussed in Chapter 4. BIPs emerged somewhat later than shelters (O'Leary, 2001). In brief, these programs aim to intervene with IPV perpetrators in order to prevent future perpetration. Many participants are mandated by the court system to participate. These programs often face restrictions and guidelines, typically referred to as standards, on their practice in order for them to be eligible to serve court-mandated clients. For court-mandated clients, facilitators typically are required to report on progress to the courts, and these reports can influence future consequences that the perpetrator may face through the legal system. As is discussed in Chapter 4, these programs may encounter high rates of dropouts and recidivism (O'Learly, 2001).

Victim Advocates. An important group of professionals who work in the area of IPV are victim advocates, who may be employed through domestic violence service agencies, shelters, or the court system (Bell & Goodman, 2001). Victim advocates work to support victims of abuse and help to ensure that their needs are met. Services they provide may include crisis intervention, case management, providing information about court processes, connecting victims with resources in the community, accompanying victims to court proceedings, and providing assistance in completing paperwork.

Advocacy Groups and National Organizations. Beyond victim advocates that work one-on-one with clients, a number of IPV-related advocacy groups exist at local, state, regional, national, and international levels. These may be grassroots organizations, or they may have formal organizational operations, and may offer training and education, local awareness and fundraising, print and media resources, and public policy work. Some well-known groups include the National Coalition Against Domestic Violence (NCADV; http://www.ncadv.org/), the Family Violence Prevention Fund (FVPF; http://www.endabuse.org/), and the National Network to End Domestic Violence (NNEDV; http://www.nnedv.org/). Additional resources for therapists to know are: (1) the National Domestic Violence Hotline (NDVH; http://www.thehotline.org/; 1.800.799.SAFE (7233) or 1.800.787.3224 (TTY); (2) the US Department of Justice's Office on Violence Against Women (http://www.ovw.usdoj.gov/); and (3) the US CDC and Prevention (http://www.cdc.gov/ViolencePrevention/intimatepartnerviolence/index.html).

Child Protective Services. Chapters 6–8 will delve further into overlaps between IPV and child maltreatment, as well as the structure and goals of Child Protective Services (CPS) systems. Here, it is important to note that victims who are parents may also be involved CPS agencies, whether resulting from the children witnessing their parental IPV or from direct experiences of children being maltreated concurrent with parental IPV. Although the links between adult IPV and child maltreatment have been well-documented (e.g., Fleck-Henderson, 2000), service delivery between domestic violence and CPS agencies often is poorly coordinated (Fleck-Henderson, 2000; Friend, 2000; Jones & Gross, 2000; Mills et al., 2000). Therefore, when such involvement is present, therapists should be alert to any concerns that clients may have about how both issues are being address by all involved parties.

Other Relevant Systems. A variety of other types of organizations that are not related specifically to IPV may address this issue, either directly or indirectly. These organizations include schools, workplaces, and other ancillary organizations. School systems have an interest in addressing IPV due to growing recognition of the negative impact that witnessing IPV can have on children (Keller, 1994). In particular, teachers may observe children who have witnessed IPV acting aggressively in the classroom (Keller, 1994). Some schools have helped teachers develop safety plans to address violence within the classroom and in the homes of the children they teach (Keller, 1994).

Due to the growing recognition that experiences with IPV can carry into the workplace, employers also have begun to develop workplace programs designed to prevent and respond to IPV among employees (Gurchiek, 2005; NDVH, n.d.). Employers have an interest in these types of programs not only because of the support they provide to employees, but also because experiences with IPV can impact employee performance and productivity (Gurchiek, 2005). IPV may spill over to work in a variety of ways, including an abuser coming to a victim's workplace, increased healthcare costs due to abuse-related injuries, and higher levels of absenteeism for victims (NDVH, n.d.). Some provisions of workplace IPV programs may include steps to increase employees' safety (e.g., escorting a victim to and from the building to their vehicles) and developing communication channels so that employees and employers can be informed about potential threats (Gurchiek, 2005).

A variety of ancillary services may be needed by individuals who have experienced IPV. First, individuals may need help in locating housing (Gorde et al., 2004), and this may be especially relevant for women without children who do not qualify for support based on the needs of children. Second, these clients may benefit from employment services and job training (Gorde et al., 2004). Third, parents may need help in accessing child care (Johnson & Zlotnick, 2009). Fourth, clients may need to identify sources of transportation (McLeod et al., 2010). Fifth, for both victims and perpetrators, substance abuse treatment may be essential (Humphreys, Regan, River, & Thiara, 2005; the links between IPV and substance abuse are explored further in Chapter 11). Victims may need help navigating the various agency policies and resources related to these services (McLeod et al., 2010).

Coordinated Community Response Systems. With all of these various social systems in place to address IPV, it should be no surprise that there have been increased calls for coordinating the services that are provided across them (Koss & White, 2008; McCollum, 2008; O'Leary, 2001). Integrated services that involve coordination between the criminal justice system, healthcare and mental health professionals, social service agencies, and other related organizations are often referred to as *coordinated community response systems* (CCRs). CCRs often are viewed as a best practice in how communities can respond to IPV (McCollum, 2008). However, collaborative efforts among professionals to address IPV can face many challenges, including time demands, training differences, limited funding to support collaborations, practical demands, and different funding streams (Campbell, Dienemann, Kub, Wurmser, & Loy, 1999; Malik, Ward, & Janczewski, 2008). Other challenges may include ensuring that staff members in different organizations have appropriate knowledge about the services and roles of other organizations, determining how best to meet the needs of families who have experienced multiple forms of victimization (e.g., IPV and child maltreatment), integrating different organizational philosophies (Malik et al., 2008), and determining which services and protections are most suitable for particular perpetrators, victims, and involved children (McCollum, 2008). In light of these challenges, the effectiveness of CCRs varies across communities.

Summary

This chapter demonstrated the complexity of the topic of IPV. It is clear that IPV is a common phenomenon within both the general population and clients in clinical settings. However, recent research on the distinctions among different types of IPV, perpetrators, and victimization underscores the importance of therapists attending to individual variations in their clients' experiences. In some regards, what matters more to therapists than the prevalence of IPV within the general population is whether and how any particular client with whom they work has experienced IPV, as well as how this relates to their concerns and goals for therapy. The following chapters in this section on IPV will further assist therapists in assessing clients' experiences with IPV and their related characteristics and in determining how best to move forward with conducting therapy with these clients.

3

GUIDELINES FOR THE ASSESSMENT OF INTIMATE PARTNER VIOLENCE

A couple presents for marital therapy, and they report that their primary goal for treatment is to stop the violence that has become more frequent in their relationship. The therapist must make a decision: Is it safe for this couple to be treated conjointly?

A male client tells his counselor during the first session, "My girlfriend said she'd leave me if I don't go to counseling to learn to control my temper. She said this after I hit her a couple weeks ago when I'd been drinking." Is it best for this client to be treated individually, or should he be referred to a batterer intervention group? Should he even be considered a "batterer"?

A single mother tells her counselor, "I am thinking about going back to my husband. Sure, he hit me once in a while, but it's too hard raising my three kids on my own without him." What safety considerations must this counselor address through the treatment process?

When working with clients impacted by IPV, therapists face many major decisions, often very early in treatment, that impact the course of treatment. It is difficult, if not impossible, for therapists to make informed decisions as to the appropriateness of treatment strategies without understanding their clients and the role that violence plays in their relationships. However, many therapists are not aware when their clients are experiencing or have experienced IPV, in part because they fail to assess for it (Aldarondo & Straus, 1994). Therefore, the first essential step for therapists to take is to conduct a thorough, multidimensional assessment. This chapter presents clinical guidelines and strategies for assessing the nature of the violence, the perpetrator, the victim/survivor, other relationship variables, and other relevant contextual characteristics.

General IPV Assessment Recommendations

We begin with 13 general recommendations to guide the assessment process.

1. *Safety considerations always should be the ultimate concern.* Safety should be a direct and indirect consideration in planning to do the assessment, and then subsequent treatment approaches (Heyman & Schlee, 2003; Schacht, Dimidjian, George, & Berns, 2009; Stith, Rosen, & McCollum, 2003). Both physical and emotional safety should be considered. For example, regarding physical safety, therapists should consider how to gather assessment data without incurring increased safety risks for victims. One strategy, assessing partners separately in conjoint treatment, is discussed below. The issue of emotional safety relates to the possibility that recounting information about traumatic victimization may contribute to emotional distress, and potentially exacerbate trauma symptoms (Lindhorst, Nurius, & Macy, 2005). The assessment should be paced to balance the need to gather information with clients' needs for emotional safety. The informed consent process can describe the pacing of disclosing information about experiences with violence. An additional recommendation is that victims' safety should be assessed during every follow-up treatment session to identify changing risks over time. This can occur during a brief "check in" and "check out" process in which safety is assessed at the beginning and end of each session.
2. *The assessment of clients impacted by IPV should include both formal and informal assessment strategies* (Aldarondo, 1998; Simpson, Doss, Wheeler, & Christensen, 2 ormal strategies involve the use of standardized assessment instruments (Aldarondo & Straus, 1994; Schacht et al., 2009; Thompson, Basile, Hertz, & Sitterle, 2006), and therapists can choose from several available instruments. Therefore, therapists must understand the advantages and disadvantages of available instruments. Several instruments relevant to IPV assessment are reviewed in the Directory of Selected Instruments in this chapter's Appendix. Formal assessment strategies can be supplemented with such informal strategies as client interviews and behavioral observations, which can add depth to information gathered through standardized instruments and offer clients an opportunity to provide information that was not directly addressed. Therapists' informal observations of clients' nonverbal behaviors and mini-mental status exams also can be considered a part of the assessment process. For example, when conducting a conjoint assessment of a couple, a therapist may notice that one partner appears nervous and does not speak without asking permission from her partner. In combination with other information, nonverbal behaviors provide insights into power imbalances that may underlie abusive dynamics.

3. *Therapists should consider cultural influences throughout the assessment process.* Astute readers likely read the above description of the couple in which one partner asks permission from her partner to speak and noted that this dynamic may reflect the clients' cultural norms rather than an abusive dynamic. Indeed, therapists should avoid pathologizing behaviors merely because they are different from one's own cultural, religious, or ethnic background (Aklin & Turner, 2006). It is not possible to determine, based solely on the information presented, whether the client's behavior reflects abuse, cultural influences, or another dynamic altogether. Therapists must apply cultural sensitivity when gathering and interpreting assessment data (Lo & Fung, 2003). Therefore, therapists should discuss clients' relevant cultural influences on the information gathered through the assessment. Also, therapists should confirm that selected standardized assessments have been validated and normed for the client's cultural group.
4. *When working with couples, it is wise to assess each partner individually for reports of violence and abuse* (Almeida & Durkin, 1999; Bograd & Mederos, 1999; Heyman & Schlee, 2003; LaTaillade, Epstein, & Werlinich, 2006; Schacht et al., 2009; Stith et al., 2003). An IPV victim may be unwilling to report victimization with the perpetrator present. Even if a victim reports violence with a perpetrator present, the reported violence may be minimized or dismissed, likely due to fear of retaliation. In addition, partners may differ in the extent to which they report prior abuse experiences (Moffitt et al., 1997). An individual assessment with each partner, therefore, provides each client with a more confidential forum than a conjoint interview for discussing potential abuse. Because of the high incidence of violence in couples who present for counseling, along with the potential risks if violence is present, a common recommendation is that universal screening for IPV (as well as other types of traumatic experiences) be conducted with all couples who present for conjoint therapy (LaTaillade et al., 2006; O'Leary, 2001; Schacht et al., 2009; Simpson et al., 2007; Stith et al., 2003).

   Bograd and Mederos (1999) presented guidelines and procedures for universal IPV screening among couples seeking counseling. Bograd and Mederos urged therapists to assume that all clients are at risk for IPV until it is clear that it is not present. According to Bograd and Mederos, "It is advisable to maintain an attitude of friendly and supportive skepticism that constantly questions the depth of the batterer's resolve and realism" (p. 296). In Bograd and Mederos's assessment protocol, the therapist begins with a conjoint meeting in which general relationship dynamics are assessed, but there is a very limited focus on IPV at this point. Next, individual meetings occur with both partners. The purposes of these individual meetings are to assess whether IPV is present, and if so, what the dynamics are of that violence. This assessment should focus on specific behaviors and the context surrounding the behaviors. For the male partner (assumed to be the perpetrator by the authors of this particular article), the assessment includes the extent to which he is willing to change his behaviors, his history of family violence exposure, his general use of violence, and psychopathology. For the female partner (assumed to be the victim), the therapist assesses depression and PTSD. Also during this meeting, the therapist discusses with the woman the safety limitations of treatment and conducts some preliminary safety planning. Bograd and Mederos note that, if violence is disclosed on the phone call before the first meeting, it would be more appropriate to begin with the victim before attempting a conjoint interview.

5. Therapists should consider in advance what steps may be taken if previously-unreported instances of violence are disclosed in the assessment. For example, a woman in couple therapy may reveal in an individual interview that she is the victim of physical abuse in the relationship and there are children in the home. As another example, an IPV perpetrator who is in court-mandated individual counseling may reveal a new, recent perpetration incident about which the court or probation officer was not aware. Both examples highlight the importance of a thorough informed consent process that outlines the nature of, and exceptions to, confidentiality for clients in therapy and assessment, particularly in cases in which there is court involvement (Knapp, 2001). Therapists must be knowledgeable of all applicable laws, ethical standards, and professional regulations pertinent to the management of confidential information.
6. Therapists should be aware of the powerful influence of social desirability with regard to reporting violence. Both perpetrators and victims may recognize that IPV is not a socially accepted behavior and be reluctant to report victimization or perpetration (Aldarondo & Straus, 1994; Arias & Beach, 1987; Heckert & Gondolf, 2000b). In many cases (i.e., when IPV includes physical and/or sexual assault), reporting violence constitutes confessing to criminal behavior. Perpetrators may have a vested interest in maintaining a reputation as an upstanding citizen, such as when they have a high profile job (Weitzman, 2000). Victims may feel ashamed or concerned that they will be blamed, thereby making them less willing to disclose. Reluctance to report victimization may be very strong if they were shunned, shamed, or admonished previously after disclosing to others. Clients also may want to wait until they have established a stronger rapport before they disclose abuse. As Jory (2004) stated, "even in a skillfully conducted one-to-one interview, therapists should not assume that victims will be forthcoming about abuse" (p. 30). For all these reasons, reports gathered through the assessment may not paint the full picture of IPV. The impact of social desirability may be minimized by normalizing IPV as a common concern for therapy clients (e.g., by including questions about abuse on intake forms and in standard assessment procedures,

mentioning it in marketing literature, and including information about violence and abuse on informed consent documents).

7. When available, therapists should consult objective records to verify clients' self-reported information. Due to the criminal nature of physical and sexual IPV, legal documents (e.g., police reports, 911 calls, court records, victim impact statements, and probation records) may be available. Other records could include case notes from prior mental health services, medical health records to demonstrate the extent of injuries, school or work records, information from other social service agencies (e.g., shelters), and reports from friends or family members. When these documents are not public records, therapists should seek appropriate permissions to obtain them in order to provide a more thorough description of clients' circumstances.
8. To the extent possible, when working with one client (i.e., a victim or perpetrator), information should be gathered about the client's current or former partner. This recommendation applies to individual counseling with one partner in which IPV is known to be present. The primary reason for gathering this information is victim safety—whether or not that person is the client. When the client has been a victim, information about the partner can provide an understanding of the likelihood of further risk of victimization. Potentially useful information includes whether the perpetrator was punished, whether and what type of treatment the perpetrator received, whether the perpetrator initiated contact with the client, the extent to which the client believes that the perpetrator accepts responsibility for the abuse, and other impressions the client holds toward the perpetrator. When working with a perpetrator, information about how the client views his or her partner may help determine whether the perpetrator continues to pose a threat to that person's safety. Other topics to assess include substance use, violence severity and duration, and involvement in other types of criminal activity that is not relationship-specific.
9. As with all forms of clinical assessment, therapists should use instruments that demonstrate sound psychometric properties and apply principles of good assessment practice throughout the process. Corcoran and Fischer (2000a) describe several basic principles of assessment practice. First, assessments should be reliable, including internally consistent (i.e., the extent to which the items on an instrument are related to one another) and stable over time (i.e., test-retest reliability, or the extent to which an instrument produces similar scores at different administrations). Test-retest reliability is particularly relevant when assessment instruments will be used as pre-test/post-test assessments of treatment progress. The Cronbach's alpha coefficient typically is used to assess internal consistency, correlation coefficients typically are used to estimate test-retest reliability, and, for both of these, coefficients above .80 generally indicate strong reliability. Second, therapists should select valid instruments. Validity refers to the extent to

which an instrument actually measures what it is purported to measure. Two types of validity that should be considered include criterion validity (i.e., whether the instrument is correlated in the expected direction with other related variables) and construct validity (i.e., whether the instrument adequately reflects the underlying theoretical construct it is designed to assess). Third, therapists should use appropriate methods for scoring and interpreting the assessment results. Finally, Corcoran and Fischer recommend that clinical assessment instruments be selected based on their practical utility. That is, an instrument should add value to the clinical process by measuring change over time, accurately reflecting the client's situation, and providing information that helps guide treatment.

10. Therapists must consider the validity of assessment instruments in light of relevant contextual factors. The use of assessment instruments that do not account for the context of violence perpetration has been the source of great controversy in both clinical and research domains (Smith, Smith, & Earp, 1999). For example, one instrument that has been used widely in the research literature is the Conflict Tactics Scales (CTS/CTS2; Straus, Hamby, Boney-McCoy, & Sugarman, 1996), which asks respondents to indicate which conflict response tactics (including violent behaviors) they and their partner have used. However, the CTS has been criticized because it does not assess the intention behind using the various conflict tactics (DeKeseredy & Schwartz, 1998). For example, an individual who hits his or her partner in self-defense would report that behavior in the same manner as an individual who hits his or her partner as part of an effort to gain power and control. As such, these individuals would appear to display the same type of violence, although clearly the nature of the violence differs. Therapists must therefore use strategies that are contextually valid representations of abusive behaviors. These strategies include using instruments designed to assess the context or supplementing behavior-specific assessments with additional sources of information that explain the context.
11. Therapists should apply sound clinical reasoning to the collection and interpretation of assessment data. The assessment process should be grounded firmly in a detailed understanding of clinical assessment procedures and knowledge about IPV. Clinical reasoning also must be applied in order to make process-related decisions to ensure that accurate information is gathered. Process-related decisions that arise in an IPV assessment include determining the following: (a) when it is appropriate to push the client for more information, and when it is appropriate to wait for the client to respond on his or her own terms; (b) how best to respond when the therapist has an inclination a client is withholding information; (c) the most appropriate way to phrase questions so as to avoid communicating judgment or shame; (d) how quickly to pace the process in order to avoid overwhelming the client and to allow for rapport to develop; and (e) whether to

ask follow-up questions to gather additional information about questions for which incomplete information was provided.

12. IPV assessment should be ongoing, and the results and implications should be updated in light of new information (Jory, 2004). Assessment information gathered at one point in time may not represent experiences at other times. Viewing IPV assessment as an ongoing process allows therapists to identify needed changes in treatment approaches over time. For example, a couple who initially presents for therapy reporting low levels of situational couple violence may appear to be suitable candidates for conjoint treatment. However, if their violence begins to escalate, conjoint treatment may become contraindicated, and other approaches (e.g., batterer intervention and referrals to victim service agencies) may be warranted. The converse situation—in which a client initially reports high levels of violence but, as treatment progresses, demonstrates consistent and sustained nonviolent and non-abusive behaviors—also could warrant modified treatment approaches. Overall, therapists should continue IPV assessment throughout all treatment phases, such as by re-administering instruments, including open-ended interview questions as a routine part of every session, and monitoring third-party records for additional information that would indicate changes in the experiences of IPV over time.
13. IPV assessment should be multidimensional and address the numerous contextual variables that impact the manner in which violence is manifested in a particular client's relationship. The remainder of this chapter describes the dimensions that therapists should assess when working with clients impacted by IPV.

Dimensions of IPV Assessment

This section provides information about several important dimensions to assess with clients impacted by IPV, including the nature of the violence, perpetrator and victim/survivor characteristics, clients' relationship functioning, and other issues that include substance abuse and mental health, family history of violence, the needs of children, and safety considerations. In many cases, it is not necessary to assess every dimension, so appropriate clinical judgment should guide which dimensions to assess with particular clients (Corcoran & Fischer, 2000a).

Within each dimension, informal and formal assessment strategies can be used. Lists of sample open-ended interview questions are included in this chapter. In adapting these questions to practice, the exact wording should be modified as appropriate to meet each client's needs. For example, therapists working with clients who do not describe violent behaviors as "violence" or "abuse" may need to use alternative language, such as by asking about specific behaviors (e.g., "When did your partner first hit you?") (Aldarondo & Straus, 1994). Furthermore, therapists should consider the listed questions to be starting points for conducting open-ended interviews.

This chapter's Appendix includes a Directory of Selected Instruments for Assessing IPV. Given space limitations, all available instruments are not able to be included. However, the included instruments provide therapists with a starting point for understanding the relative advantages and disadvantages of existing instruments across dimensions of IPV. Because some dimensions of IPV assessment (e.g., mental health disorders, general relationship functioning, substance abuse, and suicidality) are broad areas of clinical assessment in and of themselves, instruments addressing these dimensions are not included in the Directory. Rather, readers will find references to credible sources of information in the corresponding sections of this chapter. On a practical note, we remind readers to consult the original sources listed in the Directory for information about how to access and administer specific instruments that they wish to use with clients, as well as relevant copyright regulations.

This chapter addresses various clinical situations that warrant assessment of IPV and its related features. Preliminary information about clients' presenting concerns, background characteristics, and treatment goals—as well as the referral source, whether treatment is mandatory, and whether individual or couple therapy is requested—should factor into therapists' decisions as to the specific characteristics to assess. In addition, information gathered through the initial phases of the assessment can alert the therapist to what further information is needed. For example, if it is determined that violence in a couple's relationship is situational (i.e., not battering), and there is not one clear perpetrator and one clear victim, then a greater emphasis may be placed on assessing relationship variables. To illustrate how different clinical situations warrant different assessment approaches, we present three case examples, with a brief discussion of the primary characteristics that warrant assessment in each case. (Note: Other characteristics may warrant assessment based on additional information revealed about each client situation.)

Case example #1: Bob and Joanna present for therapy. Joanna insisted that her husband participate in marital therapy or else she would divorce him. The partners agree that their primary presenting concern is that Bob has become increasingly emotionally abusive toward Joanna. They report that the first and only incident of physical violence in their relationship was two weeks ago. This incident involved Bob pushing Joanna into a wall during an argument.

The assessment should determine the appropriateness of couple therapy. The therapist should assess all aspects of the violence, starting with safety considerations, to understand the presence of power and control dynamics; the severity, pattern, duration, and direction of the violence; and whether Bob accepts responsibility for his violent behaviors. The results of this initial assessment will guide the appropriate direction for treatment (i.e., couple therapy or individual treatment for one or both partners). Other characteristics that may become necessary to assess include perpetration-related characteristics for Bob, victimization-related characteristics for Joanna, the couple's relationship functioning and goals, each partner's amenability to treatment, parenting issues if the couple has children, and other background characteristics, such as the clients' mental health functioning and histories of family or other trauma.

Case example #2: Naomi, age 27, was court-mandated to attend individual counseling at a mental health agency as a result of a criminal charge she received after being physically violent toward her female partner, Jess. Jess required medical treatment for injuries sustained during the violence, in which Naomi struck her with a heavy object. Although the court typically requires a group batterer intervention program, Naomi was referred for individual counseling because there is not a program for female batterers in the community. The court system's referral sheet indicated that Naomi was intoxicated at the time of the incident and that there were two prior 911 calls about Naomi's violence toward Jess, although this was the first time charges were filed.

The initial screening of Naomi should include a safety assessment, both for potential suicidality and ongoing threats toward Jess. The primary assessment focus will be on perpetrator characteristics, such as aggressiveness and jealousy. Assessment consideration also should be given to the nature of the violence (i.e., severity, pattern, duration, and concurrence with power and control dynamics). Understanding these characteristics should provide insight into what type of perpetrator Naomi is, which allows the therapist to tailor treatment accordingly. Because substances were involved, Naomi's assessment should address the potential for substance abuse.

Case example #3: Sylvia is a 38-year-old woman who is currently living in a battered women's shelter after leaving her husband, who she reports had been physically abusive toward her throughout their 10-year marriage. At the shelter with her are her two children, ages 8 and 6. Sylvia says that she feels safe in the shelter, although she is considering returning to her husband at home, and says, "I think it would be best for the children if their parents were together."

Again, Sylvia's and her children's safety should be a primary consideration, and this includes assessing the nature of the violence to determine potential risks if she returns to her husband. This assessment can be integrated into a safety plan, which is discussed in Chapter 4. Sylvia's assessment also should include consideration of her victimization-related characteristics, including her available social support, perceptions of the violence, and coping abilities. Because she is considering remaining in the relationship with her husband, it also may be useful to assess her perceptions of her relationship functioning. Since children are living with her, the assessment also should address parenting considerations and the needs of the children.

Assessment of the Violence

In Chapter 2, we discussed distinctions made in recent research between different types of IPV, most notably situational couple violence and battering. Because these two types of violence are essentially two different phenomena

(Johnson, 2006, 2009; Johnson & Ferraro, 2000; Leone, Johnson, & Cohan, 2007), different treatment approaches likely are warranted depending on which type of IPV is, or has been, present. Therefore, therapists face the difficult task of determining which type(s) of violence their clients have experienced. This is challenging because these types of IPV are not classified based on the frequency or severity of the violence (Johnson, 2006, 2009; Johnson & Ferraro, 2000; Johnson & Leone, 2005). For example, two couples present for conjoint therapy, and both report a similar frequency and severity of violence; however, one couple is experiencing battering, while the other couple is experiencing situational couple violence. As Johnson (2009) wrote, the presence of generalized power and control dynamics within the relationship is the key feature that distinguishes battering from situational couple violence. As will be discussed in greater detail in Chapters 4 and 5, the nature of the violence is a significant factor in determining the appropriateness of treatment approaches, particularly conjoint therapy. Therefore, this feature is a crucial component of IPV assessment.

In this section, we present a five-component framework (Figure 3.1) for assessing the type of violence that is present. The five components include whether generalized power and control dynamics are present, the severity of the violence, the pattern and duration of the violence, the direction of the violence, and whether the perpetrator(s) accepts responsibility for the violent behavior. Figure 3.1 can guide therapists through deciding whether conjoint treatment is appropriate. In addition, when working with individuals—either perpetrators or victims/survivors—a therapist's understanding of these characteristics will aid in the assessment of safety issues and clients' unique potential treatment needs. Furthermore, in working with clients who are survivors of violence that occurred in the past, or with clients who witnessed IPV in their families-of-origin, identifying the features of the violence can aid clients in developing greater understanding of their experiences and how they impact their current functioning.

Generalized Power and Control Dynamics

Identifying whether power and control dynamics are present is a key task for therapists in assessing IPV, including determining whether one partner fears other partner and whether the fear extends beyond violent incidents (Leone et al., 2007; Schacht et al., 2009). The context surrounding identified fears should be explored, such as the severity of the violence (as will be discussed more fully in the next section) and size and strength differentials between partners. A strategy for identifying generalized power and control dynamics is to assess for the presence and severity of emotional/psychological abuse in the relationship. As presented in the Appendix, several instruments exist to measure these dynamics. In addition, interview and observational assessment data can provide

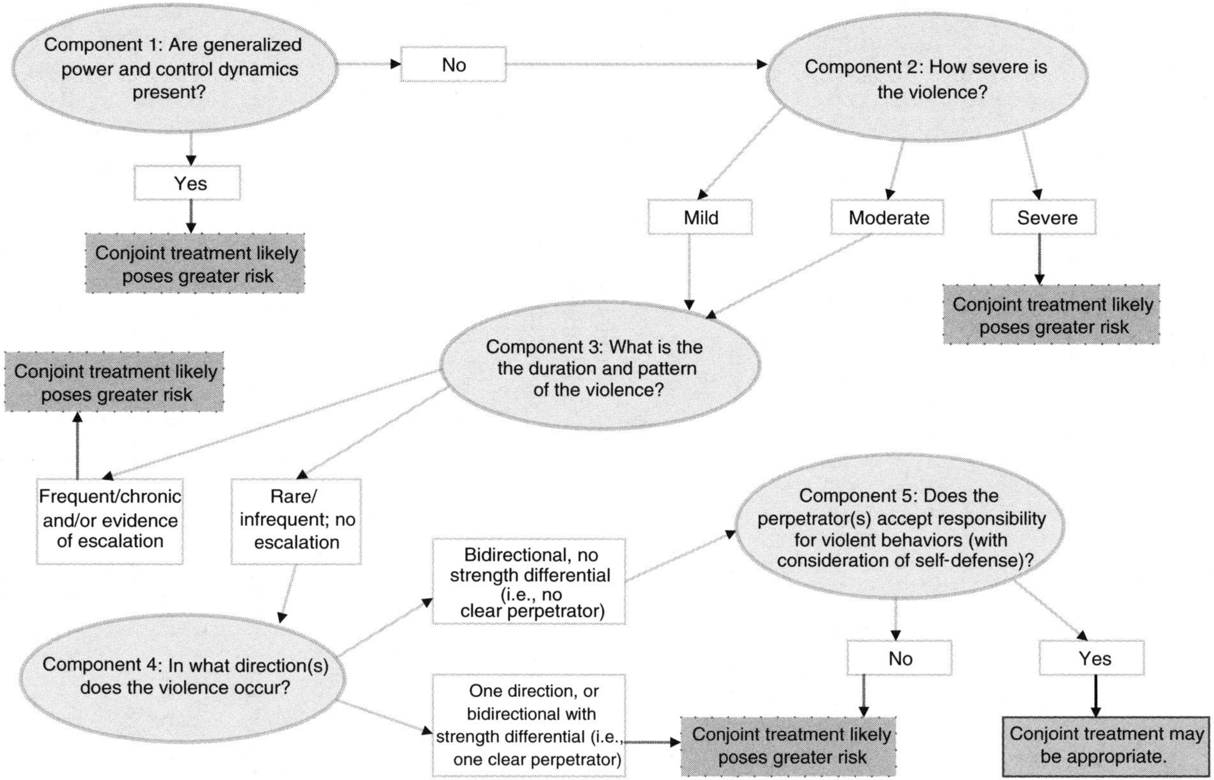

FIGURE 3.1 Five-component framework for assessing the nature of IPV: Flow chart for determining whether conjoint treatment may be appropriate.

a thorough understanding of each partner's phenomenological understanding of power and control dynamics within their relationship.

Sample Interview Questions for Assessing Generalized Power and Control Dynamics

- Overall, how would you say that you and your partner treat each other?
- Describe some of the ways that your partner shows respect for you (or you show respect for your partner) in your relationship.
- How does your partner show disrespect to you in your relationship?
- Since becoming involved in your relationship, have you been able to maintain relationships with others, such as friends and family members?
- Do you (or your partner) view yourselves as equal partners in your relationship?
- Are you afraid of your partner? If so, what is the reason for being afraid?
- Do you think that your partner is afraid of you? If so, what do you think s/he is afraid of?
- Do you ever call your partner names? If so, what kinds of names do you use?
- Does your partner ever call you names? If so, what kinds of names does your partner use?
- Does your partner ever threaten you to convince you to do something?

The Severity of the Violence

Violence severity can be considered both subjectively and objectively. For example, certainly there are people who view any form of violence as a severe violation of trust and safety in an intimate relationship. An individual with this perspective may hold such a belief as, "If he hits you once, leave him." Likewise, an individual with no personal history of violence victimization or perpetration may view even more minor forms of violence as scary and severe. Client's subjective perceptions of violence warrant consideration in an IPV assessment. In addition, they represent an important area for self-reflection among therapists who do this work.

However, therapists also must be aware of objective standards of violence severity in assessing the nature of IPV experienced by their clients. The Appendix includes descriptions of a number of instruments that provide objective standards of IPV severity. The assumption of most of these standards is that more severe forms of violence are more likely to result in (a) injury and (b) injuries that are more severe. Thus, mild or minor acts of violence have a minimal likelihood of resulting in injury, and resulting injuries would likely neither be lasting nor require medical attention. For example, an individual grabs his or her partner's upper arm roughly, but releases the arm within a few seconds and leaves a red mark that fades within minutes. Moderately severe acts of violence are more likely to result in injury, although the resulting injury would not pose a serious threat and may not require medical attention. An example of a moderate form of violence is a person who punches his or her partner in the eye, leaving a black eye that takes about one week to heal, but no lasting damage was done to the partner's facial structure or eyesight. At the severe levels, violent acts are very likely to result in severe injury to the victim. Violence perpetrated with weapons is considered severe (Campbell, 2005; Campbell, Webster, & Glass, 2009). At the extreme, victims may be killed by such forms of violence, a phenomenon known as intimate partner homicide (IPH; Garcia, Soria, & Hurwitz, 2007; Mize & Shackelford, 2008).

Thus, violence severity can be considered on a continuum from mild to moderate to severe. When multiple forms of violence occur during the same incident, it is useful to rate the severity of that incident based on the most severe level (Campbell, 2005; Campbell et al., 2009). Building on the examples in the previous paragraph, a violent incident in which an individual first grabs and releases his or her partner's arm, then punches him or her in the eye, and then finally hits the partner over the head with a heavy household object, resulting in a concussion, fits the criteria for severe violence. Because multiple forms of violence often co-occur, open-ended interview questions provide useful supplemental information about IPV severity.

Sample Interview Questions for Assessing the Severity of the Violence

- Describe the most severe incident of violence that ever occurred in your relationship. What happened before, during, and after the incident? When did this occur?
- Have you ever had to seek medical attention for an injury resulting from violence between you and your partner? Has your partner? Describe the extent of the injuries.
- Have you ever feared for your life during a violent incident in your relationship?
- Have you ever feared for your partner's life during a violent incident in your relationship? If so, please describe what happened.
- When violence has happened, were you or your partner using substances at the time?

The Pattern and Duration of the Violence

Therapists should assess both violence frequency and whether it has escalated over time. In assessing the frequency, two essential questions arise: (a) How many times has the violence occurred? and (b) How frequently has it occurred during the relationship? The length of the couple's relationship is an important consideration. For example, to state that violence happened 10 times over the course of a relationship provides incomplete information. If that couple has been together two months, a higher frequency is indicated than if the couple has been together 20 years. In addition to understanding the pattern of violence as a function of the length of the couple's relationship, it is useful to ask clients to describe the violence frequency within different time-frames (e.g., within the past week, month, six months, and year) to determine whether there have been changes in frequency over time.

Assessing for an escalation in the violence provides insight into potential safety risks. For example, consider a couple in which violence occurred 10 times during their year-long relationship. If the first three incidents were mild in severity, the next five were moderate, and the most recent two incidents were severe, this suggests that the victim is at increasing risk. Because of the potential lethality of severe violence, escalations can be viewed as indicators of a potential for increased risk to victims' safety. For this reason, ongoing assessment should identify patterns of escalation, and treatment approaches should be modified accordingly.

Sample Interview Questions for Assessing the Pattern and Duration of the Violence

- When did the first incident of violence occur? How long was this into your relationship?
- Describe the first incident of violence, including what happened before and after it.
- How soon after the first incident of violence occurred did another incident happen?
- How has the violence in your relationship changed over time? (Has it become more or less frequent? Has it become more or less severe?)
- Describe the most recent incident of violence in your relationship. What happened? When did this occur?
- Over the past six months, how often has violence occurred in your relationship? What about over the past month? The past week?
- How does a violent incident in your relationship usually end?

The Direction of the Violence

An IPV assessment challenge is determining in what direction(s) the violence occurs. To illustrate, with two partners in a relationship (e.g., Partner A and Partner B), the violence can occur with Partner A perpetrating against Partner B (A → B), with Partner B perpetrating against Partner A (B → A), or with Partners A and B perpetrating against one another (A ←→ B). In some cases, making this determination is easy, such as when there is one clear perpetrator and one clear victim. However, the direction can become complicated in light of contextual factors—particularly gender, size and strength, and the use of self-defense—surrounding the violence, especially in cases in which both partners acknowledge using violent behaviors. In such cases, therapists must use careful assessment strategies to determine whether the violence is truly mutual or whether it is a case of one partner being primarily a perpetrator and the other partner being primarily a victim. In part due to typical size differentials between women and men, female IPV victims are more likely than men to experience negative and more severe consequences resulting from IPV (Gauthier & Levendosky, 1996).

The accurate assessment of the direction of the violence is important when deciding whether conjoint treatment is appropriate. A major reason that couple therapy is considered inappropriate when IPV is present is that it implies that the violence is mutual, and therefore takes away the responsibility for changing from the perpetrator (Stith et al., 2003). As such, when the assessment reveals that IPV occurs in one direction, couple therapy should be avoided (see Figure 3.1). To assess the direction of the violence, therapists can use inventories such as the Revised Conflict Tactics Scale (Straus et al., 1996), which is reviewed in the Appendix. However, because these inventories vary in their consideration of contextual variables, this information should be supplemented by open-ended interview questions and the information gathered previously regarding the presence of generalized power and control dynamics.

Sample Interview Questions for Assessing the Direction of the Violence

- Would you say that you and your partner are equally violent toward one another? If not, who is more likely to be violent?
- In comparing you and your partner, who is physically stronger? Who is larger? (Follow-up questions might include seeking details about height, weight, and physical fitness.)
- When violence occurs, who is more likely to be injured as a result of that violence?
- Who in your relationship is more likely to use violence in self-defense?

Acceptance of Responsibility for Violent Behaviors

Whether or not the perpetrator accepts responsibility can impact the course of treatment and the prognosis for achieving nonviolence in the relationship (Heyman & Schlee, 2003; Stith et al., 2003). Perpetrators often blame their partners for their violent behaviors (Henning, Jones, & Holdford, 2005). For example, a batterer might state something to the effect of "I was only doing it because she made me so mad because she nags me all the time," or "She had it coming for the way she was talking to that other guy at the party." Therefore, information about the extent to which perpetrators accept responsibility can aid therapists in determining the most suitable type of treatment. Of course, this characteristic could change over the course of treatment (i.e., a person who does not initially accept responsibility for using violent behaviors begins to accept that responsibility as part of treatment). As such, it is wise to include this in the ongoing perpetrator assessment. A final caution regarding this characteristic is for therapists also to consider issues of self-defense with respect to accepting responsibility for the violence.

Sample Interview Questions for Assessing Acceptance of Responsibility for Violent Behaviors

- How likely do you think it is that another violent incident will occur in your relationship?
- Have you made promises that the violence will not occur again? Are these promises kept?
- After violence occurs, what usually happens? What do and your partner do?
- How have you shown that you have accepted responsibility for violence you committed?
- What do you think needs to happen in order for the violence in your relationship to end?

Assessment of the Perpetrator

As discussed in Chapter 2, a growing body of research suggests that IPV perpetrators are not all the same, and typologies have been developed to reflect the field's emerging understanding of characteristics that differentiate abusers (e.g., Holtzworth-Munroe & Stuart, 1994; Jacobson & Gottman, 1998). The primary focus of this section is on perpetrators of battering, as characteristics of perpetrators of situational couple violence have been studied much less frequently. A primary purpose of the assessment of IPV perpetrator characteristics is to understand the perpetrator's background characteristics in order to inform treatment decisions and determine the extent to which the perpetrator is likely to benefit from treatment.

Perpetrator Characteristics

Although all batterers are potentially dangerous, and batterers within any category may be amenable to treatment, distinguishing between batterers based on background characteristics can help therapists decide which treatment approaches may be helpful to a given client. A key distinguishing feature between different types of batterers is whether the batterer uses violence only in the context of the intimate relationship(s) or whether there is a history of general aggressive, potentially antisocial behaviors. Therefore, assessing levels of aggression can provide insight into whether it is generalized or relationship-specific. Therapists may use such instruments as the Aggression Questionnaire (Buss & Perry, 1992) or the Verbal Aggressiveness Scale (Infante & Wigley, 1986) to assess this trait. An additional characteristic that can aid in understanding a perpetrator's background is whether the violence stems in part from jealousy and dependence, and an instrument such as the Hypothetical, Jealousy-Producing Events Scale (Hansen, 1982) may be useful to include in the assessment of the perpetrator. Open-ended interview questions are extremely important in the assessment of IPV perpetrators, in that information gathered through these interviews can help therapists make connections among the objective data from assessment instruments, other information gathered about the nature of the violence, and other objective records that are able to be obtained (e.g., lifetime criminal records).

Sample Interview Questions for Assessing Abuse-Related Characteristics of the Perpetrator

- What are your current feelings for your partner?
- To what extent have your violent behaviors made your relationship unhealthy?
- What do you view as the reasons for your violent behavior?
- In general, tell me what you think about men (or women).
- What do you think about the term "batterer"? Do you think that term applies to you?
- Would you describe yourself as a violent person? Why or why not?
- Would you describe yourself as an abuser/batterer? Why or why not?
- How would you define the term *emotional abuse*? Do you believe that you are emotionally abusive toward your partner? If so, how?
- Tell me about past experiences you've had with using violent behaviors. Please include violence in this or other intimate relationships and in other types of situations.
- Describe to me the first time you ever used violent behavior (i.e., not just in your relationship). What happened? What, if any, consequences resulted from that incident?
- About how often do you use violent behavior in your relationship?
- Do you think your violent behaviors have become worse or better over time?
- Tell me what you experience when you are using violent behaviors. What thoughts go through your mind? What happens in your body? What emotions do you feel?
- Please describe for me a time when you felt jealousy related to something to do with your partner. How did you handle that emotion?
- Let's think of a hypothetical situation where you and your partner are out and someone starts hitting on your partner in front of you. How would respond?
- Are there "lessons" that you were attempting to teach your partner when you used violence? If so, what were those "lessons"?
- Think about people who know you in different areas of your life (e.g., work, friends, or family). How much do these people know about your use of violence in your relationship? If they don't know, how surprised do you think they would be if they found out? If they know, how did they react when they learned you had been violent?
- Tell me about the friends you spend the most time with. How common is violence in their relationships? Would you describe these people as being accepting of violent behaviors?

Likelihood of Benefitting from Treatment

This section focuses on assessing the extent to which an IPV perpetrator is likely to benefit from treatment, and this information can be useful in determining the treatment approach (e.g., group or individual) that may be most useful for a particular client. The Client Motivation for Therapy Scale (Pelletier, Tuson, & Haddad, 1997) measures a client's internal or external motivation for general therapy participation. In addition, two IPV-specific assessments exist, namely the Safe at Home Instrument (Begun et al., 2003) and the University of Rhode Island Change Assessment for Domestic Violence (Levesque, Gelles, & Velicer, 2000). These instruments may assist the therapist in understanding how amenable a client is to treatment. In addition, the interview questions below are designed to elicit perpetrators' perceptions of the negative consequences of their behaviors, their prior experiences with treatment, and perceptions of being in a group treatment format.

Sample Interview Questions for Assessing Likelihood a Perpetrator will Benefit from Treatment

- What motivates you to change your violent behaviors?
- If you were to change your behaviors, how do you think your life would be different?
- Do you think that any punishment you received for your violent behavior (e.g., probation, mandatory batterer intervention program participation) was justified? Why or why not?
- What do you think is the worst thing that has resulted from your use of violence in your relationship? Do you think that anything good has come out of this? If so, what?
- What have been some of the negative consequences of your use of violent behaviors? How have these consequences impacted your life?
- What do you think needs to happen in order for you to change your violent behavior?
- Have you ever been in any sort of program before that was aimed at changing your violent behavior? If so, was that program helpful? Did you change?
- Have you ever participated in any sort of mental health treatment (e.g., counseling, psychiatric medications) previously? If so, what did you think about that experience?
- Tell me what you think about participating in a group intervention program for batterers. What about this sort of approach do you think could be helpful or unhelpful?
- What would you like to get out of this intervention/treatment program?
- Mandated clients: How do you feel about being ordered to participate in this program?
- What is your main motivation for participating in this intervention/treatment program?

Assessment of the Victim

The focus of this section will be on victims of battering, as the needs of this population have been a much greater focus in research and practice than individuals who have experienced situational couple violence. Although research on IPV victims has not revealed distinct typologies as with perpetrators, research provides evidence that victims respond in different ways to their experiences of violence (e.g., Apsler, Cummins, & Carl, 2002; Herbert, Silver, & Ellard, 1991; Smith, Murray, & Coker, 2010). Furthermore, recent research views these individuals through a more strength- and resource-based lens than before (i.e., they previously were viewed primarily through a focus on learned helplessness and trauma). As such, greater attention is warranted on the strengths and resources available to support victims in their progress toward treatment goals (Lee, 2007; Lindhorst et al., 2005).

Level of Social Support

Therapists should determine the extent to which victims have access to a support network that may include friends, family members, community and religious organizations, neighbors, and coworkers. Available instruments related to social support include the Multidimensional Scale of Perceived Social Support (Zimet, Dahlem, Zimet, & Farley, 1988), the Perceived Social Support—Friend Scale and Perceived Social Support—Family Scale (Procidano & Heller, 1983), the Provision of Social Relations (Turner, Frankel, & Levin, 1983), and the Social Support Appraisals Scale (Vaux, Phillips, Holly, Thomson, Williams, & Stewart, 1986).

Sample Interview Questions for Assessing Social Support Available to the Victim/Survivor

- Do your family members/friends/coworkers/neighbors/etc. know about the violence you have experienced? If so, how have they responded? Have they been helpful or unhelpful?
- It is common for people who have been victims of domestic violence to become isolated from friends and family over time. Has this happened to you?
- How would you describe the current level of social support available to you?
- Can you name friends or family members that you could turn to for help if you needed it?
- Are you affiliated with any community groups or religious organizations? If so, do you think these groups could provide any support to you at this time, and how?

Perceptions of the Violence

A victim's perceptions of the violence refer to thoughts, feelings, and beliefs regarding the victimization, the abusive partner, and where s/he stands currently in relation to the violence (Lindhorst et al., 2005). An understanding of these perceptions can alert therapists to irrational beliefs the victim holds, the extent to which the victim is ready to take steps toward a life of nonviolence (e.g., seeking legal intervention, leaving the partner, or accessing resources), and the presence of ambivalent feelings toward the perpetrator or oneself. As one example, the Domestic Violence Myth Acceptance Scale (Peters, 2008) is useful for identifying irrational beliefs that may impact a client's decision to stay in the relationship. Another instrument is the Domestic Violence Survivor Assessment (Dienemann, Campbell, Landenburger, & Curry, 2002), which can provide the therapist with information about the client's progress in moving toward a violence-free life. Another dimension is the extent to which the client views the traumatic experiences associated with IPV as opportunities for growth, which can be assessed through the Posttraumatic Growth Inventory (Tedeschi & Calhoun, 1996). In addition, the following open-ended interview questions address the context for these perceptions.

Sample Interview Questions for Assessing Victim/Survivor Perceptions of the Violence

- What are your current feelings for your partner?
- Do you believe that your partner can change his/her violent behavior? Why or why not?
- If you are considering staying with your partner, what are your main reasons for staying?
- Do you still like and/or love your partner? If so, what do you like or love about him/her?
- If you want to leave your partner but feel like you have to stay with him/her, what would need to happen in order for you to really be ready and able to leave?
- What do you think it would be like for you to start a new life without your partner?
- If you left your partner, are there reasons that you would need to maintain contact with him/her (e.g., custody, finances)? If so, what would you like future contacts to be like?
- To what extent do you think that violence is a common or normal experience for people in intimate relationships? How did you come to think this way?
- What do you think are the causes of your partner's violent behavior?
- What would you like to see happen now with regard to your relationship?
- How do you think that your ability to function in other areas of life (e.g., work, school, and/or parenting) has been affected by the violence in your relationship?

Stress, Coping Strategies, and Other Available Resources and Supports

Experiencing IPV victimization can be viewed as a stressful life event involving both acute and chronic stress (Carlson, 1997; Herbert et al., 1991; Smith et al., in press; Smith et al., 1999). As such, stress management skills, coping skills, and other resources are useful to incorporate into treatment with victims/survivors (Carlson, 1997). Therefore, one area for assessment of the victim/survivor is to gather a baseline measurement of his or her level of stress, such as by using Cohen, Kamarck, and Mermelstein's (1983) Perceived Stress Scale. To determine how a victim/survivor has coped with and responded to the victimization, the therapist also may apply one of the existing coping measures, such as the Coping Resources Inventory for Stress (Matheny, Aycock, Curlette, & Junker, 1993). IPV-specific information that addresses coping with victimization is the Intimate Partner Violence Strategies Index (IPVSI; Goodman, Dutton, Weinfurt, & Cook, 2003). Open-ended interview questions also can be used to gather in-depth information about the context surrounding IPV victimization coping strategies.

Sample Interview Questions for Assessing Stress, and Coping, and Other Resources

- Do you know about local resources to help people who have been victims of domestic violence? Which of them have you used? How helpful have you found them to be?
- How have you coped with the violence in your relationship?
- Has there been involvement of the legal system (e.g., the police, the district attorney's office) in your relationship as a result of the violence? If so, how helpful or unhelpful has this involvement been? Would you turn to these sources for assistance in the future?
- Have you ever received counseling before related to experiences of abuse? If so, what was helpful and unhelpful about that treatment?
- Have you ever received other types of mental health treatment (e.g., counseling, psychiatric medications) for any other reason? If so, how helpful was it?
- How do you think that a therapist can be most helpful to you?
- What would you most like to get out of counseling at this time?

Assessment of Relationship Functioning

Clinical situations occur in which it is useful for therapists to take a broader view and assess general relationship functioning. For example, many clients who have experienced IPV remain in violent relationships (Heyman & Schlee, 2003). Other clients might use the therapeutic setting to decide whether to remain in or end their relationships. Although it may surprise some therapists, couples who have experienced IPV do not necessarily view violence as the key defining feature of their relationships (Heyman & Schlee, 2003). As such, failing to address other relationship variables through the assessment can lead to gaps in therapists' understanding of their clients and frustration for both clients and therapists. Aspects of relationship functioning addressed in this section are clients' relationship plans, goals, and skills.

Current Plans and Goals for the Relationship

The issue of whether a couple plans to remain together or end their relationship should be considered a fluid one. A commonly-cited statistic among victim advocates is that a typical battered woman leaves her partner seven times before finally making a permanent split from her abusive partner (e.g., AARDVARC, 2008). As such, a client may cycle through various phases of deciding whether to remain in a relationship in which IPV has occurred. Two instruments that assess inclinations toward terminating a relationship are the Marital Alternatives Scale (Udry, 1981) and the Marital Instability Index (Edwards, Johnson, & Booth, 1987).

Existing research indicates that experiences of IPV are associated with decreased relationship satisfaction (Kaura & Lohman, 2007; Testa & Leonard, 2001). On the other hand, some individuals who experience IPV may view violence as just one component of their relationships, and therefore their overall relationship satisfaction appears higher than if it were based solely on the violence (Johnson, 2009). This may be particularly true for couples who have experienced situational couple violence, in that the violence and power and control dynamics are not seen as the central, defining characteristic of the relationship (Johnson, 2006, 2009). Three potentially useful instruments for assessing relationship satisfaction are the Kansas Marital Satisfaction Scale (KMSS; Schumm et al., 1986), the Marital Comparison Level Index (MCLI; Sabatelli, 1984), and the Relationship Assessment Scale (RAS; Hendrick, 1988). Therapists should aim to identify factors that impact clients' current plans and goals for their relationships through a combination of structured assessments and open-ended questions.

Sample Interview Questions for Assessing Relationship Plans, Goals, and Status

- Overall, how would you describe your relationship with your partner?
- How satisfied are you currently with your relationship with your partner?
- Are you more or less satisfied with your relationship now compared to six months ago?
- How committed are you to staying in your relationship with your partner?
- Describe for me all of the ways your and your partner's lives are interconnected. As examples, think about financial assets, children you have, mutual friends, shared leisure interests, and other lifestyle issues. How do you feel about this level of interconnection?
- What would you like for this relationship to be like in five years? You do not have to assume that you would still be in this relationship.
- What do you think is the best thing about your relationship with your partner?

- What do you think is the worst thing about your relationship with your partner?
- How much do you think that the violence you have experienced in your relationship has impacted other aspects of your relationship?
- If you could change anything about your relationship, what would you like to change?
- Have you ever participated in couple therapy before? If so, was it helpful or unhelpful?
- If you participated in couple therapy before, how was the violence in your relationship addressed, if at all? Did you tell your previous therapist(s) about the violence?
- What would you most like to get out of couple therapy at this point in time?
- Is there anything that you think could happen in couple therapy that would make it an unsafe experience for either one of you? If so, what? What should happen if this occurs?

Relationship Skills

The causes of IPV have not been identified fully, although researchers have put forth several theoretical explanations (Barnett, Miller-Perrin, & Perrin, 2005). Battering is not thought to result from relationship skill deficits, but rather from one partner's desire to exert power and control over the other (Johnson, 2006, 2009; Johnson & Ferraro, 2000). On the other hand, situational couple violence is, by its very definition, rooted in specific conflict situations that escalate into violence (Johnson, 2006, 2009; Johnson & Ferraro, 2000). Therefore, skill deficits are likely at least one factor contributing to this form of IPV. Thus, an important component of assessing these couples is identifying skill deficits that are contributing to their violence.

Two relationship skills studied in relation to IPV are communication skills and conflict management (e.g., Ronan, Dreer, Dollard, & Ronan, 2004; Whitchurch & Pace, 1993). Therefore, therapists may find it useful to incorporate instruments that assess communication (e.g., the Primary Communication Inventory; Navran, 1967) and conflict management skills (e.g., the Kansas Marital Conflict Scale (KMCS; Eggeman, Moxley, & Schumm, 1985). Additional relationship skills that may be relevant to address through formal assessments or open-ended interview questions include dyadic coping and problem-solving skills.

Sample Interview Questions for Assessing Relationship Skills

- How well do you think you and your partner communicate with one another?
- When conflict arises in your relationship, how well do you think that you manage it?
- Do you ever feel like your conflicts get out of control? If so, what does that look like?

- Most couples experience some conflicts or problems. What are the most likely issues about which you and your partner are most likely to experience conflict?
- How are household chores (e.g., cooking, cleaning, child care, and yard work) divided up in your relationship? How satisfied are you with this division of the housework?
- Is one partner considered to be the "head of the household"? What does this mean to you?
- Imagine a situation in which you and your partner are having a problem that needed to be solved. For example, you need to choose between spending a holiday with one of your extended families or the other, and both sides are pressuring you to choose their side. Or, as another example, something unexpected happens (e.g., the heater breaks in the middle of winter) and it is not convenient for either one of you to address the problem right away. How well do you think you would work together to come up with a solution?

Assessment of Other Relevant Characteristics

IPV typically occurs in the context of numerous other dynamics that can impact client functioning and treatment progress. The existing research suggests that the characteristics below—including substance abuse and mental health disorders, prior experiences with trauma and violence, parenting, and safety concerns—may be intricately related to clients' IPV experiences. As such, this chapter's final section provides practical guidance for therapists who determine that any or all of these characteristics warrant attention in the clinical assessment.

Substance Abuse and Mental Health Disorders

Co-occurring substance abuse and/or mental health disorders are relevant for assessment because their presence warrants attention in treatment planning. Furthermore, there are high rates of comorbidity between IPV and substance use (e.g., Brown, Werk, Caplan, & Seraganian, 1999; Fowler, 2007; Martin, Moracco, Chang, Council, & Dulli, 2008) and mental health disorders (e.g., Helfrich, Fujiura, & Rutkowski-Kmitta, 2008; Huss & Langhinrichsen-Rohling, 2006; Mourad, Levendosky, Bogat, & von Eye, 2008; O'Campo et al., 2006). Both issues can be assessed through combining structured inventories and informal interview questions. The relationship between substance abuse and family violence is so significant that an entire chapter is devoted to this issue later in this book (see Chapter 11).

Existing research also demonstrates high rates of mental health symptoms among individuals impacted by IPV (Helfrich et al., 2008; Huss & Langhinrichsen-Rohling, 2006; Mourad, et al., 2008; O'Campo et al., 2006). As such, current functioning and past histories related to clients' mental health are relevant in the IPV assessment process. In addition to using the *Diagnostic and Statistical Manual of Mental Disorders* (American Psychiatric Association, 2000), structured instruments, such as the Minnesota Multiphasic Personality Inventory–2 (MMPI-2; Butcher et al., 2001), Millon Clinical Multiaxial Inventory–III (MCMI-III; Millon, Davis, & Millon, 1997), and Personality Assessment Inventory (PAI; Morey, 1991) may be useful for assessing psychological functioning (Wise, Streiner, & Walfish, 2010). The MCMI-III may be particularly useful in the assessment of IPV perpetrators, as it has been used in several research studies examining batterer typologies (e.g., Babcock, Costa, Green, & Eckhardt, 2004; Chase, O'Leary, & Heyman, 2001; Meehan, Holtzorth-Munroe, & Herron, 2001).

Family History and Childhood and Other Previous Trauma

An instrument such as the Lifetime Trauma and Victimization History (Widom, Dutton, Czaja, & DuMont, 2005) can be used in conjunction with open-ended questions to assess intergeneration patterns of violence (e.g., Kwong, Bartholomew, Henderson, & Trinke, 2003).

Sample Interview Questions for Assessing Intergenerational Patterns of Family Violence

- How would you describe the family environment in which you grew up?
- Did you witness abuse between your parents (or your parents and their significant others, if they were not in a steady relationship)? If so, what was that like?
- What messages did you receive in your family about relationships, abuse, and violence?
- Did you or other members of your family ever seek any sort of professional help related to any experiences of violence or abuse in your family? If so, please describe that for me.
- Are you aware of abuse that occurred in any relationships in your extended family (e.g., grandparents, aunts and uncles, etc.)? If so, what do you know about that abuse? [Note: It may be helpful to construct a genogram (McGoldrick, Gerson, & Petry, 2008).]
- How would you say your parents disciplined you and/or your siblings? Was corporal punishment used? If so, what are your feelings about that?
- How do you think your childhood experiences relate to the violence in your relationship?
- On a scale from 1 (not at all nurturing) to 10 (extremely nurturing), how do you rate the environment in the family in which you were raised?

Parenting and the Needs of Involved Children

Parenting concerns and the needs of children should be considered even if children are not participating in treatment. Parental functioning may be impacted by IPV experiences, and therefore clients' perspectives toward their parental abilities warrant assessment. For example, it may be useful to include a measure of parental satisfaction, such as the Kansas Parental Satisfaction Scale (KPSS; James et al., 1985), in the assessment of parents who have experienced IPV. Readers also may wish to refer to Chapter 7 on assessment related to child maltreatment.

Sample Interview Questions for Assessing Parenting Concerns and the Needs of Children

- How well do you think you and your partner work together in parenting your children?
- How often do you and your partner typically agree on matters of disciplining your children? When you disagree, how do you usually decide what will happen?
- How much do you think your children have been impacted by your relationship violence?
- To what extent do you think your ability to parent your children has been impacted by the violence in your relationship?
- Have you noticed recent changes in your children's behaviors or moods lately? If so, please describe these for me. How concerned are you about these changes?
- Has your child witnessed (either by seeing or hearing) the violence between you and your partner? If so, how did your child respond to this experience?
- Is your child currently receiving any form of treatment related to the violence in your relationship? Is your child currently receiving any sort of mental health or behavioral treatment services? If so, please describe these services.
- Would you say that your child has a lot of friends and gets along well with his/her peers?
- Can you name any other adults (besides you and your partner) with whom your child has a close relationship (e.g., extended family members, teachers, mentors, or neighbors)?
- Has there been recent or current involvement of Child Protective Services with your family? If so, please describe this involvement for me and what the current status of it is.

Safety Considerations

The significance of safety considerations when working with clients impacted by IPV cannot be understated. Chapter 4 includes detailed guidelines for safety planning, an important component of treatment with clients experiencing IPV. In addition, the list below includes questions designed to help therapists gather information needed to develop a detailed and thorough safety plan. The other major safety consideration for which specific assessment may be warranted is suicidal ideation. Suicidal thoughts and/or behaviors may be present among both perpetrators and/or victims of IPV (Conner, Cerulli, & Caine, 2002;

Guggisbert, 2006). Therefore, readers may wish to consult Range and Knott (1997) for a review of 20 suicide assessment instruments, and additional open-ended questions are presented in the list below.

Sample Interview Questions for Assessing Safety Considerations

- Questions for victims/survivors:
    - To what extent do you think your partner is a threat to your personal safety now?
    - Has your partner made threats to your safety within the past week? Month? Six months? Year? At any other point in time? If so, please describe those threats?
    - Do you believe your partner is capable of killing you? If so, please describe the reasons that you believe this to be true.
    - Do you think your personal safety is at more or less risk if you stay in your partner or if you attempt to leave your partner? Why?
    - Please describe the environment in and around your home in terms of your safety during a violent incident. In which areas do you think you would be more at risk? In thinking about the neighborhood in which you live, what are some factors that make that area more or less safe for you (e.g., how close you are to your neighbors and how easily you could escape your home if you needed to)?
- Questions for perpetrators:
    - At the present time, do you have intentions to do harm to your partner? If so, please describe those intentions.
    - Do you have access to weapons in your home, car, or any other location you may be with your partner? If so, what are those weapons, and where are they located?
    - Do you now believe yourself to be a threat to your partner's safety?
    - Do you believe that your partner now views you as a threat to his or her safety?
- Questions relating to suicidal ideation:
    - At the present time, do you have thoughts of doing harm to yourself or killing yourself? If so, please describe those thoughts. If so, how do you think that you would do this? Do you have access to any supplies (e.g., a weapon or pills) that are involved in this plan? When are you planning to carry out this plan?
    - In the past, have you ever considered killing yourself? If so, please describe those thoughts, when they occurred, and what you did in response to them.
    - Have you ever in the past actually attempted to kill yourself? If so, please describe when and where that happened, and what happened afterward.

Assessing for Intimate Partner Homicide (IPH)

Intimate partner homicide (IPH) occurs when a partner in an intimate relationship is murdered by the other partner. In the United States, approximately 1,500–1,700 women are killed by former or current intimate partners each year, and among all women murdered, 61% were, killed by a current or former intimate partner (Violence Policy Center, 2006). Unfortunately, children also are killed in 19% of IPH (Websdale, 1999). Often, clients are not aware of the danger that they are in with a partner. Thus, it is essential that therapists are aware of key safety concerns related to IPH and have a solid foundation of Threat Assessment and Management when working with clients experiencing IPV. Threat Assessment and Management is the examination of behaviors associated with targeted violence to identify and understand the subject's motivation and future behavior, with the goal of controlling and preventing the intended violence (Kropp, 2008). Some key pieces of information that a therapist should gather include: Does the perpetrator have access to a weapon? Is s/he using substances? Does s/he have a mental health problem? Have multiple recent stressors occurred? Is the perpetrator? Is there a long standing pattern of violence? Does s/he view violence as acceptable behavior? A questionnaire, the Danger Assessment (Campbell, Webster, & Glass, 2009), provides a 20-item assessment to understand the degree to which a person is in severe danger and at elevated risk for IPH.

Sample Interview Questions for Assessing IPH (i.e., Questions for Immediate Assessment in Escalating IPV Situations)

- Has he/she used a weapon against you or threatened you with one?
- Has he/she threatened to kill you, him(her)self, or anyone else?
- Has he/she choked/strangled you?
- Is he/she stalking you?
- Does he/she have any substance abuse or mental health issues?
- Is he/she controlling, jealous, or possessive?

Conclusion

This chapter highlighted numerous dimensions of clinical assessment that may be involved in working with clients impacted by IPV. The assessment of these dimensions should be done in a manner that accounts for the unique needs and treatment considerations of particular clients. Issues of client safety should play a major role in planning, carrying out, and interpreting the findings of the entire IPV assessment process. With safety considerations as a foundation for the process, the additional strategies addressed in this chapter provide therapists with guidance to carry out an assessment process to gather information that will be useful in formulating treatment goals, objectives, and approaches.

APPENDIX Directory of Selected Instruments for Assessing IPV

This Appendix contains an overview of several instruments that therapists may find useful to include in the clinical assessment of IPV. The source of each instrument is included so therapists can locate additional information, including scoring directions and the availability of the instrument for clinical use. Some of the full-length instruments are available in the original sources, and it is the responsibility of the therapist to ensure that copyright instructions are followed. Instruments are listed in alphabetical order within sections.

Instrument Name and Source	*Construct(s) Designed to Assess*	*Number of Items; Sample Item(s)*	*Reliability and Validity Information*	*Strengths of Instrument for Clinical Practice*	*Limitations of Instrument for Clinical Practice*
Instruments for Assessing the Violence					
Composite Abuse Scale (CAS; Hegarty, Bush, & Sheehan, 2005; Hegarty, Sheehan, & Schonfeld, 1999)	The CAS assesses multiple forms of abuse within IPV.	30 items with four subscales: Severe Combined Abuse; Emotional Abuse; Physical Abuse; and Harassment; Sample item from Emotional abuse subscale: "tried to turn my family, friends, and children against me" (Hegarty et al., 1999, p. 408).	From Hegarty et al. (2005): Severe combined abuse (Cronbach's a = .91); Emotional abuse (a = .93); Physical abuse (a = .94); and Harassment (a = .87); There is preliminary evidence for the convergent and discriminant validity of the CAS.	- The instrument has been validated on a large sample drawn from a clinical population. - The instrument is brief. - The CAS is inclusive of different types of abuse.	- The instrument was developed in Australia, so its cross-cultural applicability is not known.

Instrument Name and Source	*Construct(s) Designed to Assess*	*Number of Items; Sample Item(s)*	*Reliability and Validity Information*	*Strengths of Instrument for Clinical Practice*	*Limitations of Instrument for Clinical Practice*
Danger Assessment (DA; Campbell, 2005; Campbell et al., 2009)	The DA assesses the extent to which IPV is likely to result in lethality (i.e., femicide or attempted femicide) for female victims of IPV in heterosexual relationships.	The DA contains two sections. (1) The respondent is presented with a calendar of the past year and is asked to write on the approximate dates on which they occurred any incidents of abuse victimization, including the level of the violence on a scale from one (e.g., slapping) to five (e.g., using weapons). (2) The woman is asked to answer 20 yes/no questions about her relationship with her abusive partner (e.g., "Does he threaten to kill you?;" Campbell et al., 2009, p. 655).	The DA has been shown to demonstrate Cronbach's alphas ranging from $a = .69$ and $a = .78$; Evidence exists for the construct and predictive validity of the DA (Campbell, 2005).	- Clear scoring guidelines are available (e.g., in the second section, scores between 0 and 7 are described as *variable danger* (a term conceived to reflect that IPV may change quickly and should always be taken seriously), scores between 8 and 13 reflect *increased danger*, scores between 14 and 17 indicate severe danger, and scores 18 and above represent *extreme danger*. - The use of the calendar in Part 1 can provide therapists with detailed information about a client's recent experiences with violence. The calendar may be especially useful for identifying recent escalations in violence.	- The instrument's applicability with male victims or same-sex relationship victims has not yet been demonstrated. - Because femicide is such a rare event, there will always remain some risk of falsely categorizing clients based on their scores (i.e., some women will be at higher risk than their scores may indicate, and other women may demonstrate higher scores than reflective of their actual risk) (Campbell et al., 2009)

(*continued*)

APPENDIX Continued

Instrument Name and Source	*Construct(s) Designed to Assess*	*Number of Items; Sample Item(s)*	*Reliability and Validity Information*	*Strengths of Instrument for Clinical Practice*	*Limitations of Instrument for Clinical Practice*
Fear Scale (Sackett & Saunders, 1999)	This fear scale measures an IPV victim's fear of the abusive partner (this instrument was developed as part of the development and testing of the PPA, which is reviewed below.	6 items; "How often … do you worry that what you do will make your partner angry?" (Sackett & Saunders, 1999, p. 117).	Cronbach's $a = .84$	- This is one of the few existing measures to specifically address the presence of fear of an abusive partner.	- The instrument has been subject to minimal psychometric testing.
Intimate Justice Scale (IJS; Jory, 2004)	The IJS assesses ethical dimensions of psychological and physical abuse victimization (The theoretical framework is Intimate Justice Theory, an extension of Contextual Family Therapy).	15 items (single factor); "My partner believes he or she has the right to force me to do things" (Jory, p. 44).	Cronbach's $a = .98$; Some evidence is available for the criterion and discriminant validity of the IJS.	- The IJS is applicable for adults and adolescents. - The IJS is able to be administered and scored in 10 minutes. - The IJS uses gender-neutral language (although it was developed originally with females in heterosexual relationships).	- The IJS should be combined with other assessments due to the lack of perfect accuracy in classifying level of violence severity. - Items are not rated on a specific time-frame but rather how one's partner "usually treats" him or her.

Instrument Name and Source	*Construct(s) Designed to Assess*	*Number of Items; Sample Item(s)*	*Reliability and Validity Information*	*Strengths of Instrument for Clinical Practice*	*Limitations of Instrument for Clinical Practice*
Measure of Wife Abuse (MWA; Rodenburg & Fantuzzo, 1993)	The MWA assesses the severity, frequency, types, and emotional consequences of abusive behaviors that occur in an intimate relationship during the previous six months.	60 items with four subscales; For each item, respondents report how many times the action occurred in the past six months. Sample items in each subscale are as follows: Physical abuse ("Your partner punched you"); Sexual abuse ("Your partner tried to rape you"); Psychological abuse ("Your partner stole your possessions"); and Verbal ("Your partner told you that you weren't good enough") (Rodenburg & Fantuzzo, 1993, pp. 212–213). For each item, the respondent rates the extent to which the abusive action was hurtful or upsetting.	Cronbach's alphas: total scale (a = .93); Physical abuse subscale (a = .81), Sexual abuse subscale (a = .73), Psychological abuse subscale (a = .94), and Verbal abuse subscale (a = .83); Some evidence exists for the instrument's concurrent validity.	- Although the title of the instrument uses the term *wife*, the instrument was designed to be applicable to forms of intimate relationships other than marriage. Gender-neutral language is used. - Allows clinicians to assess multiple forms of abuse within one measure. - The instrument addresses both severity/impact and frequency. - The six-month time-frame may be useful for identifying recent escalations in violent experiences.	- The MWA is somewhat long with 60 items. - The instrument's applicability with same-sex relationships is unknown. - The bluntness of some of the items (e.g., "Your partner called you a cunt") could be emotionally distressing to some clients.

(*continued*)

APPENDIX Continued

Instrument Name and Source	*Construct(s) Designed to Assess*	*Number of Items; Sample Item(s)*	*Reliability and Validity Information*	*Strengths of Instrument for Clinical Practice*	*Limitations of Instrument for Clinical Practice*
Ongoing Violence Assessment Tool (OVAT; Weiss, Ernst, Cham, & Nick, 2003)	The focus of the OVAT is on ongoing (i.e., presently continuing) abuse victimization.	4 items (3 assess physical and 1 assesses nonphysical abuse); "My partner has no respect for my feelings" (Weiss et al., 2003, p. 138).	Cronbach's *a* = .72; The OVAT's sensitivity and specificity were both greater than 85%.	- The OVAT is brief and may be very useful for universal screening for IPV victimization.	- The sample with which OVAT was developed was nonrandom and excluded some high-risk individuals. - The OVAT may be limited in its usefulness when the respondent is in a period of less active violence (i.e., a "honeymoon" phase).
Profile of Psychological Abuse (PPA; Sackett & Saunders, 1999)	The PPA assesses four dimensions of psychological abuse: Jealous Control; Ignoring; Ridiculing Traits; and Criticizing Behaviors.	21 items (4 subscales); "How often does your partner … become angry or upset if you want to be with someone else and not with him" (from the Jealous Control subscale) (Sackett & Saunders, 1999, p. 117).	Jealous control (Cronbach's *a* = .85), Ignore (*a* = .80), Ridicule Traits (*a* = .79), and Criticize Behavior (*a* = .75); Some evidence is provided for the instrument's validity.	- The language used in the PPA appears to be easy to comprehend. - The PPA is applicable to clinical populations. - Psychological abuse is measured as a multidimensional construct.	- The PPA was developed with a small sample (60 women seeking help from a domestic violence agency; 30 were shelter residents, and 30 were receiving nonresidential services). - The instrument asks respondents to disregard physical abuse, and this may be impossible to do.

Instrument Name and Source	*Construct(s) Designed to Assess*	*Number of Items; Sample Item(s)*	*Reliability and Validity Information*	*Strengths of Instrument for Clinical Practice*	*Limitations of Instrument for Clinical Practice*
Psychological Maltreatment of Women Inventory – Short Form (PMWI-SF; Tolman, 1999)	Based on the longer (58-item) full PMWI scale, the short form of the PMWI measures two underlying dimensions of psychological maltreatment: Dominance-Isolation and Emotional-Verbal.	14 items total (7 per subscale); Dominance-Isolation subscale: "My partner monitored my time and made me account for my whereabouts"; Emotional-Verbal subscale: "My partner called me names" (Tolman, 1999, p. 37).	Cronbach's *a* = .88 for Dominance-Isolation subcale and *a* = .92 for Emotional-Verbal Subscale; Some evidence is available for the Short Form's validity, although Tolman (1999) recommends that the Short Form be used with caution for clinical purposes.	- The Short Form is most appropriate as a brief initial screening tool, which should then be followed-up with more detailed assessment. - The items address specific behavioral indicators of psychological maltreatment. - The language used is gender-neutral.	- The Short Form should be used with caution for clinical purposes due to the lack of an established cutoff score to indicate the presence of psychological maltreatment. - The full-length version of the instrument is somewhat lengthy.

(*continued*)

APPENDIX Continued

Instrument Name and Source	*Construct(s) Designed to Assess*	*Number of Items; Sample Item(s)*	*Reliability and Validity Information*	*Strengths of Instrument for Clinical Practice*	*Limitations of Instrument for Clinical Practice*
Revised Conflict Tactics Scale (CTS2; Straus et al., 1996)	The CTS2 assesses specific behaviors, including minor to severe violence, used to manage conflict within intimate relationships. Respondents are asked to report on their own and their partners' behaviors.	78 items with five subscales: Negotiation (e.g., explained side of argument); Psychological aggression (e.g., insulted or swore at partner); Physical assault (e.g., kicked, bit, or punched partner); Sexual coercion (e.g., used force to make partner have sex); Injury (e.g., partner was cut or bleeding).	- All CTS2 subscales have good internal consistency: Negotiation ($a = .86$); Psychological aggression ($a = .79$); Physical assault ($a = .86$); Sexual coercion ($a = .87$); and Injury ($a = .95$) (Straus et al., 1996). - The CTS2 has demonstrated high test-retest reliability (Vega & O'Leary, 2007). - Evidence exists for the construct and discriminant validity.	- As one of the most widely used measures of IPV (Vega & O'Leary, 2007), this instrument's psychometric properties have been studied extensively. - The instrument was designed to be readable at a 6th grade reading level. - Although the standard reference time for the instrument is 12 months, it is possible to use other reference periods (e.g., six months or since the relationship began; Straus et al., 1996) to provide the most clinically-relevant information. - A short form of the instrument exists, which may be useful in clinical situations in which time is limited, although the short form has lower sensitivity than the full scale (Straus & Douglas, 2004).	- The CTS2 has been criticized for not addressing the context surrounding IPV (e.g., DeKeseredy & Schwartz, 1998). As such, it is recommended that it be combined with other instruments and qualitative assessment procedures in order to provide a more comprehensive depiction of IPV in clients' lives. - The accuracy of the instrument may be limited if a client has difficulty remembering how many times specific behaviors were used during the previous year.

Instrument Name and Source	*Construct(s) Designed to Assess*	*Number of Items; Sample Item(s)*	*Reliability and Validity Information*	*Strengths of Instrument for Clinical Practice*	*Limitations of Instrument for Clinical Practice*
The SAFE-T Questionaire (Fulfer et al., 2007)	This instrument uses indirect questions (i.e., those that do not assess directly or specifically for abusive behaviors) in an effort to detect IPV victimization.	5 items; SAFE-T is an acronym that represents the issues assessed by the corresponding items: Secure/comfortable in home/apartment, Accepted by husband/partner, Family likes husband/partner, Even/calm disposition of husband/partner, and Talk to resolve differences.	Cronbach's *a* = .95; Some evidence is provided for the instrument's validity as a screening tool, although the researchers concluded that the instrument may be more effective at ruling out IPV than it is in ruling it in.	- The instrument is brief and time-effective. - The "SAFE-T" acronym provides a mnemonic device that could be applied informally when formal assessment instruments are not readily available (e.g., when a therapist begins to suspect in the midst of a session on another topic that IPV victimization may be present). - The SAFE-T Questionnaire offers a potentially useful way to screen for the generalized power and control dynamics that may exist within IPV with clients for whom indirect questioning may be more appropriate or useful than more direct assessments.	- The instrument is not fully reliable as a stand-alone screening tool for IPV victimization. - It was designed and tested exclusively for female IPV victims in heterosexual relationships.

(*continued*)

APPENDIX Continued

Instrument Name and Source	*Construct(s) Designed to Assess*	*Number of Items; Sample Item(s)*	*Reliability and Validity Information*	*Strengths of Instrument for Clinical Practice*	*Limitations of Instrument for Clinical Practice*
Severity of Violence Against Women Scale (SVAWS; Marshall, 1992a)/ **Severity of Violence Against Men Scale** (SVAMS; Marshall, 1992b)	These instruments are designed to be sensitive measures of the severity of threatened, attempted, and completed violence behaviors within intimate relationships. The SVAWS focuses on male-perpetrated violence against female partners, and the SVAMS focuses on female-perpetrated violence against male partners.	- The SVAWS includes 49 items with 9 factors; "How often has your partner hit or kicked a wall, door or furniture?" (Marshall, 1992a, p. 120) - The SVAMS contains 46 items with 8 factors.	- For the SVAWS subscales, Cronbach's alpha coefficients ranged from .89 to .96. - For the SVAMS subscales, Cronbach's alpha coefficients ranged from .93 to .95.	- The instruments were developed with both college students and community-based samples. - The categorizations of the levels of severity of specific acts of violence are based on empirical, rather than theoretical, derivations. - The SVAWS and SVAMS could potentially be useful for understanding clients' perceptions of the severity of different types of violence, and this could supplement information about the types they have experienced personally. -The clinically-appropriate version of the SVAWS (Marshall, 1992a) can provide information about the frequency of violent acts within a relationship.	- Although Marshall (1992a) presents a clinically-appropriate version of the SVAWS (i.e., one that asks respondents to report on their own experiences with violence), this version should be used with caution because this is not the version tested in these studies, and the instrument was not developed with clinical populations.

Instrument Name and Source	*Construct(s) Designed to Assess*	*Number of Items; Sample Item(s)*	*Reliability and Validity Information*	*Strengths of Instrument for Clinical Practice*	*Limitations of Instrument for Clinical Practice*
Women's Experience with Battering (WEB; Smith, Earp, & DeVellis, 1995; Smith et al., 1999)	The WEB assesses the victimization process associated with battering	10 items; "He has a look that goes straight through me and terrifies me" (Smith et al., 1999, p. 189*).	Cronbach's *a* = .99; Evidence exists for the validity of the WEB Scale.	- Because the instrument focuses on the presence of power and control dynamics, it could be useful for differentiating between intimate terrorism and and situational couple violence in clinical practice. - The instrument was developed based on focus groups designed to elicit information about battered women's lived experiences. -The WEB is brief.	- Because the instrument does not focus on specific behaviors, it may not provide a complete picture of violence in clients' relationships.

(*continued*)

APPENDIX Continued

Instrument Name and Source	*Construct(s) Designed to Assess*	*Number of Items; Sample Item(s)*	*Reliability and Validity Information*	*Strengths of Instrument for Clinical Practice*	*Limitations of Instrument for Clinical Practice*
Instruments for Assessing the Perpetrator					
Proximal Antecedents to Violent Episode Scale (PAVE; Babcock et al., 2004)	The PAVE is designed to assess the extent to which a man self-reports that he is likely to perpetrate intimate partner violence in response to a variety of situations.	30 items with three subscales: Violence to Control, Violence out of Jealousy, and Violence Following Verbal Abuse; "I walk in and catch my partner having sex with someone" (Babcock et al., p. 442).	- Across two samples, the total scale and factor subscales' Cronbach's alpha coefficients were all above $a = .90$, with the exception of the Violence out of Jealousy subscale, which demonstrated alpha coefficients greater than $a = .70$ across the two samples. - There is some evidence of the validity of the PAVE, although it does appear that social desirability influences respondents' reporting on the instrument.	- The PAVE is relatively brief. - The instrument could be very useful for identifying potential triggers to violent episodes. This information could be used to enhance safety planning interventions.	- If social desirability is not accounted for in the interpretation of the responses to the PAVE, the responses could be biased toward more socially desirable reporting. - The Violence out of Jealousy subscale is the least psychometrically-strong subscale of the instrument. - The scale seems to be less applicable with individuals who demonstrate lower levels of violence.

Instrument Name and Source	*Construct(s) Designed to Assess*	*Number of Items; Sample Item(s)*	*Reliability and Validity Information*	*Strengths of Instrument for Clinical Practice*	*Limitations of Instrument for Clinical Practice*
Safe at Home Instrument (SAHI; Begun et al., 2003)	Grounded in Prochaska & DiClemente's (1983) Transtheoretical Model of Change, the SAHI is designed to assess the extent to which male perpetrators of IPV in heterosexual relationships are ready to change their IPV-related behaviors.	23 items, with 3 subscales; "It's time for me to listen to the people telling me I need help" (from the Contemplation subscale; Begun et al., 2003, p. 87)	- The Cronbach's alpha coefficients for the subscales varied: Contemplation (*a* = .91), Precontemplation (*a* = .59), and Preparation/Action (*a* = .79).- Some evidence exists for the concurrent and predictive validity of the SAHI.	- The SAHI is one of the few existing instruments designed to assess readiness for change specifically within the population of IPV perpetrators. - The instrument has a strong theoretical basis. - The instrument was developed with a large-scale clinical sample.	- The instrument may not reflect behavioral change.- The instrument may not apply to IPV perpetrators other than heterosexual males. - The researchers found a relationship between pre-intervention Preparation/Action scores and social desirability, which suggests that perpetrators may misrepresent their readiness for change prior to treatment. - The instrument is not yet able to be used to guide decisions about appropriate treatment approaches for clients (Begun et al., 2003).

(*continued*)

APPENDIX Continued

Instrument Name and Source	*Construct(s) Designed to Assess*	*Number of Items; Sample Item(s)*	*Reliability and Validity Information*	*Strengths of Instrument for Clinical Practice*	*Limitations of Instrument for Clinical Practice*
Spousal Assault Risk Assessment (SARA: Kropp & Hart, 2000)	The SARA is a manual that presents professional guidelines for assessing risk for spousal violence. It includes 20 risk factors, both related to general violence and spousal violence.	20 items; Sample general violence risk factor: "Personality disorder with anger, impulsivity, or behavioral instability"; Sample spousal violence risk factor: "Attitudes that support or condone spousal assault" (Kropp & Hart, 2000, p. 103); Different scoring procedures can be used depending on the purpose of the assessment.	Cronbach's alpha coefficients of the various rating procedures ranged from $a = .62$ to $a = .83$. Interrater reliabilities varied more, ranging from $r = .22$ to $r = .84$. - Some evidence exists for the concurrent and construct validity of the SARA.	- The SARA has multiple practical applications. - The SARA was tested on a large sample. - The assessment process can be used across professional disciplines. - The SARA provides a structured process for examining the potential risk factors that may be related to spousal assault perpetration.	- As a procedure, rather than a structured assessment instrument, the SARA is open to some variation in use, and therefore the subjectivity of the rater may influence scores. - Risk factors may vary for specific individuals, and certain characteristics may be more or less relevant for some perpetrators than others (i.e., as the characteristics may relate to the different typologies of batterers discussed in this book).

Instrument Name and Source	*Construct(s) Designed to Assess*	*Number of Items; Sample Item(s)*	*Reliability and Validity Information*	*Strengths of Instrument for Clinical Practice*	*Limitations of Instrument for Clinical Practice*
University of Rhode Island Change Assessment for Domestic Violence (URICA-DV; Levesque, et al. 2000)	Grounded in Prochaska & DiClemente's (1983) Transtheoretical Model of Change, the URICA-DV is designed to measure male IPV perpetrators' readiness to end their perpetration of IPV.	20 items with four subscales; "More and more I'm seeing how my violence hurts my partner" (from the Contemplation subscale; Levesque et al., 2000, p. 187).	- Cronbach's alpha coefficients for the subscales were as follows: Precontemplation (a = .72); Contemplation; (a = .73); Action; (a = .81); Maintenance; (a = .68) - There is some evidence for the construct validity of the URICA-DV.	- The instrument was developed with a clinical sample. - The instrument has the potential to inform BIP facilitators about prospective clients' readiness to change their violent behaviors.	- The authors caution that more evidence is needed for the validity of the URICA-DV before it would be appropriate to use the instrument to match BIP clients to different treatment approaches. - The instrument may not be applicable to IPV perpetrators other than heterosexual males. - In the factor analysis, Preparation stage items did not create a unique dimension, so a separate subscale is not included for this stage. However, the Preparation stage may have clinical relevance for BIP clients and facilitators. - The URICA-DV focuses only on physical abuse and does not address psychological violence.
Instruments for Assessing the Victim/Survivor					

(continued)

APPENDIX Continued

Instrument Name and Source	*Construct(s) Designed to Assess*	*Number of Items; Sample Item(s)*	*Reliability and Validity Information*	*Strengths of Instrument for Clinical Practice*	*Limitations of Instrument for Clinical Practice*
Domestic Violence Myth Acceptance Scale (DVMAS; Peters, 2008)	The DVMAS assesses the extent to which the respondent believes in myths about the intimate terrorism form of IPV (i.e., it does not address situational couple violence). Peters (2008) defined these myths as "stereotypical beliefs about domestic violence that are generally false but are widely and persistently held, and which serve to minimize, deny, or justify physical aggression against intimate partners" (p. 5).	18 items with four factors: Character Blame, Behavior Blame, Exoneration of the Perpetrator, and Minimization; "If a woman doesn't like it, she can leave" (Peters, 2008, p. 21).	- Cronbach's alpha for the total scale was .81 in Study 1 and .88 in study 2. - The Cronbach's alphas for the factor subscales ranged from .64 to .88. - There is some evidence for the construct and criterion validity of the DVMAS.	- The DVMAS could provide therapists with an understanding of clients' acceptance of myths that may influence their experiences with IPV. - From a cognitive-behavioral therapy perspective, these myths could be viewed as harmful cognitions, and therefore those myths that clients advocate could become potential targets for cognitive restructuring. - The DVMAS measures a unique aspect of IPV experiences that many other instruments do not address.	- This instrument likely should only be used with IPV victims/survivors in later stages of treatment, as some items reflect victim-blaming attitudes and may be emotionally distressing for clients in earlier stages of treatment. - The instrument was developed with limited samples, with low response rates, using only Internet-based data collection. - The instrument addresses only male violence toward women. - The instrument had an unstable factor structure. Therefore, it appears that the most appropriate way to use the DVMAS clinically is to use the total scale only.

Instrument Name and Source	*Construct(s) Designed to Assess*	*Number of Items; Sample Item(s)*	*Reliability and Validity Information*	*Strengths of Instrument for Clinical Practice*	*Limitations of Instrument for Clinical Practice*
Domestic Violence Survivor Assessment (DVSA; Dienemann et al., 2002; Dienemann, Glass, Hanson, & Lunsford, 2007)	The DVSA was designed to measure the extent to which a survivor of IPV has moved toward a life free from violence. The instrument is grounded theoretically in Prochaska and DiClemente's (1983) Transtheoretical Model of Change.	The format of the DVSA is a clinician-scored matrix in which the professional rates the client's stage of change across 12 personal (e.g., accessing help from family, friends, and organizations) and relational (e.g., seeking legal sanctions) domains.	Dienemann and colleagues (2007) examined the reliability and validity of the DVSA in a study including 355 women. The test-retest correlation coefficient was $r = .7$, and the Cronbach's alpha coefficient was $a = .96$. An exploratory factor analysis revealed a single-factor structure. The researchers also demonstrated that the DVSA was successful at demonstrating change over time as clients progressed through treatment.	- The DVSA allows for the possibility that the relationship with the partner can continue in a nonviolent manner as a potential outcome of treatment, and this outcome may be relevant to couples who wish to remain in their relationships but have the abuse stop. - Although the instrument has only been tested with females, its use of gender-neutral language may render it an appropriate tool with male survivors or partners within same-sex relationships. - Because the clinician scores the instrument, the combination of the client's self-report the clinician's observations of the client's behavior may provide a more objective perspective on the client's situation.	- A limitation of the fact that the DVSA is clinician-scored is that a clinician could introduce bias in the scoring process through to generalizing behaviors in one domain to others or through having personal or professional motivations for demonstrating that the client is improving over time, particularly if the instrument is being used to demonstrate that clinician's effectiveness. - The matrix with 12 domains and 5 levels per domain could be viewed as cumbersome to some practitioners.

(*continued*)

APPENDIX Continued

Instrument Name and Source	*Construct(s) Designed to Assess*	*Number of Items; Sample Item(s)*	*Reliability and Validity Information*	*Strengths of Instrument for Clinical Practice*	*Limitations of Instrument for Clinical Practice*
Intimate Partner Violence Strategies Index (IPVSI; Goodman et al., 2003)	The IPVSI was developed to measure the strategies that battered women use to respond to, cope with, and maintain their safety in the face of IPV victimization.	39 items; Each item reflects a strategy that women may use to respond to IPV (e.g., ending or trying to end the relationship and working out an escape plan). For each item, respondents are asked to indicate whether they have used each strategy within the past year, and for those that they have used, they are asked to rate how helpful it was on a scale from 1 (not at all helpful) to 5 (extremely helpful).	- No information is available about the psychometric properties (e.g., internal consistency or test-retest reliability) of the IPVSI. - Based on a conceptual framework, the strategies are grouped into six categories based on the purpose, means, and involvement of others in the strategies: placating, resistance, safety planning, legal, and formal network, and informal network.	- The resources addressed in the IPVSI are specific to IPV. - The IPVSI was developed in partnership with advocates and IPV victims, and therefore the items and the language used may hold particular meaning for clients. - Goodman et al. (2003) emphasize that the underlying assumption of the instrument is that women who are victims of IPV are active and resourceful in responding to their abuse, which reflects a strengths-based perspective toward this population. - The IPVSI is useful for assessing the strategies that clients have and have not yet used in response to IPV victimization and how helpful these strategies have been.	- The instrument is in need of further examination to ensure that it is reliable and valid. - Some included strategies address resources that are not available to every IPV victim (e.g., seeking help from employers or coworkers would not apply for a woman who is not employed), so the availability of resources should be considered when interpreting clients' responses to this instrument. - The instrument was developed for women who have been victimized in heterosexual relationships, so its application to other populations may not be appropriate.

Instrument Name and Source	*Construct(s) Designed to Assess*	*Number of Items; Sample Item(s)*	*Reliability and Validity Information*	*Strengths of Instrument for Clinical Practice*	*Limitations of Instrument for Clinical Practice*
Posttraumatic Growth Inventory (PTGI; Tedeschi & Calhoun, 1996)	The PTGI assesses the respondent's perceptions of the positive benefits (e.g., improved relationships with others or perceptions of oneself) that resulted from experiencing traumatic events.	21 items with five subscales; "Knowing that I can count on people in times of trouble" (Tedeschi & Calhoun, 1996, p. 460).	- The Cronbach's alpha for the total scale was .90. - The subscale Cronbach's alphas ranged from $a = .67$ to $a = .85$. -With a subsample of participants, two-month test-retest reliability was $r = .71$ for the total scale, although the subscales were more varied from $r = .37$ to $r = .74$. - There is some evidence for the concurrent, discriminant, and construct validity of the PTGI.	- The PTGI may be especially useful when working with victims/survivors who have left abusive relationships and who are working toward finding meaning in their past experiences of traumatic victimization. - The PTGI's subscales may be useful for identifying different areas in which the client has experienced personal growth as a result of traumatic victimization. - As a more positively-oriented instrument, the PTGI may provide a refreshing perspective for assessment clients within a compendium of other instruments that may be more negatively-focused (e.g., on symptoms and stressors).	- The instrument is not specific to family violence. - The PTGI appears to have been developed mostly for research purposes, so its clinical applicability should be considered carefully by any therapist considering including it in an assessment process. - The instrument was developed with college students, and it therefore may be less applicable with other populations.

(*continued*)

APPENDIX Continued

Instrument Name and Source	*Construct(s) Designed to Assess*	*Number of Items; Sample Item(s)*	*Reliability and Validity Information*	*Strengths of Instrument for Clinical Practice*	*Limitations of Instrument for Clinical Practice*
The Lifetime Trauma and Victimization History (LTVH; Widom et al., 2005)	The LTVH assesses lifetime history of trauma, including the age it occurred, its frequency and duration, and who the perpetrator was.	30 items that assess the following seven categories of trauma: 1. General trauma; 2. Physical assault/ abuse; 3. Sexual assault/ abuse; 4. Family/ friend murdered or suicide; 5. Witnessed trauma to someone else; 6. Crime victimization; 7. Kidnapped or stalked	Evidence exists for the criterion and convergent validity of the LTVH.	- The instrument is clinically useful because clients may have histories of multiple forms of trauma that could be impacting their current functioning. - The instrument was designed to be easy to administer and understand. - The instrument can be administered by paraprofessionals who receive appropriate training. - To some extent, the LTVH assesses respondents' perceptions of the trauma and not just basic historical information.	- The instrument was designed to be used as an interview due to the potentially emotionally distressing nature of the questions. Therefore, it should not be used when only paper-and-pencil administration is possible. - Completion time can vary depending on the number of traumas the respondent has experienced. Clients who have extensive trauma histories would require a lengthy clinical interview to use this instrument. - The instrument relies on the accuracy of the respondent's recall.

4

TREATMENT FOR BATTERING

Battering involves many complex dynamics. Therapists' work with clients impacted by battering—whether victims or perpetrators—is extremely complex as well. As this chapter highlights, therapists face numerous challenges, such as determining what their role should be, deciding how safety issues can best be addressed, and using sound intervention strategies when the existing research evidence on effective strategies for both populations is relatively lacking.

Treatment approaches should be based on assessment information gathered using the guidelines presented in Chapter 3. We recommend that therapists use the most cautious approaches possible until it is clear that other approaches can be considered safely (Johnson, 2009). Adding to the complexity of IPV assessment and treatment is the fact that no hard and fast rules exist as to what type of treatment is warranted based on type of IPV. This is particularly true when determining whether conjoint couple therapy is appropriate. Conjoint therapy is, in general, not advisable in cases of battering because of the potential risk for the victim (Johnson, 2009). Although Johnson (2009) indicated that couple therapy may be "just what is needed in cases of situational couple violence" (p. 289), he also advised that any case of IPV should be treated as a possible case of intimate terrorism unless it becomes clear that it is indeed situational couple violence. Thus, therapists should view conjoint treatment with couples experiencing IPV to carry a potential risk to a victim unless it becomes clear that such a risk is not present. Therefore, we assume in this chapter that treatment will be separate for battering victims and perpetrators. The first section of this chapter addresses therapy with battering victims, and the second covers treatment for perpetrators.

Therapy with Battering Victims

This section offers research- and theory-based guidelines to therapists working with victims. We begin with recommendations for setting the stage for effective therapy, particularly by creating a climate that supports clients' helpseeking behaviors and disclosure of victimization, as well as by remaining non-judgmental and avoiding pathologizing these clients. Next, we discuss a high-priority intervention: safety planning. We then provide general considerations for interventions, followed by some specific theory-based therapy approaches. Finally, we delve deeply into one of the most complicated issues for therapists working with battering victims: supporting them as they decide whether and how to leave their abusive relationships.

Creating a Context of Support

When working with battering victims, therapists must work hard from the start to establish a therapeutic climate that can support the multifaceted and diverse needs of this population. This is consistent with the nationally developing concept of trauma-informed care that engages people with a history of trauma through five guiding principles of safety, empowerment, choice, collaboration, and trust (information about this national movement can be found at http://www.samhsa.gov/nctic). As with all forms of family violence and consistent with trauma-informed care principles, safety considerations must be at the forefront of therapists' minds when working with battering victims (Chang et al., 2006; D'Ardenne & Balakrishna, 2001). Accordingly, we devote the entire next section to safety planning. As a precursor to addressing the primarily physical safety concerns addressed through safety planning, considering emotional safety throughout the therapy process is essential. We believe that there are three key elements for promoting battering victims' emotional safety as therapy clients: supporting helpseeking, remaining nonjudgmental, and avoiding pathologizing victims.

Supporting Victims' Helpseeking. Many potential barriers challenge battering victims in their helpseeking efforts. For example, the stigma surrounding battering victimization may lead some victims not to seek help (Lynch, 2006), fearing that they will be judged or blamed for their own experiences. For many battering victims, it takes courage merely to make an appointment for therapy, whether or not they are also seeking help and support from other sources, such as friends, family members, the police, shelters, and other supportive resources in the community. Other barriers that may prevent victims from seeking help include lack of knowledge about resources, not believing that the abuse they are experiencing meets the criteria for receiving help, and views that available resources are not helpful (McLeod, Hays, & Chang, 2010).

Therapists can operate their practices in ways that address common helpseeking challenges, such as limited transportation, child care, and fear of their partners following them (Shavers, Levendosky, Dubay, Basu, & Jenei, 2005; McLeod et al., 2010). For example, therapy practices can be located in safe, secure areas accessible to public transportation, and appointments can be made available at different times of day to meet child care arrangements. Because their lives may be very chaotic, victims may cancel or forget appointments (Shavers et al., 2005), and as such, therapists may need to revisit their missed appointment policies so that clients who miss frequent appointments may not be terminated prematurely from therapy. As another basic precaution, therapists should check with clients to determine whether it would be safe to leave voice mail messages at their phone numbers (McCloskey & Fraser, 1997). All of these practical steps are consistent with the concept of creating a trauma-informed therapeutic environment to maximize treatment engagement.

There are two general types of helpseeking sources: informal and formal. Informal sources of help include such resources as friends, family members, and neighbors. Formal resources include the services and programs discussed in the section on the IPV Response System in Chapter 2. Two categories of formal helpseeking that battering victims may engage include legal helpseeking (e.g., protection orders, police contacts, and the court system) and extralegal helpseeking (e.g., counseling, hotlines, clergy, and healthcare systems; Bennett Cattaneo, Stuewig, Goodman, Kaltman, & Dutton, 2007).

In light of the many barriers to helpseeking, rates of helpseeking can be low among victims. Henning and Klesges (2002) surveyed over 1,700 female victims of heterosexual IPV to examine their patterns of seeking help from counseling and other social services. All participants were interviewed as part of court-based pretrial services based on their partners' IPV charges. Only about 15% of the women had previously sought formal counseling or supportive services, even though there were several agencies in the community that offered such services. The participants who did seek these services did so through domestic violence agencies (32%), healthcare professionals (10%), and other sources (58%).

However, helpseeking can be considered an ongoing process through which victims may seek help frequently and from difference sources, although their helpseeking behaviors may change over time (Bennett Cattaneo et al., 2007). Bennett Cattaneo et al. (2007) found that, earlier on, women were most likely to use legal help, specifically calling the police. However, one year later, women were more likely to have sought help from extralegal sources, such as clergy, hotlines, and domestic violence programs. They also found that women's helpseeking behaviors from either type of source tended to decrease over time. In examining the relationships between the different types of helpseeking (i.e., legal and extralegal), Bennett Cattaneo et al. found that seeking one of these types of help was related to seeking the other type of help. The researchers concluded that their findings support the "one-stop shopping" model of victim support agencies, through which multiple sources of support are available at one site. An important implication for therapists is that, because helpseeking behaviors may decrease over time among battering victims, efforts may be needed to reconnect victims to supportive resources if they have not accessed these sources in some time.

Battering victims may differ in their helpseeking behaviors based on their background characteristics and unique experiences with violence. Henning and Klesges (2002) found that being more likely to seek these services was related to being older, having a higher socioeconomic status, being Caucasian, being or having been married (as compared to being or having been in a relationship with a dating partner), experiencing more severe physical or psychological abuse, and having minor children. Others have focused on the type of violence experienced by victims. Leone, Johnson, and Cohan (2007) examined differences in victim helpseeking from formal and informal sources based on whether they had experienced intimate terrorism (i.e., battering) or situational couple violence. They found that battering victims, as compared to situational couple violence victims, were more likely to contact the police, seek medical help, and contact a counselor. In contrast, situational couple violence victims were more likely to seek help from friends and neighbors. There were no differences in the groups in seeking help from family members. Although situational couple violence victims were less likely to seek help from police, over 30% of the women in the situational couple violence group did call the police, and 14% sought help from a counselor. This suggests that, although battering victims may be more likely to be involved with the IPV response system, components of this system must also be set up to serve the needs of situational couple violence victims.

Among battering victims, there are times during the cycle of violence when victims are more likely to seek help, referred to as the "Open Window Phase" (Matar Curnow, 1997). Matar Curnow built on Lenore Walker's (1979) Cycle of Violence Theory about the three main phases that occur in abusive relationships: tension-building, acute battering, and the honeymoon. Matar Curnow added the Open Window Phase as a period that follows acute battering and precedes the honeymoon phase. She speculated that, during the Open Window Phase, the victim is more realistic about her victimization experiences, more likely to seek help, and more amenable to interventions. In order to examine the Open Window Phase, Matar Curnow conducted a grounded theory qualitative study with 22 women from an urban battered women's shelter. All had been assaulted by male partners during the year prior to the study. The analyses revealed six characteristics of Open Window Phase behaviors: (a) telling someone else about the abuse; (b) attempting to leave the relationship; (c) acknowledging the abusive reality of their situation; (d) seeking protective assistance from the police; (e) seeking healthcare assistance from medical professionals; and (f) seeking legal help. This Open Window Phase may present the optimal time for initiating interventions with battering victims, although the extent to which these interventions can be sustained if the cycle of violence continues remains to be determined.

Remaining Non-judgmental and Responding to Initial Disclosures of Victimization Experiences. Because victims may be afraid of being judged, counselors should start by building rapport with clients and orienting them to the nature of the counseling services to be rendered (Chronister, Linville, & Kaag, 2008). Promoting acceptance and not conveying judgment are basic requirements for creating a safe therapeutic climate for victims (Smith & Randall, 2007). Chang et al. (2004) conducted seven focus groups with 41 women with previous or current experiences of IPV victimization about how healthcare providers can best ask about and discuss victimization experiences. The women suggested that professionals should make asking about IPV experiences routine and provide a rationale for asking in order to reduce conveying judgment. These conversations should occur in a climate of kindness, safety, and support. In a similar study, Dienemann, Glass, and Hyman (2005) held five focus groups with a total of 26 female battering victims to learn how these women would have liked professionals to respond upon first disclosing IPV. An important recommendation was to avoid judging victims, but rather ensure that they are treated with respect. A professional's immediate response to a client's disclosure of victimization can have a profound impact on how safe and comfortable the victim will feel in sharing further with the professional.

Therapists must be mindful of how their personal values about battering and victims may impact their judgment of their clients (D'Ardenne & Balakrishna, 2001). For example, therapists may have strong personal reactions when working with clients involved in an abusive relationship, such as wanting to tell these clients to leave their partners. However, the role of helpers is not to insist that victims leave violent relationships (Lynch, 2006), although this issue can present an ethical dilemma for therapists (See Ethical Case Study below, as well as a related discussion later in this chapter). By helping victims maintain their right to make decisions for their own lives, therapists can empower them to make decisions for themselves and develop a greater sense of agency and empowerment (McLeod et al., 2010). It important for therapists to join with their clients and meet them where they are (McCloskey & Fraser, 1997). When victims feel understood, they are better able to make meaning of their experiences with abuse (McLeod et al., 2010). Therapists should allow these clients to take the time that they need to move through the healing process at their own pace (Wuest & Merritt-Gray, 1999).

Ethical Case Study: To Influence or Not to Influence?

Case description. Aileen, age 30, is receiving counseling through the mental health division of the agency that runs the battered women's shelter where she has been staying for two weeks. Before entering the shelter, Aileen was living with her boyfriend, Kendall, age 35. The couple has no children. Aileen entered the shelter after a violent incident in which she suffered multiple injuries, including a broken leg bone and two black eyes. A neighbor had heard the violence and called the police. Kendall was arrested, and Aileen was brought to the shelter for protection. Kendall has since been released from jail and returned to the home while awaiting prosecution. Aileen tells her counselor that she is thinking of moving back into the home with Kendall. Aileen acknowledges that she experienced physical and emotional abuse for nearly all of their four-year relationship, and she reports that the physical violence has become increasingly frequent and severe recently, after Kendall unexpectedly lost his job. Aileen seems fearful of Kendall and reports that he has made threats to hurt her again. Although she has not received a formal diagnosis, she demonstrates symptoms of a depressed mood, anxiety, and nightmares, all of which have led to sleep disturbances and impaired physical health. Nonetheless, Aileen says that she still loves Kendall, misses him, and believes that he needs her at home.

Sample Relevant Ethical Standards

AAMFT (2001) Code of Ethics.

"Marriage and family therapists respect the rights of clients to make decisions and help them to understand the consequences of these decisions. Therapists clearly advise the clients that they have the responsibility to make decisions regarding relationships such as cohabitation, marriage, divorce, separation, reconciliation, custody, and visitation." (AAMFT, 2001, Ethical Standard 1.8)

ACA (2005) Code of Ethics

"The primary responsibility of counselors is to respect the dignity and to promote the welfare of clients." (ACA, 2005, Ethical standard A.1.a)

APA (2010) Ethical Principles of Psychologists and Code of Conduct

"Principle A: Beneficence and nonmaleficence … In their professional actions, psychologists seek to safeguard the welfare and rights of those with whom they interact professionally and other affected persons… Principle E: Respect for People's Rights and Dignity. Psychologists respect the dignity and worth of all people, and the rights of individuals to privacy, confidentiality, and self-determination." (APA, 2010, General Principles A and E)

NASW (2008) Code of Ethics

"SelfDetermination: Social workers respect and promote the right of clients to selfdetermination and assist clients in their efforts to iden-

> tify and clarify their goals. Social workers may limit clients' right to selfdetermination when, in the social workers' professional judgment, clients' actions or potential actions pose a serious, foreseeable, and imminent risk to themselves or others." (NASW, 2008, Ethical Standard 1.02)

Discussion. Therapists face many potential ethical challenges when working with battering victims. Perhaps the most fundamental challenge relates to whether it is ethical for therapists to use their influence to encourage victims to leave their relationships (Huston, 1984). This issue gives rise to a potential conflict between the ethical principles of client autonomy and beneficence (Huston, 1984). The welfare and autonomy of victims as therapy clients must be supported (Kress, Protivnak, & Sadlack, 2008). However, therapists may play a role in advocating for safety (Kress et al., 2008). Huston explored this issue in depth, focusing on the extent to which victims are competent and able to engage in rational thinking. According to Huston, the traumatic consequences of victimization may render a victim to have limited competence to make decisions for him/herself. Therefore, a directive approach to recommending the client consider leaving the relationship may be warranted. However, Huston cautions that therapists cross into unethical behavior if they refuse to treat a victim who will not leave an abusive relationship, or if they otherwise attempt to force him/her to leave. As such, a prudent approach is for therapists to explore with clients the question of whether leaving an abusive partner is the wisest and safest decision at the current point in time, all while maintaining a position of being non-judgmental and supportive of the client's decisions as to what is best for him/her. Thus, therapists also should ensure that clients are informed about the potential danger involved in battering victimization, as well as about the resources that are available to help them leave the relationship (Kress et al., 2008).

An important time in the therapy process during which therapists are advised to take a non-judgmental stance is at first disclose of victimization experiences. Clients may vary in their willingness to disclose to therapists their experiences of violent victimization. Mitchell and Lacour (2001) found that the following factors led clients to be more likely to disclose previous victimization experiences: clients being female, clients having a previous history of participating in counseling, and counselors being female.

Some battering victims will disclose immediately to their therapists that they have been victimized and, for some, these experiences will be obvious even before self-disclosure occurs, such as if a client is referred from a shelter for battered women.

Other clients do not share victimization experiences immediately. Some battering experiences may be identified through the assessment process. At other times, clients may feel compelled to hide these experiences until later, perhaps once adequate rapport is established or they do not believe that their safety will be put at risk by disclosing. For example, victims may underreport abuse due to fear of retaliation from their partners (Heckert & Gondolf, 2000b). In addition, women may be likely to underreport their experiences of abuse victimization if they fear that reporting would cause problems for their partners and their relationships (Heckert & Gondolf, 2000b). Regardless of when or how therapists first learn of clients' victimization experiences, therapists should consider how their initial responses to clients' disclosures set the tone for clients' subsequent progress in therapy. Upon a client's initial disclosure of victimization, counselors must be sensitive to the language used to describe those experiences and should make efforts to make every interaction with the victim one that helps to strengthen the victim's resources (Merritt-Gray & Wuest, 1995). Therapists must avoid even subtle implications that they blame the victim for the abuse (Smith & Randall, 2007).

Avoiding Pathologizing Victims. Therapists must be cautious against further pathologizing and stigmatizing battering victims through all aspects of therapy, including diagnosing and conceptualizing their presenting symptoms, planning appropriate interventions, and defining what it means to have a successful treatment outcome. When therapists fail to assess for IPV experiences, they may assign stigmatizing labels to victims that address the symptoms of the traumatic abuse victimization experiences (Holtzworth-Munroe, Smutzler, & Sandin, 1997; Humphreys, 2008; McLeod et al., 2010). "Historically, application of diagnostic labels to battered women often focused on the psychological 'shortcomings' of these women and/or implied that they were responsible for their own victimization" (Holtzworth-Munroe et al., 1997, pp. 179–180). Mental health diagnoses may serve to blame and pathologize victims (Holtzworth-Munroe et al., 1997). Being diagnosed with a mental health disorder can lead to increased stigma for a victim, and this could play into the perpetrator's psychological abuse, in which he or she calls the victim crazy (Humphreys, 2008). As such, it is important that mental health symptoms among battering victims be considered consequences of victimization, rather than as the cause of it or as stable traits (Holtzworth-Munroe et al., 1997). As such, victims are likely to appreciate when their symptoms are considered in relation to their abuse, rather than pathologizing those symptoms as maladaptive coping strategies or inherent to the person (McLeod et al., 2010).

A need remains for greater attention to social issues and movements that can support survivors (Humphreys, 2008). We encourage therapists to attend to aspects of the service delivery organizations in and with which they work (including mental health agencies, private practice settings, and health insurance companies) that do not adequately address these clients' needs. For example, mental health reimbursement systems often emphasize shorter-term treatments, and these may not adequately address the effects of traumatization (Grigsby & Hartman, 1997). In addition, the extent of symptoms experienced by victims may hinder their ability to advance toward treatment goals or meet agency policies (Helfrich, Fujiura, & Rutkowski-Kmitta, 2008). Policies may need to be revised if organizations wish to serve victims effectively. Due to many existing therapeutic services not being attuned to the needs of victims, these clients may have previous experiences of encountering therapists who failed to assess or address for their abuse experiences (McLeod et al., 2010). Thus, clients' negative views of these experiences could impact their openness to seeking help currently or in the future. Exploring these prior experiences can be a useful area of discussion.

Safety Planning and Risk Assessment

The process of constructing a safety plan with battering victims represents a practical strategy therapists can use to address safety concerns with this client population. Safety planning is such an important process when working with victims (Chang et al., 2006; Kress et al., 2008; McLeod et al., 2010) that we describe it in detail here. It is important to note, however, that battering victims seeking therapy may already have a safety plan in place if they are also seeking help from another agency. Even in those cases, therapists should review those plans with their clients to understand the clients' unique safety needs and plans for addressing them and be alert to revisions that may need to be made over time as needs change.

What is a safety plan? We define a safety plan as a personalized, detailed document that outlines clear and specific safety strategies that a battering victim can use to promote his/her safety across a wide range of situations. Fundamental to the creation of an appropriate safety plan is a collaborative process to develop it between the client and the professional. Safety planning should not involve professionals telling victims what to do, but rather providing suggestions and empowering them to be in control of their own decisions (Dienemann et al., 2005). Although some domestic violence agencies may provide standard forms for safety plans, a safety plan is most effective when tailored to the unique needs of each client. Safety planning should not be done as a rigid, prescriptive process that does not account for the unique background of each victim (Campbell, 2001).

Safety Planning should Involve Risk Assessment. A good place to start in safety planning is assessing general safety risks that victims encounter, as well as specific risks that are present in different areas of life (e.g., home life, work settings, and using technology). A general lethality assessment should include assessing for threats of violence, the presence of weapons, and the degree to which the perpetrator demonstrates high levels of jealousy (Campbell, 2001).

Risk assessments can provide valuable clinical information to help educate clients, guide the selection of treatment interventions, and inform safety planning (Bennett Cattaneo, 2007; Bennett Cattaneo et al., 2007). However, from a practical standpoint, accurate assessment of risk is a challenging task (Bennett Cattaneo, 2007). There has been debate within the scholarly literature as to whether victims' themselves are more or less accurate predictors of risk that certain objective criteria and actuarial assessments that have been developed (Bennett Cattaneo, 2007). Bennett Cattaneo's (2007) research found that victims and advocates use different internal processes to assess risk, and advocates appeared to have more constricted risk ratings than the victims. Victims' risk ratings were related more closely to PTSD symptoms, the display of general violence by the perpetrator, and more psychological abuse while advocates' risk ratings were related more closely to the perpetrator's substance abuse and whether the victim and perpetrator had children. Bennett Cattaneo concluded that the victims' risk assessment processes may be more subtle and subjective as compared to the advocates. However, both sets of ratings demonstrated certain advantages, so Bennett Cattaneo concluded that professionals should consider victims' own assessment of their current levels of risk in their work.

In another study, Bennett Cattaneo and colleagues (2007) aimed to identify true and false positives and negatives in predicting IPV revictimization, as well as to identify predictors of women's accuracy. Among 246 female IPV victims, most of the women (69%) indicated that they were at low risk for re-abuse. Eighteen months later, the women's actual experiences of having been re-abused were assessed, and 26% of the participants actually had been re-abused by that time. Overall, 66% of participants were accurate in their risk assessments, suggesting that IPV victims are more accurate than chance in assessing their risk. Regarding predictors of accuracy, several interesting findings emerged. First, victims who met the criteria for PTSD tended to overestimate their risk levels. Second, victims with higher levels of substance abuse tended to underestimate their risk levels. Third, victims whose partners stalked them accurately perceived higher levels of risk.

Taken together, these studies highlight the complexity of accurately assessing risk. However, they also underscore the value of drawing information from multiple sources and considering numerous factors when attempting to identify general and specific risks that should be addressed in safety plans. This information can be combined with additional information gathered through assessment procedures. Once adequate information is compiled, it is time to begin planning specific safety strategies that can be used to address the identified risks.

Safety Planning should include Specific, Behavioral Safety-promoting Behaviors. Safety plans should be detailed and practical (Kress et al., 2008), and address specific situations that the victim thinks are likely to occur (Chang et al., 2006). Because each situation is different, safety planning strategies will vary, but in general, should build on victims' resources and strengths and include an evaluation of available support from friends and family members. Practical considerations, such as workplace issues and child care, should be addressed. If children are involved, safety measures should be put in place to protect the children, such as instructing children to go to a neighbor's house if they are able to do so. Other practical strategies that could be included in a safety plan include removing guns from convicted perpetrators and having documents and money in a safe and accessible place. Some actions that battering victims have used to promote their safety include seeking information about legal and social resources, discussing their situations with professionals, taking a self-defense course, working toward economic independence, gathering and hiding supplies for leaving (e.g., documents), and filing for a legal protective order (Cluss et al., 2006). Another example of a practical strategy that could be included in a safety plan is for a victim to keep car keys in an accessible place so that quick escape could be possible (Kress et al., 2008). Other variables that should be considered as part of the safety planning process include lethality, emotional issues, available resources, and the safety of any involved children (Campbell, 2001).

Another important issue that safety planning may address is safety related to the victim's use of various forms of technology. Technological devices and programs (e.g., cell phones, GPS, and the Internet) can serve as beneficial tools for victims, such as by providing social connections and allowing access to information and resources (Finn & Atkinson, 2009; Southworth, Finn, Dawson, Fraser, & Tucker, 2007). However, these also can be used by perpetrators as means of exerting control and intimidating victims (Finn & Atkinson, 2009). For example, abusers may attempt to keep track of what websites their partners visit or make threats via e-mail (Finn & Atkinson, 2009; Southworth et al., 2007).

Two additional practical strategies are useful during the safety planning process. First, for victims currently in abusive situations, professionals' documentation of victims' injuries, including pictures if feasible, can provide useful relevant information if needed later for legal proceedings (Dienemann et al., 2005). Second, using role plays to practice safety and emergency management skills, such as calling for emergency help and responding to home intrusions, can be an effective way for victims and their children to develop competence in using safety-promoting strategies (Lund & Green, 2003). Although the focus on basic survival of safety planning may feel foreign to therapists who are accustomed to addressing higher-order concerns (e.g., psychological well-being), therapists must bear in mind that this focus on basic survival is often a necessary precursor to beginning to address these deeper needs.

Safety Planning should include Providing Referrals to Appropriate Community-based Resources. Providing appropriate referrals to needed services is a key component of responding effectively to battering victims

(Dienemann et al., 2005). Therapists can help clients identify how existing sources of social support can provide practical support if the client decides to leave the abusive partner, such as by providing a place to live, being alert to a perpetrator's attempts to contact the victim, or by helping care for children. In addition, the safety planning process should identify areas in which supportive resources are needed and strategies the victim can use to connect to these resources. Some of the practical areas in which battering victims may need supportive resources include transportation, employment, housing, support with parenting concerns, and child care (Gorde, Helfrich, & Finlayson, 2004). As such, therapists must become familiar with local resources to which they could refer clients to receive practical support and protection to their clients who have been victims of battering (McLeod et al., 2010). Finally, safety plans should address how clients can gain access to supportive resources that may not be available in the local community. In particular, victims in rural communities may experience additional challenges in accessing resources based on their geographic isolation (Merritt-Gray & Wuest, 1995). Geographically isolated clients may need additional assistance in accessing state- or national-level resources for battering victims, and they also may need to look to surrounding areas to see if any resources (e.g., shelters) in nearby locations may be accessible to them.

Therapists should Convey Clearly the Limitations and Advantages of Clients' Safety Plans. Therapists must caution victims that a safety plan can only identify potentially useful safety-promoting strategies, but it cannot guarantee that the strategies will be effective in keeping them safe. This may be especially true for victims whose perpetrators are currently enrolled in batterer intervention programs, and therapists working with these victims should coordinate their efforts with staff of those programs (Campbell, 2001; Smith & Randall, 2007). Victims may view these programs as a last resort for ending the violence in their relationships (Smith & Randall, 2007). Some of victims' hopes about batterer intervention programs include that they will teach their partners how to manage their tempers, stop their jealousy, and end their controlling behaviors. However, therapists should help victims have realistic expectations about the likelihood that their partners will change as a result of participating in a batterer intervention program, especially in light of limited evidence of the effectiveness of these programs (Gelles, 2001; Smith & Randall, 2007), which is discussed later in this chapter.

Intervention Approaches

After safety assessment and planning have occurred, it is time to move toward considering general treatment strategies that may be useful for battering victims. Next, we discuss these general strategies and describe some of the specific theory- and research-based approaches proposed by scholars to meet the needs of battering victims as clients in therapy.

General Intervention Strategies. When selecting appropriate interventions, therapists should use approaches that reflect the lived experiences of battering victims, and this may mean modifying traditional approaches that do not adequately address their unique needs and experiences (Humphreys, 2008; Merritt-Gray & Wuest, 1995). For example, battering victims may face challenges that impact their ability to participate in counseling and make progress toward treatment goals, such as the extent of their partners' control over them, discomfort in groups, limited time available, and difficulties arranging child care (Chronister et al., 2008). Thus, it is important for therapists to maintain flexibility in the approaches they adopt (Chronister et al., 2008). Some broad areas of clinical focus are as follows:

Promoting Empowerment and Enhancing Self-esteem. An important goal for counseling with battering victims is promoting empowerment and enhancing victims' self-esteem (Gorde et al., 2004). Many victims' levels of self-esteem may have been lowered as they have blamed themselves for the violence, believing that they could have changed the nature of their abusive relationships by changing their own behaviors (Smith, Smith, & Earp, 1999). Sackett and Saunders (1999) suggested that practitioners can help victims evaluate the harmful impact of the character attacks that are so frequent with psychological abuse victimization, and they can also help them to be more realistic about the attacks that their abusers make on their behaviors. For example, some victims may come to think, "If I just changed how I take care of my husband (e.g., by cooking better, being a better sexual partner, or met his needs better), he would stop beating me up," if their partner frequently berates their actions. Therapists can work with such clients to understand that the perpetrator is fully responsible for his/her own behavior.

Educating Clients about Abusive Relationships. Psychoeducational approaches hold value for battering victims (Chronister et al., 2008; Hattendorf & Tollerud, 1997). Victims may benefit from learning information about the dynamics of abusive relationships (Chang et al., 2006; McLeod et al., 2010; O'Leary, Heyman, & Neidig, 1999) and the resources that are available to support them (Chang et al., 2006; Wuest & Merritt-Gray, 1999; McLeod et al., 2010). An important part of this process is making clear that the victim does not deserve to be abused (Chang et al., 2006). By educating clients about the dynamics of abusive relationships, therapists can help clients identify and label their experiences, and this may be especially true when victims experienced multiple forms of victimization (Humphreys, 2008).

Promoting Emotional Expression. Therapists can support battering victims by validating their feelings, expressing concern for their well-being, acknowledging that they have experienced pain as a result of their victimization, and allowing them to express the full range of their emotions (McLeod et al., 2010;

O'Leary et al., 1999). Two particularly strong emotions that may be experienced by victims are shame (Smith & Randall, 2007) and self-blame (Humphreys, 2008). Having their emotional responses normalized can be very a powerful experience for battering victims (Wuest & Merritt-Gray, 1999).

Strengthening Clients' Skills. Therapists can help victims develop and strengthen skills that promote their personal and relationship functioning (Gorde et al., 2004; Hattendorf & Tollerud, 1997). Therapists can model the effective use of personal and relational skills (Hattendorf & Tollerud, 1997). Some skills that have been suggested to be useful for battering victims to develop include relaxation, especially when victimization experiences are related to physical health symptoms (Kendall-Tackett, Marshall, & Ness, 2003); decision-making (Hattendorf & Tollerud, 1997); and communication (McLeod et al., 2010). Although it is important for victims to learn to use effective communication skills to ask for help (Chang et al., 2006), therapists should urge these clients to use caution in using assertive communication skills with their perpetrators in case doing so would increase their safety risks.

Incorporating Creative Approaches. Creative approaches such as art therapy offer unique potential benefits to victims. For example, Frohmann (2005) described the Framing Safety Project, which combined elements of a photography workshop and support groups for female battering victims. Through the project, women develop photos and narratives to represent their experiences with violence. First, the women generate photos. Then, they put on a community exhibit of them that educated their community about their experiences with violence. Frohmann suggested that the project appeared to stimulate positive change for the women and the community, although certain challenges (e.g., the financial cost and its potentially limited applicability in other communities) may limit its ability to be used widely.

Combining Counseling with other Supportive Programs. McFarlane, Soeken, and Wiist (2000) evaluated three levels of treatment for 329 physically abused, pregnant, Hispanic women. All women from two clinics who indicated that they had been abused either while pregnant or during the prior year were invited to participate, and women were assigned to a level of intervention based on the month in which they began the study. The first level of intervention was labeled the brief intervention, involving the provision of a resource and informational card and brochure. The second level, counseling, involved an unlimited number of counseling sessions provided by a female counselor with significant experience in domestic violence issues. The third level, outreach, provided the same access to the counselor in addition to a mentor mother, who was a non-professional woman who had received some specialized training. At a two-month follow-up, the women who received both the counseling and mentoring reported less physical violence than those who received counseling alone. However, there were no significant differences based on group in the women's use of community resources. Although this study had several methodological limitations (e.g., nonrandom assignment to groups, attrition, and the culturally homogeneous sample), it suggests that it may be useful to combine counseling with mentoring to provide more comprehensive support to battering victims.

Research- and Theory-based Treatment Approaches. Interventions for battering victims are relatively under-developed in the scholarly literature (Brosi & Rolling, 2010; Lee, 2007). However, several approaches have been proposed. As the following paragraphs demonstrate, the research and theoretical basis for these programs varies widely.

The Barriers Model. Grigsby and Hartman (1997) created the feminist-informed barriers model based on clinical experience with female battering victims. This model holds that the symptoms experienced by battering victims result not from individualized pathology, but rather from barriers they experience from four layers: (a) environment (e.g., lack of access to financial resources and supportive resources, misinformation, and problems within the criminal justice system response to battering); (b) family and social role expectation (e.g., values about relationships and religious beliefs); (c)psychological consequences of abuse (e.g., defense mechanisms and somatic consequences); and (d) childhood abuse and neglect issues (e.g., the messages learned in childhood about abuse and safety). Based on this model, therapists should begin by addressing the first level (i.e., environmental). As therapy progresses, by examining external barriers that these clients face, the focus shifts away from internalized pathology to the larger social system. This approach is advocacy-oriented, in that therapists are encouraged to work at the community-level to impact policies and practices that present barriers to battering victims' safety.

Career Counseling. Job readiness programs may benefit battering victims (Gorde et al., 2004). A career counseling program developed specifically for IPV victims is called Advancing Career Counseling and Employment Support for Survivors of Domestic Violence (ACCESS; Chronister et al., 2008). This research-based program involves five group sessions that include assessments, information, role models, and support building. The program aims to support participants' development of career knowledge, interests, skills, and long- and short-term planning while also connecting survivors to community resources. Based on a focus group evaluation of this program, some of the advantages it offered participants included providing career- and education-related information, the joint focus on IPV and career issues, and its ability to increase career motivation. However, participants indicated that it may be more beneficial if such a program is done with groups that are homogeneous groups based on education level and socioeconomic status.

Dialectical Behavior Therapy (DBT). Iverson, Shenk, and Fruzzetti (2009) pilot tested an adaptation of Linehan's DBT for female victims of IPV. They theorized that this approach would be useful with this population due to the common challenges that battering victims may face related to emotional regulation. Some of the key features of DBT in general include a focus on changing behaviors and acceptance, skills training, addressing client motivation, and supporting change within the familial and social context. The modified version of DBT tested by Iverson and colleagues involved a 12-week group program that emphasizes skills related to mindfulness, self-validation, emotional regulation, tolerating distress, and relationship skills. The program emphasizes not only learning these new skills, but also applying them to the clients' lives.

Helping to Overcome PTSD through Empowerment (HOPE). Johnson and Zlotnick (2009) developed the Helping to Overcome PTSD through Empowerment (HOPE) project as a cognitive-behavioral therapy approach to helping women in battered women's shelters. Some of the issues addressed in the HOPE program include safety, trust, power and control, esteem, intimacy, multiculturalism, empowerment, psychoeducation about PTSD, and goal setting. The program lasts for between 9 to 12 individual sessions. HOPE is not thought to be appropriate for battering victims who also demonstrate high levels of psychopathology or substance dependence. Ongoing research evaluating the effectiveness of the HOPE program demonstrates that it can lead to decreased PTSD and depressive symptoms for clients, and clients also may be more likely to use relevant community resources following the program.

Narrative Therapy. Brosi and Rolling (2010) suggested that narrative therapy is a useful framework for battering victims because it focuses on strengths and helps victims create new stories. These researchers interviewed eight female battering victims to determine the extent to which their experiences aligned with tenets of narrative therapy. The results fell into three themes: unique outcomes, dominant cultural narratives, and support for new narratives. Three unique outcomes that these women experienced were that they gained external support, they changed their views of themselves and their relationships, and they decided to leave to protect their children. The most prominent dominant cultural narratives that impacted these women's experiences included that divorce is not a desirable outcome, that women are dependent on their relationships with men, and that conflicts should be avoided. As the women experienced their new narratives, they received support from others, began to view themselves in a more positive manner, and became contemptuous and disdainful toward their abusive relationships and partners. Brosi and Rolling made several practical suggestions for using a narrative approach with this client population. First, therapists can emphasize clients' strengths and agency by highlighting unique outcomes they have created. Second, clients can work toward deconstructing dominant cultural narratives that shaped their experiences with abuse. And finally, a visual map can be created to depict resources available to support the client's new narrative.

Solution-focused Therapy (SFT). Lee (2007) proposed a solution-focused approach to working with battering victims. Lee's approach includes an emphasis on using clients' strengths and resources to help the client set and move toward solution-oriented goals. The primary goals of SFT for battering victims are "safety, empowerment, and healing" (p. 104). An intervention used involves identifying and exploring exceptions, or times when the clients views him/herself as more competent and better able to achieve safety. Rather than focusing on the past, a solution-focused therapist works with the client to envision a violence-free future. The therapist maintains a collaborative, supportive relationship with the client. Other interventions that Lee suggests hold promise for working with victims include outcome questions (e.g., the "miracle question"), task assignments, and scaling questions. An example of a scaling question is a "safety scale" (Lee, p. 107), on which the client is asked to rate the extent to which they feel safe. Lee emphasizes that victims are not held responsible for their abuse, but rather they can be helped through SFT to examine possible strategies for building increased safety in their lives.

Counseling Victims Deciding Whether and How to Leave an Abusive Relationship

One of the most challenging clinical issues for therapists working with battering victims is supporting clients when they are deciding whether and how to leave an abusive relationship. Perhaps even more challenging than this is working with clients who seemingly have no interest in leaving their abusive partners. These situations can give rise to personal frustrations and challenging questions for therapists regarding their role in working with these clients. We conclude this section on therapy for battering victims with an in-depth exploration of this issue.

Why do Victims Stay in Abusive Relationships? Contrary to common stereotypes, victims do leave abusive relationships (Holtzworth-Munroe et al., 1997). Although a commonly cited statistic is that victims attempt to leave their abusive relationships about seven times before actually doing so, the research evidence for this statistic is unclear (Frasier, Slatt, Kowlowitz, & Glowa, 2001). However, the participants in some published studies do demonstrate this trend of leaving multiple times. For example, in a sample of 84 women seeking services from a Chicago-area domestic violence agency, the average number of times that participants had left their abusers was six (Gorde et al., 2004). In another study (Helfrich et al., 2008), the participating women in shelters reported that they had left their abusive partners between one and 20 times, although over 76% of them had left between one and five times. Therefore, although it is somewhat unclear exactly what the average number of times that battering victims leave before making a permanent separation, two points appear clear: first, that many victims leave their abusive relationships, and second, leaving is a fluid process that may involve multiple returns to their abusive partners.

Victims may not leave their abusive relationships due to the increased risk of harm they may experience if they leave. Leaving an abusive partner can typically be considered a short-term risk for increased danger, but a factor that can potentially contribute to longer-term safety (Campbell, 2001). Multiple safety risks may arise for victims upon leaving (McLeod et al., 2010; McCloskey & Fraser, 1997). Based on threats that an abusive partner may have made, victims may justifiably believe that leaving is a less-safe alternative to staying in the relationship (Holtzworth-Munroe et al., 1997). If a victim is actively planning to leave a relationship, these threats must be addressed through the safety planning process.

Clients may remain in or terminate their relationships for a variety of other reasons, which may or may not relate directly to the violence. Factors that can influence a victim's decision to remain in an abusive relationship include (a) beliefs about love and commitment, (b) emotional and attachment issues, (c) feelings of entrapment and self-blame, (d) parenting concerns, (e) economic reasons, (f) cultural beliefs, (g) trauma-related symptoms, (h) a perceived lack of alternatives, and (i) beliefs about whether it is possible to stop the violence through treatment (Griffing et al., 2002; Holtzworth-Munroe et al., 1997; Martin et al., 2000; McCloskey & Fraser, 1997; McLeod et al., 2010; Rhatigan & Axsom, 2006; Short et al., 2000; Smith & Randall, 2007; Smith et al., 1999; Strube, 1988; Strube & Barbour, 1983). In addition, victims may be hesitant to leave if doing so would involve giving up the lifestyle to which they are accustomed, such as their careers, neighborhoods, and friends (McLeod et al., 2010).

With all of these potential influences making it more likely for victims to stay, when and why do they ultimately leave? To address this question, Short et al. (2000) conducted 22 focus groups with a total of 168 African American and Caucasian rural and urban IPV survivors. Reasons for leaving their abusive relationships included: a) changing how they viewed themselves and their partners; b) experiencing extremely violent incidents; c) increasing their self-esteem; d) realizing the violence would not end; and e) becoming concerned for their children. African American women were more likely to mention the importance of social support and religion. These researchers concluded that the question of why women stay in abusive relationships is different than the question of why they cannot leave them, and different interventions may be needed based on which question a client is considering.

Applicability of "Stages of Change" Models to Leaving Abusive Relationship. Notions of what it means for clients to make progress in therapy may need to be shifted when working with battering victims (Chang et al., 2006). Victims' progression through the stages of change is influenced by many factors, including the frequency and severity of the abuse, economic dependence, substance abuse, and child care issues, to name just a few (Dienemann, Glass, Hanson, & Lunsford, 2007). Chang et al. (2006) studied the application of Prochaska's transtheoretical model of change to women experiencing IPV and identified four categories of actions that victims took to change their situations. First, they engaged in education and information-seeking, such as learning about resources. Second, they engaged in interpersonal helpseeking, such as telling friends or others about the abuse. Third, they used self-empowerment strategies, including seeking or returning to employment. Fourth, they sought protection or separation, such as going to a shelter. Chang et al. found that the change process was not a direct, linear route for the victims they interviewed. For example, women often moved back and forth among stages and skipped stages. They appeared to be most likely to skip the contemplation and preparation stages and move immediately into action in response to immediate attacks. The researchers concluded that looking at how women moved between the stages was ultimately more useful than looking at what stage the women were in at a given point in time. Chang et al. suggested that creating a visual change map may be a useful clinical tool in both individual and group therapy, although the clinical use of this tool has not yet been studied.

Frasier et al. (2001) applied the stages of change framework to counseling IPV victims, suggesting that differential interventions are warranted at different stages. A victim's level of readiness for change can be assessed with two questions. First, therapists can ask, "Have you thought about making any changes in your current situation within the next six months?" (Frasier et al., 2001, pp. 215–216). If the answer is no, the victim is likely in the precontemplation stage. If the answer is yes, then the follow-up question is, "Have you thought about making changes within the next 30 days?" (p. 216). If the answer is no, then the victim is likely in the contemplation stage. If the answer is yes, and the victim is making plans for change, then s/he is in the preparation stage, and if the victim is actively making efforts to change, then s/he is in the action stage. Once the client's stage is identified, Frasier et al. suggest that potentially useful interventions for each stage are as follows. For a victim in the precontemplation stage, at which time s/he is likely to be demonstrating hopelessness and self-blame, therapists should help the client think critically about the abuse, provide safety and resources, and avoid pressuring the client to leave the relationship. If the victim is in the contemplation stage, when s/he may be aware that a problem exists but unwilling to make changes yet, therapists can ask about any changes that have been used in the past and consider the positive and negative potential consequences of keeping things the same. For victims in the preparation phase, who are likely desiring change and seeking information about how to create it, therapists can provide referrals to supportive resources and set a date at which the client may want to complete the planning process. For victims in the action stage, who probably are seeking support and making changes to promote their self-sufficiency, therapists refer them to support groups and schedule follow-up appointments. Once changes have been made, victims may experience challenges as to maintaining them, and therapists should be alert to safety risks that may arise.

Advantages of using the stages of change model are that it redefines what it means for an intervention to be successful (Frasier et al., 2001) and addresses different decision-making processes that occur across stages (Fraizer et al., 2001). The term "returning" has been used to indicate movement back to an earlier stage, and this process reflects the often non-sequential progress of battering victims (Fraizer et al., 2001). However, reasons that the transtheoretical model of change should be applied with caution to battering victims include that the perpetrator is the one responsible for the abuse and that the outcome likely to be viewed by most as healthy (i.e., leaving) may not be the safest (Chang et al., 2006; Cluss et al., 2006; Frasier et al., 2001). Positive change should not only be viewed as occurring when the victim leaves, but rather when s/he makes any changes that alter the situation for the better (Frasier et al., 2001).

The Dynamics of Leaving an Abusive Relationship. Merritt-Gray and Wuest (1995; Wuest & Merritt-Gray, 1999, 2001) conducted a qualitative study to examine the process that battering victims go through as they leave abusive relationships and rebuild their lives. Based on the interviews they conducted with women who had left abusive relationships, they developed the Reclaiming Self model, which involves four stages: counteracting abuse, breaking free, not going back, and moving on (Wuest & Merritt-Gray, 1999, 2001). The process described by this model is viewed as "a prolonged, iterative social-psychological process of reinstatement of self within the larger social context of family and community beliefs, norms, resources, and services" (Wuest & Merritt-Gray, 1999, pp. 115-116). The Reclaiming Self model was based on the experiences of rural Canadian women, so its applicability with other populations remains untested. Nonetheless, the model is useful for understanding the process of leaving and moving beyond an abusive relationship. The final stage (i.e., moving on) will be addressed further in Chapter 10 on long-term survivors of abuse. The first three stages (i.e., counteracting abuse, breaking free, and not going back; Merritt-Gray & Wuest, 1995; Wuest & Merritt-Gray, 1999, 2001) are most relevant for therapists working with victims of current or recent battering.

The first stage, *counteracting abuse*, describes the victims' resiliency from the start of the victimization, use of strategies to reduce the abuse, and efforts to develop personal strengths amidst challenges (Merritt-Gray & Wuest,

1995; Wuest & Merritt-Gray, 1999, 2001). This stage begins at the onset of the victimization, and it involves three subprocesses. The first subprocess involves the victim relinquishing parts of oneself, such as by buying into the perpetrator's negative labeling of her (Merritt-Gray & Wuest, 1995). Other common experiences in this subprocess involve self-blame and shame. Second, victims minimized the extent of the abuse they were experiencing, such as by ignoring it, attempting to reason with the abuser, and believing they could change their partners' violence by changing their own behaviors. The third subprocess was described as fortifying defenses, and this involved making early preparations to leave the relationship and beginning to access social support and increase financial resources.

All of these experiences impact the victim when s/he begins to make efforts to break free from the relationship (Merritt-Gray & Wuest, 1995; Wuest & Merritt-Gray, 1999, 2001). During the second stage, *breaking free*, the victim begins to disengage from the relationship by drawing upon growing competence, and she attempts different strategies for leaving, which result in various potential consequences. Upon initially leaving, the victim may feel free and excited, although these positive feelings may be supplanted by uncertainty and a loss of control (Wuest & Merritt-Gray, 1999). This stage was described as "eclectic, repetitive, and tortuous" (Wuest & Merritt-Gray, 1999, p. 118), in that threats to the victim's safety may be heightened. Ultimately, victims may not leave until they reach what Chang et al. (2006) labeled a turning point, which represents a major shift in the way that the victim views his or her relationship. However, even these major turning points may not immediately lead to change (Chang et al., 2006).

The third stage, *not going back*, involves the victim beginning to create a separate life from the abuser, which may involve a risk of escalating violence (Merritt-Gray & Wuest, 1995; Wuest & Merritt-Gray, 1999, 2001). Experiences that victims may have during this stage include creating boundaries and taking steps to maintain safety. Wuest and Merritt-Gray (1999) described two subprocesses in this stage: claiming and maintaining territory and relentless justifying. In claiming and maintaining territory, the victim accesses and uses resources to gain a sense of control and achieve a safe living environment. In relentless justifying, the victim defends the decisions s/he has made to oneself and others, a stage that is viewed as key to the victim's ability to sustain the separation in the long-term (Wuest & Merritt-Gray, 1999).

Summary

Therapists working with battering victims must be prepared to support these clients on multiple levels. Even basic survival needs may require attention in therapy. Therapists must work from the earliest stages of treatment to establish a supportive context for working with victims through the various emotional, safety, relational, and trauma-related concerns they bring to treatment. Ultimately, therapists have the potential to serve as a powerful resource for these clients as they move toward establishing physical and emotional safety in their lives.

Treatment with Battering Perpetrators

Treatment for battering perpetrators is a challenging and complex clinical issue. First, especially when working with clients who are court-mandated to treatment, therapists often must adhere to local or state regulations that govern the approaches they may use with this population. As such, a preliminary step for therapists working in this area is to become familiar and compliant with regulations in their area. Second, therapists must reflect on their personal perspectives toward battering perpetrators. The label "batterer" is typically applied to these clients, and therapists must consider the extent to which this label may impact their beliefs about these clients' abilities to change (Corvo & Johnson, 2003). A good place to start is for therapists to examine how biases they may hold toward perpetrators could impact their ability to work with this population. This is especially important because, as Aymer (2008) points out, "abusive men are not 'popular' clients due to the perception that they are 'bad people'" (p. 329).

Third, therapists must become clear as to the nature of interventions that they deem appropriate for working with this client population. The term typically used to describe work with this population is *batterer intervention programs* (BIPs). Although the term *intervention* may appear to be merely a semantic issue, it reflects an underlying assumption held by many in the domestic violence field, particularly victim advocates, that this work should not constitute therapy, particularly when it is being done as a criminal sanction for breaking the law (Austin & Dankwort, 1999). Fourth, therapists must apply critical thinking to evaluating and interpreting existing research on interventions for battering perpetrators in light of common methodological limitations in these studies. Some major methodological issues that limit the existing body of research on battering perpetrators include sampling and measurement issues, as well as the limitations of the correlational research designs that are typically used (Holtzworth-Munroe, Bates, Smutzler, & Sandin, 1997). Finally, further adding to the complexity of working with battering perpetrators are the diversity of client background characteristics and the multitude of approaches to working with them, both of which are discussed at length in the coming pages.

Appropriate Treatment Based on Type. The ultimate value of developing battering perpetrator typologies is that approaches may be developed to address their unique needs (Carlson & Jones, 2010; Chiffriller, Hennessy, & Zappone, 2006). Indeed, the growing body of batterer typology research, which was reviewed in Chapter 2, holds value for therapists in understanding the general features of this client population. However, therapists must be cautious in applying information on batterer typologies to practice, given that its clinical applicability has not yet been subject to rigorous evaluation (Anderson, 2010). In addition, the methodologies and measurements used in research to differentiate perpetrators by typologies are problematic in their application to individual clients (Holtzworth-Munroe et al., 2000; Lohr, Bonge, Witte, Hamberger, & Langhinrichsen-Rohling, 2005). Holtzworth-Munroe and Stuart (1994) suggested that typologies would be useful if they could be determined using a small, reliable set of instruments, but this brief assessment protocol has yet to be developed (Chiffriller et al., 2006). A challenge in differentiating among types of batterers is that individual perpetrators may demonstrate multiple motives for their violence (Anderson, 2010).

Although there is not yet hard and fast scientific evidence to support differential assignment to treatments based on perpetrator characteristics, there is an ever-increasing body of knowledge that suggests that certain approaches may be more or less useful based on predictable background characteristics (Holtzworth-Munroe, 2000; Holtzworth-Munroe & Stuart, 1994; Holtzworth-Munroe et al., 2000; Saunders, 1996). One early study by Saunders (1996) tested outcomes of both feminist-cognitive-behavioral treatment (FCBT) and process-psychodynamic treatment (PPT) models of BIP, focusing on how certain client background characteristics influence outcomes. Saunders hypothesized that men with more dependent personality traits (representing about one-third of the participants) would respond more to the PPT, and men with more antisocial personalities (representing about four-tenths of the participants) would respond more positively to the FCBT. Participants were 218 men seeking BIP services from a mental health clinic. Most were court- or probation-referred and Caucasian. Participants were randomly assigned to a treatment condition, both of which were led by clinical social workers or psychologists and lasted for 20 weeks, with 2.5 hour sessions each week. The FCBT program was structured, included homework, and focused on such topics as communication, relaxation, and sex roles and violence. The PPT program was less structured and included phases that covered the themes of addressing childhood trauma and building support among group members.

Overall, the groups led to similar outcomes, with no group differences found in recidivism, arrest rates, psychological abuse, participants' female partners' reports of change, or participants' female partners' fear levels. When looking at the interaction between treatment type and participants' characteristics, Saunders' initial hypotheses were supported partially. Among men with dependent personality traits, recidivism rates were lower for those in the PPT program than in the FCBT program. However, although there was not a statistically significant difference, there was a general trend for men with antisocial personality traits to respond more positively to the FCBT program than the PPT program. Antisocial perpetrators with substance abuse potential or hypomania appeared especially likely to benefit from the FCBT approach. Saunders cautions that, among all participants, there were high numbers of men for whom treatment did not stop reoffending. Furthermore, only 82% of participants attended their first session. Other limitations included the lack of a no-treatment control group and some questionable measurements. Nonetheless, strengths of this study were that it included multiple forms of assessment of outcomes and used random assignment. Saunders concluded that "for practitioners, this study suggests that in developing programs for men who batter, 'one size does not fit all'" (p. 411).

In a more recent study, Huss and Ralston (2008) studied treatment outcomes based on battering perpetrator types among 175 men who were either self- or court-referred for BIP. The BIP was based on the Duluth Model and integrated aspects of cognitive-behavioral therapy. Using cluster analyses, the participants were classified into three groups consistent with Holtzworth-Munroe and Stuart's (1994) typology: FO, DB, and GVA. The results revealed that the men responded differentially to treatment based on their group. For example, FO participants completed more treatment sessions and were more likely to complete treatment than participants in the other two groups. Interestingly, however, the men in the GVA group who completed treatment appeared to benefit more than men in other groups. The GVA group had more positive changes with respect to anger levels and partner violence. On the other hand, though, the GVA group was more likely to recidivate and to do so more quickly. These somewhat contradictory findings demonstrate the complexity of achieving meaningful distinctions between different types of perpetrators in actual clinical settings.

Additional researchers have speculated on the usefulness of different treatment approaches based on perpetrator characteristics. For example, Holtzworth-Munroe et al. (2000) suggested that GVA perpetrators are most appropriate for cognitive-behavioral intervention approaches, although for some psychopaths, treatment may be altogether ineffective. Both GVA and Pathological perpetrators appear to require a treatment focus on personality disorders in order to benefit (Waltz, Babcock, Jacobson, & Gottman, 2000). Waltz et al. also suggest that Pathological perpetrators require longer-term treatment. Unfortunately, therapists looking to research to find clear guidelines on differential battering perpetrator treatment based on type will find inconclusive evidence at this time. However, the growing body of research indicates that some perpetrator characteristics appear to impact treatment outcomes, including recidivism (e.g., Huss & Ralston, 2008; Scott & Wolfe, 2003), and it is expected that this topic will be the focus of much research in coming years.

At the present time, additional efforts are needed to develop guidelines for assigning perpetrators to treatment based on their background characteristics (Huss & Ralston, 2008; Saunders, 2001). Despite increased attention to this issue, research over at least two decades has provided minimal definitive guidance as to the types of BIPs that are most effective with different perpetrators (Dalton, 2007). Put simply, there just isn't yet enough evidence to support specific treatment assignments based on typologies (Holtzworth-Munroe, 2000; Holtzworth-Munroe et al., 2000). Furthermore, clinicians must guard against the temptation to view abuse perpetrated by certain types of perpetrators as less significant—battering is a crime regardless of the characteristics of perpetrator (Margolin, Gordis, Oliver, & Raine, 1995).

Overview of Batterer Intervention Program Standards, Effectiveness, and Approaches

This section will familiarize therapists who work in this area with the unique context for BIPs. First, regulatory standards often apply to BIPs, and these programs are but one aspect of community-based approaches to addressing battering. Second, several intervention approaches with battering perpetrators have been put forward, so therapists must use clinical judgment to decide which to use. Finally, the existing research on the effectiveness of BIPs is inconclusive, particularly with regard to attrition and program dropouts.

Batterer Intervention Program Standards. Therapists should familiarize themselves with mandatory or voluntary BIP standards in effect in the jurisdiction in which they practice. However, there are many common standards across different locations (Austin & Dankwort, 1999). BIP standards began to proliferate in the mid-1980s (Austin & Dankwort, 1999) to provide consistency in the services delivered across programs, raise public awareness of the issue of battering, promote victim safety, and hold perpetrators accountable (Austin & Dankwort, 1999; Maiuro & Eberle, 2008). The philosophical underpinning of BIP standards often rests in the view that battering is a manifestation of patriarchy, although they have in many cases been influenced by therapeutic advances as well (Austin & Dankwort, 1999). Many existing policies and practices related to BIPs are based on feminist theory (Carlson & Jones, 2010).

Maiuro and Eberle (2008) conducted a content analysis of BIP standards for all states for which they were able to locate standards. This study offers important insights into the criteria that are often included in these standards. At the time of their review, 45 states (including the District of Columbia) had standards in place. Across the states, there were many similarities in standards, likely reflecting that many were developed using other states' standards as models. Some common features among a majority of the existing standards include the following:

- Clients should undergo an intake assessment, including a lethality assessment, prior to beginning the intervention to determine whether they are appropriate for treatment.
- Some standards are voluntary, while others are legal requirements.

- Most standards provide guidelines about the approach and content of treatment. Most emphasize power and control dynamics and social-psychological explorations of IPV.
- Most states disallow certain approaches to BIP, such as mental health, family systems theory, or addition models.
- Programs should hold perpetrators accountable for their use of abusive behaviors.
- Programs should make the victim's safety the highest priority.
- Minimum program lengths ranged from twelve weeks to more than one year.
- Group treatment is typically preferred.
- Couples therapy is typically forbidden.
- Most standards require BIP staff to have contact with victims for the purpose of safety and not to involve the victims in treatment directly.
- Some standards put forth minimum training requirements for facilitators, although these vary across statutes.
- Many standards lack references to solid, current empirical evidence to support the recommendations they contain.

Controversies Surrounding BIP Standards. The proliferation of BIP standards has not been without debate. Benefits of standards have been noted in the literature. For example, they can serve a very important protective function, particularly related to protecting the public from unscrupulous programs or leaders (Gelles, 2001; Hamberger, 2001). Furthermore, they create a structure for holding programs accountable to the community and the larger IPV response system (Hamberger, 2001). It is our impression that the broader debate regarding BIP standards is not so much a debate as to whether regulation of programs is needed, but rather how standards have been developed and the potential negative ramifications of them. Babcock, Green, and Robie (2004) stated, "For the most part, state standards have been developed independently of empirical research" (p. 1024). Babcock et al. (2004) also wrote, "Because no one treatment model or modality has demonstrated superiority over then others, it is premature for states to issue mandates limiting the range of treatment options for batterers" (p. 1048).

Corvo and Johnson (2003) argued that batterers have been vilified by ideological movements, thereby hindering progress in the field. This vilification has resulted, in part, from an intense focus on the most severely abusive perpetrators that has been generalized to all persons who use abusive behaviors toward their partners. They suggested that innovations in research and practice have been thwarted by prohibitions on types of approaches used to treat this population. Research-inclined practitioners and scholars may be tempted to dismiss the influence of advocates and feminist theorists on the development of standards as being ideologically-driven and not grounded in research. However, the contributions of the larger battered women's movement cannot be underestimated. This movement has raised the issue of IPV to social consciousness and led to an extensive history of practice-informed knowledge (Austin & Dankwort, 1999). Austin and Dankwort (1999) stated, "Standards have been criticized because there is an absence of empirical evidence to support them, but it is also true that no conclusive evidence exists to radically change them. In the absence of such scientific proof, it appears reasonable to consider standards in the light of their historical origins, recognizing the experiential knowledge of the battered women's movement because it constitutes the very foundation of all accumulated information in the field" (p. 167). They suggest that the key criteria of keeping victims safe, holding batterers accountable, and keeping programs responsive to the community should remain fundamental aspects of any BIP standards or programs.

In sum, the controversies surrounding BIP standards challenge therapists to examine their own beliefs about how decisions should be made about intervention with battering perpetrators. As Hamberger (2001) noted, "through the process of research, knowledge is never complete" (p. 277), and thus the field is confronted with the challenge of considering when and if it is appropriate to have standards. On the one hand, definitive research evidence to provide clear guidelines for policy and practice simply did not exist at the time most standards were developed (Geffner, 1995)—and such clear, research-based guidelines continue to be unavailable. Thus, standards likely represent, in most cases, best efforts to promote victim safety and perpetrator accountability within existing service delivery systems (Hamberger, 2001). On the other hand, when standards exist in such a way that limits the development of new, potentially effective interventions, and when they are not updated to reflect emerging relevant research, they can become limiting and outdated. Thus, BIP standards should be revised and updated over time, particularly in light of new research and practice developments (Austin & Dankwort, 1999; Hamberger, 2001), and it may be useful for standards to include exemptions from standard practices for research purposes (Hamberger, 2001).

The Role of BIPs within IPV Response Systems. BIP standards typically do not advocate for BIPs to be the sole approach to intervening with batterers. Rather, these standards typically suggest coordination among BIPs, the criminal justice system, and other components of community responses to battering (Austin & Dankwort, 1999). However, the degree to which these components work together effectively varies across communities. For example, at the local level, frictions may exist between staff of BIPs and battered women's shelters (Dalton, 2007). Therefore, therapists who work with battering perpetrators will benefit from learning about local and state legal and social services and their typical responses to battering perpetrators.

BIPs generally are viewed to be most effective if they occur in the context of legal sanctions, especially for participants who fail to complete the programs

(Babcock et al., 2004). Research suggests that perpetrators are more likely to believe that they will face legal sanctions for reassault than for dropping out of the BIP (Heckert & Gondolf, 2000a). These findings raise questions about the extent to which legal sanctions promote treatment compliance and deter reassault. However, these findings do not imply that there is no value to these sanctions, but rather that the severity and certainty of these sanctions may need to be raised.

Babcock and Steiner (1999) examined the effectiveness in reducing recidivism of a coordinated community response (CCR) in Seattle, which included mandatory arrest and treatment for battering perpetrators. The mandatory BIP included 26 weekly, followed by 6 monthly, sessions that addressed anger management, responsibility for violence, power and control, problem-solving, communication, and attitudes toward violence. Rates of treatment completion were low, with only approximately one-third of participants completing the BIP. Of those assigned to substance abuse treatment, only 43% completed it. Most perpetrators who did not complete court-mandated BIP did not receive any legal punishment for this. There were statistically significant differences in the re-offense rates of the perpetrators studied. Among those who completed treatment, only 8% reoffended during the two-year follow-up period, compared with 23% of perpetrators who did not complete treatment and 62% of perpetrators who were incarcerated instead of being mandated to treatment. Babcock and Steiner concluded that their findings lend support to the potential value of BIP treatment *if it is completed.* However, there was an overall small effect size for the effectiveness of treatment, meaning that the actual clinical significance of these findings is limited. Two practice-relevant implications of their findings are that there must be increased attention to legal consequences for failure to complete court-mandated BIPs and that there may be a need for more culturally-relevant groups based on the higher rates of dropping out among non-White perpetrators.

Approaches to Batterer Intervention. Clearly, BIP approaches often are influenced heavily by relevant standards and regulations. However, the manner in which these are translated into practice varies. Before addressing specific intervention models, it is useful for therapists to understand common elements of BIPs. Dalton (2007) set out to conduct the first national survey of BIPs since the 1980s. Dalton used systematic sampling to invite 312 of the 2,131 BIPs in the United States that were able to be identified. Of these, representatives from 150 programs in 35 states participated in the survey. The following trends were among the Dalton's findings. First, almost all programs required that the clients pay their own fees to participate, and the average fee per session was $31.50. Second, the average length of the programs was 31.5 weeks, although they ranged in length from 8 to 52 weeks. Third, most programs dismissed clients from participating if they had excessive absences or did not pay for their fees. Finally, the respondents reported that an average of 62% of their clients completed their programs. Dalton suggested that some respondents likely overestimated the effectiveness of their programs, with program directors even reporting 0% recidivism, which was labeled as "disconnect from reality" (p. 72).

BIPs may address a range of topics, including the following: (a) *skill-building* (Rynerson & Fishel, 1993), such as stress management (Rynerson & Fishel, 1993) and anger management (Brown & O'Leary, 2000; O'Leary et al., 1999); (b) *information about battering*, such as types of abuse (Austin & Dankwort, 1999), the consequences of violence (Austin & Dankwort, 1999; O'Leary et al., 1999; Schmidt et al., 2007), power and control dynamics (Austin & Dankwort, 1999; Schmidt et al., 2007), and the cycle of violence (Brown & O'Leary, 2000); (c) *attitudinal and behavioral change*, including taking responsibility for one's use of violence (Austin & Dankwort, 1999; Brown & O'Leary, 2000; Gondolf, 2004; O'Leary et al., 1999; Schmidt et al., 2007), behavioral alternatives to violence (Brown & O'Leary, 2000; Gondolf, 2004), cognitions that are linked to abuse (Schmidt et al., 2007), and motivation to change (Schmidt et al., 2007); (d) *sociocultural issues* (Austin & Dankwort, 1999); (e) *substance abuse*, if applicable (Dalton, 2007); (f) *relationship enhancement* (Rynerson & Fishel, 1993); and (g) *safety* (Schmidt et al., 2007). The formats of BIPs may involve the following: (a) lecture (Rynerson & Fishel, 1993); (b) experiential activities (Rynerson & Fishel, 1993); (c) role plays (Paymar & Barnes, n.d.; Rynerson & Fishel, 1993; (d) process-oriented approaches (Gondolf, 2004); (e) confrontation (Buttell & Pike, 2002); (f) therapy (Buttell & Pike, 2002); and (e) education (Buttell & Pike, 2002). Female partners may be invited, but not required, to be involved in their male partners' BIP treatment (Rynerson & Fishel, 1993).

By far the most common approach to BIPs is group-based interventions. In fact, group approaches to BIPs are so common that "there have been no controlled, empirical studies to date testing individual therapy approaches for abusers" (Babcock et al., 2004, p. 1027). In light of the widespread use of group approaches, Waldo, Kernet, and Kerne (2007) compared the therapeutic factors at work in two different group-based BIP approaches: guidance and counseling. The guidance sessions were psychoeducational and based on the Duluth Model (described in the next section), whereas the counseling sessions focused on processing immediate experiences, examining relationship challenges and successes, and learning about oneself from others. Participants included 99 men, most of whom were court-mandated. The study occurred in the larger context of six guidance-based BIP groups, and the leaders replaced one guidance session with one counseling session during each program in different orders. When participants rated the overall value of both formats, there were no differences in their ratings, and both were viewed as worthwhile. However, different therapeutic factors emerged based on the type of session. The therapeutic factors that were viewed as most unique in the guidance sessions were hope, information, and existential factors, whereas the factors that viewed as unique to the counseling sessions were universality, cohesion, and interpersonal learning. Although limitations of this study (e.g., the single counseling sessions and the limited sample) limit this study's ability to be generalized to other populations, it lends some support to the notion that different BIP approaches may offer participants different benefits.

In general, the two intervention models that are most commonly used are the Duluth Model and cognitive-behavioral therapy-based approaches. Following an overview of each approach, other approaches that have been described in the literature are discussed.

The Duluth Model. The term "Duluth Model" is often used to describe the Domestic Abuse Intervention Project (DAIP; Feder & Wilson, 2005). The Duluth Model is perhaps the most commonly used approach to BIP (Babcock, Canady, Senior, & Eckhardt, 2005; Babcock et al., 2004; Easton, Lee, Wupperman, & Zonana, 2008; Feder & Wilson, 2005), and some states have mandated that this model be used (Babcock et al., 2004). Although the Duluth Model is the term usually applied to specific BIPs, the model actually refers to a coordinated community response approach that links legal and social service agencies (DAIP, 2008a; Paymar & Barnes, n.d.). Key components of this model include the following: (a) the safety of the victim and the accountability of the perpetrator are primary considerations; (b) relevant community organizations should work together; (c) cases of domestic violence should be monitored over time; (d) services for victims should play a primary role; and (e) the safety of the victim is the responsibility of the larger response system (DAIP, n.d.; Paymar & Barnes, n.d.). The primary focus of the model is to stop the violence (DAIP, n.d.). The Duluth Model is based on a feminist assumption that battering results from patriarchy and cultural acceptance of men using violence to maintain power over women (Babcock et al., 2005; Babcock et al., 2004; Feder & Wilson, 2005; Pence & Paymar, 1993). Another overall emphasis in the Duluth Model is that effective intervention with battering perpetrators occurs within a consistent set of messages from all aspects of the response system, and that offenders should face consequences for their abuse and if they fail to comply with the BIP (DAIP, n.d.).

Duluth Model BIPs are primarily psychoeducational and are grounded in a philosophical assumption that battering occurs as a means for the perpetrator to control his/her partner (Paymar & Barnes, n.d.). Interactive dialogue promotes participants' critical thinking about their use of violence and cultural norms about male dominance of women (Paymar & Barnes, n.d.). One intervention used in Duluth Model BIPs involves participants' completion of *control logs* in which they describe and examine their abusive behaviors (Paymar & Barnes, n.d.). The Power and Control Wheel is a widely used tool that was developed by the creators of the model (DAIP, 2008b). It describes various strategies that abusers use to exert power and control. These strategies are in contrast to the other main wheel developed by within the Duluth Model, which is the Equality Wheel (DAIP, 2008b). Other interventions in the model include learning alternatives to violence (e.g., time-outs and empathy; Feder & Wilson, 2005).

Although the Duluth model has achieved widespread dissemination and become the standard BIP in many communities, its effectiveness has been the subject of great debate (Carlson & Jones, 2010; Gelles, 2001). The Duluth Model has minimal research evidence to demonstrate its effectiveness (Easton et al., 2008). However, this may be in part due to limitations in the way that the program has been studied rather than wholly attributable to the failure of the program to produce the desired results (Gondolf, 2007). Furthermore, many existing evaluations of the Duluth Model address only the BIP component of the program and therefore do not capture the full essence of the model (Paymar & Barnes, n.d.).

Cognitive-behavioral and Integrative Approaches. Most cognitive-behavioral BIP approaches were developed by psychologists, and they hold that violence is a behavior that is learned but can be unlearned (Babcock et al., 2004). Cognitive-behavioral BIPs examine the functions played by violent behaviors and assist clients in evaluating the effects of these behaviors (Babcock et al., 2004). These programs emphasize skills training, such as communication, anger management, and relaxation skills training (Babcock et al., 2004). Evidence from Gondolf's (2000) four-site BIP evaluation provides evidence of the impact of BIPs on perpetrators' cognitions and behaviors. At two follow-up periods following 15 and 30 months, participants were asked how they avoided re-using violence. Some of the changes reported using included interruption (e.g., taking a time-out), decreasing substance abuse, and increasing their respect for women. The results were mixed, however. Thirty months following the BIPs, 19% of the men reported holding more positive attitudes toward women. On the other hand, 16% of the men held more negative attitudes toward women. Positive changes were more likely to have been reported among men who successfully completed their BIPs.

Babcock et al. (2004) point out that although BIPs may hold labels that ascribe them to one category or another (i.e., Duluth or cognitive-behavioral), there is overlap that blurs distinctions between different approaches. For example, an Idaho program evaluated by Hayward, Steiner, and Sproule (2007) was described as a cognitive-behavioral program based on the Duluth model. Therefore, although certain programs may make claims of being grounded in one tradition or another, in practice they often share many common features and content.

Interventions for Increasing Client Motivation, Participation, and Retention: Readiness to Change. A key characteristic that can impact battering perpetrators' treatment progress is their readiness to change their abusive behaviors (Alexander & Morris, 2008). Factors that impact their readiness to change include the extent to which they deny and minimize the abuse (Alexander & Morris, 2008) and whether they have been mandated to treatment by the criminal justice system (Eckhardt & Utschig, 2007). Research suggests that most batterers attend treatment only when mandated to do so by courts (e.g., Eckhardt & Utschig, 2007; Heckert & Gondolf, 2000a; Kernsmith, 2005; Musser, Semiatin, Taft, & Murphy, 2008; Roffman, Edleson, Neighbors, Mbiliny, & Walker, 2008; Taft, Murphy, Elliott, & Morrell, 2001). As such, general strategies for working with mandated clients may prove useful for working with perpetrators. These strategies include describing the process of treatment, being clear about confidentiality, anticipating that resistance may occur, and asking the client to share how she or he feels about having been required to attend treatment (Amundson & Borgen, 2000; Waldman, 1999).

Researchers have begun to apply Prochaska and DiClemente's (1984) Transtheoretical Model of Change (TTM) to this client population (e.g., Alexander & Morris, 2008; Babcock et al., 2005; Begun, Shelley, Strodthoff, & Short, 2001; Eckhardt & Utschig, 2007; Levesque, Gelles, & Velicer, 2000; Roffman et al., 2008). According to Alexander and Morris (2008), battering perpetrators may present for treatment in any stage. Those in the *precontemplation* stage will be likely to deny or minimize their abuse perpetration and blame others for it. Individuals in the *contemplation* stage may be in the early stages of acknowledging that their use of violent behaviors is harmful, although they have not made any efforts to change. Perpetrators who move into the *preparation* stage begin to consider the changes they can make to end their abusive behaviors. Once they begin to take proactive steps toward changing, they move into the *action* stage. Finally, once these clients have stopped engaging in abusive behaviors, they continue to work to prevent these behaviors from reemerging, which is known as the *maintenance* stage. The stages in the TTM are recursive, in that most people move back and forth among stages rather than progress in a neat, orderly fashion (Begun et al., 2001).

Research demonstrates support for these theoretical assumptions. For example, Levesque et al., (2000) found, among a sample of 258 men in BIPs, that men in later stages of change readiness tended to be less likely to blame their partners for their violence and more likely to identify positive reasons for ending their use of violence. However, Begun et al. (2001) urge caution in applying this model, because (a) of its minimal attention to social factors (e.g., economic and cultural issues), (b) it must be applied within the context of consistent messages of nonviolence, (c) expectations about change must be realistic, (e) perpetrators' partners must be warned about potential danger, and (f) relapse must not be viewed as an excuse for violence. As described in Chapter 3, two assessment instruments have been developed to assess this characteristic among battering perpetrators: the URICA-DV (Levesque et al., 2000) and the SAHI

(Begun et al., 2003). These instruments may be useful for informing therapists when planning appropriate interventions for battering perpetrators based on their levels of change readiness. However, Eckhardt and Utschig (2007) found that these measures have conceptual differences that complicated the identification of perpetrators based on their stages of change.

Getting an abusive individual to accept responsibility for violent behaviors is a fundamental goal in many BIPs (Heyman & Schlee, 2003), and whether such acceptance of responsibility is assumed influences whether perpetrators are likely to change (Jacobson & Gottman, 1998). One of the most promising areas of research and practical innovation in the area of batterer intervention, therefore, lies in the development and evaluation of procedures that may be useful for increasing treatment engagement. Given the importance of understanding battering perpetrators' readiness to change, researchers have suggested that differential interventions may be warranted depending on their stage of change (Alexander & Morris, 2008; Babcock et al., 2005; Begun et al., 2001; Roffman et al., 2008).

For perpetrators in the *precontemplation* stage, appropriate interventions (a) focus on having clients move toward voluntary participation, (b) avoid increasing defensiveness, (c) focus on accountability and responsibility, (d) aim to increase motivation, (e) include consistent reinforcement about the need to change from multiple sources, and (f) should educate partners about the minimal likelihood of actual change. In the contemplation stage, clients may benefit from interventions that (a) affirm recognizing the problem as a first step, (b) focus on costs and benefits of change, emphasizing benefits, (c) include success stories, and (d) incorporate culturally meaningful reasons for change. Appropriate interventions for the preparation stage should (a) focus on accountability and (b) reinforce positive steps. For clients in the action stage, interventions should (a) be adaptable to unique needs and preferences, (b) potentially be separate from those in precontemplation, (c) include learning skills, and (d) be theory-based. Finally, maintenance stage-appropriate interventions should (a) continue reinforcement, (b) potentially involve serving as mentors, and (c) focus on increasing competence for keeping up change. Begun et al. (2001) also emphasize the importance of addressing the potential for relapse to earlier stages as clients progress toward ending abusive behaviors. Therapists must be cautioned, however, that the present body of research does not provide clear evidence of differential effectiveness of interventions based on battering perpetrators' stages of change, and therefore this model is not yet ready for prescriptive guidelines as to matching perpetrators to treatment based on stage of change (Levesque et al., 2000).

Interventions designed for highly motivated clients, yet applied to clients with low motivation, have a low likelihood of success (Babcock et al., 2005; Musser et al., 2008). However, many existing BIP interventions seem most appropriate for clients in later stages of change (Begun et al., 2001; Musser et al., 2008). Indeed, much of the research reviewed in this chapter was conducted with samples of predominantly court-mandated batterers, and thus we must use caution in applying the information provided to working with individuals who voluntarily seek treatment.

In light of the research described above, motivational interviewing (MI) may be a useful precursor to treatment with this population (Babcock et al., 2005; Roffman, et al., 2008). In comparing BIP clients based on their levels of readiness to change, Alexander and Morris (2008) recommended that MI could be useful for inducing clients to perceive their use of violence as being at odds with the goals the individual holds for his or her life (e.g., having a loving partner). These researchers suggest, however, that interventions typical of MI, such as conveying acceptance and validating the clients' choices, may run counter to typical BIP approaches. Nonetheless, MI techniques that may be especially useful when working with battering perpetrators include reflective listening, reducing resistance, helping the client express a desire to change, providing individualized feedback based on assessment data, and actively planning for change (Musser et al., 2008).

The Effectiveness of Batterers Intervention Programs

Buttell and Pike (2002) concluded from the existing literature that 60% to 80% of men who complete BIPs end their use of physical abuse at the end of the program. However, other researchers suggest that the demonstrated effectiveness of BIPs in existing research is mixed at best (Feder & Wilson, 2005; Musser et al., 2008; Stith, Rosen, & McCollum, 2003), with several studies having high dropout and recidivism rates (Bennett, Stoops, Call, & Flett, 2007; Buttell & Carney, 2008; Dalton, 2007). Whether treatment is at all appropriate for IPV perpetration, which is, after all, usually a criminal behavior, also has been hotly debated (Rosenbaum & Leisring, 2001). Real change, meaning really putting an end to battering, is viewed by many to be more likely to result from change at the larger social level, rather than individual approaches such as therapy (Gelles, 2001). Even those who do believe that true change is possible for battering perpetrators do not view it as an easy task.

Meta-analyses of BIP Effectiveness. Babcock et al. (2004) conducted a meta-analysis of BIP outcome research in order to determine the effectiveness of these interventions, including only studies with pretest/posttest data, experimental or quasi-experimental designs, and the use of objective records. The studies included in the meta-analysis used the Duluth Model, cognitive-behavioral approaches, and/or other therapeutic modalities, such as conjoint groups. These researchers defined recidivism as "any report of physical violence reported by the victims and/or any domestic violence incidents reported to the police during a follow-up period" (p. 1036). Their findings reveal a bleak depiction of the demonstrated effectiveness of BIPs. They found only a small effect size on recidivism when using both police records and victim reports as indicators. Furthermore, their findings did not lend strong support to indicate that any one approach is more or less effective than others. According to Babcock et al., "Based on a partner report, treated batterers have a 40% chance of being successfully nonviolent, and without treatment, men have a 35% chance of maintaining nonviolence. Thus, there is a 5% increase in success rate attributable to treatment. To a clinician, this means that a woman is 5% less likely to be re-assaulted by a man who was arrested, sanctioned, and went to a batterers' program than by a man who was simply arrested and sanctioned" (p. 1044). Although Babcock et al. point out that this overall effect size is small, when applying their findings to the overall population, they claimed that "batterers treatment in all reported cases of domestic violence in the United States would equate to approximately 42,000 women per year no longer being battered" (p. 1044).

Feder and Wilson (2005) also conducted a meta-analysis of experimental or quasi-experimental studies of BIPs. They included 10 studies from 1996 to 2003 that used matched group designs or statistical controls, had a minimum of a six month follow-up period, and included objective measures of reoffending (e.g., complaints to police, arrests, and victim reports). Based on criminal justice data (i.e., police complaints and arrests), there was a moderate reduction in reoffenses based on treatment. Although completing treatment led to reductions in reoffending as compared to dropping out of treatment, Feder and Wilson caution that these results may be related more to the background characteristics of perpetrators that influence their motivation to complete treatment rather than to the treatment itself. When using victim report data to conduct the meta-analysis, however, there was less support for the effectiveness of BIPs. Based on victims' reports (which Feder and Wilson describe as "the best source for information on the offender's continued abuse," p. 252), no statistically significant effect sizes were found. Thus, the effectiveness of BIPs in existing research studies can be viewed as minimal, suggesting that alternative approaches to interventions with battering perpetrators are needed.

Attrition and Dropouts. Published estimates suggest that approximately 40% to 80% of battering perpetrators who are court-mandated to BIPs do not attend, drop out of, or are terminated prematurely from these programs (Buttell & Pike, 2002; Eckhardt & Utschig, 2007; Jones & Gondolf, 2002; McCloskey, Sitaker, Grigsby, & Malloy, 2003; Taft et al., 2001). Certain characteristics have been identified as decreasing the likelihood of successfully completing BIPs, including the following: being an ethnic minority, not living with family members and/or an intimate partner, being younger, having less education, having lower incomes, not being married, having more unstable employment, and having a more extensive prior criminal history (Alexander & Morris, 2008;

Babcock & Steiner, 1999; McCloskey et al., 2003; Taft et al., 2001). Additional differences may be observed based on the typologies described earlier. For example, in Huss and Ralston's (2008) study of BIP treatment completion based on batterer typology designations, FO perpetrators had the highest completion rates (78%), followed by DB (59%), and then GVA (50%).

Despite these trends, these characteristics are not very useful in their ability to predict treatment compliance for individual perpetrators. Buttell and Pike (2002) aimed to determine the demographic and personality characteristics that were associated with completion and drop out in a 12-week BIP. Participants were 91 men in Alabama who were court-mandated to a BIP. The BIP studied was developed in accordance with state standards, used a cognitive-behavioral approach, was a group treatment, and focused on anger management and skills training. 72.5% of participants completed the program. The results were discouraging in terms of predicting treatment completion: no demographic or psychological characteristics proved useful at determining which participants would complete the BIP. Due to high rates of dropout among BIP participants, increasing their retention must remain a high priority for the field (McCloskey et al., 2003). In particular, participants must be supported to attend programs long enough that they achieve the benefits they are purported to hold for participants, namely learning to become nonviolent (McCloskey et al., 2003).

Treatment for "Atypical" Cases

Although most battering appears to be perpetrated by men against women, therapists also must be able to identify and address atypical cases that do not fit this dynamic. For example, heterosexual women may perpetrate abuse against male partners (Babcock et al., 2005). BIP standards often stipulate that heterosexual female perpetrators and same-sex IPV perpetrators should receive separate treatment from heterosexual male perpetrators (Austin & Dankwort, 1999). According to Kernsmith (2005), BIP models that were developed for men may be inadequate or unsuitable for female perpetrators. In comparing a sample of 125 male and female IPV perpetrators, Kernsmith found that women were more likely than men to report that their violent behaviors were motivated by prior victimization experiences and for revenge. Kernsmith's conclusion was that many female IPV perpetrators use violence as a means of protecting personal freedoms. Some of Kernsmith's recommendations for treatment with female IPV victims included addressing the issue of self-defense when discussing accountability and providing education about nonviolent strategies for resisting domestic violence.

Dowd (2001) reviewed research on the background and treatment of female perpetrators of IPV. The topic of female perpetrators has been controversial due to common assumptions about IPV held by researchers and practitioners, and full treatment descriptions have been limited (Dowd, 2001). Some unique influences that Dowd notes may play a role in female IPV perpetration include the effects of prior trauma, attachment disorders, and substance abuse. Group, individual, and conjoint treatment approaches may be used with this population. Some other common elements of treatment approaches reviewed by Dowd include the following: (a) incorporation of the Duluth Model; (b) a focus on women's prior victimization; and (c) understanding women's socialization. Dowd went on to describe a treatment model used for an anger management group for women at the University of Massachusetts. This 20-week cognitive-behavioral and psychoeducational program covered a range of topics, including emotional awareness, conflict, relationship issues, communication, cognitive errors, and stress management. According to Dowd, additional attention is needed for future researchers and practitioners to develop parallel treatments for men and women.

As with the limited existing information about female IPV perpetrators, currently there are limited services and information available for male victims (Tsui, Cheung, & Leung, 2010). Tsui and colleague surveyed US domestic violence service organizations to learn about the availability of services for male victims of IPV. The results suggest that limited resources are available for male IPV victims, especially shelters and counseling groups. Individual counseling appears to be the most common approach for these clients. Some themes that emerged from qualitative feedback as to why men don't seek help related to IPV victimization included perceptions that services were not for them, shame, embarrassment, denial, and stigma. A limitation of this study was an extremely low (7.9%) response rate, so the study's findings should be considered preliminary. Despite this study's limitations, it provides some evidence for the need for increased services and public awareness related to the needs of male IPV victims.

Another type of battering outside the typical paradigm (i.e., male perpetrators against female victims) is battering in same-sex relationships. Fortunata and Kohn (2003) studied the characteristics of lesbian battering perpetrators, comparing a convenience sample of perpetrators to a control group of non-batterers. The lesbian perpetrators, compared with non-batterers, reported more experiences of childhood abuse, higher levels of substance abuse, and higher levels of psychopathology, including antisocial, aggressive, and borderline characteristics. Byrne (1996) suggested that different approaches may be used to treat gay male perpetrators. The first approach, *individual psychosocial* treatment, is primarily behavioral and includes safety planning, identifying violence triggers, and coping skills development. The second approach, *psychotherapeutic treatment,* has a primary emphasis on cognitions and emotions and focuses on helping the client change his negative self-concept and becoming more self-aware. The third approach, *group intervention,* is tailored to the unique needs of gay males. Byrne argues that interventions combining group and individual treatments are most likely to be effective.

Because atypical forms of battering have received less attention in the existing literature, future advances in research and practice are needed to develop a stronger knowledge base and effective intervention strategies for female heterosexual, lesbian, and gay male perpetrators.

Summary: Treatment with Battering Perpetrators

This section highlighted the complexity that therapists face when working with battering perpetrators. First, although some characteristics are common among subtypes of the population, perpetrators are diverse, and population trends must be applied cautiously to individuals. Second, therapists who facilitate BIPs likely are regulated by standards that dictate the types of interventions they may use. Third, various treatment approaches have been proposed, but minimal existing research-based guidelines can provide definitive guidance to therapists regarding how best to work with clients. Finally, especially with court-mandated clients, rates of dropout are high, and successful outcomes may be difficult to identify.

However, a broader view of the existing research and practice in this area suggests important guidelines for therapists to follow when working with this population. First, again, the value of a thorough assessment to understand clients and their use of violence cannot be understated. Second, therapists must be aware that different clients may respond differently to treatment, and therefore they should maintain some degree of flexibility, when permissible, in their approaches to treatment. Third, due to high rates of dropout among this client population, as well as research suggesting that many clients are in early stages of considering changing their violent behaviors, therapists should work hard and early to engage clients in treatment. Fourth, therapists must work collaboratively with other involved professionals (e.g., law enforcement, probation officers, and victim advocates) to ensure that perpetrators are held accountable for their behaviors and progress in treatment. In all, although many advances in approaches to treatment with battering perpetrators are likely to occur in coming years, therapists can use existing research to inform their current practices.

5

CONJOINT TREATMENT FOR COUPLES WHO HAVE EXPERIENCED IPV

We begin this chapter facing head-on the ethical dilemma posed to therapists considering whether conjoint couple therapy ever has a place when working with clients impacted by IPV. We illustrate this dilemma with a case study and review ethical principles to guide therapists in making this determination. Following this overview of the complexities of this topic, we delve into the surrounding controversies, strategies for addressing safety concerns, and approaches described in the literature, including the research basis for their effectiveness.

Ethical Issue: Determining Whether Conjoint Therapy is Appropriate

Whether conjoint therapy is appropriate for couples who have experienced IPV is both a therapeutic and ethical question. Therapists must ask themselves when considering this approach whether it is therapeutically justifiable and likely to help clients to achieve their treatment goals. Even if the approach holds potential therapeutic benefits, however, ethical issues may render it inadvisable due to safety concerns and difficulties in detecting the potential costs and benefits for all of the involved parties, as illustrated by the following case example.

Case Example: Kate and Joe

Kate (age 25) and Joe (age 28) present for couple therapy in a private practice. They have been married for two years and have no children. They report their presenting problem to be "frequent fighting and terrible communication." Kate appears quiet and nervous, and Joe does most of the talking during the intake session. When asked about experiences of violence or abuse in their relationship, Joe admits he slapped Kate across the face two times: once before they were married and once recently, which prompted them to make a counseling appointment. Kate reports that she is not afraid of Joe. Both partners indicate they are not interested in individual therapy and are only willing to come to therapy together as a couple.

Discussion and Selected Relevant Ethical Codes. Based on the limited information provided, it is impossible to determine whether it is advisable to proceed with conjoint therapy. A thorough assessment is warranted to explore the nature of the violence and each partner's needs and characteristics. As the therapist proceeds, several ethical questions are likely to arise. First, is it ethical to proceed to conjoint therapy if a safety risk is involved? Standard 1.9 of the AAMFT (2001) Code of Ethics states, "Marriage and family therapists continue therapeutic relationships only so long as it is reasonably clear that clients are benefiting from the relationship." Likewise, the ACA (2005) Code of Ethics holds that "counselors terminate a counseling relationship when it becomes reasonably apparent that the client … is being harmed by continued counseling" (Standard A.11.c). The APA (2010) Ethical Code also holds that therapy should be terminated when clients are "being harmed by continued service" (Standard 10.10). The information provided (e.g., Kate's nervous demeanor and Joe's greater participation in the session) suggests that a power imbalance may exist in the couple's relationship. Combined with the report of some physical violence, this suggests that Kate's safety may be at risk if heated issues are discussed in therapy. Even if her safety risks can be managed, the therapist also must question the extent to which she would benefit from treatment if her diminished power in the relationship renders her less likely to participate fully in therapy.

The therapist must consider the potential that the safety risk is greater than the level of violence disclosed by Kate and Joe. As stated in the IAMFC (n.d.) Ethical Codes, therapists "promote client safety, security, and a place-of-belonging in family, community, and society" (Standard I.A). Further, the ACA (2005) Code of Ethics states, "Counselors act to avoid harming their clients … and to minimize or to remedy unavoidable or unanticipated harm" (Standard A.4.a). These standards underscore the importance of taking safety and the risk of harm into consideration when deciding on an appropriate treatment approach.

Another important question is whether it is ethical for therapists to refuse to treat a couple conjointly if they request that service. In other words, what right do clients have as consumers to choose the treatment they receive? The AAMFT (2001) Code of Ethics states, "Marriage and family therapists respect the rights of clients to make decisions and help them to understand the consequences of these decisions" (Standard 1.8). Also, the IAMFC (n.d.) Ethical Codes state, "Members respect the autonomy and independent decision-making abilities of their clients" (Standard I.C). Therapists' concern for clients' autonomy and right to make decisions must be evaluated with respect to the potential risks of treatment approaches and clients' possible vulnerabilities. For example, the NASW (2008) Code of Ethics states, "Social workers may limit clients' rights to self-determination when, in the social workers' professional judgment, clients' actions or potential actions pose a serious, foreseeable, and imminent risk to themselves or others" (Standard 1.02), and the APA (2010) ethical code includes the following statement: "Psychologists are aware that special safeguards may be necessary to protect the rights and welfare of persons or communities whose vulnerabilities impair autonomous decision making" (General Principle E). The rationale for conjoint treatment, therefore, must be based on an evaluation of the clients' right to make their own decisions and the potential risks involved.

An additional concern is that, if conjoint treatment truly is the only form of treatment that Joe and Kate are willing to consider, could refusing to provide this service cut them off from a potentially valuable source of support? In particular, if the couple plans to stay together and will maintain an ongoing relationship, could withholding conjoint treatment actually increase the safety risks for the victim? For example, conjoint treatment could offer an opportunity to develop increased skills for improving their relationship functioning, and therefore decreasing the frequency of situations that may escalate into violence. This is especially relevant given the social isolation often experienced by couples experiencing IPV. If the therapist decides not to proceed with conjoint treatment, s/he has an ethical obligation to refer the clients for appropriate treatment elsewhere (See, for example: ACA, 2005, Standard A.11.d; AAMFT, 2001, Standard 1.10; APA, 2010, Standard 10.10; NASW, Standard 1.16.b).

Finally, if the therapist proceeds to conjoint treatment with Joe and Kate, what message does this send about whose responsibility it is to end the violence? Often, therapists who work with couples and families view the relationship as the "client," rather than viewing any one family member as the identified client. For example, the Ethical Codes of IAMFC (n.d.) states, "Members must determine and inform all persons involved that the primary client is the family" (Standard I.J). If this same stance is taken with couples who have experienced IPV, it may imply that the interactions between the partners (i.e., the relationship) are the locus of the violence, and thereby the responsibility for change is placed, in part, upon the victim.

In summary, promoting client welfare is a basic ethical requirement (e.g., see ACA, 2005, Standard A.1.a). A major challenge in determining whether conjoint treatment is appropriate is determining which decision is most likely to promote the welfare of the clients, and the unique needs of individual partners may be at odds in this regard. The case of Kate and Joe makes clear that risks may be associated with any potential decision as to whether and how to proceed with conjoint treatment. This area of clinical practice should never be undertaken lightly, and safety considerations must be paramount.

Although professional ethical codes offer some guidance for addressing these ethical dilemmas, they leave much room for interpretation. As such, our goal for the remainder of the chapter is to provide therapists with adequate information about this issue to guide their decisions about how best to proceed with their clients. In light of the controversies surrounding the questions of conjoint treatment for couples who have experienced IPV, therapists' professional competency is perhaps one of the most significant ethical considerations, such that any therapist engaging in this type of clinical practice must demonstrate the professional competence to do so safely. The NASW (2008) Code of Ethics provides a particularly applicable suggestion related to this area of practice: "When generally recognized standards do not exist with respect to an emerging area of practice, social workers should exercise careful judgment and take responsible steps (including appropriate education, research, training, consultation, and supervision) to ensure the competence of their work and to protect clients from harm" (1.04.c).

Conjoint Therapy: The Context of Controversy

Conjoint treatment is not appropriate in all cases for couples in which IPV has occurred, and there are some circumstances in which conjoint therapy is not advisable (O'Leary, Heyman, & Neidig, 1999). Therapists should consider every case within the context of safety concerns by asking, "Does conjoint therapy present a safety risk for one or both members of this couple?" We believe that the existing research and insights drawn from clinical practice make clear that conjoint treatment is never appropriate for couples who are experiencing current, ongoing battering. In these cases involving serious abuses of power and control within the relationship, the risks of conjoint treatment far outweigh any potential benefits. In such cases, therapists should refer to treatment guidelines for victims and perpetrators, as discussed in Chapter 4.

To some extent, the decision as to whether conjoint treatment is appropriate when battering is present is the easiest one to make. When the violence and abusive dynamics are not extreme enough to be considered battering, an expansive "gray area" exists in which it is difficult to make clear rules as to whether and when conjoint treatment is appropriate. Before we turn to existing research to guide us through this gray area, we urge readers to pause and reflect upon whether you believe that conjoint treatment could be appropriate in the following situations:

- When the couple experienced battering in the past, but no violent incidents have occurred for an extended period of time (e.g., six months or one year);
- When the couple demonstrates situational couple violence involving only relatively minor levels of physical violence that is contained to relationship conflict situations;

- When one partner is psychologically and emotionally abusive to the other partner, but there have never been any incidents of physical or sexual abuse.

We refrain from putting forth hard and fast rules about the above situations because such rules would overlook the complexity of the dynamics involved in individual relationship patterns. To demonstrate the shortcomings of such rules, consider the following holes we could poke into each of them. First, imagine that we proposed a rule related to the timing of past violent incidents, such as stating that conjoint treatment can begin once a couple demonstrates no violent incidents in the past six months. In fact, some previously-studied approaches to conjoint treatment have been developed for couples in which the perpetrator has completed treatment successfully and the abuse has stopped (e.g., Almeida & Durkin, 1999; Gauthier & Levendosky, 1996). A problem with this rule is that the violence could simply have gone under the radar, in that physical violence was replaced by psychological abuse to maintain the perpetrator's power (Gauthier & Levendosky, 1996). Second, consider if we proposed a rule that conjoint treatment is appropriate for couples whose violence fits the pattern of situational couple violence. This rule would oversimplify what we currently know to be true of this form of IPV. Even in cases of situational couple violence, the violence has the potential to be severe (Derrington, Johnson, Menard, Ooms, & Stanley, 2010), and it is difficult to predict which couples' violence will escalate. And finally, what if we were to suggest that conjoint treatment is appropriate when only psychological and/or emotional abuse was present (LaTaillade, Epstein, & Werlinich, 2006), and there was no evidence of physical or sexual abuse? Again, this rule overlooks the potential for the psychological abuse to escalate to physical or sexual violence, and it also downplays the severity of the consequences of psychological abuse. Furthermore, we must always consider the possibility that one or both partners are underreporting the true extent of the violence.

In light of current research, we believe that it is appropriate to say at this time that conjoint treatment *might* be an appropriate treatment for *some* couples, in *some* circumstances, who have experienced IPV if (a) there is no severe, ongoing pattern of battering, (b) the violence appears to be relatively minor and confined to conflict situations, and/or (c) the couple demonstrates only emotional abuse. But, then again, there are exceptions to these guidelines that would render conjoint treatment inadvisable. It is our hope that our tentativeness is not interpreted as being wishy washy. Rather, we challenge therapists to understand the full complexity of this issue so that they will be best informed when they are considering these decisions in their clinical practice, particularly given how common IPV is among couples presenting for therapy.

Reasons Conjoint Treatment Should Be Avoided

Numerous reasons have been suggested for avoiding conjoint treatment in cases involving IPV. In particular, conjoint therapy may threaten victims' safety (Bograd & Mederos, 1999; Schacht, Dimidjian, George, & Berns, 2009). Conjoint therapy may increase the risk for further and more severe violence for victims and their children (Aldarondo & Straus, 1994; Bograd & Mederos, 1999; Galvani, 2007; McCollum, 2008; Rosen, Matheson, Stith, McCollum, & Locke, 2003; Stith, Rosen, & McCollum, 2003). For example, conjoint treatment can be risky if it highlights victims' weaknesses, which perpetrators could exploit (Jory, Anderson, & Greer, 1997). As another example, perpetrators may threaten victims not to disclose certain information about them or their relationships (Jory et al., 1997). Also, therapy could lead to arguments after the session about topics discussed during the session (O'Leary, 2001; O'Leary et al., 1999; Stith et al., 2003), especially if the perpetrator views the therapist as having challenged his/her power (Galvani, 2007).

Another concern about the use of conjoint treatment relates to the implications about who is responsible for the violence. Conjoint treatment may imply that the victim is to blame because, after all, the context for conjoint treatment is a focus on the relationship (McCollum, 2008; O'Leary et al., 1999; Rosen et al., 2003; Schacht et al., 2009; Shamai, 1995; Stith et al., 2003; Stith, Rosen, McCollum, & Thomsen, 2004). Perpetrators may feel absolved of their individual responsibility for their own behaviors (Aldarondo & Straus, 1994; Galvani, 2007; O'Leary, 2001). Participating in conjoint treatment could even provide an excuse for the perpetrator, in that s/he could claim to be working on his/her problems (Jory et al., 1997).

Critics argue that traditional conjoint interventions do not adequately address power and control dynamics (Aldarondo & Straus, 1994; Jory & Anderson, 2000b), and the violence may not be the primary focus of the treatment (McMahon & Pence, 1996). Therapists inadequately prepared to provide conjoint therapy to violent couples may take too lightly any evidence of potential violence (Jory et al., 1997), and many therapists do not acknowledge that they themselves are afraid of battering perpetrators (McMahon & Pence, 1996). These dynamics may render traditional approaches and unprepared therapists ill-equipped to address safety concerns. Furthermore, victims may not feel free to express that they do not feel comfortable in conjoint treatment due to the abusive dynamics (Jory et al., 1997; McMahon & Pence, 1996; O'Leary, 2001; O'Leary et al., 1999). This limited participation may decrease couples' likelihood of positive treatment outcomes.

Finally, a reason to cautiously use conjoint approaches for couples who have experienced IPV is that this remains an area of clinical practice for which there is relatively minimal research evidence (Bograd & Mederos, 1999). Currently, clear, empirically-supported guidelines do not exist to define appropriate cutoff levels for violence (Simpson, Atkins, Gattis, & Christensen, 2008). Furthermore, even by ruling out certain couples, safety cannot be guaranteed (McMahon & Pence, 1996).

Reasons Conjoint Treatment Should be Considered

Despite the significant concerns about potential risks of conjoint therapy with couples who have experienced IPV, a number of other reasons warrant its consideration for some couples. These reasons revolve around four common themes: (a) recognition of different types of violence, (b) the importance of unique relational dynamics, (c) the view that clients are consumers, and (d) the potential that conjoint approaches can lead to positive client outcomes.

Different Types of Violence. Again, IPV can vary greatly in severity, frequency, and impact (O'Leary, 2001). Interventions targeting battering may not apply to couples experiencing other forms of violence, especially those couples who are voluntarily seeking treatment and demonstrate lower levels of violence (LaTaillade et al., 2006; O'Leary et al., 1999). Couples may not want to participate in treatment for battering if these treatments do not match their lived experiences (Simpson et al., 2008). Couples differ in their IPV experiences, and some may be fitting for conjoint approaches (Gauthier & Levendosky, 1996; Greene & Bogo, 2002; Jory & Anderson, 2000b; McCollum, 2008; O'Leary, 2001; Rosen et al., 2003; Stith et al., 2003; Stith et al., 2004). Even though low levels of abuse can have significant consequences for couples, it is also possible that some violence has minimal impact on partners (Bograd & Mederos, 1999; Lipchik, Sirles, & Kubicki, 1997).

Attention to Relationship Dynamics. Conjoint approaches offer a therapeutic advantage in that they provide greater attention to relationship dynamics that may be contributing to IPV (Bograd & Mederos, 1999; Lipchik et al., 1997). For example, conjoint therapy allows therapists to observe control tactics (Bograd & Mederos, 1999; Lipchik et al., 1997). Traditional approaches to BIP may ignore important relationship dynamics (Greene & Bogo, 2002; Rosen et al., 2003; Stith et al., 2003; Stith et al., 2004). Some relationship dynamics that conjoint therapy can address include conflicts, satisfaction, gender role expectations, reciprocal violence patterns, and belief systems. First, relationship conflict can increase the risk for IPV, so addressing those conflicts can potentially reduce risk (Heyman & Schlee, 2003; LaTaillade et al., 2006; McCollum, 2008; O'Leary, 1996; O'Leary, 2001; O'Leary et al., 1999). Second, because relationship satisfaction influences the relationship between batterers' impulsivity and perpetration of psychological abuse, improving relationship functioning through conjoint treatment may help prevent further violence (Stuart & Holtzworth-Munroe, 2005). Third, gender inequalities can be addressed in conjoint approaches (Heyman & Schlee, 2003). Fourth, because it is possible for IPV to be reciprocal, and stopping violence used by one partner could lead to the other partner's violence stopping as well (Rosen et al., 2003). Finally, a couple's underlying belief systems about relationships create a context that supports violence, and these beliefs can be address in conjoint treatment (Shamai, 1995). Indeed, some techniques used in traditional BIP approaches, notably time-outs, may be used ineffectively or even as further abuse if not considered as part of the couple's relationship dynamics (Rosen et al., 2003).

Clients as Consumers. Conjoint approaches also warrant consideration because clients may *want* this type of treatment and have a right to request it as consumers (Bograd & Mederos, 1999; Lipchik et al., 1997). Some have even gone so far as to argue that refusing to treat any couples who have experienced IPV could be considered unethical practice, especially if the violent dynamics have not been explored thoroughly and if there are minimal other resources for the couples in the community (Gauthier & Levendosky, 1996). Not providing the service may lead to further social isolation, especially for victims, and may close off a limited window for help-seeking (Derrington et al., 2010). A conjoint intervention could provide a supportive resource for the couple and valuable and useful information (Derrington et al., 2010). Some victims may feel empowered through conjoint treatment (Jory & Anderson, 2000b). Some perpetrators' partners want to be involved in treatment, such as by wanting to know what their partners are learning and to help their partners change their violent behaviors (Milner & Singleton, 2008). And finally, the fact is, many couples choose to remain in their relationships, despite the violence they experience (Jory & Anderson, 2000b; McCollum, 2008; Rosen et al., 2003). Conjoint therapy can help couples determine the viability of their relationships (Bograd & Mederos, 1999; Lipchik et al., 1997). Some advocate that denying couples from conjoint treatment based on any level of aggression may mean that couples are denied a potentially needed and beneficial source of support (Simpson et al., 2008).

Potentially Effective Interventions. Conjoint approaches have not been ruled out entirely as effective approaches for treating couples who have experienced IPV. In fact, as is discussed later in this chapter, there is evidence that these approaches can be conducted effectively and safely under the right circumstances. Conjoint treatments may be effective at producing positive outcomes, at least for some couples (Aldarondo & Straus, 1994; Fals-Stewart & Clinton-Sherrod, 2009; Gauthier & Levendosky, 1996; O'Leary, 1996). Existing research suggests that no treatments are clearly more effective than others for IPV, so all potentially useful approaches should be able to be considered (O'Leary, 2001; Rosen et al., 2003; Stith et al., 2003). In particular, conjoint approaches may be more effective at identifying and building on positive aspects of the couple's relationship to promote positive outcomes (Rosen et al., 2003). Although more research is needed to tease apart the potential costs and benefits of conjoint approaches, the possibility that these approaches may be effective in some cases remains viable.

Conditions Under Which Conjoint Treatment May Be Appropriate

Although rates of violence among couples seeking therapy are high, the severity of this violence is generally low and often not characteristic of battering (Greene & Bogo, 2002; Simpson et al., 2008). Furthermore, most couples who seek treatment and demonstrate IPV seek treatment voluntarily (O'Leary et al., 1999), and many couples seeking marital therapy experience IPV but don't necessarily report it as a problem (Greene & Bogo, 2002; Heyman & Schlee, 2003; O'Leary, 1996; O'Leary, 2001; Shamai, 1995; Simpson et al., 2008). This presents another clinical challenge for couple therapists, as even very low levels of physical violence or verbal aggression alone can have very negative impacts on clients' functioning (Aldarondo & Straus, 1994; Holtzworth-Munroe, 2000; Olson, 2002). How, then, are therapists supposed to help couples who want to enter conjoint treatment but also demonstrate IPV? We explore this question in greater depth in the remainder of this chapter.

Therapists must assess carefully whether each particular couple is suitable for conjoint treatment if IPV has been present (Carr, 2009). The professional debate surrounding the use of conjoint therapy provides a challenging context for therapists in making these decisions. Again, no hard-and-fast rules can be established to cover of the cases therapists will face. The rationale for conjoint therapy must be considered carefully, and it must be the best alternative among possible treatment approaches (Bograd & Mederos, 1999). How, then, can therapists make the best decisions as to which couples are appropriate to treat? We can turn to existing research and practices to identify some conditions under which conjoint therapy may be able to be conducted safely, as well as some conditions under which conjoint therapy should be avoided.

In our review of existing literature, we noted that, although there are some conditions for which there is general agreement, there are other conditions in which differing criteria have been suggested. For example, some scholars have suggested that violence must have stopped completely for conjoint treatment to commence, while others suggest that it may be appropriate as long as the violence is only low to moderate in severity. Therefore, we present a comprehensive list and encourage therapists to apply these criteria carefully and uniquely to each couple. The application of these criteria also must account for the unique characteristics of each couple, such as whether the type of IPV they experienced. In addition, these criteria should be considered in combination, and no single criterion should be used to make a decision for a particular client. As such, we recommend that a couple should meet the preponderance of criteria for being appropriate and should not meet the preponderance of exclusionary criteria in order for there to be a sufficient rationale to proceed with conjoint treatment. The exclusionary criteria should be weighted more heavily than the appropriateness criteria in making these decisions, and, again, therapists should err on the side of caution when no clear answer is evident.

Appropriateness Criteria. Some conditions under which conjoint treatment may be appropriate include the following:

Relationship-related criteria

- Both partners want to continue the relationship (Gauthier & Levendosky, 1996; Heyman & Schlee, 2003; Jackson-Gilfort, Mitrani, & Szapoczni, 2000; LaTaillade et al., 2006; O'Leary, 1996; O'Leary, 2001; O'Leary et al., 1999; Stith et al., 2003).
- Both partners are freely choosing to participate in the treatment (Bograd & Mederos, 1999; O'Leary, 2001; Shamai, 1995; Tolman & Bhosley, 1990).
- In many cases, both partners have completed individual treatment (Gauthier & Levendosky, 1996).
- The couple's relationship is generally stable (LaTaillade et al., 2006; Schacht et al., 2009).
- Partners view their abuse experiences as problematic (LaTaillade et al., 2006; O'Leary, 2001; O'Leary et al. 1999).
- Each individual partner has a goal of working toward a nonviolent relationship (Bartle & Rosen, 1994; Jackson-Gilfort et al., 2000; LaTaillade et al., 2006; Lipchik et al., 1997; O'Leary et al., 1999; Shamai, 1995).

Violence-related criteria

- The violence is no longer occurring (Gauthier & Levendosky, 1996; McMahon & Pence, 1996).
- The violence is low or low-to-moderate in severity (Bograd & Mederos, 1999; LaTaillade et al., 2006; Rosen et al., 2003).
- Violence is not chronic (Bograd & Mederos, 1999; Lipchik et al., 1997).
- There is minimal psychological violence (Bograd & Mederos, 1999).
- There does not appear to be an imminent risk to either partner's physical safety (LaTaillade et al., 2006).
- No lethality risk factors are present (Bograd & Mederos, 1999).

Perpetrator-related criteria

- The perpetrator assumes responsibility for violent behaviors (Bartle & Rosen, 1994; Bograd & Mederos, 1999; Gauthier & Levendosky, 1996; Tolman & Bhosley, 1990).
- The perpetrator shows a sincere interest in changing (Gauthier & Levendosky, 1996).

- The perpetrator demonstrates effective use of nonviolent behaviors prior to beginning conjoint therapy (Almeida & Durkin, 1999; Tolman & Bhosley, 1990).
- The perpetrator has successfully been nonviolent for some designated period of time (Tolman & Bhosley, 1990), such as six months (Gauthier & Levendosky, 1996).

Victim-related criteria

- The victim (individually and separately) reports being comfortable and feeling safe in conjoint treatment (Gauthier & Levendosky, 1996; Gray, 2004; Heyman & Schlee, 2003; LaTaillade et al., 2006; O'Leary, 2001; O'Leary et al. 1999; Shamai, 1995; Stith et al., 2003).
- The victim is willing to take steps to promote safety (Bartle & Rosen, 1994).
- The victim does not believe that s/he is in danger (Stith et al., 2003) and does not demonstrate a high level of fear (Bograd & Mederos, 1999; LaTaillade et al., 2006; Schacht et al., 2009).

Therapist-related criteria

- The therapist is knowledgeable and competent to provide such services (Gauthier & Levendosky, 1996; Greene & Bogo, 2002).
- The therapist has conducted a very careful assessment of the level of violence present and is willing and able to regularly reassess for safety throughout the therapeutic process (Simpson et al., 2008).
- The therapist is able to modify confidentiality rules so that information gathered in individual assessments is considered secret until the client determines otherwise (Bograd & Mederos, 1999).
- The therapist is able to maintain a professional stance and focus (Bograd & Mederos, 1999).

Exclusionary criteria. Conjoint therapy is generally not recommended when the following exclusionary criteria are present:

Relationship-related criteria

- One or both partners have a serious, untreated mental health disorder (Derrington et al., 2010; Heyman & Schlee, 2003; Lipchik et al., 1997; McCollum, 2008; O'Leary et al., 1999; Stith et al., 2003).
- Partners report IPV experiences differently from one another (Bograd & Mederos, 1999).
- One or both partners demonstrate excessive anger toward the partner (O'Leary, 2001).

Violence-related criteria

- An imminent threat of danger appears to be present (Jackson-Gilfort et al., 2000).

- The level of violence is severe (Gauthier & Levendosky, 1996; Jory & Anderson, 2000b; McCollum, 2008; O'Leary, 2001).
- The violence is ongoing (Bartle & Rosen, 1994; Gauthier & Levendosky, 1996).
- The violence results in physical injury to the victim (Brown & O'Leary, 2000; Jacobson & Gottman, 1998; McCollum, 2008; O'Leary, 1996; O'Leary, 2001; O'Leary et al., 1999; Schacht et al., 2009; Stith et al., 2003).
- Severe risk factors for lethality are present, such as previous restraining order violations, the use of weapons, and the perpetrator being obsessed with the partner (Bograd & Mederos, 1999).

Perpetrator-related criteria

- The perpetrator demonstrates characteristics of being generally violent/antisocial (Gauthier & Levendosky, 1996; Heyman & Schlee, 2003).
- The perpetrator uses substances (Bograd & Mederos, 1999; Heyman & Schlee, 2003; Lipchik et al., 1997; O'Leary, 2001; O'Leary et al., 1999; Stith et al., 2003).
- The perpetrator has a brain injury (Stith et al., 2003).
- The perpetrator is not willing to remove access to weapons (McCollum, 2008).
- The perpetrator has not made adequate progress in individual treatment (Jory & Anderson, 2000b).
- The perpetrator is court-mandated to treatment, which is significant due to the high levels of violence that typically precede such legal involvement (Bograd & Mederos, 1999).

Victim-related criteria

- The victim fears the perpetrator (Brown & O'Leary, 2000; Jacobson & Gottman, 1998; O'Leary, 1996; O'Leary, 2001; O'Leary et al., 1999; Schacht et al., 2009).

Ruling Out Clients from Conjoint Therapy. Deciding not to proceed with conjoint treatment leads to another challenge of how to communicate this decision in a safe manner. If a therapist believes that a perpetrator presents a high level of risk or danger for a victim, the therapist has a responsibility to communicate this to the victim (Bograd & Mederos, 1999). This is challenging if the decision was made based on information provided by one client alone (especially the victim) during an individual session. For example, one partner reveals to the therapist that she was severely injured by her partner as recently as two weeks ago, and she admits that she is very afraid that her partner will do it again. The therapist is in a very difficult situation in this case. On the one hand, s/he has decided that conjoint treatment will pose a safety risk for the victim, and it would not be appropriate to proceed with this approach at this time. On the other hand, telling the perpetrator the reason for this decision could also put the victim at risk, in that the perpetrator may retaliate out of anger that the victim disclosed the violence to the therapist. Bograd and Mederos (1999) suggest potentially useful wording to explain to clients that conjoint treatment would not be appropriate: "I know you want to do couples counseling, but things are pretty intense right now and we often find that when things are so hot, couples therapy makes problems work. A lot of guys feel more provoked and blow up. I would be lying to you or misleading you if I told you this could work now" (p. 307). Even this wording may be too direct, so therapists may need to find other, safer ways to convey this message. As a follow-up to making and communicating this decision, it is advisable to meet individually with the victim in order to prepare a safety plan and provide him or her with resources (Heyman & Schlee, 2003).

Setting the Stage for Safety in Conjoint Treatment

Once a decision is made to proceed with conjoint therapy, the therapist must consider carefully how best to conduct treatment in a way that adequately addresses various safety concerns. A primary focus on safety should underlie any conjoint interventions when IPV is present (Derrington et al., 2010; Greene & Bogo, 2002; Lipchik et al., 1997; McMahon & Pence, 1996; Stith et al., 2003; Stith et al., 2004). Key aims in using conjoint treatment when IPV is present are to reduce the amount of risk and promote the maximum amount of safety for clients (Bograd & Mederos, 1999; D'Ardenne & Balakrishna, 2001; McLeod, Hays, & Chang, 2010). Therapists must be mindful not to engage in practices that may increase the risk for violence (Almeida & Durkin, 1999). Another preliminary step is to take a clear stance that violence and abuse are not acceptable or healthy (Bartle & Rosen, 1994; Gauthier & Levendosky, 1996; Shamai, 1995). This stance can and should be taken without conveying judgment on the individual clients, but rather the violent behaviors (Gauthier & Levendosky, 1996). When providing conjoint treatment with clients who have experienced IPV, therapists walk a fine line between making clear that violence is not to be tolerated and maintaining a stance of respect for clients (Bograd & Mederos, 1999).

Nonviolence Contracts

A strategy for conveying to clients that violence is not acceptable is by having clients sign and abide by a no-harm contract as a precursor to conjoint treatment (Bartle & Rosen, 1994; Carr, 2009; Gauthier & Levendosky, 1996). Typically, this contract stipulates that violence must not occur, or conjoint treatment will cease (not all treatment, but conjoint treatment; Bartle & Rosen, 1994; Schacht et al., 2009). A basic contract for conducting conjoint treatment should include that (a) the primary goal of treatment is ending the violence;

(b) conjoint treatment will discontinue if violence occurs; and (c) the perpetrator will enter specialized treatment if s/he demonstrates violence (Bograd & Mederos, 1999). Some other terms that may be in a nonviolence contract include how partners will act when triggers for violence occur and terms of a couple's separation, if applicable (Perez & Rasmussen, 1997). The contract should also include a plan for using time-outs (Bartle & Rosen, 1994), which is discussed further in the next section. In addition, a safety plan for involved children should be developed.

Shamai (1995) believes that the process of developing nonviolence contracts can function as a significant ritual in the process of conjoint treatment. Shamai recommends drawing up separate contracts for the perpetrator and the victim. The perpetrator's contract includes statements regarding the damaging consequences of the abuse, that therapy can offer alternatives to violence, and that the violence must stop as a precondition to therapy. The victim's contract includes statements that the violence is not his or her fault but that s/he does bear some responsibility for making decisions to promote safety. The therapist should keep a copy of the contract and provide a copy to the clients.

Nonviolence contracts should be written documents (Perez & Rasmussen, 1997). The terms should be mutually agreeable to both partners, and both partners and the therapist should sign the contracts (Perez & Rasmussen, 1997). Therapists must be consistent in enforcing the contract's terms, and it may be helpful to review and reference contracts regularly as therapy progresses (Gauthier & Levendosky, 1996). Although this stance can put therapists into a "position of disciplinarian, ... therapists need to be prepared to be uncomfortable when setting limits like nonviolence contracts" (Gauthier & Levendosky, 1996, p. 413).

Conjoint Safety Planning

Safety planning should be conducted routinely in conjoint treatment with violent couples (Rosen et al., 2003). Conjoint safety planning holds many similarities to individual safety planning. As with individual safety plans, conjoint safety plans should be tailored to unique client needs and include resources to promote victim safety (Bograd & Mederos, 1999). In some cases, it is useful to develop one safety plan for the couple, one for the perpetrator, and one for the victim. For example, it may be useful for the therapist and victim to develop a code or code word that the victim can use to communicate to the therapist that the victim perceives his/her safety to be at risk (Galvani, 2007). This code should not be shared with the perpetrator. The safety plan also may stipulate that both partners will participate in individual sessions while conjoint treatment occurs (LaTaillade et al., 2006). This sets the tone and normalizes instances in which the therapist and victim meet without the perpetrator. Whether one or more safety plans are drawn up, they should include relevant community resources that can support clients in addressing safety needs and activate the IPV response system (LaTaillade et al., 2006; Stith et al., 2003).

Time-outs. Time-outs are a potentially useful tool to include in safety planning to deescalate conflicts that could lead to violence (Perez & Rasmussen, 1997; Rosen et al., 2003). However, time-outs should be planned carefully to ensure that they are used in a way the supports the couple's relationship, especially because this tool can be abused as part of a pattern of power and control dynamics. Possible abuses of time-outs include leaving the partner without informing him/her where one is going and never returning to finish the discussion (Perez & Rasmussen, 1997). Rosen et al. (2003) described a conjoint approach to using time-outs as a de-escalation strategy for preventing violence. In their research, these researchers learned from participants that time-out, as it is traditionally taught in BIPs, can be ineffective when considered in the relational context. For example, a perpetrator could abuse this technique to control his or her partner, such as by not having a specified time period in which it will be over (see also Perez & Rasmussen, 1997). As another example, a victim may not understand the reason for the time-outs, which could lead to confusion and disappointment. As such, Rosen et al. proposed a strategy called *negotiated time-out,* in which the partners work together to develop parameters for using time-outs during conflicts. The negotiated time-out process involves the following steps: (1) identifying a pattern of escalating anger; (2) determining that a time-out is needed; (3) using a signal to call the time-out; (4) having the partners separate physically to calm down; and (5) partners returning to continue the discussion. This procedure is taught to couples early in treatment, and therapists practice it with clients during the session. Some details of the time-out that are negotiated by the couple are how long it will last, ways to calm down, and practical strategies to manage the time out (e.g., addressing child care). If the couple's experiences reveal that the negotiated time-out is not working in practice, the original plan is revised to improve its effectiveness.

Monitoring Client Safety during Conjoint Approaches

As Gauthier and Levendosky (1996) stated, "The process of assessing for physical and emotional abuse in couples is never finished" (p. 408). The decision to conduct conjoint treatment is never a final one, and therapists who provide conjoint treatment to couples who have experienced IPV must monitor client safety as an ongoing process throughout treatment. Ongoing assessment is warranted because initial reports of violence may have been minimized (Almeida & Durkin, 1999; Bograd & Mederos, 1999), new violence may develop (Bograd & Mederos, 1999), and lower levels of violence may escalate (Aldarondo & Straus, 1994).

How should Therapists Monitor Client Safety in Ongoing Conjoint Therapy? Therapists should monitor safety in ongoing conjoint treatment (McCollum, 2008), such as by assessing for new incidents of violence and monitoring the victim's safety at all times (Stith et al., 2003; Stith et al., 2004). It is useful to plan intermittent individual sessions with each partner as standard practice (Jory et al., 1997; Stith et al., 2003; Stith et al., 2004). It also may be useful to do a brief individual check-in with each partner before and after each session to attend to new safety concerns (Rosen et al., 2003).

What should Therapists do if Clients Disclose New Incidents of Volence in Conjoint Therapy? Any reported abuse must be treated very seriously and not be minimized (Derrington et al., 2010; O'Leary, 2001). If at any point a new incident of violence is disclosed, the therapist must immediately shift the focus to addressing safety concerns (Bograd & Mederos, 1999). Any reports of violence must be followed by a thorough assessment of the safety of the victim and involved children (Gauthier & Levendosky, 1996). This may be followed by referring partners for individual services (e.g., shelter and/or legal assistance for a victim and a BIP for a perpetrator) (Gauthier & Levendosky, 1996). Therapists should be prepared to stop conjoint treatment if it becomes clear that continuing presents safety risks (Galvani, 2007; McCollum, 2008; Stith et al., 2004).

How should Therapists Address Potentially Volatile Situations in Conjoint Therapy? When working with couples who have demonstrated IPV, there is a potential for emotionally intense and volatile situations to occur in treatment (O'Leary, 2001). In the PACT approach to conjoint treatment with violent couples (described below), some added protections that are in place to address these situations include having the therapists take extra time with one or both clients following sessions when they occur, having therapists call clients following the session to check-in about the clients' safety status, and having the therapist use de-escalation strategies when perpetrators demonstrate high levels of anger during sessions (O'Leary, 2001). Crisis intervention strategies may be warranted (LaTaillade et al., 2006). Throughout treatment, therapists must manage their own emotional reactivity to the potentially intense dynamics that arise during sessions (Bartle & Rosen, 1994). In other words, stay calm!

Addressing "Secrets" in Conjoint Treatment

A major challenge in conjoint therapy is addressing secrets disclosed by one partner that the therapist is asked to keep from the other partner. During an IPV assessment or subsequent therapy, one partner may ask a therapist to keep secret a disclosure of violence victimization, and reporting that disclosure to the allegedly violent partner could increase the risk of harm for the victim. How best to address the issue of secrets in couple therapy has been debated in the professional community, with some professionals believing it is best to have a no-secrets policy, others believing that secrets should be maintained, and others calling for a middle-of-the-road position, in which the therapist maintains some discretion as to which secrets are kept and how (Bass & Quimby, 2006). It is our professional opinion that the latter approach is the most sound in light of issues of potential IPV. In general, we believe it creates a challenging bind for therapists to promise to keep one partner's secrets from the other partner; this can present both therapeutic limitations and practical difficulties (i.e., keeping straight which partner knows what). On the other hand, the potential that new incidents of IPV will be reported as a secret, as well as the potential risks that may occur from disclosing such a secret, highlight the need for therapists to maintain some right to withhold information. The following box, adapted from the first author's professional disclosure statement, contains a declaration that could be included in informed consent documents to address this issue.

Informed Consent Statement on Secrets in Couple and Family Counseling

Special note on confidentiality regarding couple and family counseling: When I provide counseling to couples or families, I view the relationship(s) as the primary client, as opposed to any particular family member(s). Therefore, as a general rule, I do not keep secrets from family members that individuals may disclose to me individually. However, I maintain the professional responsibility (a) to not disclose secrets if I believe that doing so has the potential to result in an unsafe situation for one or more family members; (b) to not disclose secrets if, in my professional opinion, there is a valid therapeutic rationale for maintaining the secret; and (c) to discontinue couple or family treatment if maintaining the secret wou ld compromise my ability to provide quality counseling services. In the latter situation, clients will have the option to either continue counseling on an individual basis with myself or another counselor, or to seek couple or family counseling from another provider. Please note that I am ethically bound to assist clients who choose to seek the services of another counselor in locating an appropriate provider.

Conjoint Treatment Approaches and Outcome Research

Conjoint treatment for couples who have experienced IPV is not "generic marital therapy" (O'Leary, 2001, p. 156; see also Heyman & Schlee, 2003). Treatment should be structured, focused on stopping the violence completely, and having perpetrators accept responsibility for violence (O'Leary, 1996). For example, conjoint treatment approaches should address IPV risk factors, including family background and psychological variables, cognitive risk factors, gender roles and power dynamics, and relational dynamics (LaTaillade et al., 2006). Treatment approaches that do not have a primary focus on stopping the violence and that do not account for safety considerations are not appropriate (D'Ardenne & Balakrishna, 2001; Jory & Anderson, 2000b; Heyman & Schlee, 2003; O'Leary, 2001).

Later in this section, we discuss specific approaches that have been proposed for conducting conjoint treatment when violence has been present. To varying degrees, these approaches address similar underlying goals, which include the following. First, therapy should address each partner's individual needs (Jackson-Gilfort et al., 2000). In many cases, this means focusing on increasing the perpetrators' assumption of responsibility for their use of violent behaviors and improving the victims' self-esteem (Bartle & Rosen, 1994). Second, therapy may help clients establish more positive relationship functioning, such as by creating healthier boundaries, examining their relationship goals, and becoming better at managing emotional reactivity (Bartle & Rosen, 1994). Part of this work may involve helping couples develop the basic relationship skills they lack (Heyman & Schlee, 2003). Skills that may be appropriate points of focus include anger management, communication, conflict resolution, and problem-solving (Bartle & Rosen, 1994; Carr, 2009; Derrington et al., 2010; LaTaillade et al., 2006; O'Leary, 1996; Stith et al., 2004, as cited in Carr, 2009). In addition, due to the tendency for conflict to escalate into violence for couples that demonstrate violence (Olson, 2002), developing de-escalation strategies may prove useful. In focusing on skills, however, therapists must assess carefully whether negative relationship behaviors represent emotional abuse or poor communication skills (Jory et al., 1997).

Third, appropriate referrals should be provided based on clients' needs. For example, couples with work-related or financial conflicts may benefit from a referral to career counseling or a financial services organization, and couples in which one or both partners abuse substances should be connected with substance abuse treatment programs (Derrington et al., 2010). Fourth, therapy can focus on examining and deconstructing the influence of larger contextual variables on couples' experiences with violence (Jory et al., 1997), such as gender role beliefs (Bartle & Rosen, 1994) and family-of-origin influences (Jory et al., 1997). Fifth, therapists can challenge perpetrators' strategies for maintaining power and control (Jory et al., 1997), as well as both partners' cognitions that promote violence (Jory et al., 1997). Finally, therapists must consider how to address memories of past abuse, which perpetrators often do not want to discuss (Jory et al., 1997). Jory et al. (1997) recommend that therapists support victims in creating space for these memories to be a part of the couple's therapy.

Empirically Studied Conjoint Treatment Approaches

A small number of studies have been done to empirically test the effectiveness of conjoint treatment for IPV (Stith et al., 2003). Together, the existing studies show that conjoint treatment approaches can reduce violence, and there has not been evidence that programs lead to increased risk to victims, although it is important to note that all studies included careful screening procedures (Greene & Bogo, 2002; Stith et al., 2003). Some key features that appear to be best practices in conducting conjoint treatment with couples who have experienced IPV include: (a) detailed screening procedures; (b) maintaining a clear and primary focus on stopping the abuse; (c) helping clients develop skills that can potentially reduce their risk for violence; and (d) emphasizing that perpetrators are responsible for any violence they use (Stith et al., 2003). Despite the first study by Dunford (2000) reviewed below, other results suggest that, when done under the right conditions (e.g., adequate screening to rule out inappropriate clients), conjoint approaches may be just as, if not more effective, than traditional, gender-specific approaches for this client population.

Comparing Conjoint, Gender-specific, and Case Management Interventions. Dunford (2000) examined the differences in effectiveness among four different types of year-long interventions for male Navy servicemen with substantiated IPV. The four types of interventions were: (a) a gender-specific treatment group based on cognitive-behavioral therapy; (b) a multi-couple conjoint group also based on cognitive-behavioral therapy (note: women were not required to participate in this treatment, and results indicated that they did so at a generally low level); (c) a "rigorous monitoring" (p. 469) group, which included regular case management and contacts with wives; and (4) a no-treatment control group. The participants, who were randomly assigned to groups, included 861 married couples in which the husband was on active duty with the Navy. Dunford found no differences on any major outcome measures (e.g., reabuse, rearrest) based on which group participants were assigned to, and recidivism was generally low across all groups. These results call into question the potential value of the interventions, none of which produced more positive outcomes as compared to a no-treatment control group.

General Couple Therapy. Simpson et al. (2008) were interested in studying whether couple therapy that was not specifically focused on the violence could be effective with couples with low levels of relationship aggression. Among 134 married couples (most of whom were Caucasian), the couples with histories of low-level violence had treatment outcomes similar to couples without such histories, and the aggression demonstrated by couples with histories of low-level violence decreased as a result of treatment.

Behavioral Couples Therapy (BCT). O'Farrell and colleagues (Fals-Stewart & Clinton-Sherrod, 2009; O'Farrell, Murphy, Stephan, Fals-Stewart, & Murphy, 2004; Schumm, O'Farrell, Murphy, & Fals-Stewart, 1999) have studied an intensive, conjoint behavioral couples therapy (BCT) with couples demonstrating substance abuse and IPV. Some behavioral skills emphasized in the manualized BCT approach include coping and communication, using safety behaviors, supporting the partner's sobriety, increasing positive relationship behaviors, conflict management, and de-escalation strategies (Fals-Stewart & Clinton-Sherrod, 2009; O'Farrell et al. 2004; Schumm et al., 1999). BCT also addresses unique considerations related to IPV if the substance-abusing partner relapses (Fals-Stewart & Clinton-Sherrod, 2009).

Three outcome studies provide evidence of the effectiveness of BCT. First, Fals-Stewart and Clinton-Sherrod (2009) studied BCT with 207 men entering outpatient substance abuse treatment and their partners. Participants were randomly assigned to either a BCT treatment or an individual treatment based on the 12-step model. Both approaches included 32 60-minute sessions, and partners were included in 12 of the BCT sessions. Following treatment, as compared to the participants in individual treatment, the couples in the BCT approach demonstrated less frequent male-perpetrated IPV and fewer incidents of male-perpetrated IPV on days when the male partner relapsed in using substances. Second, O'Farrell et al. (2004) studied BCT with 303 men entering substance abuse treatment and their partners. These researchers compared their sample to a demographically matched comparison group drawn from a national family violence survey. Participants who completed BCT showed statistically significant decreases in levels of male-perpetrated IPV in both the first and second years following treatment. Although these findings suggest that the BCT approach is effective at reducing IPV, the study's limitations (especially the nonrandom comparison group) hamper the researchers' ability to state that the treatment actually caused the changes. Third, Schumm et al. (1999) studied the effectiveness of BCT at reducing IPV among 103 women seeking alcohol abuse treatment. These women participated in BCT with their male partners, and their rates of IPV were compared with a demographically matched comparison group drawn from a national family violence survey. Generally, the results revealed that both male- and female-perpetrated IPV decreased for the participants who completed BCT and whose substance abuse was in remission. Again, the study's lack of a random no-treatment control group limits the researchers' ability to make causal attributions as to the treatment's effectiveness. However, given the consistent positive findings of these studies, together, they demonstrate the potential value of using the BCT approach for couples who have co-occurring substance abuse and IPV (Fals-Stewart & Clinton-Sherrod, 2009; O'Farrell et al., 2004; Schumm et al., 1999).

Despite these promising findings, scholars have critiqued behavioral approaches to conjoint treatment with couples who have demonstrated IPV.

For example, Gauthier and Levendosky (1996) asserted that behavioral interventions reflect an underlying assumption that partners share equal levels of power in their relationships, meaning that victims may not have the power to adequately uphold contingencies put in place in treatment. Also, the primary focus on behaviors may fail to account for underlying power and control dynamics (Gauthier & Levendosky, 1996). Other criticisms have been directed more specifically to the BCT approach. Galvani (2007) criticized BCT by suggesting that these researchers should have set a lower level of violence at which the approach should be considered in appropriate, as well as by calling into question the ethics of some of the research participant section criteria.

The Couples Abuse Prevention Program (CAPP). The Couples Abuse Prevention Program (CAPP; LaTaillade et al., 2006) is a structured conjoint treatment grounded in CBT that was designed for couples with low- to moderate-physical aggression and/or psychological abuse. This psychoeducation approach aims to increase participants' knowledge about abuse, develop participants' anger and conflict management skills, address trust and trauma consequences in participants' relationships, and promote positive relational interactions. Other CAPP interventions include cognitive restructuring, stress management, and communication skills training. The CAPP program involves 10 90-minute weekly sessions. The first session focuses on providing an overview of the program, gathering assessment data, and establishing treatment goals. During the second session, treatment goals are refined, and psychoeducation occurs, focusing on anger management and conflict management. The third and fourth sessions focus on expressive and listening skills, and the fifth through seventh sessions address problem-solving. The final three sessions help the couple apply the skills and information they have learned to their lives, with the last session addressing relapse prevention. The therapist coaches the couple throughout treatment. Based on the developers' preliminary outcome data on the CAPP program, the approach shows promise for contributing to positive outcomes for couples who complete the program.

Domestic Violence Focused Couples Treatment (DVFCT). DVFCT is designed for couples demonstrating lower-level violence (i.e., not battering) (McCollum, 2008; Stith et al., 2004). This approach is grounded in feminist, solution-focused, cognitive-behavioral, and family systems theories (Rosen et al., 2003; Stith et al., 2004). To be able to participate in the conjoint treatment involved in the DVFCT, individual partners must have already completed at least six weeks of gender-specific treatment (Stith et al., 2004). This approach takes a clear stance that perpetrators are fully accountable for their use of violent behaviors, but relationship dynamics are examined and viewed as relevant to couples' experiences with IPV (Rosen et al., 2003). DVFCT is based on a treatment manual (Stith et al., 2004), is conducted by co-therapists (Stith et al.,

2004), and may occur in either multi-couple groups or with individual couples (Stith et al., 2004). Although both formats share a similar theoretical foundation, the program content varies based on the unique needs of the participating couples (Stith et al., 2004). Important elements include focusing on accepting responsibility for the violence, challenging violence-engendering cognitions, training clients to manage anger, training clients in skills to communicate and solve problems, and preventing relapse (Carr, 2009).

Stith et al. (2004) compared the effectiveness of the individual couple therapy format with the multi-couple group format among a sample of 42 couples randomly assigned to one approach or the other, with another 9 couples comprising a no-treatment comparison group. Participants in both formats had similar levels of program completion (i.e., about 70%), which these researchers defined as having completed at least 10 of the 12 sessions. The results suggest that that the multi-couple group approach may be the most effective. For example, males who participated in the group approach demonstrated significantly lower recidivism rates than those in the no-treatment comparison group (25% vs. 66%), but there were no significant differences in recidivism between the men who participated in the individual couple therapy approach (43%) as compared to the no-treatment comparison group. Participants in the group format also demonstrated statistically significant positive outcomes related to increased marital satisfaction and less accepting attitudes about wife abuse, but these positive outcomes were not found for participants in the individual couple approach or who were in the no-treatment group. The researchers speculated that group dynamics in the multi-couple groups were key to producing the more positive outcomes. Although this study's findings must be considered with respect to methodological limitations (e.g., small sample size and use of a nonrandom comparison group), they suggest that conjoint treatment holds promise for couples who have experienced IPV when conducted in a multi-couple group format.

Physical Aggression Couples Treatment (PACT). PACT is a research-based, conjoint treatment for couples who have experienced IPV (Heyman & Schlee, 2003). The primary focus is on stopping physical and psychological abuse within the couples' relationships (O'Leary, 2001; O'Leary et al., 1999). The PACT program has been described as a "feminist social learning" approach (Heyman & Schlee, 2003, p. 140). An underlying assumption of the program is that, while each partner is fully responsible for choosing to use violent behaviors, both partners hold some responsibility for the escalation of relationship conflict (Heyman & Schlee, 2003; O'Leary, 2001; O'Leary et al., 1999).

PACT is a group-based treatment protocol involving six to eight couples, and the program is facilitated by male-female co-therapists (O'Leary, 2001; O'Leary et al., 1999). The PACT program includes 14 sessions (Greene & Bogo, 2002; Heyman & Schlee, 2003). Three main emphases of the program are increasing awareness of the violence, anger management, and improving communication (Heyman & Schlee, 2003; Greene & Bogo, 2002; LaTaillade et al., 2006; O'Leary, 2001; O'Leary et al., 1999). The first seven sessions have an intrapersonal focus on responsibility, nonviolence contracts, anger cognitions, and stress (Heyman & Schlee, 2003). The final seven sessions have an interpersonal focus on such topics as communication skills, gender, equality, conflict management, sex, jealousy, social support, and maintenance (Heyman & Schlee, 2003).

Existing evaluation data have shown that PACT participants demonstrated significant differences in physical aggression following treatment, with no differences between PACT participants and a gender-specific approach, but marital adjustment was higher for PACT participants than in gender-specific approaches (Heyman & Schlee, 2003). In comparing PACT to gender-specific treatments, both were similarly effective at reducing physical and psychological aggression (O'Leary et al., 1999). Overall, the researchers suggested that their findings support the potential viability of conjoint treatments when couples are screened appropriately and the primary treatment focus is on ending the violence.

Brown and O'Leary (2000) examined further the effectiveness of PACT by studying the role of therapeutic alliance on treatment outcomes. The results revealed that husbands' levels of therapeutic alliance were related to their success in treatment, in that their alliance ratings were statistically significant predictors of reduced mild and severe physical and psychological aggression. The husbands' therapeutic alliance levels did not differ based on the type of program they attended (i.e., conjoint or gender-specific), and the therapeutic alliance for the wives had no bearing on outcomes. These results indicate the importance of therapists working hard from the start of treatment—regardless of approach—to establish a strong alliance with the perpetrator.

Summary

Clearly, the use of conjoint therapy approaches for couples who have experienced IPV remains controversial. Therapists must establish a strong rationale for proceeding with conjoint therapy and ensure safety prior to, and throughout, engaging in conjoint therapeutic approaches. A therapist who decides to provide conjoint treatment to couples who have been violent must remain vigilant for new safety risks that may arise as treatment progresses, as well as be prepared to shift course if needed.

PART II

6

CHILD MALTREATMENT

Background and Overview of Response Systems

Child maltreatment is an extremely complex and challenging issue for therapists to address, whether they are treating child victims, perpetrators, non-offending parents, or adult survivors. Competent clinical practice begins with an in-depth understanding of the dynamics of child maltreatment, including its various forms, prevalence rates, common risk factors and consequences, and the response systems in place to address it. This chapter addresses these issues and lays the groundwork for the information about assessment, therapy, and clinical work with adult survivors found in subsequent chapters. Although our focus is on abuse perpetrated by family members, children also may be maltreated by perpetrators outside of their families. Thus, clients in counseling also may be impacted by abuse perpetrated by others, such as clergy, teachers, coaches, and others in their lives (Farrell & Taylor, 2000).

Definitions: What is Child Maltreatment?

We use the term *child maltreatment* as an umbrella term that includes a range of abusive and neglectful behaviors perpetrated against children (typically defined as individuals under the age of 18; Finkelhor, 2009; Govindshenoy & Spencer, 2006; Horton & Cruise, 1997) within a family or other caregiving context. In this book, we refer to child maltreatment in which the child victim is somehow dependent on the perpetrator (Ahmad, 2006). This is an important distinction. If therapists become aware of a child who has been harmed by a perpetrator on whom the child is not dependent (i.e., the perpetrator is not in a caregiving role, such as a stranger), the reporting requirements typically are different, as is discussed later in this chapter. Such cases may need to be reported to the police rather than child protective systems (CPS). In keeping with the topic of this book, our primary focus is on child maltreatment that occurs in a family context.

Researchers have used varying definitions of maltreatment, making it difficult to compare results across studies (Knickerbocker, Heyman, Slep, Jouriles, & McDonald, 2007). In part, this is because child maltreatment is multifaceted and difficult to reduce down to a simple, all-inclusive definition. The definition of child maltreatment is further complicated because a child's developmental age can influence the types of experiences that may be considered "abusive" or maltreatment (Manly, 2005). Therefore, we begin with an overview of child maltreatment in general, and then we will describe in greater detail several specific forms of child maltreatment.

The term *child maltreatment* describes a behavior, done either willfully or with a lack of appropriate reasoning, that endangers a child's safety and results in actual or threatened harm or injury to a child's health or well-being, including physical or emotional pain or in diminished healthy development (Bacon & Richardson, 2001; Govindshenoy & Spencer, 2006; Horton & Cruise, 1997; Peterson, Tremblay, Ewigman, & Saldana, 2003; Skowron & Reinemann, 2005; Westby, 2007; Yampolskaya & Banks, 2006). These behaviors are perpetrated by someone who holds any form of responsibility for the child's well-being (Govindshenoy & Spencer, 2006; Peterson et al., 2003; Skowron & Reinemann, 2005; Stith et al., 2009) and who holds a position involving a greater level of power over the child (Tell, Pavkov, Hecker, & Fontaine, 2006). Child maltreatment may be either an act of commission (typically considered abuse) or omission (typically considered neglect) (Peterson et al., 2003; Yampolskaya & Banks, 2006).

We use the term *perpetrator* to identify the individual who commits maltreatment. Similar to the IPV chapters, we use the term *victim* to describe a child with current or recent experiences of child maltreatment, and we use the term *survivor* to describe an individual with past experiences of maltreatment, typically adults who experienced maltreatment in childhood.

Specific forms of maltreatment include physical abuse, sexual abuse and exploitation, emotional/psychological abuse (sometimes referred to as mental abuse); and neglect, which may be emotional and physical (Allen, 2008; Govindshenoy & Spencer, 2006; Horton & Cruise, 1997; Martsolf & Draucker, 2005; Peterson et al., 2003; Skowron & Reinemann, 2005; Tell et al., 2006; Widom & Hiller-Sturmhofel, 2001). Although child maltreatment is typically thought to be perpetrated by a parent or caregiver, it also includes sibling abuse (Bass, Taylor, & Knudson-Martin, 2006; Caffaro & Conn-Caffaro, 2006; Kiselica & Morrill-Richards, 2007). Children who are maltreated often experience multiple forms of maltreatment (Holden, 2003; Sullivan & Knutson, 2000), so distinctions in types should not be considered mutually exclusive.

Each form of child maltreatment can be considered a broad category that is inclusive of a range of behaviors. Therefore, we now move to describing each of these in greater detail. Generally, physical and sexual abuse have received the most research attention (MacMillan, 2000), while neglect and emotional abuse are less well-understood (MacMillan, 2000; Smullens, 2010; Stith et al., 2009) and are thought to be difficult to measure (MacMillan, 2000). Again, these forms of maltreatment often co-occur, so clinical presentations of child maltreatment are likely to be much more complex than any simple definition can convey.

Physical Abuse

The term *physical abuse* describes threatened or actual physical violence perpetrated by another person (Tell et al., 2006) that may or may not result in the infliction of physical injuries (Brassard, Rivelis, & Diaz, 2009; Donohue, Romero, & Hill, 2006; Horton & Cruise, 1997; Widom & Hiller-Sturmhofel, 2001). Examples of injuries that may result from physical abuse include burns, broken bones, head injuries, bruises, and abrasions (Horton & Cruise, 1997; Widom & Hiller-Sturmhofel, 2001). Physical abuse is considered non-accidental (Stith et al., 2009) and an act of commission (Brassard et al., 2009). Sometimes, physical child abuse is thought to occur when a parent uses overly harsh discipline (Chaffin et al., 2004). Munchausen by Proxy Syndrome (MBPS) also may be considered a form of physical child abuse (Siegel & Fishcher, 2001). MBPS describes a parent or parent figure excessively seeking healthcare for a child, often involving the parent (who is often diagnosable with *factitious disorder by proxy*) exaggerating a child's symptoms, up to even intentionally harming the child in order to seek the healthcare attention for the intentionally-created conditions (Siegel & Fishcher, 2001).

Sexual Abuse

The term *child sexual abuse* describes forced or coerced sexual activity perpetrated against a child (Ahmad, 2006; Tell et al., 2006; Topping & Barron, 2009). Child sexual abuse victims are not sexually, cognitively, and/or emotionally mature enough to be able to consent to or fully understand the nature of the sexual activities (Ahmad, 2006; Topping & Barron, 2009). A perpetrator of child sexual abuse is older than and holds some form of power over the child (Ahmad, 2006; Tell et al., 2006; Topping & Barron, 2009), and the perpetrator's actions are intended to bring sexual pleasure to him/her or some other person(s) (Topping & Barron, 2009).

Child sexual abuse is much broader than the term *pedophilia*, although these terms are often used interchangeably (Finkelhor, 2009). Child sexual abuse occurring in a family is often referred to as *incest* (Widom & Hiller-Sturmhofel, 2001), and is considered a violation of family roles and a taboo (Ahmad, 2006). Child sexual abuse covers a broad spectrum of possible behaviors (Finkelhor,

2009) that may involve contact or no contact, genital or otherwise (Horton & Cruise, 1997; Topping & Barron, 2009). Some behaviors that may be considered child sexual abuse include fondling (Horton & Cruise, 1997; Widom & Hiller-Sturmhofel, 2001; Finkelhor, 2009) and other forms of sexual touching (Widom & Hiller-Sturmhofel, 2001), sodomy and rape (Widom & Hiller-Sturmhofel, 2001), oral sex, intercourse, voyeurism (Horton & Cruise, 1997), exhibitionism, involving children in pornography (Finkelhor, 2009), and forcing a child into prostitution (Mitchell, Finkelhor, & Wolak, 2010). Statutory rape, describing a teenaged child in a "quasi-voluntary sexual relationship" with an older adult, also can be considered a form of child sexual abuse, even when the teenager initiated the relationship (Finkelhor, 2009).

Emotional/Psychological Abuse

Emotional/psychological abuse is potentially the most difficult form of maltreatment to define and identify (Baer & Martinez, 2006). It includes verbal and nonverbal behaviors that have a negative or potentially negative impact on the child's emotional well-being and feelings of self-worth (Tell et al., 2006). Emotionally/psychologically abusive behaviors lead the child to feel unloved and unworthy of affection (Allen, 2008), as well as humiliated and shamed (Smullens, 2010). Emotional/psychological abuse may occur on its own, but it typically co-occurs with other forms of maltreatment (Allen, 2008; Widom & Hiller-Sturmhofel, 2001).

Emotional/psychological abuse may be subtle or overt. Unfortunately, there is no shortage of tactics that a perpetrator can use to inflict emotional pain on a child. These tactics include insulting the child with name-calling and verbal attacks (Horton & Cruise, 1997; Smullens, 2010; Tell et al., 2006); belittling through criticism and humiliation (Brassard et al., 2009; Horton & Cruise, 1997; Smullens, 2010); corrupting the child, or prompting the child to participate in antisocial behaviors (Allen, 2008; Brassard et al., 2009; Smullens, 2010); terrorizing, such as screaming, slamming doors, bullying, scaring the child, and making threats (Allen, 2008; Brassard et al., 2009; Horton & Cruise, 1997; Smullens, 2010; Tell et al., 2006); exploiting or putting too much pressure on the child (Allen, 2008; Brassard et al., 2009; Smullens, 2010); and conveying that the child is worthless through rejection, ignoring, isolation, spurning, and abandonment (Allen, 2008; Brassard et al., 2009; Smullens, 2010).

Neglect

Child neglect also is difficult to define (Lounds, Borkowski, & Witman, 2004). Generally, *child neglect* describes when a caregiver fails to provide basic essentials of healthy living (Allin, Wathen, & MacMillan, 2005; Goodvin, Johnson, Hardy, Graef, & Chambers, 2007; Horton & Cruise, 1997; Kaufman Kantor et al., 2004; McDaniel & Dillenburger, 2007; Stith et al., 2009; Stowman & Donohue, 2005; Tell et al., 2006; Widom & Hiller-Sturmhofel, 2001), including essentials for physical and emotional health (Tell et al., 2006) and cognitive and educational development (Goodvin et al., 2007). Typically, neglect reflects a long-standing pattern rather than an isolated incident (Stowman & Donohue, 2005), and the severity of neglect can range widely (Stowman & Donohue, 2005). Neglect results in harm for the child (Connell-Carrick, 2003) and can negatively impact the child's development (Goodvin et al., 2007).

Neglect reflects an act of omission as opposed to an act of commission (Stowman & Donohue, 2005; Yampolskaya & Banks, 2006). Neglect involves a caregiver failing to fulfill caregiving responsibilities (Yampolskaya & Banks, 2006) by providing inadequately or not at all for the child (Widom & Hiller-Sturmhofel, 2001). Although certain neglectful behaviors are easy to identify, understandings of what behaviors and conditions constitute neglect vary based on unique norms in certain communities (Goodvin et al., 2007; Kaufman Kantor et al., 2004).

Physical Neglect. Physical neglect describes caregivers not providing adequately for the child's physical needs, including food, water, and nutrition; cleanliness, hygiene, and a sanitary home; shelter; clothing, such as weather-appropriate clothes; adequate, timely medical and mental health care; and safety, protection, and stability in the home and beyond (Allen, 2008; Goodvin et al., 2007; Harrington, Zuravin, DePanfilis, Ting, & Dubowitz, 2002; Horton & Cruise, 1997; Widom & Hiller-Sturmhofel, 2001; Yampolskaya & Banks, 2006). Exposing a newborn to drugs in utero can be considered a form of neglect (Harrington et al., 2002). Also, allowing an underage child to use drugs or alcohol and/or to engage in other antisocial behaviors (e.g., delinquency) could be considered neglect (Harrington et al., 2002).

Emotional Neglect. Emotional neglect is the most challenging type to define and identify (Stowman & Donohue, 2005). Emotional neglect describes a lack of emotional responsiveness and failure to support a child's self-esteem, autonomy (at a developmentally-appropriate level), and sense of security (Goodvin et al., 2007; Horton & Cruise, 1997). This may be reflected in the absence of affection, extreme detachment, and isolation (Harrington et al., 2002). Some forms of emotional neglect may overlap with emotional/psychological abuse.

Educational and Supervisory Neglect. Caregivers who neglect a child's educational needs do not promote school attendance and do not support the child's academic success (Allen, 2008; Goodvin et al., 2007; Harrington et al., 2002). Caregivers who fail to provide adequate supervision for their child commit supervisory neglect, and this may involve not being adequately watchful of a child and/or leaving a child alone or with an unfit caregiver (Chen &

Scannapieco, 2006; Coohey, 2003; Harrington et al., 2002; Yampolskaya & Banks, 2006).

Exposing a Child to Parental IPV. Parental IPV is of great concern for child witnesses, especially because battering victims and perpetrators are at an increased risk of becoming physically abusive toward their children as well (Chang, Theodore, Martin, & Runyan, 2008; Coohey, 2004; Cox, Kotch, & Everson, 2003; Holden, 2003; Taylor, Guterman, Lee, & Rathouz, 2009). Parental IPV and child maltreatment co-occur in about 30% to 60% of cases (Kaufman Kantor & Little, 2003), and children living in homes in which parental IPV occurs are up to 15 times more likely to experience maltreatment (Haeseler, 2006). In the context of parental IPV, children also may be used as part of the perpetrators' use of control tactics, such as by harassing, stalking, and intimidating victims through their children (Beeble, Bybee, & Sullivan, 2007). Witnessing parental IPV also can be considered a form of emotional/psychological abuse, in that it leads to physical and emotional distress and may be experienced as traumatic by the child (Holden, 2003). In addition to emotional consequences, children's physical safety may be at risk if they are caught in the way when parental IPV occurs (Brassard et al., 2009).

Officially, exposing a child to parental IPV is labeled failure to protect in many jurisdictions (Kaufman Kantor & Little, 2003) and is typically reportable to CPS (Fleck-Henderson, 2000). However, the threshold as to how much and what forms of parental IPV constitutes neglect remains undetermined (Kaufman Kantor & Little, 2003). In some cases, what it means to witness IPV is unclear. For example, this could depend on the size of the home and whether the child saw or heard the abuse. Exposure to parental IPV is most commonly thought to involve the child either seeing or hearing inter-parental violence (Holden, 2003; Johnsona et al., 2002). Parents often fail to recognize the full extent to which their children observe their IPV (Dubowitz, 2009; Young, Mancuso, Faherty, Dorman, Ubrell, 2008), and children are often considered "invisible victims" of parental IPV (Osofsky, 2003).

Sibling Abuse

Sibling abuse, which may be physical, emotional, and/or sexual, has begun to receive more attention, although it often is not studied directly in association with child maltreatment (Anderson, 2010; Bass et al., 2006; Caffaro & Conn-Caffaro, 2006; Kiselica & Morrill-Richards, 2007). Sibling abuse is defined as "a repeated pattern of aggression directed toward a sibling with the intent to inflict harm, and motivated by an internal emotional need for power and control" (Caffaro & Conn-Caffaro, 2006, p. 609). Sibling abuse may occur in biological and other sibling relationships, including step- and foster siblings (Kiselica & Morrill-Richards, 2007), and between same- or different-gender siblings (Caffaro & Conn-Caffaro, 2006). Sibling abuse appears more likely to occur when there are power imbalances (Kiselica & Morrill-Richards, 2007), a lack of parental involvement in sibling relationships (Caffaro & Conn-Caffaro, 2006), and poor parental supervision (Kiselica & Morrill-Richards, 2007). Certain levels of aggression between siblings are viewed as "normal" culturally, so questions often arise as to when aggression rises to a level that is abusive (Caffaro & Conn-Caffaro, 2006).

Statistics: How Common is Child Maltreatment?

Child maltreatment is widespread. However, exactly *how* widespread is difficult to determine because rates of abuse are difficult to decipher. For example, Topping and Barron (2009) report that the range of females worldwide that have experienced sexual victimization is from 6% to 62%, and for males, the range is 3% to 24%. Also, published estimates are most likely underestimates (Donohue et al., 2006). Child maltreatment so often goes unreported (Wurtele, 2009), and statistics based on reports made to CPS are "the tip of the iceberg" (Leventhal, 2001, p. 1137). Thus, estimates may differ depending on the source of the data, such as whether the data are from official reports or from population surveys (Ards, Myers, Chung, Malkis, & Hagerty, 2003; Yampolskaya & Banks, 2006). In addition, social desirability limits the ability to obtain accurate data, in that families are likely to be hesitant to disclose abuse because of the stigma surrounding it and the likely consequences they may experience if they disclose (Manly, 2005). Therefore, the statistics presented in this section provide an incomplete yet useful picture of the prevalence of child maltreatment.

According to the United States Department of Health and Human Services (US DHHS, 2010), during the 2009 federal fiscal year, over 3 million children in the United States were reported at least once to CPS agencies. Of these, approximately one in five children was substantiated as a victim (US DHHS, 2010). The rates of maltreatment experienced by these victims were as follows: neglect (78%); physical abuse (18%); sexual abuse (10%); psychological maltreatment (8%); medical neglect (2%); and other forms of maltreatment (10%). (Note: victims could have experienced multiple forms of maltreatment at once; Yampolskaya & Banks, 2006).

Another national study over a one-year period between 2005 and 2006 showed that over 1.25 million were maltreated during that time, representing one out of every 58 children (Sedlak et al., 2010). Of these, 44% were abused, and 61% were neglected. Among children who had experienced abuse, 58% were abused physically, 24% sexually, and 27% emotionally. Among the children experiencing neglect, 47% were neglected educationally, 38% physically, and 25% emotionally. (Again, children could experience multiple forms of maltreatment.)

Consistent with the statistics above, both emotional/psychological abuse (Smullens, 2010) and neglect (Allin et al., 2005; Arias, 2004; Goodvin et al., 2007; Harrington et al., 2002; Stowman & Donohue, 2005; Sullivan & Knutson, 2000) have been described as the most common forms of child maltreatment. Both emotional/psychological abuse and neglect are difficult to define, and researchers and legal statutes have employed varying definitions across studies and jurisdictions (Black, Slep, & Heyman, 2001). Neglect is especially difficult to measure because it represents the absence of a set of behaviors (Connell-Carrick, 2003). However, neglect may be more likely to be reported to authorities, whereas emotional abuse on its own may not ever result in such a report. Neglect is the most common form of abuse reported to and substantiated by CPS (Donohue et al., 2006).

Child maltreatment apparently has decreased, in some cases extensively, from the early 1990s through the mid-2000s (Finkelhor, 2009; Finkelhor & Jones, 2006; Giardino, 2009; Leventhal, 2001; Yampolskaya & Banks, 2006). These decreases occur across virtually all forms of abuse (Finkelhor & Jones, 2006), although rates of child neglect have not decreased similarly (Giardino, 2009). Although some of these apparent decreases may reflect methodological issues, evidence suggests that these decreases do represent real reductions in rates of child maltreatment in the United States (Finkelhor & Jones, 2006). A variety of factors may explain these decreases, such as reductions in overall crime rates, changes in public policies, fertility-related factors, positive economic conditions, and changed social norms (Finkelhor & Jones, 2006).

Revictimization is relatively common among CPS populations, although the type of maltreatment experienced on subsequent occasions may not be the same as the original incident (Jonson-Reid, Drake, Chung, & Way, 2003). Within CPS systems, child maltreatment is most likely to re-occur when there have been multiple reports, when the child experienced multiple forms of abuse, and when caregivers are absent (Yampolskaya & Banks, 2006).

Other facts about child maltreatment that are relevant to clinical practice are as follows. First, most perpetrators are biological parents (Sedlak et al., 2010). Second, most cases of fatalities from child maltreatment result from neglect (Connell-Carrick, 2003). Third, statistics demonstrate the complexity of child sexual abuse in particular. Accurately measuring rates of child sexual abuse is very complex, in part because of the range of behaviors that can be considered abusive, the frequent lack of physical evidence, and the low likelihood that children and perpetrators will report it (Wurtele, 2009). Most sexual abuse cases involve fondling and/or penetration (Finkelhor, 2009). Most child sexual abuse perpetrators are known to the child (Finkelhor, 2009). Approximately one-fourth of child sexual abuse is perpetrated by a family member, 60% by someone else known to the child, and 14% by a stranger (Finkelhor, 2009). About one-third of child sexual abuse perpetrators are also under the age of 18, and statutory offenses may account for as much as one-third of child sexual abuse cases (Finkelhor, 2009).

Gender and Child Maltreatment

Girls are reported as maltreated more than boys (Donohue et al., 2006). In particular, girls are more likely to be sexually abused (Arias, 2004; Finkelhor, 2009; Sedlak et al., 2010). Girls and boys appear equally likely to be victims of other forms of maltreatment (Arias, 2004), although the traumatic stress may be manifested differently among girls versus boys (see Graves, 2007, for a full theoretical review). Perhaps because child maltreatment is often reported in mother-led, single parent families, neglect is more likely to occur with female caregivers than male (60% vs. 40%; Thomas, 2007; see also Sedlak et al., 2010), whereas male caregivers have higher rates of abuse, and especially sexual abuse (Sedlak et al., 2010).

Age and Child Maltreatment

Existing research also paints a complex picture of the intersections between age and child maltreatment. Some research shows that younger children are at the greatest risk for maltreatment, especially those between birth and the age of three, followed by those between the ages of four and seven (Chen & Scannapieco, 2006). However, in another population-based study, children between the ages of six and nine experienced the highest levels of first-time maltreatment as compared to older or younger children (Sullivan & Knutson, 2000). Perhaps these inconsistencies are related to different age-related patterns across types of maltreatment. Although some research suggests that physical abuse occurs relatively evenly across children of different ages (Donohue et al., 2006), other data indicate that physical abuse is most common among children between the ages of three and eight (Begle, Dumas, & Hanson, 2010). Regarding sexual abuse, although some data suggest that children between the ages of 7 and 13 are at the greatest risk of experiencing sexual abuse (Kenny, 2009), the teenage years also are a high-risk period, in that approximately one-half of child sexual abuse victims are between the ages of 12 to 17 (Finkelhor, 2009). Age-related data are more consistent for neglect, which is thought to be most common among children in the preschool years (Connell-Carrick, 2003; Donohue et al., 2006). In addition, age and gender interact in relation to demographic patterns of abuse. For example, girls experience an increasing risk of sexual abuse as they get older, whereas boys appear to be most at risk for sexual abuse as they enter puberty (Finkelhor, 2009).

Race and Child Maltreatment

Across the different forms of child maltreatment, African American children appear to be more likely to experience maltreatment than Caucasian and Hispanic children (Sedlak et al., 2010). Given the critical public health importance of health disparities, we devote a full chapter to culture and family violence (see Chapter 12).

Understanding Child Maltreatment Victims

Children who are victimized often present for therapy, so it is important for therapists to understand common characteristics and experiences they face. In this section, we review risk factors for maltreatment and the potential consequences of maltreatment for victims.

Risk Factors for Child Maltreatment Victimization

Researchers have identified several factors that appear to increase the likelihood of maltreatment. Families can have the following risk factors and *not* demonstrate child maltreatment, so therapists should be cautious about assuming that maltreatment occurred based on the presence or absence of risk factors alone. However, familiarity with these risk factors can alert therapists to high-risk populations and can provide a useful context for considering more direct indicators of maltreatment (e.g., suspicious bruises).

Demographic Characteristics. Although maltreatment can occur across all levels of the socioeconomic spectrum, poverty and low socioeconomic status increase a child's risk of victimization (Begle et al., 2010; Connell-Carrick, 2003; Cox et al., 2003; Widom & Hiller-Sturmhofel, 2001; Lowe, Pavkov, Casanova, & Wetchler, 2005; Schumacher, Slep, & Heyman, 2001; Stowman & Donohue, 2005). The stressors associated with poverty may contribute to an increased risk for child maltreatment, including financial stress (Cox et al., 2003), parental unemployment and housing problems (Paavilainen & Åstedt, 2003), and having more people living in the home (Connell-Carrick, 2003). In part, this may be due to the fact that lower income families are more likely to come into contact with social systems (e.g., welfare, public health departments) through which child maltreatment may come to the attention of the authorities.

Other demographic factors that have been identified as child maltreatment risk factors include younger age of parents and low parental educational attainment (Cox et al., 2003; Connell-Carrick, 2003; Donohue et al., 2006; McDaniel & Dillenburger, 2007; Paavilainen & Åstedt, 2003; Stowman & Donohue, 2005). In addition, children with special health needs, children born prematurely, and children with disabilities are at an increased risk (Donohue et al., 2006). In Chapter Ten, we address the issue of vulnerable populations in greater detail.

Family Structure. Family structure characteristics also have been identified as child maltreatment risk factors. Risk factors include having a larger family size (Cox et al., 2003; Donohue et al., 2006) and living in a single-parent household (Finkelhor, 2009; McDaniel & Dillenburger, 2007; Stowman & Donohue, 2005). Family structure characteristics also relate to the emotional climate in the family, such as an unstable or chaotic family structure (Begle et al., 2010; Connell-Carrick, 2003; Finkelhor, 2009; Paavilainen & Åstedt, 2003), less positive affect (Connell-Carrick, 2003), high levels of conflict, and low cohesion (Stith et al., 2009). In addition, children are at an increased risk when there is poor parental supervision (Finkelhor, 2009) and poor parent-child relationships (Black, Heyman, & Slep, 2001; Stith et al., 2009).

Parenting. Child maltreatment may result, in some cases, from parenting deficiencies. As such, researchers have studied characteristics that may make parents more likely to perpetrate maltreatment. First, parents with mental health problems may be at a greater risk (Paavilainen & Åstedt, 2003), including depression, anxiety (Connell-Carrick, 2003; Lewin & Bergin, 2001), and low self-esteem (Stith et al., 2009). Parents also may be at a greater risk when they have high levels of anger and are overly reactive to the child (Stith et al., 2009). In some cases, these factors are associated with the parent's own past history of trauma (Paavilainen & Åstedt, 2003). Second, high levels of parental stress also may increase the risk of child maltreatment (Baumann & Kolko, 2002; Stith et al., 2009). Parents may be more likely to maltreat their children if they view children to be less attractive or to have difficult temperaments (Donohue et al., 2006). Parents who maltreat their children may have generally poor parenting skills (Connell-Carrick, 2003) and demonstrate parental incompetence (Baumann & Kolko, 2002). Finally, other parenting-related variables associated with an increased risk of child maltreatment include parental learning difficulties (McDaniel & Dillenburger, 2007), parental substance abuse (Paavilainen & Åstedt, 2003; Scannapieco & Connell-Carrick, 2007; Widom & Hiller-Sturmhofel, 2001), and parental IPV (Anderson, 2010).

The Social Context. Community and social network variables also may increase the risk of child maltreatment. In particular, social isolation is a key risk factor (Connell-Carrick, 2003; McDaniel & Dillenburger, 2007; Paavilainen & Åstedt, 2003; Stowman & Donohue, 2005), including isolation from extended family (Paavilainen & Åstedt, 2003). Neighborhood-related risk factors also have been identified, such as being characterized by poverty, economic declines, lack of resources, and people moving in and out frequently (Ernst, 2001).

Potential Consequences of Child Maltreatment Victimization

Children who have been maltreated may experience a range of consequences in multiple aspects of their lives. Isolating the consequences of maltreatment is very complicated, however. Child maltreatment often occurs within the context of other negative family climate characteristics, such as parental substance abuse (Locke & Newcomb, 2003). As such, it can be difficult to tease apart the unique consequences of maltreatment from the consequences of these other experiences (Strathearn, 2009). Likewise, determining unique consequences of each form of child maltreatment is difficult because they so often co-occur (Allen, 2008). Additional longitudinal research is needed to help clarify the developmental pathways among various risk factors, abuse experiences, and consequences (Williams & Herrera, 2007).

The consequences of child maltreatment can vary widely from child to child (Saywitz, Mannarino, Berliner, & Cohen, 2000), and, thus, therapists should not make any assumptions as to how a victimized child will respond. Moreover, there are no simple rules as to which consequences victimized children will view as more difficult. The internal (i.e., emotional) wounds a child experiences from maltreatment may be perceived as more negative than the external (i.e., physical) ones (Crenshaw & Hardy, 2007). Some children display minimal negative outcomes following abuse and appear to be functioning quite well (Finkelhor, 2009; Hebert, Parent, Daignault, & Tourigny, 2006). These children may have numerous protective factors which buffer the impact of the abuse (Hebert et al., 2006). Ultimately, survivors of maltreatment even may view some potentially positive consequences as resulting from their maltreatment, such as more compassion for others, increased personal strength and resilience, and connections with new supportive individuals. However, the preponderance of evidence suggests that most short-term consequences have deleterious effects on victims.

Several factors mediate the relationship between victimization and later outcomes. These include (a) coping skills; (b) the attributions the child makes about the maltreatment, especially self-blame; (c) the abuse severity and frequency; (d) the level of force involved; (e) the nature of the relationship to the perpetrator; (f) the age and gender of the child (for example, girls may be more likely to experience internalizing symptoms, whereas boys may be more likely to show externalizing symptoms; Arias, 2004); (g) whether multiple forms of maltreatment co-occurred; (h) the mental health of the caregivers; (i) general family functioning; (j) the nature of the child's relationship with his or her primary caregiver(s); and (k) the presence of protective factors, such as a positive family environment (Cash & Snow, 2001; Chaffin & Shultz, 2001; English, Marshal, & Stewart, 2003; Hebert et al., 2006; Valle & Silovsky, 2002). Generally, consequences are more likely to be severe when the abuse was more severe (Freeman & Morris, 2001) and included multiple forms of victimization (Hosser, Raddatz, & Windzio, 2007).

Child Maltreatment as Trauma. Many potential consequences of child maltreatment can be understood within a scientific trauma framework termed developmental traumatology (De Bellis, 2001). Childhood trauma is often more likely to result in developmental disruptions than adulthood trauma due to the developing brain in childhood (De Bellis, 2001). Child maltreatment causes stress that changes the child's neurobiological system (i.e., brain development) (De Bellis, 2001). Some areas in which developmental delays may occur include language, cognitions, motor skills, emotions, and behavior (De Bellis, 2001). Children who have experienced trauma may develop PTSD symptoms (Brown, 2005), although studies vary widely in their findings as to rates of PTSD among children who have been abused (Brown, 2005). In addition to symptoms typically associated with PTSD (i.e., avoidance, arousal, and re-experiencing the traumatic event), children who have been traumatized may manifest these symptoms as general agitation (Brown, 2005; Horton & Cruise, 1997; Jones, 2002). Even if a formal PTSD diagnosis is not warranted, victimized children may demonstrate some features of PTSD (Brown, 2005), anxiety, or dissociation (Adams, 2006).

The trauma of child maltreatment can result in a complicated pattern of symptoms (Gold, 2008), particularly given that maltreated children often also experience co-occurring traumatic experiences (Cloitre et al., 2009). Experiencing complex trauma appears to increase the severity and complexity of trauma-related symptoms among children (Cloitre et al., 2009). This has been referred to by Bessel van der Kolk (2005, as cited in Cloitre et al., 2009) as Developmental Trauma Disorder, reflecting the impact of cumulative trauma on a child's ongoing development.

Beyond mental health symptoms, the trauma of maltreatment can impact a child's physical health and general worldview. The child may begin to feel that the world is not safe in light of the violations they experienced to their own safety, and children who experienced trauma may shift into a defensive, self-protective survival mode (Hosser et al., 2007). To date, one of the most significant studies on the impact of trauma was the Adverse Childhood Experiences study (i.e., the ACE study; see Felitti et al., 1998, for a full review). The ACE study surveyed a diverse group of over 17,000 individuals in the United States and examined the prevalence of childhood traumatic experiences, as well as the relationships among childhood exposure to trauma and adulthood health risk behaviors and diseases. Researchers found that over 50% of participants reported at least one traumatic incident, and 25% reported multiple types of childhood traumas. There was a strong and robust link among childhood trauma and a large host of negative outcomes, including alcoholism, drug abuse, depression, suicide attempts, smoking, risky sexual behaviors and sexually transmitted infections, obesity, ischemic heart disease, cancer, chronic lung disease, skeletal fractures, liver disease, and many, many others. In addition, as the number of childhood traumatic experiences increased, the risk of negative adult health risk behaviors also increased. This study substantiated that (a) childhood trauma is not as uncommon as once thought and (b) the impact of childhood trauma can have life-long consequences, not only on mental health and substance abuse, but physical health as well. We now move to discussing each of those potential negative consequences in more detail.

Mental Health Consequences. Beyond viewing child maltreatment as a traumatic experience, victimization can contribute to numerous mental health consequences. These symptoms may or may not fit neatly into diagnostic criteria or patterns, and children may display symptoms consistent with multiple diagnoses at once (Haugaard, 2004). Because the range of possible mental health consequences is so broad, and because traumatic responses can manifest differently at different ages across development, we review them in the following categories for organizational purposes. However, symptoms may not present neatly within or across these categories. Again, we are addressing these potential consequences across types of maltreatment because there is substantial overlap in the types of consequences that may result from each form.

Attachment-related Symptoms. Many children who have experienced maltreatment will demonstrate attachment difficulties (Aymer, 2008; Baer & Martinez, 2006; Cohen, 2008; Herschell & McNeil, 2005; MacMillan, 2000), especially insecure attachments (Bacon & Richardson, 2001). Some maltreated children will meet the diagnostic criteria for Reactive Attachment Disorder (RAD; Chaffin, 2008; Hanson & Spratt, 2000), which is a diagnosis that is likely to be applied to children who have been maltreated (Hanson & Spratt, 2000). RAD describes disrupted social relationship functioning that begins before a child is five years old (Buckner, Lopez, Dunkel, & Joiner, 2008; Hanson & Spratt, 2000). Two types of RAD are: (a) inhibited (i.e., the child shows restricted responses to social interactions); and (b) disinhibited (i.e., the child shows overly familiar social interactions; Buckner et al., 2008; Hanson & Spratt, 2000). RAD can only be diagnosed in the presence of having received impaired caregiving (Hanson & Spratt, 2000). Children who demonstrate RAD display impaired attachment functioning across different relationships (Hanson & Spratt, 2000). RAD is a controversial diagnosis, especially because of challenges associated with assessment (Hanson & Spratt, 2000). Children in foster care are especially likely to receive a diagnosis of RAD (Buckner et al., 2008).

Behavioral Concerns. Children who have been maltreated may begin to exhibit problematic behaviors (Crozier & Barth, 2005; English et al., 2003; Noll, 2005). Behaviors identified in the literature include externalizing behaviors, antisocial behaviors, aggression, hyperactivity, impulsivity, regression, and conduct disorders (Adams, 2006; Arias, 2004; Black et al., 2001; Cash & Snow, 2001; Crozier & Barth, 2005; English et al., 2003; Hebert et al., 2006; Horton & Cruise, 1997; Hosser et al., 2007; Jones, 2002; Price, Hilsenroth, Petretic-Jackson, & Bonge, 2001; Strathearn, 2009; Vandenberg & Marsh, 2009; Widom & Hiller-Sturmhofel, 2001; Wurtele, 2009). Maltreated children also may demonstrate inappropriate sexual behaviors (Black et al., 2001) and sexual acting out (Cash & Snow, 2001; Jones, 2002; Noll, 2005; Price et al., 2001). This may include excessive masturbation, overly mature sexual knowledge, and drawing sexually explicit images (Horton & Cruise, 1997; Merrick, Litrownik, Everson, & Cox, 2008). Sexualized behaviors are most commonly linked to sexual abuse but also may result from other forms of maltreatment (Merrick et al., 2008).

Emotional Regulation and Responses. Children who have been maltreated may have a difficult time identifying and regulating emotions (Crozier & Barth, 2005; MacMillan, 2000). Children may not feel safe to express emotions in abusive families, especially if caregivers have shamed them for displaying emotions (Wolfe, Crooks, Chiodo, & Jaffe, 2009). Emotional regulation challenges are difficult in light of the range of negative emotions that may arise. Some feelings that children may experience include the following: anger, confusion, defensiveness, fear, feeling trapped, feeling stigmatized, inadequacy, inferiority, powerlessness, sadness, self-blame, shame, and guilt (Adams, 2006; Black et al., 2001; Cash & Snow, 2001; Cohen, 2008; Deblinger & Runyon, 2005; Feiring, 2005; Follette, La Bash, & Sewell, 2010; Freeman & Morris, 2001; Hebert et al., 2006; Horton & Cruise, 1997; Hosser et al., 2007; Jones, 2002; Wurtele, 2009). The level of shame a child experiences is likely linked to the manner in which others responded to the abuse disclosure (Deblinger & Runyon, 2005).

Mood and Anxiety-related Symptoms. Perhaps due to resulting emotional responses to child maltreatment, children may meet criteria for a mood disorder, particularly depression (Adams, 2006; Black et al., 2001; Cash & Snow, 2001; Hebert et al., 2006; Horton & Cruise, 1997; Jones, 2002; Noll, 2005; Price et al., 2001; Wurtele, 2009). In addition, previously we noted that maltreated children may experience PTSD symptoms (Adams, 2006; Black et al., 2001; Widom & Hiller-Sturmhofel, 2001), but other anxiety-related symptoms also may arise (Black et al., 2001; Cash & Snow, 2001; English et al., 2003; Freeman & Morris, 2001; Hebert et al., 2006; Horton & Cruise, 1997; Jones, 2002; Strathearn, 2009; Wurtele, 2009). These may include nightmares, neuroses, and chronic hyperarousal (Adams, 2006; Black et al., 2001).

Other Mental Health Symptoms. In addition to general low self-esteem (Adams, 2006; English et al., 2003; Horton & Cruise, 1997; Jones, 2002; Noll, 2005; Price et al., 2001; Valle & Silovsky, 2002; Wurtele, 2009) and psychopathology (Maniglio, 2009), rarely-seen mental health disorders, including schizophrenia, bipolar disorder, borderline personality disorder, dissociative disorders, somatization, and somatoform disorders can occur (Haugaard, 2004). Children may develop generalized hostility (Adams, 2006) and have difficulty solving problems (English et al., 2003), may exhibit disordered eating (Adams, 2006; Young, Read, Barker-Collo, & Harrison, 2001), self-injurious behaviors (Black et al., 2001; Herschell & McNeil, 2005; Horton & Cruise, 1997), suicidality (Adams, 2006; Black et al., 2001; Herschell & McNeil, 2005; Price et al., 2001), and/or dissociation (Freeman & Morris, 2001; Jones, 2002; Noll,

2005; Wurtele, 2009). In children, dissociation may manifest as forgetfulness, depersonalization, trance-like states, and extreme behavioral regressions (Silberg, 2004). Finally, psychosomatic problems may arise (Hebert et al., 2006), and these can overlap with the physical health consequences discussed in the next section.

Physical Health Consequences. Physical health consequences may result directly from maltreatment, such as physical harm resulting from abuse. In addition, physical consequences may arise indirectly, such as through the physiological impact of chronic stress (Westby, 2007). At the most extreme, maltreatment may result in fatality for the child (Arias, 2004). Some other potential physical health consequences include the following: altered brain development, asthma, brain injury, chronic pain, digestive problems, disabilities, disruption of the body's hormonal functioning, eczema, failure to thrive, head injury, headaches, heart disease, heightened stress response, impaired language abilities, malnourishment, obesity, problems sleeping, sexually transmitted infections, urinary tract infections (especially for sexual abuse), and vaginal tears (Adams, 2006; Arias, 2004; Horton & Cruise, 1997; Jones, 2002; Kendall-Tackett, 2001; Noll, 2005; Strathearn, 2009; Taylor et al., 2009; Westby, 2007; Wurtele, 2009).

Additional Consequences. Potential consequences of child maltreatment are not limited to the child's mental and physical health. Consequences may change over time at different points in the child's social and emotional development, especially if developmental delays arise (Jones, 2002). Several categories of other potential consequences have been identified in the literature.

Academic Problems. Children may develop academic problems related to maltreatment victimization (Adams, 2006; Arias, 2004; Black et al., 2001; Crozier & Barth, 2005; English et al., 2003; Herschell & McNeil, 2005; Noll, 2005; Price et al., 2001; Wurtele, 2009). For example, they may be less likely to go to school (Westby, 2007), experience problems learning (Crozier & Barth, 2005; Westby, 2007), and have a difficult time concentrating (Arias, 2004; Wurtele, 2009). The poor behaviors in schools that children who have been maltreated may exhibit (Herschell & McNeil, 2005; Westby, 2007) can lead them to receive punishments that further isolate them (e.g., losing a privilege of playing at recess; Westby, 2007).

Relational Problems. Child maltreatment typically occurs in the context relationships that are close and significant, so it is not surprising that victims may experience interpersonal difficulties as a result (Herschell & McNeil, 2005; Valle & Silovsky, 2002; Young et al., 2001). These children may have problems in peer relationships (Adams, 2006; Crozier & Barth, 2005; MacMillan,

2000; Topping & Barron, 2009). They may engage in frequent fights with siblings and peers (Horton & Cruise, 1997), have low social competence (Valle & Silovsky, 2002), and exhibit generally poor social skills (Arias, 2004; Mathews, Fawcett, & Sheldon, 2009). Specific areas in which victims may demonstrate impaired social functioning include establishing healthy boundaries in relationships (Jones, 2002), trusting others (Follette et al., 2010; Wolfe et al., 2009; Wurtele, 2009), and accurately reading others' emotions (i.e., emotion knowledge; Sullivan, Bennett, Carpenter, & Lewis, 2008). These children may demonstrate clinginess (Adams, 2006) and/or social withdrawal (Black et al., 2001; Hebert et al., 2006; Herschell & McNeil, 2005; Horton & Cruise, 1997; Jones, 2002; Wurtele, 2009).

Negative Views of Oneself and the World. Children who have been victimized may come to hold a negative self-image (Bacon & Richardson, 2001; Horton & Cruise, 1997), and their overall personality development may be impacted by the maltreatment (Aymer, 2008). Beyond their views of themselves, they may develop distorted views of relationships (Wolfe et al., 2009), such as adopting a general victim/victimizer schema in which all people are thought to fall into one of these categories or the other (i.e., black and white thinking; Wolfe et al., 2009). They may come to view the world as a very dangerous place (Horton & Cruise, 1997). Another specific area in which victims may develop negative views is in their views about sexuality, especially in relation to child sexual abuse (Follette et al., 2010; Wurtele, 2009).

Risky Behaviors. Children, especially adolescents, who have experienced maltreatment, may demonstrate risky, self-destructive behaviors (Arias, 2004). These may include substance abuse, juvenile delinquency, and unsafe sexual behaviors that may result in teenage pregnancy and/or sexually transmitted infections (Arias, 2004; Black et al., 2001; English et al., 2003; Herschell & McNeil, 2005; Ruffolo, Evans, & Lukens, 2003; Taylor et al., 2009; Topping & Barron, 2009; Widom & Hiller-Sturmhofel, 2001; Williams & Herrera, 2007).

Violence. Experiencing maltreatment victimization may lead some children to develop a greater acceptance of violent behaviors (Wolfe et al., 2009). This may contribute to an increased risk of both revictimization and perpetration (English et al., 2003; Hosser et al., 2007; Topping & Barron, 2009). Two forms of violence that child maltreatment victims may be more likely to experience are dating violence and bullying (Adams, 2006; Wolfe et al., 2009).

Understanding Child Maltreatment Perpetrators

Many therapists struggle to understand how *anyone* could do anything to hurt a child, especially intentionally. Although understanding the background characteristics of perpetrators may not provide any easy answers to that question, it is important for therapists to become familiar with some common characteristics of perpetrators that have been identified in the existing literature. This information can provide a foundation for working with these clients in therapy. Of course, each perpetrator is an individual and may not demonstrate any or all of these characteristics. Nonetheless, they can serve as a useful foundation for considering appropriate treatment approaches, which are discussed in Chapter Eight. It is important when considering perpetrators' background characteristics to bear in mind that these characteristics should not be viewed as excuses for the perpetrators' behaviors, but rather that they can provide a context for understanding factors that may contribute to the person engaging in abusive behaviors.

Demographics

Finkelhor (2009) provided an overview of the diversity of child maltreatment (specifically sexual abuse) perpetrators. They typically are more educated and have better employment histories than perpetrators of other crimes. Most child sexual abuse perpetrators are male (Finkelhor, 2009). About one-third are under the age of 18. Two age periods have the greatest risk for child abuse perpetration. The first is adolescence, which is linked to general delinquent behaviors. Juvenile child sexual abuse offenders may be displaying transitory behaviors, which may or may not be part of larger delinquency patterns. The second higher-risk age period is during one's 30s, which may reflect being around children more frequently. Most child sexual abuse perpetrators are at a low risk for reperpetration if they are caught. Rates of reoffending among child sexual abuse perpetrators are actually lower than many other crimes.

Psychological Variables

Child maltreatment perpetrators may abuse substances and/or demonstrate symptoms of mental health disorders, such as depression (Hien, Cohen, Caldeira, Flom, & Wasserman, 2010; Widom & Hiller-Sturmhofel, 2001). Generally, they have difficulty regulating emotions (Hien et al., 2010), are emotionally needy (Black et al., 2001), and have attachment problems (Bacon & Richardson, 2001; Bugental, Ellerson, Lin, Rainey, Kokotovic, & O'Hara, 2002).

Perpetrators may hold distorted beliefs about children and parenting. For example, identified risk factors for perpetrators include being unsatisfied as a parent, feeling like one's child's behaviors are out of control, and holding negative attributions toward one's child (Begle et al., 2010). Perpetrators may misinterpret children's behaviors and view them as intentionally negative toward the parent (Bugental et al., 2002). In addition, many believe that victims are not harmed by the abuse (Adams, 2003). Child sexual abuse offenders typically are thought to demonstrate one or more of the following five psychological schemas, first proposed by Tony Ward (2000): (a) children are viewed as sexualized beings; (b) sexual abuse is not viewed as harmful to the child; (c) the abuser believes that s/he is entitled to sexual relations with children; (d) the world is viewed as being a dangerous and rejecting place; and (e) the person views the world as uncontrollable and difficult to predict (Gannon, Keown, & Rose, 2008).

Personal Trauma History

Despite common methodological problems that limit the existing body of research, evidence suggests that intergenerational patterns of family violence, including child maltreatment, do exist (Coohey, 2004; Newcomb & Locke, 2001; Widom & Hiller-Sturmhofel, 2001). Having been maltreated as a child may influence the types of parenting practices that an adult uses with his or her own children (Newcomb & Locke, 2001), and this may contribute to some parents using abusive parenting tactics with their children.

A substantial proportion of perpetrators have personal histories of childhood maltreatment (Adams, 2003; Begle et al., 2010), and perpetrators may have unresolved childhood traumas that continue to impact them into their adult lives (Bacon & Richardson, 2001). They may have experienced ongoing rejection by their family members and peers as they grew up and lacked positive, supportive relationships with adults (Bentovim, 2002). However, the pathway from having been victimized as a child to perpetrating maltreatment as an adult is a very complex, and certainly not a direct one (Bentovim, 2002). A history of childhood maltreatment does not cause one to grow up and become a perpetrator oneself. Rather, it may be combined with a number of other adverse experiences in childhood and adulthood that contribute to perpetration among a subset of the population that has been abused (Bentovim, 2002).

Understanding the Child Maltreatment Response System

Because children are vulnerable members of society, society bears some responsibility in protecting them from harm (Giardino, 2009). Child maltreatment often does not stop unless some outside intervention occurs (Cohen, 2008). The child maltreatment response system involves a complex intersection between legal and social service processes, and this reflects the fact that child maltreatment is a crime that has a variety of social and emotional impacts on the child. Therefore, it is critical for therapists to understand how they fit within the broader child maltreatment response systems that exist in communities. Informal social support networks also can be considered part of the broader child maltreatment response system, although often the roles of these networks are unclear. Members of the general population may become aware of or begin to suspect child maltreatment, such as in their neighborhood or through community groups in which they are involved. These individuals may be hesitant to act for such reasons as fear of retaliation or believing that family matters are private (Bensley et al., 2004). Nonetheless, many community members report that they would take some form of action, either formally (e.g., calling CPS) or informally (e.g., talking to the parents; Bensley et al., 2004). State laws vary in terms of who is a mandatory reporter of child maltreatment. In North Carolina, for example, all adults are mandatory reporters, and therefore the question of how community members should respond to abuse has particular relevance in states with similar policies. Therapists should be sure to be familiar with and follow their state's child maltreatment reporting laws.

Legal Systems

Finkelhor, Cross, and Cantor (2004) suggested that the legal systems in place to respond to child maltreatment constitute a complex juvenile victim justice system that does not always operate smoothly and effectively. Two subsystems combine to make up this juvenile justice system: CPS and the criminal justice system. The processes of these subsystems overlap but are generally separate, although increasingly efforts are made to coordinate their processes. Nonetheless, going through the simultaneous processes may be very challenging for young victims. CPS generally is concerned only with cases in which a child has been maltreated by a family member or some other adult with caregiving responsibilities. Such cases also may be prosecuted within the criminal justice system. Cases in which a child is maltreated by a non-caregiver or non-family member (e.g., a neighbor) often will only be able to be pursued within the criminal justice system, although CPS may become involved if a caregiver knew about and failed to protect the child from the maltreatment. In some communities, efforts have been made to promote collaboration between these two different subsystems. For example, some police departments have specialized mental health units that respond to child maltreatment cases or develop collaborative relationships with mental health agencies to address this goal (Murphy, Rosenheck, Berkowitz, & Marans, 2005).

Child Protective Services. We use the term *child protective services* (CPS) to refer to the primary agency in a jurisdiction that takes reports on suspected child maltreatment, investigates cases to determine whether maltreatment has actually occurred, and provides follow-up services and monitoring in cases when maltreatment is substantiated. These agencies are called by different names (e.g., Department of Children and Families, Department of Social Services), but generally the functions they serve are consistent across communities. CPS workers typically have a background in social work but also may have come from other backgrounds (Jones & Gross, 2000). We will now provide an overview of CPS systems, including typical services and functions at the major stages of their processes.

Reporting Suspected Maltreatment to CPS. Most states have mandatory reporting laws that require certain people (and in some cases, all adults) to report any suspected child maltreatment to the appropriate CPS authorities. Therapists typically are among those required to report to CPS agencies if they are aware that children are at risk of harm (Barnett, Miller-Perrin, & Perrin, 2005). Most reports to CPS are made by professionals who work with children, such as teachers and mental health professionals (Finkelhor et al., 2005). However, some reports are made by family members, friends, neighbors, and the victims themselves (Finkelhor et al., 2005). Typically, laws require that mandated reporters report reasonable suspicions that maltreatment has occurred (Foreman & Bernet, 2000). However, reporters may differ in their personal opinions as to what actually constitutes a reasonable suspicion (Foreman & Bernet, 2000). This is made even more complicated because states vary in their definitions of *reasonable suspicion* or other terms used to identify these criteria (Foreman & Bernet, 2000). And, of course, the unique details of any given situation often make these cases murkier and difficult to determine.

Many mandated reporters lack in-depth knowledge of relevant laws in their jurisdictions, and laws often are difficult to read and comprehend (Foreman & Bernet, 2000). Therefore, therapists must become familiar with the laws in their jurisdictions in order to both know when to make a report and when not to make an unnecessary report (Foreman & Bernet, 2000; Small, Lyons, & Guy, 2002). These statutes typically outline the reporting criteria and process, the people who are required to report, the possible consequences a mandated reporter may face for not reporting, potential consequences of making a false report, and often some form of immunity or protection for people making reports in good faith (Foreman & Bernet, 2000; Small et al., 2002). Therapists are encouraged to consult with other professionals as they make decisions about reporting suspected child maltreatment (Lawrence & Kurpius, 2000).

When making a report, therapists will likely be asked to provide information about the child, the child's family, the suspected perpetrator, the nature of the suspected maltreatment, the evidence that suggests that maltreatment occurred, and other information that may assist with the CPS investigation. Therapists are advised to document all reports made to CPS. In addition, we recommend that therapists document in the client's case file possible signs of abuse that suggest maltreatment even when these signs do not warrant an immediate report to CPS. In such cases, it is wise to document the rationale for making the decision not to make the report at that time, as well as the process used to make that decision (e.g., a review of state statutes, discussion with a supervisor, and a review of client files to determine if indicators have been noted previously).

Our general guideline when a therapist faces an ambiguous decision as to whether to make a report is as follows: *When in doubt, make the report.* We believe this to be sound practice both on the grounds of making all reasonable efforts to protect children and to protect the therapist from potential liability

(Small et al., 2002). Our clinical experience suggests that CPS will either not take the report or will not follow-through with the investigation if they do not believe that the evidence presented provides reasonable suspicion of abuse. However, sometimes a therapist sees only one small part of a case, and that small part is critical information when considered in the context of prior CPS reports that have been made by others.

Although most therapists appreciate the need for mandated child maltreatment reporting laws for the protection of children, many also are concerned how making such a report will impact the therapeutic relationship with the child and family (Adams, 2006; Burkemper, 2002; Knickerbocker et al., 2007). Of particular concern is the potential that making the report will lead to a problem in the therapist-client alliance, as well as to an increased likelihood that the clients will drop out of therapy (Knickerbocker et al., 2007). Some steps a therapist can take to minimize these negative outcomes include ensuring that clients are aware of the limits on confidentiality from the outset of therapy, reminding clients about these limitations in the case that suspicions arise, involving clients in the reporting process, and explaining what happens when a report is made (Adams, 2006).

Ethical issues abound related to the mandate to report suspected child maltreatment (Burkemper, 2002). In particular, therapists often struggle with the role of protecting a client's confidentiality with the responsibility to protect the welfare of the child (Burkemper, 2002). The following Ethical Case Study presents an illustration of these issues.

Ethical Case Study: Mandated Reporting of Suspected Child Maltreatment

Case description: Kim and Jenny. Kim is a licensed therapist working in a community agency providing school-based therapy to children diagnosed with mental health disorders. Her involvement with her clients' parents is usually limited to monthly progress meetings, and most parents are not interested in participating in family therapy. Recently, Kim has become concerned that one of her clients, six-year-old Jenny, is being emotionally, if not also physically, abused by one of her parents. However, at the present time, this concern is more of a "hunch" than solid evidence that this abuse is actually occurring. She has conferred with Jenny's teacher (a consent form has been signed), who also has a similar hunch but no solid evidence. Kim is wondering if she needs to report this suspicion to the local Department of Social Services, and if so, what that might mean for her therapeutic relationship with Jenny and her family.

Sample relevant ethical standards

AAMFT (2001) Code of Ethics

"Marriage and family therapists disclose to clients and other interested parties, as early as feasible in their professional contacts, the nature of confidentiality and possible limitations of the clients' right to confidentiality. Therapists review with clients the circumstances where confidential information may be requested and where disclosure of confidential information may be legally required." (AAMFT, 2001, Ethical Standard 1.8)

ACA (2005) Code of Ethics

"At initiation and throughout the counseling process, counselors inform clients of the limitations of confidentiality and seek to identify foreseeable situations in which confidentiality must be breached." (ACA, 2005, Ethical Standard A.2.b.)

"The general requirement that counselors keep information confidential does not apply when disclosure is required to protect clients or identified others from serious and foreseeable harm or when legal requirements demand that confidential information must be revealed. Counselors consult with other professionals when in doubt as to the validity of an exception." (ACA, 2005, Ethical Standard B.2.a)

"To the extent possible, clients are informed before confidential information is disclosed and are involved in the disclosure decision-making process. When circumstances require the disclosure of confidential information, only essential information is revealed." (ACA, 2005, Ethical Standard B.2.d)

APA (2010) Ethical Principles of Psychologists and Code of Conduct

"Psychologists may disclose confidential information with the appropriate consent of the organizational client, the individual client/patient, or another legally authorized person on behalf of the client/patient unless prohibited by law." (APA, 2010, Ethical Standard 4.05.a)

"Psychologists disclose confidential information without the consent of the individual only as mandated by law, or where permitted by law for a valid purpose such as to (1) provide needed professional services; (2) obtain appropriate professional consultations; (3) protect the client/patient, psychologist, or others from harm; or (4) obtain payment for services from a client/patient, in which instance disclosure is limited to the minimum that is necessary to achieve the purpose." (APA, 2010, Ethical Standard 4.05.b)

NASW (2008) Code of Ethics

"Social workers may disclose confidential information when appropriate with valid consent from a client or a person legally authorized to consent on behalf of a client." (NASW, 2008, Ethical Standard 1.07.b)

"Social workers should inform clients, to the extent possible, about the disclosure of confidential information and the potential consequences, when feasible before the disclosure is made." (NASW, 2008, Ethical Standard 1.07.d)

"Social workers should discuss with clients and other interested parties the nature of confidentiality and limitations of clients' right to confidentiality. Social workers should review with clients circumstances where confidential information may be requested and where disclosure of confidential information may be legally required. This discussion should occur as soon as possible in the social workerclient relationship and as needed throughout the course of the relationship." (NASW, 2008, Ethical Standard 1.07.e)

Discussion. When deciding whether to breach a client's confidentiality to make a child maltreatment report, therapists should consider relevant professional ethical standards, legal requirements, and the therapeutic relationship (Burkemper, 2002). The basic principles of professional ethics—beneficence, nonmaleficence, autonomy, fidelity, and justice—also must be considered (Burkemper, 2002). Due to the potential for harm to a child in a case of suspected child maltreatment, the highest priority will likely fall to the principle of nonmaleficence, or making the decision that is most likely to do no harm to the child (Burkemper, 2002). As the ethical codes listed above make clear, the potential of breaching Jenny's confidentiality must be handled with the utmost attention to guiding ethical principles.

In the case of Kim and Jenny, part of the challenge in determining whether and how confidentiality should be breached lies in the ambiguity of the situation. A first step for Kim is to consult the law in her jurisdiction to determine what level of information is required in order to make a report to CPS. The primary consideration for Kim should be to ensure that she is in compliance with mandatory reporting laws. Let us assume, however, that Kim consulted the law and remained uncertain as to whether a report should be made. An important next step is for Kim to consult with other professionals as she continues to consider this decision (ACA, 2005, Ethical Standard B.2.a). She already consulted with Jenny's teacher. Other professionals with whom she may consult include her supervisor, a therapist colleague, the school principal or other school personnel, and an attorney. As part of this consultation, she should review the indicators that have led Kim to develop her suspicions about Jenny. These may include behavioral changes, physical observations, statements that Jenny made, and emotional responses Jenny has shown.

Kim may decide that she needs to gather information or observe the situation for a designated time period to determine whether other potential maltreatment indicators are present. If this is the case, she should document her reasons for not making the CPS report at this time and detail a plan for the type of information she intends to seek in the future, how she will gather that information, and her time-line for reviewing the case again.

As another alternative, Kim may decide that she has sufficient information to justify making a report to CPS at this time. It is possible that she will make the report, but it will be screened out and not lead to an investigation. Regardless of the outcome (which Kim may not learn at the time of making the report), Kim should document when she made the report and the information she provided. As the ethical codes make clear, Kim should have in place an informed consent document that notified the client from the outset of treatment that suspected child maltreatment is an exception to confidentiality. Of course, Jenny's level of understanding of this exception may be limited based on her developmental age and cognitive functioning.

If appropriate, Kim may elect to inform Jenny and her caregiver(s) that the CPS report has been made (NASW, 2008, Ethical Standard 1.07.d). However, this should be done only if Kim does not believe that this information would put Jenny at risk of harm. When making the report, Kim should disclose enough information to provide sufficient detail about the case, but also the minimal amount of information needed so that Jenny's confidentiality is protected (ACA, 2005, Ethical Standard B.2.d). Depending on the outcome of the report (i.e., whether an investigation commences and whether maltreatment is substantiated), Kim may need to consider how the report could impact her therapeutic work with Jenny.

A final note in this case relates to the fact that Jenny's teacher also experienced suspicions that Jenny was being maltreated. As such, Jenny's teacher likewise will be going through a parallel decision-making and reporting process. Therapists should not rely on other professionals to make reports, and each person should make a report separately unless the professionals jointly file the report. This is a cautionary approach, in that the possibility remains that the other professional will fail to make the report that s/he was supposed to make, and therefore the opportunity to potentially protect the child will be lost (in addition to the liability issues that could arise for failing to make a mandated report to CPS).

The CPS Investigation and Determination. Once a case of alleged maltreatment is reported to CPS, the initial responder screens the report to determine whether there is adequate information to move to the next step of conducting an investigation (Finkelhor et al., 2005; Giardino, 2009; US DHHS, 2010). As the investigation proceeds, the case may be referred to the criminal justice system (e.g., the police or a district attorney), and a medical examination may be warranted (Finkelhor et al., 2005). Information gathered through the investigation will be used to determine whether the case is substantiated (Finkelhor et al., 2005). Approximately two-thirds of reports made to CPS are investigated

(Finkelhor et al., 2005), and about one-fourth to one-third of all reports are substantiated (Finkelhor et al., 2005; Young, Boles, & Otero, 2007).

The level of evidence required by CPS is generally lower than the level required in criminal justice systems, so it is possible that CPS substantiation will occur in the absence of the case being prosecuted in criminal justice systems (Finkelhor et al., 2005). If a case is pursued in the criminal justice system, possible actions may include arrest, prosecution, and sentencing (Finkelhor et al., 2005). When a case has been prosecuted, the victim may be entitled to victim compensation (Finkelhor et al., 2005). When maltreatment is substantiated, decisions will be made regarding whether and what follow-up services are needed, and a court hearing may be required to determine if the child needs to an out-of-home placement (Finkelhor et al., 2005).

CPS investigations may be more complicated when parental substance abuse is involved. Parental substance abuse does not automatically warrant removal of a child from the home unless the CPS investigation shows that the parents' use of substances poses a risk to the child's well-being (Barth, Gibbons, & Guo, 2006; Rittner & Dozier, 2000). Some considerations in determining whether substance use poses a risk include whether physiological impacts of the substance compromise the user's parenting abilities, whether aspects of the user's substance-related lifestyle put the child at risk (Kerwin, 2005), and if the child has access to the substances. Therapists must bear in mind, then, that some substance abusing parents care for their children at a level that is not considered maltreatment (Scannapieco & Connell-Carrick, 2007).

Overall, the CPS investigation process must take into account, first and foremost, the safety of the child(ren). However, a number of other potential complicating factors may influence the case. Therapists who are familiar with typical proceedings in their jurisdictions will be best equipped to assist their clients through the investigation process, as well to comply with any involvement they are required to have throughout the process.

Follow-up Services and Monitoring. If the investigation substantiates abuse, then a CPS caseworker is likely to develop a case plan that describes necessary services and treatment goals the family must meet to be discharged from the CPS caseload. Although many clients fear that CPS involvement will result in the removal of children from the home, the general philosophy underlying most CPS agencies is to preserve the family, as long as doing so can be done while providing a safe home environment for the child (Fleck-Henderson, 2000; Jouriles et al., 2010).

In a CPS case plan, clients may be linked to community resources to help them meet their parental responsibilities, such as parenting classes, social service organizations, or other support (e.g., food, housing, and educational opportunities). To provide additional support to children as they move through legal processes, some children are appointed a specialized professional advocate or volunteer guardian ad litem (Weisz, 2003). Many CPS agencies have become increasingly likely to take active steps to promote smoother coordination of services across various agencies that are involved with the families on their caseloads (Fleck-Henderson, 2000).

Despite a general aim to keep families intact, this is not always determined to be in the best interest of the child. Therefore, one possible legal outcome of child maltreatment is the termination of parental rights (TPR), meaning that a parent no longer has any parental obligations or rights to his or her child, thereby leaving the child open to adoption or in the permanent care of the CPS system (Ezzo, Evans, & McGovern-Kondik, 2004). About one-tenth of children in foster care experience TPR (Finkelhor et al., 2005).

Foster Care. Children who have been maltreated may be placed in the foster care system either temporarily, such as during a CPS investigation or while caregivers complete their case plans, or permanently, such as when parental rights are terminated or while children await adoption. Therapists should be familiar with how the foster care system functions so they will be equipped to support clients involved with this system, including children in care and foster parents. Rates of children in foster care increased from the 1980s to the 1990s (Ruffolo et al., 2003). Approximately two-thirds of children in foster care are reunified with their biological families (Finkelhor et al., 2005). Approximately one-half of children in foster care in the United States are teenagers (Ruffolo et al., 2003). Many teenagers in foster care are unable to achieve permanent placements (e.g., adoption or permanent reunification with their biological family members), and therefore many simply age out of the system (Ruffolo et al., 2003).

When possible, children are placed with extended family members (Chapman, Wall, Barth, and the National Survey of Child and Adolescent Well-Being Research Group, 2004). Other potential home-like settings include an extra-familial foster family or a group home (Chapman et al., 2004), and children appear to prefer group settings the least as compared to other types of placements (Chapman et al., 2004).

Many children in foster care face difficulty in being able to leave the foster care system and enter into a permanent placement, whether that means returning to biological families or adoption (Fisher, Kim, & Pears, 2009). A variety of reasons—including those related to the child and/or the placement—may lead some children to experience multiple placements, especially if problems arise in the original placement setting (Chapman et al., 2004). Moving into a new foster care placement often involves additional transitions for the child, such as entering a new school and leaving friends in one's neighborhood (Chapman et al., 2004). For many children, these transitions contribute to the difficulties in educational progress or social relationships, which can lead to mood and anxiety problems, as well as general psychopathology.

Negative images of the foster care system abound. However, many children have positive experiences in foster care, and they may even show positive changes in their functioning while in their foster care placements (Chapman et al., 2004). One challenge children in foster care may grapple with is how to maintain contact and connection with their biological families while living in foster care (Chapman et al., 2004), and this may especially be relevant if reunification is a likely outcome. The foster care system, at its best, offers children a supportive home environment to promote their healing from their prior abuse (Fisher et al., 2009). However, some foster care placements simply are not supportive environments for children (Fisher et al., 2009), and negative environments can contribute to a child experiencing increasingly negative consequences stemming from the abuse and the results of it (Fisher et al., 2009). Many children in foster care demonstrate multiple risk factors and face lengthy, complex challenges (Ruffolo et al., 2003). The mental health needs of children in foster care are increasingly recognized as a critical issue, in that these children demonstrate greater symptoms compared to children who are not in care, and they often face barriers to receiving needed services (Kerker & Dore, 2006). Therefore, when working with clients involved in the foster care system, therapists should help clients advocate to receive mental health and other services to promote their well-being.

Child Sex Offender Registries and Laws. Moving now to the criminal justice side of the child maltreatment response system, other legal issues are child sex offender registries and other relevant laws, especially those related to perpetrators. Today, child sexual abuse offenders who are found guilty face much steeper sentencing than in decades past (Finkelhor, 2009). Individuals who have perpetrated substantiated child sexual abuse are likely to be required to register with sexual abuse registries, which are mandated by law in many states (Finkelhor, 2009). Some jurisdictions prohibit registered sex offenders from living near or being in certain areas, such as schools or public parks (Finkelhor, 2009). In addition, employers often check to see if prospective employees are listed in these registries, especially if the work involves working with children (Finkelhor, 2009). Therefore, these laws and registries can impact perpetrators' ability to reintegrate into the community following treatment and other legal consequences (e.g., a prison sentence). These issues will be addressed in greater detail in Chapter 8.

Other Components of the Child Maltreatment Response System

Depending on their needs, other organizations may be involved in the lives of children and families who have experienced child maltreatment. These include healthcare professionals, substance abuse treatment, child advocacy centers, domestic violence agencies, and schools.

Healthcare Professionals. Therapists should work collaboratively with medical healthcare professionals when clients have experienced physical injuries resulting from abuse (Haugaard, 2004). Therapists should make efforts to understand current medical treatments or medications that their clients are receiving. Therapists may need to support their clients in locating affordable healthcare, such as through local health departments. In addition, therapists should address the emotional consequences of physical conditions resulting from the maltreatment (e.g., a sexually transmitted infection acquired through child sexual abuse).

Substance Abuse Treatment Facilities. Substance abuse treatment facilities also may be involved in the treatment of perpetrators and non-offending parents (Barth et al., 2006; Jones & Gross, 2000; McAlpine, Marshall, & Doran, 2001; Rittner & Dozier, 2000). Parents may agree to participate in substance abuse treatment as a way to avoid having their children removed from their care (Barth et al., 2006). These intersections are addressed more fully in Chapter 11.

Child Advocacy Centers. Child advocacy centers (CACs) began to emerge in the 1980s to promote collaboration among professionals involved in responding to child maltreatment (Friend, 2000). CACs are typically set up as "one-stop shops" in which children under investigation as suspected child maltreatment victims can be interviewed and treated within the same agency by multiple professionals representing different components of the child maltreatment response system. Professionals such as social workers, CPS representatives, therapists, and law enforcement personnel work together, often within the same facility, to conduct a collaborative and streamlined investigation process (Wolfteich & Loggins, 2007). The facility is designed to be child-oriented, and often children can receive follow-up services within the same facility following the investigation (Friend, 2000; Wolfteich & Loggins, 2007).

CACs are designed to help child maltreatment investigations run more smoothly (Finkelhor, 2009; Smith, Witte, & Fricker-Elhai, 2006), reduce unnecessary duplication of interview processes (Finkelhor et al., 2005), and minimize the retraumatization and negative impact of the investigation on children (Finkelhor, 2009; Wolfteich & Loggins, 2007). CACs may allow the child to experience a single investigative interview, and that interview can be recorded to reduce the need to re-interview the child (Finkelhor et al., 2005). Preliminary evidence suggests that the CAC model is effective at producing more effective outcomes for child maltreatment investigations, such as greater substantiation of abuse and more efficient investigation processes (Smith et al., 2006; Wolfteich & Loggins, 2007).

Domestic Violence Agencies. As Friend (2000) stated, "Domestic violence work in the context of child protection is enormously complicated" (p. 309).

Despite the high numbers of families involved with CPS that demonstrate parental IPV (Coohey, 2004; Fleck-Henderson, 2000; Friend, 2000; Jones & Gross, 2000), there are many barriers that prevent effective coordination of services between CPS and domestic violence agencies (Fleck-Henderson, 2000; Kaufman Kantor & Little, 2003; Mills et al., 2000). For example, IPV is often under-recognized by CPS workers (Jones & Gross, 2000). In cases when both parental IPV and child maltreatment are present, the different response systems for each issue frequently put forth different recommendations as to how the family can best achieve safety (Knickerbocker et al., 2007).

CPS and agencies supporting mothers who have been battered typically operate under different philosophies that may be at odds (Fleck-Henderson, 2000; Mills et al., 2000). Because CPS systems hold a primary goal of protecting children, they may sanction parental IPV victims for failing to protect their children (Fleck-Henderson, 2000; Jones & Gross, 2000). However, many domestic violence advocates take umbrage at this stance, as it is thought to ignore the role of the mother's own trauma and victimization (Fleck-Henderson, 2000; Jones & Gross, 2000; Landsman & Hartley, 2007). Further, CPS case plans may pressure IPV victims to make decisions that may ultimately not be in their best interest (Fleck-Henderson, 2000). For example, a mother who is an IPV victim may be forced to kick her abusive boyfriend out of the home in order to keep her children, but she may also know that her boyfriend has threatened that if she kicks him out, he will kill her. Thus, therapists can help clients in these situations to consider all relevant safety factors in order to make the best and safest decisions.

Schools. School personnel are the most frequent reporters of suspected maltreatment to CPS (Sedlak et al., 2010). The behavioral and academic consequences of child maltreatment victimization may have detrimental effects on children's school performance, so school personnel are often called upon to provide support (Brassard et al., 2009). Within schools, personnel who work with children who have been maltreated include speech-language pathologists, teachers, and administrators (Haeseler, 2006; Westby, 2007). Schools have especially focused on preventive interventions (Ko & Cosden, 2001), as discussed in Chapter 13. Likewise, children with substantiated abuse may receive counseling in their schools (Brassard et al., 2009). Schools may offer an optimal setting for counseling because the child is already there and therefore the risk of the child missing appointments is low (Mishna, 2007).

Child Maltreatment Researchers. Researchers who study child maltreatment aim to discover knowledge to enhance the understanding, prevention, and intervention of child maltreatment. Researchers who study child maltreatment come from a range of disciplines, including psychology, social work, law, medicine, and public policy (Bottoms & Quas, 2006). Some researchers have direct contact with children who have been maltreated, although unless they are conducting treatment outcome studies, their role in responding to child maltreatment is typically more indirect. However, researchers may collaborate with practitioners in other ways, such as through program evaluations, collaborative studies on client populations, and developing knowledge to inform clinical practices. Research on child maltreatment is extremely complicated (Lutzker, Tymchuk, & Bigelow, 2001). Because child maltreatment is not a socially-accepted behavior, families are often very hesitant to participate in research (Lutzker et al., 2001). Even researchers who are committed to studying this issue face potential challenges and frustrations in doing so (Lutzker et al., 2001). An ongoing struggle for researchers is to translate their findings into applications for clinical practice (Bottoms & Quas, 2006). Therefore, continued efforts are needed to increase and enhance collaborative efforts between researchers and practitioners.

Summary

Child maltreatment is an extremely challenging, complicated clinical issue. Victims may face negative consequences that lead them to seek counseling services, and it is important for therapists to understand how clients' background characteristics and experiences impact their current functioning. Therapists who work with perpetrators are likely to face many personal and professional challenges, including attempting to understand the worldview of clients who have acted in harmful ways toward children. Therapists need not work in isolation when addressing child maltreatment, as numerous legal and social service resources can provide additional support and collaboration. This chapter has provided a foundation for understanding background information about child maltreatment and the systems in place to respond to it, and the following chapters will move to clinical applications of this information for assessment and treatment.

7

GUIDELINES FOR THE ASSESSMENT OF CHILD MALTREATMENT

Conducting a thorough clinical assessment is invaluable to the subsequent treatment of child maltreatment victims, perpetrators, and other involved clients (e.g., non-offending parents). The information gathered through the assessment can guide therapists in making decisions about appropriate treatment approaches. As was discussed in Chapter 6, a victim of child maltreatment may experience consequences in multiple domains, so determining which factors to assess can be a challenge. Likewise, understanding the background characteristics and motivation for treatment of perpetrators is essential to addressing safety-related and therapeutic considerations involved in their treatment. This chapter begins with some general considerations for conducting a clinical assessment when child maltreatment is suspected or confirmed. We then discuss specific areas of clinical assessment related to child maltreatment, including strategies for assessing these areas through open-ended questions and formal assessment instruments.

General Child Maltreatment Assessment Considerations

1. *Address safety issues throughout the assessment process.* As with all work related to family violence, therapists must place primary priority on ensuring the emotional and physical safety of their clients and others who may be at risk of harm. Therapists can promote emotional safety in the assessment process by letting the client guide the pace and allowing the client to share a level of information that is manageable within their coping abilities. This may mean that the assessment needs to be broken up into several sessions. Physical safety can be promoted by developing a safety plan, addressing potential

safety risks as part of the assessment process, and connecting the client with community resources.

2. *Use appropriate approaches before and after it is determined that maltreatment has occurred.* Therapists must be alert to identify possible cases of child abuse when working with children (Giardino, 2009). In this book, we primarily address clients with whom maltreatment is suspected or identified, but maltreatment may be present when working with any clients, even when maltreatment is not disclosed. There are many reasons that children may be hesitant to disclose abuse, such as being afraid of the abuser (Paine & Hansen, 2002). Other factors can influence the extent to which children disclose maltreatment, including their age, gender, and level of support received from caregivers (Lippert, Cross, Jones, & Walsh, 2009).

   Obtaining accurate information is a primary goal. Therapists must remain alert to the possibility that assessment results may be inaccurate, in that abuse may be identified when it is not present (i.e., a false positive) or abuse may not be identified when it is occurring (i.e., a false negative) (Jones, 2001; Wood & Garven, 2000). Although a clinical assessment differs from a child protective service (CPS) or criminal justice investigation in this regard, the implications of identifying or failing to detect maltreatment are significant in terms of determining the best course of treatment. There are a number of reasons that a child or other client may provide inaccurate information in the assessment process, including that they remember experiences incorrectly, they lack adequate vocabulary to describe their experiences, or they are being intentionally deceitful to protect themselves or a family member (Sjoberg & Lindholm, 2009). False allegations of maltreatment may be especially likely when parents are engaged in bitter separations or child custody disputes, although even then rates of false allegations are relatively low (Trocme & Bala, 2005). In light of these issues, therapists should conduct child maltreatment-related assessments with appropriate (a) attention to the timing and purpose of the assessment, (b) sensitivity to concerns that may inhibit disclosure, and (c) consideration for gathering the most accurate information available.

3. *Determine the appropriate focus of the assessment.* Child maltreatment investigations may involve a forensic interview (Perron & Hiltz, 2006; Saywitz, Mannarino, Berliner, & Cohen, 2000). A forensic interview is different than a clinical assessment because the purpose of the former is to inform legal proceedings, whereas the purpose of the latter is to inform therapeutic treatment. These interviews must be done by appropriately qualified personnel and usually are done in designated settings (e.g., a child advocacy center). Forensic interviews may involve the use of anatomically correct dolls (Perron & Hiltz, 2006), which are a controversial but common practice for eliciting information from a child about body-related

experiences related to the abuse. Specialized training should be sought prior to using these dolls.

Because forensic interviews, which may or may not be conducted by therapists, are a unique subset of child maltreatment assessment, the majority of the information discussed in this chapter addresses clinical assessment related to therapy and not forensic interviewing. If a forensic investigation is ongoing when a therapist begins to work with clients, it is typically advisable to avoid directly discussing and assessing the maltreatment until that investigation is complete. Rather, therapists can focus on other aspects of the client's functioning (e.g., coping) until the clinical assessment can be done without risk of contaminating the forensic assessment.

At the start of an assessment interview, the therapist should ensure that the client understands the purpose of the interview, the expectations of the interviewer and client, that there are not necessarily "right" or "wrong" answer to the questions being asked, that the client should respond to questions using language that is comfortable to him or her, and that the client can skip questions s/he are uncomfortable with that can be returned to later (Sjoberg & Lindholm, 2009).

4. *Attend to the developmental level of the child.* Therapists should use developmentally-appropriate language and approaches throughout the assessment (Wood & Garven, 2000). For example, it may be useful to ask the client to describe his or her experiences in his or her own words (Saywitz et al., 2000), such as in a chronological story format to facilitate recall and to match a child's cognitive abilities (Wood & Garven, 2000). Even relatively young children with adequate verbal abilities are able to provide accurate information about experiences with child maltreatment (Sjoberg & Lindholm, 2009). However, therapists must understand the cognitive capacity of the clients with whom they work to ensure that assessment expectations are reasonable and interpreted correctly. Some additional child-appropriate assessment practices include being friendly, explaining the therapist's background, helping the child understand what is expected of him or her, and letting the child know that it is okay if a child does not know the answer to a particular question (Hershkowitz, 2009). Later in this chapter, we present sample open-ended interview questions that therapists may use in the assessment of child maltreatment. However, the wording of these questions should be modified based on developmental level.
5. *Address confidentiality issues throughout the assessment process.* Confidentiality issues are complex when working with minor clients, especially related to child maltreatment. Therapists must become informed about laws in their jurisdictions regarding confidentiality and minors (Lawrence & Kurpius, 2000). Therapists should ensure that both parents/guardians and children, at a developmentally-appropriate level, understand the nature of confidentiality of information discussed during therapy sessions (Lawrence &

Kurpius, 2000). Again, any suspected abuse must be reported to local CPS systems in accordance with relevant laws and regulations (Giardino, 2009; Knickerbocker, Heyman, Slep, Jouriles, & McDonald, 2007).

6. *Include both formal and informal assessment strategies.* Both formal and informal assessment strategies hold value (Horton & Cruise, 1997). It is critical to include multiple sources of information, including self-report and other more objective sources, to gain a full picture of a clients' functioning, especially because different sources of information elicit different information (Baumann & Kolko, 2002). Three major forms of information include records and information from other agencies and individuals, standardized instruments, and open-ended interviewing. If confidentiality issues can be addressed, it also can be useful to gather assessment data from others close to the child (Sjoberg & Lindholm, 2009), including those who may have witnessed abusive behaviors or who have had opportunities to observe changes in the child's behaviors. If assessment data are gathered from official sources, such as CPS databases, therapists should bear in mind that these databases often differ in the definitions used to classify maltreatment (Fallon, Trocme, Fluke, MacLaurin, Tonmyr, & Yuan, 2010).

   Regarding standardized instruments, several formats are available, such as structured interviews, checklists, and self-report questionnaires (Peters & Barlow, 2003). As such, therapists should evaluate any potentially useful instruments to ensure that they are structured to collect accurate and comprehensive information in a manner that is suitable for the designated clients. Regardless of format selected, instruments should be psychometrically sound (Sawyer, Tsao, Hansen, & Flood, 2006). Three specific features of assessments related to child maltreatment should be considered (Peters & Barlow, 2003). First, the instrument's sensitivity reflects its ability to accurately identify abuse. Second, the instrument's specificity reflects is ability to accurately identify when abuse is not occurring. Third, its positive predictive value describes the extent to which it is able to be used to effectively predict future abuse.

   Despite their potential value, clients' unique experiences may not be captured fully by standardized instruments (Horton & Cruise, 1997). Open-ended questioning that is done in a nonjudgmental way can elicit valuable information about abuse experiences and other characteristics that may have been excluded from standardized instruments (Horton & Cruise, 1997; Young, Read, Barker-Collo, & Harrison, 2001). Therefore, it may be useful simply to ask clients, "Are there other issues or concerns you have that have not been addressed so far?"

7. *Conduct the assessment within a context of rapport.* Positive rapport is essential for conducting an effective assessment (Young et al., 2001). This is true for victims, survivors, perpetrators, and other involved family members in light of the sensitive nature of this topic. First, therapists should strive to

create a comfortable climate for the interview (Wood & Garven, 2000), such as by adopting a supportive and relaxed tone (Hershkowitz, 2009). Second, the therapist should display genuine warmth toward the client (Wood & Garven, 2000). Third, at the outset, it is useful to ask the child if s/he understands the reason for meeting with the therapist (Hershkowitz, 2009). Fourth, the therapist should be mindful not to interrupt the client, unless clinically appropriate, during the assessment (Wood & Garven, 2000).

Therapists then may build stronger rapport by asking the child to begin by discussing relatively emotionally-neutral experiences (Hershkowitz, 2009). Rapport-building need not be lengthy, and in fact overly extended rapport building may decrease the amount of information a child provides because s/he may become tired and less able to sustain attention by the end of the interview (Hershkowitz, 2009). Thus, especially with a new client, a brief but effective rapport-building process should be used at the outset of the assessment (Hershkowitz, 2009). The rapport can be sustained throughout the assessment process, and the therapist should express appreciation for the client's participation at the end of the interview (Wood & Garven, 2000).

8. *Be sensitive to the discomfort that surrounds maltreatment disclosure.* Children who have been maltreated may be hesitant to disclose these experiences voluntarily (Young et al., 2001). For example, they may feel ashamed (Feiring, 2005; Lowe, Pavkov, Casanova, & Wetchler, 2005), be afraid that they won't be believed (Lowe et al., 2005), fear that disclosing will mean that they will be taken from their home and family and lose their relationship with their parent (Lowe et al., 2005), or believe, sometimes accurately, that a parent will not be supportive (Liefer, Kilbane, & Grossman, 2001). Perpetrators may not be forthcoming because they know their behaviors are not socially acceptable. For these reasons, therapists should be mindful that information disclosed initially may not reflect the full extent of maltreatment. Therapists, too, may be hesitant to ask clients about experiences of abuse (Young et al., 2001). They may lack training, be concerned about whether reported abuse is true, and/or be concerned that they will embarrass their clients (Young et al., 2001). Therefore, therapists should begin with developing self-awareness about their comfort level in discussing abuse with clients.
9. *Avoid using leading questions and other suggestive interviewing practices.* This is a critical recommendation that therapists must consider throughout all phases of the clinical assessment. When assessing children when child maltreatment is suspected, therapists must be conscientious about the language they use to ensure that they do not (a) contaminate legal proceedings and/or (b) increase the likelihood that they will elicit false information. A specific type of question to avoid is known as a *leading question*, which means that

the way that the question is asked leads the client toward being more likely to providing a certain response, whether or not that response it accurate.

Leading questions also may be referred to as *suggestive questions* and should be avoided (Hershkowitz, 2009). Children may be highly suggestive to false information, and their memories may be unreliable based on their cognitive development (Perron & Hiltz, 2006). Therefore, leading or suggestive questions must be avoided, both because they can taint an investigation and they expose the therapist to potential liability of planting ideas in the child's mind. Suggestive interviewing strategies are especially likely to prompt false allegations in younger children (Sjoberg & Lindholm, 2009). Such questions can compromise the accuracy of the assessment (Hershkowitz, 2009). One example of a suggestive question is "Did he touch you on the bottom?" (Wood & Garven, 2000, p. 110), which is inappropriate because (a) it is closed-ended, (b) it presupposes that the perpetrator is a male, (c) it introduces the idea of touching the child, and (d) it presumes which term the child would use to describe his/her "bottom."

Other suggestive interviewing practices include the interviewer using undue influence or authority to pry out information, reinforcing or rewarding the types of information that the interviewer wants to hear, and using indirect strategies that blur the line between reality and fantasy about what might have happened (Wood & Garven, 2000). Wood and Garven described two interviewing errors: either the interviewer uses improper techniques, such as leading questions, or the interviewer is clumsy in how s/he conducts the interview. The former problem is especially likely to result in the elicitation of false information, but it can often be rectified with further training for the interviewer. On the other hand, clumsy interviewing may have detrimental effects for the child and is less easily modified.

Generally, the assessment should involve very open-ended questions, instructions, and processes to help avoid leading questions (Hershkowitz, 2009; Sjoberg & Lindholm, 2009; Wood & Garven, 2000). One technique is to use free recall strategies (Hershkowitz, 2009). More specific and directive questions are appropriate only when the child has provided adequate detail to open-ended questioning (Hershkowitz, 2009). Even then, specific and directive questions should be based on information the child already provided and should avoid suggesting any new information. Specific questions that must be asked should be held for the end of the interview so they do not interfere with the open-ended process of the interview (Sjoberg & Lindholm, 2009).

10. *Remember that child maltreatment assessment is a multidimensional process.* Whether a therapist is assessing a potential or confirmed victim, survivor, perpetrator, or other family member impacted by child maltreatment, therapists should be thorough in their work (Giardino, 2009). Assessment

should focus on gathering information about multiple aspects of the client's life and from multiple sources (Horton & Cruise, 1997). Of course, even a well-planned, comprehensive assessment can miss certain pieces of information. However, the more comprehensive a process the therapist takes from the beginning, the greater the likelihood that pertinent information will be revealed to help guide treatment and provide information about client background characteristics. As treatment progresses, assessment should be ongoing in order to identify changes that occur over time in different areas of clients' lives (Horton & Cruise, 1997). As we move to the next section on specific areas of clinical assessment, we encourage readers to consider how each of the following areas combine to develop a complete and detailed clinical picture of the client's presenting concerns and treatment needs.

Dimensions of Child Maltreatment Assessment

Specific focus areas for the clinical assessment of child maltreatment are the nature of the maltreatment, the victim, general family functioning and non-offending parents, and the perpetrator. In each section below, we discuss general assessment considerations, specific variables to assess (with relevant structured instruments reviewed in this chapter's Appendix), and possible open-ended questions. The assessment of adult survivors of childhood abuse is addressed in Chapter 9. Safety concerns also should be assessed, and we refer readers to the section on safety consideration in Chapter 3 for additional information on this topic.

Assessment of the Abuse

Assessment of a child's experience with maltreatment goes far beyond a simple yes or no question as to whether abuse occurred (English, 2003). Aspects of child maltreatment that should be assessed include the child's age currently and at the onset of maltreatment; how much force was used; the nature of the relationship with the perpetrator(s); whether the maltreatment resulted in out-of-home placements; whether the child also witnessed parental IPV; and the severity, frequency, pattern, duration, and type of maltreatment (Bentovim, 2002; English, 2003; Locke & Newcomb, 2003; Manly, 2005; Tell, Pavkov, Hecker, & Fontaine, 2006; Wolfe, Crooks, Chiodo, & Jaffe, 2009). The assessment of neglect in particular should account for the child's unique developmental stage, as experiences considered neglectful at one stage may not be so for other ages (Stowman & Donohue, 2005). Special attention should be paid to understanding the severity of maltreatment the child experienced (Higgins, 2004).

Different assessment approaches may be used, including observation, risk factor identification, behavior-focused reports, and self-report measures

(Stowman & Donohue, 2005). Children's artwork also may provide clues about experiences with maltreatment (Veltman & Browne, 2001). Art therapy theories hold that certain images (e.g., inclement weather) symbolize negative family experiences (Veltman & Browne, 2001). However, children's drawings alone are not suitable for identifying maltreatment, as they are highly susceptible to being improperly classified (Veltman & Browne, 2001). Although in the past some therapists have used projective techniques to assess for child maltreatment, sexual abuse in particular, these are not considered sound, thorough assessment strategies by themselves (Garb, Wood, & Nezworski, 2000).

Standardized instruments can provide an objective measure of maltreatment severity. For example, the Mother-Child Neglect Scale (MCNS; Lounds, Borkowski, & Witman, 2004) and the Multidimensional Neglectful Behavior Scale—Child Report (MNBS-CR; Kaufman Kantor et al., 2004) may be useful for assessing neglect, and the Parent-Child Conflict Tactics Scales (CTSPC; Straus, Hamby, Finkelhor, Moore, & Runyon, 1998) can be used to assess the severity of abuse. These are reviewed in this chapter's Appendix. To supplement these standardized instruments, therapists may wish to ask open-ended questions similar to those in the list below.

Sample Interview Questions for Assessing Child Maltreatment

- Tell me what happened to you that led you to get involved with CPS.
- You seem to be feeling sad. Would you like to tell me what's been going on?
- Sometimes adults do things that make kids uncomfortable. Has that ever happened to you? Tell me about what happened. (Therapists could also frame this question as, "Do you have friends or know anyone who had something uncomfortable happen to them?)
- I see you have a bruise on your arm [or other physical indicator]. How did that get there?
- I wonder what led you to feel the way you are feeling now. Can you tell me about it?
- I heard from your teachers that you've been having a difficult time in school lately. What's going on?
- *When the nature of the maltreatment is known, such as when the CPS investigation has been completed and maltreatment has been substantiated, more specific questions, such as the following, may be useful. We use the example of a child getting hit, and this should be replaced with the specific form of maltreatment, if that information is known.*
    - How badly did getting hit hurt your body?
    - How did you feel after you were hit?
    - Who was it that hit you?
    - How often did they hit you?
    - Did they say anything to you when they were hitting you? If yes, what?

- Did they tell other people about their hitting you? If yes, who did they tell?
- What did you do after you were hit?
- Did anything else happen to you that also hurt your body or feelings? If so, what?

Assessment of the Victim

Other areas of the victim's functioning to assess include their experience of trauma, social support, current mental health symptoms (including risk for harming self and others), perceptions of the maltreatment, coping resources and strengths, and other areas of functioning.

Trauma. Assessing the trauma(s) the child has experienced is a necessary precursor to understanding symptoms that may have resulted from it (Brown, 2005). Therapists should assess the severity, frequency, and duration of a child's PTSD symptoms (Brown, 2005). Therapists also should determine whether the client has re-experienced the trauma, such as through nightmares or play (Brown, 2005). Three instruments for assessing the child's experience of the trauma are the UCLA PTSD Index for *DSM-IV* (Rodriguez, Steinberg, & Pynoos, 1999), the Children's Impact of Traumatic Events Scale-Revised (CITES-R, Chaffin & Shultz, 2001), and the Trauma Symptom Checklist for Children (TSCC; originally constructed by Briere, 1996, as cited in Sadowski & Friedrich, 2000), all of which are reviewed in this chapter's Appendix.

Sample Interview Questions for Assessing a Child Victim's Experience of Trauma
- What has it been like for you to have gone through that experience?
- How are you sleeping?
- Do you ever have nightmares? If so, tell me about what they're like.
- Do you ever have thoughts that scare you or make you upset? If so, tell me about them.
- Are there things that remind you or make you think about what happened?
- When something reminds you of what happened, what happens in your mind and body?

Social Support. The availability of social support can have a powerful impact on child functioning following maltreatment. Supportive parents can buffer negative impacts of child abuse (Liefer et al., 2001). Even when children's fathers do not live in the home, a supportive adult male figure can have a positive impact on a child victim's life (Bellamy, 2009). By assessing a victim's level of social support, the therapist can identify potential resources to help the client, as well as potentially problematic relationships that may impede treatment progress. A useful technique for assessing the child's social support is to ask the child to name three adults they view as helpful (Cox, Kotch, & Everson, 2003).

If the child does not name a parent, this can provide valuable insight into the child's perceptions of support from family (Cox et al., 2003). Several additional questions that can be helpful to ask are provided below.

Sample Interview Questions for Assessing a Child Victim's Social Support

- Can you draw me a picture of your favorite friends? Tell me about the people you drew.
- Can you draw me a picture of your family? What are each of these people like?
- If something upset you, who could tell about it? How do you think they'd respond?
- Who do you think you can go to when you need help to solve a problem you are facing?

Mental Health Symptoms. Children's mental health symptoms are important to assess across affective, cognitive, and behavioral domains (Horton & Cruise, 1997). Commonly used measures such as the Global Assessment of Functioning (GAF) and Children's Global Assessment Scale (CGAS) also are likely to be used (Blake, Cangelosi, Johnson-Brooks, & Belcher, 2007). However, the complexity of the lived experiences of children who have experienced trauma may render these measures less reliable with this population (Blake et al., 2007). Therapists can combine standardized instruments with open-ended questions to gather a comprehensive picture of clients' current mental health functioning. For children who have trouble verbalizing feelings, therapists can show pictures of feelings and ask them to pick the picture that shows how they feel.

Sample Interview Questions for Assessing a Child Victim's Mental Health Symptoms

- How have you been feeling lately?
- How long have you been feeling this way?
- Can you pinpoint any one thing or number of things that are leading you to feel this way?
- What do you usually do when you start to feel this way?
- Sometimes, when people go through things that are really difficult for them, they start to feel like their mind isn't working like it usually does. Have you ever had that happen to you? How does your mind feel like it's working right now?
- When you start to feel down, how easy is it for you to help yourself feel better?
- Where and how in your body can you tell where your feelings are? What does your body feel like right now?
- Within the past week [or other designated time-frame], have you been feeling like you've had the same amount of energy as usual?
- Have you noticed lately that you've been interested in doing different things than you usually are interested in? If so, what changes have you noticed?

Perceptions of the Maltreatment. The way a child views her/his victimization experiences can influence the outcomes s/he experiences (Kolko, Brown, & Berliner, 2002). Perceptions are useful to understand from a clinical standpoint because they are potentially modifiable in treatment (Kolko et al., 2002). Examples of relevant perceptions include the extent to which the child views the maltreatment as positive or negative, how much the child blames him/herself for the abuse, the significance of the maltreatment compared to other areas of the child's life, and how harmful the child thinks the maltreatment experiences will be for his/her future. The Children's Abuse-Specific Perceptions (CASP; Kolko et al., 2002) measure, reviewed in this chapter's Appendix, may be useful in this part of the assessment.

Sample Interview Questions for Assessing a Child Victim's Perceptions of the Maltreatment

- Who do you think is responsible for this happening to you?
- On a scale from 1 to 10, where 1 means that it didn't hurt you at all and 10 means that it hurt you the worst it could possibly hurt you, how much does it hurt that this happened?
- What is the best thing about your life right now? What is the hardest thing?
- Sometimes, when kids are abused or hurt, they feel like it's their fault. Do you ever feel like that?
- Can you imagine what your life will be like five years from now? Do you think that the abuse that happened to you recently will still be affecting you then? If so, how?

Related Stress and Coping. Children may experience stressors related to the maltreatment and in other areas of their lives. Therefore, it is useful to gain a sense of a child victim's general perceptions of stress and coping. Assessing related stressors has important implications for treatment planning. For example, some children may have to move to a new school if they were removed from their home, which can create changes in peer relationships. In addition to understanding clients' coping resources, the therapist should identify other strengths and resources. These include resources available from various sources, such as trusting relationships with other adults, formal social systems, peers (Osofsky, 2003), and spiritual and/or religious resources (Reinert & Edwards, 2009; Walker, Reese, Hughes, & Troskie, 2010). Children's talents, skills, personal qualities, and life goals also may serve as important resources. Therefore, therapists should include a focus on strengths during the assessment process.

Sample Interview Questions for Assessing a Child Victim's Strengths and Resources

- What happens to you in your body and mind when you feel stressed? How much have you been feeling this way lately?
- When you're going through hard times, what are some things you do to feel better?

- What are some things you like about yourself?
- What are some things that you are really good at?
- What is your best subject in school?
- What do you want to be when you grow up?
- What are your religious/spiritual beliefs? How are those helping you during this time?

Other Areas of Child Functioning (e.g., academic, social, and behavioral). Although it may not be possible to identify all unique consequences at the start of therapy, therapists should ensure that they are comprehensive in the areas of a child's life they assess. Some specific areas that may warrant consideration include the following:

The child's basic needs. Therapists may need to help victims meet their basic needs (e.g., food, safety) before they will be prepared to address higher-order psychological and relational needs. Typically, therapists can work with other involved professionals (e.g., a CPS caseworker) to address these needs. However, a child's needs may change or new needs may be identified through the course of the assessment and treatment. An instrument that may prove useful for assessing a child's level of needs is the Inventory for Assessing Maslow's Needs in Children (Harper, Harper, & Stills, 2003), which is reviewed in this chapter's Appendix.

Problematic behaviors. Therapists should assess the child's behaviors in a range of domains. Some specific behavioral domains that are relevant for children who have been maltreated, along with potential instruments to assess each domain (all of which are reviewed in the Appendix), are as follows: general behavioral problems [Weekly Problems Scale—Child Version (WPSC) and Weekly Problems Scale—Parent Version (WPSP) (Sawyer et al., 2006)], social behaviors (Social Behavior Inventory; SBI; Gully, 2001), and problematic sexual behaviors (Modified Child Sexual Behavior Inventory-II; Modified CSBI-II; Merrick, Litrownik, Everson, & Cox, 2008). Therapists also may want to assess whether a child, especially an adolescent, has begun to display any aggression or delinquent behaviors across various settings.

The child's attachment style. Due to the likelihood that the child's attachment style was impacted by the maltreatment, it is useful to assess for any problematic attachment patterns demonstrated by a victim (Baer & Martinez, 2006). Different strategies can be used to assess attachment, including self-report and observational approaches such as the Ainsworth Strange Situation protocol (Crittenden, Claussen, & Kozlowska, 2007). Different attachment assessment approaches have unique advantages and limitations, so therapists must consider carefully the assessment strategy that is most applicable to a particular client in relation to the goals of the assessment (Crittenden et al., 2007). Generally, it is useful to determine whether the child demonstrates a secure versus insecure attachment style, and if an insecure style is identified, to classify whether it is avoidant or ambivalent (Crittenden et al., 2007). It may be useful to ask victims to describe their perceptions of their parents, both custodial and noncustodial, which can provide additional clues about a child's attachment with significant caregivers (Dubowitz, 2009).

School functioning. A child's performance in school should be assessed (Brown, 2005), especially any recent changes that have occurred. A child's relationships with peers and teachers at school should be considered (Brown, 2005). It may be useful to include official school records as part of the assessment data if these records can be obtained.

Sample Interview Questions for Assessing a Child Victim's Functioning

- What kind of food do you eat each day?
- How much sleep do you get each day?
- How safe do you feel in your home?
- How often do you get in trouble for misbehavior at home? At school? What kinds of behaviors tend to get you in trouble? What kinds of punishment do you usually get?
- How close do you feel to your mother? How close do you feel to your father?
- Can you name some adults, not your parents, in your life—such as a teacher or coach—that you have a relationship with? What is your relationship like with those people?
- In general, how well do you think you can trust other people in your life?
- How well would you say you are doing in school?
- What is the hardest thing for you in school?
- Who is your favorite teacher? What do you like about that teacher?
- Tell me about the kinds of kids you hang out with at school.

Assessment of Non-Offending Parents and General Family Functioning

Whether the child alone is the client, the child and the non-offending parent are participating together, or the clinician is providing family therapy with other involved family members, it is important to assess the functioning of the non-offending parent(s) and the general family functioning. Specific areas to assess include: the non-offending parent's general functioning, parenting skills, and resources; reactions to the disclosure of maltreatment in the family; and general family dynamics.

The Non-Offending Parent's General Functioning. Non-offending parents' functioning impacts their ability to provide support for their maltreated children and nurture their own self-care. Therapists may therefore find it worthy to assess the following domains with non-offending parents: available resources and information needs (Horton & Cruise, 1997); substance abuse (Scannapieco & Connell-Carrick, 2007); mental health (Brown, 2005; Lewin & Bergin,

2001); and intergenerational patterns of family violence (Naughton & Heath, 2001; Lewin & Bergin, 2001; Scannapieco & Connell-Carrick, 2007). Chapter 9 provides information on treatment of adult survivors of child maltreatment in cases in which abuse histories are identified.

The Non-Offending Parent's Parenting Skills and Resources. It is important to assess parental functioning among non-offending parents (Horton & Cruise, 1997). Parenting domains that are relevant to assess include attitudes toward child rearing, how parents interpret their children's behavior (Naughton & Heath, 2001), the quality of interactions between parents and their children (Naughton & Heath, 2001), and general patterns of responding to the child (Elliott & Carnes, 2001). Non-offending parents may experience numerous stressors that impact parental functioning. As such, it may be useful to assess their levels of parenting stress. An instrument for this purpose, the Parenting Stress Index—Short Form (PSI-SF; Abidin, 1995, Haskett, Ahern, Ward, & Allaire, 2006), is described in the Appendix. In addition, parents' level of satisfaction with their parenting role and responsibilities are important to assess. We refer readers to Carpenter and Donohue (2006) for a review of standardized instruments assessing this domain.

Reactions to the Disclosure of Maltreatment within the Family. In some cases, maltreatment is identified when a child discloses it, either to a family member, professional, or other person in the child's life. The disclosure may set off a chain of reactions that can be more or less supportive to the child. Research is mixed regarding the percentage of parents who believe and support their children when the child discloses abuse (Liefer et al., 2001). Although exact percentages are difficult to decipher, it is clear that a substantial proportion of parents do believe and support their children, but a substantial proportion do not (Liefer et al., 2001). Of course, parents could have an ambivalent response, such as by partially believing their children or by providing only inconsistent emotional support (Elliott & Carnes, 2001). It is therefore important for therapists to ascertain the extent to which the child's initial disclosure was believed (Horton & Cruise, 1997). Furthermore, therapists should assess how the disclosure of the maltreatment impacted different members of the child's family, including the child. In particular, focus should be given to the level of support the child received from the parent(s) and other family members before and after the abuse was disclosed (Horton & Cruise, 1997).

General Family Functioning. Family dynamics can support or hinder clients' progress toward therapy goals. Some family dynamics warrant modifying treatment approaches to ensure that they are appropriate for the family context. Family dynamics that may be useful to assess include the family's view of the current presenting problem (Pardeck, 2004), level of cohesion (Bass, Taylor,

& Knudson-Martin, 2006), structure, communication processes, relationship roles, developmental history (Pardeck, 2004), level of conflict (Brown, 2005), and risk and protective factors (Bentovim, 2002). A child's relationship with his or her father and other important adult male figures also should be assessed (Bellamy, 2009). Although they may be challenging to assess at first, it is useful to ascertain the degree of secrets within the family (Bass et al., 2006) and whether sibling abuse is present (Kiselica & Morrill-Richards, 2007). The family's home environment should be assessed (Scannapieco & Connell-Carrick, 2007), and a related instrument reviewed in this chapter's Appendix is the Home Observation for Measurement of the Environment Inventory (HOME; Bradley, Caldwell, Rock, Hamrick, & Harris, 1988; Linver, Brooks-Gunn, & Cabrera, 2004). Beyond the immediate family context, therapists should assess how the family interacts with their social environment (Pardeck, 2004; Scannapieco & Connell-Carrick, 2007), including their view of external systems involved in their lives (Bass et al., 2006).

Sample Interview Questions for Assessing Non-Offending Parents and Family Functioning

- How have you been handling all of the challenges that you have been facing lately?
- What has been the most difficult thing you've been facing lately?
- Are you currently facing any specific challenges that you need help with?
- How would you describe yourself as a parent?
- How do you typically discipline your child?
- What do you think are your greatest strengths as a parent?
- What do you think are your biggest challenges as a parent?
- How did you first respond when you heard that your child said that s/he had been abused?
- What feelings did you have about the disclosure of the abuse?
- Did you have any doubts about whether your child was telling the truth? If so, tell me about those doubts.
- Tell me about your family.
- How do people in your family get along with one another?
- When there's a conflict in your family, what usually happens?
- How do you think people who know your family would describe your family?
- What do you think your family will be like five years from now? What do you think will happen between now and then to get to that point?

Assessment of Child Maltreatment Perpetrators

Perhaps one of the most difficult and least understood areas of child maltreatment assessment is the assessment of perpetrators. Currently, there is a mismatch between theoretical understandings of child maltreatment perpetrators and the instruments available to assess them (Gannon, Keown, & Rose, 2008). Likewise, research findings provide limited clear guidance as to how to use assessment findings to predict whether a perpetrator will reoffend. Therefore, therapists must conduct the assessment of perpetrators with attention to existing theory and research, but also be mindful of the limitations of existing approaches. Sound clinical judgment must be combined with theory- and research-based guidelines in this area in particular. In this section, we discuss key aspects of the clinical assessment of perpetrators, including the potential for perpetrating future maltreatment, personal characteristics, and treatment-related variables.

Assessing the Potential for Future Perpetration. Both researchers and therapists have attempted to develop strategies to predict whether a caregiver is likely to perpetrate abuse, which is referred to in the literature as *child abuse potential* (Begle, Dumas, & Hanson, 2010). Theoretically, this could help stop abuse before it occurs and prevent recidivism. Some researchers assert that the cumulative level or number of risk factors is most important in determining child abuse potential, while others argue that certain types of risk factors are more or less influential on child abuse potential (Begle et al., 2010).

Milner's Child Abuse Potential Inventory (CAPI; Milner, 1986) has some evidence to support is validity (Begle et al., 2010). Another instrument is the Adult Adolescent Parenting Inventory—2 (AAPI-2, Originally developed by Bavolek & Keene, 1999, as cited in Conners, Whiteside-Mansell, Deere, Ledet, & Edwards, 2006), and both of these are reviewed in the Appendix. However, existing instruments designed to predict the perpetration of child maltreatment are limited in their predictive abilities, so currently they are best used to inform treatment directions rather than as part of punishment for offenders (Peters & Barlow, 2003). Clearly, predicting child abuse perpetration is extremely complex and not able to be narrowed down to a small number of variables (Peters & Barlow, 2003). Therefore, therapists should evaluate cautiously any information suggestive of predictions of future abuse.

Physiological measures also have been utilized in the assessment of child sex offenders, in particular a penile plethysmograph, which measures sexual arousal to different sexual stimuli (Tong, 2007). These physiological measures offer the advantage of providing information beyond that which is self-reported by the perpetrator, but they are considered invasive. A similar, yet less invasive assessment strategy has been to examine perpetrator's visual response time to a variety of potentially stimulating images to determine which ones are associated with higher levels of sexual interest. Existing evidence suggests that less-invasive techniques provide similar information than more invasive ones, so a prudent approach would be to use the least invasive assessment strategy that is appropriate for any given client. Therapists should not use physiological assessment strategies unless they have received the proper training to do so. It may be wise to identify professionals in the local community to whom therapists can make a referral for these assessment approaches if they are warranted for certain clients.

Assessing Perpetrators' Personal Characteristics. The perpetrator's use of substances (Locke & Newcomb, 2003) and mental health symptoms (Stith et al., 2009) should be assessed. It also may be useful to assess the presence and extent of abuse victimization experienced by the perpetrator as a child (Bentovim, 2002). This can include all forms of maltreatment, as well as exposure to interparental IPV (Bentovim, 2002). It is important this not be conveyed so as to imply that the childhood victimization is an excuse for the perpetration. However, this information can show whether current perpetration occurred in the context of longstanding patterns of maltreatment in the perpetrator's extended family. Another perpetrator characteristic to assess is parental empathy, such as by using the Parental Empathy Measure (PEM; Kilpatrick, 2005), which is reviewed in the Appendix. A parent perpetrator's level of empathy toward his/ her child can impact parenting abilities, and lower levels of parental empathy suggest an increased likelihood of reoffending.

Assessing Treatment-related Variables. Perpetrator variables that can impact treatment responsiveness include the extent to which the perpetrator accepts responsibility for the maltreatment, motivation for seeking treatment, and perceptions of past experiences in treatment. In addition, a perpetrator's willingness to acknowledge the harm that the abuse has caused for the child can impact his/her responsiveness to treatment (Bentovim, 2002). Therefore, these variables should be assessed, especially through the use of open-ended questions to gain an in-depth understanding of perpetrators' beliefs. Other assessment strategies may be useful to employ through ongoing treatment, such as diaries to track their progress. For example, because brief self-report instruments can be subjective to social desirability bias, another approach to documenting change over time among potential or substantiated child maltreatment perpetrators is to ask them to keep a daily diary of their parenting experiences to document their use of positive and negative parenting strategies (Peterson, Tremblay, Ewigman, & Popkey, 2002).

Sample Interview Questions for Assessing Child Maltreatment Perpetrators

- How do you feel about the consequences you've faced as a result of being convicted of child abuse perpetration? How fair do you believe these consequences are?
- How fairly do you think you have been treated through the CPS investigation process?
- How willing are you to comply with the terms of your CPS case plan?

- What steps have you taken to seek out services that you are required to get based on your CPS case plan (e.g., counseling, substance abuse treatment, parenting classes)?
- What has your mood been like within the past two weeks?
- How much anxiety have you experienced recently? How do you manage this anxiety?
- Tell me about your use of alcohol or drugs, including prescription medications, in the past two weeks.
- When you were a child, did you experience any form of abuse or know about any abuse happening in your family? If so, tell me about those experiences.
- How do you feel currently toward the child you are accused of maltreating?
- What do you think life has been like lately for the child you are accused of maltreating?
- How do you feel about being required to participate in this therapy?
- Have you been in therapy before? What was helpful about it? What would you have liked to have been different about it?

Conclusion

The specific focus of a child maltreatment-related clinical assessment depends on the purpose of the assessment and the client's needs and characteristics. Clinical assessments should be comprehensive so that important client needs are not overlooked. Because child maltreatment impacts victims in so many domains, clients' needs may be many, and an accurate assessment can help therapist be in the best position to meet those needs. Other clients who have been impacted by or who have been perpetrators of child maltreatment also may exhibit a range of clinical needs that can influence their progress in therapy and impact the safety of children who have been maltreated. Therefore, therapists must conduct a child maltreatment-related clinical assessment to gather information that will guide and enhance subsequent treatment.

APPENDIX Directory of Selected Instruments for Assessing Child Maltreatment

This Appendix contains brief reviews of several available instruments that therapists may find useful to use in the clinical assessment of child mal treatment. The original source of each instrument is included so that therapists can locate additional information, including scoring directions and the availability of the instrument for clinical use. Some full-length instruments are available in the original sources, and it is the responsibility of the therapist to ensure that copyright instructions are followed. Instruments are listed in alphabetical order within each section, and the chart is organized into four sections: Assessing the Maltreatment, Assessing the Child Victim, Assessing the Non-offending Parent and General Family Functioning, and Assessing the Perpetrator.

Instrument Name and Source	*Construct(s) Designed to Assess*	*Number of Items; Sample Item(s)*	*Reliability and Validity Information*	*Strengths of Instrument for Clinical Practice*	*Limitations of Instrument for Clinical Practice*
Instruments for Assessing the Maltreatment					
Community Norms of Child Neglect Scale (CNCNS; Goodvin, Johnson, Hardy, Graef, & Chambers, 2007)	The CNCNS assesses respondents' perceptions of the types of behaviors and situations that constitute child neglect.	21 items with four subscales: Emotional Neglect; Physical Neglect—Failure to Provide; Physical Neglect—Lack of Supervision; and Educational Neglect; Sample item from the Lack of Supervision subscale: "An 8-year-old is left at home alone for several hours while the parents are shopping" (Goodvin et al., 2007, p. 82).	The total scale internal consistency was $a = .94$, and the subscale internal consistency coefficients ranged from $a = .82$ to .85. Minimal validity information is available.	- This instrument could be used to measure outcomes in psychoeducational programs about neglect and positive parenting practices. - The CNCNS may be useful for understanding community norms about neglectful parenting practices, which could help therapists target psychoeducational programming to unique community needs.	- The CNCNS is primarily a measure of the respondent's attitudes about neglect, and this does not necessarily correspond with their own behaviors. The instrument was not originally designed for use with clinical samples.

Instrument Name and Source	*Construct(s) Designed to Assess*	*Number of Items; Sample Item(s)*	*Reliability and Validity Information*	*Strengths of Instrument for Clinical Practice*	*Limitations of Instrument for Clinical Practice*
Mother-Child Neglect Scale (MCNS; Lounds et al., 2004)	The MCNS assesses "the type and severity of past neglectful behaviors" used by mothers (Lounds et al., 2004, p. 371).	The MCNS has 20 items with four subscales: Emotional Needs, Cognitive Needs, Supervision Needs, and Physical Needs. A sample item is as follows: "I helped my child with homework" (Lounds et al., 2004, p. 375).	The MCNS demonstrates strong internal consistency (with subscale coefficients ranging from *a* = .78 to .91) and moderate test-retest reliability (*a* = .60 for the total scale). Some evidence exists for the instrument's convergent validity.	- The MCNS is brief and easy to administer. An 8-item short form of the scale also was created. The positive wording of many of the items may promote more honest responses.	-The MCNS was developed for research purposes, so its applicability to clinical practice remains unclear.
Multi-dimensional Neglectful Behavior Scale—Child Report (MNBS-CR; Kaufman Kantor et al., 2004)	The MNBS-CR is administered on a computer and assesses four types of child neglect: cognitive, emotional, physical, and supervisory. Other neglectful experiences addressed include exposing a child to violence, neglect related to substance use, and abandonment.	The main constructs of the MNBS-CR are assessed through 36 items with four types of child neglect, plus 19 other items assessing the other neglectful experiences. A sample item is "The girl's mother does not make sure she takes a bath … Is this: A little like you?; Sort of like you?; A lot like you?; Really a lot like you?" (Kaufman Kantor et al., 2004; pp. 415–416).	The MNBS-CR has been shown to be more reliable with older (ages 10 to 15; *a* = .94) than younger (ages 6 to 9; *a* = .66) children. The internal consistency coefficients of the subscales ranged widely, suggesting that some subscales are less reliable than others. Some evidence exists for the instrument's construct validity.	- There are two versions of the MNBS-CR based on the child's age. - The computer-based technology and visual imagery used in the instrument may help children completing it be more engaged in the assessment process.	- The entire program through which the MNBS-CR is assessed takes approximately 30 to 40 minutes to complete, so it may be cumbersome for clinical use. - The lower internal consistency among younger children suggests that the instrument is less applicable with this population.

(*continued*)

APPENDIX Continued

Instrument Name and Source	*Construct(s) Designed to Assess*	*Number of Items; Sample Item(s)*	*Reliability and Validity Information*	*Strengths of Instrument for Clinical Practice*	*Limitations of Instrument for Clinical Practice*
Parent-Child Conflict Tactics Scales (CTSPC; Straus et al., 1998)	The CTSPC assesses various forms (i.e., physical, psychological, and neglect) of parent-perpetrated child maltreatment and whether they resulted in injury to the child. Nonviolent discipline tactics also are assessed.	22 items with ** subscales: Nonviolent Discipline, Psychological Aggression, Physical Assault, and Neglect; Sample item from the Psychological Aggression subscale: "Said you would send him/her away or kick him/her out of the house" (Straus et al., 1998, p. 267) .	Subscale Cronbach's alpha coefficients ranged from $a = .22$ to .70, although these low coefficients may be explained, at least in part, due to the forms of child maltreatment being relatively rare events more than as a reflection of poor psychometric properties of the scale; There is evidence for the CTSPC's discriminate and construct validity.	- The CTSPC is brief and therefore feasible for clinical settings. - The CTSPC items reflect specific behavioral items that provide an objective understanding of some of the behaviors that indicate maltreatment. - The CTSPS is easy to score.	- Conceptually, the CTSPC was created from the Conflict Tactics Scales (CTS/CTS2), which were designed to assess adult intimate partner violence. Although the CTS/CTS2 have been studied extensively, they also have been criticized for their lack of attention to the context of the behaviors assessed, as discussed in Chapter 3 of this book. - This self-report instrument may be highly influenced by social desirability.

Instrument Name and Source	*Construct(s) Designed to Assess*	*Number of Items; Sample Item(s)*	*Reliability and Validity Information*	*Strengths of Instrument for Clinical Practice*	*Limitations of Instrument for Clinical Practice*
Instruments for Assessing the Child Victim					
Children's Abuse-Specific Perceptions (CASP; Kolko et al., 2002)	The CASP assesses the perceptions that a child holds toward a specific experience of maltreatment.	16 items; Sample item: "I think that the person who abused me did this … (with the following response options: by accident, somewhat accidental, somewhat on purpose, and on purpose") (Kolko et al., 2002, p. 44)	- The CASP has not been subjected to rigorous psychometric evaluation.	- The instrument was developed with input from practitioners.	- There is no clear standard for scoring and interpreting the CASP.
Children's Impact of Traumatic Events Scale-Revised (CITES-R, Chaffin & Shultz, 2001)	The CITES-R is a child-report instrument that assesses PTSD, sexualization, and mediating factors in relation to child sexual abuse.	78 items with 11 subscales: Intrusive Thoughts, Avoidance, Hyperarousal, Sexual Anxiety, Eroticism, Self-blame and Guilt, Empowerment, Personal Vulnerability, Dangerous World, Negative Reactions by Others, and Social Support.	The mean Cronbach's alpha coefficient for the subscales was a = .69. Some evidence supports the instrument's construct validity.	- The CITES-R is easy to administer. - The CITES-R assesses multiple domains of interest (i.e., PTSD, attributions) at once and therefore may prove more useful than combining separate instruments for each of these variables.	- The CITES-R is in need of further investigation into its psychometric properties. Some of the subscales demonstrate especially weak psychometric properties.

(*continued*)

APPENDIX Continued

Instrument Name and Source	*Construct(s) Designed to Assess*	*Number of Items; Sample Item(s)*	*Reliability and Validity Information*	*Strengths of Instrument for Clinical Practice*	*Limitations of Instrument for Clinical Practice*
Inventory for Assessing Maslow's Needs in Children (Harper et al., 2003)	This inventory is designed to assess the needs of a child based on Maslow's hierarchy of human needs.	16 items: Sample item: "Does the child have an adequate home or adequate shelter for living?" (Harper et al., 2003, p. 18).	No psychometric information is available about this inventory.	- This inventory can alert the therapist to basic needs of a child that may not be met. These basic needs may need to be met before the child is able to address higher-order concerns in counseling. - The inventory is brief and easy to complete.	- This inventory lacks a solid research basis.
Modified Child Sexual Behavior Inventory-II (Modified CSBI-II; Merrick et al., 2008)	The Modified CSBI-II assesses problematic sexualized behaviors in children.	25 items with five subscales; Sexual Knowledge, Sexual Intrusiveness, Boundary Problems, Displaying Private Parts, and Sexual Interest; Sample item from Sexual Intrusiveness subscale: "Imitates acts of sexual intercourse" (Merrick et al., 2008, p. 125).	Subscale Cronbach's alpha coefficients ranged from a = .43 to a = .75, demonstrating mixed support for subscale internal consistency.	- The Modified CSBI-II is based on a preexisting measure. - The behaviorally-specific items are useful for providing an objective assessment of sexualized behaviors in children. - The Modified CSBI-II may be useful for identifying patterns of sexualized behaviors and differentiating those patterns from developmentally-appropriate sexual exploration.	- The instrument's clinical utility is in need of further investigation.

Instrument Name and Source	*Construct(s) Designed to Assess*	*Number of Items; Sample Item(s)*	*Reliability and Validity Information*	*Strengths of Instrument for Clinical Practice*	*Limitations of Instrument for Clinical Practice*
Social Behavior Inventory (SBI; Gully, 2001)	The SBI was developed to assess social behaviors among children who are participating in treatment related to child abuse.	30 items with five subscales: Aversive-Miscommunication, Prosocial-Genuine, Aversive Insensitive, Prosocial-Direct, and Aversive-Argumentative (Note: No sample items were identified in Gully, 2001).	Subscale Cronbach's alpha coefficients ranged from $a = .72$ to .86. There is some evidence for the test-retest reliability and validity of the SBI.	- The SBI can be completed by parents or therapists to rate the children being assessed. - The SBI is brief and easy to administer. - The SBI addresses both positive and negative behaviors.	- Additional research is needed to provide more information about the psychometric properties of the SBI.
Trauma Symptom Checklist for Children (TSCC; originally constructed by Briere, 1996, as cited in Sadowski & Friedrich, 2000)	The TSCC assesses responses to traumatic events among youth between the ages of 8 and 15.	54 items with six clinical subscales: Anger, Sexual Concerns, Anxiety, Posttraumatic Stress, Dissociation, Depression, and Anger.	Subscale internal consistency coefficients range from $a = .71$ to .91, with the total scale coefficient of a - .97.	- The TSCC is relatively brief. - The TSCC addresses sexuality-related impacts of trauma.	- The age range for which this instrument is appropriate may not meet the needs of all clinical populations.

(*continued*)

APPENDIX Continued

Instrument Name and Source	*Construct(s) Designed to Assess*	*Number of Items; Sample Item(s)*	*Reliability and Validity Information*	*Strengths of Instrument for Clinical Practice*	*Limitations of Instrument for Clinical Practice*
Weekly Problems Scale—Child Version (WPSC) and Weekly Problems Scale—Parent Version (WPSP) (Sawyer et al., 2006)	The WPS is designed to assess problematic behaviors among children in treatment for sexual abuse.	**WPSC**: 11 items with three factors: Negative Moods and Behaviors, Problem Peer and Parental Interactions, and Self-Esteem; **WPSP**: 15 items with four factors: Problem Behaviors, Parenting and Family Problems, Sex and Sexual Abuse Communication Issues, and Negative Moods (Sample item: "During the past 7 days my child appeared unhappy, sad, or depressed;" Sawyer et al., 2006, p. 38).	There is evidence for the internal consistency (WPSP total scale $a = .86$; WPSC total scale $a = .79$), temporal stability ($r = .88$ across one to three sessions and $r = .72$ across 10 to 11 sessions), and construct validity of the WPSC and WPSP.	- An advantage of these scales is that they address both the child's and parents' perspectives about the child's behaviors. - The scales are relatively brief and easy to administer and score. - The WPSC and WPSP show promising for measuring clients' progress over time.	- The instrument was tested on a sample of children and adolescents between the ages of 6 and 17, so the applicability with children of other ages remains uncertain.

Instrument Name and Source	*Construct(s) Designed to Assess*	*Number of Items; Sample Item(s)*	*Reliability and Validity Information*	*Strengths of Instrument for Clinical Practice*	*Limitations of Instrument for Clinical Practice*
Instruments for Assessing the Non-offending Parent and General Family Functioning					
Home Observation for Measurement of the Environment Inventory (HOME; Bradley et al., 1988; Linver et al., 2004)	The HOME assesses a child's home environment, particular in the areas of emotional support and cognitive stimulation.	The number of items and subscales varies based on the age level of the child being assessed, but all versions contain between 45 and 60 items; A sample item is as follows: "Parent spontaneously praises child at least twice during visit" (Linver et al., 2004; p. 101).	The HOME subscales were derived through factor analysis. The different forms of the HOME have been subject to analysis of their psychometric properties and found to be acceptable.	- The home is a semi-structured interview format, meaning that it could be integrated into the therapy process. - There are multiple forms of the HOME for different age levels, including infancy and toddlers, up to early adolescence. - The HOME uses both parental self-report and direct observation, such that it overcomes limitations of using each of these approaches on its own.	- Administration of the HOMC takes about one hour, which may be impractical for clinical use.

(*continued*)

APPENDIX Continued

Instrument Name and Source	*Construct(s) Designed to Assess*	*Number of Items; Sample Item(s)*	*Reliability and Validity Information*	*Strengths of Instrument for Clinical Practice*	*Limitations of Instrument for Clinical Practice*
Parenting Stress Index—Short Form (PSI-SF; Abidin, 1995; Haskett et al., 2006)	The PSI-SF assesses distress related to the parenting role and problematic parent-child interactions.	36 items. The original scale had three subscales (Parental Distress, Parent-Child Dysfunctional Interaction, and Difficult Child), but subsequent testing by Haskett et al. revealed two stable subscales (i.e., Parent Domain and Child Domain). Sample item: "My efforts for child aren't appreciated" (Haskett et al., 2006, p. 307).	There is some evidence for the reliability and validity of the PSI-SF. However, the underlying factor structure appears to be in need of additional refinement.	- The instrument is brief and easy to administer. - The PSI-SF addresses different domains of parenting stress that may be relevant to clinical practice with families in which maltreatment has occurred.	- The subscale structure is in need of further investigation, so currently it may be most prudent to use the instrument in its total scale.

Instrument Name and Source	*Construct(s) Designed to Assess*	*Number of Items; Sample Item(s)*	*Reliability and Validity Information*	*Strengths of Instrument for Clinical Practice*	*Limitations of Instrument for Clinical Practice*
Adult Adolescent Parenting Inventory—2 (AAPI-2, Originally developed by Bavolek & Keene, 1999, as cited in Conners et al., 2006)	The AAPI-2 is designed to measure a parent's potential for perpetrating child abuse or neglect.	40 items with five subscales: Inappropriate Expectations of Children; Parental Lack of Empathy toward Children; Belief in Corporal Punishment for Discipline; Reversing Parent-Child Roles; and Oppressing Children's Power and Independence. A sample item from the "Role Reversal" subscale is "Children should offer comfort when their parents are sad" (p. 47).	The full scale internal consistency coefficient was a = .85, and subscale coefficients ranged from a = .50 to .79 (Conners et al., 2006*).	- The AAPI-2 is relatively brief and easy to administer. - Two forms are available to increase the utility as a pretest-posttest measure in clinical practice.	- The factor/subscale structure of the instrument remains in question due to some conflicting findings from different analyses.

(continued)

APPENDIX Continued

Instrument Name and Source	*Construct(s) Designed to Assess*	*Number of Items; Sample Item(s)*	*Reliability and Validity Information*	*Strengths of Instrument for Clinical Practice*	*Limitations of Instrument for Clinical Practice*
Child Abuse Potential Inventory (CAPI; Milner, 1986, cited in Begle et al., 2010; McNary & Black, 2003; and Walker & Davies, 2010)	The CAPI is a self-report instrument that assesses for risk factors for child abuse perpetration.	160 items, with a primary Abuse Risk Scale with 77 items that contains six sub-scales (Distress, Rigidity, Unhappiness; Problems with the Child and Self; Problems with Family; and Problems from Others). Sample item: "I always try to check on my child when it's crying" (Ondersma, Chaffin, Mullins, & LeBreton, 2005, p. 302).	The CAPI has demonstrated good internal consistency, test-retest reliability, test-retest reliability, construct validity, and concurrent validity across a number of studies. The instrument's predictive validity remains unclear (McNary & Black, 2003; Walker & Davies, 2010).	- The CAPI may be useful for identifying risk factors that can become a focus point for clinical interventions. - The length of the CAPI may be burdensome for clinical practice. However, a brief, 24-item version of the CAPI is available (Ondersma et al., 2005). - The CAPI has been studied extensively and is used widely in clinical settings (Walker & Davies, 2010).	- The CAPI is certainly not a fail-proof way to predict future child maltreatment perpetration. - The instrument may misclassify some respondents as 'at-risk' or 'not at-risk' when in fact they fall into the other category.

Instrument Name and Source	*Construct(s) Designed to Assess*	*Number of Items; Sample Item(s)*	*Reliability and Validity Information*	*Strengths of Instrument for Clinical Practice*	*Limitations of Instrument for Clinical Practice*
Parental Empathy Measure (PEM; Kilpatrick, 2005)	The PEM is a semi-structured interview that assesses four aspects of parental empathy toward one's child: attending to the child's emotional responses, making accurate attributions about the child, having a positive emotional response to the child, and having a helpful behavioral response.	The PEM includes four sections: (1) a demographic questionnaire, (2) a beliefs section with 13 items about parenting and children, (3) 10 parenting scenarios, about which the respondent is asked to indicate how s/he would be likely to respond, and (4) open-ended questions about various background experiences. A "Faking Good" social desirability scale also is included.	There is evidence that the PEM demonstrates good internal consistency (with subscale coefficients ranging from $a = .73$ to .93), interrater reliability, and construct and concurrent validity.	- The PEM includes both qualitative and quantitative data to provide a comprehensive description of the parent's experience of empathy. - The PEM's "Faking Good" scale is useful for detecting malingering.	- Additional research is needed to examine how parental empathy is linked to child maltreatment outcomes.

8

THERAPY TO ADDRESS CHILD MALTREATMENT

Therapy clients may be impacted by child maltreatment in a variety of ways, as victims, survivors (which we address in Chapter 9), and/or perpetrators. Due to the complicated experiences of these clients, therapists may feel challenged personally and professionally in their work with them. However, therapists have an opportunity to help victims and survivors process and heal from their experiences of victimization. Likewise, therapists may be able to help perpetrators accept responsibility for their abusive behaviors and stop future abuse. Therefore, the potential impact of this therapeutic work is great. We begin this chapter by discussing general considerations for clinical work with clients impacted by child maltreatment. We then move to reviewing several theory- and research-based interventions that have been outlined in the literature, focusing on interventions for victims, family members, and perpetrators.

General Treatment Considerations

Determine Treatment Plans based on the Assessment Outcomes. Treatment for victims and perpetrators should be tailored to the unique client needs identified through the assessment (Herschell, Calzada, Eyberg, & McNeil, 2002; Horton & Cruise, 1997; Locke & Newcomb, 2003; Saxe, Ellis, Fogler, Hansen, & Sorkin, 2005). Therapy should build on existing supportive resources and social support (Haugaard, 2004). Assessment should be ongoing throughout treatment (Horton & Cruise, 1997), so new information can guide treatment decisions at all phases of therapy. Assessment information can help therapists decide when the client has met treatment goals and is ready to terminate therapy (Horton & Cruise, 1997). The assessment process also can help identify clients' unique developmental needs and characteristics that may influence treatment, potentially including their cognitive abilities (Allin, Wathen, & MacMillan, 2005). Treatment also should be consistent with a client's cultural and religious/spiritual background (Nelson, Laurendeau, & Chamberland, 2001; Walker, Reese, Hughes, & Troskie, 2010).

Children's needs should be assessed and guide treatment, and treatment should focus on the most basic level of needs (e.g., food, clothing, shelter) before moving on to higher-order issues (Harper, Harper, & Stills, 2003). Maslow's hierarchy of human needs provides a useful framework for considering a child's current level of needs (Harper et al., 2003). Children and their families should be connected to outside resources—such as medical or parental substance abuse treatment—as needed (Cohen, Mannarino, Murray, & Igelman, 2006). This is true both during and after treatment, such that families may need additional support once they complete their participation in a formal intervention program but still have needs that place them at risk of further maltreatment (Staudt, Scheuler-Whitaker, & Hinterlong, 2001). Even children demonstrating relatively minimal symptoms may benefit from receiving education about abuse and resources available to support them (Hebert, Parent, Daignault, & Tourigny, 2006).

Therapy should be Coordinated with Broader Child Maltreatment Response Systems. Effective coordination of services for maltreated children should promote more effective and less restrictive services (Ruffolo, Evans, & Lukens, 2003). Ideally, all systems working to protect children from new or recurring maltreatment strive to meet the needs of children, strengthen families, and be responsive to children's cultural backgrounds (Ruffolo et al., 2003). Therapy treatment plans may need to be developed with consideration of requirements of other agencies involved in clients' lives. For example, when working with CPS-involved clients, treatment plans should reflect stated goals in the CPS case plan and the required time-lines for meeting those goals (Kerwin, 2005; McAlpine, Marshall, & Doran, 2001).

Provide a Safe Context for Exploring the Maltreatment-related Trauma. A therapist's office may prove to be a relatively safe context for a child compared to the negative environment in which he or she lives (Saxe et al., 2005). Positive rapport between the therapist and client is essential for effective treatment with children who have been traumatized (Feather & Ronan, 2006). However, due to impaired attachment functioning that may result from maltreatment, therapists may find it difficult to establish rapport with child maltreatment victims early in therapy (Haugaard, 2004). Some clients feel more comfortable with a therapist of a particular gender, although definitive rules cannot be made in this regard (Moon, Wagner, & Kazelskis, 2000).

Therapists should be sensitive to the shame a child may be feeling related to the abuse (Deblinger & Runyon, 2005). To help minimize this shame, therapists can discuss experiences openly, match the client's language, and display comfort in talking about abuse (Deblinger & Runyon, 2005). In addition, therapists can invite clients to share their experiences through different forms of expression (e.g., writing, art, and talking) so that children can express themselves in ways that are comfortable to them (Deblinger & Runyon, 2005). A key question to consider is the level of detail a child needs to share about his/her abuse experiences in order for treatment to be effective (Jones & Morris, 2007). Jones and Morris suggest that, although retelling the story of maltreatment in therapy can be healing for some clients, this is not necessary for all clients. Thus, some clients may be able to be helped without recounting their abuse, and therapists should respect this decision when it is appropriate.

Finally, termination should be handled sensitively, in that it may be experienced as very stressful (Deblinger & Runyon, 2005). Some clients may even feel a sense of abandonment. Thus, it may be useful to begin to discuss termination a few sessions prior to it and to plan a celebration of the client's progress in the final session (Deblinger & Runyon, 2005).

Attend to Safety Issues Throughout. Some unique aspects of safety planning with children who have been traumatized include helping them learn how to label, identify, and express their feelings, educating them about how to report any future abuse, learning to be alert to potential warning signs of unsafe situations, and role playing safety strategies (Walker et al., 2010). Another aspect of promoting the child's safety may be to report newly revealed incidents of abuse that arise during treatment (Vickerman & Margolin, 2007).

One way for a therapist to promote a safe context for therapy is to allow the client to move at his/her own pace (Cash & Snow, 2001). The pace can be influenced by the timing of therapy in relation to the abuse, the extent to which the child has internal coping resources, other stressors the child faces, general family functioning, parental support, the strength of the child's relationship with the therapist, and the overall level of social support (Crenshaw & Hardy, 2007).

Therapists also must consider how the work they do in session may relate to the child's safety needs outside of the session (Saxe et al., 2005). These environmental safety needs may be especially pronounced if the child does not live in a safe home or community (Saxe et al., 2005). For example, children's trauma symptoms may be triggered by negative experiences in their environment, such as neighborhood violence (Saxe et al., 2005).

Conduct Home-based Therapy Safely. Home visitations are frequently used in the treatment of children who have been maltreated (Naughton & Heath, 2001; Nelson et al., 2001; Ruffolo et al., 2003; Thomlison, 2003). Therapists must be conscientious of their own and their clients' safety when conducting home-based therapy. Children who have experienced trauma often live in unsafe environments that are characterized by numerous potential risks, such as parental substance abuse, poverty, and community violence (Saxe et al., 2005). Therefore, therapists are encouraged to take precautionary steps to promote their safety when working with clients in their homes, such as traveling with a colleague, ensuring that a supervisor knows where the therapist is, carrying a mobile phone, and identifying quick exit routes from the home. Other treatment settings may include the school (including preschool) and other community settings (Murphy, Rosenheck, Berkowitz, & Marans, 2005; Thomlison, 2003). Therapists should be mindful of safety considerations across any of these settings.

Theory- and Research-Based Therapy Approaches for Victims

A broad range of theory- and research-based approaches have been proposed for working with child maltreatment victims. In this section, we propose general suggestions for clinical work with this population, review existing research limitations and findings, and describe several specific approaches that have been developed. Clinical interventions with child maltreatment victims should be grounded in a strong conceptual and/or research foundation (Thomlison, 2003). Approaches that build on the client's family resources, when family involvement is appropriate, are beneficial (Thomlison, 2003). Interventions also should be of sufficient duration to meet the needs of the child, which may be extensive (Thomlison, 2003). Throughout treatment, therapists should focus on safety issues and address the clients' presenting symptoms, as well as promote positive functioning in the future (Borrego, Gutow, & Reicher, 2008). In addition, interventions should be culturally- and gender-responsive (Gershater-Molko, Lutzker, & Sherman, 2002; Graves, 2007; Graves, Frabutt, & Kaslow, 2010). As appropriate, treatment should address community-level and social issues contributing to child maltreatment and further negative outcomes from it (e.g., poverty, unsafe neighborhoods) (Lutzker, Tymchuk, & Bigelow, 2001; Nelson et al., 2001; Saxe et al., 2005; Thomlison, 2003; Toth & Cichetti, 2006).

Many questions remain about the appropriate duration, frequency, and content of therapy (Nurcombe, Woodling, Marrington, Bickman, & Roberts, 2000). Typically, the length of treatment lasts from about two months to two years (Thomlison, 2003). Lengthier treatment may be associated with better outcomes (Schewe, 2008). Regarding the timing of the interventions in relation to the maltreatment, earlier interventions have a greater potential for effectively helping a child victim (Toth & Cichetti, 2006; Wolfe, Crooks, Chiodo, & Jaffe, 2009).

Treatment Modalities

A number of treatment formats have been used with victims of child maltreatment. Two of the most common approaches are individual therapy and group therapy (Cash & Snow, 2001; Nurcombe et al., 2000; Schewe, 2008). Group therapy may be especially helpful for children to begin to understand that they are not alone (Jones, 2002), although the modality may be difficult for children who are uncomfortable in social interactions (Vickerman & Margolin, 2007). Thus, it is important that children receive an orientation to the group so that they will know what to expect (Schewe, 2008). Some scholars assert that group therapy may be more effective than individual (Nurcombe et al., 2000). However, Nolan et al. (2002) compared individual therapy alone with combined individual and group therapy for child sexual abuse victims and found that both approaches were effective, with no significant difference between the groups.

Other modalities that have been used with victims include the following, either alone or in some combination (Nurcombe et al., 2000; Thomlison, 2003): (a) therapeutic day care (MacMillan, 2000); (b) play therapy (Cash & Snow, 2001; Crenshaw & Hardy, 2007; Jones, 2002; Nurcombe et al., 2000; Schewe, 2008); (c) psychoeducation (Schewe, 2008); (d) support groups (Schewe, 2008); (e) multiple-family groups (Schewe, 2008); (f) case management (Schewe, 2008); (g) family support services (Schewe, 2008); (h) family therapy (Cash & Snow, 2001; Nurcombe et al., 2000); (i) early intervention foster care (Thomlison, 2003); (j) parent education program (Thomlison, 2003); (k) peer-mediated treatment to promote social integration (Fantuzzo, Manz, & Atkins, 2005; Mathews, Fawcett, & Sheldon, 2009); (l) role-play (Taban & Lutzker, 2001); (m) exposure-based interventions that view the re-exposure process as important to helping the child to reduce distress related to the trauma and to help the child develop new understanding of his or her experiences (Vickerman & Margolin, 2007); and (n) psychopharmacological interventions (Cohen, Berliner, & Mannarino, 2003). In addition to community agencies and other traditional clinical settings, therapeutic interventions may be delivered in other settings, such as domestic violence shelters (Vickerman & Margolin, 2007) and schools (Brassard, Rivelis, & Diaz, 2009; Mishna, 2007).

Topics Addressed in Treatment

In general, treatment should focus on changeable aspects of the child's life (Nurcombe et al., 2000). In addition, abuse-specific interventions may be more effective than more general counseling approaches to address the unique needs of children who have been maltreated (Saywitz, Mannarino, Berliner, & Cohen, 2000). Some commonly addressed topics in therapy with child maltreatment victims include the following:

Client Safety. An important topic to address is the safety of the child (Adams, 2006; Kenny, 2009). Interventions may specifically aim to increase the child's safety skills (Schewe, 2008; Skowron & Reinemann, 2005), including learning to identify when they may be in a potential unsafe situation and how to get out (Deblinger & Runyon, 2005), safety planning (Lewin & Bergin, 2001), addressing safety risks in the child's home (Taban & Lutzker, 2001), and ensuring that the child has needed health care services (Taban & Lutzker, 2001).

The Trauma of Maltreatment. Treatment may focus directly on the trauma of maltreatment and provide a forum for victims to retell the story and process their thoughts and feelings (Schewe, 2008; Skowron & Reinemann, 2005). Trauma-focused therapy may involve education about abuse (Deblinger & Runyon, 2005; Schewe, 2008; Skowron & Reinemann, 2005), including the dynamics of maltreatment, symptoms following abuse, and coping skills (Vickerman & Margolin, 2007).

Trauma-focused treatment also may allow the child to process events that occurred after the abuse (Nurcombe et al., 2000), such as CPS involvement and investigation-related interviewing (Finkelhor, 2009), as well as family members' responses and support (Liefer, Kilbane, & Grossman, 2001). Other therapeutic elements that may be addressed during trauma-focused treatment include levels of support from parents, parents blaming the children for being abused, and the child blaming him- or herself for the abuse (Nurcombe et al., 2000). Therapists also may help the child process the manner in which his or her disclosure of abuse was received, especially if this disclosure was not believed by significant others (Freeman & Morris, 2001).

Beyond the maltreatment they experienced, clients may need to address other forms of victimization (Cohen et al., 2006). For example, children may also have experienced abuse perpetrated by adults who are not family members (e.g., a neighbor, friend of the family, clergy person, or stranger; Grosz, Kempe, & Kelly, 2000; Jones & Morris, 2007). Ultimately, a goal of trauma-focused treatment is to help the child identify, understand, and integrate their traumatic experiences into their life stories without being dictated, or impaired, by them (Adams, 2006; Crenshaw & Hardy, 2007). By doing so, children begin to reclaim their empowerment, choice, and control over their lives, which are all key aspects of trauma-informed care.

Managing Symptoms. Another potential focus is to reduce mental health symptoms (Maniglio, 2009), such as anxiety, fear, depression, other mood problems, and/or PTSD (Cohen et al., 2006; Finkelhor, 2009; Schewe, 2008; Skowron & Reinemann, 2005). Often, these may manifest as somatic complaints (e.g., stomachaches), trouble sleeping, trouble concentrating, or agitated behaviors. It is important that therapists understand these symptoms, particularly when making differential diagnoses such as PTSD versus attention deficit-hyperactivity disorder (AD/HD), oppositional defiant disorder (ODD), and other childhood behavioral disorders.

Clients' Cognitions. Therapy may focus on changing maladaptive thinking patterns, perceptions, and attributions that increase distress (Kolko, Brown, & Berliner, 2002). In particular, therapists may work with clients to reduce their sense of self-blame (Finkelhor, 2009; Nelson et al., 2001; Schewe, 2008) and shame (Deblinger & Runyon, 2005). This may be achieved through cognitive restructuring (Kolko, Cohen, Mannarino, Baumann, & Knudsen, 2009).

Clients' Behaviors. Therapy may address problematic behaviors the child is demonstrating (Adams, 2006; Cohen et al., 2006). In particular, therapists should consider a child's intention (e.g., attention-seeking) for engaging in behaviors that may be viewed as problematic (Cash & Snow, 2001). Equipped with this understanding, therapists may be able to help clients develop more adaptive ways of achieving their desired results.

Clients' Emotions. Therapy may provide a space for the client to process and express emotions (Nelson et al., 2001; Schewe, 2008). Through therapy, clients may learn to better regulate their emotions (Adams, 2006), such as through anger management (Schewe, 2008). In addition, therapists may help the child process ambivalent feelings toward the perpetrator, especially if the perpetrator is a family member (Celano, Hazzard, Campbell, & Lang, 2002).

Personal Resources. From a strengths-based perspective, interventions help build clients' personal protective resources. Some resources include coping skills (Merrick, Litrownik, Everson, & Cox, 2008; Skowron & Reinemann, 2005), self-esteem (Adams, 2006; Allin et al., 2005; Maniglio, 2009), problem-solving skills (Kolko et al., 2009), general life skills (Maniglio, 2009), and greater insight (Kolko et al., 2009). Therapists also may address spirituality as a potential resource to help the child make meaning of their experiences (Walker et al., 2010).

Positive Relationship Skills. Therapy can help victims develop relationship and social skills (Ruffolo et al., 2003), which can serve as protective factors and reduce the negative impact of the abuse (Cox, Kotch, & Everson, 2003). These include communication skills (Kenny, 2009), learning to more accurately recognize the emotions of others (Sullivan, Bennett, Carpenter, & Lewis, 2008), understanding "safe touching" and appropriate physical affection, and helping children understand the difference between privacy and secrecy (Crenshaw & Hardy, 2007).

Social Support. A goal of therapy may be to increase the child's available social support (MacMillan, 2000). This may be achieved through enhancing the child's attachment relationships with others (Adams, 2006), connecting clients to community resources (Haeseler, 2006), and promoting positive change in the child's social environment (Mishna, 2007).

Parent and Family Concerns. Therapy may address parenting deficiencies in order to increase child functioning and decrease the likelihood of the child being removed from the home (Thomlison, 2003), thereby reducing additional transitions for the child. Parenting and family-related concerns that may be addressed include parenting skills (MacMillan, 2000), reducing family conflict (Kolko et al., 2009), promoting an appropriate family hierarchy (Kolko et al., 2009), and strengthening parent-child bonding (Taban & Lutzker, 2001).

Sexuality. Clients may benefit from interventions that address sexuality concerns (Skowron & Reinemann, 2005), especially when the maltreatment was sexual abuse or when the client demonstrates sexual acting out behaviors. Clients may benefit from learning sexuality-related language and terms to communicate about their maltreatment experiences (Kenny, 2009).

Termination. At the end of treatment, the focus may shift to a positive and smooth termination. Because the end of the therapeutic relationship may be very difficult for the child, the therapist should give special care to addressing issues that arise related to therapy termination (Schewe, 2008). Some therapists find it useful to implement post-treatment booster sessions in which the child and family return after a designated period of time for additional support.

General Research on Child Maltreatment Interventions

Increasingly, therapists are called upon to deliver interventions that are grounded in research that supports their effectiveness (Dufour & Chamberland, 2004). However, child maltreatment interventions are relatively understudied (Lutzker et al., 2001). More research has been done on interventions addressing physical and sexual abuse or neglect as compared to those that target psychological abuse (Allin et al., 2005; Dufour & Chamberland, 2004; Gershater-Molko et al., 2002; James & Mennen, 2001; Toth & Cichetti, 2006). Methodologically strong studies are difficult to design and conduct (Lutzker et al., 2001). Five common limitations in existing research include a failure to distinguish among subtypes of abuse, lack of attention to the heterogeneity of the population, minimal attention paid to the context surrounding maltreatment, high attrition, and lack of follow-up studies to determine the persistence of treatment gains over time (James & Mennen, 2001). Thus, a gap persists between research and practice in the area of child maltreatment interventions (James & Mennen, 2001; Kolko et al., 2009). Programs that have some empirical support for their efficacy often lack evidence that they may be applied effectively in the community (Nurcombe et al., 2000).

Despite this gap, a number of evidence-based approaches to working with maltreated children exist, and therapists should take care to ensure that appropriate treatments are selected based on the clients' needs and backgrounds (Brassard et al., 2009; Chaffin & Friedrich, 2004). Generally speaking, existing research suggests that therapeutic approaches promote positive outcomes in clients who have experienced child maltreatment, although much more research is needed in this area (James & Mennen, 2001). Skowron and Reinemann (2005) conducted a meta-analysis of research studies published between 1974 and 2000 on psychological treatment for child maltreatment. The results suggest that clients participating in child or family therapy to address child maltreatment fared better than about 70% of those with similar experiences but who were not treated. Thus, in general, therapy appears to be beneficial for most clients impacted by child maltreatment. Therapists are encouraged to put in place systems to monitor the effectiveness of the interventions they use with this population (Thomlison, 2003), such as by regularly assessing the target symptoms for changes throughout the therapeutic process.

Individual Approaches to Therapy with Child Maltreatment Victims

A range of approaches have been used with maltreated children, including cognitive-behavioral, child-parent psychotherapy, behavioral therapy, play therapy (Cohen et al., 2006; Mishna, 2007), psychodynamic, nondirective supportive therapy (Brown, 2005), solution-focused, and narrative therapies (Myers, McLaughlin, & Warwick, 2003). In this section, we summarize some approaches that have been described in greater detail in the existing literature.

Cognitive-Behavioral Therapy (CBT). The most available research evidence supports the use of CBT with this population because of its direct ability to impact the child's experience of trauma (Dufour & Chamberland, 2004; Nurcombe et al., 2000; Ross & O'Carroll, 2004; Runyon, Deblinger, Ryan, & Thakkar-Kolar, 2004; Saywitz et al., 2000; Skowron & Reinemann, 2005). However, the preponderance of support for CBT may not necessarily reflect its superiority over other approaches, but may simply reflect that these models are more amenable to empirical research and thus have been studied more extensively (Saywitz et al., 2000). Commonly used CBT strategies include promoting emotional expression, correcting cognitive distortions, psychoeducation, stress and anger management training, gradual exposure to traumatic material, and teaching behavioral skills (Ross & O'Carroll, 2004; Runyon et al., 2004).

As one example of a CBT approach, Deblinger, Stauffer, and Steer (2001) compared structured CBT groups and supportive self-help groups for young children who had been sexually abused and their non-offending caregivers. The focus of the parents' CBT groups was on coping skills, parent education, and behavior management skills, and the focus of the children's CBT groups was on communication about feelings, acceptable and unacceptable forms of touch, and abuse response skills. The supportive groups were relatively unstructured and followed a more self-help model. Overall, the clients who participated in the CBT groups demonstrated more positive outcomes than those in the supportive groups.

Attribution Retraining. One type of cognitive restructuring that may be used with maltreated children is called attribution retraining. Attribution retraining aims to help the child move from blaming him/herself for the abuse to appropriately attribute responsibility for it to the perpetrator (Celano et al., 2002). These techniques first focus on examining and then modifying the child's irrational beliefs about the abuse and self-blame (Celano et al., 2002). Attribution retraining examines different aspects of self-blame, which may include feeling at fault for stopping the abuse, not asking for help, experiencing some pleasure for it (especially if the abuse was sexual), not protecting siblings who also may have been abused, or causing problems in the family as a result of disclosing abuse (Celano et al., 2002). Specific techniques that may be included in attribution retraining include keeping a thought record, challenging negative thoughts, using the Socratic Method, educating clients about common attributions, therapeutic story-telling, and reminding the child that s/he is not to blame (Celano et al., 2002). Attribution training may be a primary focus of treatment or may occur in a broader context for therapy (Celano et al., 2002). Despite the common use of attribution retraining, limited research is available to determine the extent to which it is effective (Celano et al., 2002).

Trauma-Focused CBT. Trauma-focused CBT holds promise for child victims of abuse (Williams & Herrera, 2007), especially those demonstrating PTSD symptoms (Brown, 2005). Trauma-focused CBT involves psychoeducation, reprocessing of the trauma, development of affect regulation skills, and in-vivo desensitization strategies (Cohen et al., 2006; Deblinger, Mannarino, Cohen, & Steer, 2006; Walker et al., 2010). Through trauma-focused CBT, a client develops new coping resources and relaxation strategies (Walker et al., 2010). This approach often involves the parent when appropriate, such as through parent training and conjoint sessions with the parent and child (Walker et al., 2010).

The phases of TF-CBT include strengthening the client's psychosocial resources, building coping skills, reprocessing the trauma, addressing unique concerns, and terminating (Feather & Ronan, 2006). According to Cohen et al. (2006), the TF-CBT process is reflected in the acronym, PRACTICE: Parenting Skills, Psychoeducation, Relaxation skills, Affective modulation skills, Cognitive processing, Trauma narration, In vivo desensitization, Conjoint child-parent sessions, and Enhancing safety. Parent-child sessions with the non-offending parent focus on improving communication between the parties (Cohen et al., 2006; Walker et al., 2010). Parent training emphasizes four strategies: praising the child, using selective attention, using time-out, and developing contingency reinforcements (Walker et al., 2010).

Psychoeducation includes information about abuse and its potential consequences, the client's diagnosis, and available treatment options (Walker et al., 2010). Relaxation skills that are addressed include mindfulness, meditation, and breathing exercises (Walker et al., 2010). Clients learn to express and regulate their emotions through learning to identify and express emotions (Walker et al., 2010). Other central components of TF-CBT include exposure, processing memories, and expressive techniques, including drawing and writing (Deblinger et al., 2006). Through treatment, clients retell the trauma narrative as a means of desensitizing them to their related symptoms (Walker et al., 2010). As clients tell their trauma narratives, the therapist helps them identify and restructure cognitive errors that are contributing to distress (Walker et al., 2010). TF-CBT has been shown to be superior to child-centered therapy in reducing PTSD symptoms among sexually abused children in a study of 183 children and their caregivers, and the treatment gains appeared to sustain over a one-year period (Deblinger et al., 2006).

Play Therapy. Play therapy may be used because children often lack the words to verbalize their thoughts and feelings (Crenshaw & Hardy, 2007). Through play therapy, metaphors can emerge that provide an understanding of children's inner lives (Crenshaw & Hardy, 2007). The symbolism involved in play can help children access a broader range of emotions (Crenshaw & Hardy, 2007). Play therapy also builds on children's natural needs to engage their senses (Mishna, 2007). Play therapy is especially therapeutic when done by an empathetic therapist (Crenshaw & Hardy, 2007), and parents also can be involved (Hill, 2006). Through play therapy, children can experiment with different roles in their abuse experiences in order to process and understand those experiences (Cash & Snow, 2001). For example, the child may experiment with the role of the perpetrator (Cash & Snow, 2001).

Play therapy may be conducted in groups (Jones, 2002). Jones (2002) recommends that play therapy groups for preschoolers who have been abused address the following issues. First, the groups should be small with around three to four children. Second, the children should be similar in age. Third, the group should not last long, perhaps up to 40 minutes. Fourth, toys should be selected carefully to promote the child's expression through play. Examples of potentially useful toys include telephones, puppets, and sand play. Fifth, groups can include education about relationship and self-management skills. Finally, the dynamics that arise through the group process are opportunities to address abuse-related issues and symptoms.

Creative Therapy Approaches. Children also may benefit from other creative therapy approaches, such as visual techniques, coloring pages, drama, role play, music, art therapy, and therapeutic games, and these may reach children in ways that more traditional therapies cannot (Celano et al., 2002; Ostertag, 2002; Pifalo, 2002; Pifalo, 2007; Robarts, 2006; Strehlow, 2009).

Equine-Assisted Psychotherapy. Another non-traditional approach that has been used with child maltreatment victims is equine-assisted psychotherapy (EAP; Schultz, Remick-Barlow, & Robbins, 2007). EAP allows children to interact with horses as a means of increasing self-esteem, developing their capacities for communication and relationships, learning empathy and problem-solving, and experiencing success. The child's interaction with the horses provides opportunities for children to experience and express emotions, and the therapist helps the child process and understand those emotions. Safety and body-related issues can be addressed through the child's interactions with the horses and in the outdoors environment in which EAP occurs. At the present time, only minimal evidence exists to document the effectiveness of this approach.

Adlerian Therapy. Cash and Snow (2001) suggested that Adlerian therapy is especially useful for child victims of sexual abuse. Key features of this approach include positively reframing the reason for children's problematic behaviors and helping the child shift to more adaptive behaviors. An Adlerian therapist aims to help a child overcome shame through encouragement, develop realistic goals, and adopt more positive beliefs. An important element of this approach is for the therapist to educate the client about more positive ways of being in relationships. The therapist may include play therapy, family therapy, and group therapy as a complement to the individual therapy conducted within this framework (Cash & Snow, 2001).

Peer-Mediated Programs. In light of the relational challenges that children who have been maltreated often experience, peer-mediated programs have been used to help them become better integrated in their social surroundings (Mathews et al., 2009). Mathews et al. (2009) outlined the Peer Engagement Program (PEP), which combines peer mentoring and social skills training. The PEP model uses specially trained peers who meet regularly with the client to talk, work together, or do projects together. In addition, PEP participants take part in a social skills training program that includes such skills as manners, managing conflict and anger, and engaging in conversations. In addition, participants receive a small incentive to reinforce their participation in the program. Mathews et al. studied PEP with three children, and all three demonstrated improved social functioning through their participation. Although more rigorous research is needed to determine the effectiveness of this approach, it holds promise to address the unique social interaction needs of children who have experienced maltreatment.

Trauma Systems Therapy (TST). Saxe et al. (2005) proposed Trauma Systems Therapy (TST) as a comprehensive approach to treating children who have been traumatized. This approach has a dual focus on the child's trauma symptoms, especially through emotional regulation, and social environmental factors (Saxe et al., 2005). The therapist begins by assessing the safety of the child's environment and the child's emotional regulation abilities (Saxe et al., 2005). Assessment information is used to determine which of five treatment phases (i.e., surviving, stabilizing, enduring, understanding, or transcending) a child is in currently, and a treatment plan is developed in line with the current phase (Saxe et al., 2005). From there, treatment often progresses in a nonlinear fashion as the child's needs emerge. The impact of TST was studied with a pilot sample of 61 boys and 49 girls between the ages of 5 and 20. The children who participated in TST had decreased trauma symptoms and positive changes in their social environments following treatment. Although more rigorous research is needed to examine this approach further, its unique contribution is its dual focus on the child's symptoms and the environment, and thus this approach warrants future attention by researchers and therapists.

Treatment for Specific Concerns. We conclude this section with recommendations for addressing unique concerns related to specific forms of maltreatment: neglect, sibling abuse, Munchausen by Proxy Syndrome, Reactive Attachment Disorder, and dissociative symptoms.

Neglect. Specific interventions that may benefit children and/or families who have experienced neglect include behavioral interventions (e.g., skills training), safety and hazard prevention training, strength-based approaches, and linking families to needed community resources (Gershater-Molko et al., 2002). Play therapy, therapeutic day treatment programs, and multisystemic therapy also have received empirical support for their effectiveness for treating clients impacted by child neglect (Allin et al., 2005).

Sibling Abuse. In cases of sibling abuse, Kiselica and Morrill-Richards (2007) recommend that the counseling process involve three phases. First, the therapist builds rapport with the family. Second, the therapist conducts a thorough assessment of the family environment. Third, family system-focused interventions are used to promote positive change in the family. Approaches that may prove useful include: parenting interventions to help the parents create a safe, developmentally-appropriate family context; establishing serious consequences should any future abusive behaviors continue; framing sibling abuse as a form of bullying that will not be tolerated; helping siblings develop more positive and cooperative relationships; and promoting positive relationship and problem-solving skills. A potential challenge in treating sibling abuse is that the perpetrator also may be a victim of other forms of child maltreatment, so addressing the dual issues in these dual roles can be very complicated (Caffaro & Conn-Caffaro, 2006).

Munchausen by Proxy Syndrome. Treatment for Munchausen by Proxy Syndrome should include intensive individual therapy for the offending parent, in combination with play therapy for the child and ongoing monitoring of the child's health (Siegel & Fishcher, 2001).

Reactive Attachment Disorder. Treatments for Reactive Attachment Disorder (RAD) are relatively underdeveloped (Buckner, Lopez, Dunkel, & Joiner, 2008; Hanson & Spratt, 2000), and most existing approaches lack a strong theoretical or empirical basis (Hanson & Spratt, 2000). Some existing approaches are very controversial and may carry a risk of harming a child. For example, an approach often referred to as holding therapy involves restraining a child and subjecting them to unpleasant conditions with a supposed goal of ultimately strengthening their attachment to a primary caregiver (Buckner et al., 2008; Hanson & Spratt, 2000). Evidence as to whether the risks involved in such an approach actually promote positive outcomes is currently lacking (Hanson & Spratt, 2000). Thus, we recommend that therapists use more conventional treatment approaches, including parenting education, promoting coping skills and safety, and less intrusive attachment-focused interventions (Hanson & Spratt, 2000).

Another approach that may be used effectively and safely with children with RAD is behavior management training (BMT; Buckner et al., 2008). BMT involves a manualized psychoeducational program for parents to increase parenting skills and promote positive child outcomes (Buckner et al., 2008). Although additional research is needed to examine the effectiveness of BMT with children who have been diagnosed with RAD, it holds promise as a less controversial and potentially effective approach. Children with attachment problems, such as RAD, also may benefit from structured and attachment-focused CBT (Chaffin, 2008).

Dissociative Symptoms. Treatment for dissociative symptoms may include enhancing emotional regulation and self-awareness and accepting responsibility for one's behaviors (Silberg, 2004). Treatment should focus on helping the child develop age-appropriate self-management strategies (Silberg, 2004).

Because children's experiences of dissociation may not fit neatly into diagnostic criteria, therapists can focus on addressing and reducing symptoms and promoting a positive family context to support the child's further development (Silberg, 2004).

Family-Focused Treatments for Child Maltreatment Victims

Increasingly, the importance of engaging the child's family in treatment has been recognized (Thomlison, 2003). The ultimate aims of any treatment for maltreating parents are for them to be nonviolent (Adams, 2006) and, in the case of non-offending parents, increase their ability to promote their children's safety. Families in which maltreatment has occurred may demonstrate a range of presenting concerns, including a lack of affection and support and/or high levels of control (Gold, 2008). Families with more severe and a greater number of co-occurring problems may be less likely to have positive treatment outcomes, such as reunification if the child was removed from the home (Marsh, Ryan, Choi, & Testa, 2006). Therefore, therapists should consider carefully whether family involvement is appropriate for each client.

Family approaches can occur in groups or with individual families (Runyon et al., 2004). Some applicable family-based models include behavioral therapy, cognitive-behavioral family therapy, general family systems therapy, social network therapy (Corcoran, 2000), psychoanalytic family therapy, integrative family therapy, interactional family therapy (Pardeck, 2004), strategic, solution-focused, and narrative family therapy (Price, 2004). Therapists may need to consider practical sources of support when involving family members in treatment—such as helping clients get transportation or dealing with unpredictable schedules (Hughes & Gottlieb, 2004). When conducting family therapy, it is important to provide information to the family members at the outset so that they will know what to expect from treatment, as well as to establish a collaborative relationship with other involved professionals (Pardeck, 2004). In addition to approaches involving parents, siblings also may be included when appropriate, and this can offer many potential practical and therapeutic advantages (Baker, Tanis, & Rice, 2001).

Family therapy may be useful when the family is dealing with the initial experiences following recent disclosure of maltreatment (Price, 2004). Family approaches also may be beneficial when the family is moving toward reunification if the child was removed from the home (e.g., placed in foster care) due to maltreatment (Price, 2004). Reunification generally should occur only after the abuser has accepted responsibility for the abuse, the family has reached a stable environment, and the victim desires that reunification occur (Price, 2004). Currently, there is minimal research evidence to suggest therapy practices in reunification processes (Saywitz et al., 2000). However, some interventions that may prove useful include the abuser writing a sincere apology letter to the child, reorganizing the family structure, promoting positive communication within the family, linking the family to a wider social network, planning a celebration to mark the reunification, safety planning, and relapse prevention planning (Price, 2004). If appropriate, a therapy session may serve as a forum for the perpetrator to apologize to the victim and other family members who have been impacted (Nelson et al., 2001).

In the remainder of this section, we provide a brief review of several specific approaches to family-based intervention for child maltreatment victims and their caregivers.

Attachment-focused Interventions. Attachment-focused interventions are becoming increasingly common and aim to promote a more secure attachment between the caregiver and child (Bacon & Richardson, 2001). Some points of focus in attachment-focused interventions include improving parenting behaviors, addressing parents' inner working models of relationships, changing maternal attributions of child behavior, and positive communication skills training (Lewin & Bergin, 2001).

Family Preservation Services. A range of services fall under the heading of *family preservation services* (Dufour & Chamberland, 2004; Littell, 2001). Generally, family preservation services are designed to keep children in families at risk of maltreatment in their homes and to improve the conditions of their home lives so that the risks are reduced and protective factors are increased. Ideally, the therapist or case manager works collaboratively with the family to develop an individualized treatment plan that outlines treatment goals and the responsibilities of each party involved (Littell, 2001). When families are involved in treatment planning, they are more likely to comply with treatment and correspondingly are more likely to experience positive outcomes (Littell, 2001). Current research provides only mixed support for the effectiveness of family preservation services (Dufour & Chamberland, 2004).

Filial Relationship Enhancement Therapy. A form of family-based play therapy is Filial Relationship Enhancement therapy (Ginsberg, 2002). In this approach, parents are instructed to engage in play therapy sessions in their homes. The therapist trains the parent(s) how to conduct these sessions and then provides support throughout the process. The parent is viewed as the primary change agent, which builds on the child's natural existing support system. Booster sessions occur once formal treatment has been completed. Filial therapy also has applications for children who have been maltreated and are currently in adoptive or foster homes.

Multisystemic Therapy (MST). MST is an intensive, family-based treatment that may be used with families of victims of child maltreatment (Finkelhor,

2009; Thomlison, 2003). MST views behavior as the result of influences from various interconnected systems, including families, peers, and the community (Locke & Newcomb, 2003). Issues addressed in MST include parenting, peer relationships, and academic functioning (Finkelhor, 2009).

Parent-Child Interaction Therapy (PCIT). PCIT holds promise for children who have experienced family violence due to its emphasis on improving the parent-child relationship (Borrego et al., 2008; Hakman, Chaffin, Funderburk, & Silovsky, 2009; Herschell et al., 2002; Herschell & McNeil, 2005). This may especially be true in cases in which a child witnessed parental IPV (Borrego et al., 2008). PCIT is a behavioral treatment that focuses on helping parents address problematic behaviors of young children between two and seven years old (Borrego et al., 2008). PCIT typically lasts between 10 to 14 sessions (Herschell & McNeil, 2005). A dual focus is to reduce negative and increase positive parenting behaviors (Hakman et al., 2009), and PCIT occurs in two phases: Child-Directed Interaction and Parent-Directed Interaction (CDI and PDI, respectively; Herschell et al., 2002; Herschell & McNeil, 2005).

Through PCIT, a parent learns skills to enhance the parent-child relationship, such as positive reinforcement, play, and discipline (Borrego et al., 2008; Chaffin et al., 2004). For example, a parent may learn how to give children specific, positive directions related to disciplinary issues (Hakman et al., 2009). The therapist coaches the parent through learning these skills, and skills are practiced in session (Chaffin et al., 2004; Hakman et al., 2009; Herschell & McNeil, 2005). Other issues that can be addressed through PCIT include aggressive behaviors, attachment problems, unemotional parenting, and nurturing (Borrego et al., 2008). PCIT is promising for helping parents become more responsive to their children's needs (Borrego et al., 2008; Hakman et al., 2009). A growing body of research supports the effectiveness of PCIT, including among physically abusive parents (Chaffin et al., 2004; Hakman et al., 2009; Herschell & McNeil, 2005; Timmer, Urquiza, Zebell, & McGrath, 2005) and among children in foster care (Timmer et al., 2006). PCIT may be made more effective if a motivational intervention is done prior to therapy, especially with families who mandated to treatment (Chaffin et al., 2004). However, this approach is not appropriate in cases in which either the parent or child demonstrates severe symptoms and/or violence is ongoing in the family (Borrego et al., 2008).

Parent Education Programs. Parent education programs are used widely in the treatment of families in which child maltreatment has occurred (Hughes & Gottlieb, 2004; Runyon et al., 2004), and there is empirical support that they can lead to positive outcomes (Hughes & Gottlieb, 2004). Parent education programs are most beneficial when combined with services for the child (Runyon et al., 2004). It is useful to gradually increase the level of parent-child interactions as the child's symptoms are reduced and the parent's skills and resources are enhanced (Runyon et al., 2004). Topics addressed in these programs fall into the following five categories.

1. *Promoting parents' strengths.* Education programs should aim to help parents increase positive resources to support healthy parenting (Thomlison, 2003) and improve family functioning (Schewe, 2008). These include enhancing social support (Schewe, 2008) and healthy habits, such as nutrition (Thomas, 2007) and time management (Pardeck, 2004).
2. *Behavioral skills.* Skills that parent education programs may address include stress management, anger management, coping skills, and communication skills (Brown, 2005; Pardeck, 2004; Runyon et al., 2004; Skowron & Reinemann, 2005; Thomas, 2007). Communication-related topics that programs may address include how parents can talk with their children about trauma and abuse (Brown, 2005) and, in cases of child sexual abuse, how to better communicate about sexuality and sex (Kenny, 2009).
3. *Improving parenting competence* (Nelson et al., 2001). A primary focus is to help parents become better equipped to manage the demands of parenting. Relevant topics include general parenting skills and information (McDaniel & Dillenburger, 2007; Ruffolo et al., 2003), child development (Kerwin, 2005; Nelson et al., 2001; Schewe, 2008; Thomas, 2007), discipline (Thomas, 2007) and behavior management strategies (especially related to reducing aggressive behaviors and antisocial behaviors; Pardeck, 2004; Skowron & Reinemann, 2005; Williams & Herrera, 2007), consistency of parenting behaviors (Huebner, 2002), conveying empathy for children (Brown, 2005; Pardeck, 2004), and helping parents anticipate how to respond to children in a range of possible situations (Huebner, 2002). In addition, programs may help parents manage their emotional responses to their children (Brown, 2005) and challenge parents' distorted thoughts about parenting (Skowron & Reinemann, 2005).
4. *Problematic issues in the parents' lives.* Programs often reflect the fact that child maltreatment often occurs in a context of multiple problematic family dynamics. As such, education may address such topics as IPV, marital problems, legal and financial issues, parent's own trauma experiences, and substance abuse (Pardeck, 2004; Schewe, 2008; Thomas, 2007).
5. *Abuse-related topics.* Some topics that may be addressed include the parents' distress related to the disclosure of the maltreatment (MacMillan, 2000), including self-blame (Celano et al., 2002), and the impact of abuse on children (Adams, 2006; Schewe, 2008).

Preschooler-Parent Psychotherapy. Toth, Maughan, Manly, Spagnola, and Cichetti (2002) described preschooler-parent psychotherapy (PPP), which is an attachment-focused intervention for young children who have been maltreated.

PPP addresses parenting skills within a the parent-child attachment relationship. A focus is on promoting positive attachment in the mother through a positive therapeutic relationship. Through this context, the therapist helps the mother develop supportive, positive attachment-enhancing interactions with her child. Toth et al. compared PPP with a psychoeducational home visit program and nonmaltreating comparison group and found that the children in the PPP group demonstrated the most positive outcomes.

Substance Abuse Treatment. Perpetrators and/or non-offending parents may have needs for substance abuse treatment in conjunction with other forms of treatment (Barth, Gibbons, & Guo, 2006; Donohue, Romero, & Hill, 2006; Jones & Gross, 2000; Marsh et al., 2006; McAlpine et al., 2001; Rittner & Dozier, 2000; Scannapieco & Connell-Carrick, 2007). Although more are needed, some coordinated treatment programs exist, and these typically include mentoring, parent education, and practical support for housing, transportation, and food (Kerwin, 2005; Scannapieco & Connell-Carrick, 2007). Some residential substance abuse programs allow children to stay with their parents, although the extent to which these programs address the needs of these children varies (Huebner, 2002). This topic is addressed in greater detail in Chapter 11.

Therapeutic Foster Care. Children in foster care may benefit from family-based approaches that enlist the support of their foster families, such as therapeutic foster care (also referred to as treatment foster care) (Kerker & Dore, 2006). This approach involves foster parents receiving specialized training to help the child and parents work together with professionals to meet the child's specialized mental health needs (Kerker & Dore, 2006). Therapeutic foster care offers children a supportive context for receiving treatment while in foster care (Fisher, Kim, & Pears, 2009). For example, Fisher et al. (2009) described the multidimensional treatment foster care for preschoolers (MTFC-P) model that uses a team approach and involves the children, foster parents, and other supportive resources. Foster parents participating in this program complete an intensive 12-hour training program before taking a child into their care. Once the child comes into their home, a trained professional serves as a consultant to the family and provides parents with support and supervision. Foster parents also participate in a weekly support group, and they have access to on-call services to address issues that arise at all hours of the day. Participating children receive treatment over a lengthy period of time. In an initial study with 117 preschool-aged children in foster care, those who participated in the MTFC-P intervention were more likely to be placed in a permanent home by adoption during the study's two-year follow-up period. This is significant given the potential benefits to children of being placed in a permanent setting rather than remaining permanently in foster care.

Another program for foster parents is the KEEP intervention that was developed and implemented in San Diego County (Price et al., 2008). Groups of foster parents participated in a 16-week intervention that addressed behavior management strategies (e.g., positive reinforcement), appropriate discipline, and monitoring children's social relationships. The KEEP intervention included didactic, interactive, and out-of-session homework components. The children whose families participated in the program were more likely than others to have exited the foster care system by the end of the intervention.

Therapy for Non-Offending Parents. Non-offending parents often are enlisted to provide support to maltreated children (Lewin & Bergin, 2001). The extent to which non-offending parents support maltreated children plays a powerful role in children's adjustment (Elliott & Carnes, 2001). Non-offending parents may need support in addressing their emotional responses to the disclosure of the maltreatment (Hebert et al., 2006). For example, non-offending parents may benefit from processing their ambivalent feelings about the abuse and disclosure (Elliott & Carnes, 2001). Therapists should not make assumptions as to how non-offending parents will respond to the disclosure, as parents can display a wide range of responses (Hill, 2005). In particular, the immediate time following disclosure of abuse may be very stressful and challenging for non-offending parents (Elliott & Carnes, 2001).

The mental health needs of non-offending parents also may need to be addressed (Lewin & Bergin, 2001), and non-offending parents may be especially likely to benefit from CBT (Elliott & Carnes, 2001). In cases in which IPV is present, safety planning can help the non-offending parent develop strategies for promoting his/her safety and the children's safety (Jones & Gross, 2000). Because children are often caught up in parental IPV dynamics (Beeble, Bybee, & Sullivan, 2007), supervised visitation centers may be useful when custody disputes arise.

Treatment for Child Maltreatment Perpetrators

Many in society believe that offenders should be punished rather than treated (Finkelhor, 2009). However, therapy and other therapeutic interventions often are indicated, even required, for perpetrators. It is possible that perpetrators will recognize their need to change and voluntarily seek services. However, the bulk of the information in the existing literature, and accordingly this section of this chapter, addresses perpetrators whose abusive and/or neglectful behaviors have been discovered by someone else, and therefore the perpetrators are not seeking services voluntarily. In this section, we explore some general issues related to therapists' treatment of child maltreatment perpetrators and describe a few specific treatment approaches.

Working with child maltreatment perpetrators is very complex and challenging. Therefore, readers are encouraged to seek additional resources, training, and information before engaging in this work. Therapists often are undertrained in working with child abuse perpetrators (Finkelhor, 2009), and many therapists are hesitant to work with this population (Adams, 2003). In part, this may be due to perpetrator clients being especially prone to challenging and testing their therapists (Drapeau, Korner, Granger, Brunet, & Caspar, 2005). Therapists may benefit from completing the Attitudes Toward Treatment of Sex Offenders assessment (ATTSO; Wnuk, Chapman, & Jeglic, 2006) to aid in their self-reflection as to whether they are competent to work with this population.

A gap exists between research and practice in the area of child maltreatment perpetrator treatment (Ricci & Clayton, 2008). However, although it is widely believed among professionals and the general public that sex offenders are not responsive to treatment, there is some evidence that treatment can reduce recidivism (Wnuk et al., 2006). Existing evidence is inconclusive as to whether child sexual abuse perpetrator treatments are effective, with some studies showing no effect on recidivism, but other studies demonstrating some positive outcomes (Finkelhor, 2009). Treatment may be more beneficial for juvenile offenders than adults (Finkelhor, 2009).

Although it is recommended that offender treatment be adapted to the unique needs of the offender, minimal research evidence exists currently to provide solid recommendations for doing so (Drapeau et al., 2005). Different strategies should be used depending on whether a perpetrator is at higher or lower risk of reoffending (Finkelhor, 2009), although determining which perpetrators fall into which category remains questionable. Some perpetrators are not suitable candidates for treatment. Some contraindications include serious cognitive deficits (Scott & Crooks, 2004), untreated substance abuse, and lack of accepting any responsibility for the maltreatment. Treatment compliance is especially relevant in working with perpetrators. Offenders who drop out prematurely likely will not reap the full benefits of treatment and may actually become more likely to reoffend (Drapeau et al., 2005). Therefore, therapists should conduct a careful assessment with prospective perpetrator clients prior to beginning treatment.

Therapists should consider how legal considerations may impact a perpetrator client's ability to reach treatment goals. Child sexual abuse perpetrators who have been convicted are likely to be required to register with a sex offender registry in their jurisdictions (Hill, 2005; Finkelhor, 2009; Malesky & Keim, 2001). Because these registries often are publicly available through electronic channels, they likely will influence the perpetrator's ability to make a smooth transition back into the community (Hill, 2005; Finkelhor, 2009). Therapists should work with offender clients to determine how such registration may impact their ability to make progress in therapy and other areas of their lives, such as employment (Hill, 2005). Moreover, therapists may benefit from examining how their own biases and beliefs about sex offender registries might impact their ability to work with this population (Malesky & Keim, 2001).

Treatment Format and Content

Perpetrator treatments often occur in group formats (Beech & Fisher, 2002; Frost, 2004), although individual approaches may be used as well (Drapeau et al., 2005). Treatments may be provided in community settings or in prisons (Drapeau et al., 2005). Commonly used theory-based approaches to sex offender treatment include CBT, psychodynamic therapy, group therapy, and relapse prevention (Drapeau et al., 2005; Winton, 2005). Juvenile child sexual abuse offenders may be especially likely to benefit from multisystemic therapy or CBT (Finkelhor, 2009). The most common form of treatment for child sexual abuse perpetrators is grounded in CBT and include components such as confronting denial, cognitive restructuring, building skills, addressing social deficits, and planning for relapse prevention (Beech & Fisher, 2002; Finkelhor, 2009). Common topics addressed in these interventions include those described below.

Motivational interventions. Perpetrators may have vastly different motivations for seeking treatment, and this can influence their participation and progress in treatment (Frost, 2004). Early in treatment, assessing and increasing the perpetrator's motivation to change is essential (Drapeau et al., 2005). Although understanding a perpetrator's motivation is valuable, it may not predict how a client will respond to treatment, so this information should be considered one part of the case conceptualization process (Littell & Girvin, 2005).

Client-specific Needs. Therapy may address unique client characteristics that could impact treatment, such as one's locus of control and level of fixation on inappropriate sexual stimuli (Beech & Fisher, 2002), as well as other problems that may lead the person to offend (Finkelhor, 2009). Clients may need treatment to address substance abuse (Locke & Newcomb, 2003), as well as their own personal histories of trauma (Adams, 2003; Bentovim, 2002; Ricci & Clayton, 2008). However, this is controversial because it may convey to the perpetrator that s/he is excused for his behaviors because of a past history of victimization. Thus, trauma-focused treatment for perpetrators is best used as an adjunctive service (Ricci & Clayton, 2008).

Skill Development. Therapy may aim to help perpetrators develop skills to reduce their risk of reoffending and enhance their functioning. Some skills that may be targeted include problem-solving, anger management, coping, emotional regulation, behavioral self-regulation, and parenting (Beech & Fisher, 2002; Bentovim, 2002; Bugental et al., 2002; Drapeau et al., 2005; Finkelhor,

2009). Caregivers who have maltreated children may need to learn more accurate ways of interpreting children's behaviors (Bugental et al., 2002), such as by learning about developmentally-appropriate behaviors.

Relationship Functioning. Therapy may address different aspects of a perpetrator's relationship functioning, such as social skills (Drapeau et al., 2005), boundaries (Bentovim, 2002), empathy (Drapeau et al., 2005), and attachment injuries (Bentovim, 2002).

Dysfunctional Thinking Patterns. Therapists may challenge perpetrators' dysfunctional thinking patterns related to the maltreatment (Beech & Fisher, 2002). In particular, treatment may focus on challenging the perpetrator's denial (Beech & Fisher, 2002; Bentovim, 2002).

Sexuality. Especially with sexual abuse perpetrators, treatment may include some form of sex education (Drapeau et al., 2005). In addition, treatment may focus on challenging clients' sexual arousal to deviant stimuli (Beech & Fisher, 2002).

Relapse Prevention. Relapse prevention planning involves having the perpetrator identify potential triggers for abuse and planning how to respond in non-abusive ways, particularly by helping the perpetrator develop necessary skills and resources (Beech & Fisher, 2002; Drapeau et al., 2005; Fisher, Beech, & Browne, 2000; Frost, 2004). Relapse prevention is appropriate only when clients have demonstrated progress in treatment (Fisher et al., 2000).

Theory- and Research-Based Therapy Approaches for Perpetrators

Fewer comprehensive treatment descriptions are available in the professional literature to describe interventions for perpetrators compared with interventions for victims and non-offending parents. We conclude this section with a brief review of two approaches to illustrate how programs may incorporate the topics and treatment modalities described above.

Caring Dads. When working with fathers who have maltreated their children, Scott and Crooks (2004) provide several recommendations to guide treatment. First, an initial focus should be on addressing fathers' sense of control and entitlement. Second, the fathers' motivation to change should be considered at the outset of treatment. Third, fathers' gender-role expectations related to abuse perpetration should be addressed. Fourth, therapy should address the relationship between the fathers and the mothers of the victimized children. Finally, an emphasis should be placed on rebuilding trust between the father and child. As a reflection of these guidelines, Scott and Crooks (2007; Crooks, Scott,

Francis, Kelly, & Reid, 2006) developed the *Caring Dads: Helping Fathers Value Their Children* program for fathers who have perpetrated maltreatment against their children. This 17-week group program educates fathers about healthy attitudes, parenting behaviors, and how children are impacted by family violence. Some interventions used in the program include making a family genogram, providing education about child development, and discussing nurturing versus abusive parenting (Crooks et al., 2006). The initial program evaluation demonstrated that fathers who participated in the program demonstrated such positive outcomes as becoming less hostile and less rejecting of their children.

Juvenile Sex-Offender Treatment. Longo (2004) proposed an integrated, experiential approach for treating juvenile sexual abuse offenders. This approach was designed to be more effective than traditional, relapse prevention-focused treatments that are often used for adult offenders. Longo suggests that therapy should focus on clients' overall well-being, such as by emphasizing their needs for generosity, belonging, and independence. Clients are viewed positively and are supported in promoting positive changes in their emotions, mental and physical health, and spirituality. The therapist aims to help the client develop greater self-awareness and more effective ways of relating to others. Clients may especially benefit from learning skills to help them function and solve problems more effectively (Longo, 2004).

Conclusion

Therapy focusing on child maltreatment is both personally and professionally challenging for therapists. Victims, offenders, and other family members may have very complex clinical needs, and treatment may be complicated further by the need to coordinate services with other involved organizations, professionals, and legal requirements. This chapter provided readers with an overview of commonly-used approaches to therapy with clients impacted by child maltreatment. Clearly, there is a need for further efforts to develop effective interventions for these populations. Overall, when child maltreatment is a topic of focus in therapy, therapists must maintain a primary focus on safety issues and use trauma-informed treatment approaches that are likely to promote the safety and welfare of children impacted by maltreatment.

9

TREATMENT OF ADULT SURVIVORS OF CHILDHOOD MALTREATMENT

In light of the profound impact of childhood maltreatment, it is no surprise that these experiences can have a lifelong influence on survivors. Although we continue to use the term *survivor* to refer to adults who experienced maltreatment as children, we want to emphasize that therapists should not view these individuals solely in light of their prior victimization experiences. Phillips and Daniluk (2004) conducted a qualitative study that examined, in part, how seven female survivors of childhood sexual abuse defined themselves in relation to their abuse experiences. These authors suggest that those who were abused in childhood move from viewing themselves as *victims* to *survivors*, but eventually even the *survivor* label becomes limiting because it still defines the person in relation to their abuse. As such, even the *survivor* label can be considered stigmatizing and not reflective of the true depth of their experiences as human beings. A positive aspect of the survivor label is that it may help the person feel connected to others with similar experiences. However, as survivors heal, they may come to view their abuse experiences as being just one aspect of their personal identities.

Of course, there is wide individual variation on how people respond to childhood abuse victimization (Bogar & Hulse-Killacky, 2006), so we must be cautious in making assumptions about how these experiences will play out as survivors reach adulthood. Some people who experience child abuse function well and lead positive, resilient lives (Leonard & Follette, 2002; Mersky & Topitzes, 2010; Miltenburg & Singer, 2000). In addition, some may not recall their experiences of abuse as traumatic or overly negative (Hall, 2008). Furthermore, therapists must never lose sight of the strengths and resilience demonstrated by survivors. Indeed, much of this chapter will focus on negative consequences and experiences faced by survivors. This is in part due to the fact that this is the lens used in so much research (Bogar & Hulse-Killacky, 2006), and also in part due to the fact that these challenges are likely what will bring clients to the offices of therapists. However, mere survival in the face of the multiple challenges associated with childhood maltreatment is an indication of survivors' strength and resourcefulness.

Therapists also should be familiar with the concept of post-traumatic growth, which addresses potential growth and benefits that are byproducts of traumatic events (Tedeschi & Calhoun, 1996). Some areas in which people may experience posttraumatic growth include more positive views about oneself, stronger relationships, and a renewed life philosophy (Tedeschi & Calhoun, 1996). Many survivors are able to view themselves as resilient and identify positive growth that they experienced as a result of their recovery process (Choate & Henson, 2003; Connor & Higgins, 2008a; Grossman, Sorsoli, & Kia-Keating, 2006; Phillips & Daniluk, 2004).

This chapter begins with a review of possible client characteristics and presenting concerns that adult survivors may demonstrate. The rest of the chapter provides in-depth coverage of treatment and assessment concerns. A sampling of some specific approaches that have been developed will then be presented. The chapter concludes with an integrative three-phase process for therapy with child maltreatment survivors.

Possible Client Characteristics and Presenting Concerns

Childhood maltreatment survivors may experience a range of hardships that persist into adulthood. The depth of challenges faced by survivors can be so great that Mersky and Topitzes (2010) concluded, "That any maltreated children are able to function well is seemingly remarkable" (p. 1086). When working with survivors, it is helpful for therapists to consider the function that any experienced symptoms may serve for these clients, even if the adaptive function of these symptoms are no longer present (Wright, Crawford, & Del Castillo, 2009).

The lifelong consequences of childhood maltreatment can be far-reaching and impact the survivor's physical and mental health, socioeconomic status, and relationships (Macmillan, 2009; Mersky & Topitzes, 2010). This section reviews symptoms and consequences in each of these areas that existing research links to a history of childhood maltreatment. Different forms of abuse may be linked more closely with certain outcomes. However, because multiple forms of abuse often co-occur (e.g., Ahmad, 2006; Allen, 2008; Cloitre et al., 2009; Maker & Buttenheim, 2000), it is difficult to identify each type's unique influence on adult outcomes. Furthermore, children often experience maltreatment within the context of other challenging life circumstances (e.g., parental IPV or substance abuse), making it even more difficult to isolate specific consequences in adulthood (Maker & Buttenheim, 2000). These interconnections add to the difficulty of isolating specific effects within and between categories. Therefore, we discuss consequences broadly and do not link them specifically to any particular form of maltreatment.

The consequences addressed below must be considered in the context of common methodological limitations in existing research (Peleikis & Dahl, 2005; Price, Hilsenroth, Callahan, Petretic-Jackson, & Bonge, 2004). Common design-related limitations include the primary use of cross-sectional and retrospective designs (Ahmad, 2006; Arias, 2004; Mersky & Topitzes, 2010; Noll, 2005), as well as insufficient controlling for potentially confounding variables (Maniglio, 2009). Common limitations related to samples include the frequent use of small, nonrepresentative samples (Maniglio, 2009; Mersky & Topitzes, 2010), particularly drawn from clinical populations (Arias, 2004; Mersky & Topitzes, 2010), a primary focus on women such that limited research addresses male survivors (Ahmad, 2006; Arias, 2004; Havig, 2008; Widom & Hiller-Sturmhofel, 2001), culturally limited samples (Ahmad, 2006), and lack of adequate control groups (Maniglio, 2009). A variety of measurement problems also are frequently found (Hulme, 2004; Maniglio, 2009). For example, researchers often rely solely on self-report data (DiLillo & Damashek, 2003) and do not corroborate abuse reports with objective records (Noll, 2005). In addition, researchers use different definitions across studies (Ahmad, 2006; Leonard & Follette, 2002) or provide no clear definitions (Peleikis & Dahl, 2005), making it difficult to compare results across studies. Thus, although existing research provides some useful information about potential adulthood consequences, methodological limitations necessitate that therapists use caution in applying these findings to any particular clients.

Physical Health Concerns

Child maltreatment is both a direct and indirect (through its connection to further adulthood victimization) risk factor for adulthood physical health problems (Arias, 2004). Although survivors may be more likely to use healthcare services that non-survivors, many healthcare providers are under-equipped to respond effectively to survivors (Havig, 2008). Survivors may be less compliant with healthcare treatment, and seeking healthcare may be challenging for survivors for whom touch and being unclothed triggers traumatic memories (Havig, 2008), so clients may benefit from addressing these concerns in therapy.

Physical health consequences may be mediated by psychological consequences (Arias, 2004). Indeed, many researchers list somatization as a psychological consequence of childhood maltreatment (Allen, 2008; Arias, 2004; Follette, La Bash, & Sewell, 2010; Giles et al., 2007; Maniglio, 2009; Mersky & Topitzes, 2010; Price et al., 2004). Other possible health outcomes include substance abuse, risky behaviors, immune functioning, and the physiological and brain-based responses to trauma (Havig, 2008). Some physical health concerns associated with childhood sexual abuse noted in the literature include cancer, chronic pain, gastrointestinal conditions, gynecological problems, headaches, heart problems, impaired immune system functioning, sexually transmitted diseases (although the evidence for this is not very strong; Maniglio, 2009), non-epileptic seizures, obesity, and pelvic pain (Havig, 2008; Maniglio, 2009; Noll, 2005).

Educational and Economic Status

Childhood maltreatment may increase a survivor's risk for poor educational performance and attainment (Arias, 2004; Mersky & Topitzes, 2010). Some possible links between child abuse and later socioeconomic outcomes include decreased educational attainment, psychopathology, and physical health problems (Zielinski, 2009). Potential education-related consequences of childhood maltreatment include being less likely to complete high school or attend or complete college (Mersky & Topitzes, 2010; Wright et al., 2009). Survivors also may demonstrate learning problems (Maniglio, 2009) and increased absenteeism in school (Tell, Pavkov, Hecker, & Fontaine, 2006). A variety of indicators suggest that survivors may face a variety of economic hardships as adults. For example, survivors may have lower income levels (Mersky & Topitzes, 2010) and be at higher risk for poverty (Zielinski, 2009). They may be more likely to be unemployed as adults (Zielinski, 2009) or to be arrested and/or incarcerated (Mersky & Topitzes, 2010). Finally, they may be more likely to use Medicaid and less likely to have adequate health insurance coverage as adults (Zielinski, 2009).

Mental Health

A variety of adult mental health conditions have been linked to childhood maltreatment. Before listing these, we emphasize that a number of factors influence whether and how severe mental health symptoms develop. First, symptoms may differ based on the type of maltreatment. For example, certain types of psychological abuse are linked more closely with specific mental health outcomes (Allen, 2008; Gibb, Butler, & Beck, 2003). In one study of college students, terrorizing was most likely to be related to anxiety and somatization, ignoring was most likely to be related to depression and borderline personality disorder, and degrading was most likely to be related to borderline personality disorder (Allen, 2008). Another interesting finding of this study, that physical abuse only predicted somatic complaints, suggested that psychological maltreatment has a more negative impact on mental health than physical abuse (Allen, 2008).

In another study of over 550 psychiatric outpatients, emotional abuse was related most closely to depression, physical abuse was linked most closely with anxiety, and sexual abuse did not appear to be tied uniquely to a particular disorder (Gibb et al., 2003). Other research, however, suggests that sexual abuse is linked more closely than other types to dissociation (Wright et al., 2009). Furthermore, other characteristics of sexual abuse, such as whether penetration occurred and whether physical force was used, may contribute to more severe mental health outcomes (Ahmad, 2006). Generally, more severe abuse leads to more negative consequences (Campbell, Greeson, Bybee, & Raja, 2008).

In addition to distinctions made in mental health outcomes based on type of abuse, the lasting mental health impacts can vary based on the age at which the individual experienced abuse as a child (Kaplow & Widom, 2007). In particular, adults who experienced abuse very early in life, such as between birth and age two, appear most likely to experience internalized mental health symptoms, such as depression and anxiety, whereas those who experienced abuse later in childhood may be more at risk for antisocial behaviors, such as substance abuse and diminished educational attainment (Kaplow & Widom, 2007).

The list of possible mental health symptoms of abuse is extensive. Symptoms discussed in the literature generally fall into the following categories: anxiety-related symptoms; mood-related and other psychiatric symptoms; self-destructive behaviors; and negative self-attributions.

Anxiety-related Symptoms. Survivors' anxiety may be manifest in a variety of ways. First, they may experience general anxiety (Ahmad, 2006; Allen, 2008; Anda, 2007; Arias, 2004; Callahan, Price, & Hilsenroth, 2004; Choate & Henson, 2003; Classen, Koopman, Nevill-Manning, & Spiegel, 2001; Colangelo, 2007; DiLillo & Damashek, 2003; Gibb et al., 2003; Giles et al., 2007; Havig, 2008; Hodges & Myers, 2010; Horton & Cruise, 1997; House, 2006; Kaplow & Widom, 2007; Leonard & Follette, 2002; Maniglio, 2009; Mersky & Topitzes, 2010; Moller & Steel, 2002; Pearson, 1994; Peleikis & Dahl, 2005; Price et al., 2004; Rowan & Foy, 1993; Wright et al., 2009). They also may exhibit specific disorders, such as obsessive-compulsive disorder (Maniglio, 2009) or phobias (Choate & Henson, 2003; Hodges & Myers, 2010; Rowan & Foy, 1993).

The anxiety disorder that has been studied most extensively among survivors is PTSD (Arias, 2004; Chard, 2005; Choate & Henson, 2003; Classen et al., 2001; Cloitre, Miranda, Stovall-McClough, & Han, 2005; Cloitre et al., 2009; Cohen, 2008; Colangelo, 2007; DiLillo & Damashek, 2003; Giles et al., 2007; Havig, 2008; Hodges & Myers, 2010; House, 2006; Kaplow & Widom, 2007; Maker & Buttenheim, 2000; Maniglio, 2009; Noll, 2005; Moller & Steel, 2002; Paivio, Hall, Holowaty, Jellis, & Tran, 2001; Peleikis & Dahl, 2005; Price et al., 2004; Rowan & Foy, 1993; Tell et al., 2006). PTSD symptoms appear to have the potential to impair survivors' functioning in many areas of life (Cloitre et al., 2005).

Researchers speculate that PTSD associated with childhood maltreatment differs from the traditional definition of PTSD as outlined in the *DSM-IV-TR* (American Psychiatric Association, 2000). In part, this is due to unique features of the trauma of childhood abuse, such as the child's relationship to the perpetrator and the repeated and multiple forms of trauma it often involves (Cloitre et al., 2009; Cohen, 2008; Connor & Higgins, 2008a; Etherington, 2000; Gleiser, Ford, & Fosha, 2008; Malmo & Laidlaw, 2010; Rowan & Foy, 1993; Spitzer, Chevalier, Gillner, Freyberger, & Barnow, 2006). In addition, there is evidence that there is a positive relationship between the severity of abuse experienced and the complexity of symptoms in adulthood (Cloitre et al., 2009). Although not an official diagnosis in the *DSM-IV-TR*, the term *Complex PTSD* (Herman, 1992), is frequently used to describe the combination of typical PTSD symptoms (i.e., avoidance, arousal, and re-experiencing) with additional common symptoms in survivors, such as difficulty regulating emotions, impaired social functioning, and dissociation (Cloitre et al., 2009; Connor & Higgins, 2008a; Dorrepaal et al., 2010; Gleiser et al., 2008; Spitzer et al., 2006). There are six specific criteria for Complex PTSD: impaired emotional regulation, dissociation, feelings of guilt and shame, impaired and mistrustful relationships, somatic symptoms, and a negatively altered personal meaning system (Spitzer et al., 2006). Complex PTSD may co-occur with personality disorders (Dorrepaal et al., 2010). Scholars who advocate for increased recognition of Complex PTSD assert that this singular diagnosis is a more coherent and less stigmatizing way to describe the symptoms that survivors may experience (Cloitre et al., 2009).

Mood-related and Other Psychiatric Symptoms. Survivors often demonstrate difficulty regulating emotions (Cloitre et al., 2005; Giles et al., 2007). This may, in part, explain the strong links found between childhood maltreatment and depressive symptoms in adulthood (Ahmad, 2006; Allen, 2008; Anda, 2007; Arias, 2004; Callahan et al., 2004; Chard, 2005; Choate & Henson, 2003; Chu, 1992; Classen et al., 2001; DiLillo & Damashek, 2003; Havig, 2008; Gibb et al., 2003; Giles et al., 2007; Hodges & Myers, 2010; Horton & Cruise, 1997; House, 2006; Kaplow & Widom, 2007; Leonard & Follette, 2002; Maniglio, 2009; Mersky & Topitzes, 2010; Moller & Steel, 2002; Noll, 2005; Pearson, 1994; Peleikis & Dahl, 2005; Price et al., 2004; Rowan & Foy, 1993; Tell et al., 2006; Wright et al., 2009).

Dissociation may occur in some survivors (Chard, 2005; Choate & Henson, 2003; Chu, 1992; Classen et al., 2001; Etherington, 2000; Giles et al., 2007; Havig, 2008; Hodges & Myers, 2010; Leonard & Follette, 2002; Maker & Buttenheim, 2000; Maniglio, 2009; Mersky & Topitzes, 2010; Miltenburg & Singer, 2000; Moller & Steel, 2002; Noll, 2005; Peleikis & Dahl, 2005; Tell et al., 2006; Wright et al., 2009). Dissociation is often considered a defense mechanism for dealing with the overwhelming experience of trauma linked maltreatment (Chu, 1992; Lord, 2008). The function of dissociation for children experiencing abuse may be to provide separate schemas to keep the abuse experiences from overtaking all aspects of the child's life (Miltenburg & Singer,

2000). Another way of understanding dissociation is as a lack of integration of one's identity, memory, and perceptual systems (Lord, 2008). Dissociation may occur at different levels, and at the most extreme is manifest as Dissociative Identity Disorder (Lord, 2008).

Additional adulthood psychiatric symptoms linked to childhood maltreatment include psychosis and paranoia, sexual dysfunction, sleep disruptions and nightmares, and suicidality (Ahmad, 2006; Anda, 2007; Arias, 2004; Callahan et al., 2004; Choate & Henson, 2003; Classen et al., 2001; Colangelo, 2007; Follette et al., 2010; Havig, 2008; Hodges & Myers, 2010; Leonard & Follette, 2002; Maniglio, 2009; Miller, Cardona, & Hardin, 2007; Pearson, 1994; Peleikis & Dahl, 2005; Price et al., 2004; Rowan & Foy, 1993; Wright et al., 2009). Survivors also may exhibit personality disorders (Arias, 2004; Callahan et al., 2004; Chard, 2005; Maniglio, 2009; Mersky & Topitzes, 2010; Moller & Steel, 2002; Peleikis & Dahl, 2005; Tell et al., 2006), most notably borderline (Classen et al., 2001; Maniglio, 2009; Wright et al., 2009) and antisocial (Kaplow & Widom, 2007). The trauma associated with childhood maltreatment also may result in memory disruption (Anda, 2007; Malmo & Laidlaw, 2010; Pearson, 1994), which may be a further manifestation of dissociative symptoms (Malmo & Laidlaw, 2010). In light of these potential psychiatric symptoms, it is no surprise that survivors exhibit an increased use of psychotropic medications compared to non-survivors (Anda, 2007).

Self-destructive Behaviors. Survivors may be more likely to engage in self-destructive behaviors, including disordered eating and risky sexual behaviors (Arias, 2004; Choate & Henson, 2003; Colangelo, 2007; DiLillo & Damashek, 2003; Follette et al., 2010; Hall, 2008; Havig, 2008; Hodges & Myers, 2010; Horton & Cruise, 1997; Maniglio, 2009; Mersky & Topitzes, 2010; Moller & Steel, 2002; Noll, 2005; Peleikis & Dahl, 2005; Tell et al., 2006; Wright et al., 2009). Survivors also may engage in self-injurious behaviors (Ahmad, 2006; Choate & Henson, 2003; Chu, 1992; Follette et al., 2010; Hodges & Myers, 2010; Horton & Cruise, 1997; House, 2006; Maniglio, 2009; Noll, 2005; Pearson, 1994; Peleikis & Dahl, 2005; Yates, Carlson, & Egeland, 2008), which are "self-inflicted, direct, socially unacceptable destruction or alteration of body tissue that occurs in the absence of suicidal intent or pervasive developmental disorder" (Yates et al., 2008, p. 652). Adults with histories of sexual abuse or physical neglect may be especially likely to engage in self-injury more frequently, whereas those with physical abuse only may be more likely to engage in these behaviors only rarely (Yates et al., 2008).

In addition, adult substance abuse has been linked to childhood maltreatment (Ahmad, 2006; Arias, 2004; Bernstein, 2000; Choate & Henson, 2003; Classen et al., 2001; Colangelo, 2007; Easton, Swan, & Sinha, 2000; Follette et al., 2010; Havig, 2008; Hodges & Myers, 2010; Horton & Cruise, 1997; House, 2006; Kaplow & Widom, 2007; Leonard & Follette, 2002; Maniglio,

2009; Mersky & Topitzes, 2010; Noll, 2005; Moller & Steel, 2002; Pearson, 1994; Peleikis & Dahl, 2005; Price et al., 2004; Rowan & Foy, 1993; Widom & Hiller-Sturmhofel, 2001). The relationship between childhood maltreatment and substance abuse will be addressed in greater detail in Chapter 11. For adult survivors, substance abuse may serve a variety of functions, including as a coping mechanism, a way to avoid feeling lonely, a form of "self-medication," a way to temporarily feel better about oneself, and as part of a pattern of self-destructive behaviors (Widom & Hiller-Sturmhofel, 2001).

Negative Attributions toward Self and Others. In light of their abuse histories, survivors may develop negative emotional states and cognitive perceptions that impact their views of themselves and others (Giles et al., 2007). They may exhibit low self-esteem (Chu, 1992; Choate & Henson, 2003; DiLillo & Damashek, 2003; Giles et al., 2007; Havig, 2008; Horton & Cruise, 1997; House, 2006; Maniglio, 2009; Moller & Steel, 2002; Paivio et al., 2001; Pearson, 1994; Peleikis & Dahl, 2005; Rowan & Foy, 1993; Tell et al., 2006; Wright et al., 2009) and negative cognitions about themselves, such as viewing themselves as defective and vulnerable (Wright et al., 2009). They may blame themselves for their abuse (Grossman et al., 2006; Hodges & Myers, 2010; Leonard & Follette, 2002; Miller et al., 2007).

Other feelings they may experience include anger (Hodges & Myers, 2010; Leonard & Follette, 2002; Maniglio, 2009; Rowan & Foy, 1993; Wright et al., 2009), fear (Ahmad, 2006; Callahan et al., 2004; Follette et al., 2010; Pearson, 1994; Rowan & Foy, 1993), guilt (Leonard & Follette, 2002; Moller & Steel, 2002; Paivio et al., 2001; Pearson, 1994; Peleikis & Dahl, 2005; Rowan & Foy, 1993), helplessness and hopelessness (Pearson, 1994), hostility (Maniglio, 2009), and shame (Maker & Buttenheim, 2000; Paivio et al., 2001; Pearson, 1994; Wright et al., 2009). They may display a primarily external locus of control (Tell et al., 2006), have low levels of optimism (Mersky & Topitzes, 2010), and have difficulty making decisions and trusting themselves (Choate & Henson, 2003).

Finally, it is not uncommon for survivors to experience deeply conflicted and ambivalent feelings toward their abuser. For example, consider the following quote from a case study presented by Arnd-Caddigan (2006): "After I got grown, and after I started having all my babies … I still was the one that was crying about the fact that I couldn't have a decent relationship with my mother … I just want her to understand what's going on …" (p. 298). In part, continuing to hold positive feelings towards one's abuser may serve a protective function of maintaining hope for a more positive future (Miltenburg & Singer, 2000). Dissociation may contribute further to ambivalence, in that the survivor has separate schema relating to the abuse experiences and other dimensions of his or her relationship with the perpetrator (Miltenburg & Singer, 2000).

Relationship Concerns

Survivors typically long for healthy, positive relationships with others (MacIntosh & Johnson, 2008). However, survivors may experience unique relational challenges (Allen, 2008; Classen et al., 2001; Cloitre et al., 2005; Colangelo, 2007; DiLillo, Peugh, Walsh, Panuzio, Trask, & Evans, 2009; Giles et al., 2007; Havig, 2008; Hodges & Myers, 2010; House, 2006; Maniglio, 2009; Moller & Steel, 2002; Pearson, 1994; Price et al., 2004; Tell et al., 2006). Survivors may have a general sense of isolation (Callahan et al., 2004; Choate & Henson, 2003; Rowan & Foy, 1993) or loneliness (Einhorn, 2000; Miltenburg & Singer, 2000; Tell et al., 2006) across areas of their lives. Impaired relationship functioning may be a byproduct of trauma-related symptoms, such as PTSD (DiLillo et al., 2009).

Survivors may exhibit attachment problems (Callahan et al., 2004; Chard, 2005; Cohen, 2008; MacIntosh & Johnson, 2008), fear intimacy (Tell et al., 2006), and be emotionally disengaged (Tell et al., 2006). Reduced trust in others (Arias, 2004; Choate & Henson, 2003; Classen et al., 2001; DiLillo et al., 2009; Hall, 2008; Horton & Cruise, 1997; Paivio et al., 2001; Pearson, 1994; Rowan & Foy, 1993; Tell et al., 2006) may lead them to difficulty in establishing healthy intimate relationships in particular (Ahmad, 2006; Arias, 2004; Basham, 2004; Feiring, Simon, & Cleland, 2009; Leonard & Follette, 2002; Lord, 2008; Pearson, 1994; Reyome, 2010). In a study of over 200 newly married couples recruited randomly from the community, DiLillo et al. (2009) found that a history of childhood maltreatment was associated with lower martial satisfaction, especially for husbands, and this effect became even greater over time.

Survivors may exhibit impaired communication (Chard, 2005; Tell et al., 2006), have a difficult time asserting themselves (Cloitre et al., 2005), and feel uncomfortable when interacting with others (Maniglio, 2009). In addition, survivors may be extremely sensitive to others' criticism (Cloitre et al., 2005) and display increased negativity during conflict (Tell et al., 2006). Perhaps in part due to communication problems, partners of survivors may have a difficult time understanding their partners' experiences, potentially leaving them feeling confused, isolated, and unhappy in their relationships (MacIntosh & Johnson, 2008).

In addition to general concerns, researchers have studied relationship functioning of survivors in three areas: sexual functioning, parenting, and intergenerational patterns.

Sexual Functioning. A great amount of research attention has focused on adult sexual functioning as it relates to childhood sexual abuse (Ahmad, 2006; Hall, 2008; Leonard & Follette, 2002). People who have been sexually abused in childhood may demonstrate impaired sexual functioning as adults (Ahmad, 2006; Hall, 2008; Callahan et al., 2004; Classen et al., 2001; Leonard & Follette,

2002; Maniglio, 2009; Moller & Steel, 2002; Pearson, 1994; Rowan & Foy, 1993; Tell et al., 2006). In addition, they may be more likely to engage in risky or compulsive sexual behaviors (Follette et al., 2010; Maniglio, 2009). Some specific sexuality-related concerns that sexual abuse survivors may experience include having sexual activity trigger dissociation or the re-experiencing of abuse, acting in sexually compulsive ways, and experiencing extreme anxiety or aversion to sex (Hall, 2008). In addition, it may be difficult for these survivors to be able to experience pleasure related to sexual activities (Hall, 2008).

Possible connections between childhood sexual abuse and impaired adulthood sexual functioning include the use of avoidant coping strategies and impaired attachments (Ahmad, 2006; Leonard & Follette, 2002). Additional links may relate to feelings of being abnormal and having a lack of access to credible information about sexuality and health (Hall, 2008). In addition, these outcomes may result, in part, due to the fact that the sexual abuse experiences often were among the person's earliest sexual experiences, which increases the potential long-term impact on his or her understanding of sexuality (Leonard & Follette, 2002).

There are some mixed and controversial findings as to whether childhood sexual abuse survivors are more likely to develop same-sex attractions as adults (Ahmad, 2006). As such, therapists should refrain from making assumptions about sexual orientation based on knowledge of an abuse history (Grossman et al., 2006). However, it may be worth exploring survivor clients' perceptions of connections between their abuse histories and their sexual orientation and any same-sex experiences or attractions they experienced.

Parenting Concerns. Survivors may find that their experiences of prior abuse impact them in their roles and experiences with parenting (Basham, 2004; DiLillo & Damashek, 2003; Maker & Buttenheim, 2000; Price et al., 2004). Some parenting experiences that have been linked to parental histories of childhood abuse include unclear boundaries between the parent and children, permissive parenting styles, and harsh discipline practices, although research in this area has been inconclusive (DiLillo & Damashek, 2003). Parenting abilities may be impacted by direct psychological consequences of the childhood abuse, such as PTSD or depressive symptoms, as well as through attachment problems (DiLillo & Damashek, 2003). Existing research suggests that survivors may have unrealistic expectations about children's developmental capacities (Maker & Buttenheim, 2000).

Parenting challenges may be especially prominent at certain developmental stages, particularly those connected to survivors' age when maltreated (Maker & Buttenheim, 2000). Another time when parenting concerns may arise is if a survivor is the non-offending parent of an abused child. In such cases, the survivor's abuse history may impact their response to their child and their ability to support their child in therapy s/he receives (DiLillo & Damashek, 2003).

Abuse Perpetration and/or Victimization. Being maltreated as a child is a risk factor for being victimized as an adult (Ahmad, 2006; Arias, 2004; Callahan et al., 2004; Campbell et al., 2008; Classen et al., 2001; DiLillo et al., 2009; Giles et al., 2007; House, 2006; Leonard & Follette, 2002; Lord, 2008; Maniglio, 2009; Moller & Steel, 2002; Noll, 2005; Peleikis & Dahl, 2005; Price et al., 2004; Rowan & Foy, 1993; Tell et al., 2006), as well as for perpetrating IPV (DiLillo et al., 2009; Rowan & Foy, 1993). Individuals who perpetrate battering as adults may have experienced or witnessed abuse in their families of origin (Aymer, 2008), and having been sexually abused as a child may increase one's risk of perpetrating sexual violence as an adult (Maniglio, 2009). However, there are mixed research findings as to whether individuals who were abused as children are more likely to perpetrate child abuse on their own children (DiLillo & Damashek, 2003).

Treatment Considerations

The range of potential consequences of childhood maltreatment underscores the complexities often involved in therapy with this population. The remainder of this chapter addresses goals, strategies, and approaches to treatment with survivors. We begin by discussing general treatment issues, and then we move to discussing assessment considerations. Next, we present brief reviews of some specific approaches to therapy with survivors. Finally, we integrate our treatment recommendations into a three-phase process for therapy. Our goal is not to put forth narrow prescription for therapy with this population, but rather to address the range of approaches and interventions that may be useful to guide therapy for survivors.

General Considerations

According to Chu (1992), "the therapy of childhood abuse survivors is both a science and an art" (p. 369). A range of treatment approaches have been developed and tested for survivors, and many of these have potential to be beneficial for clients (Martsolf & Draucker, 2005; Price et al., 2004). The experiences and consequences of childhood abuse are complex, and treatments should reflect the complexity of the lived experiences of survivors (Hodges & Myers, 2010; Noll, 2005). As a basic foundation for treatment with survivors, therapists should consider how to establish appropriate treatment goals and a strong therapeutic relationship, determine the most suitable format of treatment, and be aware of relevant outcome research supporting the effectiveness of therapy with this population.

Treatment Goals. A range of treatment goals may be addressed in therapy with survivors. According to Paivio and Laurent (2001), "The overall goal of therapy for resolving child abuse issues is to facilitate emotional engagement with trauma memories in order to process the trauma" (p. 218). As we discuss later in this chapter, however, some questions remain as to whether focusing primarily on traumatic memories is the most suitable approach for all survivors. More broadly, general goals for therapy with survivors include helping them address their emotional responses to their abuse, identify how past abuse impacts them currently, develop life skills, challenge distorted beliefs, reduce self-blame, become more accepting of themselves, and develop more positive behaviors, coping strategies, and relationship patterns (Choate & Henson, 2003; Peleikis & Dahl, 2005). Consideration should be given to survivors' socioeconomic backgrounds and how these relate to the resources they have available to them to support them in making progress toward their treatment goals (Hall, 2008).

Therapeutic Relationship. A positive, supportive therapeutic relationship between the client and therapist is fundamental to treatment with survivors (Arnd-Caddigan, 2006; Pearson, 1994). First and foremost, counselors should maintain a hopeful stance about the possibility of survivors being able to heal and move forward from past experiences with abuse (Bogar & Hulse-Killacky, 2006). In addition, it is useful to maintain a strong professional and therapeutic boundary when working with survivors (Chu, 1992). The therapist's competence and professionalism also can contribute to a more positive therapeutic relationship. Abuse survivors appear to be most comfortable receiving healthcare services when practitioners are open, professional, and genuinely concerned for their well-being (Havig, 2008). Finally, since this work often involves a high level of listening to clients' traumatic memories, therapists should maintain a focus on their own self-care throughout treatment (see Chapter 14). Therapists may find it useful to receive competent supervision when working with survivors due to the multiple challenges that may arise (Harper & Steadman, 2003).

Treatment Format. Two pertinent considerations for therapists working with survivors is whether group or individual therapy is most appropriate and whether survivors' partners should be included in treatment (e.g., through couples counseling). Group therapy is very common for survivors and shows promise as an effective means for helping survivors improve their psychological functioning, especially longer-term groups (Callahan et al., 2004; Cohen, 2008; DiLillo & Damashek, 2003; Lundqvist, Svedin, Hansson, & Broman, 2006; Price et al., 2004; Valerio & Lepper, 2010). Potential benefits of group approaches include helping survivors overcome the shame and secrecy surrounding abuse (Valerio & Lepper, 2010), providing a forum for survivors to learn new, more adaptive ways of interacting with others (Callahan et al., 2004), and allowing group members to offer each other mutual support (Choate & Henson, 2003; House, 2006).

However, there is a risk in groups that clients' disclosure of traumatic memories will negatively impact other group members, such as by triggering flashbacks of others' own abuse (Chard, 2005; Valerio & Lepper, 2010). As such, it is important that group members are addressing similar goals so that their experiences will be in line with general group processes (Cohen, 2008). The most effective approach may involve a combination of group and individual therapy (Chard, 2005; Connor & Higgins, 2008a; Einhorn, 2000; Giles et al., 2007), with individual therapy focusing on extensive discussion of trauma experiences, and group therapy focusing on normalizing clients' experiences and developing coping strategies (Chard, 2005).

Therapists should discuss the extent to which clients wish to include significant others in therapy. Although traditionally couple therapy does not occur until later in the therapeutic process, partners may be valuable supporters in survivors' recovery process (MacIntosh & Johnson, 2008). Later, we describe some couple-based approaches to therapy with survivors.

Outcome Research. Generally, research supports the potential benefits that survivors can receive from therapy, although much more research is still needed in this area. After a review of 26 outcome studies of treatment for adult child sexual abuse survivors, Martsolf and Draucker (2005) concluded that both individual and group treatments can be effective in reducing mental health symptoms. In another review of 24 studies examining therapy outcomes for childhood sexual abuse survivors, Peleikis and Dahl (2005) concluded that these clients can experience moderate gains through their participation in therapy, and these gains are likely to remain in place over time. There is inconclusive evidence regarding the length of treatment that is most likely to produce positive outcomes (Callahan et al., 2004; Martsolf & Draucker, 2005). Providing some structure regarding treatment length can provide clients with a much-needed sense of structure and control in their otherwise potentially chaotic lives (Einhorn, 2000). However, any structure should be introduced with flexibility if clients' needs change over time.

Assessment Considerations

As Horton and Cruise (1997) wrote, "Knowing that an individual has been abused is only the beginning of clinical evaluation" (p. 96). This statement illustrates the importance and complexity of conducting a comprehensive clinical assessment with adult survivors. Treatment should be tailored to unique client needs (Morrison & Ferris, 2002), and a comprehensive assessment can help identify these needs. Three recommendations for assessment with survivors include viewing the assessment as an ongoing process, being sensitive to clients' discussion of maltreatment experiences, and assessing a broad range of potentially related factors.

The Assessment Process. Assessment should begin early and continue throughout therapy (McGregor, Thomas, & Read, 2006). Therapists should maintain a stance of professionalism, respect, and support throughout the process (Bernstein, 2000). In particular, ongoing attention should be paid to safety (Connor & Higgins, 2008b) to ensure that any new risks are addressed. Also, symptoms should be monitored throughout treatment, especially as new phases of treatment begin, to ensure that clients do not become overwhelmed by them (Horton & Cruise, 1997). Clients' needs are likely to change as therapy progresses, so ongoing assessment will help the therapist stay alert to changes that may impact the therapy process.

Assessment of the Maltreatment. Maltreatment-specific areas to assess include how clients describe the abuse, the impact of the abuse on clients' current and past functioning, and coping resources (Bernstein, 2000; Higgins Kessler, Nelson, Jurich, & White, 2004). Disclosing abuse histories can be very difficult (Farmer, Khurgin-Bott, & Feldman, 2009; Follette et al., 2010), and clients may take time before they are able to fully disclose their experiences (Lock, Lewis, & Rourke, 2005; McGregor et al., 2006). A variety of factors can contribute to clients' discomfort in disclosing their abuse histories. These include shame, guilt, avoidance, fear of being disbelieved, and feeling unsafe with their therapists (Follette et al., 2010; Lock et al., 2005). It is not necessary for clients to reveal every single detail of their abuse experiences in order for them to make progress in therapy, so therapists should help their clients discover the best balance of disclosure and privacy (Farmer et al., 2009). Bernstein (2000) suggests that therapists avoid using direct language as "abuse" and "victim," which may decrease a client's willingness to disclose. Rather, therapists can inquire about abuse experiences with questions such as "When you were growing up, did anyone ever tough you in a sexual way or make you touch them?" or "When you were a child or teenager, did anyone ever hit you or beat you?" (Bernstein, 2000, pp. 27-28).

Many therapists rely solely on their clients' self-reported information to assess for childhood maltreatment histories (Lock et al., 2005). In addition, self-report instruments may be used to supplement the assessment. For example, see Hulme (2004) for a review of instruments related to childhood sexual abuse, although the primary focus of Hulme's review is instruments used for research, not clinical purposes. However, there are some common measurement problems in these instruments, so they should be combined with other assessment strategies (Hulme, 2004). Therapists should evaluate any potentially useful instrument to ensure that it asks questions in ways that are likely to elicit accurate and complete information. For example, instruments that include language that is specific and behavioral can be more informative than those that use broad-based terms and questions (Hulme, 2004).

An example of a potentially useful instrument for addressing childhood history of sexual abuse is the Sexual Abuse Questionnaire (SAQ; Lock et al., 2005). A unique feature of the SAQ is that it is designed to measure not just specific historical information about abuse, but also common characteristics among clients in clinical populations with histories of childhood sexual abuse. The final version of the instrument has 43 items, examples of which include "I did not have a happy childhood"; "There are periods of my life (past the age of 5) for which I have no memory"; and "When I was an adolescent or young adult, I acted out sexually more than I wanted" (p. 17). Across two studies with university students, Lock et al. provided some support for the psychometric properties (e.g., test-retest reliability, internal consistency, and discriminant validity) of the SAQ. Thus, the SAQ shows promise to be a valuable assessment tool.

Assessment of Related Factors. Our review earlier in this chapter of consequences of childhood maltreatment in adulthood suggests potentially useful areas for clinical assessment. For example, therapists may assess such issues as mental health symptoms, developmental issues, self-esteem, emotional regulation abilities, relationship patterns, interpersonal skills, and resilience factors. Therapists can also assess coping resources (Higgins Kessler et al., 2004), including those that no longer serve an adaptive function, such as substance abuse (Bernstein, 2000). Intergenerational patterns of maltreatment may be useful to identify, such as through a genogram focusing on patterns of abuse (Pearson, 1994).

Another useful area for assessment relates to how childhood maltreatment experiences relate to clients' other trauma and victimization experiences. Widom, Dutton, Czaja, and DuMont (2004) created the Lifetime Trauma and Victimization History (LTVH) interview guide. This 30-item instrument can provide therapists with a more comprehensive view of their clients' trauma histories, including physical and sexual assault, in addition to other categories, such as general trauma, witnessing someone else's trauma, and being kidnapped or stalked. When respondents indicate that they experienced a traumatic experience listed on the LTVH, they are asked to report the age it first occurred, the number of times it occurred, the age at which it last occurred, and its severity, based on its dangerousness and fear. There is some evidence for the validity and sensitivity of the instrument. Because it is comprehensive and detailed, it could take a long time to complete with clients with extensive trauma histories. However, the LTVH provides a structured process that therapists can use to gather relevant, detailed information about their clients' experiences with trauma. This can be useful in putting any experiences with childhood maltreatment in the context of other childhood or adult trauma experiences.

Specific Approaches

Although some researchers (e.g., Pearson, 1994) suggest that nondirective approaches are most appropriate, a range of more structured approaches are described in the literature to offer therapists guidance in working with survivors. We review several approaches here, although this list is intended to be illustrative, not exhaustive. After discussing specific approaches, we outline a general, integrative process that can be used when working with survivors.

Accelerated Experiential Dynamic Psychotherapy (AEDP). AEDP integrates emotion-focused therapy with an emphasis on affect regulation to address symptoms of Complex PTSD (Gleiser et al., 2008). The therapist plays an important role as a trustworthy companion throughout therapy, as the client and therapist together explore the client's traumatic memories. The therapist and client first focus on the symptoms leading the client to seek treatment. Next, intense emotional responses are explored and processed in the context of the strong therapeutic relationship. Ultimately, the therapist and client collaborate to help the client make meaning of the trauma experiences. Some clinical evidence exists for the effectiveness of ADEP.

Acceptance and Commitment Therapy. A couple therapy approach to treating childhood sexual abuse survivors is Acceptance and Commitment Therapy (ACT; Hayes et al., 1999). This approach combines behavioral approaches (e.g., exposure) and relationship enhancement, emphasizing the importance of accepting oneself, others, and one's abuse history (Follette et al., 2010; Leonard & Follette, 2002). Additional emphasis is placed on clients developing mindfulness and behavioral flexibility (Follette et al., 2010).

Affect Management Group. Wolfsdorf and Zlotnick (2001) proposed an affect management group for clients coping with the effects of childhood sexual abuse and PTSD. Three goals of this group are to help clients develop skills, reduce presenting symptoms, and become more stabilized. This approach addresses the problems many survivors experience related to regulating their emotions and may be especially useful early in therapy by helping clients to become more stable and better able to manage emotions. Participants engage in 15 structured sessions of 90 minutes each. The sessions involve psychoeducation, skills rehearsal, and homework assignments. Specific interventions used in this group include mindfulness, planning for crises, and challenging maladaptive thinking strategies. The researchers evaluated this approach with 48 female survivors, and the results showed promising benefits related to symptom reduction. Although additional research is needed on this approach, it may offer practical strategies for the early phases of therapy with survivors.

Cognitive Processing Therapy. Chard (2005) studied the effectiveness of a sexual abuse-specific modification of cognitive processing therapy (CPT-SA) among a sample of 71 female clients. This model's theoretical foundations are in information processing, developmental psychology, and trauma. The manualized CPT-SA treatment combined group and individual therapy over a 17-week period. Two unique interventions are writing an impact statement in which the clients detail the range of impacts that traumatic experiences had on their lives and using questions to challenge negative thinking patterns. One way that CPT-SA differs from traditional CPT is through its focus on communication skills and sexual intimacy. In Chard's study, CPT-SA helped reduce clients' trauma symptoms (i.e., PTSD, depression, and dissociation), and symptom reductions persisted at the one-year follow-up.

Cognitive Restructuring. Cognitive restructuring interventions help clients identify and challenge maladaptive thinking patterns and develop more positive ones (Moller & Steel, 2002). Moller and Steel examined the impact of cognitive restructuring in a 10-week group-based rational-emotive behavior therapy intervention for childhood sexual abuse survivors. Their results indicated that, among clients participating in this intervention, many demonstrated clinically-significant symptom reductions after participating in the group.

Emotion-focused Therapy. Emotion-focused therapy (EFT; MacIntosh & Johnson, 2008) also has been applied to survivors of childhood sexual abuse (Leonard & Follette, 2002; MacIntosh & Johnson, 2008; Paivio et al., 2001). EFT aims to help clients access emotions and develop more positive relationships (Leonard & Follette, 2002). EFT is experiential and grounded in attachment theory (Cohen, 2008; MacIntosh & Johnson, 2008). A goal of EFT is to help clients experience "corrective emotional experiences" (MacIntosh & Johnson, 2008, p. 301) so they can move toward more positive relationship dynamics. MacIntosh and Johnson did a mixed-methodology study to examine the experience and effects of EFT for 10 couples involving survivors of childhood sexual abuse and their partners. The quantitative outcome data revealed a trend for participants to experience fewer symptoms and increased relationship satisfaction following treatment. The data also showed that the therapy process was, at times, very challenging for participants, especially related to emotional flooding and numbing. As such, the researchers recommended that therapists ensure that the therapy process move slowly and address dynamics of shame and self-blame as they arise.

Enhanced Cognitive-Behavioral Therapy (CBT). Cohen (2008) suggested that CBT can be made more relevant to survivors' unique needs by integrating feminist, emotion-focused, and developmental perspectives. Cohen's conceptual article lists suggestions for therapists when working with survivors. These include the importance of focusing on attachment concerns and a strong therapeutic relationship, emphasizing and highlighting clients' strengths and resources, challenging clients' beliefs about personal blame for the abuse and clients' assumptions about sex and gender, and considering whether clients would like to get involved with broader social advocacy efforts as part of their healing process.

Eye Movement Desensitization and Reprocessing (EMDR). EMDR was developed by Francine Shapiro (1989). Despite some controversy regarding its effectiveness, it has been used with clients with histories of childhood maltreatment (Edmond & Rubin, 2004). EMDR uses interventions to stimulate eye movements in order to reprocess traumatic experiences (Edmond & Rubin, 2004). Edmond and Rubin followed 42 survivors of childhood sexual abuse for 18 months following either completion of an EMDR intervention, routine treatment, or participation in a control group. The participants who completed EMDR demonstrated slight improvements during the follow-up period. Although the differences were not statistically significant, the participants in the control group actually demonstrated some symptom deterioration during the follow-up period. Although these findings offer only minimal support to the potential effectiveness of EMDR in treatment for survivors, this remains a popular approach among some therapists and warrants future research.

Group Psychoeducation. Survivors may benefit from psychoeducational groups that help them develop knowledge and skills to help them manage the effects of their abuse. For example, Choate and Henson (2003) suggested that a psychoeducational group program is useful for survivors, especially in the latter stages of healing when they are attempting to make positive changes in their lives. Both males and females participated in an implementation of this group, and the group was not specific to any one form of maltreatment. Some of this group's goals were to help participants build support and connection, examine the influence of their maltreatment on their current lives, develop adaptive beliefs about themselves and others, and develop and practice relationship and coping skills. Each of 10 weekly sessions began with a check-in with all group members, followed by interactive psychoeducational activities, and concluding with a closing ritual. Psychoeducational activities included cognitive restructuring, skills training, and brainstorming discussions. Topics addressed included trust, self-esteem, emotional boundaries, and conflict management. Minimal outcome data were collected in the form of anonymous evaluation questionnaires. The researchers suggest that the approach provided a useful forum for clients, although additional research is needed to study the outcomes of this approach further.

Another approach to group psychoeducation for survivors was proposed by Dorrepaal et al. (2010). This 20-week, complex-PTSD focused approach incorporates CBT interventions in a structured format. Participants receive information about symptoms of Complex PTSD and their links to childhood trauma. Skills emphasized through CBT include self-regulation and relationships. Additional goals are to help clients develop hope, normalize their symptoms, and reduce isolation and shame. Dorrepaal et al. studied the effects of treatment among 36 female participants. Participants who completed treatment demonstrated decreased symptoms of PTSD and Complex PTSD. Although the researchers did not use a control group and their study demonstrated other methodological limitations, their findings suggest that this approach may hold value for survivors.

Seeking Safety. One of the most studied and commonly used evidence-based approaches for addressing co-occurring trauma and substance abuse is Seeking Safety (Najavits, 2001), a 25-session, present-focused coping skills model that is grounded in CBT and uses coping skills to integrate trauma-specific and substance abuse treatment. Over 17 completed research studies of randomized controlled trials, multisite trials, and dissemination studies document its effectiveness across a wide variety of populations (gender, age, race) and settings (individual outpatient, inpatient, group, etc.). Readers are encouraged to go to www.seekingsafety.org for full information on these studies.

The HEALTH Model. Connor and Higgins (2008a, b) developed the HEALTH model to address Complex PTSD related to childhood maltreatment. The HEALTH model incorporates six treatment stages. First, the therapist establishes a supportive relationship with the client. Second, the client's personal safety is addressed. Third, the therapist helps the client enhance his/her daily functioning. Fourth, the client learns self-regulation strategies for managing primary symptoms of PTSD. Fifth, symptoms of complex PTSD are treated. Sixth, the emphasis is on ego strengthening for the client. Although based on detailed treatment guidelines, the HEALTH model maintains flexibility to be adapted to the unique needs of individual clients (Connor & Higgins, 2008b). Data from a pilot study (Connor & Higgins, 2008a) and a case illustration (Connor & Higgins, 2008b) provide some evidence of this approach's utility.

Integrative Couple and Family Therapy. Basham (2004) proposed a framework for working with couples and families that integrates social constructionism, feminism, narrative therapy, and intergenerational, trauma and attachment theories. Three treatment phases are (a) safety and stabilization, (b) reflecting on the trauma narrative, and (c) consolidating and developing a new perspective. Basham presented a clinical vignette to illustrate this approach.

Short-term Psychodynamic Therapy. Price et al. (2004) proposed a short-term psychodynamic approach for the treatment of child sexual abuse survivors. Treatment goals include helping the client express emotions, examining patterns in the clients' lives, establishing a strong therapeutic alliance, and exploring clients' dreams, fantasies, and avoidance strategies. They conducted a pilot study of this approach with 27 outpatient clients, 12 of whom had a history of childhood sexual abuse. The results provided preliminary support for the approach's ability to lead to positive outcomes in clients' psychological and relational functioning. Even though the approach was non-specific to the abuse, clients with histories of child sexual abuse experienced greater benefits in some areas as compared to those clients without such histories.

Wellness Approach. A wellness approach focuses on the strengths and resources of survivors (Hodges & Myers, 2010). Hodges and Myers assert that such a holistic, strength-based approach can empower and destigmatize survivors and promote healing. Therapists emphasize clients' personal choices and how these choices can create positive changes. Interventions target different aspects of wellness, such as physical and spiritual. Although this approach may help orient clients toward the positive aspects of their lives, Hodges and Myers assert that it is not appropriate for clients in extreme distress, such as those demonstrating suicidal ideation.

Women Recovering from Abuse (WRAP). WRAP was developed by Giles et al. (2007) as an outpatient therapy program for women maltreated in childhood. This two-phase program integrates individual and group therapy with psychopharmacology. First, participants go through a four- to six-week Building Resources Group that prepares them for the more intense second phase. The second phase includes different types of group therapy, including interpersonal process groups, body-oriented groups, skills-focused groups, and art therapy. Participants also receive psychoeducation about the impact of trauma. WRAP is an intensive eight-week program that participants attend for four half-days each week. New participants are admitted to the program continuously, so it is not a closed-group format. Although more research is needed to examine the effectiveness of this approach, preliminary qualitative data support its usefulness in helping clients reduce symptoms of trauma and develop more adaptive coping strategies.

An Integrative Three-Phase Process for Therapy

Therapy with survivors is often conducted in a stage-based approach (Cohen, 2008). In the last section, we outline a three-phase therapy process that can serve as a broader lens for using the specific approaches described above or other approaches with survivor clients. The three phases we address are as follows: Phase One: Stabilization and relationship building; Phase Two: Addressing traumatic memories; and Phase Three: Integration and moving forward. Our goal in describing this phase-based approach is to integrate a range of interventions often used with this population into the general phase-based approaches described in the literature. According to Cohen (2008), many existing stage-based models fail to provide adequate direction regarding appropriate interventions at each stage. Therefore, our goal is to offer readers a cohesive set of recommendations that follows the general phases of treatment recommended for survivor clients.

We derived our three phases from a variety of approaches described in the literature. As examples, several of the specific approaches described above (e.g., Basham, 2004; Connor & Higgins, 2008a; Giles et al., 2007; Lord, 2008; Miller et al., 2007) incorporate a phase or stage approach. Other examples can be found in the literature. For example, citing Herman (1992), Wolfsdorf and Zlotnick (2001) refer to a three-phase approach to treatment, with the first phase focusing on safety, the second focusing on addressing trauma memories, and the third phase on building social supports. Emotion-focused therapy and more general trauma-focused therapy also tend to follow three stages of treatment: "stabilization, the building of self and relationship capacities, and integration" (Leonard & Follette, 2002, p. 376). Another three-stage approach was described by Cohen (2008), in which the earliest stage emphasizes safety and emotional regulation, the middle stage focuses on processing the trauma, and the third stage focuses on developing life skills and refocusing on other aspects of life. In addition, Chu (1992) suggested that different therapeutic tasks are warranted for survivors at different stages of therapy. The early stage focuses on helping the client to develop coping skills, the middle stage focuses on the traumatic memories, and the later stage focuses on broader personal and relational growth. Finally, Bernstein (2000) suggests that, across several different phase-based treatment approaches for clients with trauma histories, there are four common phases: "(1) assessment, (2) stabilization, (3) working through traumatic memories, and (4) resolution" (p. 26). Thus, therapy with survivors is often viewed as being carried out in different phases or stages, and the three-phase process we describe here represents an integration of these frameworks.

We intentionally use the term *phases* instead of *stages* to describe the therapy process with survivors. Viewing these processes as phases implies a fluid transition between phases, and these phases may not be able to be discretely defined. In addition, although we list these phases in a sequential manner, therapy may progress in a non-sequential manner, with clients moving back and forth in their needs to focus on the various issues addressed at different phases of the process. Throughout all treatment phases, clients may benefit from being provided with information about what they can expect to be the general process of therapy (Chard, 2005; McGregor et al., 2006), especially related to their rights and responsibilities as clients (McGregor et al., 2006) and as a preliminary orientation to the therapy process (Classen et al., 2001).

Phase One: Stabilization and Relationship Building. In Phase One, there are four early therapy tasks: (a) establishing the therapeutic relationship; (b) conveying empathy; (c) helping the client regulate emotions and stabilizing the client's symptoms; and (d) building the client's resources to support the challenges involved in subsequent phases of treatment. Generally, going in-depth into clients' trauma memories is not a focus at this phase, although certainly these experiences cannot be ignored.

Establishing the Therapeutic Relationship. Earlier, we discussed the importance of a strong therapeutic relationship when working with survivors. The assessment process provides a context for establishing this relationship (McGregor et al., 2006). Therapists can facilitate the therapeutic relationship by validating and encouraging clients, as well as by establishing clear professional boundaries around and within the relationship (Pearson, 1994).

Therapists should be sensitive to clients' potential discomfort in seeking help (Lord, 2008). Early in treatment, clients may be vigilant of therapists and their responses to the clients' disclosures of abuse, in part because they are sensitive to how therapists may respond to them throughout treatment (McGregor et al., 2006). Some clients may even test their therapists to see how they respond to minimal disclosures of abuse before they share their full histories (McGregor et al., 2006). Some use of self-disclosure can help build the therapeutic relationship; however, therapists must be cautious that such disclosures are made in the best interest of the client and not the therapist (Harper & Steadman, 2003).

Establishing a strong professional boundary with survivor clients is a key early task (Harper & Steadman, 2003). However, this task can be complicated. Harper and Steadman (2003) conducted two qualitative studies to learn about the unique challenges therapists face when working with childhood sexual abuse survivors. The results underscored that although boundaries should be clear, therapists must maintain some degree of flexibility in order to respond to the clients' changing needs throughout treatment. In particular, safety concerns may warrant that therapists shift the therapeutic boundaries in order to support clients through a crisis. Due to the personal demands faced by therapists when working with survivors, therapists may struggle to maintain an appropriate level of professional distance from clients while also remaining genuinely concerned for their clients' well-being. Two boundary-related challenges identified in Harper and Steadman's study included when clients made it difficult to end sessions on time, such as by raising new and significant issues at the end of sessions, and when clients made excessive contacts (especially telephone calls) with therapists outside of sessions.

Finally, it may be useful to discuss with the client his or her perceptions about how gender may impact the therapeutic relationship (Simpson & Fothergill, 2004). Clients, at least initially, may hold expectations about their level of comfort in discussing their abuse histories with a therapist of one gender or another (Simpson & Fothergill, 2004). As such, addressing these expectations from the outset may help the therapist and client determine how best to move forward in a manner in which the client feels safe and comfortable. Overall, creating a context of trust and safety are important for clients during this first phase of treatment (Bernstein, 2000; Classen et al., 2001; Harper & Steadman, 2003; Lord, 2008), and this context will be a strong resource for clients as they progress to subsequent phases.

Conveying Empathy. Empathic responses are one means of establishing a positive and trusting therapeutic relationship (Paivio et al., 2001). Even though directly addressing traumatic memories is likely not a major focus as this phase, therapists must convey an understanding of what a significant and impactful experience the abuse was for the client (Chu, 1992). Early in treatment, it is important for therapists to normalize clients' experiences with abuse and their reactions to it (McGregor et al., 2006). By conveying empathy for the client's current functioning and emotional responses to past abuse, therapists can lay a foundation for more intense and in-depth discussions of abuse that occur in the middle and later phases of treatment (Paivio & Laurent, 2001). Therapists demonstrate empathy for survivors by conveying that they understand their clients' perspectives and meanings about their lives and experiences (Paivio & Laurent, 2001). Therapists further demonstrate empathy by remaining present, nonjudgmental, and authentic in their interactions with clients (Paivio & Laurent, 2001).

Therapists should maintain a focus on survivors' strengths (Bogar & Hulse-Killacky, 2006; Higgins Kessler et al., 2004; Hodges & Myers, 2010). Therapists can bear witness to clients' stories of childhood abuse, offering validation and hope (Cohen, 2008; Lord, 2008). However, therapists must strike a balance between acknowledging the weight of clients' experiences with maltreatment and yet also holding out hope that clients can experience more fulfilling, healthy lives (Lord, 2008). Therapists must be cautious about being overly positive, which could lead clients to feel like the depth of their challenges are not understood (Lord, 2008). McGregor et al. (2006) interviewed 20 women with histories of childhood sexual abuse to ask them to describe positive and negative experiences they had in prior therapy. Based on their findings, errors that therapists are encouraged to avoid include being overly distant or overly intrusive, imposing the therapists' own interpretations on the clients' experiences, and being unable to manage the therapists' personal emotional responses to the clients' abuse stories.

Emotional Regulation and Symptom Stabilization. Learning to regulate emotions is an important component of treatment for survivors, especially those with PTSD symptoms (Cloitre et al., 2005; Cohen, 2008). Adequate emotional regulation is a precursor to being able to proceed to traumatic memory work involved in Phase Two (Paivio & Laurent, 2001). Clients can demonstrate emotional regulation by experiencing a wide range of emotions, demonstrating appropriate emotional responses, and managing emotional responses effectively (Paivio & Laurent, 2001). Therefore, therapists can implement interventions to help clients increase skills in mindfulness, self-soothing, tolerating emotional distress, and managing emotions (Giles et al., 2007; House, 2006; Lord, 2008).

Another Phase One task is to establish safety and stability in clients' lives

(Cohen, 2008). Therapists may wish to examine potentially unhealthy coping strategies that survivors are using. It may be necessary to include specific interventions to help clients stop such problematic behaviors, such as self-injury, substance abuse, disordered eating patterns, and other risky behaviors (Bernstein, 2000; Bogar & Hulse-Killacky, 2006; Chu, 1992; Connor & Higgins, 2008a; Giles et al., 2007; Horton & Cruise, 1997). In this phase, therapists should help clients achieve safety in current relationships, such as by addressing any potential IPV (Cohen, 2008). To further help clients stabilize symptoms, therapists can help clients learn to manage distressing thoughts (Giles et al., 2007), such as through cognitive therapy.

Building Resources. The first phase of therapy is a period of building up clients' resources so that they will be equipped to engage in the difficult challenges that lie ahead in addressing directly the effects of prior trauma (Connor & Higgins, 2008a). In the early stages, clients should be supported to develop self-care skills to help them manage symptoms and maintain an adequate level of functioning throughout treatment (Connor & Higgins, 2008a; Giles et al., 2007). Some potentially useful coping strategies include relaxation training, writing, setting boundaries, and self-soothing strategies (Bogar & Hulse-Killacky, 2006). Clients' available social support should be considered as well. Being able to express emotion genuinely may help survivors be more authentic and adaptive in relationships (Bonanno et al, 2007), which may help them increase the social support available to them as they progress through treatment. Finally, also during this phase, it can be useful to set clear and specific goals for treatment (Classen et al., 2001). Such clarity and focus also can serve as a resource for clients, such that they may feel empowered by having a clear sense of purpose in moving forward with treatment.

Phase Two: Addressing Traumatic Memories. Once a strong therapeutic relationship is established, the client feels understood and supported by the therapist, his/her symptoms are stabilized, and increased emotional regulation strategies and resources have been developed, clients may be ready to move to Phase Two, in which the focus shifts to addressing directly the trauma they experienced through childhood maltreatment. Some pertinent considerations during this phase include determining whether direct trauma work is needed, using appropriate strategies for processing trauma memories, knowing how to proceed in the case of newly recalled memories, and determining whether and how clients may confront their perpetrators.

Determining whether Direct Trauma Work is Needed. It is widely thought that working through traumatic memories is a key step in recovering from childhood maltreatment (Colangelo, 2007; Paivio & Laurent, 2001). However, Paivio and Laurent (2001) suggest that this may not be the case for all clients. A rationale for addressing clients' traumatic memories in therapy is that it directly counters clients' tendencies to avoid thinking about and feeling emotions related to these memories, which is thought to lead to their perpetuation. However, memory work is surrounded by controversy, especially because of the distress this work can create for survivors. As such, it may not be suitable for all clients, although some may find it helpful to reprocess their experiences and learn how to tolerate their memories and emotions surrounding them.

Despite the widespread assumption that therapy for survivors should hold a primary focus on their abuse, research evidence remains inconclusive as to whether clients can receive equal benefits from therapy that is focused more broadly on their overall functioning. Classen et al. (2001) conducted a pilot study in which they randomly assigned 55 female survivors of childhood sexual abuse to receive either trauma-focused (i.e., past-focused) or non-trauma-focused (i.e., present-focused) group therapy or to a wait-list control group. The primary goals of the trauma-focused therapy group were to help clients process and reconstruct their abuse experiences, as well as to develop a more cohesive integration of their trauma histories into their current lives. In contrast, the present-focused group's primary goals were to examine and alter current maladaptive behavior patterns. Because the sample was so small, the researchers were not able to compare the effects of the different groups to determine whether one was superior to the other. However, participants in both approaches demonstrated positive outcomes, such as reduced symptoms and increased social functioning. Therefore, therapists should remain open to the potential benefits of different approaches, and therapists and clients should collaborate to determine the most suitable approach for a given client's needs. Overall, for some clients, processing traumatic memories IS a necessary component of treatment (Cohen, 2008), but therapists should not force clients to engage in this type of work if they do not wish to do so. Psychoeducation about different approaches is important to empower clients and help them choose the extent to which they believe these treatment strategies would be helpful to them (Chu, 1992). Bibliotherapy may be a useful adjunct to this psychoeducation (Pearson, 1994).

Treatment Strategies for Processing Traumatic Memories. Common approaches in this phase include psychodynamic, exposure, narrative, or cognitive processing therapies (Bernstein, 2000; Cohen, 2008). A strong therapeutic relationship must serve as the foundation for traumatic memory work (Paivio & Laurent, 2001). When moving into memory work, therapists should build on the relationship established in the first phase and continue to demonstrate empathy (Paivio & Laurent, 2001). Paivio and Laurent list several important benefits from maintaining empathic responses while engaging in memory work. For example, empathic responses help clients regulate the pace of therapy, promote therapist-client collaboration, convey the therapist's support, help clients label emotions, demonstrate compassion, reduce clients' anxieties while increasing their emotional experiences, and help clients focus on their inner experiences. At a basic level, clients benefit when their therapists are able to listen to their stories about their abuse (McGregor et al., 2006). Being able to use words to describe abuse experiences, and develop a language for doing so, can be very healing (Einhorn, 2000). It is useful for clients at this phase to be able to verbalize and otherwise express emotions related to their prior trauma(s) (Chu, 1992).

This can be a very distressing aspect of therapy for clients (Chu, 1992). Therefore, this therapeutic work is contraindicated in some cases. Clients should not progress to addressing traumatic memories until they develop some capacity to manage dissociative symptoms (Cohen, 2008). Addressing traumatic memories may not be appropriate if the client is currently in any sort of unsafe living environment (e.g., IPV or homelessness) (Bernstein, 2000). It also is important to assess the extent to which memory work may impact clients' daily functioning in order to establish strategies for completing this work safely (Cohen, 2008). Clients may be ready to address traumatic memories once they establish a basic sense of safety and trust in the therapy process (Bernstein, 2000; Chu, 1992), and clients may move spontaneously into this phase by beginning to disclose abuse experiences that they did not discuss previously (Bernstein, 2000).

According to Chu (1992), *abreaction* is a term often used to describe the process of clients re-experiencing traumatic memories in a supportive therapeutic context, with the goal of helping clients learn to tolerate memories and integrate them into their overall broader psychological processes in a more adaptive way. One way that these memories may be brought out is through exposure techniques. These techniques may actually retraumatize clients, so they must be used with caution and always within the context of very high levels of emotional support.

Prolonged exposure therapies often are used with clients experiencing PTSD (Gleiser et al., 2008). These therapies involve therapists supporting clients as they recall memories of past trauma in great detail, with the assumption that clients' distress will eventually reduce as the exposure continues (Gleiser et al., 2008). Clients' initial distress in relation to remembering the trauma is thought to reduce as they become increasingly accustomed to facing their memories directly (Gleiser et al., 2008). Some clients may become too overwhelmed by prolonged exposure strategies, and these approaches are not appropriate for all clients (Gleiser et al., 2008). A general goal of this memory work is for clients to become increasingly able to tolerate their memories and emotional responses to them over time (Chu, 1992). This work should be viewed as an ongoing process rather than a one-time event (Chu, 1992).

When addressing traumatic memories, therapists may use grounding techniques (Chu, 1992) to help clients maintain a sense of safety and being in the present moment. Grounding techniques reduce dissociation by focusing attention on the present moment and the "senses" around the person. These are often visual, auditory, or tactile. For example, keeping lights up in the room, maintaining eye contact, and keeping a familiar object nearby are common grounding strategies (Chu, 1992). Two additional techniques to use when clients experience memory-related distress are to have clients focus on their immediate senses to create more of an observer stance and to have clients use self-talk to remind themselves that they are safe, in the presence of the therapist, and not actually experiencing the trauma currently (Gleiser et al., 2008).

Therapists should help clients have a sense of control over the therapeutic process and move through this phase at their own pace (Bernstein, 2000; Horton & Cruise, 1997). In an effort to "get it over with" (Lord, 2008, p. 122), some clients may feel compelled to move through this phase rapidly, and this may lead them to attempt to take on more than they can handle emotionally at any given point in time (Lord, 2008). Generally, it is wise to proceed slowly through this phase to ensure that traumatic memories are processed with adequate safety and support (Lord, 2008). It is useful to assess throughout the phase the extent to which symptoms re-emerge or become more intense as traumatic memories are addressed (Bernstein, 2000; Chu, 1992). For some clients, a temporary increase in symptoms may be a necessary precursor to increased acceptance and integration of oneself and one's traumatic memories (Chu, 1992). However, therapists should regularly "check in" with clients to assess distress levels so as to monitor the level of distress experienced during memory work.

Understanding and Addressing Newly Recalled Memories. We base this section on the following Ethical Case Study to illustrate some of the challenges involved in this issue.

Case Example: Jerry and Donna. Jerry, 40, and Donna, 39, have been coming to you for couple therapy, focusing on improving their sexual relationship, for about two months. During a conjoint session, Jerry asks if he can come to you for an individual session before the next conjoint session. Donna does not express any concerns with this, so you agree to meet with him alone before the next conjoint session. During that individual session, Jerry reports that he has begun to have recurrent ("almost every night") and distressing dreams about having been sexually abused by his grandmother (now deceased) when he was a young child. He says to you, "I'm so confused about these dreams. I don't remember this ever happening to me, but it also seems possible since I spent so much time alone with my grandmother while I was growing up."

Discussion and Relevant Codes. The therapist in this situation faces a critical ethical dilemma, primarily reflecting the tension between desiring to believe one's client and considering the potential for false memories. We draw upon the AAMFT (2001) Code of Ethics as illustrative of the professional ethical considerations that should be addressed in this situation. The AAMFT (2001)

Code of Ethics states, "Marriage and family therapists do not diagnose, treat, or advise on problems outside the recognized boundaries of their competencies" (Standard 3.11). Accordingly, therapists should understand current professional understanding of the notion of repressed memories, or memories that at one time were forgotten but are newly recalled. The disruption of memories of abuse remains a controversial and relatively poorly understood issue in the mental health professions (Brown et al., 2007; Colangelo, 2007, 2009; Geraerts et al., 2009). On the one hand, some professionals are wary of the notion of recovered memories because of the potential that these memories may be false, which can expose therapists to liability issues (Colangelo, 2009). On the other hand, there is evidence that memories can be forgotten for a period of time and then recovered (Colangelo, 2009). Current consensus among most professional groups is that it is possible for previously-forgotten memories to be remembered, but that there is a potential for false memories to arise, especially through suggestive therapy techniques (Colangelo, 2007, 2009; Geraerts et al., 2009). Therapists should avoid attributing mental health symptoms to abuse histories if clients do not present these histories (Colangelo, 2007).

Memory loss may be evident for survivors of childhood abuse (Bogar & Hulse-Killacky, 2006; Henderson, Hargreaves, Gregory, & Williams, 2002; Malmo & Laidlaw, 2010). Clients who experienced many problematic experiences in childhood may be especially prone to memory loss (Brown et al., 2007). Memories can be disrupted through changes to the brain's structure (Brown et al., 2007; DeBellis et al., 1999) or deficiencies in survivors' cognitive processing abilities (Henderson et al., 2002). Other theorized links between abuse and memory loss are more psychological in nature, such as the defense mechanism of repression or dissociation symptoms (Colangelo, 2009). Memories of trauma experiences are thought to be different than more general memories, and their retrieval may be more state-dependent, such that these memories may be more or less likely to arise in certain situations (Malmo & Laidlaw, 2010). Both external (e.g., being touched, hearing about abuse in the media) and internal (e.g., nightmares or physical sensations) cues may be triggers for abuse memories (Malmo & Laidlaw, 2010). Clients may report experiencing memories as feelings rather than visual images or narrative stories (Malmo & Laidlaw, 2010).

Another ethical consideration relates to the potential influence of a therapist upon his/her clients. As stated in the AAMFT (2001) Code of Ethics, "Marriage and family therapists are aware of their influential positions with respect to clients, and they avoid exploiting the trust and dependency of such persons.... When the risk of impairment or exploitation exists due to conditions or multiple roles, therapists take appropriate precautions" (Standard 1.3). Some techniques that may be especially likely to lead to false memories, and therefore should be avoided in relation to traumatic memory work, include dream interpretation and hypnosis (Colangelo, 2007). A free recall approach may be the most ethically responsible way to proceed with addressing potentially forgotten memories in therapy (Colangelo, 2007, 2009). For example, the therapist can begin by asking the client to discuss memories that are known (with acknowledgement that even these memories may not reflect the full facts of the situation) and then discuss other possibly linked experiences to this known information (Colangelo, 2007, 2009). Colangelo (2007) makes a useful distinction between historical memory, reflecting the actual facts of past experiences, and narrative memory, reflecting how these experiences are remembered, which may or may not be fully true.

If new memories arise, clients can try to obtain objective verification of these memories, such as by interviewing family members about circumstances surrounding the memories (Colangelo, 2007, 2009). According to Colangelo (2007), therapists should inform clients about the limitations of human memory, especially related to trauma recall. Although difficult, it may be necessary to simply accept that the full truth of some memories may never be able to be known. Therapists generally should not offer specific advice to clients about what actions they should take in relation to their past abuse and their memories of it. Clients who wish to take action (e.g., confronting a suspected abuser or legal action) based on newly recovered memories should consider potential legal issues that could arise from these actions, such as a defamation lawsuit.

Confrontation. It is not necessary to confront one's abuser in order to heal (Colangelo, 2007; Freshwater, Ainscough, & Toon, 2002). Whether or not clients confront abusers should be their own decisions (Colangelo, 2007; Freshwater et al., 2002). Potential benefits of direct or symbolic confrontation include helping clients overcome fear and self-blame, increase assertiveness and self-esteem, and develop confidence in their personal power (Freshwater et al., 2002). However, direct confrontation can be counterproductive if clients have doubts as to whether abuse occurred and the alleged perpetrator denies it (Freshwater et al., 2002).

Clients can confront abusers in a variety of ways, both directly (e.g., by speaking to the abuser in person or writing a letter) or indirectly or symbolically (e.g., by role plays) (Freshwater et al., 2002). Other forms of abuse-related confrontation may involve pursuing legal action, confronting other family members, and confronting others who have perpetrated abuse but not one's own abuser (Freshwater et al., 2002). Paivio et al. (2001) described the use of an imaginal confrontation intervention, though which the client expresses his/her thoughts and emotions to an imagined version of the perpetrator. Similar to an empty chair technique, this intervention involves the client imagining and talking to the perpetrator while s/he talks about the experience of doing so. In a study of the impact of this intervention, Paivio and colleagues found that it reduced trauma symptoms, helped clients develop a new understanding of their experiences and relationships, and made a unique contribution to their healing above and beyond the basic influence of the therapeutic relationship. However, the positive therapeutic alliance was essential for providing adequate safety to engage in this potentially distressing intervention. In addition, this type of intervention is not appropriate for all clients. Writing activities, such as letter writing and journaling, also could be used as tools in the imaginal confrontation process (Pearson, 1994). Although writing activities can provide survivors with some benefits, these activities appear to be most useful in combination with other intervention strategies rather than as stand-alone interventions (Batten, Follette, Rasmussen Hall, & Palm, 2002).

If a client wants to engage in some form of confrontation, the therapist can help prepare the client beforehand and debrief the client afterward (Freshwater et al., 2002). Clients who wish to confront their abusers must prepare to face any outcome that may result from it (Colangelo, 2007; Freshwater et al., 2002). That is, they should not expect that the abuser will respond in the way that they would like for them to respond.

Phase Three: Integration and Moving Forward. According to Miltenburg and Singer (2000), "Building a good life after a bad childhood often proceeds through small steps and with great difficulty" (p. 505). Phase Three involves consolidating gains the client made through treatment, considering how best to move forward in one's life and relationships, and ultimately terminating the current therapy. Although in some ways this phase represents an "ending" for the client, it can also be considered a beginning of the next phases of therapy or the beginning of the client's future, which will not be defined primarily by his or her history of maltreatment.

Consolidating Treatment Gains. In the later phases of treatment, therapists can help clients consolidate gains made in treatment and transfer these into other areas of their lives (Classen et al., 2001). At this phase, clients may benefit from developing new skills to help them continue to have positive growth in their lives. For example, therapists can work with clients to further develop a range of life skills, such as communication, assertiveness, and parenting skills (Pearson, 1994). Survivors who are parents may benefit from learning parenting strategies, such as self-soothing related to parenting stressors and appropriate discipline strategies (DiLillo & Damashek, 2003; Maker & Buttenheim, 2000). Clients in the later stages of recovery may be surprised to experience new areas of their lives in which they now notice that they were impacted by their abuse, and these may be new areas to address in therapy (Chu, 1992).

In this final phase, clients may benefit from reflecting on the growth they experienced as they went through the recovery and healing process. Key aspects of the recovery process from childhood sexual abuse identified by Phillips and Daniluk (2004) included developing increased feelings of safety and security in the world, accepting sadness over time and experiences that they may lost to the abuse, and developing a more positive self-perception overall. Other areas of growth may include developing adaptive attachment styles, emotional regulation, and more positive interpersonal relationships (Cloitre et al., 2009). By exploring gains they made in these areas, clients can identify needs for further growth and plan strategies to maintain their progress.

Attaining some sense of closure is a common goal in the latter phases of treatment (Edmond & Rubin, 2004). The use of a creative therapeutic ritual may facilitate the process of the survivor gaining this sense of closure (Phillips & Daniluk, 2004). According to Bogar and Hulse-Killacky (2006), "Achieving closure does not imply that participants forgot about the abuse they experienced but, rather, that they were able to integrate that aspect of their lives into their personal life stories without undue emotional pain" (p. 323). As such, therapists may wish to explore what *closure* means to survivor clients who reach this phase of treatment.

Moving Forward in One's Life and Relationships. By this phase, clients likely achieved a clinically significant reduction in symptoms and have begun to feel that they are well-equipped to manage the impact of their abuse histories on their current and future lives. At this point, they may begin to grapple with broader issues, such as integrating their abuse histories into their self-identities, making meaning of their experiences, and developing stronger relationships.

Identity Concerns. Clients in the later stages of healing may benefit from discussing how they want to view their abuse experiences as related to their self-identity, as continuing to view oneself as a survivor may eventually feel limiting and constraining (Phillips & Daniluk, 2004). Becoming more authentic is a common goal for survivors, as they often have previously not allowed their true selves to be known to others in light of past violations of trust (Lord, 2008). Therefore, in Phase Three, clients may grapple with establishing a positive and authentic self-identity that incorporates the abuse history but is not defined by it. To make further progress, clients may find it useful to refocus their energy and attention to positive aspects of their lives, such as their careers, families, faith, or social relationships (Bogar & Hulse-Killacky, 2006).

Making Meaning. Clients may continue to struggle to make meaning of their experiences, but doing so can be an important and normal aspect of treatment (Grossman et al., 2006; Horton & Cruise, 1997). Perhaps one of the greatest challenges for clients nearing the "end" of the healing process to make meaning of their abuse experiences (Grossman et al., 2006). Survivors may make sense of their abuse experiences through a variety of lenses, including spiritual beliefs or philosophical considerations (Grossman et al., 2006). Survivors also may make meaning of their experiences through active efforts to help others, by expressing themselves creatively through art or writing, or by examining underlying relational or cultural explanations for abuse (Grossman et al., 2006). Forgiving one's abuser may or may not be an essential to feeling closure and making meaning of the abuse (Bogar & Hulse-Killacky, 2006). However, when it occurs, forgiveness may help the survivor release anger and shame that s/he had been holding on to (Bogar & Hulse-Killacky, 2006). Finally, for some survivors, healing is enhanced as they begin to view their abuse experiences as part of larger societal trends regarding social dynamics that contribute to abuse being an unfortunately common experience (Phillips & Daniluk, 2004).

Strengthening Relationships. Developing more positive relationships is often an important consideration at this phase. In particular, it may be useful to include the client's partner in treatment to address relationship concerns, such as trust and power dynamics (Cohen, 2008). Clients' intimate partners can provide valuable support during the therapy process (Higgins Kessler et al., 2004). In addressing problems related to sexual functioning at this phase, elements of traditional sex therapy (e.g., sensate focus) can be combined with abuse-specific interventions and information (Leonard & Follette, 2002). In particular, therapists can provide clients with educational information about sexuality and relationships (Leonard & Follette, 2002). Abuse survivors also may need assistance in developing relationship skills, such as communication and negotiation (Cloitre et al., 2005). Finally, it may be useful to develop groups or other educational strategies to inform family members, friends, and significant others about the potential consequences of victimization and the healing process (Bogar & Hulse-Killacky, 2006).

Therapy Termination. Therapists should pay special attention to termination with survivor clients, particularly because the end of the relationship can give rise to feelings of abandonment (Classen et al., 2001; Einhorn, 2000). Therapists should be open and supportive through the termination process. By discussing the client's thoughts and feelings about termination, supports can be mobilized to help the process be another therapeutic element of treatment for the client. Although it may be important to establish a clear ending and termination to therapy, therapists may wish to leave the door open for the client to return if new issues arise in the future, whether or not they relate to the abuse history. In particular, new life transitions, such as entering adulthood, marriage, or having children, may give rise to new challenges in coping with one's abuse history (Bonanno et al., 2007). Therapists can discuss with clients upon termination what circumstances might arise that would warrant further therapy. At termination, special attention should be paid to highlighting the gains the client made throughout treatment, and the therapist can express appreciation for the work they completed together.

Conclusion

A large number of challenges may result from childhood maltreatment as survivors navigate their adult lives. A range of therapy approaches can be used to help survivors create positive lives and relationships. Some goals of therapy are to help the client develop safety and stability, manage traumatic memories, and move forward in life with more positive beliefs about oneself and relationship functioning. Despite the potential challenges they face, therapists must never lose sight of the strengths and resources of survivors of childhood maltreatment. By holding out hope for the potential growth these clients may experience, and combining this hope with sound clinical practices, therapists can offer survivors a relationship in which remarkable growth and support can emerge.

PART III

10

ABUSE OF VULNERABLE POPULATIONS

As discussed throughout this book, family violence presents major challenges for individuals who experience it. Consider, then, the additional challenges that family violence presents to individuals with other vulnerabilities, such as physical or cognitive impairments and/or disabilities, or chronic health conditions. In this chapter, we examine three populations that are uniquely vulnerable to family violence: individuals with disabilities, individuals infected with HIV/AIDS, and the elderly. This chapter's focus is on understanding the dynamics of these phenomena as they relate to assessment and therapy.

Family Violence and Disabilities

The consequences of family violence victimization can create lasting disabilities for victims, such as physical or mental health conditions that limit one's ability to fully function (Ansello & O'Neill, 2010; Westcott & Jones, 1999). Thus, a disability can be considered a potential consequence of family violence victimization. However, having a disability also can increase a person's risk of experiencing abuse (Westcott & Jones, 1999). When abuse occurs, a person's disability also may make it more difficult for that person to seek help. In this section, we explore unique considerations for people with disabilities who experience abuse, and briefly explore abuse perpetrated by individuals with disabilities.

The term *disability* refers to a chronic impairment that limits an individual's functioning in one or more areas, such as being able to care for oneself, learning abilities, physical development, psychological functioning, hearing, vision, and/or language (Ansello & O'Neill, 2010; Govindshenoy & Spencer, 2006). Disabilities may be congenital or acquired, such as through a traumatic injury

(Ansello & O'Neill, 2010). Examples of disabilities include autism, limited hearing or vision, epilepsy, and Down syndrome (Ansello & O'Neill, 2010). Therapists are encouraged to use "person-first" language to describe individuals with disabilities, meaning that they should be described first as people and not defined solely by their disability (Ansello & O'Neill, 2010). For example, the term "person with a disability" should be used instead of "disabled person" (Ansello & O'Neill, 2010, p. 122). As with all clients, therapists should strive to highlight the strengths and resources of clients with disabilities (Ansello & O'Neill, 2010).

Maltreatment of Individuals with Disabilities

Individuals with disabilities appear to be at a higher risk of being abused than people without disabilities (Cooke & Standen, 2002; Howe, 2006; Kelley & Moore, 2000; Peckham, Corbett, Howlett, McKee, & Pattison, 2007). For example, in a population-based study in Omaha, Nebraska, 9% of children without disabilities had been maltreated, whereas 31% of children with disabilities had been, making children with disabilities 3.4 times more likely to have been maltreated (Sullivan & Knutson, 2000). When these researchers looked at specific forms of abuse, as compared with children without disabilities, children with disabilities were nearly 3.8 times more likely to be neglected, 3.8 times more likely to be physically abused, 3.1 times more likely to be sexually abused, and 3.9 times more likely to be emotionally abused. Children with disabilities are more likely to be abused at younger ages than non-disabled, abused children, thus signifying the importance of early intervention and prevention (Sullivan & Knutson, 2000). In addition, rates of abuse among women with disabilities are at least as high as, but likely higher than, rates of women in the general population (Hassouneh-Phillips & Curry, 2002; Yoshida, Odette, Hardie, Willis, & Bunch, 2009). Regarding IPV among adults with disabilities, most victims are female and most perpetrators are male (Hassouneh-Phillips & Curry, 2002).

The type of disability an individual has may be linked with different forms of abuse. For example, Govindshenoy and Spencer (2006) discussed the following associations: conduct disorder and emotional abuse; learning disorders and sexual abuse; and communication disorders and all forms of abuse except for sexual. Children with intellectual and psychological disabilities may be at a greater risk for abuse than those with physical disabilities (Cooke & Standen, 2002; Govindshenoy & Spencer, 2006; Howe, 2006; Sullivan & Knutson, 2000). In fact, in the Sullivan and Knutson study, children with behavior disorders had rates of neglect, physical abuse, and emotional abuse that were seven times higher than children without disabilities. Having an intellectual disability can increase one's risk of sexual abuse victimization up to 10 times compared to the general population (Ansello & O'Neill, 2010). Overall, individuals with disabilities who have been abused often experience severe, lengthy, and multiple forms of abuse (Ansello & O'Neill, 2010; Hassouneh-Phillips & Curry, 2002; Sullivan & Knutson, 2000), especially those with multiple forms of disabilities (Howe, 2006).

However, given a limited body of research on this issue, many questions remain unanswered, and the quality of existing studies varies (Govindshenoy & Spencer, 2006; Hassouneh-Phillips & Curry, 2002; Westcott & Jones, 1999). Most research on IPV among women with disabilities is qualitative (Hassouneh-Phillips & Curry, 2002), and therefore the ability to generalize findings is limited. Further, the increased risk may be better explained by some other common characteristics and not necessarily related directly to the disability (Govindshenoy & Spencer, 2006). Many people with disabilities live healthy, satisfying, and productive lives (Ansello & O'Neill, 2010). Thus, therapists should avoid assuming that individuals with disabilities have been abused, although it is essential to remain alert for signs of it (Govindshenoy & Spencer, 2006).

Why are Individuals with Disabilities at an Increased Risk of Abuse? Individuals with disabilities may experience the same forms of abuse as non-disabled individuals—physical, sexual, and emotional. In addition, some forms of abuse are uniquely related to their disability status (Hassouneh-Phillips & Curry, 2002; Westcott & Jones, 1999). For example, a perpetrator may limit a victim's mobility by dismantling his or her wheelchair, or an abusive caregiver may withhold medications or other treatments needed to address the disability (Hassouneh-Phillips & Curry, 2002; Lynch, 2006). A form of emotional abuse is for a caregiver to shame an individual with a disability into believing that she or he would not be able to function without the caregiver's help (Lynch, 2006). Sexual abuse may occur when a caregiver inappropriately touches an individual with disability during such caregiving activities (Hassouneh-Phillips & Curry, 2002; Lynch, 2006). In addition, features of the individual's disability may present unique barriers to leaving an abusive situation (Yoshida et al., 2009). For example, abuse hotlines may not be accessible to individuals who are deaf (Yoshida et al., 2009).

Another category of contributing factors relates to the potential for abuse in a caregiving relationship. Individuals' disabilities may render them dependent on a greater number of helpers, and thereby increase the number of potential perpetrators with whom they have contact (Ansello & O'Neill, 2010; Cooke & Standen, 2002; Kelley & Moore, 2000; Oosterhoorn & Kendrick, 2001; Westcott & Jones, 1999). Caregivers of individuals with disabilities may experience high levels of stress, which may lead them to become overwhelmed and prone to maltreatment (Westcott & Jones, 1999). Individuals with disabilities may have learned to be compliant with caregivers (Ansello & O'Neill, 2010) and have a level of emotional dependence on their caregivers that makes them hesitant to disclose if abuse occurs (Oosterhoorn & Kendrick, 2001).

Social factors also may contribute, as disabilities may be associated with decreased community involvement, such as being unable to work (Ansello & O'Neill, 2010; Kelley & Moore, 2000). Isolation also may be related to living in an institution as opposed to living in the community (Westcott & Jones, 1999). Further, individuals may have low self-esteem associated with their disability (Ansello & O'Neill, 2010), and may have internalized societal messages that people with disabilities are less valuable than people without disabilities (Cooke & Standen, 2002; Westcott & Jones, 1999), sometimes referred to as *ableism* (Yoshida et al., 2009). Being marginalized by society may contribute to viewing themselves as deserving to abused (Kelley & Moore, 2000; Peckham, Howlett, & Corbett, 2007).

Clinical Assessment. Abuse of individuals with disabilities is underreported (Ansello & O'Neill, 2010). Protective Service systems often do not document disabilities of the individuals they investigate (Ansello & O'Neill, 2010; Cooke & Standen, 2002). When investigators do note disabilities, they may view the disability as contributing to the abuse and therefore treat the case differently than if they were investigating someone without a known disability (Manders & Stoneman, 2009). Even when abuse is detected, victims may be retraumatized by their experiences with systems that are supposed to protect them (Ansello & O'Neill, 2010). For example, cases may be dismissed because they are difficult to investigate, they may be unable to access useful treatments, and perpetrators may not be punished due to perceptions that individuals with disabilities are not credible witnesses (Ansello & O'Neill, 2010). Thus, therapists should assess for abuse experiences if clients have had interactions with Protective Services, even if the investigation did not result in formal intervention. Therapists should understand the laws in their jurisdictions regarding whether, when, and how they are required to report suspected abuse of individuals with disabilities to the appropriate authorities.

Identifying maltreatment among individuals with disabilities can be a challenge, especially since signs may be unclear or difficult to differentiate from features of the disability (Ansello & O'Neill, 2010). Some physical disabilities render an individual prone to injury, and so it can be difficult to distinguish injuries resulting from accidents and from abuse (Ansello & O'Neill, 2010; Cooke & Standen, 2002). In addition, some individuals with disabilities engage in self-injurious behaviors, with resulting injuries that can be difficult to differentiate from abuse-related injuries (Ansello & O'Neill, 2010; Westcott & Jones, 1999). Some professionals also overlook abuse of disabled individuals due to being overly empathetic of the challenges faced by caregivers (Ansello & O'Neill, 2010; Cooke & Standen, 2002; Manders & Stoneman, 2009).

We recommend three considerations in the clinical assessment of individuals with disabilities when abuse is suspected or known. First, be comprehensive in the information included. Potentially useful sources of information include interviewing caregivers, observing clients, and using existing measures to assess for risk (Westcott & Jones, 1999). Therapists should note inconsistencies in caregivers' stories related to potential abuse indicators (Ansello & O'Neill, 2010). Second, consider clients' cognitive capacity and level of knowledge. Many individuals with disabilities lack information about abuse, so they may not identify abuse they are experiencing as such (Ansello & O'Neill, 2010). Therapists therefore should seek to understand through the assessment process the extent of the client's knowledge about maltreatment. Third, adapt the assessment to meet the client's unique needs and characteristics. Individuals with disability-related communication impairments may be unable to effectively report their abuse experiences due to these impairments (Ansello & O'Neill, 2010). Therapists must be especially vigilant for potential signs of abuse when working with clients who lack the communication capacity to report the abuse themselves (Oosterhoorn & Kendrick, 2001).

Treatment. There is a lack of available research and programming designed to meet the needs of individuals with disabilities who were abused. On the basis of existing information, we advise therapists to consider the following suggestions when working with this population.

Develop Increased Competence in this Area. Many professionals lack training in understanding the unique needs of individuals with disabilities (Cooke & Standen, 2002; Yoshida et al., 2009). Some topics to learn about include identifying healthy aspects of families and individuals with disabilities, understanding service delivery systems to assist individuals with disabilities, and assessment approaches to differentiate abuse symptoms from disability features (Manders & Stoneman, 2009). Therapists looking to increase their competence with this population may want to develop such skills as sign language (Cooke & Standen, 2002).

Focus on Clients' Strengths throughout the Therapy Process. Individuals with disabilities may be hesitant to seek counseling (Kelley & Moore, 2000). To engage these clients, therapists should involve the client as an active partner in the therapy process (Westcott & Jones, 1999). All interventions should be tailored to the client's unique developmental level (Ansello & O'Neill, 2010) and mobilize the client's personal and social strengths. Development occurs on many levels, and therapists should bear in mind that adults with cognitive impairments may have a level of emotional maturity that is more advanced than their IQ or mental age or vice versa (Ansello & O'Neill, 2010). When possible, treatment should involve interdisciplinary collaborations to ensure that professionals are involved who understand and address clients' unique disability-related needs (Manders & Stoneman, 2009; Westcott & Jones, 1999). This may include using an interpreter during sessions, as in the case of sign language.

Develop Strategies for Working with Clients with Communication Impairments. Many therapists are not adequately prepared to work with individuals with communication impairments (Ansello & O'Neill, 2010). Individuals with communication-related disabilities may understand language better than they can speak it (Ansello & O'Neill, 2010). Therapists may use adaptive technologies to assist with communication (Ansello & O'Neill, 2010). However, these technologies often must be adapted to be suitable for treatment of abuse experiences (Oosterhoorn & Kendrick, 2001). For example, some communication-related technologies do not include abuse-related vocabulary (Oosterhoorn & Kendrick, 2001). Therapists also may introduce pictures to augment the capacity of individuals to communicate about their abuse (Oosterhoorn & Kendrick, 2001; Peckham et al., 2007). Non-language-based approaches, such as expressive therapies (e.g., art or dance therapy) and play therapy may be useful for individuals with limited communication abilities (Ansello & O'Neill, 2010; Peckham et al., 2007).

Address Trauma Experiences within a Climate of Safety and Support. Trauma-related symptoms that clients with disabilities may experience in relation to abuse include depression, PTSD, anxiety, and dissociation (Ansello & O'Neill, 2010). Similar to individuals without disabilities, those with disabilities benefit from feeling supported and validated by therapists as they re-tell the stories of their abuse (Peckham et al., 2007).

Empower Clients through Education. Therapists may provide psychoeducational interventions to help clients learn about abuse and its impact (Hassouneh-Phillips & Curry, 2002; Kelley & Moore, 2000; Oosterhoorn & Kendrick, 2001; Peckham et al., 2007), as well as strategies for coping with it (Peckham et al., 2007). Information must be provided in a developmentally-appropriate manner (Peckham et al., 2007). In addition to general information about abuse, individuals with disabilities may not be familiar with community resources available to them (Ansello & O'Neill, 2010), and therefore therapists can link them to these sources of support. Clients may need assistance in understanding legal issues, so therapists should link them to qualified legal personnel to assist with this need (Kelley & Moore, 2000).

Understand the Accessibility of Local Abuse-related Resources. Therapists must familiarize themselves with relevant resources so that they can pass this information along to clients (Hassouneh-Phillips & Curry, 2002). For example, adult IPV victims can benefit from knowing how and where to locate shelters, especially those that are accessible (Kelley & Moore, 2000). Unfortunately, many battered women's shelters are not accessible for individuals with disabilities (Hassouneh-Phillips & Curry, 2002; Yoshida et al., 2009). Despite the importance of making resources accessible to individuals with disabilities, it is an unfortunate reality that many programs have very limited resources available (Yoshida et al., 2009). Therefore, increased funds and policies are needed to ensure that all relevant community resources are made accessible to individuals with disabilities (Yoshida et al., 2009).

Consider Treatment Strategies for Caregivers. Treatment for caregivers of individuals with disabilities can address what Ansello and O'Neill (2010) referred to as "the three R's" (p. 118): (1) Recognizing their roles as caregivers; (2) Reinforcing their ability to provide care; and (3) Resources to help them function most effectively. It is important to connect caregivers with resources to better equip them to provide care effectively (Howe, 2006). Other potentially useful areas of treatment for caregivers include learning to accurately interpret the individuals' emotional responses and providing information about the nature of the disability (Howe, 2006).

Address Systemic Issues Related to Clients' Disabilities and Abuse. Therapeutic interventions may address different levels, including the individual, family, and broader social context (Westcott & Jones, 1999). Clients may benefit from a discussion related to the intersections of their disability status, abuse, and other forms of oppression they experienced, such as due to gender or race (Yoshida et al., 2009). Therapists may help clients develop self-advocacy skills to enable them to better recognize abuse if it occurs and to feel empowered to ask for what they need (Ansello & O'Neill, 2010). Family interventions can improve the relationship dynamics between the client and family members, especially those who are caregivers (Westcott & Jones, 1999). Advocacy to improve the living conditions and value of individuals with disabilities within society remains necessary (Westcott & Jones, 1999). Preventive approaches to reducing the abuse of individuals with disabilities in society include building public awareness of the issue, building the community's capacity to support individuals with disabilities, helping them learn how to advocate for their needs, and increasing training for professionals who may work with them (Ansello & O'Neill, 2010).

Maltreatment Perpetrated by Individuals with Disabilities

Another issue related to abuse and disabilities is abuse perpetrated *by* individuals with disabilities, in particular those with developmental disabilities and cognitive impairments. Individuals with developmental disabilities may display aggressive behaviors associated with their disabilities (Antonacci, Manuel, & Davis, 2008; Ayland & West, 2006; Murphy, Powell, Guzman, & Hays, 2007), and these behaviors can lead to higher use of psychotropic medications (Antonacci et al., 2008). The link between developmental disabilities and aggression can be further complicated if mental health disorders also are present (Antonacci et al., 2008).

The most common characteristics of sexual abuse perpetrators with intellectual disabilities include: being male; having a relatively mild disability; perpetrating against a known victim (i.e., not a stranger); coming from a chaotic family; demonstrating other problematic behaviors; and having a history of mental health disorders (Murphy et al., 2007). Sexual offences perpetrated by this population often involve victims who also have intellectual disabilities (Murphy et al., 2007). Especially in these cases, such sexual offences often are not prosecuted (Murphy et al., 2007). Reoffending is common among this population (Murphy et al., 2007).

Treatment. There is limited research evidence regarding effective treatments for individuals with developmental disabilities who demonstrate aggressive behavior (Antonacci et al., 2008). Potentially useful treatment topics include the following: (a) sex education (Hays, Murphy, Langdon, Rose, & Reed, 2007; Murphy et al., 2007); (b) relevant laws (Hays et al., 2007; Murphy et al., 2007); (c) developing empathy for a potential victim (Ayland & West, 2006; Hays et al., 2007; Murphy et al., 2007); (d) problem-solving skills (Hays et al., 2007); and (e) relapse prevention (Ayland & West, 2006). Cognitive-behavioral therapy (CBT) (Murphy et al., 2007), strengths-based, and narrative approaches may prove useful to working with this population (Ayland & West, 2006).

Intimate Partner Violence among Individuals with HIV/AIDS

There is growing recognition that IPV is linked with being infected with HIV/AIDS in at least four ways. First, experiencing IPV may place a victim at risk of HIV infection (Heintz & Melendez, 2006; Rose, House, & Stepleman, 2010). An IPV victim may feel disempowered to engage in safer sex practices if his/her partner is abusive (Heintz & Melendez, 2006; Toro-Alfonso & Rodriguez-Madera, 2004). For example, negotiation about safer sex practices may be limited in a relationship characterized by abuse (Heintz & Melendez, 2006). The risk-related abusive relationship dynamics may include partners who have additional sexual partners and/or who fail to use condoms (Molina & Basinait-Smith, 1998). Reflecting these dynamics, in one study of 40 randomly selected women in battered women's shelters, 50% reported that their partner had infected them with at least one sexually transmitted infection (Molina & Basinait-Smith, 1998). HIV infection also may be a direct consequence of IPV, such as when an infected partner forces his or her uninfected partner to have unprotected sex (Heintz & Melendez, 2006; Rountree, Pomeroy, & Marsiglia, 2008; Toro-Alfonso & Rodriguez-Madera, 2004). Even with these risks, women may not view themselves as being at risk for HIV (Molina & Basinait-Smith, 1998). This is troubling, in that more severe forms of abuse appear to be related to greater risk of HIV infection (Molina & Basinait-Smith, 1998). The risks are considered great for females in heterosexual relationships and gay and bisexual males who are IPV victims (e.g., Rountree et al., 2008; Toro-Alfonso & Rodriguez-Madera, 2004).

Second, having HIV/AIDS can increase one's risk for experiencing IPV. For example, Ramachandran and colleauges (2010) interviewed 56 HIV-positive men who have sex with men and found that 73% reported experiencing IPV in their lifetimes and 20% reported current experiences of IPV. Rose et al. (2010) studied the links between IPV and HIV among a sample of 40 HIV-positive African American women in Georgia. 60% of the women indicated that they experienced IPV in their lifetimes. These studies demonstrate that rates of IPV among individuals infected with HIV are high.

Third, for individuals infected with HIV/AIDS, experiencing IPV victimization can lead to negative health outcomes and more rapid progression of the infection (Lichtenstein, 2006; Rose et al., 2010). Reasons for this include that an abusive partner may limit a victim's ability to seek healthcare and that the chaotic nature of the IPV may make it difficult for the victim to keep up with a prescribed medication regimen (Lichtenstein, 2006; Rose et al., 2010). Medication adherence is critical in treatment regimens for HIV, so the challenges that arise in this area related to IPV victimization are crucial to address (Rose et al., 2010). Both HIV infection and IPV independently can lead to a host of negative outcomes, and the combination of the two can seriously impact individuals' quality of life (McDonnell, Gielen, O'Campo, & Burke, 2005).

Fourth, HIV/AIDS and IPV can be related through one's disability status. Many individuals infected with HIV are classified as having an HIV-related disability (Rose et al., 2010), and therefore information discussed above regarding abuse and disabilities may apply to this population. Along these lines, Rose et al. (2010) referred to women with HIV infections and women with disabilities as "overlapping risk groups for IPV" (p. 315). As a disability, HIV may become increasingly limiting as it progresses (Rose et al., 2010).

Assessment and Treatment Considerations

Therapists should avoid stereotypical assumptions about which IPV victims may be at risk for HIV infection, as HIV crosses all sociodemographic backgrounds (Molina & Basinait-Smith, 1998). When working with clients who have experienced IPV or who are HIV-positive, it is advised that therapists assess for the other phenomenon (Ramachandran, Yonas, Silvestre, & Burke, 2010; Rose et al., 2010; Rountree et al., 2008). Therapists should address the potential of HIV infection with all clients who have experienced IPV (Molina & Basinait-Smith, 1998).

More research and clinical work are needed to develop effective strategies to address IPV among clients at risk for or infected with HIV (Lichtenstein, 2006; Ramachandran et al., 2010). Further consideration is warranted for other potentially-related issues, such as substance abuse, as HIV-positive clients' experiences of IPV may be complicated by substance abuse (Burke, Thieman, Gielen, O'Campo, & McDonnell, 2005; McDonnell et al., 2005). Therapists also can assist with managing challenges to medication adherence by identifying strategies to increase the likelihood that they will adhere to medication regimens within the context of abuse (Rose et al., 2010). Another component of a comprehensive treatment approach relates to sexual behaviors, and therapists should talk with HIV-infected clients or clients whose partners are HIV-positive regarding safer sex practices (Heintz & Melendez, 2006). As such, IPV safety plans should address safer sex strategies (Heintz & Melendez, 2006).

According to Rountree et al. (2008), when working with clients who have been abused and who are at risk for or infected with HIV, therapists should connect clients to resources in the community through which they can receive supportive services and education related to HIV. Battered women's shelters have increasingly been identified as important sites for HIV/AIDS education and referral. However, despite growing recognition of the links between HIV and IPV, many are ill-equipped to address HIV risk behaviors. Even when they do assess for HIV risk, shelter staff may fail to provide services and referrals to ensure that women who have been battered receive support they need in this area. Again, limited financial and other resources often prevent shelters from being able to effectively address the compound issues faced by individuals who have been battered. Overall, the strong links between HIV/AIDS and IPV, within the context of limited information and resources for comprehensive treatment, indicate that this is an important area for future developments in research and practice.

Elder Abuse

Professional attention to elder abuse became most prominent in the 1970s and 1980s (Anetzberger, 2005a). The phenomenon once known as "granny battering" has now become recognized as a major threat to the well-being of older adults (Anetzberger, 2005a). With the baby boomer generation growing into older age, the percentage of elderly individuals in the population is likely to grow for years to come (Krienert, Walsh, & Turner, 2009; Lundy & Grossman, 2004; Powell & Berman, 2006), and thus, elder abuse is likely to become an increasingly significant concern (Donohue, Dibble, & Schiamberg, 2008; Just, 2007; Krienert et al., 2009; Mouton et al., 2005; Ploeg, Fear, Hutchison, MacMillan, & Bolan, 2009; Teaster, Stansbury, Nerenberg, & Stanis, 2009). In addition, individuals with lifelong disabilities have experienced longer life spans with recent advances in medical treatments for many of these conditions (Ansello & O'Neill, 2010). Thus, there are some intersections with the disability-related issues discussed earlier and elder abuse.

What is Elder Abuse?

Varying definitions have been used to describe elder abuse, leading to inconsistencies in research and practice (Anetzberger, 2005a; Malks, Schmidt, & Austin, 2002). The terms *elder maltreatment* and *elder abuse* are umbrella terms for a wide range of forms of abuse and neglect of elderly adults (Krienert et al., 2009), and these terms are used interchangeably throughout this chapter. Elder abuse refers to acts of commission or acts of omission (Krienert et al., 2009), and can occur in home or institutional settings (Welfel, Danziger, & Santoro, 2000).

In the literature, an *elder* generally refers to someone over the age of 65 (e.g., Kaye, Kay, & Crittenden, 2007), although sometimes it refers to someone over the age of 60 (e.g., Anetzberger, 2005a; Krienert et al., 2009), and even state laws differ in this regard (Welfel et al., 2000). Although they may not meet specific criteria for elder abuse, individuals between the ages of 50 and 60 may be viewed as uniquely vulnerable to abuse, in that they often do not have dependent children that render them eligible for Medicaid and other welfare-related programs, and yet they typically do not qualify for Medicare and other protective services for older adults (Leisey, Kupstas, & Cooper, 2009). Often, an elder abuse perpetrator is in a position of trust to the victim (Donohue et al., 2008), although this is not always the case. Elder abuse may involve several different specific types of abuse, including the following:

Physical abuse involves a perpetrator inflicting physical harm on a victim (Anetzberger, 2005a; Mouton et al., 2005; Welfel et al., 2000). This can include hitting, beating, shaking, or slapping (Choi & Mayer, 2000; Page, Conner, Prokhorov, Fang, & Post, 2009; Welfel et al., 2000), and can result in physical injuries (e.g., bruises or broken bones) (Choi & Mayer, 2000). The term *caretaking abuse* describes maltreatment that reflects the failure of a caregiver to perform necessary functions of this role, such as by giving too much medication, using physical restraints excessively, or using unacceptable toileting practices (Page et al., 2009).

Neglect refers to the failure of a presumed caregiver to provide for an elderly person. *Physical neglect* involves failing to provide for the physical needs of an elder (Anetzberger, 2005a; Donohue et al., 2008; Mouton et al., 2005; Welfel et al. 2000), such as by failing to provide nourishment or medical care (Choi & Mayer, 2000) or by ignoring an elderly person when s/he requests assistance (Page et al., 2009). *Emotional neglect* involves failing to provide emotional and social support for an elder (Anetzberger, 2005a). Neglect may be unintentional if the presumed caregiver does not know about the needs of the elderly person or lacks the resources to provide the needed care (Choi & Mayer, 2000; Welfel et al., 2000).

Psychological/emotional abuse involves a perpetrator inflicting emotional or psychological distress (Anetzberger, 2005a; Choi & Mayer, 2000; Mouton et al., 2005; Welfel et al., 2000), such as isolation, threatening, violating one's rights, treating the person like a child, harassment, and intimidation (Anetzberger, 2005a; Choi & Mayer, 2000; Page et al., 2009). It also may relate to violating the rights of the elderly person, which is sometimes viewed as its own category of abuse. *Violating rights* includes such actions as forcing an elderly into an institutional setting when the person does not want to go (Choi & Mayer, 2000) or denying the elder privacy or free speech (Welfel et al., 2000). This category also addresses verbal abuse, or such behaviors as yelling, insulting, or humiliating an elderly person (Page et al., 2009).

Financial abuse, sometimes referred to as *material abuse*, involves a perpetrator using an elderly person's financial resources in an illegal or improper manner that is not in that person's best interest but that benefits the abuser (Anetzberger, 2005a; Choi & Mayer, 2000; Mouton et al., 2005; Page et al., 2009). This may include theft (the most common form of financial abuse; Welfel et al., 2000), using resources without permission, or using deception to acquire resources (Malks et al., 2002). Possible signs of financial abuse include unexplained changes in financial status, suspicious changes in legal documents (e.g., a will or power of attorney), unexplained loss of resources, and forged signatures (Malks et al., 2002).

Sexual abuse, which is sometimes subsumed under the category of physical abuse (Anetzberger, 2005a; Chihowski & Hughes, 2008; Choi & Mayer, 2000; Kaye et al., 2007), involves forced or coerced, nonconsensual sexual activity or molestation (Anetzberger, 2005a; Choi & Mayer, 2000; Mouton et al., 2005; Page et al., 2009). Attempted, threatened, or completed rape or sexual assault fall under this category (Chihowski & Hughes, 2008, p. 380). Other examples include exposing one's genitals, "taking sexually oriented photographs of an elder, or performing sexual acts in front of an elder without ... consent" (Chihowski & Hughes, 2008, p. 380). Elder sexual abuse also can include overly intrusive, painful genital practices that are not performed for a justifiable purpose (Chihowski & Hughes, 2008).

Self-abuse and *self-neglect* occur when an elderly person does not adequately care for his/her personal health or safety (Choi & Mayer, 2000). Self-abuse refers to engaging in behaviors that result in the self-infliction of injury (Anetzberger, 2005a), and self-neglect refers to failing to adequately provide for one's own physical needs (Anetzberger, 2005a; Donohue et al., 2008). Self-neglect may include not seeking medical care, not performing basic self-care, not caring for pets, and living in unclean conditions (Donohue et al., 2008). Three aspects of self-neglect include being unable to maintain a healthy living environment, having inadequate hygiene, and having impaired mental functioning (Donohue et al., 2008). The latter issue is complicated because it is often difficult to determine the point at which a person is no longer competent to make choices about being living independently (Donohue et al., 2008).

Self-neglect is understandably quite a controversial issue (Anetzberger, 2005a; Kaye et al., 2007). The issue of whether elder abuse requires a perpetrator other than oneself has been debated (Anetzberger, 2005a). Some professionals view self-neglect as a form of neglect by others, in that others are not adequately overseeing or caring for the person (Anetzberger, 2005a). Further, self-neglect may better be viewed as a reflection of an underlying mental illness rather than a form of maltreatment (Kaye et al., 2007; Teaster et al., 2009). Most states include self-neglect in elder abuse laws, and so this issue warrants attention by therapists and is often addressed within adult protective systems (APSs) (Anetzberger, 2005a). Elders who self-neglect may be more likely to be socially isolated, and their self-neglectful behaviors may emerge after a period of gradual decline in physical and/or cognitive capacity (Choi & Mayer, 2000).

How Common is Elder Abuse?

Most elderly individuals are able to live independently and are cared for lovingly and appropriately (Choi & Mayer, 2000; Donohue et al., 2008; Just, 2007). However, a certain segment of the elderly adult population experiences maltreatment. Elder abuse occurs among approximately 1% to 10% of older Americans, although studies provide different estimates within that range (e.g., Just, 2007; Krienert et al., 2009; Mouton et al., 2005; Nahmiash & Reis, 2000; Page et al., 2009; Ploeg et al., 2009; Welfel et al., 2000). Krienert et al. (2009) examined data from the Federal Bureau of Investigations (FBI's) National Incident-Based Reporting System (NIBRS) from 2000 to 2005 to identify patterns of elder abuse. During this time frame, 87,422 incidents of elder abuse were reported to law enforcement agencies. However, reported rates of elder abuse are likely underestimates due to extensive underreporting (Just, 2007; Malks et al., 2002; Ploeg et al., 2009).

Some forms of elder abuse are more common. Choi and Mayer (2000) examined cases of elder abuse in Erie County, New York, between 1992 and 1997. Among these cases, 22% were self-neglect, 8% neglect by others, and 7% neglect by self and others. Financial abuse occurred in 38% of the cases. Nearly 52% of the cases reflected cases of endangerment by self, as in self-neglect, financial mismanagement, or self-harm, and the other 48% involved an identified perpetrator. Of the cases involving perpetrators, many involve multiple forms of abuse. A similar rate of self-neglect (52%) was found in substantiated APS cases in an Ohio county during 2001 (Dayton, 2005). Across other studies, the more common forms of elder abuse identified were self-neglect (Anetzberger, 2005a; Donohue et al., 2008), financial abuse (Anetzberger, 2005a; Boldy, Hornder, Crouchley, Davey, & Boylen, 2005), and emotional abuse (Anetzberger, 2005a). Sexual abuse is the least commonly-reported form of elder abuse, accounting for only 1% of confirmed elder abuse cases substantiated by APS systems (Chihowski & Hughes, 2008).

Elder Abuse Response Systems

Laws regarding elder abuse vary across states (Just, 2007; Welfel et al., 2000) and are controversial in that some view them as limiting the older adults' independence (Anetzberger, 2005a). Regardless, therapists must learn about reporting requirements in their jurisdiction, and therapists are often required to report suspected elder abuse (Anetzberger, 2005a; Choi & Mayer, 2000; Welfel et al., 2000).

Similar to Child Protective Service (CPS) systems, Adult Protective Service (APS) systems became common in the 1970s (Anetzberger, 2005a). Once a case is reported to APS, an investigation occurs, and investigators must find reasonable cause or reasonable suspicion to substantiate elder abuse (Chihowski & Hughes, 2008). Reasonable cause means that elder abuse likely occurred, based on available facts and evidence (Chihowski & Hughes, 2008; Malks et al., 2002). A social work model underlies APS systems, such that the goals are to involve clients in making decisions about their cases and providing the least restrictive level of services (Dayton, 2005; Teaster et al., 2009). These systems aim to both protect victims and help them maintain autonomy (Teaster et al., 2009). APS processes are somewhat different than CPS ones in that, assuming an elderly person has the cognitive capacity to make a decision for him-/herself, the person has the right to choice to live at risk of harm (Dayton, 2005; Teaster et al., 2009; Welfel et al., 2000). Depending on state law, if an elder is competent, s/he may refuse services offered through APS (Just, 2007).

Despite the availability of APS systems, the majority of elder abuse incidents are not reported (Anetzberger, 2005a; Choi & Mayer, 2000). Cases often do not reach the level of APS investigation until they have become extremely severe and the abuse has been occurring for a long time (Dayton, 2005). Therefore, a range of other entities may be involved in addressing and preventing elder abuse, both in collaboration with APS systems and through other activities such as: (a) law enforcement (Anetzberger, 2005a; Choi & Mayer, 2000; Falk et al., 2010; Teaster et al., 2009); (b) domestic violence agencies and shelters (Anetzberger, 2005a; Leisey et al., 2009; Lundy & Grossman, 2004; Teaster et al., 2009), although many individuals are reluctant to seek such services (Anetzberger, 2005a); (c) medical professionals (Anetzberger, 2005a; Falk et al., 2010) and public health agencies (Teaster et al., 2009); (d) financial institutions (Choi & Mayer, 2000; Malks et al., 2002); (e) social workers (Falk et al., 2010); (f) district attorneys (Malks et al., 2002; Teaster et al., 2009); (g) private attorneys (Malks et al., 2002); (h) religious organizations (Podnieks & Wilson, 2003; Sherr & Ellor, 2009); and (i) mental health agencies. Increasingly, APS systems have developed collaborative relationships with mental health service systems (Teaster et al., 2009). In addition to these formal sources of support, older adults may turn first to informal sources of support (e.g., friends) before more formal protective systems in response to abuse victimization (Leisey et al., 2009). Thus, individuals impacted by elder abuse are likely to have several potential supportive resources available to them in their communities.

Risk Factors for and Consequences of Elder Abuse

Elders may be especially vulnerable to abuse if they have impairments, either physically or cognitively, and poor health is linked to abuse risk (Anetzberger, 2005a; Choi & Mayer, 2000; Donohue et al., 2008; Just, 2007; Kaye et al., 2007; Powell & Berman, 2006; Welfel et al., 2000). As adults age, they may develop increasing impairments that require them to become dependent on others, which is another major risk factor (Donohue et al., 2008). For example, requiring caregiving in the areas of bathing and toileting has been identified as a risk factor for sexual abuse (Chihowski & Hughes, 2008).

Certain demographic characteristics are linked to an increased risk of elder abuse. A typical elder abuse victim is female (Anetzberger, 2005a; Boldy et al., 2005; Chihowski & Hughes, 2008; Choi & Mayer, 2000; Just, 2007; Krienert et al., 2009), although this may be due in part to women outnumbering men in older age (Lundy & Grossman, 2004). Although females are at greater risk, the needs and experiences of older males who have been abused should not be ignored (Kaye et al., 2007). A typical victim also is over 75 (Anetzberger, 2005a; Boldy et al., 2005; Chihowski & Hughes, 2008; Choi & Mayer, 2000) or 80 (Just, 2007).

An elderly person's living situation may contribute to his/her risk level. For example, a typical victim lives in his/her own home (Anetzberger, 2005a), especially in cases of self-neglect or financial exploitation (Choi & Mayer, 2000). Many victims live with their perpetrators (Choi & Mayer, 2000; Krienert et al., 2009; Powell & Berman, 2006), especially in cases involving physical or emotional/psychological abuse or neglect (Choi & Mayer, 2000). Social isolation is another risk factor (Anetzberger, 2005a; Choi & Mayer, 2000; Just, 2007; Kaye et al., 2007). Other risk factors include substance abuse (Choi & Mayer, 2000), fewer financial resources (Choi & Mayer, 2000; Just, 2007; Kaye et al., 2007), a history of childhood trauma (Kaye et al., 2007), and mental illness (Choi & Mayer, 2000). In particular, depression is linked to self-neglect (Donohue et al., 2008; Just, 2007; Kaye et al., 2007; Powell & Berman, 2006).

Perpetration Risk Factors. Generally, elder abuse perpetrator characteristics are more accurate predictors than victim ones (Anetzberger, 2005a; Choi & Mayer, 2000). Of course, perpetrators are diverse and may perpetrate for different reasons (Chihowski & Hughes, 2008). Nonetheless, several categories of perpetrator risk factors have been identified.

First, the nature of the relationship between perpetrators and victims has been explored. A perpetrator is usually a family member (Anetzberger, 2005a; Donohue et al., 2008; Just, 2007; Kaye et al., 2007; Welfel et al., 2000), most commonly an adult child (Anetzberger, 2005a; Boldy et al., 2005; Choi & Mayer, 2000; Donohue et al., 2008; Krienert et al., 2009; Lundy & Grossman, 2004; Welfel et al., 2000), followed by a spouse (Anetzberger, 2005a; Lundy & Grossman, 2004) or other family member (Boldy et al., 2005). However, perpetrators also may be from outside the family (Choi & Mayer, 2000; Kaye et al., 2007; Krienert et al., 2009) and are especially likely to be outside the family for financial abuse, such as a neighbor, tenant, guardian, handyman, home health aide, or supposed friend (Choi & Mayer, 2000). Even in those cases, family members are still the most likely perpetrators of financial elder abuse (Malks et al., 2002). Different types of perpetration are more likely depending on whether the victim is male or female. Perpetrators against females are more likely to be family members, whereas those against males are more likely to be strangers or acquaintances (Krienert et al., 2009).

Another aspect of the perpetrator-victim relationship that increases the risk for elder abuse includes the perpetrator being dependent on the victim. This includes financial and other forms of dependence (Anetzberger, 2005a; Choi & Mayer, 2000; Lundy & Grossman, 2004; Powell & Berman, 2006; Welfel et al., 2000). For example, a perpetrator usually lives with the elder (Anetzberger, 2005a; Donohue et al., 2008). Conflict-ridden family relationships also increase the risk (Anetzberger, 2005a), and elder abuse may stem from longstanding problematic family relationship patterns (Choi & Mayer, 2000; Just, 2007).

Second, caregiving stress and burnout often are discussed in relation to elder abuse (Anetzberger, 2005a; Choi & Mayer, 2000; Donohue et al., 2008; Just, 2007; Teaster et al., 2009). A caregiver is defined as a person "offering help to an older adult on a regular basis. They may or may not live with the older adult. Caregivers are usually family members but could also be a friend, a neighbor, a janitor, or even a person, who until recently, had been a stranger but has begun to offer services ... to the older adult... Most caregivers do an excellent job with little support or assistance" (Nahmiash & Reis, 2000, p. 54). People differ in their attitudes toward caregiving based on how they view the responsibility of caring for elders within one's family (Mouton et al., 2005). Some challenging aspects of caregiving include ongoing losses associated with the elder's continued declines, difficult caregiving instructions involved in managing medical regimens, and the potential for increased social isolation over time (Drossel, Fisher, & Mercer, 2011). In light of these demands, caregiving has been linked to a variety of negative mental and physical health outcomes for caregivers (Drossel et al., 2011). Caregivers at an increased risk of perpetrating elder abuse include those with inexperience with caregiving (Anetzberger, 2005a) and those who are overwhelmed with the responsibilities involved (Chihowski & Hughes, 2008).

Third, dysfunctional personal and behavioral patterns, as well as demographic characteristics, are linked to the risk of elder abuse perpetration. These include mental illness (Anetzberger, 2005a; Lundy & Grossman, 2004; Teaster et al., 2009; Welfel et al., 2000), substance abuse (Anetzberger, 2005a; Choi &

Mayer, 2000; Lundy & Grossman, 2004; Welfel et al., 2000), low self-esteem (Cook-Daniels, 1997), a history of violent behavior (Anetzberger, 2005a), and social isolation (Lundy & Grossman, 2004). Research suggests that elder abuse perpetrators are usually male (Anetzberger, 2005a; Krienert et al., 2009) and usually under the age of 60 (Donohue et al., 2008), often between the ages of 40 and 49 (Krienert et al., 2009).

Intersection with IPV Risk Factors. Risk factors for IPV apply to elder abuse, in that elder abuse also may reflect IPV, either new cases or cases that have simply aged into later life (Leisey et al., 2009; Lundy & Grossman, 2004). A unique feature of IPV within elder abuse is the abusive partner's ability to physically neglect the victim, which is not typically a dynamic associated with IPV at younger ages (Leisey et al., 2009). Lundy and Grossman (2004) studied 1,057 adults aged 65 and older who received services from domestic violence agencies in Illinois between July 1990 and June 1995. Over 90% of these adults were female, and they ranged in age from 65 to 94. Most of their abusers were relatives, especially spouses. The types of abuse they experienced included emotional (96%), physical (71%), and sexual (5%). Very few of these adults had any major physical impairments. An implication of this study is that older adults who enter into the service delivery system through domestic violence agencies may have unique characteristics and needs as compared to those who enter through APS or other channels.

Consequences of Elder Abuse Victimization. Elder abuse can result in a host of negative outcomes for victims, including the following physical, mental health, and other consequences.

Physical Consequences. An elderly person's physical health can be compromised as a result of abuse. One result could be physical injury (Anetzberger, 2005a; Choi & Mayer, 2000), including genital injuries resulting from sexual abuse (Chihowski & Hughes, 2008). Neglect may lead to dehydration and malnutrition (Anetzberger, 2005a; Choi & Mayer, 2000). Victims also may experience problems sleeping (Anetzberger, 2005a; Chihowski & Hughes, 2008). Elder abuse also may increase a victim's risk of mortality (Choi & Mayer, 2000; Donohue et al., 2008; Ploeg et al., 2009). Together, these physical consequences can contribute to more rapid cognitive and physical declines than if the abuse were not present (Choi & Mayer, 2000).

Mental Health Consequences. Elder abuse victimization is linked to an array of possible mental health outcomes. Mental health disorders that victims may experience include depression, PTSD, and other anxiety disorders (Anetzberger, 2005a; Chihowski & Hughes, 2008; Choi & Mayer, 2000; Welfel et al., 2000). Other negative emotions also may be experienced, including anger, helplessness, denial, fear, alienation, guilt, and shame (Anetzberger, 2005a; Chihowski & Hughes, 2008; Choi & Mayer, 2000; Welfel et al., 2000). These feelings may be generalized or specific to abuse-related situations. For example, an elderly person who has been sexually abused may become distressed when receiving body-oriented care, such as baths or a physical health exam (Chihowski & Hughes, 2008). Victims also may be at an increased risk of suicidality (Anetzberger, 2005a). All of these symptoms can be especially difficult in the face of impaired coping abilities that victims often demonstrate (Anetzberger, 2005a).

Other Consequences. Victims may become socially withdrawn (Anetzberger, 2005a), and some may display aggressive behaviors (Chihowski & Hughes, 2008). Elder abuse, especially financial, may lead to negative economic impacts, such as losing assets (Choi & Mayer, 2000).

Assessment Considerations

The assessment of elder abuse may involve detecting previously unidentified cases or understanding the dynamics and related features in cases that are already known. Several challenges can arise through the assessment, and we present the following recommendations to help therapists gather accurate and comprehensive information in suspected or known cases.

Recognize that Elder Abuse is often Difficult to Detect. Many forms of elder abuse are not readily identifiable because they lack visible consequences (Choi & Mayer, 2000; Welfel et al., 2000). Sexual abuse in particular is often underreported and very difficult to substantiate (Chihowski & Hughes, 2008). Victims and perpetrators may be hesitant to disclose elder abuse for a variety of reasons (Choi & Mayer, 2000). First, they may believe that reporting will reflect negatively on their families (Mouton et al., 2005; Welfel et al., 2000). If the perpetrator is a family member, a victim may be hesitant to disclose for fear of potential negative consequences to family relationships (Chihowski & Hughes, 2008). Victims also may fear that if they disclose abuse, they will be institutionalized (Choi & Mayer, 2000; Kaye et al., 2007). Elderly adults from marginalized populations, such as lesbian, gay, bisexual, transgender, and questioning (LGBTQ) individuals, may be especially hesitant to disclose abuse (Cook-Daniels, 1997). Clients who have been abused may provide hints of their abuse prior to making a full disclosure in order to test how the therapist might respond to such a disclosure (Chihowski & Hughes, 2008). Therefore, even minor indications that abuse may have occurred signify a need for further assessment.

Comply with Legal Reporting Requirements. If a new incident of elder abuse is identified through the assessment, the therapist must report the incident to the appropriate authorities (Chihowski & Hughes, 2008). Any information that may be considered evidence of abuse during an APS investigation must be handled appropriately (Chihowski & Hughes, 2008). A therapist may be concerned about the potential that reporting suspected abuse could lead to increased risk for the victim (Anetzberger, 2005a), and mandatory reporting requirements can strain the trust between a therapist and client (Kaye et al., 2007). Therefore, such reports should be handled sensitively. Some suggestions for doing so include involving the client in making the report, educating the client about the reporting and investigating processes, addressing clients' emotional reactions to the report being made, maintaining as much of the client's confidentiality as possible, and following up on the referral after it has been made (Welfel et al., 2000). Addressing the limitations of confidentiality with regards to suspected elder abuse within a therapist's informed consent document also is advised (Welfel et al., 2000).

Assess for Signs and Symptoms of Elder Abuse Therapists should be alert to the potential for abuse when one or more of the risk factors listed above are present (Anetzberger, 2005b). However, the presence of risk factors does not guarantee that abuse is present. It is important to consider alternative explanations for clients' presenting characteristics, such as medication side effects or physical health conditions (Falk et al., 2010; Anetzberger, 2005b). For sexual abuse, a therapist must make efforts to determine whether a client consented to the sexual activity (Chihowski & Hughes, 2008). This is especially complicated if the alleged perpetrator is the victim's spouse (Chihowski & Hughes, 2008). When abuse is detected, it should be described in terms of its frequency, type, severity, and duration (Anetzberger, 2005b).

Determine the Client's Cognitive Capacity. Due to cognitive impairments, elderly victims may have a limited ability to understand the consequences of their choices (Anetzberger, 2005b; Choi & Mayer, 2000), as well as the extent to which they recognize abuse if they are experiencing it. Therefore, it is important to determining the client's cognitive capacity for making decisions as part of the assessment process (Chihowski & Hughes, 2008). Psychologists and other professionals may be called upon to assess elderly individuals' cognitive capacities for making decisions and providing accurate information (Falk et al., 2010; O'Connor, Hall, & Donnelly, 2009). Therapists without the competence to conduct these assessments should refer clients to an appropriate professional in the community (Falk et al., 2010). A client whose case has been investigated by APS may have already had a cognitive capacity assessment completed as part of the investigation, and therapists may be able to obtain that assessment. An additional challenge in assessing cognitive capacity in the context of potential abuse is that the abuse itself may result in changes to the individual's cognitive capacity (O'Connor et al., 2009).

The Assessment of Elder Abuse should combine Open-Ended Interview Questions with more Standardized Measurement Instruments. The formal assessment may be enhanced by using nondirective questioning, such as by asking whether the client feels safe in his/her home (Welfel et al., 2000). The quality of existing standardized assessments varies (Anetzberger, 2005b). Assessment instruments and approaches must be selected with consideration for clients' characteristics, such as age and cognitive capacity (Falk et al., 2010). As one example of a structured assessment relevant to elder abuse, Dyer et al. (2006) developed the Self-Neglect Severity Scale (SSS) as a home-based observation and interview assessment procedure to determine the severity of an elderly person's self-neglect. The SSS assesses levels of self-neglect related to physical care, the environment, and functional status in the areas of health and safety. Items were developed through interviews with APS workers and refined through extensive field testing. Administration of the SSS takes five to ten minutes in the client's home. Although further testing is needed, the SSS appears to provide a useful and objective way to assess for self-neglect. The researchers have made a draft of the SSS available on-line at http://www.bcm.edu/crest/?PMID=0.

Draw on Multiple Sources of Information. These can include clients' self-report (Chihowski & Hughes, 2008), reports of caregivers or other family members (Anetzberger, 2005b), and a medical examination (Chihowski & Hughes, 2008). Specialized physicians, called geriatricians, may be called upon to examine a client's medical history in the assessment of elder abuse (Falk et al., 2010). Involving multiple forms of information is especially important if there are questions about the client's cognitive capacity to provide accurate information (Chihowski & Hughes, 2008). Home visits can be telling about a client's living situation, although these can be challenging if strong odors are present (Anetzberger, 2005a). Visiting a client's home can help to either verify or disconfirm information that the client provided in the office setting (Falk et al., 2010; Anetzberger, 2005b). When interviewing members of the client's family, family members should be assessed separately (Welfel et al., 2000). Because other professionals may be involved with the care and assessment of the elderly client, efforts should be made to make the assessment be cohesive and coordinated among involved personnel. Interdisciplinary assessments can reduce the burden of interviewing on the victim, and therefore it may be beneficial for therapists to conduct their assessments in conjunction with other involved professionals (Falk et al., 2010).

Assess Multiple Levels of the Client's Functioning and Environment. Therapists should assess how elder abuse affects clients across different areas of their lives. Relevant areas of assessment include existing health problems, changes over time in the client's cognitive or physical functioning, available financial resources, and recent significant life events (Anetzberger, 2005b). Across domains, therapists should seek to determine the level and immediacy of their needs (Anetzberger, 2005b). The assessment also should address the needs and characteristics of the caregiver(s). Some perpetrators may view abusive behaviors as their only alternatives related to managing the tasks of caregiving, such as if they overmedicate clients to sedate them and keep them from wandering (Anetzberger, 2005b). As such, the assessment may reveal important areas for the caregivers to develop new skills and information to help them provide care in more adaptive ways. The assessment should not focus exclusively on problematic areas and should therefore address clients' strengths and resources as well (Anetzberger, 2005b).

Maintain Cultural Sensitivity. Depending on clients' cultural backgrounds or socioeconomic status, they may differ in what behaviors they view to be abusive (Anetzberger, 2005b; Mouton et al., 2005; Sherr & Ellor, 2009). Clients' help-seeking behaviors may be influenced by their cultural backgrounds (Anetzberger, 2005a). For example, some cultural groups prefer seeking help from informal sources, such as friends, whereas others are more likely to use formal sources of support, such as law enforcement (Anetzberger, 2005a).

Ethical Case Study: Client Self-Determination in Light of a Potential Cognitive Impairment

Case description. Ross, a 76-year-old Caucasian man, lives alone in the same apartment he used to share with his wife, who died over 15 years ago. Ross has two adult children, both of whom are married, have children, and live nearby. Ross meets with a therapist once a month, which is a requirement of the mental health agency through which he meets quarterly with a psychiatrist in order to be prescribed antidepressant medications. Each visit, the therapist talks with Ross about his life and specific challenges he faces currently. Ross is generally a very likeable and reserved man, and he does not share many details about his life with his therapist. He acknowledges that he would not meet with the therapist if he was not required to do so.

The same therapist has met with Ross for about eight months. This therapist learned that Ross sees his children and grandchildren about every other week, when one of his children picks him up at his home to takes him to dinner. Aside from those visits, Ross does not have much social interaction and mostly prefers to stay in his apartment and sit on his balcony to watch people go by. Ross stated that he is content with this lifestyle. Due to increasingly poor eyesight, Ross no longer drives, but he has a paid aide who comes once a week to drive him to the store for groceries and other necessities, as well as to drive him to medical and other appointments.

For the last two counseling sessions, Ross presented as disheveled and, at times, confused. The therapist noticed that Ross had significant body odor of urine on each visit. Ross admitted that his home is "very messy." Also, Ross appeared to be losing weight, and he informed the therapist that he "doesn't have the energy to cook" and often skips meals. During the both sessions, Ross showed occasional memory loss, such as repeating things he had just said multiple times and failing to be able to describe how he spent time over the past few days.

The therapist expressed concern and asked Ross if he feels like he is getting the help he needs and is able to care for himself in his own home. Ross replied defensively, "I know what you're suggesting—that I shouldn't be living on my own—and I take great offense. I have more than enough help, I can take care of myself, and I have no intention of changing." The therapist asks Ross to sign a release form so the therapist can contact Ross's children, but he refuses.

Discussion. Ethical dilemmas are common when addressing elder abuse (Anetzberger, 2005a). The major ethical dilemma faced by Ross's therapist is whether to respect Ross's autonomy (e.g., refusal to allow the therapist to reach out to his children) or whether Ross's welfare is compromised by his apparent declining ability to care for himself. Professional ethical codes value each of these goals. For example, the NASW (2008) code emphasizes a client's right to self-determination (1.02). Likewise, the AAMFT (2001) ethical code validates clients' rights to make decisions about their own lives. Nonetheless, promoting the client's welfare is the fundamental goal underlying all professional therapists' ethical codes (e.g., AAMFT, 2001, Principle 1; ACA, 2005, A.1.a; APA, 2010, Preamble; NASW, 2008, 1.01). The therapist in this situation must consider whether Ross's welfare is at risk in light of the indicators described. Consulting with Ross's psychiatrist may offer additional insights, although the therapist is likely to have more information than the psychiatrist due to their more frequent meetings.

Does the therapist have a responsibility to report Ross to APS, assuming that the therapist is a mandatory reporter of elder abuse? In our opinion, the answer is yes. Again, mandatory reporters are not obligated to know for certain that maltreatment occurred, but rather to report suspected abuse when the known facts provide reasonable suspicion that it is occurring. In this case, some of the indicators that warrant the therapist reporting the abuse to APS include Ross's disheveled and confused demeanor, his weight loss and acknowledgement that he is not adequately preparing food for himself, and his memory loss, indicating a possible decline in cognitive functioning. Ross's body odor of urine suggests that his home may not be adequately cleaned and hygienic. Timing considerations offer additional support to the need to make the report. Presumably, Ross was not demonstrating these indicators during the first six months of his counseling, so there is evidence of a potential decline in his self-care abilities.

Further, since the therapist noticed these indicators during two separate sessions, a month apart, there is evidence that they may not be isolated events. Therefore, the therapist should call APS to make a report, and the outcome of their investigation will be determined by the additional details they uncover. In particular, if maltreatment is substantiated, APS will need to determine whether Ross's situation reflects self-neglect or whether one of his caregivers (e.g., his children or his paid aide) are liable, which is often a difficult determination to make (Choi & Mayer, 2000).

At least two additional ethical responsibilities for the therapist in this case study are significant. First, the therapist should not assess Ross's cognitive capacity unless s/he is competent to do so (e.g., ACA, C.2.a). Therefore, unless the therapist is trained, experienced, and has appropriate credentials to conduct a cognitive capacity assessment, the therapist should refer Ross to another professional to do so. Second, because reporting to APS will involve breaking confidentiality, the therapist should ensure that this is handled in an ethically responsible manner (e.g., AAMFT, 2001, 2.2; APA, 2010, 4.05.a). In particular, the therapist should disclose only the minimal information that is pertinent to the case (NASW, 2008, 1.07.c) and should likely discuss the disclosure with Ross and remind him of the therapist's obligation to report suspected abuse, which should have been addressed in the informed consent document and discussed at the outset of treatment (e.g., ACA, 2005, B.1.d; NASW, 2008, 1.07.e).

Treatment Considerations

The assessment findings should guide treatment (Anetzberger, 2005b; Nahmiash & Reis, 2000). Elder abuse interventions are relatively underdeveloped and understudied (Nahmiash & Reis, 2000; Ploeg et al., 2009). Existing research demonstrates common methodological limitations that hinder the quality of previous studies (Ploeg et al., 2009). Although there are few programs with strong evidence for their effectiveness, this, of course, does not signify that interventions to address elder abuse are not warranted (Ploeg et al., 2009).

Two goals underlying interventions should be to promote the client's safety and help the client maintain as much autonomy as possible (Anetzberger, 2005b). The general process for elder abuse intervention is as follows: (a) address acute or crisis needs; (b) ensure safety, such as through safety planning; (c) help the victim feel empowered and in control, such as by providing information about their options; and (d) address underlying issues that may contribute to further abuse (Anetzberger, 2005b). Clients who experienced elder abuse should receive long-term follow-up to ensure that their safety is maintained over time (Anetzberger, 2005b). The remainder of this section presents recommended approaches for therapists working with clients impacted by elder abuse, focusing especially on treatment of victims.

Tailor Treatment to Clients' Unique Needs. Therapy for elder abuse victims offers some general benefits, including emotional support (Lundy & Grossman, 2004; Teaster et al., 2009) and helping to manage abuse-related symptoms (Kaye et al., 2007). To complement these general goals, additional areas of treatment should be tailored to clients' unique needs. For example, clients with trauma-related symptoms should be supported in reducing the negative impacts of the trauma (Teaster et al., 2009), as well as in addressing additional past traumas the person experienced prior to the elder abuse (Kaye et al., 2007). Clients using maladaptive coping strategies, such as substance abuse (Nahmiash & Reis, 2000), can be supported in developing new, more positive coping skills (Kaye et al., 2007). Some clients benefit from educational information about abuse, especially to alert them to the potential for further abuse (Kaye et al., 2007). Some approaches that may prove useful in addressing clients' unique needs include a life review, solution-focused therapy, and narrative therapy to help the client reconstruct a new narrative that is not centrally focused on the abuse (Kaye et al., 2007).

Focus on the Client's Strengths. A strengths-based perspective is useful when working with elder abuse victims (Dayton, 2005). This may include building upon existing strengths (Nahmiash & Reis, 2000) and developing new ones, such as positive coping strategies, self-esteem, and self-care behaviors (Kaye et al., 2007). Generally, interventions with elder abuse victims aim to promote self-determination and independence (Dayton, 2005), and one way to do this is to ensure that clients' strengths are highlighted throughout treatment.

Address the Client's Relationship with a Known Perpetrator and Ambivalent Feelings about that Relationship. Because so many cases of elder abuse involve family members as perpetrators, clients with close relationships to their perpetrators may benefit from processing their ambivalent feelings toward them (Chihowski & Hughes, 2008). Many victims have long minimized the extent of the abuse (Anetzberger, 2005a), and consequences such as APS involvement may bring to light the severity of the abuse they faced. Therapists can help clients to explore mixed feelings they may have about their abuser, such as feeling love for them but also confusion about how they could treated them in an abusive manner. When relationships are ongoing, therapists can help clients create more adaptive relationship patterns (Teaster et al., 2009). To the extent possible, this may involve supporting victims to develop resources to become less dependent on others (Just, 2007). Therapists also can help clients decide what types of future relationships they would like to have with previously abusive family members.

Consider Clients' Preconceptions about Therapy. Mental health counseling can be helpful for elder abuse victims (Boldy et al., 2005; Choi & Mayer, 2000;

Just, 2007). Therapy offers a potentially safe environment in which the client feels comfortable to discuss his or her experiences (Welfel et al., 2000). However, older adults in general are less likely to seek mental health services than their younger counterparts (French, Wiener, & Mosher-Ashley, 2000). These clients may be hesitant to trust a helping professional (Just, 2007), and elder abuse victims often refuse help (Anetzberger, 2005a). In part, this may be due to the tendency for other professionals with whom they come into contact, physicians especially, to fail to refer them to mental health services (French et al., 2000). Physicians may view elderly patients as not being receptive to therapy, and therefore they do not think to refer them even if these patients are, in fact, open to such services (French et al., 2000). Thus, many physicians rely solely on psychiatric medications to treat older patients' mental health symptoms (French et al., 2000).

Consider the Unique Needs of Male Clients. Treatment options for male elder abuse victims are especially limited (Kaye et al., 2007). In particular, there is a lack of emergency shelter options available in a crisis situation (Kaye et al., 2007). Kaye et al. suggest that gender-sensitive intervention approaches for male victims of elder abuse are warranted. Strategies Kaye and colleagues recommend include multisystemic approaches and male-only groups. In addition, suicide risk should be addressed, as this has been found to be elevated among older adult males.

Collaborate with Multidisciplinary Teams. Additional training for professionals who work with elderly adults is needed (Chihowski & Hughes, 2008; Choi & Mayer, 2000; Podnieks & Wilson, 2003). For example, professionals who work in elder care settings should learn to recognize signs of sexual abuse (Chihowski & Hughes, 2008). One way to help ensure that clients' needs are met effectively is for therapists to collaborate with professionals from other relevant disciplines. Therapists are likely to work together as part of multidisciplinary teams when addressing elder abuse (Anetzberger, Dayton, Miller, McGreevey, & Schimer, 2005; Falk et al., 2010; Malks et al., 2002; Nahmiash & Reis, 2000; Ploeg et al., 2009), whether these are formal or informal networks (Teaster et al., 2009). Such multidisciplinary teams have a long history in the area of addressing elder abuse and can bring together multiple perspectives to work toward a common goal of supporting clients affected by elder abuse (Anetzberger et al., 2005). Benefits of multidisciplinary elder abuse response teams include that they offer a more holistic approach, share the responsibility of care among a number of professionals, and provide more seamless service provision (Anetzberger et al., 2005).

Include Home Visitation as Appropriate. Home visitations are challenging, especially if clients' homes are unkempt (Falk et al., 2010). Therapists are advised not to go on home visits alone, especially on the first visit, in case safety risks are present (Falk et al., 2010). Home-based services offer the advantage of reducing the stigma the client may feel at seeking services from an agency (Kaye et al., 2007) and increasing access to care. Therefore, when feasible and appropriate, home-based therapy may prove useful to clients impacted by elder abuse.

Support Clients through Transitions They Face Related to the Outcomes of Elder Abuse. Therapists can help clients make tough decisions, such as deciding whether elders have the ability to care for themselves due to physical or cognitive impairments or whether they may need to move into assisted living facilities to stay safe (Choi & Mayer, 2000; Just, 2007). In the latter case, therapists may be called upon to help the client and family members adjust to this new living arrangement. Many elderly individuals are resistant to moving to an institutional setting (Just, 2007; Kaye et al., 2007). Additional protections may need to be put in place to ensure that an institutional setting is safe. Sadly, elderly individuals may face continued risk for maltreatment in institutional settings, with Page et al. (2009) reporting that "moving from paid home care to nursing homes is shown to more than triple the odds of neglect" (p. 239).

Help Clients Develop Increased Social Connectedness (Kaye et al., 2007). Social isolation and withdrawal can be both risk factors for and consequences of elder abuse. Victims may have previously hidden their abuse from friends and family members, further isolating them (Leisey et al., 2009). When available, therapists should build on the client's existing social support system (Dayton, 2005), and it also may be useful to help clients identify new sources of support, such as community organizations and neighbors. Support groups offer another potentially beneficial resource for elder abuse victims to reduce feelings of isolation (Just, 2007; Nahmiash & Reis, 2000; Welfel et al., 2000). These groups can address self-blame, education about the dynamics of elder abuse, and coping strategies (Nahmiash & Reis, 2000).

Refer Clients to Additional Services and Resources. Clients often lack awareness of community resources available to them (Choi & Mayer, 2000; Just, 2007). Services and resources designed to meet specific, concrete needs may be especially useful (Nahmiash & Reis, 2000). Additional services an elder abuse victim may need include: (a) medical care (Chihowski & Hughes, 2008); (b) financial advising (Choi & Mayer, 2000; Just, 2007; Welfel et al., 2000); (c) substance abuse treatment (Just, 2007); (d) volunteer home visiting programs (Nahmiash & Reis, 2000); (e) legal consultation (Anetzberger, 2005b; Lundy & Grossman, 2004); (f) case management (Powell & Berman, 2006); and (g) housing assistance (Welfel et al., 2000) or assistance with keeping their houses clean (Nahmiash & Reis, 2000).

Address Broader Social Issues that Continue to keep Elder Abuse Under-recognized. Increased public awareness is needed about elder abuse (Boldy et al., 2005; Choi & Mayer, 2000; Kaye et al., 2007), and this issue receives far less public attention than other forms of family violence (Choi & Mayer, 2000; Welfel et al., 2000). Thus, efforts are needed to help inform the general public and potential victims about the dynamics of abuse and resources to seek help (Leisey et al., 2009). An additional broader issue is that many organizations that help the general population of elderly individuals are not adequately prepared to address elder abuse (Just, 2007). Vinton (2003) described an innovative arrangement for providing emergency shelter for older domestic violence victims that was established between a domestic violence agency and an assisted living facility. The latter facility agreed to provide such a victim with assisted living care for a designated brief period of time. Therefore, therapists are encouraged to take an active role in advocating for more innovative approaches such as these to building more appropriate community resources for clients impacted by elder abuse.

Assist Caregivers in Developing Resources to Reduce Their Risk of Abuse. Therapists may be called upon to conduct therapy with elder abuse perpetrators or those at risk of becoming so. Generally, treatment for an elder abuse perpetrator should be tailored to perpetrators' unique needs, characteristics, and motivations (Chihowski & Hughes, 2008). The type of perpetrator that has been the focus of most existing research is the caregiver-turned-perpetrator. Therapists may work with caregivers who face caregiving-related stressors that either increase their likelihood of perpetrating elder abuse or have led them to do so already. At any point in working with caregivers, APS should be notified if a caregiver who has been determined to be unsuitable to provide caregiving support has begun to do so again (Just, 2007).

Caregivers may demonstrate a wide range of needs in therapy. Some issues that caregivers may need to address in counseling include anxiety and depression (Nahmiash & Reis, 2000), feeling overwhelmed by their responsibilities (Just, 2007), coping skills to manage the stresses associated with caregiving (Donohue et al., 2008), burnout and stress, legal considerations, and supportive resources (Sherr & Ellor, 2009). Interventions that increase positive relationship functioning in the elderly person's family (i.e., communication skills) can increase caregiving resources and buffer against stress (Donohue et al., 2008). As such, family counseling may be beneficial for caregivers and elder abuse victims (Nahmiash & Reis, 2000).

One approach that has been adapted for elder caregivers is Dialectical Behavior Therapy (DBT). Drossel et al. (2011) proposed a modified DBT group for caregivers who are at risk for perpetrating elder abuse. The group aimed to reduce harmful behaviors and increase caregivers' quality of life. Some topics addressed in the nine-week program included mindfulness, emotion regulation, interpersonal effectiveness, and distress tolerance. In a pilot evaluation of the program with 16 caregivers, it showed promise for helping caregivers reduce their risks of elder abuse perpetration. For example, they showed more positive psychosocial adjustment, more problem-focused coping, more positive emotional well-being, increased use of supportive services, and reduced fatigue. The intervention's long-term benefits were enhanced when caregivers participated in follow-up booster sessions. Although additional research is needed to examine the effectiveness of this program with larger populations and using more rigorous methods, it holds promise for addressing elder abuse potential among at-risk caregivers.

In addition to counseling interventions for these issues, caregivers may benefit from educational and resource referral interventions (Nahmiash & Reis, 2000). Caregivers may benefit from developing a formal support team to more proactively manage the tasks of caregiving (Sherr & Ellor, 2009). Therapists should connect caregivers with potentially helpful sources of support in the community (Donohue et al., 2008), as often caregivers are not referred to the services they need (Drossel et al., 2011). Interventions that may benefit caregivers include respite care (Boldy et al., 2005) and support groups (Nahmiash & Reis, 2000).

Conclusion

Therapists working with clients impacted by the abuse of vulnerable populations face significant challenges in this work. One of the greatest challenges is balancing respect for the client's autonomy with the need to protect some of the most vulnerable members of our society. Because these individuals have limited abilities to protect themselves from abuse and to report abuse once it has occurred, therapists must remain vigilant for potential abuse when working with clients from vulnerable populations. Therapists also must be flexible when working with clients from vulnerable populations, in that approaches they use likely will need to be adapted to meet the unique needs of clients. Collaboration with other professionals is important in addressing all areas of family violence, but building on multidisciplinary approaches is especially important among vulnerable populations. Moreover, because many members of these populations require the assistance of caregivers, therapists should work to ensure that caregiving relationships are positive and supportive resources for helping those in need of care. As always, the ultimate goal of therapists' work with vulnerable populations is to help these clients achieve personal safety in their lives and communities.

11

FAMILY VIOLENCE AND CO-OCCURRING SUBSTANCE ABUSE

Research demonstrates a clear and consistent, yet complicated, link between family violence and substance abuse (Easton, Swan, & Sinha, 2000a). For example, Easton et al. (2000a) studied the family violence histories of 130 outpatient substance abuse treatment clients over a two-month timeframe. Among these clients, 37% reported some history of physical family violence, with 22% reporting adulthood victimization, 14% reporting childhood abuse, and 18% reporting physical violence perpetration. These researchers compared clients with a history of physical family violence to the clients without such a history, and those with the family violence history generally demonstrated more severe problems than those without. For example, clients with family violence histories had higher levels of alcohol use, cocaine use, and depression.

Violence and substance use and abuse are linked in both direct and indirect ways (Hoaken & Stewart, 2003). Directly, violence can be induced by the physiological effects of a substance. Indirectly, violence can be used as a means of acquiring a drug (Hoaken & Stewart, 2003). The relationship between substance abuse and family violence is bidirectional, in that each one can be considered a risk factor for, and outcome of, the other one (Acierno, Coffey, & Resnick, 2003; Bennett & O'Brien, 2007; El-Bassel, Gilbert, Schilling, & Wada, 2000; Ullman, Najdowski, & Filipas, 2009; Widom & Hiller-Sturmhofel, 2001). Substance abuse is a risk factor for more severe family violence (Easton, Swan, & Sinha, 2000b; Thomas & Bennett, 2009) and may precipitate an incident of violence (Easton et al., 2000a). Likewise, family violence is a risk factor for substance abuse (Easton et al., 2000b), as a victim may turn to substances as a means of coping with difficulties resulting from victimization (Cruz & Peralta, 2001; Steele, 2000).

Given the overlap between family violence and substance abuse, perhaps it is no surprise that this overlap has been the focus of theoretical and research attention (Bednar, 2003; Galvani, 2007; Hoaken & Stewart, 2003; Humphreys, Regan, River, & Thiara, 2005; Klostermann & Fals-Stewart, 2006). Many questions about the nature of the relationship between substance abuse and family violence are likely to remain forever unanswered, especially because it is ethically impossible for researchers to randomly assign participants to these experiences (Fals-Stewart & Kennedy, 2005; O'Leary & Schumacher, 2003). Nonetheless, researchers have studied a number of explanations for the relationship between family violence and substance abuse, including situational, physiological, and underlying contextual explanations.

Regarding situational explanations, researchers speculate that individuals who abuse substances experience situations and circumstances that inherently involve risk for violence. For example, substance users may use violence to access substances, such as committing a violent robbery to get money to buy drugs (Hoaken & Stewart, 2003). The physiological effects of substances can impact users' inhibitions and biologically based impulses toward aggression (Bednar, 2003), thus potentially increasing the risk for violence in the family. More broadly, researchers have speculated that the relationship between family violence and substance abuse is explained by a range of underlying characteristics. These researchers speculate that people who experience family violence and substance use may share common underlying characteristics (such as sensation seeking) that make them prone to these behaviors (Hoaken & Stewart, 2003).

This chapter addresses the overlap and intersections of substance abuse with family violence, although it is beyond the scope of this book to provide comprehensive coverage of substance abuse counseling approaches. We begin with general treatment considerations that apply to all forms of family violence. Next, we explore links among family violence and specific forms of family violence: intimate partner violence (IPV), child maltreatment, and elder abuse.

General Treatment Considerations

Common themes underlie treatment for any form of family violence. These relate to the ongoing need to maintain a primary focus on safety, the coordination of treatment, which may be hampered by different philosophical orientations of treatment programs or a general lack of truly integrated treatment models, and the need to consider overlaps with mental health issues.

General Consideration 1: The Primary Focus in Treatment Must Remain on Safety

As we emphasize in this book, the primary focus in treatment for overlapping substance abuse and family violence issues must be on safety (Bennett

& O'Brien, 2007; Steele, 2000). One approach to integrated treatment that takes safety considerations into account is found in Steele's (2000) stage-based approach to treatment with substance-abusing trauma survivors. The first stage focuses on stabilizing the client's symptoms, including behaviors, substance use, and emotional reactions. Next, clients learn about the recovery process and develop skills to manage stress and regulate emotions. As clients move through the middle and later stages of recovery, they address the trauma experiences more directly and ultimately focus on broader issues, such as enhancing self-esteem and relationships. Relapses are addressed as a potential part of the recovery process. Moving beyond Steele's approach, other safety considerations for working with clients with these multiple problems include developing safety strategies specific to substance use (e.g., leaving the immediate environment if a perpetrator becomes intoxicated and knowing where to seek help when one's substance use becomes a threat to the safety of oneself or others), and considering differential safety risks that may emerge as treatment progresses.

General Consideration 2: There is a Need for Increased Coordination of Treatment

Different Philosophical Views. Differing philosophical understandings of the links among substance abuse and family violence have hindered collaboration because professionals often differ in how they understand and explain these links (Bednar, 2003; Bennett & O'Brien, 2007; Chartas & Culbreth, 2001; Dalton, 2009; Fals-Stewart & Kennedy, 2005; Humphreys et al., 2005; McAlpine, Marshall, & Doran, 2001; Steele, 2000). For example, differences in child welfare and substance abuse treatment paradigms may stem from who is the identified client, what outcomes are considered acceptable, and differential time-lines for progress (McAlpine et al., 2001). As another example, mental health professionals may view substance abuse problems as secondary to other psychological issues (Steele, 2000). Thus, professionals in different focus areas may hold unique beliefs as to which issues warrant highest priority in treatment.

A critical area in which philosophical differences have hindered collaboration is in the overlap between IPV and substance abuse. Although some have viewed IPV as a sort of addiction (e.g., Serritella, 1992), this view is controversial (Ronel & Claridge, 2003). Almeida and Durkin (1999) cautioned that 12-step models should be used with caution with IPV perpetrators due to several key features of these models, including the emphasis on privacy, the view that substance abuse is the primary problem, and the perspective that one is powerless over the substance. A fundamental premise of many existing substance abuse treatment programs is that the individual does not have control over the disease of addiction (Bednar, 2003). The notion that violence and substance abuse may both reflect the person's experience of powerlessness is a controversial stance (Ronel & Claridge, 2003). However, advocates of this view suggest that a byproduct of admitting powerlessness is the ultimate acceptance of personal responsibility for making change (Ronel & Claridge, 2003). Nevertheless, many domestic violence advocates are concerned that substance abuse can be used to excuse or justify IPV perpetration (Bednar, 2003). The predominant feminist-informed ideology regarding IPV holds that perpetrators are fully responsible for, and in control of their violent behaviors (Bednar, 2003; Humphreys et al., 2005).

Two other common assumptions among substance abuse treatment providers run counter to widely held assumptions about treatment of IPV perpetrators and victims. First, many substance abuse professionals believe that establishing sobriety is a necessary precursor to beginning other aspects of treatment (Steele, 2000). Second, in view of a medical model, some substance abuse treatment providers view people with addictions as having a sickness, and this could limit their beliefs in these clients' abilities to change (Rogers, McGee, Vann, Thompson, & Williams, 2003). An additional challenge is an overarching assumption among many domestic violence and substance abuse providers that, given their limited available time and resources, they do not have the capacity to address issues other than those on which their organizations are directly focused (Fals-Stewart & Kennedy, 2005). Even when these issues are addressed, professionals may apply different paradigms for understanding substance use among victims and perpetrators (Chartas & Culbreth, 2001).

Lack of Widespread Availability of Truly Integrated Programs. Despite the importance of integrated treatment for family violence and substance abuse (Easton et al., 2000a; Rogers et al., 2003; Steele, 2000), there is a lack of widespread availability of truly integrated programs. Coordinated and collaborative approaches to treatment are sorely needed (Bennett & O'Brien, 2007; Thomas & Bennett, 2009). Staff of many programs lack training in the other area (Clay, Olsheski, & Clay, 2000; Martin, Moracco, Chang, Council, & Dulli, 2008; Ogle & Baer, 2003), and increased training for professionals working in each area remains a critical need (Humphreys et al., 2005; Galvani, 2007; Steele, 2000). Organizational or governmental policies, as well as funding agency restrictions, further contribute to the singular focus of treatment (Humphreys et al., 2005). For example, in a statewide survey of domestic violence agencies in North Carolina, only one-half of the agencies had formal policies addressing clients who abuse substances (Martin et al., 2008). As another example, many batter intervention programs (BIP) do not permit active substance users to participate (Bednar, 2003).

Each issue often is addressed separately (Bednar, 2003; Easton et al., 2000b); however, neither of these mutually occurring problems can be treated fully and effectively by focusing solely on one or the other (Fals-Stewart & Kennedy, 2005). It is important to treat these issues in an integrated way because, left untreated, each experience may contribute to relapse in progress in the other area (Easton et al., 2000a). In addition, by addressing only one issue at a time, important information about the context of both experiences can be ignored (Thomas & Bennett, 2009). However, an additional challenge in establishing integrated treatment programs is that clients often differ in the extent to which they want to address each issue. Steele (2000) suggests that substance-abusing trauma victims/survivors may present differently based on the extent to which they want to address each issue.

Not only are integrated treatment programs in short supply, but programs often fail to refer clients for adjunct services, even when the other needs are identified (Fals-Stewart & Kennedy, 2005). Many programs operate, in effect, with a "don't ask, don't tell" policy (Fals-Stewart & Kennedy, 2005, p. 14), such that they do not assess for experiences of their nonspecialized issue and therefore do not consider these other issues in treatment (Fals-Stewart & Kennedy, 2005; Ogle & Baer, 2003; Schumacher, Fals-Stewart, & Leonard, 2003; Thomas & Bennett, 2009). Some may fear asking because they are concerned that they do not have the resources to address these issues if they are identified (Kail, 2010). Even when substance abuse programs ask about IPV, this assessment may be limited to a single question and be asked in such a way that is not likely to produce accurate information (Schumacher et al., 2003).

There are some problems with a primary practice of referring out clients to other service providers for treatment for the issue not addressed in the primary treatment setting. For example, BIP services may not be set up to be appropriate for the needs of voluntary clients, especially if they are court-mandated (Fals-Stewart & Kennedy, 2005). Often, when referrals are made, clients do not follow through and seek out services to which they are referred (Schumacher et al., 2003). Clients who follow through with referrals and seek services simultaneously from multiple agencies may face challenges in navigating the policies and procedures of each agency (Kail, 2010), which may at times be at odds with one another. For example, some domestic violence shelters do not permit women to enter the shelter if they are intoxicated (Martin et al., 2008).

However, when integrated treatments are not feasible, agencies are recommended to develop strong referral networks to ensure that clients can get the ancillary services they need (Dalton, 2009; Fals-Stewart & Kennedy, 2005; Kail, 2010; Thomas & Bennett, 2009). In addition, agencies should routinely assess for violence and substance abuse and make appropriate referrals as needed (Stuart, Moore, Ramsey, & Kahler, 2004; Thomas & Bennett, 2009). Given the strong links between substance abuse and family violence, therapists working in treatment settings focusing on one of these issues should assess for experiences of the other (Easton et al., 2000a; Fals-Stewart & Kennedy, 2005; Galvani, 2007). Organizations can establish collaborative networks to address these issues cohesively, if not in a single integrated program (Dalton, 2009). In addition, agencies may work to develop memoranda of agreements to spell out conditions for coordinating and exchanging services between them (Martin et al., 2008).

The U.S. Department of Health and Human Services, Substance Abuse and Mental Health Services Administration (SAMHSA) published two relevant resources that readers may consult for further discussion of treatment linkages between substance abuse and IPV (2003, 2008). As of the writing of this book, both of these resources are available at no cost.

General Consideration 3: Therapists Need to Consider Potential Overlaps with Mental Health Issues

Although in this chapter we are focused primarily on the overlaps between the two phenomena of family violence and substance abuse, therapists must bear in mind that a third phenomenon often is at play: mental health symptoms. Psychiatric diagnoses often co-occur with substance abuse disorders and family violence (Bernstein, 2000; Langeland, Draijer, & van den Brink, 2004; Smith, 2007). Some specific symptoms that may co-occur include depression (Lee, Lyvers, & Edwards, 2008), PTSD, other anxiety disorders, and suicidality (Langeland et al., 2004; Langeland, van den Brink, & Draijer, 2002). Family violence, substance abuse, and impaired mental health often present simultaneously for clients seeking treatment for one or the other issues (Walton-Moss et al. 2003), and more extensive problems in any one of these areas can contribute to poorer treatment outcomes (Bernstein, 2000). Thus, every client's unique background and combination of life experiences and current symptoms warrant consideration, and treatment should be tailored to reflect these unique needs to the extent possible (Steele, 2000).

Intimate Partner Violence

As indicated in Figure 11.1, the relationship between IPV and substance abuse is complex. Acute (i.e., substance use) and chronic (i.e., substance abuse) dynamics influence the underlying links between these experiences. We explore these dynamics further in this section.

Immediate events. Immediate situational dynamics surrounding substance use may precipitate IPV (Cruz & Peralta, 2001), and relationship conflicts can stem from one partner's substance abuse, which can then precipitate more violence (Fals-Stewart & Clinton-Sherrod, 2009; H. R. White & Chen, 2002). Alcohol has been referred to as "the world's biggest magnifying glass" (Rolfe et al., 2006, p. 350), in that it may lead some who consume it to escalate minor infractions to serious issues rather quickly. Thus, conflicts may escalate more quickly when substances are involved, and the negativity surrounding conflictual relationship patterns may be exacerbated by the influence of substances (Fals-Stewart, 2003).

Excuses. Therapists and advocates often are concerned that perpetrators may use substance abuse as an excuse for violent behaviors, and the relationship

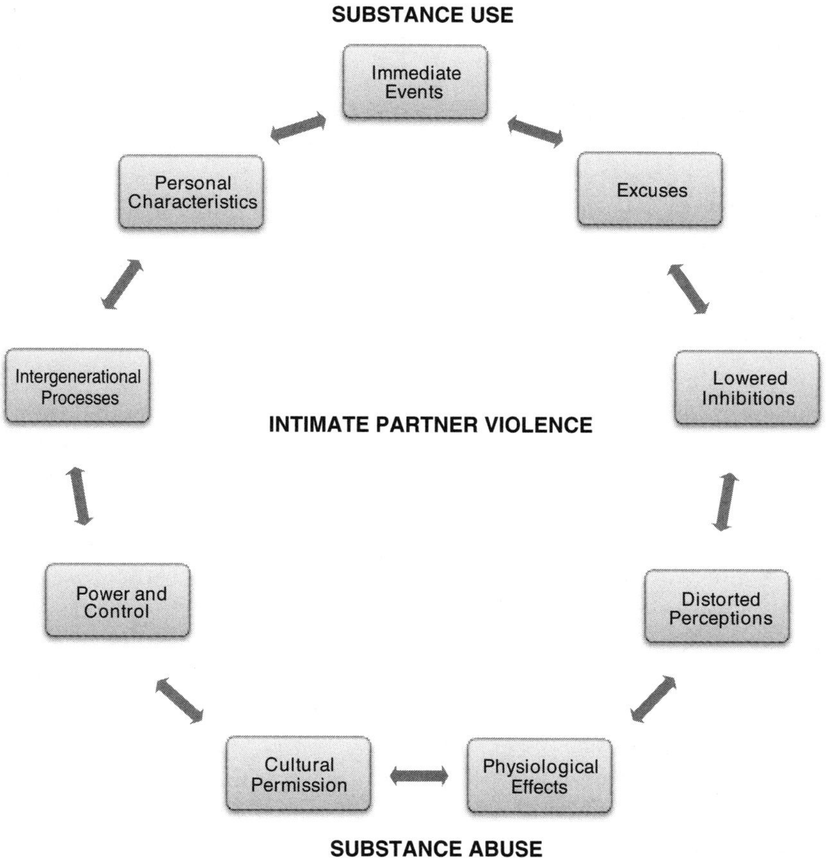

FIGURE 11.1 The cycle of intimate partner violence and substance abuse.

between substance abuse and IPV should be considered correlational and not causal (Chartas & Culbreth, 2001). However, for some people, using substances serves as a "socially acceptable excuse for aggressive behavior" (Rolfe et al., 2006, p. 344). Victims may not explicitly blame substances for their partners' use of violence (Humphreys et al., 2005). Nonetheless, they may hold beliefs that allow them to justify violent behaviors or believe that their partners will change once they cease using substances. Perpetrators may use substances because they know that their partners are likely to excuse their violent behaviors if they do so (Dalton, 2009; Sabia, 2004). The belief that substance use is a viable excuse for violent behavior can lead to higher rates of engaging in these behaviors (Thomas & Bennett, 2009). However, the notion that substance use is an excuse for violence does not bear out, in that even when substance abuse occurs in violent relationships, perpetrators may use violence both when using and when not using substances (Cruz & Peralta, 2001).

Lowered inhibitions. A common explanation for the link between IPV and substance abuse is the notion that individuals experience decreased behavioral inhibitions following substance consumption (Chartas & Culbreth, 2001; Dalton, 2009). Reduced inhibitions may result from the direct physical effects of substances or from a complex subset of thoughts and beliefs about substance use and behavior that contribute to a person feeling less inhibited after consuming (Rolfe et al., 2006). Many substances reduce a user's anxiety-related internal inhibitions, which may be linked to increased use of aggressive behaviors (Hoaken & Stewart, 2003). Other potential inhibition-related effects of substance use include becoming more excitable and feeling more courageous (Sabia, 2004). Parks, Huquembourg, and Dearing (2008) conducted an interesting experiment in which they assigned 42 women to drink either a high or low level of alcohol, and then they observed the behavior of these women interacting with men in a bar laboratory setting. The women who drank higher levels of alcohol displayed more behaviors suggestive of intoxication and romantic interest compared to those who drank lower levels. These findings suggest that, especially with higher levels of alcohol consumption, people may behave differently in social situations. These researchers in particular believe that such behaviors may be linked to increased vulnerability to potential abuse perpetrators.

Distorted perceptions. As a result of intoxication, substance users' cognitive capacities and problem-solving skills may become impaired and impact their perceptions of situations they encounter (Bednar, 2003; Fals-Stewart, 2003; Fals-Stewart & Clinton-Sherrod, 2009; Fals-Stewart, Golden, & Schumacher, 2003; Thomas & Bennett, 2009; White & Chen, 2002). Ways that a user's perceptions can become distorted are through paranoia and misinterpreting social cues (Easton et al., 2000a). This could relate to jealousy that sometimes precipitates IPV.

Physiological effects. Substances can have a direct physical effect on violence through immediate intoxication, physiological consequences of prolonged usage, and the effects of withdrawal (Hoaken & Stewart, 2003). Some physiological effects that substance use can have that can increase the likelihood of aggressive behaviors include the impact of the substance on the user's pain sensitivity and on the user's cognitive functioning (Hoaken & Stewart, 2003). In addition to immediate physiological effects, long-term substance abuse can lead to chronic health conditions that may contribute to violence (Thomas & Bennett, 2009).

Hoaken and Stewart (2003) provided a comprehensive review of research on the physiological effects of substances on aggressive behaviors. The effects vary for different classes of substances. For example, alcohol intoxication is linked most directly with violence elicitation, whereas certain other categories of substances (e.g., benzodiazepines, opiates, and psychostimulants) are linked to violence more through underlying personal characteristics rather than the direct effects of intoxication. Some substances, such as cannabis, may actually result in a decreased likelihood of perpetrating violence during intoxication, although the agitation experienced during withdrawal could prompt aggression. Physiological linkages between abuse of prescription medications and violence remain understudied (Humphreys et al., 2005).

Cultural permission. People may receive cultural messages that substance use and violence are related (Dalton, 2009). This may lead them to hold culturally based expectations that substance use leads to aggressive, violent behaviors, and as such, they may feel more justified for using such behaviors while intoxicated (Bednar, 2003; Fals-Stewart et al., 2003). In many communities and cultures, there is an implied norm that substances lead to violence, and therefore violence perpetrated while under the influence of substances is more excusable (Humphreys et al., 2005). In particular, cultural beliefs may surround masculinity, violence, and substances, and these may perpetuate violence perpetration (Humphreys et al., 2005; Rolfe et al., 2006). Some people simply expect that substance use leads to violence, and this expectation may lead them to behave in accordance with those expectations (Rolfe et al., 2006).

Power and control. Both substance abuse and IPV can occur in the context of power and control dynamics, and both can be viewed as ways that a person exerts power in social interactions (Bednar, 2003). Substance abuse by one partner can contribute to relationship problems related to the distribution of power in the relationship, especially when this occurs for a long period of time and is the source of conflict for a couple (Fals-Stewart, 2003).

Intergenerational processes. Both IPV and substance abuse have been documented to occur in the context of intergenerational family patterns (Bednar, 2003). People who grew up in violent homes in which substance abuse also occurred may come to view these experiences as normal and may play out these patterns in their own adult lives (Steele, 2000). Similarly, experiencing parental substance abuse as a child can impact IPV perpetrators' use of violence, potentially even as much as the impact of witnessing violence as a child (Corvo & Carpenter, 2000). These patterns may be explained by social learning theory, or the ways that people learn to interact with others through their family-of-origin experiences (Bednar, 2003).

Personal characteristics. The notion that substance use and IPV are related as a result of other underlying factors is referred to as the spurious model (Dalton, 2009; Fals-Stewart, 2003; Fals-Stewart et al., 2003; White & Chen, 2002) or the "unobserved bum hypothesis" (Sabia, 2004), which suggests that there are some underlying negative characteristics of perpetrators that contribute to both issues. Personal characteristics that may underlie both IPV and substance use include the following: antisocial personality, blaming, low self-esteem, feeling out of control, having a high need for control, history of childhood abuse, impaired conflict resolution abilities, impaired stress management abilities, isolation, more permissive attitudes about substances and violence, psychological problems, risky lifestyles, sociopathy, and underlying relationship problems and dissatisfaction (Bednar, 2003; Bell, Harford, Fuchs, McCarroll, & Schwartz, 2006; Bennett & O'Brien, 2007; Dalton, 2009; Fals-Stewart, 2003; Humphreys et al., 2005; Klostermann & Fals-Stewart, 2006; Testa, Livingston, & Leonard, 2003; White & Chen, 2002).

Substance Abuse among IPV Perpetrators

IPV perpetrators often demonstrate substance abuse problems (Easton, Mandel, Babuscio, Rounsaville, & Carroll, 2007; Easton et al., 2000b; Parrott, Drobes, Saladin, Coffey, & Dansky, 2003; Sabia, 2004; Stuart et al., 2008). Even when controlling for common risk factors, substance use is predictive of IPV perpetration and victimization (White & Chen, 2002). For example, having general problems with alcohol can increase the likelihood that alcohol will be a factor in a particular incident of IPV (Bell et al., 2006), with male-perpetrated IPV being substantially more likely to occur on days when men drink alcohol, and violence also is more likely to be severe on those days (Fals-Stewart, 2003). In particular, alcohol and cocaine use are associated with higher incidents of IPV, but neither opiates nor cannabis increase the likelihood of violence (Fals-Stewart et al., 2003), at least in this particular study.

Existing evidence suggests that IPV perpetration is especially problematic among those who abuse substances. For example, Parrott et al. (2003) examined the intersections between alcohol or cocaine use, IPV perpetration, and PTSD among a sample of 233 men and women in South Carolina. Rates of perpetration were highest among participants with PTSD diagnoses and cocaine dependence. Perpetrators with ongoing substance abuse also may be more likely to reoffend (Hirschel, Hutchinson, & Shaw, 2010). Furthermore, adjudicated perpetrators with substance abuse histories may be more likely violate conditions of their sentencing (Olson & Stalans, 2001). In addition, IPV perpetration may occur more frequently (Stuart et al., 2008) and be more severe among substance abusing perpetrators. Perpetrators may be especially dangerous while under the influence of substances (Humphreys et al., 2005).

O'Leary and Schumacher (2003) studied whether the relationship between alcohol use and IPV is linear (meaning that as the amount of alcohol consumed increases, so does the risk for IPV), a threshold effect (meaning that alcohol consumption does not increase IPV risk until there is a certain level of intake), or a combination of these explanations. Using analyses of large secondary data sets, O'Leary and Schumacher demonstrated a weak linear relationship, but men reporting the highest levels of alcohol consumption were more likely to report IPV. Thus, these results support a combination of both of these potential links between consumption and IPV.

At least half of men who seek alcohol treatment may demonstrate IPV (Fals-Stewart & Clinton-Sherrod, 2009; Fals-Stewart & Kennedy, 2005; Schumacher et al., 2003; Thomas & Bennett, 2009). Men who demonstrate both substance abuse and IPV perpetration have been referred to as *dual-problem men* (Thomas & Bennett, 2009). Thomas and Bennett (2009) studied whether dual-problem men can be differentiated based on whether they first enter treatment settings through substance abuse or IPV channels. They suggested that there are two possible phenomena at play. Either those entering through these channels display more severe problems in the area through which they enter (called a rational perspective) or these men will demonstrate the same levels of each problem but merely be entering through a different channel (referred to as the *different door hypothesis*). Among the 49 participants drawn from substance abuse or domestic violence treatment settings, there were no differences based on point of entry in the levels of violence, but the participants from substance abuse settings demonstrated more substance abuse problems. Thus, both the rational perspective and different door hypotheses were partially supported.

Compared to males, female IPV perpetrators may demonstrate fewer substance abuse problems and are less likely to be using substances during a violent incident (Simmons, Lehmann, & Cobb, 2008). However, among another sample of 103 adult females who had been arrested on domestic violence perpetration causes, those with higher levels of alcohol abuse—representing nearly half of the sample—experienced more frequent IPV perpetration and victimization than those with lower levels (Stuart et al., 2004). Among another sample of 35 women arrested for domestic violence, over half could be considered hazardous drinkers and had very high levels of drinking (Stuart, Moore, Ramsey, & Kahler, 2003). Compared to women in the sample who demonstrated lower levels of drinking, the hazardous drinkers were more aggressive in their relationships and in general, and they were less satisfied with their marriages.

Treatment. Few integrated treatment approaches have been developed thus far (Easton, Mandel, Hunkele, Nich et al., 2007). Often, courts mandate perpetrators to receive both IPV and substance abuse treatment as part of sentencing or probation, and it is typical that perpetrators must seek these services from different agencies (Easton et al., 2007; Easton et al., 2000b). In standard BIPs, substance use may be viewed as an ancillary problem and not addressed directly (Fals-Stewart, 2003). Likewise, substance abuse treatments may only address IPV if the client raises the issue, and even then the treatment approach may be to refer the client to another source for treatment to address that issue (Fals-Stewart, 2003).

Coordinated efforts are warranted because substance abuse can influence a perpetrators' success in treatment (Easton et al., 2000b). Perpetrators may be less likely to complete treatment successfully if they have an untreated substance abuse problem (Stalans & Ritchie, 2008; Stuart et al., 2008). Easton, Mandel, Babuscio et al. (2007) studied whether there were differences in treatment outcomes between two groups of substance abusing IPV perpetrators:

those who demonstrated alcohol use only and those who demonstrated both alcohol and illicit drugs. Those who used both alcohol and drugs, as compared to those using alcohol only, were less compliant with treatment, less abstinent from alcohol, and had more anger management problems, although there were no significant differences between the groups on their levels of physical or verbal aggression. This suggests that use of multiple forms of substances can contribute to poorer treatment outcomes.

Assessment and referral are commonly suggested for IPV perpetrators who abuse substances (Stuart et al., 2003). However, breakdowns can occur in these areas and hinder efforts to coordinate treatment. For example, Dalton (2009) surveyed 150 BIP directors nationally to learn about their experiences with perpetrators who abuse substances. 84% of these program directors reported that they assess for substance abuse, and they reported that they referred about 32% of their clients for substance abuse treatment. However, the average percentage of male perpetrator clients that directors reported were substance abusers was 49%, whereas the average percentage for females was 41%. These results suggest that BIP staff do not refer all clients with potential substance abuse problems for treatment to address that issue. In another sample of 1,496 men seeking substance abuse treatment, 44% reported that they had perpetrated at least one act of physical IPV within the previous year (Schumacher et al., 2003). Among these, only 17% were referred for domestic violence treatment (Schumacher et al., 2003).

Easton and colleagues (Easton, Mandel, Babuscio et al., 2007; Easton, Mandel, Hunkele et al., 2007) developed the Substance Use and Domestic Violence (SADV) intervention for substance abusing perpetrators. This manualized treatment involves 12 weeks of group therapy, with each session lasting 90 minutes, with a maximum of 10 participants per group. SADV is grounded in cognitive-behavioral therapy (CBT) and addresses such topics as examining substance use and aggression patterns, problem-solving and conflict management, mood regulation, anger management, and planning to manage triggers that may prompt aggression or substance use.

SADV has been compared to Twelve Step Facilitation (TSF) approaches to substance abuse treatment (Easton, Mandel, Babuscio et al., 2007; Easton, Mandel, Hunkele et al., 2007). TSF focuses primarily on substance abuse and involves education about alcoholism and recovery, participation in support groups, and building support systems. In the Easton, Mandel, Babuscio et al. (2007) study, TSF also involved 12 weeks of weekly group therapy; 78 male IPV perpetrators who abused substances were randomly assigned to either SADV or TSF. Prospective participants who demonstrated suicidal or homicidal ideation, who demonstrated severe psychopathology or had acute detoxification needs were excluded from this study. Generally, those who completed SADV demonstrated more positive treatment outcomes. For example, the SADV group demonstrated less alcohol use throughout treatment and had somewhat less frequent violence perpetration, although it is important to note that these differences did not persist at the six-month follow-up assessment. Therefore, increased efforts may be needed to help participants sustain positive changes they make in treatment over time.

Although not supported by empirical research, another model outlined in the literature, grace therapy, illustrates how both IPV perpetration and substance abuse can be treated simultaneously. Ronel and Claridge (2003) proposed a model in Israel called grace therapy to address dual IPV perpetration and substance abuse for males. This model is grounded conceptually in twelve-step approaches and is built on an assumption that both IPV perpetration and substance use share common underlying themes, such as denial, manipulation, the increasing severity of the problem, the self-centeredness of the person engaging in these behaviors, and a feeling of powerlessness that drives both of these behaviors (Ronel & Claridge, 2003). Early in treatment, the approach focuses on motivating clients to change their behaviors and engage in treatment. As treatment progresses, both substance abuse and violence are examined at the levels of behavior, thought processes, and spirituality. Although this approach attempts to integrate substance abuse and IPV perpetration interventions, its use is likely to remain controversial due to its focus on powerlessness. Furthermore, an approach such as this may not be permitted within some state BIP requirements that restrict the application of addiction-based models of battering.

Bednar (2003) suggested several general guidelines for integrated treatment of battering perpetrators who abuse substances. These include beginning with a thorough assessment of both issues, having staff members who are adequately trained to address both concerns, using such cognitive-behavioral strategies as motivational interviewing and relapse prevention, maintaining a clear stance that substance use is not an excuse for violence, and focusing on perpetrators' responsibility for his or her behaviors. Given that CBTs are commonly used to treat both issues, these approaches hold promise for future development of integrative models (Bednar, 2003). Other suggestions for coordinated treatment include: (a) addressing the unique needs of substance-abuse female IPV perpetrators (Simmons et al., 2008), for whom treatment options are especially limited (Wupperman et al., 2009); (b) focusing primarily on the clients' needs to take personal responsibility for both of these concerns (Chartas & Culbreth, 2001); and (c) avoiding acceptance of a perpetrator's use of alcohol as a justification or excuse for violence (Chartas & Culbreth, 2001).

Substance Abuse among IPV Victims

Research on substance use among IPV victims is not as extensive as research on perpetrators (Humphreys et al., 2005), although existing evidence demonstrates consistent links between the two (Bennett & O'Brien, 2007; Ogle &

Baer, 2003). For example, Bennett and O'Brien (2007) sampled 255 women seeking substance abuse and IPV victimization services from community agencies that offered either integrated or collaborative services to address both issues simultaneously. Through treatment, participants generally increased in their beliefs in their abilities to address the violence in their lives and decreased their use of substances. However, they also appeared to become increasingly aware of their vulnerability to IPV. These findings suggest that decreasing substance use may lead to more awareness of the threat one faces, or that victims' partners may respond with increased threats to positive changes they make in treatment. In either case, the practical implication is that even positive changes can be met with unintended challenges that may arise.

Rates of IPV among women seeking treatment for substance abuse are very high, perhaps even as high as 60% to 75% (El-Bassel et al., 2000), and these rates may be three times higher than the general population (El-Bassel et al., 2000). In a study of 145 women seeking services from methadone clinics in New York City (El-Bassel et al., 2000), approximately 75% of the women had lifetime histories of abuse, and about 33% had experienced IPV victimization in the previous year. The women who had been victimized in the past year were more likely to live with another person with substance abuse problems, to have acquired money or drugs by exchanging sex, and to have lower incomes (El-Bassel et al., 2000), illustrating the complexity of these women's lives.

Rates of substance abuse among IPV victims also are high and have ranged from 35% to 85% (Fowler, 2007). For example, in a sample of women in battered women's shelters (Fowler, 2007), about 66% of the women were at moderate to high risk for substance abuse, nearly 60% were dependent on alcohol, and over half were dependent on drugs. The links between IPV victimization and substance abuse also have been found in general population surveys. Testa et al. (2003) conducted a longitudinal study of substance use and IPV among a sample of 724 women between the ages of 18 and 30 who were in relationships with male partners. The use of marijuana and hard drugs was related to being more likely to experience IPV in a new relationship, although heavy drinking was not.

Reasons that substance abuse can be considered a risk factor for IPV victimization include that using substances can impact a victim's judgment, that victims may become financially dependent on their abusers, or that victims may be involved with other substance abusers who also use violence (Bennett & O'Brien, 2007). Substance abuse can make it more difficult for victims to leave an abusive relationship, such as by impairing their problem-solving, alienating them from social support, or reducing financial resources (Dalton, 2009). Substance abusers also may be at increased risk of victimization due to the stigma they face related to their use of illicit substances (El-Bassel et al., 2000). Perhaps the most common explanation for the link between IPV victimization and substance use relates to coping, in that victims are thought to turn to substances as a mechanism for coping with the impact of their traumatic victimization (Chartas & Culbreth, 2001; Dalton, 2009; El-Bassel et al., 2000; Humphreys et al., 2005; Stuart et al., 2002). In particular, victims may use substances as a form of self-medication to cope with the negative consequences of the abuse (Testa et al., 2003).

Treatment. There is a critical need for coordinated treatment for substance abuse among IPV victims (Klostermann & Fals-Stewart, 2006; Ogle & Baer, 2003). Substance abuse treatment alone may help reduce IPV victimization, but it is not thought to be able to eliminate it completely (Stuart et al., 2002). Victims of IPV who abuse substances may not be interested in changing their substance use behaviors (Ogle & Baer, 2003). The transtheoretical model of change (Prochaska & DiClemente, 1983) has been applied to therapeutic work with substance abusing victims of IPV (Kail, 2010). Kail's application holds that victims may differ in their levels of readiness to address each issue. In other words, they may be more or less ready to change their abuse situation, and they may be more or less ready to change their substance abuse habits. Kail provided specific suggestions, especially focusing on motivational strategies, for working with victims with different levels of readiness for each issue. For example, victims who are interested in becoming sober but do not want to change their relationships should be assisted in developing safety plans and in discussing the pros and cons of making potential relationship changes. Some victims will be interested in taking steps toward safety from abuse but not in becoming sober. For these, Kail recommends addressing possible pros and cons of changing and connecting victims with support groups. For clients who want to both become sober and become safer, Kail suggests that therapists should help clients develop strategies to manage possible triggers for each issue. As with most applications of the stages of change framework, Kail emphasizes that relapses may occur and should be viewed as an opportunity to learn.

Couple Therapy when IPV is Present

As discussed in chapter 5, appropriate safeguards must always be used if conducting couple therapy when IPV has occurred (Fals-Stewart & Kennedy, 2005; Galvani, 2007). One of the most researched approaches to conjoint therapy for couples who have experienced IPV and substance abuse is behavioral couple therapy (BCT; Fals-Stewart & Clinton-Sherrod, 2009). This approach is only appropriate if both partners want to remain in the relationship (Wupperman et al., 2009). BCT helps clients develop skills, such as conflict management, communication, and coping skills, which can minimize relationship problems and increase victims' safety (Fals-Stewart & Clinton-Sherrod, 2009; Fals-Stewart & Kennedy, 2005). Although BCT encourages abstinence from substances, it focuses on safety-promoting strategies that are not fully reliant on abstinence

(Fals-Stewart & Clinton-Sherrod, 2009; Fals-Stewart & Kennedy, 2005). In a study by Fals-Stewart and Clinton-Sherrod (2009), participants completed 32 treatment sessions, of which 12 were conjoint. Other applications of BCT involved weekly sessions for 20 to 22 weeks (O'Farrell, Murphy, Stephan, Fals-Stewart, & Murphy, 2004). BCT involves the non-substance-abusing partner as a support for the other partner's abstinence (Fals-Stewart & Kennedy, 2005). Other aspects of BCT include the use of a daily recovery contract, the couple verbally agreeing to not use any form of angry physical contact, the partners using time-outs to de-escalate conflicts, and a safety plan (Fals-Stewart & Clinton-Sherrod, 2009; Schumm, O'Farrell, Murphy, & Fals-Stewart, 2009). Throughout treatment, communication and negotiation skills are emphasized (O'Farrell et al., 2004; Schumm et al., 2009).

Existing research demonstrates BCT's potential positive outcomes (O'Farrell, Van Hutton, & Murphy, 1999). Fals-Stewart and Clinton-Sherrod (2009) randomly assigned 201 male substance abusers to either BCT or an individual treatment. In this study, participants were excluded if the female partner also had a substance abuse disorder or if either partner displayed severe psychopathology. A year after the men completed treatment, those in BCT demonstrated fewer IPV incidents and less severe IPV compared to those in the individual treatment.

In an earlier study, O'Farrell et al. (2004) studied the effects of BCT on IPV among a sample of 303 male alcoholic substance abuse treatment clients. These researchers used a demographically similar comparison group of men who did not abuse substances, with the comparison group drawn from an existing dataset. BCT participants demonstrated clinically significant reductions in violence that persisted into the two-year follow-up assessment. However, although the BCT participants' rates of violence were lower than before they started treatment, their rates did remain higher than the comparison group following treatment. Participants who achieved remission of alcoholism demonstrated comparable rates of IPV to participants with no history of alcoholism, whereas those who experienced relapse demonstrated higher rates of IPV. The BCT model appears to be especially likely to benefit clients when they actively attend sessions and apply the behaviors they learn in the model to their relationships.

In yet another study on the effectiveness of BCT (Schumm et al., 2009), 103 women in treatment for alcohol dependence, along with their partners, were followed for two years after completing BCT. This study's findings were similar to those of O'Farrell et al. (2004), in that the women whose alcoholism went into remission through participation in BCT demonstrated clinically significant reductions in IPV perpetration and victimization, although the reductions in victimization were somewhat less than expected.

Although these findings demonstrate the potential contributions of BCT to co-occurring IPV and substance abuse, conjoint therapy is not appropriate in all cases. A criticism of BCT is that it sets too loose a restriction around the level of violence at which treatment is considered appropriate (Galvani, 2007). BCT is only appropriate when the couple wants to stay together. Its applicability is limited only to couples for whom conjoint treatment is appropriate (Easton et al., 2007). With appropriate screening and ongoing attention to the conjoint treatment considerations outlined in chapter 5, therapists may find BCT to be a useful model to use with some clients.

Child Maltreatment

Two main links between child maltreatment and substance abuse have been studied: the increased risk of perpetration among adults who abuse substances and the increased risk of substance abuse among people who experienced childhood maltreatment (Widom & Hiller-Sturmhofel, 2001). In this section, we focus on three topics within these links: substance abuse among child maltreatment perpetrators, substance abuse among children and adolescents who have been victimized, and substance abuse among adult survivors of childhood maltreatment.

Substance Abuse among Child Maltreatment Perpetrators

Existing research indicates that parents who abuse substances are more likely to mistreat their children than parents who do not (Dawe & Harnett, 2007; Donohue, Romero, & Hill, 2006; Hien, Cohen, Caldeira, Flom, & Wasserman, 2010; McAlpine et al., 2001; Rittner & Dozier, 2000; Walsh, MacMillan, & Jamieson, 2003; Worcel, Furrer, Green, Burrus, & Finigan, 2008). Furthermore, children with parents who abuse substances face an increased risk of physical and sexual abuse, as well as neglect (Hien et al., 2010; Kerwin, 2005). However, parents can use substances, even on a regular basis, without it necessarily impacting their children (McAlpine et al., 2001; Nair, Schuler, Black, Kettinger, & Harrington, 2003). Thus, the mere presence of parental substance use or abuse does not automatically signify that children are experiencing harm as a result of that use or abuse. However, there are several ways that parental substance abuse can contribute to negative child outcomes, such as through fetal alcohol syndrome, acute incidents such as parents driving while intoxicated, physical or psychological abuse, and more chronic effects, such as neglect and poverty (McAlpine et al., 2001; Young, Boles, & Otero, 2007).

In light of the overlap between substance abuse and child maltreatment, there have been increasing efforts to coordinate substance abuse treatment and child protective service (CPS) systems (Barth, Gibbons, & Guo, 2006). As many as two-thirds (Barth et al., 2006) to 90% (McAlpine et al., 2001) of children in CPS systems have parents with substance abuse problems. Published rates vary due to different approaches to assessment and data collection across different types of treatment and CPS settings (Rittner & Dozier, 2000; Young et al., 2007). Children involved with CPS whose parents abuse substances may be especially likely to end up in the foster care system (Barth et al., 2006), and they may remain out of their homes for longer periods of time (McAlpine et al., 2001; Worcel et al., 2008).

In a study of CPS-involved families listed in a national dataset (Barth et al., 2006), the outcomes of 224 clients in which parents had substance abuse problems who received substance abuse treatment were compared to the outcomes of 224 clients in which the parents had substance abuse problems but were not treated. The major, and perhaps counterintuitive, finding was that the parents who received substance abuse treatment were about two times more likely to have another child abuse report in the 18-month follow-up period. The authors speculated that these results stem from parents feeling coerced into receiving substance abuse treatment. Furthermore, the increased rate of re-reports may simply result from the parents in treatment being in more contact with professionals who are legally mandated to make such reports.

The research as to how parental substance abuse is linked to a greater likelihood of child maltreatment perpetration is inconclusive (Widom & Hiller-Sturmhofel, 2001). In particular, questions remain regarding what explains the links between parental substance abuse and child maltreatment perpetration, although several potential mechanisms have been proposed. Several of these parallel the potential links between substance abuse and IPV discussed earlier in this chapter. At least nine mechanisms have been proposed, and these include the following.

First, parents who abuse substances may have impaired social functioning, creating greater family conflict, stress, and chaos (Anda et al., 2002; Widom & Hiller-Sturmhofel, 2001). Second, parents may blame abusive behaviors on the substance and do not accept responsibility for those behaviors (Widom & Hiller-Sturmhofel, 2001). Third, under the influence of substances, parents' inhibitions are reduced, thereby making them more likely to engage in such undesirable behaviors as maltreatment perpetration (Widom & Hiller-Sturmhofel, 2001).

Fourth, parents with addictions may place a higher priority on acquiring and using substances than on caring for their children (Barth et al., 2006). For example, risky behaviors associated with substance use (e.g., prostitution) can inhibit parental functioning (Kerwin, 2005; Nair et al., 2003). Fifth, parents who abuse substances may be less attentive to other dynamics in their homes, and therefore they may be less likely to protect their children from abuse from others (Barth et al., 2006). Sixth, parental substance abuse may relate to child abuse perpetration as part of a broader pattern of impaired functioning in many areas of life (Dawe & Harnett, 2007). Seventh, the psychophysiological effects of substances (e.g., increased paranoia and irritability) may increase the risk of aggression (Donohue et al., 2006; Kerwin, 2005).

Eighth, underlying mental health disorders may contribute to both substance use and child maltreatment perpetration (Kerwin, 2005). The relationship between substance abuse and perpetration may, in part, be explained by the parents' depression and other difficulties in mood regulation (Hien et al., 2010). Finally, substance abuse is associated with higher levels of chronic stress, which in turn contributes to parents being more harsh and punitive in their interactions with children (Nair et al., 2003). Higher levels of stress and a greater number of chronic stressors, which may serve as the backdrop for substance abuse, appear to place parents at higher risk for becoming abusive toward their children (Nair et al., 2003).

Treatment. The treatment of substance-abusing child maltreatment perpetrators remains understudied (Donohue et al., 2006; Kerwin, 2005), and there is a need for integrated interventions (Kerwin, 2005; Walsh et al., 2003). Treatment for males in this population is especially underdeveloped (Kerwin, 2005). Substance abusing perpetrators may be unwilling to voluntarily enter treatment for either issue for fear that their children will be taken from them (Kerwin, 2005). Therefore, many clinical challenges may arise.

Special considerations are warranted for CPS-involved clients, as there often is a lack of coordination between CPS systems and substance treatment (Barth et al., 2006; Kerwin, 2005). In addition, a need remains for more adequate assessment of parental substance abuse in CPS cases (Rittner & Dozier, 2000). Perpetrators involved in the CPS system may need assistance in navigating different time-lines for substance abuse treatment and key decisions made with regard to their CPS cases (Kerwin, 2005). These perpetrators may experience caseworkers as unsympathetic to the nature of their addictions (Barth et al., 2006). Efforts are being made to develop and implement more integrated service delivery approaches. For example, McAlpine et al. (2001) described the integrated approach they used in a Maryland county to address and to coordinate requirements of both the CPS system and substance abuse treatment. Key components of this approach included cross-training of staff, enhanced and tailored interventions for substance-abusing parents, the creation of clear policies, and coordinated assessment and referral procedures.

Home-based therapies may be especially useful with this population (Donohue et al., 2006; Nair et al., 2003) given that the multitude of problems that may coexist can create practical challenges, such as child care and transportation. CBT, family-based behavioral therapy, and parenting interventions also hold promise for substance abusing, child maltreatment-perpetrating parents, as do parenting interventions (Donohue et al., 2006; Hien et al., 2010; Kerwin, 2005; Romero, Donohue, & Allen, 2010).

The Parenting Under Pressure program (PUP; Dawe & Harnett, 2007) has been used with substance-abusing parents on methadone maintenance treatment. The PUP program is delivered as an intensive, in-home treatment, and it addresses multiple levels of family functioning (e.g., individuals' mental health, relationships between parents and children, and the social context) (Dawe & Harnett, 2007). Some skills, topics, and strategies emphasized in the PUP program include mindfulness, parenting relationships, discipline, managing relapse, social support networks, and affect regulation (Dawe & Harnett, 2007). Weekly, one- to two-hour therapy sessions are combined with case management throughout treatment, which typically lasts for 10 to 12 weeks. The program is adapted to the family's unique needs based on the findings of the preliminary assessment. Dawe and Harnett compared 22 parents who went through the PUP program with a control group of 23 parents receiving a standard parent education program, both in Australia. The PUP program produced positive results for participating families, with parents demonstrating decreased child abuse potential and more flexible attitudes about parenting and children demonstrating fewer behavior problems. Some families in the PUP program, however, did continue to remain at high risk of additional child victimization. In comparison, the group receiving the standard intervention demonstrated only moderate reductions in the parents' child abuse potential, and many of these families deteriorated over the course of the study. These findings demonstrate the potential value of the PUP program, although more research currently is needed, and especially to determine whether the program is applicable in the United States.

Moving beyond treatment models, potentially useful issues for general treatment with substance-abusing perpetrators include self-control training, increasing pleasant family interactions, building social support, emotional regulation, anger management, and job, problem-solving, parenting, and home safety skills (Donohue et al., 2006; Hien et al., 2010).

Substance Abuse among Children and Adolescents Who Have Been Victimized

More limited research addresses children and adolescents with substance abuse problems related to their previous victimization. In a study of adult survivors of child abuse seeking substance abuse treatment (Smith, 2007), the range of ages at which participants had first used substances was 8 to 18 years. In another study, Bailey and McCloskey (2005) studied substance use among girls who either had or had not been sexually abused. The girls who had been sexually abused had higher rates of drug use, including cocaine, marijuana, and hallucinogens. There was a significant difference between the two groups in whether they reported having ever used drugs, with 18% of the girls with sexual abuse histories claiming to have never used drugs, but 55% of the girls without sexual abuse histories making such a claim.

Adolescents may be susceptible to abusing substances due to low self-esteem and impaired social and cognitive development (Bailey & McCloskey, 2005). Substance abuse may be part of broader behavioral problems among maltreated adolescents (Bailey & McCloskey, 2005). Substance abuse and child maltreatment also may be linked through the development of PTSD (Cohen, Mannarino, Zhitova, & Capone, 2003). In particular, substance use may serve as a form of avoidance that helps adolescents keep intrusive memories at bay (Cohen et al., 2003). Finally, substance abuse may be a byproduct of antisocial and externalizing behaviors that are direct consequences of child maltreatment (Widom & Hiller-Sturmhofel, 2001).

Treatment. According to Cohen et al. (2003), there is a need for more integrated treatments in this area. Clients presenting with one of these issues should be assessed for experiences of the other. Treatment plans should address each issue but in an integrated manner. This population may require intensive intervention services in light of their complex symptoms and histories. CBT, family therapy, and systemic therapies (i.e., multisystemic therapy or MST) appear to hold the most promise for treating co-occurring substance abuse and PTSD related to child maltreatment among adolescents. Other interventions include eye movement desensitization and reprocessing (EMDR), psychodynamic psychotherapy, and psychopharmacological treatment.

Several elements appear crucial to successful treatment outcomes for adolescents demonstrating abuse-related trauma symptoms and substance abuse (Cohen et al., 2003). These include maintaining a flexible and collaborative therapeutic relationship, improving stress management and mood regulation, using cognitive restructuring, enhancing safety, improving social functioning, involving parents in treatment when appropriate, and educating clients about both issues. If appropriate, random drug screening and psychopharmacological interventions should be used. Therapists working with this population should have adequate knowledge and experience in both issues. In addition, therapists must work with these clients in a manner that reflects their unique developmental needs.

Substance Abuse among Adult Survivors of Childhood Maltreatment

Adults seeking substance abuse treatment demonstrate high rates of childhood abuse (Burnette et al., 2008; Clay et al., 2000; Lee et al., 2008; Millar & Stermac, 2000; Sacks, McKendrick, & Banks, 2008; Smith, 2007), perhaps even greater than 80% (Bernstein, 2000). Although there are some mixed research findings in this regard (Langeland et al., 2002; Zlotnick et al., 2006), more severe childhood maltreatment may be especially likely to contribute to substance abuse problems in adulthood (Downs, Capshew, & Brindels, 2004; Felitti et al., 1998; Westermeyer, Wahmanholm, & Thuras, 2001). For example, Westermeyer and colleagues (2001) examined substance abuse severity as a function of childhood physical abuse history in a sample of 642 substance abuse treatment clients. Approximately 30% of participants had histories of childhood physical abuse.

Compared to participants without this history, these clients had more severe substance abuse problems. Similarly, Zlotnick et al. (2006) studied the severity of alcohol problems among 336 treatment-seeking adults, and childhood sexual abuse was related to an earlier onset of alcohol abuse, and childhood physical abuse was related to more negative consequences of drinking. Adults whose parents abused substances themselves in addition to maltreating them may be especially prone to mental health and substance use problems (Anda et al., 2002). Survivors may be more likely to develop substance abuse problems if they were older at the time of the abuse, if they experienced more severe and longer-lasting abuse, and if they experienced multiple forms of victimization (Clay et al., 2000). The Adverse Childhood Experiences (ACE) study documented that a history of negative childhood experiences such as maltreatment also has been linked to daily cigarette smoking (Felitti et al., 1998; Topitzes, Mersky, & Reynolds, 2010), as well as a greater likelihood of illicit street drug use and earlier age of first use of all substances (Felitti et al., 1998).

There are several possible explanations for increased rates of substance abuse among survivors of child maltreatment. First, adults may use substances to self-medicate and cope with harmful effects of their victimization, such as trauma flashbacks (Millar & Stermac, 2000; Smith, 2007; Ullman et al., 2009; Widom & Hiller-Sturmhofel, 2001; Zlotnick et al., 2006). Second, survivors may view substance use as a way to connect with others and feel less isolated (Widom & Hiller-Sturmhofel, 2001). Third, survivors may feel better about themselves while under the influence (Widom & Hiller-Sturmhofel, 2001). Finally, survivors may use substances in a larger pattern of risky, self-destructive behaviors (Widom & Hiller-Sturmhofel, 2001).

Treatment. Millar and Stermac (2000) interviewed six women with histories of childhood maltreatment and prior substance abuse to learn about their recovery process. The researchers labeled the major process these women went through as reshaping the concept of self, which involved emotional management, identity development, and the construction of positive attachment styles. Key tasks that these women reported having gone through to move toward recovery from both substance abuse and childhood trauma included addressing their trauma-related emotions, developing more positive emotional responses, becoming more connected with themselves and others, and learning new ways of relating to others. A particular challenge was learning to regulate emotions without the use of substances.

Again, more work is needed to develop and study integrative treatments for survivors who abuse substances (Clay et al., 2000; Sacks et al., 2008). Many existing substance abuse treatment facilities fail to adequately treat the consequences of childhood maltreatment (Clay et al., 2000). Failing to address these issues in a coordinated manner can inhibit clients' progress. Adults in substance abuse treatment with childhood maltreatment histories may be less likely to progress in treatment than those with no such histories (Sacks et al., 2008). In addition, some commonly used substance abuse treatment interventions, especially confrontational ones, may be counterproductive with abuse survivors, but rather more supportive approaches should be used (Clay et al., 2000). Proper assessment is key, especially since many abuse histories go undetected among substance using adults (Clay et al., 2000; Millar & Stermac, 2000).

As discussed in chapter 9, therapy with substance abusing survivors typically progresses through stages of stabilization, direct work on the traumatic memories, and integration (Bernstein, 2000). Abstaining from substance use is an important part of the stabilization process (Bernstein, 2000). Due to the multiple stigmatizing experiences these clients have had, therapists should remain nonjudgmental (Smith, 2007). These clients may benefit from a combination of individual therapy and support groups (Smith, 2007), and such approaches have been documented as effective with treatment such as Seeking Safety (Najavits, 2001). Survivors may view the "culture of recovery" (Millar & Stermac, 2000, p. 179) to be extremely beneficial and supportive of their growth. Therapists can help these clients connect with positive social networks in order to enhance their recovery (Smith, 2007). Potentially useful treatment focuses include helping survivors develop a sense of empowerment and self-esteem, emotional management, and sexuality problems (Clay et al., 2000). Substance abusing survivors also may benefit from exploring the impact of gender on their experiences of child maltreatment, as the effects can vary based on whether the perpetrator was a mother or father (Downs et al., 2004).

Elder Abuse

The literature on elder abuse and substance abuse is limited. However, it suggests that substance abuse is related to elder abuse in two ways. First, elder abuse perpetrators may have more substance abuse problems compared to elder caregivers who are not abusive (Anetzberger, Korbin, & Austin, 1994; Hwalek, Neale, Goodrich, & Quinn, 1996; Just, 2007; National Center on Elder Abuse, 2004). As such, elder abuse perpetrator interventions may benefit from including a focus on substance abuse (Anetzberger et al., 1994). Given the potential for financial exploitation (Just, 2007), caregivers with substance abuse problems may exploit elderly family members in order to get money to pay for substances. Interestingly, when elder abuse victims' perpetrators have substance abuse problems, the victims may actually be more willing to seek help (Powell & Berman, 2006). Therefore, it may be worthwhile for therapists to explore the victims' views as to how their abusers' substance abuse patterns relate to their experiences of elder abuse.

Second, elder abuse victims may abuse substances, possibly to cope with their victimization, and this could put them at greater risk for further victimization (Hwalek et al., 1996; Just, 2007; National Center on Elder Abuse, 2004). In particular, elderly persons who abuse substances may be at risk for self-neglect and come to the attention of authorities because they fail to take proper care of themselves (Just, 2007; National Center on Elder Abuse, 2004). Therapists who work with elder abuse victims should assess these clients for substance use and abuse (National Center on Elder Abuse, 2004). Elderly victims with substance abuse problems may be especially difficult to engage in substance abuse treatment (Just, 2007). If possible, they may appreciate being able to participate in treatment that is with others around the same age (Just, 2007). In addition, it can be beneficial to engage the elderly person's supportive social networks, such as neighbors, to help monitor the person's safety (Just, 2007).

Conclusion

Substance abuse among perpetrators, victims, and survivors adds another level of clinical complexity to the already challenging issue of family violence. Because substance abuse is linked so closely to many cases of IPV, child maltreatment, and elder abuse, therapists must be competent to address these dual issues. A pattern across these clinical populations is the lack of existing coordinated treatments, so therapists and clients alike may struggle to address both issues within existing treatment paradigms. Therefore, therapists are encouraged to continue to advocate and work toward more comprehensive, integrative treatment approaches that can benefit clients who have experienced both family violence and substance abuse.

12

FAMILY VIOLENCE AND CULTURAL ISSUES

Family violence can occur in virtually any segment of the population. It crosses racial, ethnic, socioeconomic, religious, and geographic differences. Many dynamics of different forms of family violence—including child maltreatment, intimate partner violence (IPV), and elder abuse—are the same across cultures. In many cases, clients' unique individual characteristics exert a more powerful influence than their cultural background on their experiences with family violence. However, cultural dynamics can indeed have a powerful impact on how clients experience abuse—including cultural norms about what types of violence are acceptable, perceptions of violence experienced, and availability of culturally responsive resources to help end the abuse. Therefore, therapists must be mindful of cultural considerations when working with clients impacted by family violence.

In this chapter, we use the term *culture* broadly to address a range of social-contextual variables that influence clients' lives, such as racial and ethnic backgrounds, socioeconomic status, immigration status, religious beliefs, professional affiliations, and geographic locations. Elements of culture include social traditions, art, dance, language, rituals, stories, beliefs about individualism and collectivism, and religious beliefs (Almeida & Durkin, 1999). Culture is not static, but rather it changes and evolves over time (Korbin, 2002). Some cultural groups are at a higher risk for experiencing family violence. However, our primary focus in this chapter is on cultural dynamics, influences, and norms as they relate to family violence, rather than on exploring differences in prevalence rates across segments of the population. We believe that the former issues are of greater relevance to therapists in their work with clients impacted by family violence. In working with this population, therapists must strive to be culturally competent, meaning that the clinician "combines general knowledge with specific information provided by the patient about his or her culture, incorporates an awareness of one's biases, and approaches the definition of culture with a critical eye and open mind" (Weil & Lee, 2004, p. 219).

We begin with a caution for therapists to practice in a culturally responsive manner when working with all clients of any background. In the next section, we discuss cultural norms within some groups that may be associated with family violence. However, all clients of a particular cultural background will not experience these norms in the same way, or at all. Therefore, therapists should avoid applying these norms as stereotypes to clients from these backgrounds. Rather, we encourage therapists to approach each client with a strong sense of curiosity about their backgrounds, including how they may have been impacted by their cultural affiliations. After we provide an overview of some potential cultural dynamics that impact clients' experiences of family violence, the chapter concludes with general recommendations for culturally responsive therapy with clients impacted by family violence.

Examples of Cultural Norms and Experiences Related to Family Violence

Cultural groups may hold different norms regarding the types of behaviors that are considered abusive (Fontes, Cruz, & Tabachnick, 2001; Lowe, Pavkov, Casanova, & Wetchler, 2005). These differential norms may impact whether clients believe that certain experiences need to be reported to the appropriate authorities (Lowe et al., 2005). Any cultural group may be hesitant to acknowledge that family violence is a problem in their culture due to fearing that this could lead that group to be further disenfranchised from the mainstream culture (Kulwicki, Aswad, Carmona, & Ballout, 2010). Space limitations preclude a complete description of all cultural dynamics that may impact family violence. Therefore, in this section, we review research that we view as credible and illustrative of the types of cultural norms that may surround family violence in several cultural subgroups. The norms discussed in this section can serve as a backdrop for exploring how the client experiences his or her cultural influences. Cultural dynamics may be a positive resource or a negative barrier to their efforts to achieve safety in their relationships. The cultural influences we consider here are ethnicity, geography, professional affiliation, religion, and socioeconomic status.

Ethnicity and Family Violence

One's ethnicity can uniquely influence experiences with family violence. As the information reviewed in this section demonstrates, areas in which the influence of ethnicity may be found include norms about family relationships and violence, willingness to seek help from supportive resources, and the appropriateness of available community resources.

African American Families. There is mixed evidence regarding whether family violence is more common in African American families compared to families of other ethnic backgrounds. For example, African Americans are overrepresented among children involved in child protective services (CPS) systems (Ards, Myers, Chung, Malkis, & Hagerty, 2003). In part, this may be the result of biases in reporting, such that reports are more likely to be made for African American than Caucasian children (Ards et al., 2003). However, reporting bias does not appear to account for all of this overrepresentation, as there are differences in the rates of substantiation as well, and this may be due in part to socioeconomic differences, such as whether the child's family is on welfare (Ards et al., 2003).

Due to the historical legacy of institutional racism directed toward African Americans, some members of this group are hesitant to report suspected maltreatment or seek criminal justice or social services resources to assist them when they have experienced abuse (Lowe et al., 2005). African American perpetrators of family violence may face harsher treatment in the criminal justice system compared to Caucasians (Lowe et al., 2005), therefore leading victims to be more hesitant to report violence to the authorities out of fears of the possible consequences for their family member.

Many African Americans rely heavily on religious institutions to provide social, spiritual, and practical support in response to family problems (Lowe et al., 2005; Potter, 2007). African American victims may be more likely to turn to religious leaders than other professional helpers to help them with their abuse (Dyer, 2010). As such, the assistance that victims who turn to clergy receive from other sources may depend on the extent to which these leaders are knowledgeable about and willing to refer to other community-based resources (Dyer, 2010).

Gillum (2008) suggested that some culture-specific factors that may be related to IPV among African American communities include jealousy, extramarital affairs, norms about male and female roles, negative stereotypes about mates, economic difficulties, social isolation, societal acceptance of violence toward African Americans, and institutional racism. These and other values should be addressed in culture-specific prevention and response interventions in African American communities. Some cultural values relevant to African American culture-specific interventions include collectivism, social support networks, the inclusion of individual and group approaches, and the importance of addressing spirituality and religion (Gillum, 2008). Other culturally responsive approaches include addressing issues of oppression, discrimination, experiences with racism, and building connections with informal support networks (West, 2008).

Arab and Islamic Families. Family violence generally has not been considered a significant social issue in Arab and Islamic countries (Douki, Nacef, Belhadj,

Bouasker, & Ghachem, 2003). Individuals in these cultures may view violence as a private family matter (Douki et al., 2003). High value may be placed on the solidarity, unity, and positive reputation of the family (Douki et al., 2003), including prohibitions against divorce (Kulwicki et al., 2010). Social norms may therefore prevent victims from seeking help or leaving abusive situations (Kulwicki, 2002; Kulwicki et al., 2010). Members of this cultural group also may ascribe to a cultural belief that IPV in particular is justifiable for women who do not behave in accordance with social norms and customs (Douki et al., 2003). Muslim religious leaders may actively encourage IPV victims to stay in their abusive relationships (Kulwicki et al., 2010). At times, excerpts from the Koran have been taken out of context to justify that men are sanctioned to abuse their wives and their children (Douki et al., 2003). According to Douki et al., however, the justification of abuse in Arab cultures is culturally, not religiously, based.

In patriarchal Arab cultures, women are viewed as subordinates to men (Douki et al., 2003). Some Arab countries follow a patrilineal family structure, in which male relatives are responsible for females, and males have greater rights (Kulwicki, 2002). This structure can provide both advantages and disadvantages for females in IPV situations. On the positive side, females may receive protection by other male family members if their husbands abuse them (Kulwicki, 2002; Kulwicki et al., 2010). However, women may face harsh penalties from male relatives or husbands for demonstrating perceived dishonorable behaviors (Kulwicki, 2002).

Honor killings are a form of family violence that is somewhat unique to Arab cultures. An honor killing is a "crime committed against women by their male family members because the women had violated the honor of their family" (Kulwicki, 2002, p. 77). Typically, honor killings are done by one of the woman's male family members, especially brothers (Kulwicki, 2002). Honor killings may occur due to adultery, becoming pregnant outside of wedlock, having premarital sex, and developing a questionable reputation (Kulwicki, 2002). Honor killings may even occur in cases when a woman becomes impregnated through rape or incest (Meetoo & Mirza, 2007). Other forms of violence also may be carried out in the name of "honor," such as giving women lashes (Kulwicki, 2002). Within some Arab countries, laws may permit these acts or provide minimal sanctions for men who carry them out (Kulwicki, 2002). It should be noted that honor killings have occurred in non-Arab countries as well (Meetoo & Mirza, 2007).

Asian American Families. The term *Asian American* is an umbrella term for a diverse group of people from over 50 countries and ethnic backgrounds (Weil & Lee, 2004). Family violence among Asian American populations has been studied less than other cultural groups (Weil & Lee, 2004). Cultural values in Asian American communities that may influence family violence experiences include interdependence, respect for authority, the importance of the family, avoidance of conflict, perseverance, preserving the honor of the family, and traditional gender roles (Weil & Lee, 2004). In some Asian cultures, parents view children as the property of the parents, leading them to believe they have the right to control their children as they see fit (Deb, 2005). Asian American victims may be hesitant to disclose abuse due to shame and fear that it will lead to being cut off from family and friends (Weil & Lee, 2004). In addition, Asian Americans often value respect for elders, which may make it less likely that Asian American clients in therapy will feel comfortable discussing maltreatment perpetrated by parents (Kenny & McEachern, 2000). In relation to seeking therapy, Asian Americans may be suspicious of mental health professionals and other social service agencies, including criminal justice agencies (Weil & Lee, 2004). They may view seeking help as a sign of personal weakness (Weil & Lee, 2004).

Caucasian Families. Perhaps due to historical ethnocentricism, researchers have devoted substantially less attention to studying Caucasian family's experiences of family violence through a lens of multiculturalism. Much research on cultural groups other than Caucasians is conducted through the lens of comparing other groups' experiences to those of Caucasians (Rivers, 2005). This means that findings may be biased toward viewing other groups' experiences as non-normative. Furthermore, many existing interventions in the US have been developed to reflect dominant values of the Caucasian culture, such as individualism and women's empowerment (Rivers, 2005). These values may be inconsistent with norms of other groups. As such, it is useful to consider Caucasians as a cultural group and be mindful of how general understandings about family violence have been shaped through the lens of this group. For example, some cultural norms among Caucasian, and especially White Anglo-Saxon Protestant (WASP), families that may be associated with an increased risk of child sexual abuse include one or both parents being frequently outside of the home and a lack of emotionally close relationships within the family (Lowe et al., 2005).

Latino/Hispanic Families. Cultural values in Latino/Hispanic families that may influence family violence include familism and machismo (Elliott & Urquiza, 2006). Familism is "a commitment to provide an emotional support system for family members, and emphasizes the importance of the family" (Ferrari, 2002, pp. 794–795). Machismo relates to strong traditional gender roles, viewing males as aggressive and dominant, and holding back emotionally, although it also may relate to self-respect and the importance of being responsible to one's family (Ferrari, 2002). Latino cultures may value family and community over individuality (Parra-Cardona, Meyer, Schiamberg, & Post, 2007). Members of this cultural group may face numerous challenges to accessing mental health services (Parra-Cardona et al., 2007). In particular, Hispanic women appear less likely than women from other ethnic backgrounds to seek help when they experience IPV (Lee, Sanders Thompson, & Mechanic, 2002).

Native American Families. In Native American tribes, family violence may be viewed as a social ill resulting from the infiltration of U.S. colonialism and values (DeBruyn, Chino, Serna, & Fullerton-Gleason, 2001). Native Americans have struggled to maintain cultural traditions in light of external challenges (Rivers, 2005). Each tribe has different customs and traditions, but in general, many Native Americans retain a very strong cultural identity despite some of the challenges faced by this cultural group (DeBruyn et al., 2001).

Family violence typically is considered taboo in Navajo culture (Rivers, 2005). Navajo women who have been abused in their marriages may be reluctant to leave due to strong cultural messages about the importance of remaining together, even when these women have the resources to leave (Rivers, 2005). Native American values that may be relevant to address in child maltreatment interventions include pride and shame in one's culture, the influence of intergenerational traumas, and a collectivist value on family and community (DeBruyn et al., 2001). Risk factors for child maltreatment in the Native American cultures include parental alcohol use and depression, frequent moves, and chaotic families (DeBruyn et al., 2001).

In treatment, therapists should strive to incorporate culturally relevant traditions and resources when working with Native American clients. In particular, Native Americans may place a strong value on traditional healthy methods, as well as on the importance of elders and tribal spiritual leaders (DeBruyn et al., 2001).

Geography and Family Violence: Focus on Rural Culture

One's geographic location can impact experiences with family violence. The geographic influence that has been studied most extensively is that of rural communities. Thus, to illustrate potential geographic influences on family violence, we review existing research on this. Potential influences of rural cultural on family violence include isolation, economic opportunities and farming, and cultural values. First, isolation may limit rural victims of family violence from accessing resources to help them leave their violent situations (Bosch & Schumm, 2004; Few, 2005; Murty et al., 2003; Riddell, Ford-Gilboe, & Liepert, 2009; Teaster, Roberto, & Dugar, 2006). Isolation is especially intense if extended family members are not nearby (Few, 2005). Second, economic opportunities are often more limited in rural areas (Teaster et al., 2006). A major economic driver of many rural economies is farming. Working and living in a rural farm community could serve as both a protective factor (i.e., due to regular contact with others working on the farm) or a risk factor (i.e., the stressful working conditions and economic uncertainty) for family violence (Murty et al., 2003). If an IPV victim lives on a farm that provides the family's income, then leaving the abusive relationship may lead to financial jeopardy (Riddell et al., 2009). Third, cultural values often held in rural communities include traditional gender roles, strong religious faith, ownership of firearms, and privacy (Few, 2005; Riddell et al., 2009; Teaster et al., 2006). Rural communities may be characterized by residents knowing a lot about the daily lives of other residents, which often heightens the emphasis on privacy within families (Riddell et al., 2009).

Clients in rural areas may be more likely to rely on informal support than formal service agencies (Few, 2005; Riddell et al., 2009). The support or lack thereof that victims receive from their social networks can influence whether they will gain access to supportive resources (Bosch & Schumm, 2004). Ethnic minority residents of rural communities may experience racism when seeking assistance from formal sources of support, such as the police (Few, 2005). In addition, victims in rural communities may be especially hesitant to report experiences of abuse to the police (Few, 2005). It may take a long time for police to respond to calls related to family violence if the home in which it has occurred is located far out in the country (Riddell et al., 2009).

Family violence resources, such as shelters, may not be geographically close to rural residents (Few, 2005; Riddell et al., 2009; Teaster et al., 2006). For example, victims may need to go to a different county to receive such support. In addition, rural agencies may have more limited resources available to support victims (Eastman, Bunch, Williams, & Carawan, 2007), such as emergency departments in hospitals (Choo et al., 2010). Because of the limited resources available in rural communities, it may take longer for victims to prepare to leave abusive relationships (Riddell et al., 2009).

Community outreach may be especially needed in rural areas to make residents aware of available services (Few, 2005). A promising approach to addressing family violence in rural communities involves building collaborative relationships among various aspects of the response system, such as service agencies and the police (Sudderth, 2003, 2006). Newly emerging telemedicine technologies (e.g., videoconferencing) also may be useful for making services available to rural clients (Edwards & Patel, 2003; Thomas, Miller, & Speck, 2005).

Professional Affiliation and Family Violence: The Cases of Military and Police Families

Values and norms in various professional groups also may influence the experiences of family violence for victims and perpetrators. Two examples of professional groups whose values and traditions have been studied in relation to family violence are the military and the police.

Military Culture. Military families appear to be at an increased risk for experiencing family violence (Rentz et al., 2006). Rates of child maltreatment among military families have increased in recent years, whereas the rates have remained relatively stable among the general population (Campbell, Brown, & Okwara, 2011). In addition, military couples are at an increased risk for severe IPV, and children therefore also may face a greater risk of witnessing parental IPV (Campbell et al., 2011). However, existing research is mixed (Rentz et al., 2006), so it remains unclear as to how similar or different rates of family violence are between military and civilian families. Limitations in the existing research on family violence in military families include the unavailability of some key data and differences in data collection methods across military branches (Rentz et al., 2006).

Certain aspects of military culture could be considered unique protective resources, such as the likelihood of clear and swift punishment, employment benefits that military personnel receive, and services and programs that support military personnel and their family members (Rentz et al., 2006). However, other aspects of military culture may increase the risk of family violence. Military personnel encounter high levels of job stress, including being separated from family and friends, challenging work conditions, and the dangerous nature of the job (Rentz et al., 2006). Deployments are times in which military families face especially high levels of stress (Campbell et al., 2011; Stanley & Appleton, 2008). Aspects of the military culture may spillover into family life, such as the authoritarian hierarchical nature of relationships (Campbell et al., 2011). Other components of military culture that may influence family violence include frequent transitions, such as moving or deployment, and suspicions about the extent to which confidentiality will be maintained regarding difficult life experiences (Campbell et al., 2011). Children in military families who have been maltreated also may experience other traumas that children without a military background will encounter, such as separation from one's parent during a deployment or a parent becoming disabled or killed in battle (Campbell et al., 2011).

Many members of the military and their family members fear seeking help because they fear being stigmatized or facing serious consequences for doing so (Campbell et al., 2011). For example, perpetrating family violence may result in being discharged from the military (Campbell et al., 2011), which could hurt the family's economic status. In recent years, the Department of Defense has made increasing efforts to address the mental health and relational needs of military personnel and their family members (Campbell et al., 2011). In particular, Family Advocacy Programs (FAPs) were established in each military branch to address family violence (Campbell et al., 2011; Rentz et al., 2006). These FAPs receive reports of suspected abuse (including child maltreatment and IPV), investigate whether abuse occurred, coordinate treatment (if needed), and make recommendations for employment decisions (Rentz et al., 2006).

Regarding mental health treatment, Campbell et al. (2011) suggested that some potentially effective treatments for military children who experienced trauma include trauma-focused cognitive-behavioral therapy and child–parent psychotherapy. They also suggested that treatment is enhanced through collaboration with professionals from civilian and military organizations.

Police Culture. Although significantly less has been written about police families as compared to military families, common features of police culture may influence family violence among police officers (Johnson, Todd, & Subramanian, 2005). According to Johnson et al. (2005), police culture tends to value authoritarian hierarchical relationships. Other common values among police officers include camaraderie, secrecy, and family privacy. Police officers may be exposed to high levels of violence and trauma on the job, which may be linked to high levels of job stress and burnout. Johnson and colleagues surveyed 413 police officers, including 351 males and 62 females. The found that exposure to violence, burnout, and authoritarian spillover combined to lead to higher rates of family violence. In addition, to cope with high levels of job stress they experience, some police officers engage in heavy alcohol drinking during off-duty hours. Police officers may be particularly dangerous as abusers because their job-related training may help them learn to become more intimidating, aggressive, and dominant. In police families, loyalty to one's spouse leads to the department helping to protect the spouse and family, although this may be limited when a police spouse becomes a victim. In that case, camaraderie among officers may take a higher precedence over this loyalty-based protection.

Religion and Family Violence

A client's religious and spiritual beliefs, practices, and organizational affiliations can serve as a protective resource against or a contributing factor toward their experiences with family violence (Bottoms, Nielsen, Murray, & Filipas, 2003; Giesbrecht & Sevcik, 2000; Nason-Clark, 2009; Popescu et al., 2009; Potter, 2007; Ringel & Park, 2008; Wang, Horne, Levitt, & Klesges, 2009). In addition, family violence victims' religious or spiritual beliefs may be impacted negatively by their abuse experiences (Bottoms et al., 2003; Kvarfordt, 2010).

Kvarfordt (2010) suggested that spiritual abuse and neglect are unique forms of child maltreatment. They involve "experiences or environments that detrimentally affect the development of meaning, purpose, connection/belonging, faith, or moral and ethical guidelines" (p 143). Experiences that may fall under this category include forcing a child to participate in religious practices against their wishes, failing to provide spiritual or religious guidance or opportunities for exploration, and teasing a child about his or her religious beliefs (Kvarfordt, 2010). Another form of religion-related emotional child abuse involves parents telling children they will be punished or unloved by God if they misbehave

(Bottoms et al., 2003). Child abuse also may relate directly to victims' religions, such as if the perpetrator is a faith leader, if religious texts are used to justify the abuse, and if the perpetrator threatens that God will hurt or punish the child if s/he tells others about the abuse (Bottoms et al., 2003). Another form of maltreatment related to religion and spirituality is cultic or Satanic ritualized abuse of children (Kvarfordt, 2010; Whitsett & Kent, 2003), which involves "summoning or invoking the name, image, or concept of Satan in order to fulfill a prescribed ritual" (Kvarfordt, 2010, p. 152).

Religion-Related Barriers. Religion-related barriers may be internal (e.g., beliefs about marriage) or external (e.g., pressure from social norms) (Popescu et al., 2009; Ringel & Park, 2008). Examples of religion-related barriers associated with family violence are as follows.

Religious teachings. Religious teachings that promote male power and female submission cross different faiths, including Jewish, Christian, and Islamic teachings (Levitt & Ware, 2006a). Selected religious texts may be taken out of context as another means of justifying abuse (Potter, 2007). For example, some Christians may justify physical abuse by citing Bible verses that condone corporal punishment (Bottoms et al., 2003; Rodriguez & Henderson, 2010). In addition, literal interpretations of some religious texts may not view IPV as an acceptable reason for divorce (Levitt & Ware, 2006b; Popescu et al., 2009). Religious teachings about forgiveness also may perpetuate abuse if victims interpret them as a need to forgive and return to abusive relationships (Jones & Fowler, 2009; Popescu et al., 2009; Wang et al., 2009).

Religion-based shame and pressure. IPV victims may feel shame and pressure from religious organizations to maintain their family relationships (Dyer, 2010). IPV victims with strong, conservative religious beliefs may be unlikely to leave abusive relationships due to religious-based prohibitions against divorce (Popescu et al., 2009). The pressure to remain silent about abuse may be especially strong if the perpetrator is a leader in one's faith community (Dyer, 2010). IPV victims also may feel discouraged by differences in their own relationships compared to ideals for marriage and family promoted in their churches (Giesbrecht & Sevcik, 2000). In addition, traditional gender role expectations and beliefs that women should submit to men may exacerbate their experiences with IPV (Giesbrecht & Sevcik, 2000).

Unsupportive responses from religious leaders and organizational members. Victims may find that their faith communities minimize their abuse (Giesbrecht & Sevcik, 2000). Some clergy deny that family violence could occur in their faith communities (Homiak & Singletary, 2007; Levitt & Ware, 2006b). Some religious leaders encourage reconciliation over divorce in cases of IPV, although divorce may be an acceptable as an option of last resort (Levitt & Ware, 2006b; Nason-Clark, 2009). Pastors also may be inclined to counsel couples conjointly, even though this is generally not advisable when IPV is present (Dyer, 2010).

Religion-Related Resources. Religion and spirituality also may provide supportive resources for clients experiencing family violence, including those described below.

Supportive responses from religious leaders and organizational members. Victims may turn to religious leaders after experiencing abuse (Levitt & Ware, 2006b; Potter, 2007). Although some clergy are underprepared to address family violence, many are open to collaborating with other professionals to address family violence in their congregations (Dyer, 2010; Jones & Fowler, 2009; Nason-Clark, 2009; Ringel & Park, 2008). Beyond formal leaders, victims may find support from informal networks in their faith communities (Nason-Clark, 2009).

Organizational prevention and response initiatives. Some faith communities have initiated family violence prevention programs (Bottoms et al., 2003). Other ways that religious organizations can address family violence include teaching members about nonviolent relationships, providing a context for discussing gender roles and ideals for family life, offering financial support to victims, and helping to connect members with local resources (Giesbrecht & Sevcik, 2000; Homiak & Singletary, 2007; Nason-Clark, 2009).

Support while coping with and healing from abuse. Faith communities can serve as an important source of social support when coping with or leaving an abusive relationship (Giesbrecht & Sevcik, 2000). In addition, many victims turn to prayer to help them cope (Wang et al., 2009). Victims healing from abusive relationships in which religious beliefs contributed to the victim remaining in the relationship may need to restructure some of their religious beliefs as they heal from their relationships (Wang et al., 2009). As victims move toward healing, they may experience a transformation in their religious and spiritual beliefs, such as coming to a new view of how God may view abuse and marriage (Giesbrecht & Sevcik, 2000). Giesbrecht and Sevcik (2000) conducted a qualitative study to explore experiences of female IPV victims in the conservative evangelical culture. They found that these women's faiths helped them make meaning of their experiences with abuse and provided them with hope.

Implications for Therapists. Due to the powerful influence that one's religious beliefs may have upon experiences of family violence, therapists should invite clients to explore the impact of these beliefs on their own lives (Popescu et al., 2009; Ringel & Park, 2008). In addition, therapists can benefit from self-reflection on their values and beliefs about religion, spirituality, and family violence and how these may impact their work (Popescu et al., 2009). Therapists should become familiar with potentially useful resources for religious clients. Some communities offer faith-based women's shelters that could be appropriate for victims with strong religious beliefs (Giesbrecht & Sevcik, 2000). Likewise, faith-based batterer intervention programs are available in some communities (Nason-Clark, 2009; Todhunter & Deaton, 2010).

Some clergy lack training and experience to be able to respond competently to family violence (Homiak & Singletary, 2007; Levitt & Ware, 2006b; Ringel & Park, 2008). Therapists may play a role in providing this type of training to clergy (Homiak & Singletary, 2007; Jones & Fowler, 2009; Popescu et al., 2009; Ringel & Park, 2008). Clergy may be more receptive to programs framed as education about promoting positive family relationships, rather than preventing or addressing family violence (Jones & Fowler, 2009). Clergy should be encouraged to provide potential victims with information about community resources immediately, rather than waiting until they determine whether or not abuse actually occurred (Wang et al., 2009).

Socioeconomic Status and Family Violence

Another contextual factor that may influence clients' experiences of family violence and culture is socioeconomic status (SES). Although some research suggests that there are racial differences in rates of family violence, many of these differences can be better explained by SES than race (Gillum, 2008). Poverty is a risk factor for family violence (Cunradi, Caetano, Clark, & Schafer, 2000; Kenny & McEachern, 2000; Lowe et al., 2005), and it may impact family violence differentially based on the racial composition of lower-income neighborhoods (Cunradi et al., 2000). On the other end of the economic spectrum, individuals from wealthy backgrounds may find that their upscale lifestyles present unique challenges if they experience family violence (Weitzman, 2000). For example, they may fear that disclosing abusive experiences would damage their reputations and may find that existing resources for clients impacted by family violence are geared toward the needs of lower income clientele (Weitzman, 2000).

General Guidelines for Culturally Responsive Therapy Related to Family Violence

Programs should be responsive and accessible to the needs of different cultural groups (Pan et al., 2006). Cultural competence describes "practice that is geared towards knowledge of and skills in working with cultural groups other than one's own. It also has a political and activist component in promoting empowerment and inclusion of culturally diverse professionals in decision-making positions" (Korbin, 2002, p. 639). In addition to reflecting cultural customs, such as through food or art (DeBruyn et al., 2001), interventions should reflect the cultural group's underlying values and be responsive to historical and social influences impacting them (DeBruyn et al., 2001).

First, therapists should ensure that the language used in treatments and related materials are appropriate to clients' cultural backgrounds (Cohen, Deblinger, Mannarino, & de Arellano, 2001). Second, it may be useful to incorporate traditional healing methods when working with clients with backgrounds that value these traditions (Cohen et al., 2001). Third, when working with clients from cultural groups that place a high value on privacy, therapists should take extra precautions to ensure that clients are aware of confidentiality rights and limitations (Kulwicki et al., 2010). Fourth, therapists should consider how a client's cultural background may impact his or her willingness to participate in therapy. A client's cultural background may influence his or her responsiveness to therapy in many ways, including willingness to seek treatment, the types of treatment that are viewed as acceptable, and treatment prognosis (Cohen et al., 2001).

Fifth, interventions designed to help victims leave abusive relationships may not reflect the core values of collectivist cultures (Weil & Lee, 2004). Providing culturally relevant services may require shifting the focus from helping victims leave abusive relationships to developing interventions that focus on stopping the violence but keep relationships intact (Weil & Lee, 2004). Sixth, therapists should consider how cultural values about not speaking openly about sexuality may impact clients' willingness to discuss their sexuality in therapy, and this could impact treatment progress if clients experienced sexual abuse or sexual consequences of other forms of abuse (Kenny & McEachern, 2000). Overall, additional culturally responsive services are needed for victims and perpetrators of family violence (Simbandumwe et al., 2008), and this need is likely to continue to grow in coming years.

Help Clients Overcome Culture-Related Barriers to Useful Services

Clients' cultural backgrounds may present unique barriers that make it more difficult for them to receive services. For example, language barriers may prevent victims from seeking the help they need (Kulwicki et al., 2010; Pan et al., 2006; Meetoo & Mirza, 2007; Weil & Lee, 2004). It is useful to make available the services of a professional who speaks the client's language if at all possible (Pan et al., 2006). Other culturally relevant barriers may include the following: a lack of agencies that are culturally appropriate, such as lack of availability of food that is in line with religious or cultural restrictions; transportation limitations; economic barriers, which could potentially be addressed through job skills training; co-occurring problems, such as substance abuse; and limited trust in service providers (DeBruyn et al., 2001; Kulwicki et al., 2010; Pan et al., 2006).

Be Mindful of Immigration Issues

Immigrants face unique issues that can impact their experiences of family violence and their ability to seek help. First, the experience of immigration may be linked to clients' experiences of family violence. The time immediately surrounding immigration to the United Sates is likely to involve heightened stress (Weil & Lee, 2004; Westby, 2007). Refugees from war-plagued countries may have experienced trauma in their home countries that inhibits their functioning (Weil & Lee, 2004). Some immigrants view being separated from their home country as a disconnect from cultural norms and taboos that reduce the likelihood of family violence (Fontes et al., 2001). Immigrants often experience tension between values of their home countries and those in the United States (Pan et al., 2006), and they may be separated from social support systems that could have provided protection from their perpetrators (Kulwicki et al., 2010). Generational influences are important to consider, in that the experiences of a first-generation immigrant can be very different than those of a fourth-generation immigrant (Lowe et al., 2005).

Second, perpetrators may use victims' immigration status to control them. For example, abusive partners may isolate victims by forbidding them to learn to speak English (Weil & Lee, 2004). Also, perpetrators may threaten or attempt to thwart a victim's attempts to gain legal status as part of abuse (Weil & Lee, 2004). Immigrants may be economically dependent on their perpetrators (Kulwicki et al., 2010), so victims may fear that they have no other options than to remain in a relationship with an abusive partner. Third, some legal or social services may not be available to illegal immigrants (Kulwicki et al., 2010). Immigrants may fail to report domestic violence for fear of being deported (Pan et al., 2006; Weil & Lee, 2004).

Give Careful Consideration to Delicate Ethical Issues

Culturally sanctioned forms of violence challenge the mental health professions' value of multiculturalism and respect for clients' cultural beliefs and practices (Meetoo & Mirza, 2007). For example, different cultural groups may hold different attitudes toward whether physical discipline constitutes child maltreatment (Durrant, 2008; Ferrari, 2002). For example, traditionally corporal punishment is viewed as more acceptable in African American than Caucasian families (Durrant, 2008; Ferrari, 2002). Likewise, cultural understandings of elder abuse vary (Kosberg, Lowenstein, Garcia, & Biggs, 2003; Patterson & Malley-Morrison, 2006). In some cultures, even disrespect of one's elders may be considered abusive (Kosberg et al., 2003; Patterson & Malley-Morrison, 2006). Therapists therefore may struggle to discuss culturally sanctioned violence with their clients (Durrant, 2008). We encourage therapists ultimately to consider family violence to be a human rights issue (Durrant, 2008; Meetoo & Mirza, 2007; Patterson & Malley-Morrison, 2006), meaning that clients' rights to safety and protection must be the primary consideration with clients impacted by family violence.

Consider Culture Intersectionally Rather Than Unidimensionally

Given that most cultural groups are very heterogeneous (Cousineau & Rondeau, 2004; Kosberg et al., 2003), which is often overlooked in research and clinical practice related to family violence (Kosberg et al., 2003), therapists should explore with clients the ways that cultural discrimination and oppression contributed to their experiences of family violence with respect to the variety of intersecting contextual influences in their lives (Almeida & Durkin, 1999; Chavis & Hill, 2009).

Conclusion

We encourage therapists to be on a never-ending quest to learn more about cultural dynamics and groups in the local communities in which they work (Weil & Lee, 2004). As the information contained in this chapter makes clear, cultural influences can profoundly and deeply influence clients' experiences of family violence. Failing to address these issues may lead therapists to provide inadequate or inappropriate services. We believe therapists will find it invaluable to their work to have greater understanding of the intersections of cultural influences, geography, resources, and dynamics in their local community as they assist clients impacted by family violence.

13
FAMILY VIOLENCE PREVENTION

Increasingly, therapists are called upon to engage in professional activities that move beyond the therapy room and address the social context (Slep & Heyman, 2008). Psychotherapy represents just one component of a broad range of actions to respond to and reduce family violence and its corresponding outcomes. One way to conceptualize this range of responses is on a continuum of care as depicted in Figure 13.1 below (Slep & Heyman, 2008).

Although the continuum depicts preventive categories as discrete and separate from psychotherapy, the content and skills involved in preventive interventions often are similar to those of psychotherapy.

Why Prevention?

For those who believe that no form of family violence should exist, the answer to the question of why prevent is self-evident. However, there are always limited resources—time, energy, personnel, to name a few—to address family violence (Guterman, 2004). Thus, we must consider the relative value of preventive initiatives when those same resources could be allocated to responding to and protecting clients in crisis. Indeed, because many prevention efforts are done by the same agencies that provide intervention services, prevention is often viewed as a secondary priority (Saul, Duffy et al., 2008). However, there is value in addressing the source of problems through prevention, as treatment alone has a limited ability to eliminate family violence (Flaherty, 2010; Straus & Smith, 1995). Engaging in preventive interventions is a professional responsibility for therapists, although many therapists lack training and experience in this area (Murray, 2005). Professional ethical codes address therapists' responsibility to engage in prevention work (e.g., International Association of

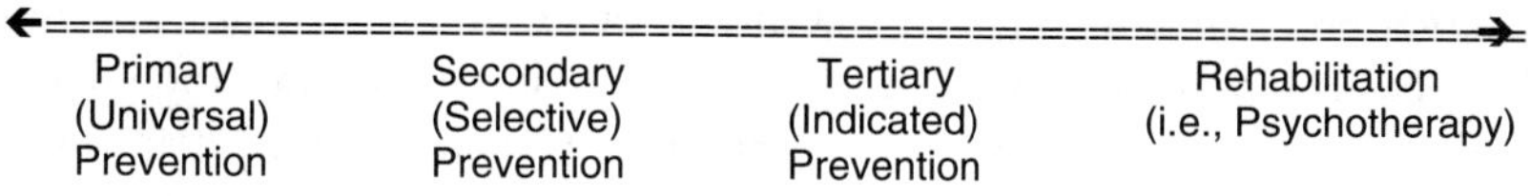

FIGURE 13.1 Continuum of care for family violence prevention.

Marriage and Family Counselors [IAMFC], n.d., I.L; National Association of Social Workers [NASW], 2008, 6.01). In addition, preventive approaches are in line with developmental theories that underlie many therapy theories (Murray, 2005). Even with an increased focus on prevention, there always will be a place for therapy (Murray, 2005; Slep & Heyman, 2008). Thus, by viewing preventive interventions on a continuum with therapy, the spectrum that includes all of these interventions offers an array of options for helping to reduce the impact of family violence on clients and society.

Research on risk factors for various forms of family violence has become extensive, so we now know many of the personal and relationship characteristics that lead to a heightened risk of victimization or perpetration (Antle, Sullivan, Dryden, Karam, & Barbee, 2011; Slep & Heyman, 2008). However, although risk factors can inform preventive interventions, they should not completely dictate approaches that are used. Risk factors for specific forms of family violence were reviewed in several previous chapters.

Understanding Prevention and General Recommendations for Prevention Work

Prevention operates on at least one of two assumptions: interventions can reduce risk factors for the target problem, or interventions can increase strengths and protective factors that buffer against the target problem (Hamby, 2006; Murray, 2005; Slep & Heyman, 2008; Wolfe, Wekerle et al., 2003). Three categories of preventive initiatives are universal/primary, selective/secondary, and indicated/tertiary. *Universal prevention initiatives* aim to prevent a particular problem from developing to begin with (Murray, 2005; Topping & Barron, 2009). Another term often used to describe this form of prevention is *primary prevention* (Campbell & Manganello, 2006; Hamby, 2006), and these terms are used interchangeably in this chapter. Universal initiatives are aimed at the general population (Campbell & Manganello, 2006; Geeraert, Van den Noortgate, Grietens, & Onghena, 2004; Murray, 2005; O'Leary, Woodin, & Fritz, 2006; Whitaker et al., 2006), aim to reach the widest number of people (Hamby, 2006; Slep & Heyman, 2008), and often are viewed as the most cost-effective approach (Topping & Barron, 2009). *Selective preventive*, also termed *targeted* or *secondary, initiatives* are aimed at a specific group of people thought to be at high risk for developing the target problem (Murray, 2005; O'Leary et al., 2006; Topping & Barron, 2009; Whitaker et al., 2006) but who have not yet experienced the target problem (Murray, 2005; Whitaker et al., 2006). *Indicated*, also often referred to as *tertiary*, preventive interventions are aimed at a population that has already begun to experience the target problem (Geeraert et al., 2004; Murray, 2005; Topping & Barron, 2009; Whitaker et al., 2006), with the goal of reducing the negative consequences of the problem (Geeraert et al., 2004; Murray, 2005). Battered women's shelters and law enforcement responses can be considered tertiary preventive interventions related to IPV (Coker, 2004).

Unfortunately, it often takes an extreme and visible crisis to mobilize a community to preventive action (Chan, Lam, & Cheng, 2009), and then sustaining motivation can become a challenge. To design and implement effective and sustainable family violence prevention initiatives is a challenging, complex task. Generally, prevention programs should address a range of issues, include different approaches to imparting information, be based on theory and research, occur at an appropriate time and for an adequate length of time, and be implemented by qualified personnel (Russell, Britner, & Woolard, 2007). In addition, the following recommendations should be considered when planning and implementing family violence prevention initiatives: (a) consider relevant ethical issues; (b) focus on multiple levels of interventions, especially the community level; (c) develop population-specific content, format, and intervention settings; (d) build on existing research; and (e) forge interdisciplinary partnerships.

Consider Ethical Issues

There are several important ethical considerations for therapists who wish to engage in prevention work (Murray, 2005). First, therapists must ensure that they are competent to deliver such services (e.g., AAMFT, 2001, III.3.7; American Psychological Association [APA], 2010, 2.01.a; NASW, 2008, 1.04.a), especially given that many lack training in this area. Second, therapists must ensure that they monitor their personal values and the values they impart through preventive interventions (e.g., American Counseling Association [ACA], 2005, A.4.a; IAMFC, n.d., I.F; NASW, 2008, Preamble). This is a challenge, because such interventions typically are based on inherent assumptions about what *health* means in relationships and families. As such, therapists should ensure that the assumptions underlying prevention programs are appropriate to clients' cultural backgrounds. In addition, therapists must consider potential dual relationships, such as when a therapy client also participates in a preventive program led by the therapist. Professional ethical codes dictate that dual relationships be handled responsibly (e.g., APA, 2010, 3.05.a; NASW, 2008, 1.06.c).

Maintain a Multilevel Focus, Especially Community

> Incremental changes in institutions in the shape of legal reform and service provision, as well as transformed social expectations and norms may prove to have a greater effect in reducing interpersonal violence in the

> long haul than strategies that target victims and perpetrators. Such primary prevention approaches should at the very least be seen as requisite adjuncts to programs that seek to influence intimate partners themselves.
> *(Wray, 2006, p. 57)*

Preventive interventions can occur on many levels (Chan et al., 2009; Flaherty, 2010; Black, Heyman, & Slep, 2001; Peterson, Tremblay, Ewigman, & Saldana, 2003; Sanders, Cann, & Markie-Dadds, 2003; Slep & Heyman, 2008; Wurtele, 2009), such as the individual, family, organizational, and community levels (Chan et al., 2009; Coker, 2004; Galano & Schellenbach, 2007; Sabol, Coulton, & Korbin, 2004; Teten, Ball, Valle, Noonan, & Rosenbluth, 2009). A critical need remains for more family-focused family violence prevention initiatives (Hamby, 2006). Program developers should consider the appropriate level(s) to target with their interventions (Slep & Heyman, 2008). Ideally, multiple levels can be addressed at once (Sabol et al., 2004; Wurtele, 2009), and family violence prevention programs can be combined with other forms of community-based violence prevention initiatives (Bowen, Gwiasda, & Brown, 2004).

Some efforts aim to educate the public about family violence, such as through public awareness campaigns (Slep & Heyman, 2008). Public health and communication science offer useful guidelines for developing effective public communication campaigns, including the following: (a) initiatives should be grounded theoretically, and there should be a clear rationale for the content and focus; (b) they should address social norms and conditions that perpetuate family violence; (c) they must be effective at reaching the target population; and (d) campaigns should mobilize social networks (Wray, 2006). Community-based events also can be planned to address this awareness-raising goal. For example, Frohmann (2005) described the Framing Safety Project (FSP), which was done in part to educate the community about the lived experiences of women who had been battered. This project involved women taking photographs to depict their experiences and then putting on a community exhibit to share the photos and corresponding narratives with the community. An advantage of a project such as FSP is that it uses the voices of the actual victims to tell their stories and educate the public.

Some preventive interventions are aimed at the community level (Slep & Heyman, 2008). At this level, two important aims are to build the community's capacity to respond to family violence and increase collaboration among various parts of family violence response systems (Chan et al., 2009). Key components of community capacity building include promoting positive social norms, increasing community members' sense of responsibility, engaging stakeholders, and helping residents access existing resources (Chan et al., 2009). Bowen et al. (2004) proposed a five-stage model for developing primary violence prevention programs in communities: (a) creating safety; (b) understanding violence; (c) building community; (d) promoting peace; and (e) building democracy and social justice. Generally, communities with stronger interconnections and greater access to resources may be better equipped to prevent violence, and it is important to help communities feel empowered to believe that they have the capacity to take action against family violence (Sabol et al., 2004).

All preventive interventions should be planned, implemented, and evaluated with consideration to the unique community characteristics of the target population (Chan et al., 2009; Slep & Heyman, 2008). Across communities, a common goal is to increase social capital to protect community members from family violence. Both formal (i.e., legal sanctions) and informal (i.e., social norms) forms of social control can be strengthened to help prevent family violence (Sabol et al., 2004). Another focus is increasing informal social support to serve as a protective factor against family violence (Budde & Schene, 2004; Sabol et al., 2004), although the effectiveness of informal social support interventions is not clearly supported by existing research (Budde & Schene, 2004). Other relevant social and community-level factors include media coverage, attitudes held by community members toward available services, neighborhood characteristics, social norms, and general public attitudes toward family violence (Wray, 2006). Although comprehensive community-based programs require a good deal of time and resources, their potential is very powerful (Fullwood, 2002; Mitchell-Clark & Autry, 2004).

Finally, advocacy can be considered a form of prevention, in that it can lead to social or political changes that reduce the likelihood of the target problem (Coker, 2004; Humphreys, 2008; Murray, 2005). Therapists may need to advocate for increased resources for preventive initiatives (Murray, 2005) or engage in media advocacy, such as by communicating with the news media to ensure adequate and accurate coverage of family violence issues (Campbell & Manganello, 2006). Advocacy efforts also may be needed to address social conditions, such as poverty and other negative economic conditions, which are relevant to the prevention of family violence (Chan et al., 2009; Sotelo, 2009). Gil (1996) wrote that prevention efforts are futile if they do not actively aim to change the elements of the larger social structure that contribute to violence (e.g., economic conditions, social norms, and the oppression of groups of people).

Develop Programs with Content, Format, and Settings Appropriate to the Population

When selecting or designing the content, format, and setting of prevention programs, therapists should consider the needs and characteristics of the target population (Avery-Leaf & Cascardi, 2002). The content should be delivered in a manner that is not stigmatizing for the target population (Simbandumwe et al., 2008). Programs may be most effective when they target individuals most in need of the information they contain, use interactive formats, include both skills training and address social norms, have longer durations, and are appropriate for the developmental level and cultural backgrounds of participants (O'Leary et al., 2006; Simbandumwe et al., 2008; Wolfe & Jaffe, 1999). Especially among immigrant populations, programs should be sensitive to participants' levels of cultural adaptation (Simbandumwe et al., 2008). Immigrants may need information about relevant laws in their new communities (Simbandumwe et al., 2008).

Prevention programs can occur in a variety of formats (Murray, 2005), but most programs include both didactic and interactive components (Whitaker et al., 2006). Some other format-related considerations include ensuring that the personnel who deliver programs are adequately trained (Avery-Leaf & Cascardi, 2002), considering whether booster sessions can sustain gains made in shorter-term programs (Avery-Leaf & Cascardi, 2002; Murray & Kardatzke, 2007), and incorporating technologies with which members of the target population are comfortable (Slep & Heyman, 2008). Programs must be developed with costs in mind, because a very expensive program is unlikely to become sustainable (Slep & Heyman, 2008).

Finally, regarding the intervention setting, many people do not voluntarily seek family violence prevention programs, even if they demonstrate risk factors (O'Leary et al., 2006). Therefore, it may be useful to build prevention efforts into sites that reach broad segments of the population, such as schools, colleges, or health care offices (O'Leary et al., 2006).

Build on Existing Research

Research on IPV prevention lags far behind other areas of IPV research (Stith, 2006), and conducting high-quality research on family violence prevention is extremely costly and challenging methodologically (O'Leary et al., 2006; Whitaker et al., 2006). However, it is important that family violence prevention initiatives build on existing research (Wurtele, 2009). Given that limited funds are typically available to support preventive initiatives, existing research findings can help increase program effectiveness (Kilpatrick, Resick, & Williams, 2001). Furthermore, there are many different potential points of focus for prevention work, and research findings can help developers make decisions about the content and format of their programs. Research findings can help practitioners identify new and promising approaches to family violence prevention (Kilpatrick et al., 2001).

Increasingly, funding agencies require collaborations between practitioners and researchers in the area of violence prevention and intervention (Edleson & Bible, 2001; Gondolf, Yllö, & Campbell, 1997; Riger, 1999), although such partnerships face challenges (Edleson & Bible, 2001). Researchers and practitioners face different demands in their work settings, and these can contribute to challenges in the two groups working together effectively (Galano & Schellenbach, 2007; Gondolf et al., 1997; Kilpatrick et al., 2001; Riger, 1999; Saul,

Duffy et al., 2008; Williams, 2004). Nonetheless, researchers and practitioners each can bring unique and valuable resources, skills, and knowledge to advance research and practice in family violence prevention (Gondolf et al., 1997; Mouradian, Mechanic, & Williams, 2001; Wurtele, 2009).

Prevention program developers also should conduct ongoing evaluations of their efforts in order to identify approaches that are and are not effective. Program evaluations, especially those that consider multiple perspectives and use reflexive research methods, can provide valuable information about the impact of prevention work (Levin, 1999; Williams, 2004). Determining appropriate outcome evaluations for prevention programs is complicated, however (Ko & Cosden, 2001). Some potential outcomes to measure include changes in attitudes toward family violence, reductions in behaviors associated with abuse, increases in positive relationship or parenting behaviors, greater knowledge about and usage of available community resources, and increased personal, relationship, and social resources to protect people from violence (Antle et al., 2011; Foshee et al., 1998; Meyer & Stein, 2004; Whitaker et al., 2006). Although there is some value in assessing attitude changes as an outcome of prevention programs, these changes do not necessarily lead to behavior changes (Campbell & Manganello, 2006; Ko & Cosden, 2001; Nabi, Southwell, & Hornik, 2002; O'Leary et al., 2006; Schewe & Bennett, 2002). Of course, the ideal goal of family violence prevention programs is to end the violence. However, measuring this goal is difficult, especially if only a short-term follow-up is possible. As such, Schewe and Bennett (2002) suggested that the most useful research questions to consider when evaluating family violence prevention programs address the relative merits and drawbacks of the program, the most appropriate population to target, and how the program impacts participants.

Forge Interdisciplinary Partnerships

There is an urgent need for new, interdisciplinary perspectives and interventions aimed at ending family violence (Gondolf et al., 1997; Russo, 2008). Therapists simply cannot work in isolation in any area of family violence work, including prevention. Collaborations are needed with such groups as police officers, domestic violence shelters and advocacy agencies, universities, and other community-based organizations (Smith, 2005). In addition, there is a need to move beyond collaborations among groups traditionally involved with addressing family violence. For example, as advances in technology expand rapidly, information technology professionals can contribute to ensure that technologies are used for the maximal protection and safety of prospective and current victims of family violence (Self-Brown & Whitaker, 2008; Wurtele, 2009). Training of professionals who work with families but whose work does not specifically address family violence can help these professionals be better equipped to identify and respond to clients who are victimized (Murray & Kardatzke, 2007).

Examples of Prevention for Different Types of Family Violence

Now that general considerations related to family violence prevention work have been explored, we will discuss prevention work as it relates to specific forms of family violence. Although most of the information available currently addresses IPV and child maltreatment, and we discuss those first, we also address elder abuse briefly at the end of the chapter.

IPV Prevention

Although the rationale for IPV prevention is clear, many questions remain about how to develop and implement effective IPV prevention programs (Hamby, 2006; O'Leary et al., 2006). However, there is preliminary evidence to suggest that IPV prevention programs can be effective (Whitaker et al., 2006). First, IPV prevention efforts are especially useful when they target adolescents and young adults (Hamby, 2006). Second, some topics that are important to address in IPV prevention programs include anger management, power and control dynamics, types of IPV, conflict and communication skills, and substance abuse issues (Murray & Kardatzke, 2007; O'Leary et al., 2006). Third, general relationship enhancement programs, such as the Prevention and Relationship Enhancement Program (PREP), may hold promise for preventing IPV (Low, Monarch, Hartman, & Markman, 2002; O'Leary et al., 2006; Slep & Heyman, 2008). Others include employer-based programs, initiatives involving men, the potential to address IPV within general violence prevention efforts, and secondary prevention strategies.

Employer-Based Programs. A growing number of employers have policies and programs that reflect IPV prevention, such as educational trainings for employees to learn about IPV (Lindquist et al., 2010). In particular, Employee Assistance Programs (EAPs) often are called upon by employers to promote employee wellness and refer employees to community resources (Lindquist et al., 2010). Although some EAP services are intervention-focused (e.g., assessment and referral for victims and perpetrators), the prevention-related services they may provide include training for employees and supervisors and consulting with employers on IPV policies (Lindquist et al., 2010). These employer- and EAP-initiated activities may also help with early detection and intervention of IPV (i.e., indicated prevention).

Initiatives that Involve Men. There is increasing recognition of the importance of involving men in IPV prevention (DeKeseredy, Schwarts, & Alvi, 2000; Fullwood, 2002; Simbandumwe et al., 2008; Stith, 2006). Men can play an important role in changing social norms in male social networks to be less supportive and more shaming of attitudes and behaviors that promote IPV (DeKeseredy et al., 2000). In particular, men have been involved in IPV prevention efforts at colleges, such as trainings and advocacy efforts (DeKeseredy et al., 2000).

Addressing IPV Prevention in General Violence Prevention. Matthews (2000) described the Choosing Non-Violence Program, which was unique in that it addresses IPV prevention within a broader focus on general violence. This interactive program was developed through a battered women's shelter and involved a series of training workshops in community organizations. Each workshop lasted between six to ten hours and addressed the topics of stress management, the media, relationships, communication, and prevention. Only part of that time, at least one hour, was devoted specifically to addressing IPV. A relatively small proportion of participants completed follow-up questionnaires, but these individuals indicated that they remembered the IPV-related content and developed the new knowledge and skills through the program. This study had several methodological limitations, but it suggests that it may be possible to include a focus on IPV within more broadly-focused preventive interventions.

Secondary Prevention. McFarlane, Groff, O'Brien, and Watson (2006) studied a secondary prevention initiative aimed at screening and providing resources for IPV in primary care healthcare clinics. These researchers tested two levels of interventions, and both led to positive outcomes. Both interventions involved screening female participants for IPV and providing them with a referral card with community resources. The more intense intervention added a 20-minute nursing case management meeting, which involved providing support, guidance, and personalized referrals. Among the 319 women in the study, over a 2-year follow-up period, participants in both groups reported fewer threatened and actual assaults, decreased homicide risk markers, less harassment at work, and increased use of safety-promoting behaviors. There were no differences in these outcomes between the two conditions, suggesting that either approach can lead to positive outcomes.

IPV-Focused Public Awareness Campaigns. A variety of creative strategies have been suggested and attempted toward changing attitudes toward IPV among the general population. Straus and Smith (1995) even went so far as to suggest that marriage licenses could come with a Surgeon General's warning about the potential risk to people's well-being if they do not take steps to avoid violence in their relationships. More common approaches, however, use campaigns to raise awareness of the problem of IPV and promote attitudes and social norms that can reduce violence (Campbell & Manganello, 2006; Wolfe & Jaffe, 1999). Another potential aim of public awareness campaigns is to help victims learn about community resources (Campbell & Manganello, 2006). Two examples of public awareness campaigns, both done by the Family

Violence Prevention Fund, are the "Philadelphia: Let's Stop Domestic Violence" campaign, which focused on advocacy in the media and neighborhood mobilization, and the "It's Your Business" campaign, which used a radio drama to illustrate IPV (Wray, 2006). Although both were well-conceived, neither was particularly effective because they failed to reach the target audience at the desired level (Campbell & Manganello, 2006; Wray, 2006).

Dating Violence Prevention. Perhaps no area of IPV prevention has received as much attention as dating violence prevention programming for adolescents and college students. Some general dating violence prevention strategies include educating adolescents about dating violence, training adults who work with adolescents, support groups, and peer counseling programs (Smith & Donnelly, 2001). Peer counseling components are viewed as especially beneficial aspects (Avery-Leaf & Cascardi, 2002; Murray & Kardatzke, 2007; Noonan & Charles, 2009; Schwartz, Griffin, Russell, & Frontaura-Duck, 2006). Dating violence prevention programs often combine some mixed-gender groups with some same-gender groups (Avery-Leaf & Cascardi, 2002), and gender-neutral language is often used in either approach (Antle et al., 2011; Avery-Leaf & Cascardi, 2002).

In an effort to learn about adolescents' needs and characteristics to guide future dating violence prevention initiatives, the Centers for Disease Control (CDC) conducted a series of 12 focus groups with middle school-age students (i.e., 6th, 7th, and 8th graders) in the Atlanta area (Noonan & Charles, 2009). The findings suggest that students at these ages are just starting to engage in dating relationships, but that involvement in dating increases over these years and students often hold gender-stereotypes about appropriate ways of behaving in dating relationships. Focus group participants identified various forms of verbal and emotional abuse that occur in dating relationships at this age, although recognition of physical and sexual abuse was less common. Most participants believed that relationship abuse is wrong, and most reported that they would be most likely to turn to their friends and older siblings for relationship advice. They varied in the extent to which they would be likely to consult adults like teachers or parents. This study's findings suggest that these years may be a critical time for preventive interventions.

Safe Dates. One of the most extensively studied teen dating violence prevention programs is the Safe Dates program (Foshee et al., 1998). Safe Dates was tested among 1,700 eighth- and ninth-grade students in a rural county in eastern North Carolina. Fourteen public schools were randomly assigned to either a treatment (involving the entire Safe Dates program) or control condition (involving only the community-based program components) (Foshee et al., 1998). Safe Dates, which is inclusive of both a primary and secondary prevention framework, involves both school- and community-based initiatives, including a peer-performed theatre performance, a 10-session educational program, a poster contest, community services for adolescents involved in abusive relationships, and professional training for community-based service providers (Foshee et al., 1998). The program's outcomes have been studied over time. In its initial implementation, participants in the treatment condition showed significantly less psychological abuse, sexual violence, and violence in current relationships as compared to those in the control condition. At the posttest, participants in the treatment condition (compared to those in the control condition) also reported decreased acceptance of dating violence norms, improved use of constructive communication and responses to anger, decreased gender stereotyping, and increased awareness of services for victims and perpetrators of dating violence (Foshee et al., 1998).

To follow-up on this preliminary support for the effectiveness of Safe Dates (Foshee et al., 1998), additional follow-up studies were conducted after one year and again after four years. One year following the intervention, there were no differences between the treatment and control groups in behavioral indicators of violence, but there were significant differences between groups on the attitudinal measures, such as dating violence norms and awareness of community resources (Foshee, Bauman, Greene et al., 2000). At the four-year follow-up, participants in the treatment condition showed significantly less violence victimization and perpetration compared to participants in the control condition, although a booster intervention did not impact treatment outcomes (Foshee, Bauman, Ennett et al., 2004). A limitation of these studies is that they relied primarily on self-report data (Foshee, Bauman, Arriaga et al., 1998). However, Safe Dates demonstrates many strengths, especially because it is so comprehensive and involves the school and the community (Foshee, Bauman, Arriaga et al., 1998).

Youth Relationships Project. The Youth Relationships Project (YRP; Wolfe et al., 2003) is an empirically supported dating violence prevention program (Teten et al., 2009; Whitaker et al., 2006) that maintains a dual focus on reducing dating violence risk and promoting healthy relationships. Across 18 two-hour sessions, participants learn about relationship abuse, develop relationship skills, and engage in social action activities (e.g., visiting community agencies relevant to dating violence). The mixed-gender groups are led by a male-female cofacilitator team and include a variety of interactive activities. Wolfe et al. tested the effectiveness of this program with a group of 14- to 16-year-olds identified as at risk for dating violence due to histories of childhood maltreatment victimization. The researchers recruited 191 teenagers, approximately half of whom were male and half were female, who were then randomly assigned to participate in the YRP or a no-treatment control group. Across the two-year study period, the YRP participants, as compared to the control group, demonstrated more positive outcomes, including reduced perpetration of abusive behaviors and greater reductions in emotional distress.

Other Examples of Dating Violence Programs. Avery-Leaf, Cascardi, O'Leary, and Cano (1997) evaluated a school-based dating violence primary prevention program. This five-session program focused on psychological and social aspects of dating violence, and its goals were to help participants develop equitable relationships, decrease violence-condoning attitudes, become more adept at using positive communication skills, and learn about resources for victims. Mostly 11th- and 12th-grade high school students (n=193) in health classes were randomly assigned based on which health class they were in to receive the prevention program curriculum or to be in the control group. Health class teachers delivered the curriculum. Compared to students in the control group, those in the intervention group showed significant reductions in attitudes condoning dating violence shortly after the program was complete. Despite some methodological limitations, this study demonstrates that a school-based program, delivered by an established teacher, can promote attitudes that are less conducive to dating violence.

The CDC developed the Choose Respect campaign (see www.chooserespect.org) to educate 11- to 14-year-olds about healthy relationships and dating violence (Teten et al., 2009). It uses a multilateral approach and includes resources, media advocacy, and educational programming (Teten et al., 2009). Choose Respect resources can be integrated into school- and community-based dating violence prevention programming.

The Love U2 healthy relationship program teaches adolescents about healthy and unhealthy relationship dynamics and skills, such as communication and conflict management (Antle et al., 2011). Antle et al. (2011) studied a brief (i.e., 12 hours over two days) version of this program among a group of teenagers identified as at risk for dating violence. Participants reported high levels of satisfaction with the program, increased likelihood of using positive communication and conflict strategies, and less supportive attitudes toward dating violence.

Child Maltreatment Prevention

As with IPV, most professionals and members of the general population would agree that preventing child maltreatment is a worthy goal (Daro & Donnelly, 2002). However, the most effective strategies for doing so have yet to be clearly defined (Daro & Donnelly, 2002). Public attention and widespread initiatives to prevent child maltreatment have experienced waves of momentum (Daro & Donnelly, 2002), with interest in this area generally growing over time (Geeraert et al., 2004). Clearly, a multilateral approach to child maltreatment prevention is needed, and efforts should address both the family and the societal level (Sanders et al., 2003). Parents should be increasingly involved in prevention efforts (Wurtele, 2009), and child maltreatment programs that are focused on the entire family are especially needed (Kumpfer, 2008). In particular, efforts are needed to promote positive, adaptive parenting practices and resources at a community level (Sanders et al., 2003).

Although a number of child maltreatment prevention programs have been developed, research supporting many of them is lacking (Daro & Donnelly, 2002; Kumpfer, 2008; Peterson et al., 2003). In addition, many programs lack a clear theoretical foundation (Geeraert et al., 2004; Topping & Barron, 2009), although attachment, cognitive-behavioral, social cognitive, and ecological theories are most common (Geeraert et al., 2004; Topping & Barron, 2009). Although some questions remain about the most appropriate program format, programs that are more intensive are likely to be more effective, but these programs are costly (Peterson et al., 2003). Many child maltreatment prevention programs are very lengthy, perhaps even up to five years (Geeraert et al., 2004). However, the actual interventions during that time can range from very frequent to more spread out (Geeraert et al., 2004). Programs may be very intensive early in the intervention and when the families experience the greatest needs (Geeraert et al., 2004). Child maltreatment programs may even work with families prior to childbirth (Geeraert et al., 2004).

There is a need for much more advancement in the area of child maltreatment prevention (Leventhal, 2005). To review trends in this area, we first discuss common themes in programs for parents, then for children. We then discuss three other major areas of attention for child maltreatment prevention, including child sexual abuse prevention efforts, home visitation programs, and community-strengthening efforts.

Programs for Parents. Programs targeting parents are based on an assumption that helping parents become better equipped to manage the responsibilities of parenting will reduce the likelihood that they will perpetrate abuse or neglect. In addition, these programs may train parents to recognize signs of abuse so that they can respond to their children if they are harmed by someone else (e.g., a teacher, neighbor, or stranger). Corresponding with these aims, topics often addressed in these programs include appropriate discipline, building supportive peer networks, communication and coping skills, economic considerations (e.g., jobs and housing), how parents can talk about abuse with their children so that children will know they can come to the parents if they are victimized, reducing isolation, education about child development, and common challenges involved in parenting, increasing parent-child bonding, community resources, managing one's home, problem-solving skills, and self-control (Daro & Donnelly, 2002; Geeraert et al., 2004; Kenny, 2009).

Another potential target for child maltreatment prevention programs is the cognitions that parents hold toward their children (Bugental et al., 2002; Sanders et al., 2003). For example, abusive parents may make negative attributions toward their children's behaviors, such as believing that their children are intentionally misbehaving in order to harm their parents (Bugental et al., 2002). In a prevention framework, changing the parents' maladaptive thinking patterns should reduce the risk for maltreatment perpetration (Bugental et al., 2002). Bugental et al. described a cognitive-focused program that helps parents learn to interpret children's behaviors more positively and accurately, as well as develop more effective problem-solving skills. Bugental et al.'s evaluation of this program's effectiveness found that the program led to significant reductions in physical abuse perpetration, and it was made even more effective through the addition of a home visitation program. Although this program is in need of further study, it holds promise for preventing child abuse perpetration, both on its own and combined with other interventions.

Programs for Children. In addition to programs targeting parents, initiatives have been developed to reach children directly. These programs aim to help children learn how to protect themselves from victimization. In addition to a primary goal to prevent future violence, a secondary goal of these programs is to prompt participants to disclose previous maltreatment so that those who have been abused can receive needed treatment (Barron & Topping, 2010). Because some participants may not feel comfortable disclosing these experiences in front of other participants, all participants should be provided with a resource for disclosing in private after the program, such as a hotline number or a school counselor (Barron & Topping, 2010). Topics often addressed in child-focused child maltreatment prevention programs include how children can protect themselves, helping children process emotional responses to abuse, personal safety skills, how to disclose when abuse occurs, and communication skills (Barron & Topping, 2010; Kenny, 2009; Topping & Barron, 2009). Whatever their focus, programs for children must be designed to reflect children's unique developmental needs (Topping & Barron, 2009).

Child Sexual Abuse Prevention. Two types of child sexual abuse prevention initiatives are school-based programs for children and tracking of offenders (Finkelhor, 2009).

School-Based Child Sexual Abuse Prevention Programs. Child sexual abuse prevention programs for children have received the most examination by researchers (Finkelhor, 2009). These programs typically are offered in schools, although they may occur in other organizations that serve youths, including religious institutions (Finkelhor, 2009). Schools offer the advantages of reaching large segments of the population and providing a nonstigmatizing setting for those who have been abused already (Finkelhor, 2009; Wurtele, 2009). Two types of child sexual abuse education programs are information-based and behavioral skills training programs (Kopp & Miltenberger, 2009).

Information-based programs are didactic and content-focused, whereas behavioral skills training programs involve training and practice in skills, such as through role plays (Kopp & Miltenberger, 2009). Skills training strategies include practicing new skills, modeling, and reinforcing positive behaviors (Davis & Gidycz, 2000; Kenny, 2009; Topping & Barron, 2009). Programs that are interactive, participatory, and focused on behavioral skills are thought to be more effective (Davis & Gidycz, 2000; Kenny, 2009; Kopp & Miltenberger, 2009).

Topics addressed in these programs include rights about one's body (e.g., private parts), good and bad forms of touch, communication skills (i.e., learning to say no), characteristics of abuse, reducing victims' self-blame, understanding good and bad secrets to keep, and knowing to tell an adult if abuse occurs (Davis & Gidycz, 2000; Finkelhor, 2009; Kenny, 2009; Kopp & Miltenberger, 2009; Topping & Barron, 2009; Wurtele, 2009). The content of these programs has been summarized as the "Three 'Rs'": Recognizing, Resisting, and Reporting (Wurtele, 2009, p. 4). The content is often more in line with stranger-perpetrated abuse than abuse perpetrated by someone known to the child (Ko & Cosden, 2001; Kopp & Miltenberger, 2009).

Some programs incorporate training for adults who interact with children (e.g., teachers, family members) to recognize and respond to newly identified instances of child sexual abuse (Finkelhor, 2009). Indeed, many professionals who work with children lack knowledge about the topic (Wurtele, 2009). Programs may be done with groups that include parents and their children together, although it can be useful to separate parents and children so that unique concerns can be addressed in separate groups (Kenny, 2009). Including parents and children in programs has both advantages and disadvantages that are in need of further study (Topping & Barron, 2009).

Topping and Barron (2009) reviewed 22 studies on the effectiveness of school-based child sexual abuse prevention programs. A number of common methodological limitations were found in these studies, therefore limiting our ability to draw conclusions about the effectiveness of these programs. Although Topping and Barron noted that many researchers purported to show positive outcomes, the overall evidence for the immediate and long-term effectiveness of these programs is very limited currently. Common elements found among the small number of studies with the most promising evidence included modeling, group discussion, and role-playing new skills. In another study examining the impact of these programs, Gibson and Leitenberg (2000) used a retrospective design that involved asking college students about their past participation in a child sexual abuse prevention program. These researchers found that, among the 62% of the 825 female college students they surveyed who reported they had participated in such a program, 8% reported having been sexually abused. In contrast, 14% of the students who had not participated in such a program reported sexual abuse victimization.

Child-focused sexual abuse prevention programs have been criticized for a number of reasons, including that they address information that is not developmentally appropriate for young children, can lead to anxiety in children, may interfere with normal sexual development, and place too much responsibility on children for stopping abuse by adults (Finkelhor, 2009; Gibson & Leitenberg, 2000; Topping & Barron, 2009; Wurtele, 2009). Existing research, however, suggests that some of these criticisms are unfounded, in that children do not appear to become more anxious after participating (Finkelhor, 2009). Further, there do not appear to be long-term ramifications for participants' sexual development (Gibson & Leitenberg, 2000). However, in their review of existing research, Topping and Barron (2009) noted that several program evaluation studies noted that some participating children experienced negative outcomes, such as anxiety, fear, aggression, embarrassment, and triggering bad memories. Therefore, due to the documented potential for negative outcomes of these programs, we urge therapists to consider how to mitigate and respond to these outcomes if they arise.

Offender Tracking. According to Finkelhor (2009), increased efforts to track prior child sexual abuse offenders have been undertaken in an effort to prevent further perpetration. These efforts include sex offender registries (including public information about where offenders live), employee background checks for positions that involve working with children, and lengthened prison sentences. Although many community residents view these efforts as important, there is minimal evidence that they are effective. One reason for this is that they do not address a significant proportion of offenders who never come into contact with law enforcement.

Finkelhor (2009) suggests that more broad-based prevention initiatives are needed to move beyond the two areas of school-based programs and offender tracking, such as public awareness campaigns and programs to empower bystanders to help. However, limited funding and a lack of leadership currently hinder child sexual abuse prevention efforts (Wurtele, 2009). Finkelhor (2009) notes, "It would have to be said that, as yet, no true evidence-based programs or policies exist in the area of preventing child sexual abuse" (p. 170). Therefore, despite the efforts that have been made to date, much more work is needed in this area.

Home Visitation Programs. Home visitation programs have long been used in child maltreatment prevention (Daro & Donnelly, 2002; Geeraert et al., 2004). These programs often have the dual aims of preventing child abuse and connecting families to community resources (Russell et al., 2007). An underlying goal is to help parents become more self-confident and self-sufficient in their parenting competencies (Russell et al., 2007). These programs can help families create positive climates for children's physical, social, and emotional development (Russell et al., 2007). Home visitation programs offer different types of support to families, including basic social support, education, and links to other agencies to address acute needs, and these programs can be highly personalized to families' unique needs (Russell et al., 2007).

There have been inconsistent research findings regarding the effectiveness of home visitation programs for preventing child maltreatment (Daro & Donnelly, 2002; Russell et al., 2007). Geeraert et al. (2004) conducted a meta-analysis to determine whether child maltreatment prevention programs targeting families with children between the ages of 0 and 3, which typically involve home visitation, are effective at preventing abuse and reducing risk factors. They included 40 studies in their meta-analysis, including 17 that examined the Health Families America (HFA) model. The meta-analysis demonstrated that the programs are generally effective at producing positive outcomes, and HFA programs were no more effective than non-HFA programs. However, the researchers classified the effect size as "relatively small" (p. 286) and urged that guarded optimism is the best way to interpret these findings. A limitation is that many studies did not provide specific information about the actual interventions used in the programs.

Community-Strengthening Programs. Broad-based child maltreatment prevention efforts are needed to promote stronger social norms around safety, respect, justice, and healthy relationships among all children, families, and communities (Wurtele, 2009). Kimbrough-Melton and Campbell (2008) described a comprehensive, community-based approach, called Strong Communities for Children (SCC). An underlying assumption of SCC is that safe, strong neighborhoods are essential for the protection of children. Carried out in South Carolina through Clemson University, SCC involves two major strategies. First, community building outreach efforts are undertaken. Second, the initiative brings together existing community resources. A range of activities reflected these strategies, including creating a new playground, helping families connect to local agencies, promoting more positive social norms, enhancing parents' sense of leadership, providing career and financial counseling, and ensuring that involved professionals (e.g., pediatricians) are linked to the program. The overarching goal is to mobilize all segments of the community to unite in efforts to promote safety for children and families. This SCC initiative is viewed as particularly innovative (Leventhal, 2005).

Peterson et al. (2003) described another multilevel initiative. Participants were mothers with toddler and preschool-age children who were recruited from a Women, Infants, and Children's (WIC) agency. Women participated in weekly interactive group therapy sessions. A focus was on cognitive restructuring and role-playing. In addition to group therapy, the women received weekly home visits that focused on consolidating and applying information discussed in group therapy. Specific topics and skills addressed in this program included parenting, problem-solving, time management, discipline, anger management, child safety, and social support. Compared with members of a control group, participants demonstrated positive outcomes across several domains, including improved discipline, greater nurturing, and improved parenting self-efficacy, and many of their gains persisted for at least a year following the program.

Clearly, these multilateral, community-based approaches to child maltreatment prevention are complex and require significant time and money. However, they have the potential to address social issues (e.g., poverty, unsafe neighborhoods) that contribute to child risk. As such, their potential to reduce child maltreatment is promising.

Elder Abuse

Far less has been written about the prevention of elder abuse compared to other forms of family violence. However, strategies mentioned in the literature are worth noting, especially because some aspects of elder abuse prevention are different from other forms of family violence. Four specific strategies have been identified, in addition to considerations for preventing financial exploitation and involving religious institutions. First, vulnerable elderly individuals, especially those with physical or cognitive impairments, should be monitored to ensure that their safety needs are met, and case management can be useful in this regard (Choi & Mayer, 2000). Second, it can be a protective factor for vulnerable elderly individuals to have increased access to and use of supportive services and organizations (Choi & Mayer, 2000). Third, caregiver support groups and other resources, such as temporary relief from caregiving responsibilities, can help reduce stresses that may lead some caregivers to perpetrate maltreatment (Choi & Mayer, 2000). Fourth, substance abuse assessment for elders can be considered a preventive measure, in that it may identify individuals at risk for self-neglect (Choi & Mayer, 2000).

Regarding prevention of financial exploitation, financial institutions and other agencies may be able to put protections in place to fend off financial abuse (Choi & Mayer, 2000). Santa Clara County (CA) developed an early response system for dealing with suspected financial abuse, the Financial Abuse Specialist Team (FAST) program (Malks, Schmidt, & Austin, 2002). The FAST program can be considered both indicated prevention in that it addresses abuse that occurred already and universal prevention, in that the developers hoped that the program's visibility would deter future abuses. Key program components include weekly interdisciplinary case reviews, legal interventions when needed, investigation of evidence, and recovery of lost assets.

Elder abuse prevention also has been addressed in religious organizations (Podnieks & Wilson, 2003; Sherr & Ellor, 2009). Faith leaders may be able to promote safety for elders by emphasizing religious beliefs that support the care for and respect of elderly people (Podnieks & Wilson, 2003). Religious organizations also may serve as key channels for disseminating educational information about elder abuse, both to raise awareness about the issue and connect individuals with needed services (Podnieks & Wilson, 2003; Sherr & Ellor, 2009). Finally, clergy and other church officials could benefit from additional training and support in learning to identify and respond to elder abuse in their congregations (Sherr & Ellor, 2009).

Conclusion

A shift from psychotherapy into the realm of family violence prevention offers both challenges and rewards for therapists. Prevention will remain an extremely complex undertaking as long as family violence remains entrenched in social forces and intergenerational family patterns. The challenges involved in this type of work are too numerous to list in entirety. To name just a few, effective prevention work involves motivating and mobilizing vast segments of the community, changing major social systems and behavior patterns with limited time and resources, working with interdisciplinary colleagues who may hold different perspectives about family violence and preventing it, and choosing from a limited body of knowledge how best to design the content, format, timing, and setting of prevention programs and initiatives. Despite these challenges, the potential rewards are great, and the actual long-term outcomes of preventive initiatives may never be able to be fully known.

PART IV

14

SELF-CARE FOR THERAPISTS WORKING WITH CLIENTS IMPACTED BY FAMILY VIOLENCE

There is no way to sugar-coat it: doing therapy with clients impacted by family violence is *hard work*. Personally, professionally, and organizationally, therapists who do this work face a number of challenges, as is evident on every page of this book. What, then, is the line between acknowledging our natural, human responses to such situations and risking that these personal reactions get in the way of effective therapy? How can therapists prepare for and respond to situations like feeling like one is going to cry during a counseling session, being afraid for one's own safety during a session, or becoming increasingly disillusioned and burnt out toward one's job? These issues are crucial to address, and yet they often are so overlooked in the training of professionals who work with clients impacted by family violence (e.g., Goldblatt, Buchbinder, Eisikovits, & Arizon-Mesinger, 2009; Iliffe & Steed, 2000; Nelson-Gardell & Harris, 2003; Winefield & Barlow, 1995).

What Makes This Work So Personally and Professionally Challenging?

Being a therapist is inherently challenging for a variety of reasons, including challenging client situations, the inconsistent progress clients demonstrate, and a host of organizational demands (Azar, 2000; Baird & Jenkins, 2003; Carroll, Gilroy, & Murra, 2003; Neumann & Gamble, 1995; O'Halloran & Linton, 2000; Rosenberg & Pace, 2006). Challenges can arise for both new and experienced clinicians (Azar, 2000). New therapists can become quickly overwhelmed by the demands of their work, while experienced therapists may struggle to stay excited about and engaged in their work after facing these challenges over time.

Therapeutic work with clients impacted by family violence and other trauma presents unique challenges beyond those experienced in non-trauma-focused therapy. Hearing detailed stories of trauma and abuse is challenging for therapists, but telling these stories is often viewed as an essential part of therapy for these clients (Azar, 2000; Dekel & Peled, 2000; Lord, 2008; Slattery & Goodman, 2009). Stories about the abuse of children can be particularly harrowing (Iliffe & Steed, 2000; Shapiro, Dorman, Burkey, & Welker, 1999; Walker, 2004). The often shocking and horrific details associated with traumatic experiences are different from the material often discussed in non-trauma-focused therapy (Follette, Polusny, & Milbeck, 1994).

As we emphasize throughout this book, safety is paramount. These safety considerations give rise to additional challenges for therapists, such as by leading them to question the safety risks involved with potential interventions (Azar, 2000). The safety of therapists themselves may be placed at risk through some aspects of this work, such as in-home therapy and direct threats to therapists made by violent clients (Azar, 2000; Csiernik, Smith, Dewar, Dromgole, & O'Neill, 2010; Dekel & Peled, 2000). In addition, if new incidents of abuse for clients or family members arise during treatment, therapists may question their decisions and whether they have done enough to help protect their clients (Azar, 2000). Unique and complex confidentiality issues also may arise, as well more frequent situations that may warrant breaking confidentiality (e.g., suspected child maltreatment and threats of imminent harm) (Iliffe & Steed, 2000).

Additional challenges are associated with certain types of family violence. For example, working with adult survivors of childhood sexual abuse has been described as a "therapeutic roller coaster" (Chu, 1992, p. 351). Chu asserts that therapy with these clients may lead therapists to feel that they lack control of the therapy process. Other examples relate to working with maltreated children. Specific challenges of working with this population include low prestige, less training, and relatively less influence on clients as compared to their families and home lives (Azar, 2000). Some therapy approaches for maltreated children involve intensive in-home services (e.g., multisystemic therapy; Henggeler & Borduin, 1990), and the on-call responsibilities involved in this work can create major challenges for professionals striving to maintain work–life balance (Anderson, 2000). Finally, some challenges related to working with IPV-impacted clients include that related service agencies often are underfunded and that conflicts may arise between one's personal ideologies and clients' experiences (Dekel & Peled, 2000). IPV perpetrators in particular tend to be unpopular clients with therapists (Aymer, 2008), and perpetrators are notoriously, although not necessarily, thought to be difficult to engage in therapy (Iliffe & Steed, 2000). In addition, because gender dynamics can be heightened in IPV cases, unique challenges may arise for female counselors working with male perpetrators (Tyagi, 2006). Furthermore, therapists may experience frustrations and anger related to IPV dynamics, including victims returning to abusive relationships and perpetrators denying responsibility for their actions (Brown & O'Brien, 1998). Respecting a client's decision to remain in a violent relationship, especially when safety risks appear clear, can be immensely challenging for therapists (Iliffe & Steed, 2000; McCloskey & Fraser, 1997).

Conceptualizations of Therapists' Work with Clients Impacted by Family Violence

There is wide recognition of the personal toll of these challenges on therapists, although this phenomenon is conceptualized in different ways by different scholars. The terms used to describe the impact of working with clients impacted by trauma include secondary traumatic stress/compassion fatigue, vicarious traumatization, countertransference, and burnout. Although there is some overlap between these terms, each has a slightly different emphasis and offers a unique perspective on understanding how therapists are impacted by this work.

Secondary Traumatic Stress/Compassion Fatigue. Charles Figley (1996) is the researcher most closely associated with the terms *secondary traumatic stress and compassion fatigue.* Although these terms are used to describe the same general phenomenon (Baird & Jenkins, 2003; Chouliara, Hutchison, & Karatzias, 2009; Conrad & Kellar-Guenther, 2006), the term *compassion fatigue* is considered a less stigmatizing term (Jenkins & Baird, 2002). However, *secondary traumatic stress* is used more widely in existing literature. Other related terms are *covictimization* (Nelson-Gardell & Harris, 2003) and *empathy fatigue* (Stebnicki, 2007). For consistency, we use the term *secondary traumatic stress* in this chapter.

Secondary traumatic stress is the experience of emotional distress as a result of being in close contact with a person who directly encountered a traumatic experience (Baird & Jenkins, 2003; Ben-Porat & Itzhaky, 2009; Bride, 2007; Bride, Robinson, Yedigis, & Figley, 2004; Chouliara et al., 2009; Gates & Gillespie, 2008; Jenkins & Baird, 2002; Nelson-Gardell & Harris, 2003; O'Halloran & Linton, 2000; Perron & Hiltz, 2006; Slattery & Goodman, 2009). Thus, close significant others (e.g., friends, family members, and helping professionals) may be subject to secondary traumatic stress (Baird & Jenkins, 2003; Jenkins & Baird, 2002; Nelson-Gardell & Harris, 2003). Many researchers view secondary traumatic stress as an unavoidable and natural consequence of working with people who experienced trauma (Conrad & Kellar-Guenther, 2006; Jenkins & Baird, 2002; Nelson-Gardell & Harris, 2003; O'Halloran & Linton, 2000), leading some scholars to describe secondary traumatic stress as an occupational hazard for professionals working with traumatized clients (Bride, 2007; Bride et al., 2004; Slattery & Goodman, 2009). In one study of IPV counselors (Iliffe & Steed, 2000), even experienced counselors acknowledged that they at times experienced "horror" in listening to clients tell stories of abuse (p. 400).

Although not an official diagnosis in the *DSM-IV-TR*, researchers speculate that secondary traumatic stress can lead to a cluster of symptoms, such as intrusion, avoidance, and arousal that closely resemble those of PTSD (Goldblatt, 2009; Nelson-Gardell & Harris, 2003). When symptoms are severe and persistent, they have been described as secondary traumatic stress disorder (STSD). One way to distinguish between secondary traumatic stress and STSD is the length of time the symptoms have been present. If they have been present for more than one month, they can be considered STSD, whereas symptoms lasting less than one month can be considered secondary traumatic stress (O'Halloran & Linton, 2000).

Vicarious Traumatization. Vicarious traumatization also is viewed as a normal response to hearing clients' traumatic experiences (Chouliara et al., 2009; Neumann & Gamble, 1995). *Vicarious traumatization* (McCann & Pearlman, 1990) describes a process through which a therapist's cognitive schemas are modified, leading to negative emotional, relational, and occupational consequences (Baird & Jenkins, 2003; Chouliara et al., 2009). Therapists may experience diminished feelings of safety, trust, and control (Baird & Jenkins, 2003; Chouliara et al., 2009). In addition, therapists may generalize clients' experiences to the wider population, leading to a belief that abuse is more common than it actually is (Dekel & Peled, 2000).

Countertransference. *Countertransference* refers to the extent to which a therapist experiences personal reactions (e.g., thoughts and feelings) in response to clients' counseling processes that impact the process of counseling (Iliffe & Steed, 2000; Nelson-Gardell & Harris, 2003; Walker, 2004). Countertransference, especially when unacknowledged, can hinder therapeutic progress if not managed (Arnd-Caddigan, 2006; Walker, 2004). In recent years, transference and countertransference have come to be understood more in terms of a function of the therapist–client relationship, rather than solely the result of one or the other's underlying psychological functioning (Arnd-Caddigan, 2006).

The countertransferential responses therapists may experience include overidentifying with clients, emotionally distancing oneself from clients, and becoming curiously fascinated with the details of clients' traumatic experiences (Neumann & Gamble, 1995). Therapists may view their emotional responses to clients as distressing, especially if they feel ashamed of them or believe that they reflect their ineffectiveness as therapists (Etherington, 2000; Neumann & Gamble, 1995; Walker, 2004). Countertransference may be especially likely among new therapists (Neumann & Gamble, 1995) or therapists with personal experiences of trauma (Tyagi, 2006), particularly when working with clients impacted by family violence (Chu, 1992).

Burnout. Burnout is common in interpersonally challenging jobs, especially within organizational settings that lack adequate resources (Baird & Jenkins, 2003; Chouliara et al., 2009). Burnout is not limited to work with trauma-impacted clients and often is linked to unfavorable working conditions (Iliffe & Steed, 2000; Jenkins & Baird, 2002; Nelson-Gardell & Harris, 2003). Burnout can occur when an individual's personal resources and energy become overwhelmed by their work-related demands (O'Halloran & Linton, 2000). Azar (2000) defined burnout as "an exhaustion of a practitioner's mental and physical resources attributed to his or her prolonged and unsuccessful striving toward unrealistic expectations (internally or externally derived)" (p. 645). Burnout may be especially likely to arise when professionals' expectations about their work are frequently unmet over time (Baker, O'Brien, & Salahuddin, 2007).

Maslach (1996) conceptualized burnout as involving three components (Anderson, 2000; Azar, 2000; Baird & Jenkins, 2003; Baker et al., 2007; Brown & O'Brien, 1998; Conrad & Kellar-Guenther, 2006; Jenkins & Baird, 2002; Perron & Hiltz, 2006). First, the professional becomes emotionally exhausted and feels as though his or her emotional resources are overdrawn (Anderson, 2000), which is often viewed as the key defining feature of burnout (Anderson, 2000). Second, the professional experiences depersonalization, which means that she or he feels and acts impersonally and emotionally detached, especially toward clients (Anderson, 2000; Baker et al., 2007). And third, the professional feels a diminished sense of personal accomplishment through his or her work, viewing him- or herself to be less competent and successful (Anderson, 2000).

Burnout develops gradually over time (Rosenberg & Pace, 2006). It can negatively impact a professional's ability and motivation to perform quality work (Anderson, 2000; Shapiro, Burkey, Dorman, & Welker, 1996; Shapiro, Dorman et al., 1999; Stevens & Higgins, 2002). The associated exhaustion may lead a therapist to have a negative outlook toward work, diminished concern for clients, and a sense that his or her work does not make any difference (Rosenberg & Pace, 2006).

Overlaps and Differences among These Concepts. Clearly, the above concepts describe similar phenomena. Although similarities exist, each concept addresses unique features (Nelson-Gardell & Harris, 2003), so we will now highlight some of key similarities and differences.

Symptom Focus vs. Cognition Focus. Both secondary traumatic stress and vicarious traumatization may involve the therapist reexperiencing clients' traumatic memories, such as through flashbacks and nightmares (Baird & Jenkins, 2003). However, vicarious traumatization can be viewed as cognition-focused, while secondary traumatic stress may be viewed as symptom-focused (Baird & Jenkins, 2003; Jenkins & Baird, 2002). In other words, secondary traumatic stress describes the symptoms experienced by the therapist (e.g., intrusion, avoidance, and arousal), whereas vicarious traumatization describes changes to a therapists' cognitions and worldview. Jenkins and Baird (2002) asked 104 sexual assault and domestic violence counselors to complete measures of vicarious traumatization, secondary traumatic stress, and burnout. Their findings supported the notion that these are distinct, yet overlapping experiences for therapists. They suggested that it may be important to evaluate each of these phenomena among therapists to determine the nature of the struggles that they may be facing in response to this type of work.

Timing Factors. Burnout is viewed as a longer-term process than secondary traumatic stress, both in terms of development and amelioration (Bell, 2003). Secondary traumatic stress can occur quickly, even in response to exposure to just one trauma, whereas burnout typically develops over a longer period of time (Conrad & Kellar-Guenther, 2006). Likewise, vicarious traumatization also typically is considered to develop over a longer time-period than secondary traumatic stress, given its focus on underlying cognitive structures.

Trauma-Specific vs. General Focus. As compared to secondary traumatic stress and vicarious traumatization, burnout is more general and not necessarily linked directly to therapists' engagement with their clients about traumatic experiences (Baird & Jenkins, 2003). Burnout may be linked more closely to characteristics of one's job setting, such as level of pay, workload, and institutional support (Baird & Jenkins, 2003).

Impact on Therapist and Client. Finally, these concepts can be distinguished based on whether they are likely to have a negative or normative impact on therapists or clients. Countertransference and STSD are viewed as more problematic, whereas secondary traumatic stress and vicarious traumatization are viewed as normative or expected (Geller, Madsen, & Ohrenstein, 2004). In addition, countertransference relates to how therapists' experiences impact the client (e.g., by diminished progress in therapy), whereas secondary traumatic stress and vicarious traumatization primarily address therapists' experiences (Baird & Jenkins, 2003).

Specific Impacts of This Work

Therapists' experiences of this work may not fit neatly into one of the above categories (i.e., secondary traumatic stress, vicarious traumatization, countertransference, or burnout) (Bell, 2003; Jenkins & Baird, 2002; Stebnicki, 2007; Walker, 2004). As Walker (2004) stated, "What is crucial for practitioners and supervisors is to recognize that becoming traumatized at one remove is a real possibility, and most will have less interest in how this is labeled: it is its manifestations and its sources that are significant" (p. 179). Thus, in this section, we review ways that therapists may be impacted by work with clients who experienced family violence. A variety of physical, emotional/psychological, relational, and work-related symptoms have been noted in the literature to be possible results of working with clients impacted by family violence. Although the following list is not exhaustive, it may be useful for therapists as a checklist for identifying possible symptoms they are experiencing and to alert them to the potential need to increase their use of self-care strategies, as will be discussed in the next section.

Physical Symptoms. Physical symptoms include: physical problems, exhaustion, fatigue, insomnia, and unhealthy eating habits (Arnold, Calhoun, Tedeschi, & Cann, 2005; Azar, 2000; Baker et al., 2007; Ben-Porat & Itzhaky, 2009; Chu, 1992; Conrad & Kellar-Guenther, 2006; Csiernik et al., 2010; Gates & Gillespie, 2008; Iliffe & Steed, 2000; Nelson-Gardell & Harris, 2003; Neumann & Gamble, 1995; Perron & Hiltz, 2006; Shapiro, Dorman et al., 1999; Stebnicki, 2007).

Emotional/Psychological Symptoms. Emotional/psychological symptoms include: PTSD-like symptoms, intrusive thoughts, nightmares, substance abuse, sadness, depression, suicidal ideation, anxiety, stress, fear, irritability, helplessness, hopelessness, anger, having a difficult time containing one's emotions, difficulty sustaining concentration, engaging in high-risk behaviors, and low self-esteem (Arnold et al., 2005; Azar, 2000; Baker et al., 2007; Ben-Porat & Itzhaky, 2009; Bober, Regehr, & Zhou, 2006; Bride, 2007; Chouliara et al., 2009; Chu, 1992; Conrad & Kellar-Guenther, 2006; Csiernik et al., 2010; Etherington, 2000; Gates & Gillespie, 2008; Goldblatt, 2009; Iliffe & Steed, 2000; McCloskey & Fraser, 1997; Nelson-Gardell & Harris, 2003; Perron & Hiltz, 2006; Shapiro et al., 1999).

Relational Symptoms. Relational symptoms include: relationship problems in personal life, withdrawing from social interactions, being skeptical of others' motives, difficulty trusting others, and sexual difficulties (Azar, 2000; Baker et al., 2007; Ben-Porat & Itzhaky, 2009; Conrad & Kellar-Guenther, 2006; Etherington, 2000; Geller et al., 2004; Iliffe & Steed, 2000; Neumann & Gamble, 1995; Shapiro et al., 1999; Walker, 2004).

Work-Related Symptoms. Work-related symptoms include: poor work functioning; missing work; considering leaving one's job or the profession; low morale and a negative attitude toward work; loss of hope in work; being cynical; impaired decision-making; withdrawing from clients or developing negative attitudes toward them; being frustrated with flaws in systems set up to support victims; overly identifying with clients (e.g., victims); fantasizing about rescuing clients; being angry at people not present in therapy (e.g., abusers when a victim is the clients); and low self-confidence in one's ability to address family violence issues (Arnold et al., 2005; Azar, 2000; Baker et al., 2007; Conrad & Kellar-Guenther, 2006; Etherington, 2000; Gates & Gillespie, 2008; Geller et al., 2004; Goldblatt, 2009; Iliffe & Steed, 2000; McCloskey & Fraser, 1997; Nelson-Gardell & Harris, 2003; Neumann & Gamble, 1995; Perron & Hiltz, 2006; Shapiro et al., 1999; Stebnicki, 2007; Tyagi, 2006; Walker, 2004).

The serious nature of these symptoms demonstrates the importance of therapists and administrators identifying and addressing the potential for vicarious trauma, secondary traumatic stress, and burnout (Azar, 2000).

Self-Care Strategies

Although the challenges associated with working with clients impacted by family violence can take a toll on therapists, therapists can respond effectively to these vicarious stressors and other work demands so they do not negatively impact their work (Clemans, 2004; Neumann & Gamble, 1995). Self-care is both a professional and ethical obligation for therapists (Neumann & Gamble, 1995; Stebnicki, 2007), especially when working with such challenging populations as clients impacted by family violence. As Neumann and Gamble (1995) stated, "If therapists do not care for themselves, they are at much greater risk of hurting their clients" (p. 345). In this section, we discuss strategies therapists may use to engage in self-care in their personal and professional lives, as well as within their organizations.

Personal Self-Care Strategies. Therapists can implement personal self-care strategies to promote their wellness and health in the face of work-related challenges. These include building coping resources, addressing unresolved personal traumas, building social support resources, engaging in wellness activities, and creating boundaries between work and home life.

Building Coping Resources. Coping resources can buffer between demanding job experiences and work-related stress (Dekel & Peled, 2000). Although some research (e.g., Baker et al., 2007; Stevens & Higgins, 2002) suggests that coping strategies may not be entirely effective in warding off burnout or secondary traumatic stress, these strategies have the potential to help therapists. Generally, more active coping strategies, compared to passive ones, are most useful for therapists to use to manage these types of stressors (Gates & Gillespie, 2008; Shapiro et al., 1999). Using avoidant coping strategies may increase one's risk of burnout, whereas more active emotion-focused and problem-focused coping strategies can help prevent burnout (Brown & O'Brien, 1998). In a study of long-term CPS workers (Anderson, 2000), those workers who used more active coping strategies (e.g., problem-solving and seeking social support) experienced less depersonalization and a greater sense of personal accomplishment than those who used avoidant coping strategies (e.g., wishful thinking and self-criticism). However, neither type of coping strategy appeared to protect the workers from experiencing emotional exhaustion, the other key component of burnout.

Addressing Unresolved Personal Trauma. Unresolved personal traumas may increase a therapist's likelihood of experiencing secondary traumatic stress or vicarious traumatization (Baird & Jenkins, 2003). Therapists may be especially likely to experience secondary traumatic stress or vicarious traumatization if a client reminds them of a family member associated with unresolved personal trauma (Gates & Gillespie, 2008). Some scholars (e.g., Etherington, 2000) believe that it is essential for therapists resolve their personal traumas in order to effectively do this work. Resolving issues surrounding therapists' personal experiences with trauma may increase their ability to believe in healing and growth (Bell, 2003).

Building Personal Social Support. A strong social support network can buffer the impact of work stress and reduce burnout (Brown & O'Brien, 1998; Shapiro et al., 1999), although some research has not shown a clear buffering effect of social support on burnout (Baker et al., 2007). Nonetheless, we recommend that therapists who work with clients impacted by family violence make it a priority to carve out time to connect with friends and family members (Iliffe & Steed, 2000; Neumann & Gamble, 1995). Therapists may wish to consider the extent to which they want to and can (given confidentiality issues) share information about their work with friends and family members. In addition, therapists may need to educate members of their social support networks who are not directly involved in this type of work about the unique demands of their jobs.

Engaging in Wellness Activities. Both during and outside of the workday, therapists are encouraged to develop a repertoire of activities that promote their personal wellness. At work, therapists may find it helpful to use brief relaxation exercises after stressful sessions. Therapists may benefit by keeping a special file with remembrances of positive work experiences and outcomes. Other wellness strategies include the following: allowing for free time, creating art, dancing, eating healthful foods, engaging in leisure and stress management activities, exercising, focusing on positive aspects of life, gardening, reading wellness-oriented books, resting, and watching nonviolent forms of entertainment (Gates & Gillespie, 2008; Iliffe & Steed, 2000; Neumann & Gamble, 1995; O'Halloran & Linton, 2000). Therapists benefit from taking advantage of leave time by taking vacations and seeking other opportunities for personal and professional renewal (Iliffe & Steed, 2000). Therapists should seek personal therapy when warranted (Neumann & Gamble, 1995). Worksite Employee Assistance Programs (EAPs) may provide therapists with benefits that can be of assistance in coping with job demands (Gates & Gillespie, 2008). Finally, therapists can focus on spiritual wellness and draw upon spiritual resources. Spirituality can be a crucial component of wellness for therapists in dealing with the work challenges they face (Brooks & Matthews, 2000).

Professional Self-Care Strategies. A number of work-related self-care strategies can help therapists prevent and address negative consequences of experiences with clients impacted by family violence. Key strategies include managing one's caseload, managing potentially unhelpful responses to clients, developing realistic expectations, seeking quality supervision, recognizing early signs of burnout or secondary traumatic stress, maintaining an appropriate professional stance, being attuned to gender considerations, and increasing work-based social support.

Managing Client Caseloads. Working long hours and having a heavy caseload may contribute to increased burnout risk, although there have been some mixed findings in this regard (Baird & Jenkins, 2003; Gates & Gillespie, 2008). Maintaining a manageable caseload may help to prevent burnout (Winefield & Barlow, 1995). If possible, therapists may benefit from not taking on too many clients at one time who have experienced family violence or other trauma (Iliffe & Steed, 2000; Neumann & Gamble, 1995; O'Halloran & Linton, 2000).

Managing Potentially Unhelpful Responses to Clients. Therapists must monitor their personal, possibly countertransferential, responses to clients. Failing to acknowledge these responses may lead therapists to subtle behaviors that are counterproductive to therapy, such as becoming distant and acknowledging only certain aspects of clients' experiences (Chu, 1992). Therapists must maintain a high level of awareness of how their values and beliefs may impact their responses to clients who are perpetrators or victims of family violence (Gauthier & Levendosky, 1996). In particular, therapists should challenge stereotypical beliefs they hold about family violence and the people who experience it (Gauthier & Levendosky, 1996).

Developing Realistic Expectations. The reality of this work is that it can be wrought with difficulties. By being realistic about these challenges, therapists may be better equipped to manage them (Azar, 2000). Over the long-term, experiencing frequently unmet unrealistic expectations may lead therapists to feel helpless, defensive, and negatively about themselves (Winefield & Barlow, 1995). Some realistic expectations that therapists can develop when working with clients impacted by family violence include that it may be difficult to empathize with some clients, some clients will be resistant, some clients will deny the extent of their problems or that their problems exist at all, and many decisions faced in this work are difficult to make (Azar, 2000). Redefining the notion of "failure" can be useful for therapists (Rosenberg & Pace, 2006). Simply because a client does not make progress does not necessarily mean that the therapist has failed in his or her work. Focusing on clients' strengths and resources can help therapists remain attuned to clients' positive growth and change (Iliffe & Steed, 2000; O'Halloran & Linton, 2000), even if such growth does not occur as quickly or substantially as the therapist would like. Appreciating clients' positive changes and maintaining realistic expectations may promote greater work self-efficacy, which can mitigate the impact of work-related stress on professionals' mental health (Baker et al., 2007; Perron & Hiltz, 2006).

Seeking Quality Supervision. Quality supervision is essential for managing the challenges involved in work with clients impacted by family violence (Aymer, 2008; Etherington, 2000; Neumann & Gamble, 1995; O'Halloran & Linton, 2000; Slattery & Goodman, 2009; Walker, 2004). Supervision that attends to respect, safety, and trust considerations is particularly valuable for therapists (Slattery & Goodman, 2009). Because many therapists received minimal training in family violence (Iliffe & Steed, 2000), we encourage therapists to seek other training opportunities, including supervision, to further their understanding of family violence issues and become better equipped for this type of work (Anderson, 2000). Some important focuses for supervision include examining countertransference, processing emotions (Walker, 2004), normalizing vicarious traumatic stress, and educating therapists about trauma (Slattery & Goodman, 2009).

Azar (2000) proposed a cognitive-behavioral therapy (CBT)-based approach for the clinical supervision of professionals working with child maltreatment cases. Azar wrote that some trauma-related dynamics of abuse cases can be seen in the context of clinical supervision, even though this is somewhat removed from the direct experiences of the client's traumatization. The focus of Azar's cognitive-behavioral approach to supervision is identifying therapists' unmet (and often unrealistic) expectations about their work, and how these expectations are linked to negative thoughts about oneself, clients, and other aspects of therapists' work. For example, an unrealistic belief that Azar asserts therapists may hold is that "Family problems are always manageable and we have the tools to be helpful" (p. 652). Azar suggests that therapists benefit from identifying rigid beliefs about their work and the families they serve and ultimately restructuring their beliefs into more realistic, flexible ones. The overall goal of this approach to supervision is to help therapists function more adaptively and flexibly by being able to find meaning in the work despite its challenges.

Recognizing Early Signs of Burnout, Vicarious Traumatization, or Secondary Traumatic Stress. Therapists should remain alert to symptoms of burnout, secondary traumatic stress, and vicarious traumatization (Gates & Gillespie, 2008). Failing to acknowledge and address early signs may lead these emotional responses to grow and become increasingly incapacitating (Etherington, 2000). These experiences must be addressed appropriately so that they will not negatively impact one's work functioning (Walker, 2004).

In addition to informally identifying one's symptoms, standardized instruments exist and may be useful for identifying problematic experiences. The Maslach Burnout Inventory (Maslach, 1996) is a widely used measure of burnout. Another potentially useful instrument is the Human Services Job Satisfaction Questionnaire (HSJSQ; Shapiro et al., 1996), which measures the extent to which human service professionals, especially those working with maltreated children, experience work satisfaction in several areas, including self-actualization, support for achievement, working conditions, and professional self-esteem. There is some evidence for the validity and reliability of the 45-item HSJSQ. Figley's (1996) Compassion Fatigue Self-Test for Psychotherapists (CFST) is commonly used to measure two components of secondary traumatic stress: burnout and compassion fatigue (Baird & Jenkins, 2003; Jenkins & Baird, 2002). Finally, another instrument therapists can use is the Secondary Traumatic Stress Scale (STSS), developed by Bride et al. (2004). This 17-item instrument assesses three categories of STS symptoms: intrusion, avoidance, and arousal. Unlike instruments measuring PTSD, the STSS is specific to helping professionals' experiences with clients' trauma. For example, two items are "It seemed as if I was reliving the trauma(s) experienced by my client(s)" and "I wanted to avoid working with some clients" (Bride et al., 2004, p. 33). Bride et al. (2004) provided preliminary support for the instrument's reliability and validity.

As is evident from the Ethics Case Study below, recognizing the signs of potential burnout and secondary stress is the first step toward managing these symptoms effectively.

Ethics Case Study: Burnout?

Tameka considers herself a "success story" and, until lately, thought she knew what she wanted to do with her life. At age 6, following being a victim of physical and emotional abuse at the hands of her single mother, Tameka was removed from the family home and spent the rest of her childhood and adolescent years in various foster care placements. She went on to graduate with honors from college, and she received a prestigious scholarship to attend graduate school. In light of her personal experiences, her dream was to become a family therapist working with abused and maltreated children, and she was thrilled to land a position doing just that upon graduating from a marriage and family therapy master's degree program.

Having worked in this position for about two years, Tameka has begun to wonder if she can—and really wants to—keep up this type of work for her entire career. She remains as committed as ever to the cause of helping children who've been abused, and she still feels "called" to do this work. However, she's begun to notice that she's having a hard time coping with the personal impact the work has on her. She reports that she's been withdrawing from her social network, saying she just doesn't "have the energy to do anything but go home and watch TV after work, and I sleep almost all weekend." Tameka also recently revealed to her clinical supervisor that, sometimes, when working with clients and hearing stories of their victimization and challenges in the CPS system, it triggers memories of her own abuse and some bad experiences in foster care. She says that she's able to set these aside in session, but she sometimes has nightmares and intrusive thoughts about them outside of work.

Ethical Considerations. A number of ethical guidelines are relevant to Tameka's situation, as well as for her clinical supervisor. Although her background is in marriage and family therapy, we consider other relevant professional codes because her situation could occur across professions. Tameka clearly is experiencing a negative impact from her work with children who have been maltreated. Based on the information provided, it remains unclear whether and how her symptoms impact her work. However, because we know that burnout, secondary traumatic stress, and vicarious traumatization can negatively impact a therapist's work functioning, we must assume that the potential for such an impact exists.

We begin by considering the role of Tameka's clinical supervisor in responding to the information Tameka provided. First, because Tameka's supervisor is aware that she is experiencing these symptoms (i.e., social withdrawal, fatigue, and triggered memories of personal trauma), the supervisor has an obligation to work with Tameka to explore the extent to which these impact her work. For example, the NASW (2008) ethical code states that "Social workers who have direct knowledge of a social work colleague's impairment that is due to personal problems, psychosocial distress, substance abuse, or mental health difficulties and that interferes with practice effectiveness should consult with that colleague when feasible and assist the colleague in taking remedial action" (2.09.a). A challenge will be to ensure that this exploration remains within the realm of supervision, in that supervisors should not provide personal therapy to current supervisees (e.g., AAMFT, 2001, 4.2; and ACA, 2005, F.5.c.). Therefore, the supervisor likely should refer Tameka to seek personal therapy to ensure that the processing that the supervisor does relates directly to Tameka's professional functioning, while also ensuring that Tameka has a forum for exploring the personal aspects of these concerns.

Together with her clinical supervisor, and possibly with her personal therapist, Tameka's primary ethical obligation is to acknowledge and address her symptoms in order to ensure that they do not impair her professional functioning. The imperative for therapists to address potential impairment is stressed in all major professional ethical codes (see AAMFT, 2001, 3.3 and 3.4; ACA,

2005, C.2.g; APA, 2010, 2.06.a and 2.06b; NASW, 2008, 4.05.a). In particular, Tameka must ensure that her symptoms and memories of her personal experiences with abuse do not negatively harm her clients, given that a therapist's primary professional obligation is to promote the welfare of his or her clients (e.g., ACA, 2005, A.1.a). Tameka may benefit from a thorough assessment of her symptoms and experiences to determine whether she is experiencing secondary traumatic stress, vicarious traumatization, countertransference, or burnout. Reviewing a symptom checklist similar to the one earlier in this chapter, in combination with one or more of the formal assessment instruments described above, can help in this regard.

Once she understands the extent to which her work is impacting her life, Tameka has an ethical obligation to determine her best course of action in terms of continuing her work. As stated in the NASW (2008) ethical code, "Social workers whose personal problems, psychosocial distress, legal problems, substance abuse, or mental health difficulties interfere with their professional judgment and performance should immediately seek consultation and take appropriate remedial action by seeking professional help, making adjustments in workload, terminating practice, or taking any other steps necessary to protect clients and others" (4.05.b.). Some possible outcomes may include: (a) continuing this work and implementing a self-care plan to help manage her personal reactions to it; (b) managing her caseload so that it is not so heavily based in trauma-impacted clients (either in her same work setting or at another agency); or (c) deciding that she needs to either take a break or permanently leave the therapy profession.

Each option would carry additional ethical considerations. Option (a) would require that Tameka remain vigilant of any indicators that her personal issues get in the way of her work to ensure that she is able to address these concerns immediately, again ensuring that her ultimate focus is on the welfare of her clients (e.g., ACA, 2005, A.1.a). Even if Tameka selects option (b) and shifts to working with a less trauma- and abuse-focused client population, she must still address personal issues that arise through this type of work. Given how high family violence incidence and prevalence rates are, it is likely that she will be unable to avoid these issues completely. Furthermore, she cannot abandon clients if they disclose experiences of abuse (NASW, 2008, 1.16.b). If Tameka decides to transfer some cases, take an extended break from her work, or leave the profession as in option (c), then she must handle the termination or transfer of her clients in an ethically responsible manner. She must ensure a limited disruption to her clients' services (e.g., see APA, 2010, 3.12) and should provide appropriate referrals in order for clients to continue to receive services they need (ACA, 2005, A.11.b.).

Maintaining an Appropriate Professional Stance. Higher levels of empathy, although useful for understanding clients, can increase the risk of vicarious trauma or secondary traumatic stress (Bober et al., 2006; Conrad &

Kellar-Guenther, 2006; Gates & Gillespie, 2008; Geller et al., 2004; Nelson-Gardell & Harris, 2003; Stebnicki, 2007). It is appropriate for therapists to demonstrate both genuine empathy and a strong therapeutic boundary in order to maintain a proper professional perspective (Chu, 1992; O'Halloran & Linton, 2000). Some therapists find it helpful to "slightly distance themselves from" stories of abuse (Iliffe & Steed, 2000, p. 201), although becoming too distant may have a negative impact on one's clinical effectiveness. Etherington (2000) shared an image of a former supervisor who imagined a "blue light surrounding her as protection" when working with severely abused clients, and this image helped the supervisor maintain both connection and therapeutic distance from clients' experiences (p. 387).

Being Attuned to Gender Considerations. Male and female therapists must be attuned to how their perceptions of gender can influence how they perceive clients (Gauthier & Levendosky, 1996). Using male–female cotherapists is a frequent practice in BIPs, based on an assumption that the therapists can model balanced communication and responsibilities (Tyagi, 2006). However, challenges can arise for female therapists working with male abuse perpetrators. Examples of unhelpful dynamics that can arise include gender stereotyping, credibility issues, modeling of unhelpful communication patterns, and perpetuating sexist behaviors (Tyagi, 2006). As such, these situations require added attention to gender and power dynamics, strong mechanisms for communication and feedback, adequate debriefing and supervision, and ongoing professional development (Tyagi, 2006).

Increasing Work-Based Social Support. Positive relationships with coworkers can buffer against burnout (Csiernik et al., 2010; Slattery & Goodman, 2009). Therapists who are the only ones in their workplaces addressing family violence issues may feel especially isolated (Iliffe & Steed, 2000). Strategies for increasing work-based social support include seeking out a mentor or a peer support group (Csiernik et al., 2010). Postincident debriefing sessions with other therapists can be a useful forum for processing reactions to challenging cases (Aymer, 2008; Gates & Gillespie, 2008; Iliffe & Steed, 2000; O'Halloran & Linton, 2000). These may include discussing therapists' reactions to the event and addressing strategies for coping effectively with them (Gates & Gillespie, 2008). Therapists should be cautioned, however, to avoid helping other therapists debrief when they themselves have depleted personal resources (Iliffe & Steed, 2000). These debriefings can help therapists increase their objectivity with clients, process frustrations, and ensure that the primary focus remains on the clients and their safety (Aymer, 2008).

Organizational Self-Care Strategies. Even when therapists implement personal and professional self-care strategies, they may be limited in their effectiveness if their work settings contribute to, or fail to address, burnout, vicarious traumatization, and secondary traumatic stress. Therefore, this section reviews workplace strategies and conditions that can support the personal and professional needs and growth of therapists. Therapists are encouraged to work with administrators in their workplaces to implement these strategies and conditions.

Whenever possible, it is advisable to address working conditions that increase the risk for burnout (Azar, 2000; Baker et al., 2007). More positive work conditions contribute to more positive work experiences for therapists (Baird & Jenkins, 2003; Csiernik et al., 2010). Work conditions that can reduce the potential for burnout include effective working teams, attention to safety issues, and adequate connections with other community organizations (Anderson, 2000). Other positive work conditions include clear policies, opportunities for feedback, appropriate hierarchies, managing dual relationships, and healthy workloads (Walker, 2004). Workplaces can be structured to help therapists to focus on positive aspects of their work and celebrate progress that clients make, even if it is relatively small (Bell, 2003). Work environments in which there is shared power among various constituents can be especially empowering for employees (Slattery & Goodman, 2009). Employees may be more likely to feel supported when they believe that they play a role in organizational decision-making and when they have support in completing mandatory administrative tasks (e.g., paperwork) (Baker et al., 2007; Brown & O'Brien, 1998).

Organizations can implement training programs to prepare and support staff in addressing the personal demands of this work (Baker et al., 2007; Gates & Gillespie, 2008; Goldblatt et al., 2009; Nelson-Gardell & Harris, 2003; Way, VanDeusen, & Cottrell, 2007; Winefield & Barlow, 1995). New employee programs may be useful to develop to orient them to the potential demands of this work and suggest self-care strategies (Csiernik et al., 2010).Useful topics to address include time management and relaxation strategies (Baker et al., 2007). Therapists and organizations looking to initiate or engage in formal self-care strategies may draw upon approaches described in the literature. Two existing models are the Clinical Risk Management Team approach (CRMT; Geller et al., 2004) and the Vicarious Trauma Seed Group Project (Clemans, 2004).

Geller et al. (2004) developed a Clinical Risk Management Team (CRMT) protocol to provide a supportive, structured process for professionals working with traumatized victims to discuss and reflect upon their reactions to these cases. The CRMT model uses 45-minute sessions that are divided into structured time-frames for discussing a case, considering the case from different viewpoints, allowing the professional to reflect on his or her feelings related to the case, and considering case conceptualization issues. Geller et al. suggest that the structured elements of the process (i.e., time limits and standard format) are useful given the extent to which trauma cases usually involve a sense of chaos. Based on preliminary feedback received from pilot testing participants, the model shows promise for supporting professionals and helping them work more effectively with clients.

Clemans (2004) developed a single-session, psychoeducational group intervention, called the Vicarious Trauma Seed Group Project, to address vicarious traumatization among professionals working with traumatized clients. The goals of this intervention are to educate participants about vicarious trauma, allow participants to discuss their stress reactions, and identify strategies to respond to vicarious trauma. In the pilot evaluation of the program, many participants noted that the group format was useful because it helps remove the stigma that professionals may experience related to vicarious trauma. In fact, many participants indicated that they would have preferred that the program last longer than one session.

Rewards from Working with Clients Impacted by Family Violence

Rich rewards are possible through this work, which may be part of therapists' overall path toward personal and professional fulfillment. The term *compassion satisfaction* describes positive feelings and outcomes that result from helping others who experienced suffering or trauma (Conrad & Kellar-Guenther, 2006; Stamm, 2002). Other aspects of compassion satisfaction include feeling successful and supported by work colleagues (Conrad & Kellar-Guenther, 2006). Compassion satisfaction protects professionals from experiencing burnout, although this relationship is in need of further exploration (Conrad & Kellar-Guenther, 2006).

Vicarious Posttraumatic Growth. Just as therapists can experience negative symptoms of trauma, researchers have begun to study *vicarious posttraumatic growth* among therapists working with trauma-impacted populations (Arnold et al., 2005; Ben-Porat & Itzhaky, 2009). There has been growing attention to the notion of posttraumatic growth in trauma research (Ben-Porat & Itzhaky, 2009). Researchers studying posttraumatic growth generally believe that people who experience traumas can grow as a result of those experiences, particular in how they view themselves, relate to others, and their outlook on life (Ben-Porat & Itzhaky, 2009). This growth also is referred to as *positive self-transformation* (Chouliara et al., 2009). Growth may especially be seen in therapists' spiritual lives (Chouliara et al., 2009).

Arnold et al. (2005) did a qualitative study on vicarious posttraumatic growth experienced among a small sample of therapists, although not all participants specifically addressed family violence in their work. Positive areas in which participants reported growth were being able to witness the growth of clients, developing appreciation for one's personal strengths and good fortunes, becoming more tolerant of others, and developing a deeper sense of spirituality. Strengths identified in another study of domestic violence counselors (Bell, 2003) included increased feelings of competence, being able to sustain one's motivation for work, coming to terms with traumas the counselors had experienced in their own lives, and maintaining a positive belief system. Counselors believed that their work helped them become more compassionate and appreciative, as well as less judgmental (Bell, 2003). By grappling with the existential issues that can arise when doing this sort of work, therapists ultimately may experience growth (Chouliara et al., 2009; Goldblatt, 2009; Goldblatt et al., 2009). This growth may result from finding meaning in the traumatic experiences (Etherington, 2000). Other areas of growth may involve becoming clearer in one's own gender identity and experiencing positive changes in one's intimate relationship (Goldblatt et al., 2009).

Conclusion

We began this chapter by emphasizing that conducting therapy with clients impacted by family violence presents many challenges. The extent to which secondary traumatic stress, vicarious traumatization, and burnout have been studied in the literature provides evidence that these are common, perhaps even normative, experiences. Thus, therapists working with clients impacted by family violence are at some risk for experiencing related symptoms in different aspects of their lives. Therapists need not remain passive recipients of these symptoms, however. They can implement personal, professional, and organizational strategies to promote self-care among themselves and their colleagues. This chapter concluded by emphasizing that therapists, like their clients, can experience growth and renewal through this work in the form of rewarding aspects of this work. It is our belief that therapists who are aware of the potential challenges that can arise through this work and who are equipped to address those challenges will be in the best position to experience the meaningful rewards that can result from helping clients address and overcome experiences with family violence.

15

CONCLUSION

The Role of Therapists in Responding to Family Violence

Our aim for this book was to provide information to support therapists in becoming more knowledgeable, comfortable, and competent to work with clients impacted by family violence. In this final chapter, we summarize the major themes addressed throughout previous chapters.

Review of Major Themes in this Book

Several underlying messages were repeated in different ways across the chapters of this book. To underscore the importance of these themes, we consolidate them here as important takeaway messages for applying the information in this book to clinical practice.

The Utmost Priority of Safety Considerations

If we were asked to summarize in two words our advice to therapists addressing family violence, the answer would be very easy: *Safety first*! The intense focus on safety is somewhat unique to clinical work related to family violence. In many aspects of clinical practice, therapists must consider how to provide an emotionally safe climate in which clients comfortably and securely examine challenging problems in their lives. A focus on emotional safety certainly is relevant to clinical work addressing family violence. Family violence often carries additional risk of actual physical harm for victims, and at times this risk even extends to therapists. Therapists must therefore be proactive to ensure the safety of both themselves and their clients.

We addressed a number of practical strategies for promoting safety throughout this book, and we review some of the most critical ones in the following list.

- Whenever appropriate, help clients develop a detailed safety plan that includes strategies to promote their safety (and that of their children, if applicable) in a range of circumstances. Throughout treatment, review and update this plan often.
- Take seriously any threats reported to therapists or revealed in other contexts. Gather more information about these threats, and determine whether further action is warranted.
- Become familiar with local laws and requirements for reporting threatened or actual violence to the appropriate authorities.
- Create a list with contact information with important safety-related resources, and keep this list in an easily accessible location.
- Be alert to signs of potential self-inflicted harm (e.g., self-injury or suicidal ideation) and harm inflicted by other perpetrators. Develop clinical competence in addressing these issues or refer clients with these concerns to other competent professionals.
- As much as possible, anticipate possible safety implications of therapy interventions. When identified, work with clients to plan ways to reduce the risk of harm.
- Increase the therapy office's safety, such as by ensuring therapists are not alone in the office, getting a security system, and using a video surveillance system in common areas.
- Home-based therapy should be conducted safely. Appropriate strategies may include carrying a cell phone, traveling with a fellow professional, and ensuring that at least one other person knows where the therapist is at all times.

There is no way to guarantee complete safety for any potential victim of family violence or other forms of violence, short of completely isolating them from society for the rest of their lives. However, steps can be taken to promote safety and minimize risks. In addition, clients and therapists can become better prepared to respond quickly to promote increased safety within a violent incident that occurs. Therefore, therapists should maintain a primary focus on safety promotion throughout all aspects of clinical work with clients impacted by family violence.

The Importance of Trauma-Informed Care

Given the different manifestations of traumatic stress, the rule of "first do no harm" demands that therapists ensure that the delivery of services does not further violate clients. Instead, therapists must be aware of the core principles of trauma-informed care. Trauma-informed care is a philosophical framework based on the recognition that many behaviors and responses expressed by survivors are directly related to their traumatic experiences (National Center for Trauma-Informed Care, 2011). Trauma-informed care is not a specific model of treatment, but rather the creation of a supportive environment that is grounded in awareness that clients' characteristics and behaviors often are expressions of traumatic responses (Jennings, 2004). The creation of a safe environment is emphasized, alongside building skills and empowerment, rather than symptom management in isolation. A trauma-informed environment focuses on understanding what happened to the person rather than what is wrong with the person (Harris & Fallot, 2001; Saakvitne, 2000), and integrates and delivers services based on five key elements, including (a) safety, (b) empowerment, (c) trust, (d) collaboration, and (e) choice (Harris & Fallot, 2001). The trauma-informed care framework sets the stage for evidence-based, trauma-specific assessment and treatment to occur.

The Importance of Thorough Clinical Assessment to Guide Treatment

Thorough clinical assessment is critical for a number of reasons. First, the dynamics of family violence can vary greatly from one client to the next, so it is important to understand each client's unique experiences with various forms of family violence. Second, clients may not disclose initially a complete description of the violence they have experienced. Missing information that is not disclosed can be extremely influential on clients' work in therapy. Thus, therapists must aim to develop a comprehensive understanding of their clients' experiences through the assessment process. Third, the assessment process provides a good starting point for conducting therapy and offers an opportunity for rapport-building with the client.

Sound practices have been established to guide clinical assessment with psychometrically sound instruments and open-ended interview approaches. Together, these multiple forms of assessment can provide therapists with a wealth of information that can guide important decisions about how best to conduct treatment with clients. Furthermore, ongoing assessment through treatment can track clients' progress over time and alert therapists to clients' needs for adjunct services. For these reasons, we encourage therapists to include a thorough clinical assessment in their treatment of all clients who experienced family violence, and to regularly reassess to examine potential shifts in symptom severity or safety.

The Need to View and Treat Family Violence in Context

For the sake of writing an organized, readable book, authors must break down information into smaller chapters that are organized around a central theme. This approach certainly offers clarity and a manageable differentiation of ideas. However, it also presents an overly simplified view of a topic as complex as family violence. Although we may speak of IPV, child maltreatment, and elder abuse as though they are distinct phenomena, in many cases, a single family may experience all these dynamics at once. We cannot easily parcel out the unique contributions of such other factors as culture, mental health, substance abuse, and intergenerational patterns on experiences of family violence. Although we aimed to address many major influences on family violence, certainly we were not able to give full attention to every possible variable. Therefore, therapists should consider not only the issues discussed in this book, but also other unique dynamics that impact the lives of clients with whom they work.

Nearly every chapter of this book underscored the importance of therapists not viewing family violence in isolation, but rather considering how it relates to a range of other contextual variables and client experiences. With this in mind, we urge therapists to view clients who have experienced family violence with at least two lenses. The first lens is the one that is grounded in professional knowledge about the dynamics, contributing factors, and potential consequences of family violence. This lens is informed by existing research and professional knowledge about family violence and interventions designed to address it. However, this lens is limited in that it can blind therapists to the nuances of individual clients' lives. Therefore, the second lens aims to understand clients' unique experiences and understandings of family violence and its impact on their lives. Although we reviewed many common patterns that exist in violent family relationships (e.g., the *cycle of violence* within battering), these trends often play out in idiosyncratic ways in the lives of individual clients that may or may not resemble the most common patterns of violence. Thus, even though existing literature provides good information to guide therapists, they must never lose sight of the individual variation in clients' lives.

Coordinating Clinical Work with Broader Family Violence Response Systems

Therapists need not, and should not, work in isolation when providing treatment to clients who have experienced family violence. For virtually every form of family violence, a number of adjunct services and resources may be available to support clients and help them move toward nonviolence in their relationships and lives. The response systems available for each type of family violence and in each local community vary, but we encourage therapists to draw upon the following categories of resources in their work.

Legal Resources. Many forms of family violence not only have the potential to be emotionally and physically damaging, but they are also violations of the law. The criminal justice system is set up to hold perpetrators accountable for their illegal actions and to afford victims legal protections to promote their safety. In order for therapists to help their clients navigate various legal systems and regulations that apply to their situation, we encourage therapists to become knowledgeable about relevant laws and criminal justice organizations and policies in their local communities.

Social Service Agencies. Therapists should identify social service agencies in their communities that provide tangible and other forms of support to clients impacted by family violence. This includes mental health agencies, but also extends to agencies that address other potential client needs. For example, relevant agencies may include those that offer shelter, food, transportation, educational assistance, job training, and healthcare.

Advocacy and Outreach Organizations. Advocacy and outreach organizations provide a valuable resource to communities. For example, these organizations may advocate for policymakers to create safety-promoting laws, host educational events to increase community residents' knowledge about family violence, and promote other social changes that lead to nonviolent environments for families. In addition, these organizations often provide valuable educational materials for therapists to use themselves or give to clients.

General Community Organizations. We encourage therapists to become aware of local organizational efforts in their communities to address family violence, such as in religious institutions, schools, and college and university campuses. Not only can these organizations provide a referral source for therapists, but they may present opportunities for collaborations to promote safe and healthy relationships within the community.

Informal Support Systems. Therapists must never underestimate the important role that informal support systems play in clients' lives. Clients often turn to people in these systems—such as friends, family members, church members, and neighbors—before seeking help from formal sources of support. Experiences with these initial contacts can impact how clients make meaning of their family violence experiences. Supportive responses may provide clients with the needed support to seek safety, whereas unsupportive responses may lead clients back into unsafe, isolated situations. Therefore, we encourage therapists to help clients identify positive sources of support in their informal support systems so they can build on this support in treatment.

The Potential Insights and Limitations of Existing Research on Family Violence

In this book, we aimed to consolidate current research on family violence into sound guidelines for clinical practice. Existing research provides valuable insights for practitioners who aim to provide competent, ethical, and helpful services to clients. Clearly, however, research does not provide all the answers.

Much existing research demonstrates significant limitations, such as nonrepresentative samples and unclear definitions and measurement of key constructs. Therefore, therapists should exercise caution in blindly applying existing research to clinical work. We urge therapists to read existing research with a critical eye and consider how research findings may require translation before they can be applied appropriately to clinical practice.

We encourage therapists to engage in strategies to remain up-to-date on new, practice-relevant research findings. We are aware that many practitioners lack easy access to a university library that provides comprehensive access to published research. Therefore, we offer the following suggestions as possible ways for practitioners to stay current with existing research

- *Develop partnerships with local family violence researchers.* Researchers can benefit from the clinical knowledge of practitioners (i.e., How does this research finding play out in clinical practice? What research questions are important to study from a practice standpoint?). Likewise, practitioners may benefit from researchers' familiarity with existing research that can provide insights into clinical practice. Therapists may even find that there are opportunities to join a family violence-related research team or group, especially if they live near to a university.
- *Subscribe to one scholarly journal relevant to family violence.* The cost of subscriptions to scholarly journals is prohibitive for many practicing therapists. However, we urge therapists to identify at least one scholarly journal that addresses topics relevant to the client populations with whom they work and purchase a subscription if they can afford to do so. Groups of therapists may even pool resources to share journals. Therapists also may be able to receive scholarly journals by joining professional organizations with subscription benefits.
- *Seek out resources through the local public library.* Local public libraries are often underutilized. Libraries with interlibrary loan privileges may offer users comparable access to scholarly databases that is available through college and university libraries.
- *Attend trainings and professional conferences.* Most therapists are required to complete continuing education in order to maintain professional credentials, and we encourage therapists to use this as an opportunity to seek out additional training related to family violence.

The Importance of Self-Care and Personal and Professional Reflection

There is no way around the fact that the topic of family violence is emotionally challenging for many therapists, whether they have minimal or extensive experience in working with these issues. Family violence issues may prompt therapists to consider challenging existential questions about relationships, life, and healing from abusive life experiences. Observing the harmful effects of family violence on the lives of clients can be emotionally exhausting for therapists. In addition, many therapists have experiences of family violence in their own lives and families, so working with clients can trigger personal responses that are psychologically challenging for therapists. As such, our final overarching message of this book is to remind therapists to take care of themselves when engaging in this difficult work. We presented a number of specific strategies for doing so in chapter 14, and we encourage readers to make self-care and personal and professional reflection an ongoing part of their work.

Summary

Family violence is an extremely challenging clinical topic that can perplex even the most experienced therapists. This remains an issue that many therapists are underprepared to address, making the clinical challenges even more difficult to face. However, we believe that within the challenges associated with clinical work with clients impacted by family violence lies a vast array of opportunities. Therapists have an opportunity to support clients in powerful healing and personal growth opportunities that allow them to transform their experiences of violence and abuse into peaceful, nonviolent, and positive relationships and lifestyles. Therapists also can assist clients in making meaning of their experiences in ways that allow them to better understand the world and live at peace with themselves. In addition, therapists can serve as a stable, positive presence in the lives of their clients. The potential power of this positive relationship cannot be underestimated for clients who have experienced such immensely difficult close relationships. Therefore, our final word of encouragement for therapists working with clients impacted by family violence is to remain focused on the hope and transformation that therapy may provide for these clients.

REFERENCES

Abidin, R. R. (1983). *The Parenting Stress Index*. Charlottesville, VA: Pediatric Psychology Press.

An Abuse, Rape, and Domestic Violence Aid and Resource Collection. (AADVARC, 2008). *Long term planning for a violence-free life*. Retrieved October 16, 2009, from http://www.aardvarc.org/dv/longterm.shtml

Acierno, R., Coffey, S. F., & Resnick, H. S. (2003). Introduction to the special issue: Interpersonal violence and substance use problems. *Addictive Behaviors, 28,* 1529–1532.

Adams, C. M. (2006). The consequences of witnessing family violence on children and implications for family counselors. *The Family Journal, 14,* 334–341.

Adams, M. J. (2003). Victim issues are key to effective sex offender treatment. *Sexual Addictions & Compulsivity, 10,* 79–87.

Adelman, M. (2004). The battering state: Towards a political economy of domestic violence. *Journal of Poverty, 8,* 45–64.

Ahmad, S. (2006). Adult psychosexual dysfunction as a sequel of child sexual abuse. *Sexual and Relationship Therapy, 21,* 405–418.

Aklin, W. M., & Turner, S. M. (2006). Toward understanding ethnic and cultural factors in the interviewing process. *Psychotherapy: Theory, Research, Practice, Training, 43,* 50–64.

Aldarondo, E. (1998). Perpetrators of domestic violence. In A. Bellack & M. Hersen (Eds.), *Comprehensive clinical psychology* (pp. 437–452). New York: Pergamon.

Aldarondo, E., & Straus, M. A. (1994). Screening for physical violence in couple therapy: Methodological, practical, and ethical considerations. *Family Process, 33,* 425–439.

Alexander, C. J. (2002). Violence in gay and lesbian relationships. *Journal of Gay and Lesbian Social Services, 14,* 95–98.

Alexander, P. C., & Morris, E. (2008). Stages of change in batterers and their response to treatment. *Violence and Victims, 23,* 476–492.

Allen, B. (2008). An analysis of the impact of diverse forms of childhood psychological maltreatment on emotional adjustment in early adulthood. *Child Maltreatment, 13,* 307–312.

Allin, H., Wathen, C. N., & MacMillan, H. (2005). Treatment of child neglect: A systematic review. *Canadian Journal of Psychiatry, 50,* 497–504.

Almeida, R. V., & Durkin, T. (1999). The cultural context model: Therapy for couples with domestic violence. *Journal of Marital and Family Therapy, 25,* 313–324.

Amar, A. F., & Gennaro, S. (2005). Dating violence in college women: Associated physical injury, healthcare usage, and mental health symptoms. *Nursing Research, 54,* 235–242.

American Association for Marriage and Family Therapy (AAMFT). (1997). Legal issues surrounding false memories. Retrieved February 6, 2009, from http://www.aamft.org/resources/LRM_Plan/Legal/lgl_Memories.htm

American Association for Marriage and Family Therapy (AAMFT). (2001). AAMFT Code of Ethics. Retrieved February 6, 2009, from http://www.aamft.org/resources/LRM_Plan/Ethics/ethicscode2001.asp

American Counseling Association (ACA). (2005). ACA Code of Ethics. Retrieved February 3, 2010, from http://www.counseling.org/Resources/CodeOfEthics/TP/Home/CT2.aspx

American Psychiatric Association. (2000). *Diagnostic and statistical manual of mental disorders, fourth edition, text revision (DSM-IV-TR).* Washington, DC: Author.

American Psychological Association (APA). (2010). Ethical Principles of Psychologists and Code of Conduct: 2010 Amendments. Retrieved October 27, 2010, from http://www.apa.org/ethics/code/index.aspx

Amundson, N. E., & Borgen, W. A. (2000). Mandated clients in career or employment counseling. *Journal of Employment Counseling, 37*(4), 204–216.

An Abuse, Rape, and Domestic Violence Aid and Resource Collection (AADVARC, 2008). *Long term planning for a violence-free life.* Retrieved October 16, 2009, from http://www.aardvarc.org/dv/longterm.shtml

Anda, R. F. (2007). Adverse childhood experiences and prescribed psychotropic medications in adults. *American Journal of Preventive Medicine, 32,* 389–394.

Anda, R. F., Whitfield, C. L., Felitti, V. J., Chapman, D., Edwards, V. J., Dube, S. R., & Williamson, D. F. (2002). Adverse childhood experiences, alcoholic parents, and later risk of alcoholism and depression. *Psychiatric Services, 53,* 1001–1009.

Anderson, D. G. (2000). Coping strategies and burnout among veteran child protection workers. *Child Abuse and Neglect, 24,* 839–848.

Anderson, K. L. (2010). Conflict, power, and violence in families. *Journal of Marriage and Family, 72,* 726–742.

Anderson, P .L., Tiro, J. A., Price, A. W., Bender, M. A., & Kaslow, N. J. (2002). Additive impact of childhood emotional, physical, and sexual abuse on suicide attempts among low-income African American women. *Suicide and Life-Threatening Behavior, 32,* 131–145.

Anetzberger, G. J. (2005a). The reality of elder abuse. *Clinical Gerontologist, 28,* 1–25.

Anetzberger, G. J. (2005b). Clinical management of elder abuse: General considerations. *Clinical Gerontologist, 28,* 27–41.

Anetzberger, G. J., Dayton, C., Miller, C. A., McGreevey, J. F., & Schimer, M. (2005). Multidisciplinary teams in the clinical management of elder abuse. *Clinical Gerontologist, 28,* 157–171.

Anetzberger, G., Korbin, J., & Austin, C. (1994). Alcoholism and elder abuse. *Journal of Interpersonal Violence, 9,* 184–193.

Ansello, E. F., & O'Neill, P. (2010). Abuse, neglect, and exploitation: Considerations in aging with lifelong disabilities. *Journal of Elder Abuse and Neglect, 22,* 105–130.

Antle, B. F., Sullivan, D. J., Dryden, A., Karam, E. A., & Barbee, A. P. (2011). Healthy relationship education for dating violence prevention among high-risk youth. *Children and Youth Services Review, 33,* 173–179.

Antonacci, D. J., Manuel, C., & Davis, E. (2008). Diagnosis and treatment of aggression in individuals with developmental disabilities. *Psychiatric Quarterly, 79,* 225–247.

Aosved, A. C., & Long, P. J. (2005). College women's experiences of psychological maltreatment and sexual assault. *Violence and Victims, 20,* 577–587.

Apsler, R., Cummins, M. R., & Carl, S. (2002). Fear and expectations: Differences among female victims of domestic violence who come to the attention of the police. *Violence and Victims, 17,* 445–452.

Archer, J. (2000). Sex differences in aggression between heterosexual partners: A meta-analytic review. *Psychological Bulletin, 126,* 651–680.

Ards, S., D., Myers, S. L., Chung, C., Malkis, A., & Hagerty, B. (2003). Decomposing Black-White differences in child maltreatment. *Child Maltreatment, 8,* 112–121.

Arias, I. (2004). The legacy of child maltreatment: Long-term health consequences for women. *Journal of Women's Health, 13,* 468–473.

Arias, I., & Beach, S. R. (1987). Validity of self-reports of marital violence. *Journal of Family Violence, 2,* 139–149.

Arnd-Caddigan, M. (2006). Transference and countertransference in the treatment of adult survivors of abuse with somatoform disorder. *Clinical Social Work Journal, 34,* 293–302.

Arnold, D., Calhoun, L. G., Tedeschi, R., & Cann, A. (2005). Vicarious posttraumatic growth in psychotherapy. *Journal of Humanistic Psychology, 45,* 239–263.

Austin, J. B., & Dankwort, J. (1999). Standards for batterer programs: A review and analysis. *Journal of Interpersonal Violence, 14,* 152–168.

Avery-Leaf, S., & Cascardi, M. (2002). Dating violence education: Prevention and early intervention strategies. In P. A. Schewe (Ed.), *Preventing violence in relationships: Interventions across the life span* (pp. 79–105). Washington, DC: American Psychological Association.

Avery-Leaf, S., Cascardi, M., O'Leary, K. D., & Cano, A. (1997). Efficacy of a dating violence prevention program on attitudes justifying aggression. *Journal of Adolescent Health, 21,* 11-17.

Ayland, L., & West, B. (2006). The Good Way model: A strengths-based approach for working with young people, especially those with intellectual difficulties, who have sexually abusive behavior. *Journal of Sexual Aggression, 12,* 189–201.

Aymer, S. R. (2008). Beyond power and control: Clinical interventions with men engaged in partner abuse. *Clinical Social Work Journal, 36,* 323–332.

Azar, S. T. (2000). Preventing burnout in professionals and paraprofessionals who work with child abuse and neglect cases: A cognitive behavioral approach to supervision. *JCLP: In Session: Psychotherapy in Practice, 56,* 642–663.

Babcock, J. C., Canady, B. E., Senior, A., & Eckhardt, C. I. (2005). Applying the transtheoretical model to female and male perpetrators of intimate partner violence: Gender differences in stages and processes of change. *Violence and Victims, 20,* 235–250.

Babcock, J. C., Costa, D. M., Green, C. E., & Eckhardt, C. I. (2004). What situations induce intimate partner violence? A reliability and validity study of the Proximal Antecedents to Violent Episodes (PAVE) Scale. *Journal of Family Psychology, 18,* 433–442.

Babcock, J. C., Green, C. E., & Robie, C. (2004). Does batterers' treatment work? A meta-analytic review of domestic violence treatment. *Clinical Psychology Review, 23,* 1023–1053.

Babcock, J. C., Green, C. E., Webb, S. A., & Graham, K. H. (2004). A second failure to replicate the Gottman et al. (1995) typology of men who abuse intimate partners...and possible reasons why. *Journal of Family Psychology, 18,* 396–400.

Babcock, J. C., Green, C. E., Webb, S. A., & Yerington, T. P. (2005). Psychological profiles of batterers: Autonomic emotional reactivity as it predicts the antisocial spectrum of behavior among partner abusers. *Journal of Abnormal Psychology, 114,* 444–455.

Babcock, J. C., & Steiner, R. (1999). The relationship between treatment, incarceration, and recidivism of battering: A program evaluation of Seattle's coordinated community response to domestic violence. *Journal of Family Psychology, 13,* 46–59.

Bacon, H., & Richardson, S. (2001). Attachment theory and child abuse: An overview of the literature for practitioners. *Child Abuse Review, 10,* 377–397.

Baer, J. C., & Martinez, C. D. (2006). Child maltreatment and insecure attachment: A meta-analysis. *Journal of Reproductive and Infant Psychology, 24,* 187–197.

Bailey, J. A., & McCloskey, L. A. (2005). Pathways to adolescent substance use among sexually abused girls, *Journal of Abnormal Child Psychology, 33*(1), 39–53.

Baird, S., & Jenkins, S. R. (2003). Vicarious traumatization, secondary traumatic stress, and burnout in sexual assault and domestic violence agency staff. *Violence and Victims, 18,* 71–86.

Baker, J. N., Tanis, H. J., & Rice, J. B. (2001). Including siblings in the treatment of child sexual abuse. *Journal of Child Sexual Abuse, 10,* 1–16.

Baker, L. M., O'Brien, K. M., & Salahuddin, N. M. (2007). Are shelter workers burned out?: An examination of stress, social support, and coping. *Journal of Family Violence, 22,* 465–474.

Balenovich, J., Grossi, E., & Hughes, T. (2008). Toward a balanced approach: Defining police roles in responding to domestic violence. *American Journal of Criminal Justice, 33,* 19–31.

Balsam, K. F. (2001). Nowhere to hide: Lesbian battering, homophobia, and minority stress. *Women and Therapy, 23,* 25–37.

Barnett, O., Miller-Perrin, C. L., & Perrin, R. (2005). *Family violence across the lifespan: An introduction (2nd ed.).* Thousand Oaks, CA: Sage.

Barron, I. G., & Topping, K. J. (2010). School-based abuse prevention: Effect on disclosures. *Journal of Family Violence, 25,* 651–659.

Barth, R. P., Gibbons, C., & Guo, S. (2006). Substance abuse treatment and the recurrence of maltreatment among caregivers with children living at home: A propensity score analysis. *Journal of Substance Abuse Treatment, 30,* 93–104.

Bartle, S. E., & Rosen, K. (1994). Individuation and relationship violence. *The American Journal of Family Therapy, 22,* 222–236.

Bartone, P. T., Ursano, R. J., Wright, K. M., & Ingraham, L. H. (1989). The impact of a military air disaster on the health of assistance workers. *Journal of Nervous and Mental Disease, 177,* 317–328.

Basham, K. (2004). Transforming the legacies of childhood trauma in couple and family therapy. *Social Work in Health Care, 39,* 263–285.

Bass, B. A., & Quimby, J. L. (2006). Addressing secrets in couples counseling: An alternative approach to informed consent. *The Family Journal, 14,* 77–80.

Bass, L. B., Taylor, B. A., & Knudson-Martin, C. (2006). Making sense of abuse: Case studies in sibling incest. *Contemporary Family Therapy, 28,* 87–109.

Batten, S. V., Follette, V. M., Rasmussen Hall, M. L., & Palm, K. M. (2002). Physical and psychological effects of written disclosure among sexual abuse survivors. *Behavior Therapy, 33,* 107–122.

Baumann, B. L., & Kolko, D. J. (2002). A comparison of abusive and nonabusive mothers of abused children. *Child Maltreatment, 7,* 369–376.

Bednar, S. G. (2003). Substance abuse and woman abuse: A proposal for integrated treatment. *Federal Probation, 67,* 52–57.

Beeble, M. L., Bybee, D., & Sullivan, C. M. (2007). Abusive men's use of children to control their partners and ex-partners. *European Psychologist, 12,* 54–61.

Beech, A. R., & Fisher, D. D. (2002). The rehabilitation of child sex offenders. *Australian Psychologist, 37,* 206–214.

Begle, A. M., Dumas, J. E., & Hanson, R. F. (2010). Predicting child abuse potential: An empirical investigation of two theoretical frameworks. *Journal of Clinical Child & Adolescent Psychology, 39,* 208–219.

Begun, A. L. (1999). Intimate Partner Violence: An HBSE perspective. *Journal of Social Work Education, 35,* 239–252.

Begun, A. L., Murphy, C., Bolt, D., Weinstein, B., Strodthoff, T., Short, L., & Shelley, G. (2003). Characteristics of the Safe at Home Instrument for assessing readiness to change intimate partner violence. *Research on Social Work Practice, 13,* 80–107.

Begun, A. L., Shelley, G., Strodthoff, T., & Short, L. (2001). Adopting a stages of change approach for individuals who are violent with their intimate partners. *Journal of Aggression, Maltreatment, and Trauma, 5,* 105–127.

Bell, H. (2003). Strengths and secondary trauma in family violence work. *Social Work, 48,* 513–522.

Bell, M. E., & Goodman, L. A. (2001). Supporting battered women involved with the court system: An evaluation of a law school-based advocacy intervention. *Violence Against Women, 7,* 1377–1404.

Bell, N. S., Harford, T. C., Fuchs, C. H., McCarroll, J. E., & Schwartz, C. E. (2006). Spouse abuse and alcohol problems among white, African American, and Hispanic U.S. army soldiers. *Alcoholism: Clinical and Experimental Research, 30*(10), 1721–1733.

Bellamy, J. L. (2009). A national study of male involvement among families in contact with the child welfare system. *Child Maltreatment, 14,* 255–262.

Ben-Porat, A., & Itzhaky, H. (2009). Implications of treating family violence for the therapist:

Secondary traumatization, vicarious traumatization, and growth. *Journal of Family Violence, 24,* 507–515.

Bennett, L., & O'Brien, P. (2007). Effects of coordinated services for drug-abusing women who are victims of intimate partner violence. *Violence Against Women, 13,* 395–412.

Bennett, L. W., Stoops, C., Call, C., & Flett, H. (2007). Program completion and re-arrest in batterer intervention system. *Research on Social Work Practice, 17,* 42–54.

Bennett Cattaneo, L. (2007). Contributors to assessments of risk in intimate partner violence: How victims and professionals differ. *Journal of Community Psychology, 35,* 57–75.

Bennett Cattaneo, L., Bell, M. E., Goodman, L. A., & Dutton, M. A. (2007). Intimate partner violence victims' accuracy in assessing their risk of re-abuse. *Journal of Family Violence, 22,* 429–440.

Bennett Cattaneo, L., Stuewig, J., Goodman, L. A., Kaltman, S., & Dutton, M. A. (2007). Longitudinal helpseeking patterns among victims of intimate partner violence: The relationship between legal and extralegal services. *American Journal of Orthopsychiatry, 77,* 467–477.

Bensley, L., Simmons, K. W., Ruggles, D., Putvin, T., Harris, C., Allen, M., & Williams, K. (2004). Community responses and perceived barriers to responding to child maltreatment. *Journal of Community Health, 29,* 141–153.

Bentovim, A. (2002). Preventing sexually abused young people from becoming abusers, and treating the victimization experiences of young people who offend sexually. *Child Abuse & Neglect, 26,* 661–678.

Berg, A. O. (2004). Screening for family and intimate partner violence: Recommendation statement. *Annals of Family Medicine, 2,* 156–160.

Berkowitz, C. D. (2010). Sex offender registration: Balancing the rights of the individual with the public good—A commentary on Comartin, Kernsmith, and Miles. *Journal of Child Sexual Abuse, 19,* 226–230.

Berliner, L. (1996). Intervening in domestic violence: Should victims and offenders or couples be the focus? *Journal of Interpersonal Violence, 11,* 449–455.

Bernstein, D. P. (2000). Childhood trauma and drug addiction: Assessment, diagnosis, and treatment. *Alcoholism Treatment Quarterly, 18,* 19–30.

Black, D. A., Heyman, R. E., & Slep, A. M. S. (2001). Risk factors for child sexual abuse. *Aggression and Violent Behavior, 6,* 203–229.

Black, D. A., Slep, A. M. S., & Heyman, R. E. (2001). Risk factors for child psychological abuse. *Aggression and Violent Behavior, 6,* 189–201.

Blake, K., Cangelosi, S., Johnson-Brooks, S., & Belcher, H. M. E. (2007). Reliability of the GAF and CGAS with children exposed to trauma. *Child Abuse & Neglect, 31,* 909–915.

Blasko, K. A., Winek, J. L., & Bieschke, K. J. (2007). Therapists' prototypical assessment of domestic violence situations. *Journal of Marital and Family Therapy, 33,* 258–269.

Bober, T., Regehr, C., & Zhou, Y.R. (2006). Development of the coping strategies inventory for trauma counselors. *Journal of Loss and Trauma, 11,* 71–83.

Bogar, C. B., & Hulse-Killacky, D. (2006). Resiliency determinants and resiliency processes among female adult survivors of childhood sexual abuse. *Journal of Counseling and Development, 84,* 318–327.

Bograd, M. (1999). Battering and couples therapy: Universal screening and selection of treatment modality. *Journal of Marital and Family Therapy, 25,* 291–312.

Bograd, M., & Mederos, F. (1999). Battering and couples therapy: Universal screening and selection of treatment modality. *Journal of Marital and Family Therapy, 25,* 291–312.

Boldy, D., Hornder, B., Crouchley, K., Davey, M., & Boylen, D. (2005). Addressing elder abuse: Western Australian case study. *Australasian Journal on Ageing, 24,* 3–8.

Bonanno, G. A., Colak, D. M., Keltner, D., Shiota, M. N., Papa, A., Noll, J. G., Putnam, F. W., & Trickett, P. K. (2007). Context matters: The benefits and costs of expressing positive emotion among survivors of childhood sexual abuse. *Emotion, 7,* 824–837.

Borrego, J., Jr., Gutow, M. R., & Reicher, S. (2008). Parent-child interaction therapy with domestic violence populations. *Journal of Family Violence, 23,* 495–505.

Bosch, K., & Schumm, W. R. (2004). Accessibility to resources: Helping rural women in abusive partner relationship become free from abuse. *Journal of Sex and Marital Therapy, 30,* 357–370.

Bottoms, B. L., Nielsen, M., Murray, R., & Filipas, H. (2003). Religion-related child physical abuse: Characteristics and psychological outcomes. *Journal of Aggression, Maltreatment, & Trauma, 8,* 87–114.

Bottoms, B. L., & Quas, J. A. (2006). Recent advances and new challenges in child maltreatment research, practice, and policy: Previewing the issues. *Journal of Social Issues, 62,* 653–662.

Bowen, L. K., Gwiasda, V., & Brown, M. M. (2004). Engaging community residents to prevent violence. *Journal of Interpersonal Violence, 19,* 356–367.

Bozorg-Omid, R. (2007). Counselors and domestic violence: Training, competence, practice, and knowledge. *Dissertation Abstracts International: Section A: Humanities and Social Sciences, 67,* 2890.

Bradley, R. H., Caldwell, B. M., Rock, S. L., Hamrick, H. M., & Harris, P. (1988). Home Observation for Measurement of the Environment: Development of a home inventory for use with families having children 6 to 10 years old. *Contemporary Educational Psychology, 13,* 58–71.

Brassard, M. R., Rivelis, E., & Diaz, V. (2009). School-based counseling of abused children. *Psychology in the Schools, 46,* 206–217.

Bride, B. E. (2007). Prevalence of secondary traumatic stress among social workers. *Social Work, 52,* 63–70.

Bride, B. E., Robinson, M. M., Yegidis, B., & Figley, C. R. (2004). Development and validation of the Secondary Traumatic Stress Scale. *Research on Social Work Practice, 14,* 27–35.

Brooks, C. W., & Matthews, C. O. (2000). The relationship among substance abuse counselors' well-being, values, and self-actualizing characteristics and the impact on clients' well-being. *Journal of Addictions & Offender Counseling, 21*(1), 23–33.

Brosi, M. W., & Rolling, E. S. (2010). A narrative journey for intimate partner violence: From victim to survivor. *The American Journal of Family Therapy, 38,* 237–250.

Brown, C., & O'Brien, K. M. (1998). Understanding stress and burnout in shelter workers. *Professional Psychology: Research and Practice, 29,* 383–385.

Brown, D. W., Anda, R. F., Edwards, V. J., Felitti, V. J., Dube, S. R., & Giles, W. H. (2007). Adverse childhood experiences and childhood autobiographical memory disturbance. *Child Abuse & Neglect, 31,* 961–969.

Brown, E. (2005). Correlates and treatment of stress disorder in children and adolescents. *Psychiatric Annals, 35,* 759–765.

Brown, P. D., & O'Leary, K. D. (2000). Therapeutic alliance: Predicting continuance and success in group treatment for spouse abuse. *Journal of Consulting and Clinical Psychology, 68,* 340–345.

Brown, T. G., Werk, A., Caplan, T., & Seraganian, P. (1999). Violent substance abusers in domestic violence treatment. *Violence and Victims, 14,* 179–190.

Buchbinder, E., & Eisikovits, Z. (2008). Doing treatment: Batterers' experience of intervention. *Children and Youth Services Review, 30,* 616–630.

Buckner, J. D., Lopez, C., Dunkel, S., & Joiner, T. E. (2008). Behavior management training for the treatment of Reactive Attachment Disorder. *Child Maltreatment, 13,* 289–297.

Budde, S., & Schene, P. (2004). Informal social support interventions and their role in violence prevention: An agenda for future evaluation. *Journal of Interpersonal Violence, 19,* 341–355.

Bugental, D., Ellerson, P., Lin, E., Rainey, B., Kokotovic, A., & O'Hara, N. (2002). A cognitive approach to child abuse prevention. *Journal of Family Psychology, 16*(3), 243–258. doi:10.1037/0893-3200.16.3.243.

Burke, J. G., Thieman, L. K., Gielen, A. C., O'Campo, P., & McDonnell, K. A. (2005). Intimate partner violence, substance use, and HIV among low-income women: Taking a closer look. *Violence Against Women, 11,* 1140–1161.

Burke, T. W., Jordan, M. L., & Owen, S. S. (2002). A cross-national comparison of gay and lesbian domestic violence. *Journal of Contemporary Criminal Justice, 18,* 231–256.

Burke, T. W., & Owen, S. S. (2006). Same-sex domestic violence: Is anyone listening? *The Gay & Lesbian Review, January-February,* 6–7.

Burkemper, E.M. (2002). Family therapists' ethical decision-making processes in two duty-to-warn situations. *Journal of Marital & Family Therapy, 28,* 203–212.

Burnette, M. L., Ilgen, M., Frayne, S. M., Lucas, E., Mayo, J., & Weitlauf, J. C. (2008). Violence perpetration and childhood abuse among men and women in substance abuse treatment. *Journal of Substance Abuse Treatment, 35,* 217–222.

Busby, D. M. (1996). *The impact of violence on the family: Treatment approaches for therapists and other professionals.* Boston: Allyn & Bacon.

Buss, A. H., & Durkee, A. (1957). An inventory for assessing different kinds of hostility. *Journal of Consulting Psychology, 21,* 343–349.

Buss, A. H., & Perry, M. (1992). The Aggression Questionnaire. *Journal of Personality and Social Psychology, 63,* 452–459.

Butcher, J., Graham, J., Ben-Porath, Y., Tellegen, A., Dahlstrom, W., & Kaemmer, B. (2001). *MMPI-2 manual for administration, scoring and interpretation* (Rev. ed). Minneapolis: University of Minnesota Press.

Buttell, F. P., & Carney, M. M. (2008). A large sample investigation of batterer intervention program attrition: Evaluating the impact of state program standards. *Research on Social Work Practice, 18,* 177–188.

Buttell, F. P., & Pike, C. K. (2002). Investigating predictors of treatment attrition among court-ordered batterers. *Journal of Social Service Research, 28,* 53–68.

Byrne, D. (1996). Clinical models for the treatment of gay male perpetrators of domestic violence. *Journal of Gay & Lesbian Social Services, 4*(1), 107–116.

Caffaro, J. V., & Conn-Caffaro, A. (2006). Treating sibling abuse families. *Aggression and Violent Behavior, 10,* 604–623.

Callahan, K. L., Price, J. L., & Hilsenroth, M. J. (2004). A review of interpersonal-psychodynamic group psychotherapy outcomes for adult survivors of childhood sexual abuse. *International Journal of Group Psychotherapy, 54,* 491–519.

Campbell, C. L., Brown, E. J., & Okwara, L. (2011). Addressing sequelae of trauma and interpersonal violence in military children: A review of the literature and case illustration. *Cognitive and Behavioral Practice, 18,* 131–143.

Campbell, J. C. (2001). Safety planning based on lethality assessment for partners of batterers in intervention programs. *Journal of Aggression, Maltreatment, and Trauma, 5,* 129–143.

Campbell, J. C. (2005). *The danger assessment.* Retrieved September 21, 2009, from www.dangerassessment.org

Campbell, J. C., Dienemann, J., Kub, J., Wurmser, T., & Loy, E. (1999). Collaboration as partnership. *Violence Against Women, 5,* 1140–1157.

Campbell, J. C., & Manganello, J. (2006). Changing public attitudes as a prevention strategy to reduce intimate partner violence. *Journal of Aggression, Maltreatment, & Trauma, 13,* 13–39.

Campbell, J. C., Webster, D. W., & Glass, N. (2009). The danger assessment: Validation of a lethality risk assessment instrument for intimate partner femicide. *Journal of Interpersonal Violence, 24,* 653–674.

Campbell, R., Greeson M. R., Bybee D., & Raja, S. (2008). The co-occurrence of childhood sexual abuse: Adult sexual assault, intimate partner violence, and sexual harassment: A meditational model of posttraumatic stress disorder and physical health outcomes. *Journal of Counseling and Clinical Psychology, 76*(2), 194–207.

Carlson, B. E. (1997). A stress and coping approach to intervention with abused women. *Family Relations, 46,* 291–299.

Carlson, R. G., & Jones, K. D. (2010). Continuum of conflict and control: A conceptualization of intimate partner violence typologies. *The Family Journal, 18,* 248–254.

Carpenter, A., & Donohue, B. (2006). Parental satisfaction in child abuse and neglect: A review of standardized measures. *Aggression and Violent Behavior, 11,* 577–586.

Carr, A. (2009). The effectiveness of family therapy and systemic interventions for adult-focused problems. *Journal of Family Therapy, 31,* 46–74.

Carr, J. L., & VanDeusen, K. M. (2002). The relationship between family of origin violence and dating violence in college men. *Journal of Interpersonal Violence, 17,* 630–646.

Carroll, L., Gilroy, P.J., & Murra, J. (2003). The effect of gender and self-care behaviors on counselors' perceptions of colleagues with depression. *Journal of Counseling & Development, 81,* 70–77.

Cash, R., & Snow, M. (2001). Adlerian treatment of sexually abused children. *The Journal of Individual Psychology, 57,* 102–115.

Cattaneo, L. B., Bell, M. E., Goodman, L. A., & Dutton, M. A. (2007). Intimate partner violence victims' accuracy in assessing their risk of re-abuse. *Journal of Family Violence, 22,* 429–440.

Celano, M., Hazzard, A., Campbell, S., & Lang, C. (2002). Attribution retraining with sexually abused children: Review of techniques. *Child Maltreatment, 7,* 65–76.

Centers for Disease Control and Prevention, National Center for Injury Prevention and Control (CDC; 2003). Costs of intimate partner violence against women in the United States. Retrieved December 3, 2010, from http://www.cdc.gov/ncipc/pub-res/ipv_cost/IPVBook-Final-Feb18.pdf

Chaffin, M. (2008). Commentary on Buckner and implications for treatment selection among foster children with RAD. *Child Maltreatment, 13,* 313–314.

Chaffin, M., & Friedrich, B. (2004). Evidence-based treatments in child abuse and neglect. *Children and Youth Services Review, 26,* 1097–1113.

Chaffin, M., & Shultz, S. K. (2001). Psychometric evaluation of the Children's Impact of Traumatic Events Scale-Revised. *Child Abuse & Neglect, 25,* 401–411.

Chaffin, M., Silovsky, J. F., Funderburk, B., Valle, L. A., Brestan, E. V., Balachova, T., ... Bonner, B. L. (2004). Parent-Child Interaction Therapy with Physically abusive parents: Efficacy for reducing future abuse reports. *Journal of Consulting and Clinical Psychology, 72,* 500–510.

Chan, Y-c., Lam, G. L. T., & Cheng, H. C. H. (2009). Community capacity building as a strategy of family violence prevention in a problem-stricken community: A theoretical formulation. *Journal of Family Violence, 24,* 559–568.

Chang, J. C., Dado, D., Ashton, S., Hawker, L., Cluss, P. A., Buranosky, R., & Scholle, S. H. (2006). Understanding behavior change for women experiencing intimate partner violence: Mapping the ups and downs using the stages of change. *Patient Education and Counseling, 62,* 330–339.

Chang, J. C., Decker, M. R., Moracco, K. E., Martin, S. L., Peterson, R., & Frasier, P. Y. (2004). Asking about intimate partner violence: Advice from female survivors to health care providers. *Patient Education and Counseling, 59,* 141–147.

Chang, J. C., Theodore, A. D., Martin, S. L., & Runyan, D. K. (2008). Psychological abuse between parents: Associations with child maltreatment from a population-based sample. *Child Abuse & Neglect, 32,* 819–829.

Chapman, M. V., Wall, A., Barth, R. P., & The National Survey of Child and Adolescent Well-Being Research Group. (2004). Children's voices: The perceptions of children in foster care. *American Journal of Orthopsychiatry, 74,* 293–304.

Chard, K. M. (2005). An evaluation of cognitive processing therapy for the treatment of posttraumatic stress disorder related to childhood sexual abuse. *Journal of Consulting and Clinical Psychology, 73,* 965–971.

Chartas, N. D., & Culbreth, J. R. (2001). Counselor treatment of coexisting domestic violence and substance abuse: A qualitative study. *Journal of Addictions and Offender Counseling, 22,* 2–11.

Chase, K. A., O'Leary, K. D., & Heyman, R. E. (2001). Categorizing partner-violent men within the reactive-proactive typology model. *Journal of Consulting and Clinical Psychology, 69,* 567–572.

Chavis, A. Z., & Hill, M. S. (2009). Integrating multiple intersecting identities: A multicultural conceptualization of the Power and Control Wheel. *Women & Therapy, 32,* 121–149.

Chen, S., & Scannapieco, M. (2006). Early childhood maltreatment: Substantiation related to family risk and intervention factors. *Child & Adolescent Social Work Journal, 23,* 343–355

Chiffriller, S. H., Hennessy, J. J., & Zappone, M. (2006). Understanding a new typology of batterers: Implications for treatment. *Victims and Offenders, 1,* 79–97.

Chihowski, K., & Hughes, S. (2008). Clinical issues in responding to alleged elder sexual abuse. *Journal of Elder Abuse and Neglect, 20,* 377–400.

Choate, L. H., & Henson, A. (2003). Group work with adult survivors of childhood abuse and neglect: A psychoeducational approach. *Journal for Specialists in Group Work, 28,* 106–121.

Choi, N. G., & Mayer, J. (2000). Elder abuse, neglect, and exploitation: Risk factors and prevention strategies. *Journal of Gerontological Social Work, 33,* 5–25.

Choo, E. K., Spiro, D. M., Lowe, R. A., Newgard, C. D., Hall, M. K., & McConnell, K. J. (2010). Rural-urban disparities in child abuse management resources in the emergency department. *The Journal of Rural Health, 26,* 361–365.

Chouliara, Z., Hutchison, C., & Karatzias, T. (2009). Vicarious traumatisation in practitioners who work with adult survivors of sexual violence and child sexual abuse: Literature review and directions for future research. *Counselling and Psychotherapy Research, 9,* 47–56.

Chronister, K. M., Linville, D., & Kaag, K. P. (2008). Domestic violence survivors' access of career counseling services: A qualitative investigation. *Journal of Career Development, 34,* 339–361.

Chu, J. A. (1992). The therapeutic roller coaster: Dilemmas in the treatment of childhood sexual abuse survivors. *Journal of Psychotherapy Practice and Research, 1,* 351–370.

Classen, C., Koopman, C., Nevill-Manning, K., & Spiegel, D. (2001). A preliminary report comparing trauma-focused and present-focused group therapy against a wait-listed condition among childhood sexual abuse survivors with PTSD. *Journal of Aggression, Maltreatment, & Trauma, 4,* 265–288.

Clay, K. M., Olsheski, J. A., & Clay, S. W. (2000). Alcohol use disorders in female survivors of childhood sexual abuse. *Alcoholism Treatment Quarterly, 18,* 19–29.

Clemans, S. E. (2004). Recognizing vicarious traumatization: A single session group model for trauma workers. *Social Work with Groups, 27,* 55–74.

Clements, C., Ogle, R., & Sabourin, C. (2005). Perceived control and emotional status in abusive college student relationships: An exploration of gender differences. *Journal of Interpersonal Violence, 20,* 1058–1077.

Clements, K., & Holtzworth-Munroe, A. (2008). Aggressive cognitions of violent versus nonviolent spouses. *Cognitive Therapy Review, 32,* 351–369.

Cloitre, M., Miranda, R., Stovall-McClough, K. C., & Han, H. (2005). Beyond PTSD: Emotion regulation and interpersonal problems as predictors of functional impairment in survivors of childhood abuse. *Behavior Therapy, 36,* 119–124.

Cloitre, M., Stolbach, B. C., Herman, J. L., van der Kolk, B., Pynoos, R., Wang, J., & Petkova, E. (2009). A developmental approach to complex PTSD: Childhood and adult cumulative trauma as predictors of symptom complexity. *Journal of Traumatic Stress, 22,* 399–408.

Cluss, P. A., Chang, J. C., Hawker, L., Hudson Scholle, S., Dado, D., Buranosky, R., & Goldstrohm, S. (2006). The process of change for victims of intimate partner violence: Support for a psychosocial readiness model. *Women's Health Issues, 16,* 262–274.

Coffey, P., Leitenberg, H., Henning, K., Bennett, R. T., & Jankowski, M. K. (1996). Dating violence: The association between methods of coping and women's psychological adjustment. *Violence and Victims, 11,* 227–238.

Cohen, J. A., Berliner, L., & Mannarino, A. P. (2003). Psychosocial and pharmacological interventions for child crime victims. *Journal of Traumatic Stress, 16,* 175–186.

Cohen, J. A., Deblinger, E., Mannarino, A. P., & de Arellano, M. A. (2001). The importance of culture in treating abused and neglected children: An empirical review. *Child Maltreatment, 6,* 148–157.

Cohen, J. A., Mannarino, A. P., Murray, L. K., & Igelman, R. (2006). Psychosocial interventions for maltreatment and violence-exposed children. *Journal of Social Issues, 62,* 737–766.

Cohen, J. A., Mannarino, A. P., Zhitova, A. C., & Capone, M. E. (2003). Treating child abuse-related posttraumatic stress and comorbid substance abuse in adolescents. *Child Abuse & Neglect, 27,* 1345–1365.

Cohen, J. N. (2008). Using feminist, emotion-focused, and developmental approaches to enhance cognitive-behavioral therapies for posttraumatic stress disorder related to childhood sexual abuse. *Psychotherapy: Theory, Research, Practice, Training, 45,* 227–246.

Cohen, S., Kamarck, T., & Mermelstein, R. (1983). A global measure of perceived stress. *Journal of Health and Social Behavior, 24,* 385–396.

Coker, A. L. (2004). Primary prevention of intimate partner violence for women's health: A response to Plichta. *Journal of Interpersonal Violence, 19,* 1324–1334.

Coker, A. L., Davis, K. E., Arians, I., Desai, S., Sanderson, M., Brandt, H. M., & Smith, P. H. (2002). Physical and mental health effects of intimate partner violence for men and women. *American Journal of Preventive Medicine, 23,* 260–268.

Coker, A. L., Smith, P. H., McKeown, R. E., & King, M. J. (2000). Frequency and correlates of intimate partner violence by type: Physical, sexual, and psychological battering. *American Journal of Public Health, 90,* 553–559.

Colangelo, J. J. (2007). Recovered memory debate revisited: Practice implications for mental health counselors. *Journal of Mental Health Counseling, 29,* 93–120.

Colangelo, J. J. (2009). The recovered memory controversy: A representative case study. *Journal of Child Sexual Abuse, 18,* 103–121.

Connell-Carrick, K. (2003). A critical review of the empirical literature: Identifying correlates of child neglect. *Child & Adolescent Social Work Journal, 20,* 389.

Conner, K. R., Cerulli, C., & Caine, E. D. (2002). Threatened and attempted suicide by partner-violent male respondents petitioned to family violence court. *Violence and Victims, 17,* 115–125.

Conners, N. A., Whiteside-Mansell, L., Deere, D., Ledet, T., & Edwards, M. C. (2006). Measuring the potential for child maltreatment: The reliability and validity of the Adult Adolescent Parenting Inventory—2. *Child Abuse & Neglect, 30,* 39–53.

Connor, P., & Higgins, D. J. (2008a). The "HEALTH" model—Part 1: Treatment program guidelines for complex PTSD. *Sexual and Relationship Therapy, 23,* 293–303.

Connor, P., & Higgins, D. J. (2008b). The "HEALTH" model—Part 2: Case study of a guideline-based treatment program for complex PTSD relating to childhood sexual abuse. *Sexual and Relationship Therapy, 23,* 401–410.

Conrad, D., & Kellar-Guenther, Y. (2006). Compassion fatigue, burnout, and compassion satisfaction among Colorado child protection workers. *Child Abuse & Neglect, 30,* 1071–1080.

Coohey, C. (2003). Defining and classifying supervisory neglect. *Child Maltreatment, 8,* 145–156.

Coohey, C. (2004). Battered mothers who physically abuse their children. *Journal of Interpersonal Violence, 19,* 943–952.

Cook-Daniels, L. (1997). Lesbian, gay male, bisexual and transgendered elders: Elder abuse and neglect issues. *Journal of Elder Abuse & Neglect, 9*(2), 35–49.

Cooke, P., & Standen, P. J. (2002). Abuse and disabled children: Hidden needs...? *Child Abuse Review, 11,* 1–18.

Corcoran, J. (2000). Family Interventions with child physical abuse and neglect: A critical review. *Children and Youth Services Review, 22,* 563–691.

Corcoran, J. (2002). The transtheoretical stages of change model and motivational interviewing for building maternal supportiveness in cases of sexual abuse. *Journal of Child Sexual Abuse, 11,* 1–17.

Corcoran, K., & Fischer, J. (2000a). *Measures for clinical practice: Volume 1: Couples, families, and children.* New York: The Free Press.

Corcoran, K., & Fischer, J. (2000b). *Measures for clinical practice: Volume 2: Adults.* New York: The Free Press.

Corvo, K., & Carpenter, E. H. (2000). Effects of parental substance abuse on current levels of domestic violence: A possible elaboration of intergenerational transmission processes. *Journal of Family Violence, 15,* 123–135.

Corvo, K., & Johnson, P. J. (2003). Vilification of the "batterer": How blame shapes domestic violence policy and interventions. *Aggression and Violent Behavior, 8,* 259–281.

Cousineau, M-M., & Rondeau, G. (2004). Toward a transnational and cross-cultural analysis of family violence: Issues and recommendations. *Violence Against Women, 10,* 935–949.

Cox, C., Kotch, J., & Everson, M. (2003). A longitudinal study of modifying influences in the relationship between domestic violence and child maltreatment. *Journal of Family Violence, 18*, 5–17.

Crenshaw, D. A., & Hardy, K. V. (2007). The crucial role of empathy in breaking the silence of traumatized children in play therapy. *International Journal of Play Therapy, 16*, 160–175.

Crittenden, P. M., Claussen, A. H., & Kozlowska, K. (2007). Choosing a valid assessment of attachment for clinical use: A comparative study. *ANZJFT, 28*, 78–87.

Crooks, C. V., Scott, K. L., Francis, K. J., Kelly, T., & Reid, M. (2006). Eliciting change in maltreating fathers: Goals, processes, and desired outcomes. *Cognitive and Behavioral Practice, 13*, 71–81.

Crozier, J., & Barth, R. (2005). Cognitive and academic functioning in maltreated children. *Children & Schools, 27*, 197–206.

Cruz, J. M., & Peralta, R. L. (2001). Family violence and substance use: The perceived effects of substance use within gay male relationships. *Violence and Victims, 16*, 161–172.

Csiernik, R., Smith, C., Dewar, J., Dromgole, L., & O'Neill, A. (2010). Supporting new workers in a child welfare agency: An exploratory study. *Journal of Workplace Behavioral Health, 25*, 218–232.

Cunradi, C. B., Caetano, R., Clark, C., & Schafer, J. (2000). Neighborhood poverty as a predication of intimate partner violence among White, Black, and Hispanic couples in the United States: A multilevel analysis. *Annals of Epidemiology, 10*(5), 297–308.

Daignault, I. V., & Hébert, M. (2009). Profiles of school adaptation: Social, behavioral and academic functioning in sexually abused girls. *Child Abuse and Neglect, 33*, 102–115.

Dalton, B. (2007). What's going on out there? A survey of batterer intervention programs. *Journal of Aggression, Maltreatment, and Trauma, 15*, 59–74.

Dalton, B. (2009). Batterer program directors' views on substance abuse and domestic violence. *Journal of Aggression, Maltreatment, & Trauma, 18*, 248–260.

D'Ardenne, P., & Balakrishna, J. (2001). Domestic violence and intimacy: What the relationship therapist needs to know. *Sexual and Relationship Therapy, 16*, 229–246.

Daro, D., & Donnelly, A. C. (2002). Charting the waves of prevention: Two steps forward, one step back. *Child Abuse & Neglect, 26*, 731–742.

Davis, M., & Gidycz, C. (2000). Child sexual abuse prevention programs: A meta-analysis. *Journal of Clinical Child Psychology, 29*(2), 257–265.

Dawe, S., & Harnett, P. (2007). Reducing potential for child abuse among methadone-maintained parents: Results from a randomized controlled trial. *Journal of Substance Abuse Treatment, 32*, 381–390.

Dayton, C. (2005). Elder abuse: The social worker's perspective. *Clinical Gerontologist, 28*, 135–155.

Deb, S. (2005). Child abuse and neglect: The Indian scenario. *Social Science International, 21*, 3–19.

De Bellis, M. D. (2001). Developmental traumatology: The psychobiological development of maltreated children and its implication for research, treatment, and policy. *Development and Psychopathology, 13*, 539–564.

De Bellis, M.D., Keshavan, M.S., Clark, D.B., Casey, B.J., Giedd, J.N., Boring, A.M., Frustaci, K., & Ryan, N.D. (1999). Developmental traumatology part II: Brain development. *Society of Biological Psychiatry, 45*, 1271–1284.

Deblinger, E., Mannarino, A. P., Cohen, J. A., & Steer, R. A. (2006). A follow-up study of a multisite, randomized, controlled trial for children with sexual abuse-related PTSD symptoms. *Journal of the American Academy of Child and Adolescent Psychiatry, 45*, 1474–1484.

Deblinger, E., & Runyon, M. K. (2005). Understanding and treating feelings of shame in children who have experienced maltreatment. *Child Maltreatment, 10*, 364–376.

Deblinger, E., Stauffer, L. B., & Steer, R. A. (2001). Comparative efficacies of supportive and cognitive behavioral group therapies for young children who have been sexually abused and their nonoffending mothers. *Child Maltreatment, 6*, 332–343.

DeBruyn, L., Chino, M., Serna, P., & Fullerton-Gleason, L. (2001). Child maltreatment in American Indian and Alaska Native communities: Integrating culture, history, and public health for intervention and prevention. *Child Maltreatment, 6*, 89–102.

Dekel, R., & Peled, E. (2000). Staff burnout in Israeli battered women's shelters. *Journal of Social Service Research, 26,* 65–76.

DeKeseredy, W. & Schwartz, M. (1998, February). Measuring the extent of woman abuse in intimate heterosexual relationships: A critique of the Conflict Tactics Scales. Harrisburg, PA: VAWnet, a project of the National Resource Center on Domestic Violence/Pennsylvania Coalition Against Domestic Violence. Retrieved October 14, 2009, from: http://www.vawnet.org

DeKeseredy, W. S., Schwartz, M. D., & Alvi, S. (2000). The role of profeminist men in dealing with women abuse on the Canadian college campus. *Violence Against Women, 6,* 918–935.

Demaris, A., & Kaukinin, C. (2005). Violent victimization and women's mental and physical health: Evidence from a national sample. *Journal of Research in Crime and Delinquency, 42,* 384–411.

Derrington, R., Johnson, M., Menard, A., Ooms, T., & Stanley, S. (2010). *Making distinctions among different types of intimate partner violence: A preliminary guide.* National Health Marriage Resource Center and National Resource Center on Domestic Violence. Retrieved August 25, 2010, from http://www.healthymarriageinfo.org/docs/MakingDistinctions_web2.pdf

DeVoe, E. R., & Kantor, G. K. (2002). Measurement issues in child maltreatment and family violence prevention programs. *Trauma, Violence, and Abuse, 3,* 15–39.

Dienemann, J., Campbell, J., Landenburger, K., & Curry, M. A. (2002). The domestic violence survivor assessment: A tool for counseling women in intimate partner violence relationships. *Patient Education and Counseling, 46,* 221–228.

Dienemann, J., Glass, N., Hanson, G., & Lunsford, K. (2007). The Domestic Violence Survivor Assessment (DVSA): A tool for individual counseling with women experiencing intimate partner violence. *Issues in Mental Health Nursing, 28,* 913–925.

Dienemann, J., Glass, N., & Hyman, R. (2005). Survivor preferences for responses to IPV disclosure. *Clinical Nursing Research, 14,* 215–233.

DiLillo, D., & Damashek, A. (2003). Parenting characteristics of women reporting a history of childhood sexual abuse. *Child Maltreatment, 8,* 319–333.

DiLillo, D., Peugh, J., Walsh, K., Panuzio, J., Trask, E., & Evans, S. (2009). Child maltreatment history among newlywed couples: A longitudinal study of marital outcomes and mediating pathways. *Journal of Consulting and Clinical Psychology, 77,* 680–692.

Dobash, R. E., & Dobash, R. P. (1979). *Violence against wives.* New York: Free Press.

Domestic Abuse Intervention Programs (DAIP, n.d.). Duluth Model on public intervention. Retrieved September 20, 2010, from http://www.theduluthmodel.org/research.php

Domestic Abuse Intervention Programs (DAIP, 2008a). What is the Duluth Model? Retrieved September 20, 2010, from http://www.theduluthmodel.org/duluthmodel.php

Domestic Abuse Intervention Programs (DAIP, 2008b). Wheel gallery. Retrieved September 20, 2010, from http://www.theduluthmodel.org/wheelgallery.php

Donohue, B., Romero, V., & Hill, H. H. (2006). Treatment of co-occurring child maltreatment and substance abuse. *Aggression and Violent Behavior, 11,* 626–640.

Donohue, W. A., Dibble, J. L., & Schiamberg, L. B. (2008). A social capital approach to the prevention of elder mistreatment. *Journal of Elder Abuse & Neglect, 20,* 1–23.

Dorrepaal, E., Thomaes, K., Smit, J. H., van Balkom, A. J. L. M., van Dyck, R., Veltman, D. J., & Draijer, N. (2010). Stabilizing group treatment for Complex Posttraumatic Stress Disorder related to childhood abuse based on psycho-education and cognitive behavioral therapy: A pilot study. *Child Abuse & Neglect, 34,* 284–288.

Douki, S., Nacef, F., Belhadj, A., Bouasker, A., & Ghachem, R. (2003). Violence against women in Arab and Islamic countries. *Archives of Women's Mental Health, 6,* 165–171.

Dowd, L. (2001). Female perpetrators of partner aggression: Relevant issues and treatment. *Journal of Aggression, Maltreatment, and Trauma, 5,* 73–104.

Downs, W. R., Capshew, T., & Brindels, B. (2004). Relationships between adult women's alcohol problems and their childhood experiences of parental violence and psychological aggression. *Journal of Studies on Alcohol, 65,* 336–344.

Downs, W. R., Rindels, B., & Atkinson, C. (2007). Women's use of physical and nonphysical self-defense strategies during incidents of partner violence. *Violence Against Women, 13,* 28–45.

Drapeau, M., Korner, A., Granger, L., Brunet, L., & Caspar, F. (2005). A plan analysis of pedophile sexual abusers' motivations for treatment: A qualitative pilot study. *International Journal of Offender Therapy and Comparative Criminology, 49,* 308–324.

Drossel, C., Fisher, J. E., & Mercer, V. (2011). A DBT skills training group for family caregivers of persons with dementia. *Behavior Therapy, 42,* 109–119.

Dubowitz, H. (2009). Commentary on fathers and children and maltreatment: Relationships matter most. *Child Maltreatment, 14*(3), 291–293.

Dufour, S., & Chamberland, C. (2004). The effectiveness of selected interventions for previous maltreatment: Enhancing the well-being of children who live at home. *Child and Family Social Work, 9,* 39–56.

Dunford, F. W. (2000). The San Diego Navy Experiment: An assessment of interventions for men who assault their wives. *Journal of Consulting and Clinical Psychology, 68,* 468–476.

Dunn, J. L. (2005). "Victims" and "survivors": Emerging vocabularies of motive for "battered women who stay." *Sociological Inquiry, 75,* 1–30.

Durrant, J. E. (2008). Physical punishment, culture, and rights: Current issues for professionals. *Journal of Developmental and Behavioral Pediatrics, 29,* 55–66.

Dutton, D. G., & Corvo, K. (2006). Transforming a flawed policy: A call to revive psychology and science in domestic violence research and practice. *Aggression and Violent Behavior, 11*(5), 457–483.

Dutton, D. G., & Corvo, K. (2007). The Duluth model: A data-impervious paradigm and a failed strategy. *Aggression and Violent Behavior, 12,* 658–667.

Dyer, C. B., Kelly, P. A., Pavlik, V. N., Lee, J., Doody, R. S., Regev, T., ... Smith, S. M. (2006). The making of a Self-Neglect Severity Scale. *Journal of Elder Abuse and Neglect, 18,* 13–23.

Dyer, J. (2010). Challenging assumptions: Clergy perspectives and practices regarding intimate partner violence. *Journal of Religion & Spirituality in Social Work: Social Thought, 29,* 33–48.

D'Zurilla, T. J., & Nezu, A. M. (2001). Problem-solving therapies. In K. S. Dobson (Ed.), *Handbook of cognitive-behavioral therapies (2nd ed.)* (pp. 211–245). New York: Guilford.

Eastman, B. J., & Bunch, S. G. (2007). Providing services to survivors of domestic violence: A comparison of rural and urban service provider perceptions. *Journal of Interpersonal Violence, 22(*4), 465–473.

Eastman, B. J., Bunch, S. G., Williams, A. H., & Carawan, L. W. (2007). Exploring the perceptions of domestic violence service providers in rural localities. *Violence Against Women, 13,* 700–716

Easton, C. J., Lee, B., Wupperman, P., & Zonana, H. (2008). Letter to the editor: Substance abuse and domestic violence interventions: The need for theoretical based research. *The American Journal on Addictions, 17,* 341–342.

Easton, C. J., Mandel, D., Babuscio, T., Rounsaville, B. J., & Carroll, K. M. (2007). Differences in treatment outcome between male alcohol dependent offenders of domestic violence with and without positive drug screens. *Addictive Behaviors, 32,* 2151–2163.

Easton, C. J., Mandel, D. L., Hunkele, K. A., Nich, C., Rounsaville, B. J., & Carroll, K. M. (2007). A cognitive behavioral therapy for alcohol-dependent domestic violence offenders: An integrated substance abuse-domestic violence treatment approach (SADV). *The American Journal of Addictions, 16,* 24–31.

Easton, C. J., Swan, S., & Sinha, R. (2000a). Prevalence of family violence in clients entering substance abuse treatment. *Journal of Substance Abuse Treatment, 18,* 23–28.

Easton, C., Swan, S., & Sinha, R. (2000b). Motivation to change substance use among offenders of domestic violence. *Journal of Substance Abuse Treatment, 19,* 1–5.

Eckhardt, C. L., & Utschig, A. C. (2007). Assessing readiness to change among perpetrators of intimate partner violence: Analysis of two self-report measures. *Journal of Family Violence, 22,* 319–330.

Edleson, J. L., & Bible, A. L. (2001). Collaborating for women's safety: Partnerships between research and practice. In C. M. Renzetti, J. L. Edleson, & R. K. Bergen (Eds.), *Sourcebook on violence against women* (pp. 73–95). Thousand Oaks, CA: Sage.

Edmond, T., & Rubin, A. (2004). Assessing the long-term effects of EMDR: Results from an 18-month follow-up study with adult female survivors of CSA. *Journal of Child Sexual Abuse, 13,* 69–86.

Edwards, J. N., Johnson, D. R., & Booth, A. (1987). Coming apart: A prognostic instrument of marital breakup. *Family Relations, 36,* 168–170.

Edwards, M. A., & Patel, A. C. (2003). Telemedicine in the state of Maine: A model for growth driven by rural needs. *Telemedicine Journal and e-Health, 9,* 25–39.

Eggeman, K., Moxley, V., & Schumm, W. R. (1985). Assessing spouses' perceptions of Gottman's Temporal Form in marital conflict. *Psychological Reports, 57,* 171–181.

Ehrensaft, M. K. (2008). Intimate partner violence: Persistence of myths and implications for intervention. *Children and Youth Services Review, 30,* 276–286.

Einhorn, S. (2000). Containing the secret: Time-limited groups for women who were sexually abused as children. *Psychodynamic counseling, 6,* 5–16.

El-Bassel, N., Gilbert, L., Schilling, R., & Wada, T. (2000). Drug abuse and partner violence among women in methadone treatment. *Journal of Family Violence, 15,* 209–228.

Elliott, A. N., & Carnes, C. N. (2001). Reactions of nonoffending parents to the sexual abuse of their child. A review of the literature. *Child Maltreatment, 6,* 314–331.

Elliott, K., & Urquiza, A. (2006). Ethnicity, culture, and child maltreatment. *Journal of Social Issues, 62,* 787–809.

English, D. J. (2003). The importance of understanding a child's maltreatment experience cross-sectionally and longitudinally. *Child Abuse & Neglect, 27,* 877–882.

English, D., Marshall, D., & Stewart, A. (2003). Effects of family violence on child behavior and health during early childhood. *Journal of Family Violence, 18,* 43–57.

Ernst, J. (2001). Community-level factors and child maltreatment in a suburban community. *Social Work Research, 25,* 133–142.

Escriba-Aguir, V., Ruiz-Perez, I., & Saurel-Cubizolles, M. J. (2007). Screening for domestic violence during pregnancy. *Journal of Psychosomatic Obstetrics & Gynecology, 28*(3), 133–134.

Etherington, K. (2000). Supervising counselors who work with survivors of childhood sexual abuse. *Counselling Psychology Quarterly, 13,* 377–389.

Evans, W. N. (1998). Assessment and diagnosis of substance use disorders (SUDS). *Journal of Counseling and Development, 76,* 325–333.

Ezzo, F. R., Evans, T. M., & McGovern-Kondik, M. (2004). Termination of parental rights: Integration of theory, practice, and demographics. *American Journal of Forensic Psychology, 22,* 29–42.

Falk, E., Landsverk, E., Mosqueda, L., Olsen, B. J., Schneider, D. C., Bernatz, S., & Wood, S. (2010). Geriatricians and psychologists: Essential ingredients in the evaluation of elder abuse and neglect. *Journal of Elder Abuse & Neglect, 22,* 281–290.

Fallon, B., Trocme, N., Fluke, J., MacLaurin, B., Tonmyr, L., & Yuan, Y-Y. (2010). Methodological challenges in measuring child maltreatment. *Child Abuse & Neglect, 34,* 70–79.

Fals-Stewart, W. (2003). The occurrence of partner physical aggression on days of alcohol consumption: A longitudinal diary study. *Journal of Consulting and Clinical Psychology, 71,* 41–52.

Fals-Stewart, W., & Clinton-Sherrod, M. (2009). Treating intimate partner violence among substance-abusing dyads: The effect of couples therapy. *Professional Psychology: Research and Practice, 40,* 257–263.

Fals-Stewart, W., Golden, J., & Schumacher, J. A. (2003). Intimate partner violence and substance use: A longitudinal day-to-day examination. *Addictive Behaviors, 28,* 1555–1574.

Fals-Stewart, W., & Kennedy, C. (2005). Addressing intimate partner violence in substance-abuse treatment. *Journal of Substance Abuse Treatment, 29,* 5–17.

Fantuzzo, J., Manz, P., & Atkins, M. (2005). Peer-mediated treatment of socially withdrawn maltreated preschool children: Cultivating natural community resources. *Journal of Clinical Child and Adolescent Psychology, 34,* 320–325.

Farmer, B. A., Khurgin-Bott, R., & Feldman, S. (2009). The benefits and risks of patient self-disclosure in the psychotherapy of women with a history of childhood sexual abuse. *Psychotherapy Theory, Research, Practice, Training, 46,* 52–67.

Farrell, D. P., & Taylor, M. (2000). Silenced by God—An examination of unique characteristics within sexual abuse by clergy. *Psychology Review, 15,* 22–31.

Feather, J. S., & Ronan, K. R. (2006). Trauma-focused cognitive-behavioral therapy for abused children with posttraumatic stress disorder: A pilot study. *New Zealand Journal of Psychology, 35,* 132–145.

Feder, L., & Wilson, D. B. (2005). A meta-analytic review of court-mandated batterer intervention programs: Can courts affect abusers' behavior? *Journal of Experimental Criminology, 1,* 239–262.

Feiring, C. (2005). Emotional development, shame, and adaptation to child maltreatment. *Child Maltreatment, 10,* 307–310.

Feiring, C., Simon, V. A., & Cleland, C. M. (2009). Childhood sexual abuse, stigmatization, internalizing symptoms, and the development of sexual difficulties and dating aggression. *Journal of Consulting and Clinical Psychology, 77,* 127–137.

Felitti, V. J., Anda, R. F., Nordenberg, D., Williamson, D. F., Spitz, A. M., Edwards, V., … Marks, J.S. (1998). Relationship of childhood abuse and household dysfunction to many of the leading causes of death in adults: The Adverse Childhood Experiences (ACE) study. *American Journal of Preventative Medicine, 14,* 245–258.

Ferrari, A. M. (2002). The impact of culture upon child rearing practices and definitions of maltreatment. *Child Abuse & Neglect, 26,* 793–813.

Few, A. L. (2005). The voices of Black and White rural battered women in domestic violence shelters. *Family Relations, 54,* 488-500.

Field, C. A., Caetano, R., & Nelson, S. (2004). Alcohol and violence related cognitive risk factors associated with the perpetration of intimate partner violence. *Journal of Family Violence, 19,* 249–253.

Figley, C. R. (1996). *Compassion fatigue: Coping with secondary traumatic stress disorder in those who treat the traumatized.* New York: Brunner/Mazel.

Finkelhor, D. (2009). The prevention of childhood sexual abuse. *The Future of Children, 19,* 169–194.

Finkelhor, D., Cross, T. P., & Cantor, E. N. (2005). The justice system for juvenile victims: A comprehensive model of case flow. *Trauma, Violence, and Abuse, 6,* 83–102.

Finkelhor, D., & Jones, L. (2006). Why have child maltreatment and child victimization declined? *Journal of Social Issues, 62,* 685–716.

Finn, J. (2000). A survey of domestic violence organizations on the World Wide Web. *Journal of Technology in Human Services, 17,* 83–102.

Finn, J., & Atkinson, T. (2009). Promoting the safe and strategic use of technology for victims of intimate partner violence: Evaluation of the Technology Safety Project. *Journal of Family Violence, 24,* 53–59.

Finn, J., & Banach, M. (2000). Victimization online: The downside of seeking human services for women on the Internet. *CyberPsychology & Behavior, 3,* 785–796.

Fisher, D., Beech, A., & Browne, K. (2000). The effectiveness of relapse prevention training in a group of incarcerated child molesters. *Psychology, Crime, & Law, 6,* 181–195.

Fisher, P. A., Kim, H. K., & Pears, K. C. (2009). Effects of multidimensional treatment foster care for preschoolers (MTFC-P) on reducing permanent placement failures among children with placement instability. *Children and Youth Services Review, 31,* 541–546.

Flaherty, M. P. (2010). Constructing a world beyond intimate partner abuse. *Affilia: Journal of Women and Social Work, 25,* 224–235.

Flay, B. R., Biglan, A., Boruch, R. F., Castro, F. G., Gottfredson, D., Kellam, S., … Ji, P. (2005). Standards of evidence: Criteria for efficacy, effectiveness, and dissemination. *Prevention Science, 6,* 151–175.

Fleck-Henderson, A. (2000). Domestic violence in the child protection system: Seeing double. *Children and Youth Services Review, 22,* 333–354.

Folette, V. M., La Bash, H. A. J., & Sewell, M. T. (2010). Adult disclosure of a history of childhood sexual abuse: Implications for behavioral psychotherapy. *Journal of Trauma & Dissociation, 11,* 228–243.

Follette, V. M., Polusny, M. M., & Milbeck, K. (1994). Mental health and law enforcement professionals: Trauma history, psychological symptoms, and impact of providing services to child sexual abuse survivors. *Professional Psychology: Research and Practice, 25,* 275–282.

Fong, R., & Cardoso, J. B. (2010). Child human trafficking victims: Challenges for the child welfare system. *Evaluation and Program Planning, 33,* 311–316.

Fontes, L. A., Cruz, M., & Tabachnick, J. (2001). Views of child sexual abuse in two cultural communities: An exploratory study among African Americans and Latinos. *Child Maltreatment, 6,* 103–117.

Foreman, T., & Bernet, W. (2000). A misunderstanding regarding the duty to report suspected abuse. *Child Maltreatment, 5,* 190–196.

Fortunata, B., & Kohn, C. S. (2003). Demographic, psychosocial, and personality characteristics of lesbian batterers. *Violence and Victims, 18,* 557–568.

Foshee, V. A., Bauman, K. E., Arriaga, X. B., Helms, R. W., Koch, G. G., & Linder, G. F. (1998). An evaluation of Safe Dates, an adolescent dating violence prevention program. *American Journal of Public Health, 88,* 45–50.

Foshee, V. A., Bauman, K. E., Ennett, S. T., Linder, G. F., Benefield, T., & Suchindran, C. (2004). Assessing the long-term effects of the Safe Dates Program and a booster in preventing and reducing adolescent dating violence victimization and perpetration. *American Journal of Public Health, 94,* 619–624.

Foshee, V. A., Bauman, K. E., Greene, W. F., Koch, G. G., Linder, G. F., & MacDougall, J. E. (2000). The Safe Dates Program: 1-year follow-up results. *American Journal of Public Health, 90,* 1619-1622.

Fowler, D. (2007). The extent of substance use problems among women partner abuse survivors residing in a domestic violence shelter. *Family & Community Health/Supplement 1,* S106–S108.

Frank, E., Elon, L., Saltzman, L. E., Houry, D., McMahon, P., & Doyle, J. (2006). Clinical and personal intimate partner violence training experiences of U.S. medical students. *Journal of Women's Health, 15,* 1071–1079.

Frasier, P. Y, Slatt, L., Kowlowitz, V., & Glowa, P. T. (2001). Using the stages of change model to counsel victims of intimate partner violence. *Patient Education and Counseling, 43,* 211–217.

Freedner, N., Freed, L. H., Yang, Y. W., & Austin, S. B. (2002). Dating violence among gay, lesbian, and bisexual adolescents: Results from a community survey. *Journal of Adolescent Health, 31,* 469–474.

Freeman, K., & Morris, T. (2001). A review of conceptual models explaining the effects of child sexual abuse. *Aggression and Violent Behavior, 6,* 357–373.

French, E. M., Wiener, C. B., & Mosher-Ashley, P. M. (2000). Referral patterns of elderly persons to psychotherapy by primary care providers at a community health center. *Clinical Gerontologist, 21,* 65–71.

Freshwater, K., Ainscough, C., & Toon, K. (2002). Confronting abusers: The opinions of clinicians and survivors. *Journal of Child Sexual Abuse, 11,* 35–52.

Friedrich, W. N., Fisher, J. L., Dittner, C. A., Acton, R., Berliner, L., Butler, J., Damon, L., Davies, W. H., Gray, A., & Wright, J. (2001). Child Sexual Behavior Inventory: Normative, psychiatric, and sexual abuse comparisons. *Child Maltreatment, 6,* 37–49.

Friend, C. (2000). Woman abuse and child protection: A tumultuous marriage (Volume II). *Children and Youth Services Review, 22,* 309–314.

Frohmann, L. (2005). The Framing Safety project: Photographs and narratives by battered women. *Violence Against Women, 11,* 1396–1419.

Frost, A. (2004). Therapeutic engagement styles of child sexual offenders in a group treatment program: A grounded theory study. *Sexual Abuse: A Journal of Research and Treatment, 16,* 191–208.

Fulfer, J. L., Tyler, J. J., Choi, N. J. S., Young, J. A., Verhulst, S. J., Kovach, R., & Dorsey,

J. K. (2007). Using indirect questions to detect intimate partner violence: The SAFE-T Questionnaire. *Journal of Interpersonal Violence, 22,* 238–249.

Fullwood, P. C. (2002). *Preventing family violence: Community engagement makes the difference.* San Francisco: Family Violence Prevention Fund. Retrieved September 29, 2005, from http://endabuse.org/programs/children/files/Preventing.pdf

Galano, J., & Schellenbach, C. J. (2007). Healthy Families America® Research Practice Network: A unique partnership to integrate prevention science and practice. *Journal of Prevention & Intervention in the Community, 34,* 39–66.

Galvani, S. A. (2007). Safety in numbers? Tackling domestic abuse in couples and network therapies. *Drug and Alcohol Review, 26,* 175–181.

Gannon, T. A., Keown, K., & Rose, M. R. (2008). An examination of current psychometric assessments of child molesters' offense-supportive beliefs using Ward's implicit theories. *International Journal of Offender Therapy and Comparative Criminology, 53,* 316–333.

Garb, H. N., Wood, J. M., & Nezworski, M. T. (2000). Projective techniques and the detection of child sexual abuse. *Child Maltreatment, 5,* 161–168.

Garcia, L., Soria, C., & Hurwitz, e. L. (2007). Homicides and intimate partner violence: A literature review. *Trauma, Violence, and Abuse, 8,* 370–383.

Gates, D. M., & Gillespie, G. L. (2008). Secondary traumatic stress in nurses who care for traumatized women. *Journal of Obstetric, Gynecologic, & Neonatal Nursing, 37,* 243–249.

Gauthier, L. M., & Levendosky, A. A. (1996). Assessment and treatment of couples with abusive male partners: Guidelines for therapists. *Psychotherapy, 33,* 403–417.

Geeraert, L., Van den Noortgate, W., Grietens, H., & Onghena, P. (2004). The effects of early prevention programs for families with young children at risk for physical child abuse and neglect: A meta-analysis. *Child Maltreatment, 9,* 277–291.

Geffner, B. (1995). Standards in the family violence field. *Family Violence & Sexual Assault Bulletin, 11,* 3.

Geller, J. A., Madsen, L. H., & Ohrenstein, L. (2004). Secondary trauma: A team approach. *Clinical Social Work Journal, 32,* 415–430.

Gelles, R. J. (2001). Standards for programs for men who batter?: Not yet. *Journal of Aggression, Maltreatment, & Trauma, 5,* 11–20.

Gelles, R. J. (2007). The politics of research: The use, abuse, and misuse of social science data: The cases of intimate partner violence. *Family Court Review, 45,* 42–51.

Geraerts, E., Lindsay, D. S., Merckelbach, H., Jelicic, M., Raymaekers, L., Arnold, M. M., & Schooler, J. W. (2009). Cognitive mechanisms underlying recovered-memory experiences of child sexual abuse. *Psychological Science, 20,* 92–98.

Gerlock, A. A. (1999). Health impact of domestic violence. *Issues in Mental Health Nursing, 30,* 373–385.

Gershater-Molko, R. M., Lutzker, J. R., & Sherman, J. A. (2002). Intervention in child neglect: An applied behavioral perspective. *Aggression and Violent Behavior, 7,* 103–124.

Gershater-Molko, R. M., Lutzker, J. R., & Wesch, D. (2003). Project SafeCare: Improving health, safety, and parenting skills in families reported for, and at-risk for child maltreatment. *Journal of Family Violence, 18,* 377–386.

Giardino, A. (2009). Child maltreatment: Is the glass half full yet? *Journal of Forensic Nursing, 5,* 1–4.

Giardino, A. P., Hudson, K. M., & Marsh, J. (2003). Providing medical evaluations for possible child maltreatment to children with special health care needs. *Child Abuse & Neglect, 27,* 1179–1186.

Gibb, B. E., Butler, A. C., & Beck, J. S. (2003). Childhood abuse, depression, and anxiety in adult psychiatric outpatients. *Depression and Anxiety, 17,* 226–228.

Gibson, L. E., & Leitenberg, H. (2000). Child sexual abuse prevention programs: Do they decrease the occurrence of child sexual abuse? *Child Abuse & Neglect, 24,* 1115–1125.

Giesbrecht, N., & Sevcik, I. (2000). The process of recovery and rebuilding among abused women in the conservative evangelical subculture. *Journal of Family Violence, 15,* 229–248.

Gil, D. G. (1996). Preventing violence in a structurally violent society: Mission impossible. *American Journal of Orthopsychiatry, 66,* 77–84.

Giles, M. D., Nelson, A. L., Shizgal, F., Stern, E-M., Fourt, A., Woods, P., Langmuir, J., & Classen, C. C. (2007). A multi-modal treatment program for childhood trauma recovery: Women recovering from abuse program (WRAP). *Journal of Trauma & Dissociation, 8,* 7–24.

Gilfus, M. E., Fineran, S., Cohan, D. J., Jensen, S. A., Hartwick, L., & Spath, R. (1999). Research on violence against women: Creating survivor-informed collaborations. *Violence Against Women, 5,* 1194–1212.

Gillum, T. L. (2008). The benefits of a culturally specific intimate partner violence intervention for African American survivors. *Violence Against Women, 14,* 917–943.

Ginsberg, B. G. (2002). The power of filial relationship enhancement therapy as an intervention in child abuse and neglect. *International Journal of Play Therapy, 11,* 65–78.

Gladue, B. A. (1991). Qualitative and quantitative sex differences in self-reported aggressive behavior characteristics. *Psychological Reports, 68,* 675–684.

Gleiser, K., Ford, J. D., & Fosha, D. (2008). Contrasting exposure and experiential therapies for complex posttraumatic stress disorder. *Psychotherapy: Theory, Research, Practice, Training, 45,* 340–360.

Glowa, P. T., Frasier, P. Y., & Newton, W. P. (2002). Increasing physician comfort level in screening and counseling patients for intimate partner violence: Hands-on practice. *Patient Education and Counseling, 46,* 213–220.

Gold, S. N. (2008). Benefits of a contextual approach to understanding and treating complex trauma. *Journal of Trauma & Dissociation, 9,* 269–292.

Goldblatt, H. (2009). Caring for abused women: Impact on nurses' professional and personal life experiences. *Journal of Advanced Nursing, 65,* 1645–1654.

Goldblatt, H., Buchbinder, E., Eisikovits, Z., & Arizon-Mesinger, I. (2009). Between the professional and the private: The meaning of working with intimate partner violence in social workers' private lives. *Violence Against Women, 15,* 362–384.

Goldner, V. (1999). Morality and multiplicity: Perspectives on the treatment of violence in intimate life. *Journal of Marital and Family Therapy, 25,* 325–336.

Gondolf, E. W. (1999). A comparison of four batterer intervention systems: Do court referral, program length, and services matter? *Journal of Interpersonal Violence, 14,* 41–61.

Gondolf, E. W. (2000). How batterer program participants avoid reassault. *Violence Against Women, 6,* 1204–1222.

Gondolf, E. W. (2004). Evaluating batterer counseling programs: A difficult task showing some effects and implications. *Aggression and Violent Behavior, 9,* 605–631.

Gondolf, E. W. (2007). Theoretical and research support for the Duluth Model: A reply to Dutton and Corvo. *Aggression and Violent Behavior, 12,* 644–657.

Gondolf, E.W., Yllö, K., & Campbell, J. (1997) Collaboration between researchers and advocates. In G. K. Kantor & J. L. Jasinski (Eds.), *Out of darkness: Contemporary perspectives on family violence* (pp. 255–267). Thousand Oaks, CA: Sage.

Goodman, L., Dutton, M. A., Weinfurt, K., & Cook, S. (2003). The Intimate Partner Violence Strategies Index: Development and application. *Violence Against Women, 9,* 163–186.

Goodman, L., & Epstein, D. (2005). Refocusing on women: A new direction for policy and research on intimate partner violence. *Journal of Interpersonal Violence, 20,* 479–487.

Goodrum, S., Umberson, D., & Anderson, K. L. (2001). The batterer's view of the self and others in domestic violence. *Sociological Inquiry, 71,* 221–240.

Goodvin, R., Johnson, D. R., Hardy, S. A., Graef, M. I., & Chambers, J. M. (2007). Development and confirmatory factor analysis of the Community Norms of Child Neglect Scale. *Child Maltreatment, 12,* 68–85.

Gorde, M. W., Helfrich, C. A., & Finlayson, M. L. (2004). Trauma symptoms and life skill needs of domestic violence victims. *Journal of Interpersonal Violence, 19,* 691–708.

Gottman, J. M. (2001). Crime, hostility, wife battering, and the heart: On the Meehan et al. (2001) failure to replicate the Gottman et al. (1995) typology. *Journal of Family Psychology, 15,* 409–414.

Gottman, J. M., Jacobson, N. S., Rushe, R. H., Shortt, J. W., Babcock, J. C., LaTaillade, J. J., & Waltz, J. (1995). The relationship between heart rate reactivity, emotionally aggressive behavior, and general violence in batterers. *Journal of Family Psychology, 9,* 227–248.

Govindshenoy, M., & Spencer, N. (2006). Abuse of the disabled child: A systematic review of population-based studies. *Child: Care, Health, and Development, 33,* 552–558.

Graves, K.N. (2007). Not always sugar and spice: Expanding theoretical and functional explanations for why females aggress. *Aggression and Violent Behavior, 12,* 131–140.

Graves, K.N., Frabutt, J.M., & Kaslow, N.J. (2010). A culturally-informed approach to trauma, suicidal behavior, and overt aggression in African American adolescents. *Aggression and Violent Behavior, 15,* 36–41.

Graves, K. N., Hunt, E., Sumner, M., Varner, L., Fluggee, L., & Casterine, L. (2011). *Understanding the arrest profiles of domestic violence offenders: Phase one findings of the offender-focused domestic violence initiative.* Manuscript submitted for publication.

Graves, K. N., Sechrist, S., White, J., & Paradise, M. (2005). Examining intimate partner violence perpetrated by women within the context of victimization history. *Psychology of Women Quarterly, 29,* 278–289.

Gray, I. (2004). Working with a couple after violence: Reflections on a differentiation-based approach. *Australian and New Zealand Journal of Family Therapy, 25,* 206–211.

Greene, K., & Bogo, M. (2002). The different faces of intimate violence Implications for assessment and treatment. *Journal of Marital and Family Therapy, 28,* 455–466.

Greenwald, R., & Rubin, A. (1999). Assessment of posttraumatic symptoms in children: Development and preliminary validation of parent and child scales. *Research on Social Work Practice, 9,* 61–75.

Greenwood, G. L., Relf, M. V., Bu Huang, Pollack, L. M., Canchola, J. A., & Catania, J. A. (2002). Battering victimization among a probability-based sample of men who have sex with men. *American Journal of Public Health, 92,* 1964–1969.

Grigsby, N., & Hartman, B. R. (1997). The barriers model: An integrated strategy for intervention with battered women. *Psychotherapy, 34,* 485–497.

Griffing, S., Ragin, D. F., Sage, R. E., Madry, L., Bingham, L. E., & Primm, B. J. (2002). Domestic violence survivors' self-identified reasons for returning to abusive relationships. *Journal of Interpersonal Violence, 17,* 306–319.

Grossman, F. K., Sorsoli, L., & Kia-Keating, M. (2006). A gale force wind: Meaning making by male survivors of childhood sexual abuse. *American Journal of Orthypsychiatry, 76,* 434–443.

Grosz, C. A., Kempe, R., S., & Kelly, M. (2000). Extrafamilial sexual abuse: Treatment for child victims and their families. *Child Abuse & Neglect, 24,* 9–23.

Guggisbert, M. (2006). The interconnectedness and causes of female suicidal ideation with domestic violence. *AeJAMH: Australian e-Journal for the Advancement of Mental Health, 5,* no page numbers provided.

Gully, K. J. (2001). The Social Behavior Inventory for children in a child abuse treatment program: Development of a tool to measure interpersonal behavior. *Child Maltreatment, 6,* 260–270.

Gurchiek, K. (2005). Study: Domestic violence spills over into workplace. *HR Magazine, 50,* 32, 38.

Guterman, N. B. (2004). Advancing prevention research on child abuse, youth violence, and domestic violence: Emerging strategies and issues. *Journal of Interpersonal Violence, 19,* 299–321.

Haeseler, L. A. (2006). Children of abuse and school discourse: Implications for teachers and administration. *Education, 126,* 534–540.

Hakman, M., Chaffin, M., Funderburk, B., & Silovsky, J. F. (2009). Change trajectories for parent-child interaction sequences during parent-child interaction therapy for child physical abuse. *Child Abuse & Neglect, 33,* 461–470.

Hall, K. (2008). Childhood sexual abuse and adult sexual problems: A new view of assessment and treatment. *Feminism and Psychology, 18,* 546–556.

Halpern, C. T., Young, M. L., Waller, M. W., Martin, S. L., & Kupper, L. L. (2004). Prevalence of partner violence in same-sex romantic and sexual relationships in a national sample of adolescents. *Journal of Adolescent Health, 35,* 124–131.

Hamby, S. L. (2006). The who, what, when, where, and how of partner violence prevention research. *Journal of Aggression, Maltreatment, & Trauma, 13,* 179–201.

Hamel, J. (2007). Domestic violence: A gender-inclusive conception. In J. Hamel & T. L. Nicholls (Eds.), *Family interventions in domestic violence: A handbook of gender-inclusive theory and treatment* (pp. 3–26). New York: Springer.

Hamberger, L..K. (2001) Musings of a state standards committee chair. *Journal of Aggression, Maltreatment, and Trauma, 5,* 265–286.

Hamberger, L. K., & Ambuel, B. (1997). Training psychology students and professionals to recognize and intervene into partner violence: Borrowing a page from medicine. *Psychotherapy, 34,* 375–385.

Hansen, G. L. (1982). Reactions to hypothetical, jealousy-producing events. *Family Relations, 31,* 513–518.

Hanson, R. F., & Spratt, E. G. (2000). Reactive Attachment Disorder: What we know about the disorder and implications for treatment. *Child Maltreatment, 5,* 137–145.

Hare, S. C. (2006). What do battered women want? Victims' opinions on prosecution. *Violence and Victims, 21,* 611–628.

Harper, F. D., Harper, J. A., & Stills, A. B. (2003). Counseling children in crisis based on Maslow's hierarchy of basic needs. *International Journal of the Advancement of Counselling, 25,* 11–25.

Harper, K., & Steadman, J. (2003). Therapeutic boundary issues in working with childhood sexual-abuse survivors. *American Journal of Psychotherapy, 57,* 64–79.

Harrington, D., Zuravin, S., DePanfilis, D., Ting, L., & Dubowitz, H. (2002). The Neglect Scale: Confirmatory factor analyses in a low-income sample. *Child Maltreatment, 7,* 359–368.

Harris, M., & Fallot, R. (2001). *Using trauma theory to design service systems.* New Directions for Mental Health Services. San Francisco: Jossey-Bass.

Haskett, M. E., Ahern, L. S., Ward, C. S., & Allaire, J. C. (2006). Factor structure and validity of the Parenting Stress Index—Short Form. *Journal of Clinical Child and Adolescent Psychology, 35,* 302–312.

Hassouneh-Phillips, D., & Curry, M. A. (2002). Abuse of women with disabilities: State of the science. *Rehabilitation Counseling Bulletin, 45,* 96–104.

Hattendorf, J., & Tollerud, T. R. (1997). Domestic violence: Counseling strategies that minimize the impact of secondary victimization. *Perspectives in Psychiatric Care, 33,* 14–23.

Haugaard, J. J. (2004). Recognizing and treating rare behavioral and emotional disorders in children and adolescents who have been severely maltreated: Introduction. *Child Maltreatment, 9,* 123–130.

Havig, K. (2008). The health care experiences of adult survivors of child sexual abuse: A systematic review of evidence on sensitive practice. *Trauma, Violence, and Abuse, 9,* 19–33.

Hayes, S. C., Strosahl, K., & Wilson, K. G. (1999). *Acceptance and commitment therapy: An experiential approach to behavior change.* New York: Guilford

Hays, S-J., Murphy, G. H., Langdon, P. E., Rose, D., & Reed, T. (2007). Group treatment for men with intellectual disability and sexually abusive behavior: Service user views. *Journal of Intellectual and Developmental Disability, 32,* 106–116.

Hayward, K. S., Steiner, S., & Sproule, K. (2007). Women's perceptions of the impact of a domestic violence treatment program for male perpetrators. *Journal of Forensic Nursing, 3,* 77–83.

Hebert, M., Parent, N., Daignault, I. V., & Tourigny, M. (2006). A typological analysis of behavioral profiles of sexually abused children. *Child Maltreatment, 11,* 203–216.

Heckert, D. A., & Gondolf, E. W. (2000a). The effect of perceptions of sanctions on batterer program outcomes. *Journal of Research in Crime and Delinquency, 37,* 369–391.

Heckert, D. A., & Gondolf, E. W. (2000b). Predictors of underreporting of male violence by batterer program participants and their partners. *Journal of Family Violence, 15,* 423–443.

Hegarty, K., Bush, R., & Sheehan, M. (2005). The Composite Abuse Scale: Further development and assessment of reliability and validity of a multidimensional partner abuse measure in clinical settings. *Violence and Victims, 20,* 529–547.

Hegarty, K., Sheehan, M., & Schonfeld, C. (1999). A multidimensional definition of partner abuse: Development and preliminary validation of the Composite Abuse Scale. *Journal of Family Violence, 14,* 399–415.

Heintz, A. J., & Melendez, R. M. (2006). Intimate partner violence and HIV/STD risk among lesbian, gay, bisexual, and transgender individuals. *Journal of Interpersonal Violence, 21,* 193–208.

Helfrich, C. A., Fujiura, G. T., & Rutkowski-Kmitta, V. (2008). Mental health disorders and functioning of women in domestic violence shelters. *Journal of Interpersonal Violence, 23,* 437–453.

Henderson, D., Hargreaves, I., Gregory, S., & Williams, J. M. G. (2002). Autobiographical memory and emotion in a non-clinical sample of women with and without a reported history of childhood sexual abuse. *British Journal of Clinical Psychology, 41,* 129–141.

Hendy, H. M., Weiner, K., Bakerofskie, J., Eggen, D., Gustitus, C., & McLeod, K. C. (2003). Comparison of six models for violent romantic relationships in college men and women. *Journal of Interpersonal Violence, 18,* 645–665.

Henggeler, S. W., & Borduin, C. M. (1990). *Family therapy and beyond: A multisystemic approach to treating the behavior problems of children and adolescents.* Pacific Grove, CA: Brooks/Cole.

Henning, K., Jones, A. R., & Holdford, R. (2005). 'I didn't do it, but if I did I had a good reason': Minimization, denial, and attributions of blame among male and female domestic violence offenders. *Journal of Family Violence, 20,* 131–139.

Henning, K. R., & Klesges, L. M. (2002). Utilization of counseling and supportive services by female victims of domestic abuse. *Violence and Victims, 17,* 623–636.

Hendrick, C., & Hendrick, S. S. (1990). A relationship-specific version of the Love Attitudes Scale. *Journal of Social Behavior and Personality, 5,* 239–254.

Hendrick, S. S. (1988). A generic measure of relationship satisfaction. *Journal of Marriage and the Family, 50,* 93–98.

Herbert, T. B., Silver, R. C., & Ellard, J. H. (1991). Coping with an abusive relationship: How and why do women stay? *Journal of Marriage and the Family, 53,* 311–325.

Herman, J. L. (1992). Complex PTSD: A syndrome in survivors of prolonged and repeated trauma. *Journal of Traumatic Stress, 5,* 377–391.

Herschell, A. D., Calzada, E. J., Eyberg, S. M., & McNeil, C. B. (2002). Clinical issues in Parent-Child Interaction Therapy. *Cognitive and Behavioral Practice, 9,* 16–27.

Herschell, A. D., & McNeil, C. B. (2005). Theoretical and empirical underpinnings of Parent-Child Interaction Therapy with child physical abuse populations. *Education and Treatment of Children, 28,* 142–162.

Hershkowitz, I. (2009). Socioemotional factors in child sexual abuse investigations. *Child Maltreatment, 14,* 172–181.

Heyman, R. E., & Schlee, K. (2003). Stopping wife abuse via Physical Aggression Couples Treatment. *Journal of Aggression, Maltreatment, and Trauma, 7,* 135–157.

Hickman, L. J., Jaycox, L. H., & Aronoff, J. (2004). Dating violence among adolescents: Prevalence, gender distribution, and prevention program effectiveness. *Trauma, Violence, and Abuse, 5,* 123–142.

Hien, D., Cohen, L. R., Caldeira, N. A., Flom, P., & Wasserman, G. (2010). Depression and anger as risk factors underlying the relationship between maternal substance involvement and child abuse potential. *Child Abuse & Neglect, 34,* 105–113.

Higgins, D. J., (2004). The importance of degree versus type of maltreatment: A cluster analysis of child abuse types. *Journal of Psychology: Interdisciplinary and Applied, 138,* 303–324.

Higgins Kessler, M. R., Nelson, B. S., Jurich, A. P., & White, M. B. (2004). Clinical decision-making strategies of marriage and family therapists in the treatment of adult childhood sexual abuse survivors. *The American Journal of Family Therapy, 32,* 1–10.

Hill, A. (2005). Patterns of non-offending parental involvement in therapy with sexually abused children: A review of the literature. *Journal of Social Work, 5,* 339–358.

Hill, A. (2006). Play therapy with sexually abused children: Including parents in therapeutic play. *Child & Family Social Work, 11,* 316–324.

Hirschel, D., Hutchison, I. W., & Shaw, M. (2010). The interrelationship between substance abuse and the likelihood of arrest, conviction, and re-offending in cases of intimate partner violence. *Journal of Family Violence, 25,* 81–90.

Hoaken, P. N. S., & Stewart, S. H. (2003). Drugs of abuse and the elicitation of human aggressive behavior. *Addictive Behavior, 28,* 1533–1554.

Hodges, E. A., & Myers, J. E. (2010). Counseling adult women survivors of childhood sexual abuse: Benefits of a wellness approach. *Journal of Mental Health Counseling, 32,* 139–154.

Holden, G. (2003). Children exposed to domestic violence and child abuse: Terminology and taxonomy. *Clinical Child and Family Psychology Review, 6,* 151–160.

Holtzworth-Munroe, A. (2000). A typology of men who are violent toward their female partners: Making sense of heterogeneity in husband violence. *Current Directions in Psychological Science, 9,* 140–143.

Holtzworth-Munroe, A. (2005). Male versus female intimate partner violence: Putting controversial findings into context. *Journal of Marriage and Family, 67,* 1120–1125.

Holtzworth-Munroe, A., Bates, L., Smutzler, N., & Sandin, E. (1997). A brief review of the research on husband violence: Part I: Maritally violent versus nonviolent men. *Aggression and Violent Behavior, 2,* 65–99.

Holtzworth-Munroe, A., Meehan, J. C., Herron, K., Rehman, U., & Stuart, G. L. (2000). Testing the Holtzworth-Munroe and Stuart (1994) batterer typology. *Journal of Consulting and Clinical Psychology, 68*, 1000–1019.

Holtzworth-Munroe, A., Meehan, J. C., Herron, K., Rehman, U., & Stuart, G. L. (2003). Do subtypes of martially violent men continue to differ over time? *Journal of Consulting and Clinical Psychology, 4,* 728–740.

Holtzworth-Munroe, A., Smutzler, N., & Bates, L. (1997). A brief review of the research on husband violence: Part III: Sociodemographic factors, relationship factors, and differing consequences of husband and wife violence. *Aggression and Violent Behavior, 2,* 285–307.

Holtzworth-Munroe, A., Smutzler, N., & Sandin, E. (1997). A brief review of the research on husband violence: Part II: The psychological effects of husband violence on battered women and their children. *Aggression and Violent Behavior, 2,* 179–213.

Holtzworth-Munroe, A., & Stuart, G. L. (1994). Typologies of male batterers: Three subtypes and the differences among them. *Psychological Bulletin, 116,* 476–497.

Homiak, K. B., & Singletary, J. E. (2007). Family violence in congregations: An exploratory study of clergy's needs. *Social Work & Christianity, 34,* 18–46.

Horton, C. B., & Cruise, T. K. (1997). Clinical assessment of child victims and adult survivors of child maltreatment. *Journal of Counseling and Development, 76,* 94–104.

Hoskins, C. N. (1986). Measuring perceived dominance-accommodation: Development of a scale. *Psychological Reports, 58,* 627–642.

Hosser, D., Raddatz, S., & Windzio, M. (2007). Child maltreatment, revictimization, and violent behavior. *Violence and Victims, 22*, 318–333.

House, A. S. (2006). Increasing the usability of cognitive processing therapy for survivors of child sexual abuse. *Journal of Child Sexual Abuse, 15,* 87–103.

Howe, D. (2006). Disabled children, maltreatment, and attachment. *British Journal of Social Work, 36,* 743–760.

Hudson, W. W. (1997). *The WALMYR assessment scales scoring manual.* Tallahassee, FL: WALMYR Publishing.

Huebner, C. (2002). Evaluation of a clinic-based parent education program to reduce the risk of infant and toddler maltreatment. *Public Health Nursing, 19*, 377–389.

Hughes, J. R., & Gottlieb, L. N. (2004). The effects of the Webster-Stratton parenting program on maltreating families: Fostering strengths. *Child Abuse & Neglect, 28,* 1081–1097.

Hulme, P. A. (2004). Retrospective measurement of childhood sexual abuse: A review of instruments. *Child Maltreatment, 9,* 201–217.

Humphreys, C. (2008). Responding to the individual trauma of domestic violence: Challenges for mental health professionals. *Social Work in Mental Health, 7,* 186–203.

Humphreys, C., Regan, L., River, D., & Thiara, R. K. (2005). Domestic violence and substance use: Tacking complexity. *British Journal of Social Work, 35,* 1303–1320.

Huss, M. T., & Langhinrichsen-Rohling, J. (2006). Assessing the generalization of psychopathology in a clinical sample of domestic violence perpetrators. *Law and Human Behavior, 30,* 571–586.

Huss, M. T., & Ralston, A. (2008). Do batterer subtypes actually matter? Treatment completion, treatment response, and recidivism across a batterer typology. *Criminal Justice and Behavior, 35,* 710–724.

Huston, K. (1984). Ethical decisions in treating battered women. *Professional Psychology: Research and Practice, 15,* 822–832.

Hwalek, M., Neale, A., Goodrich, C., & Quinn, K. (1996). The association of elder abuse and substance abuse in the Illinois Elder Abuse System. *The Gerontologist, 36,* 694–700.

Iliffe, G., & Steed, L. G. (2000). Exploring the counselor's experience of working with perpetrators and survivors of domestic violence. *Journal of Interpersonal Violence, 15,* 393–412.

Infante, D. A., & Wigley, C. J., III. (1986). Verbal aggressiveness: An interpersonal model and measure. Communication Monographs, 53, 61–69.

International Association of Marriage and Family Counselors (IAMFC, n.d.). IAMFC Ethical Codes. Retrieved November 29, 2010, from http://www.iamfconline.com/index.php?option=com_content&view=article&id=85&Itemid=109

Iverson, K. M., Shenk, C., & Fruzzetti, A. E. (2009). Dialectical Behavior Therapy for women victims of domestic abuse: A pilot study. *Professional Psychology: Research and Practice, 40,* 242–248.

Jackson-Gilfort, A., Mitrani, V. B., & Szapoczni, J. (2000). Conjoint couple's therapy in preventing violence in low income, African American couples: A case report. *Journal of Family Psychotherapy, 11,* 37–60.

Jacobson, N. (1994). Rewards and dangers in researching domestic violence. *Family Process, 33,* 81–85.

Jacobson, N., & Gottman, J. (1998). *When men batter women: New insights into ending abusive relationships.* New York: Simon & Schuster.

James, D. E., Schumm, W. R., Kennedy, C. E., Grigsby, C. C., Shectman, K. L., & Nochols, C. W. (1985). Characteristics of the Kansas Parental Satisfaction Scale among two samples of married parents. *Psychological Reports, 57,* 163–169.

James, S., & Mennen, F. (2001). Treatment outcome research: How effective are treatments for abused children? *Child and Adolescent Social Work Journal, 18,* 73–95.

Jeanjot, I., Barlow, P., & Rozenberg, S. (2008). Domestic violence during pregnancy: Survey of patients and healthcare providers. *Journal of Women's Health,* 17(4), 557–567

Jehu, D., Klassen, C., & Gazan, M. (1986). Cognitive restructuring of distorted beliefs associated with childhood sexual abuse. *Journal of Social Work and Human Sexuality, 4,* 49–69.

Jenkins, D. A., & Smith, T. E. (1994). Applying Delphi methodology in family therapy research. *Contemporary Family Therapy, 16,* 411–430.

Jenkins, P. (1996). Threads that link community and family violence: Issues for prevention. In R. L. Hampton, P. Jenkins, & T. P. Gullotta (Eds.), *Preventing violence in America* (pp. 33–52). Thousand Oaks, CA: Sage.

Jenkins, P., Hampton, R. L., & Gullotta, T. P. (1996). Understanding the social context of violent behaviors in families: Selected perspectives. In R. L. Hampton, P. Jenkins, & T. P. Gullotta (Eds.), *Preventing violence in America* (pp. 13–31). Thousand Oaks, CA: Sage.

Jenkins, S. R., & Baird, S. (2002). Secondary traumatic stress and vicarious trauma: A validational study. *Journal of Traumatic Stress, 15,* 423–432.

Jennings, A. F. (2004). *The Damaging Consequences of Violence and Trauma: Facts, Discussion points, and Recommendations for the Behavioral Health System.* Alexandria, VA. National Association of State Mental Health Program Directors (NASMHPD)/National Technical Assistance Center (NTAC).

Johnson, D. M., & Zlotnick, C. (2009). HOPE for battered women with PTSD in domestic violence shelters. *Professional Psychology: Research and Practice, 40,* 234–241.

Johnson, L. B., Todd, M., & Subramanian, G. (2005). Violence in police families: Work-family spillover. *Journal of Family Violence, 20,* 3–12.

Johnson, M. P. (2006). Gender symmetry and asymmetry in domestic violence. *Violence Against Women, 12,* 1003–1018.

Johnson, M. P. (2009). Differentiating among types of domestic violence: Implications for health marriages. In H. E. Peters & C. M. Kamp Dush (Eds.), *Marriage and family: Perspectives and complexities* (pp. 281–297). New York: Columbia University Press.

Johnson, M. P., & Ferraro, K. J. (2000). Research on domestic violence in the 1990s: Making distinctions. *Journal of Marriage and the Family, 62,* 948–963.

Johnson, M. P., & Leone, J. M. (2005). The differential effects of intimate terrorism and situational couple violence: Findings from the National Violence Against Women Survey. *Journal of Family Issues, 26,* 322–349.

Johnsona, R. M., Kotch, J. B., Catellier, D. J., Winsor, J. R., Dufort, V., Hunter, W., Amaya-Jackson, L. (2002). Adverse behavioral and emotional outcomes from child abuse and witnessed violence. *Child Maltreatment, 7,* 179–186.

Jones, A. S., & Fowler, T. S. (2009). A faith community-domestic violence partnership. *Social Work & Christianity, 36,* 415–429.

Jones, A. S., & Gondolf, E. W. (2001). Time-varying risk factors for reassault among batterer program participants. *Journal of Family Violence, 16,* 345–359.

Jones, A. S., & Gondolf, E. W. (2002). Assessing the effect of batterer program completion on reassault: An instrumental variables analysis. *Journal of Quantitative Criminology, 18,* 71–98.

Jones, D. P. H. (2001). False positives in the field of child maltreatment. *Child Abuse & Neglect, 25,* 1395–1396.

Jones, F., & Morris, M. (2007). Working with child sexual abuse: A systematic perspective on whether children need to tell their therapist details of the abuse for healing to take place. *Journal of Family Therapy, 29,* 222–237.

Jones, K. (2002). Group play therapy with sexually abused preschool children: Group behaviors and interventions. *Journal for Specialists in Group Work, 27,* 377–389.

Jones, L. P., & Gross, E. (2000). Perceptions and practice with domestic violence among child protective service workers. *Children and Youth Services Review, 22,* 355–371.

Jonson-Reid, M., Drake, B., Chung, S., & Way, I. (2003). Cross-type recidivism among child maltreatment victims and perpetrators. *Child Abuse & Neglect, 27,* 899–917.

Jory, B. (2004). The Intimate Justice Scale: An instrument to screen for psychological and physical violence in clinical practice. *Journal of Marital and Family Therapy, 30,* 29–44.

Jory, B., & Anderson, D. (2000a). Intimate justice II: Fostering mutuality, reciprocity, and accommodation in therapy for psychological abuse. *Journal of Marital and Family Therapy, 25,* 349–364.

Jory, B., & Anderson, D. (2000b). Intimate justice III: Healing the anguish of abuse and embracing the anguish of accountability. *Journal of Marital and Family Therapy, 26,* 329–340.

Jory, B., Anderson, D., & Greer, C. (1997). Intimate justice: Confronting issues of accountability, respect, and freedom in treatment for abuse and violence. *Journal of Marital and Family Therapy, 23,* 399–419.

Jouriles, E. N., McDonald, R., Rosenfield, D., Spiller, L., Corbitt-Shindler, D., Norwood, W. D., ... Ehrensaft, M. (2010). Improving parenting in families referred for child maltreatment: A randomized controlled trial examining effects of Project Support. *Journal of Family Psychology, 24,* 328–338.

Just, M. M. (2007). Issues in caregiving: Elder abuse and substance abuse. *Journal of Human Behavior in the Social Environment, 14,* 117–137.

Kahler, C. W., McCrady, B. S., & Epstein, E. E. (2003). Sources of distress among women in treatment with their alcoholic partners. *Journal of Substance Abuse Treatment, 24,* 257–265.

Kail, B. L. (2010). Motivating women with substance abuse and intimate partner violence. *Journal of Social Work Practice in the Addictions, 10,* 25–43.

Kaplow, J. B., & Widom, C. S. (2007). Age of onset of child maltreatment predicts long-term mental health outcomes. *Journal of Abnormal Psychology, 116,* 176–187.

Kaschak, E. (2001). Intimate betrayal: Domestic violence in lesbian relationships. *Women and Therapy, 23,* 1–5.

Kaufman Kantor, G., Hold, M. K., Mebert, C. J., Straus, M. A., Drach, K. M., Ricci, L. R., ... Brown, W. (2004). Development and preliminary psychometric properties of the Multidimensional Neglectful Behavior Scale—Child Report. *Child Maltreatment, 9,* 409–428.

Kaufman Kantor, G., & Little, L. (2003). Defining the boundaries of child neglect: When does domestic violence equate with parental failure to protect. *Journal of Interpersonal Violence, 18,* 338–355.

Kaura, S. A., & Lohman, B. J. (2007). Dating violence victimization, relationship satisfaction, mental health problems, and acceptability of violence: A comparison of men and women. *Journal of Family Violence, 22,* 367–381.

Kaye, D. K., Mirembe, F. M., Bantebya, G., Johansoon, A., & Ekstrom, A. M. (2006). Domestic violence during pregnancy and risk of low birthweight and maternal complications: A prospective cohort study at Mulago Hospital, Uganda. *Tropical Medicine and International Health, 11,* 1576–1584.

Kaye, L. W., Kay, D., & Crittenden, J. A. (2007). Intervention with abused older males: Conceptual and clinical perspectives. *Journal of Elder Abuse & Neglect, 19,* 153–172.

Kazmierczak, D. A., Smyth, N. J., & Wodarski, J. S. (1999). Screening and assessment instrument for alcohol and other drugs. *Family Therapy, 26,* 103–119.

Keller, K. (1994). Instructors take on domestic violence. *Women's Sports and Fitness, 16*(7), 20–26.

Kelley, S. D. M., & Moore, J. E. (2000). Abuse and violence in the lives of people with low vision: A national survey. *RE:view, 31,* 155–164.

Kellner, R. (1987). A symptom questionnaire. *The Journal of Clinical Psychiatry, 48,* 268–274.

Kelly, V. A. (2004). Psychological abuse of women: A review of the literature. *The Family Journal: Counseling and Therapy for Couples and Families, 12*(4), 383-388.

Kelly, J. B., & Johnson, M. P. (2008). Differentiation among types of intimate partner violence: Research update and implications for interventions. *Family Court Review, 46,* 476–499.

Kendall-Tackett, K. (2001). Chronic pain: The next frontier in child maltreatment research. *Child Abuse & Neglect, 28,* 997–1000.

Kendall-Tackett, K., Marshall, R., & Ness, K. (2003). Chronic pain syndromes and violence against women. *Women & Therapy, 26,* 45–56.

Kenny, M. (2009). Child sexual abuse prevention: Psychoeducational groups for preschoolers and their parents. *Journal for Specialists in Group Work, 34*(1), 24–42.

Kenny, M. C., & McEachern, A. G. (2000). Racial, ethnic, and cultural factors of childhood sexual abuse: A selected review of the literature. *Clinical Psychology Review, 20,* 905–922.

Kerker, B. D., & Dore, M. M. (2006). Mental health needs and treatment of foster youth: Barriers and opportunities. *American Journal of Orthopsychiatry, 76,* 138–147.

Kern, R., Libkuman, T. M., & Temple, S. L. (2007). Perceptions of domestic violence and mock jurors' sentencing decisions. *Journal of Interpersonal Violence, 22*(12), 1515–1535.

Kernsmith, P. (2005). Exerting power or striking back: A gendered comparison of motivations for domestic violence perpetration. *Violence and Victims, 20*(2), 173–185.

Kerwin, M. E. (2005). Collaboration between child welfare and substance-abuse fields: Combined treatment programs for mothers. *Journal of Pediatric Psychology, 30,* 581–597.

Kilpatrick, K. L. (2005). The Parental Empathy Measure: A new approach to assessing child maltreatment risk. *American Journal of Orthopsychiatry, 75,* 608–620.

Kilpatrick, D. G., Resick, P. A., & Williams, L. M. (2001). Fostering collaborations between violence against women researchers and practitioners. *Social Insight, 6,* 29–36.

Kimbrough-Melton, R. J., & Campbell, D. (2008). Strong communities for children: A community-wide approach to prevention of child abuse and neglect. *Family and Community Health, 31,* 100–112.

Kimmel, M. S. (2002). 'Gender symmetry' in domestic violence: A substantive and methodological research review. *Violence Against Women, 8,* 1332–1363.

Kiselica, M. S., & Morrill-Richards, M. (2007). Sibling maltreatment: The forgotten abuse. *Journal of Counseling and Development, 85,* 148–160.

Klostermann, K.C. & Fals-Stewart, W. (2006). Intimate partner violence and alcohol use: Exploring the role of drinking in partner violence and its implications for intervention. *Aggression and Violent Behavior: A Review Journal, 11,* 587–597.

Knapp, S. (2001). Ethical issues in personality assessment in forensic psychology. *Journal of Personality Assessment, 77,* 242–254.

Knickerbocker, L., Heyman, R., Slep, A., Jouriles, E., & McDonald, R. (2007). Co-occurrence of child and partner maltreatment definitions, prevalence, theory, and implications for assessment. *European Psychologist, 12,* 36–44

Ko, S., & Cosden, M. (2001). Do elementary school-based child abuse prevention programs work? A high school follow-up. *Psychology in the Schools, 38*(1), 57–66.

Kolko, D. J., Brown, E. J., & Berliner, L. (2002). Children's perceptions of their abusive experiences: Measurement and preliminary findings. *Child Maltreatment, 7,* 41–53.

Kolko, D. J., Cohen, J. A., Mannarino, A. P., Baumann, B. L., & Knudsen, K. (2009). Community treatment of child sexual abuse: A survey of practitioners in the National Child Traumatic Stress Network. *Administration and Policy in Mental Health, 36,* 37–49.

Kopp, B., & Miltenberger, R. G. (2009). Evaluating the acceptability of four versions of a child sexual abuse prevention program. *Child & Family Behavior Therapy, 31,* 192–202.

Korbin, J. E. (2002). Culture and child maltreatment: Cultural competence and beyond. *Child Abuse & Neglect, 26,* 637–644.

Kosberg, J. I., Lowenstein, A., Garcia, J. L., & Biggs, S. (2003). Study of elder abuse within diverse cultures. *Journal of Elder Abuse & Neglect, 15,* 71–89.

Koss, M. P., & White, J. W. (2008). National and global agendas on violence against women: Historical perspectives and consensus. *American Journal of Orthopsychiatry, 78,* 386–393.

Kotrla, K. (2010). Domestic minor sex trafficking in the United States. *Social Work, 55,* 181–187.

Krienert, J. L., Walsh, J. A., & Turner, M. (2009). Elderly in America: A descriptive study of elder abuse examining National Incident-Based Reporting System (NIBRS) data, 2000–2005. *Journal of Elder Abuse & Neglect, 21,* 325–345.

Kress, V.E., Protivnak, J.J., & Sadlack, L. (2008). Counseling clients involved with violent intimate partners: The mental health counselor's role in promoting client safety. *Journal of Mental Health Counseling, 30(*3), 200–210.

Kropp, P. (2008). Intimate partner violence risk assessment and management. *Violence and Victims, 23,* 202-220.

Kropp, R., & Hart, S. D. (2000). The Spousal Assault Risk Assessment (SARA) Guide: Reliability and validity in adult male offenders. *Law and Human Behavior, 24,* 101–118.

Kulwicki, A. D. (2002). The practice of honor crimes: A glimpse of domestic violence in the Arab world. *Issues in Mental Health Nursing, 23,* 77–87.

Kulwicki, A., Aswad, B., Carmona, T., & Ballout, S. (2010). Barriers in the utilization of domestic violence services among Arab immigrant women: Perceptions of professionals, service providers & community leaders. *Journal of Family Violence, 25,* 727–735.

Kumpfer, K. L. (2008). Why are there no effective child abuse prevention parenting interventions? *Substance Use and Misuse, 43,* 1262–1265.

Kvarfordt, C. L. (2010). Spiritual abuse and neglect of youth: Reconceptualizating what is known through an investigation of practitioners' experiences. *Journal of Religion & Spirituality in Social Work: Social Thought, 29,* 143–164.

Kwong, M. J., Bartholomew, K., Henderson, A. J. Z., & Trinke, S. J. (2003). The intergenerational transmission of relationship violence. *Journal of Family Psychology, 17,* 288–301.

Landsman, M. J., & Hartley, C. C. (2007). Attributing responsibility for child maltreatment when domestic violence is present. *Child Abuse & Neglect, 31,* 445–461.

Langeland, W., Draijer, N., & van den Brink, W. (2004). Psychiatric comorbidity in treatment-seeking alcoholics: The role of childhood trauma and perceived parental dysfunction. *Alcoholism: Clinical and Experimental Research, 28,* 441–447.

Langeland, W., van den Brink, W., & Draijer, N. (2002). Trauma, trauma-related distress, and perceived parental dysfunction: Associations with severity of drinking problems in treated alcoholics. *The Journal of Nervous and Mental Disease, 190,* 337–340.

Langhinrichsen-Rohling, J., Huss, M. T., & Ramsey, S. (2000). The clinical utility of batterer typologies. *Journal of Family Violence, 15,* 37–53.

LaTaillade, J. J., Epstein, N. B., & Werlinich, C. A. (2006). Conjoint treatment of intimate partner violence: A cognitive behavioral approach. *Journal of Cognitive Psychotherapy: An International Quarterly, 20,* 393–410.

Lawrence, G., & Kurpius, S. (2000). Legal and ethical issues involved when counseling minors in nonschool settings. *Journal of Counseling & Development, 78,* 130–136.

Lazarus, R. S., & Folkman, S. (1984). *Stress, appraisal, and coping.* New York: Springer.

Lee, M-Y. (2007). Discovering strengths and competencies in female domestic violence survivors: An application of Roberts' Continuum of the Duration and Severity of Woman Battering. *Brief Treatment and Crisis Intervention, 7,* 102–114.

Lee, M. Y., Uken, A., & Sebold, J. (2004). Accountability for change: Solution-focused treatment with domestic violence offenders. *Families in Society, 85,* 463–476.

Lee, R. K., Sanders Thompson, V. L., & Mechanic, M. B. (2002). Intimate partner violence and women of color: A call for innovations. *American Journal of Public Health, 92,* 530–534.

Lee, S., Lyvers, M., & Edwards, M. S. (2008). Childhood sexual abuse and substance abuse in relation to depression and coping. *Journal of Substance Use, 13,* 346–360.

Leisey, M., Kupstas, P. K., & Cooper, A. (2009). Domestic violence in the second half of life. *Journal of Elder Abuse and Neglect, 21,* 141–155.

Leonard, L. M., & Follette, V. M. (2002). Sexual functioning in women reporting a history of child sexual abuse: Review of the empirical literature and clinical implications. *Annual Review of Sex Research, 13,* 346–388.

Leone, J. M., Johnson, M. P., & Cohan, C. L. (2007). Victim help seeking: Differences between intimate terrorism and situational couple violence. *Family Relations, 56,* 427–439.

Leslie, R. S. (2003, March/April). Duty to report child abuse. *Family Therapy Magazine, 2*(2), 44–45. Retrieved February 6, 2009, from http://www.aamft.org/members/Resources/LRM_Plan/Legal/lgl_Child%20Abuse%20Rpt%20(2003).asp

Leventhal, J. J. (2001). A decline in the substantiated cases of child sexual abuse in the United States: Good news or false hope? *Child Abuse & Neglect, 25,* 1137–1138.

Leventhal, J. M. (2005). Getting prevention right: Maintaining the status quo is not an option. *Child Abuse & Neglect, 29,* 209–213.

Levesque, D. A., Gelles, R. J., & Velicer, W. F. (2000). Development and validation of a stages of change measure for men in batterer treatment. *Cognitive Therapy and Research, 34,* 175–199.

Levin, R. (1999). Participatory evaluation: Researchers and service providers as collaborators versus adversaries. *Violence Against Women, 5,* 1213–1227.

Levitt, H. M., & Ware, K. (2006a). 'Anything with two heads is a monster': Religious leaders' perspectives on marital equality and domestic violence. *Violence Against Women, 12,* 1169–1190.

Levitt, H. M., & Ware, K. N. (2006b). Religious leaders' perspectives on marriage, divorce, and intimate partner violence. *Psychology of Women Quarterly, 30,* 212–222.

Lewin, L., & Bergin, C. (2001). Attachment behaviors, depression, and anxiety in nonoffending mothers of child sexual abuse victims. *Child Maltreatment, 6,* 365–375.

Lewis, C. S., Griffing, S., Chu, M., Jospitre, T., Sage, R. E., Madry, L., & Primm, B. J. (2006). Coping and violence exposure as predictors of psychological functioning in domestic violence survivors. *Violence Against Women, 12,* 340–354.

Lewis, S. F., & Fremouw, W. (2000). Dating violence: A critical review of the literature. *Clinical Psychology Review, 21,* 105–127.

Lewis, S. F., Travea, L., & Fremouw, W. J. (2002). Characteristics of female perpetrators and victims of dating violence. *Violence and Victims, 17,* 593–606.

Lichtenstein, B. (2006). Domestic violence in barriers to health care for HIV-positive women. *AIDS Patient Care and STDS, 20,* 122–132.

Liefer, M., Kilbane, T., & Grossman, G. (2001). A three-generational study comparing the families of supportive and unsupportive mothers of sexually abused children. *Child Maltreatment, 6,* 353–364.

Lindhorst, T., Nurius, P., & Macy, R. J. (2005). Contextualized assessment with battered women: Strategic safety planning to cope with multiple harms. *Journal of Social Work Education, 41,* 331–352.

Lindquist, C. H., McKay, T., Clinton-Sherrod, A. M., Pollack, K. M., Lasater, B. M., & Hardison Walters, J. L. (2010). The role of employee assistance programs in workplace-based intimate partner violence intervention and prevention activities. *Journal of Workplace Behavioral Health, 25,* 46–64.

Linehan, M. M., Goldstein, J. L., Neilsen, S. L., & Chiles, J. A. (1983). Reasons for staying alive when you are thinking of killing yourself: The Reasons for Living Inventory. *Journal of Consulting and Clinical Psychology, 51,* 276–286.

Linver, M. R., Brooks-Gunn, J., & Cabrera, N. (2004). The Home Observation for Measurement of the Environment (HOME) Inventory: The derivation of conceptually designed subscales. *Parenting Science and Practice, 4,* 99–114.

Lipchik, E., Sirles, E. A., & Kubicki, A. D. (1997). Multifaceted approaches in spouse abuse treatment. *Journal of Aggression, Maltreatment, and Trauma, 1,* 131–148.

Lippert, T., Cross, T. P., Jones, L., & Walsh, W. (2009). Telling interviewers about sexual abuse: Predictors of child disclosure at forensic interviews. *Child Maltreatment, 14,* 100–113.

Littell, J. H. (2001). Client participation and outcomes of intensive family preservation services. *Social Work Research, 25,* 103–114.

Littell, J. H., & Girvin, H. (2005). Caregivers' readiness for change: Predictive validity in a child welfare sample. *Child Abuse & Neglect, 29,* 59–80.

Lloyd, S. A., & Emery, B. C. (2000). *The dark side of courtship: Physical and sexual aggression.* Thousand Oaks, CA: Sage.

Lo, H-T., & Fung, K. P. (2003). Culturally competent psychotherapy. *Canadian Journal of Psychiatry, 48,* 161–170.

Lock, T. G., Levis, D. J., & Rourke, P. A. (2005). The Sexual Abuse Questionnaire: A preliminary examination of a time and cost efficient method in evaluating the presence of childhood sexual abuse in adult patients. *Journal of Child Sexual Abuse, 14,* 1–26.

Locke, T., & Newcomb, M. (2003). Childhood maltreatment, parental alcohol/drug-related problems, and global parental dysfunction. *Professional Psychology: Research and Practice, 34,* 73–79.

Lohr, J. M., Bonge, D., Witte, T. H., Hamberger, L. K., & Langhinrichsen-Rohling, J. (2005). Consistency and accuracy of batterer typology identification. *Journal of Family Violence, 20,* 253–258.

Longo, R. (2004). An integrated experiential approach to treating young people who sexually abuse. *Journal of Child Sexual Abuse, 13,* 193–213.

Lord, S. A. (2008). Therapeutic work with trauma, revictimization, and perpetration: Bearing witness, offering hope, embracing despair. *Psychoanalytic Social Work, 15,* 110–131.

Lounds, J. J., Borkowski, J. G., & Whitman, T. L. (2004). Reliability and validity of the Mother-Child Neglect Scale. *Child Maltreatment, 9,* 371–381.

Lovibond, P. F., & Lovibond, S. H. (1995). The structure of negative emotional states: Comparison of the Depression Anxiety and Stress Scales (DASS) with the Beck Depression and Anxiety Inventories. *Behaviour Research and Therapy, 33,* 335–342.

Low, S. M., Monarch, N. D., Hartman, S., & Markman, H. (2002). Recent therapeutic advances in the prevention of domestic violence. In P. A. Schewe (Ed.), *Preventing violence in relationships: Interventions across the life span* (pp. 197–221). Washington, DC: American Psychological Association.

Lowe, W., Pavkov, T., Casanova, G., & Wetchler, J. (2005). Do American ethnic cultures differ in their definitions of child sexual abuse? *American Journal of Family Therapy, 33,* 147–166.

Lund, C. J., & Green, B. F. (2003). Developing a capacity for self-preservation and emergency management among battered families. *Journal of Family Violence, 18,* 181–192.

Lundqvist, G., Svedin C. G., Hansson, K., & Broman, I. (2006). Group therapy for women sexually abused as children: Mental health before and after group therapy. *Journal of Interpersonal Violence, 21,* 1665–1677.

Lundy, M., & Grossman, S. F. (2004). Elder abuse: Spouse/intimate partner abuse and family violence among elders. *Journal of Elder Abuse & Neglect, 16,* 85–102.

Lutzker, J., Tymchuk, A., & Bigelow, K. (2001). Applied research in child maltreatment: Practicalities and pitfalls. *Children's Services: Social Policy, Research, & Practice, 4,* 141–156.

Lynch, E. (2006). Home is where the hate is. *Nursing Standard, 20,* 26–27.

MacIntosh, H. B., & Johnson, S. (2008). Emotionally focused therapy for couples and child sexual abuse survivors. *Journal of Marital and Family Therapy, 34,* 298–315.

MacMillan, H. (2000). Child maltreatment: What we know in the year 2000. *The Canadian Journal of Psychiatry / La Revue canadienne de psychiatrie, 45,* 702–709.

Macmillan, R. (2009). The life course consequences of abuse, neglect, and victimization: Challenges for theory, data collection, and methodology. *Child Abuse & Neglect, 33,* 661–665.

Maiuro, R. D., & Eberle, J. A. (2008). State standards for domestic violence perpetrator treatment: Current status, trends, and recommendations. *Violence and Victims, 23,* 133–155.

Maiuro, R. D., Hagar, T. S., Lin, H., & Olson, N. (2001). Are current state standards for domestic violence perpetrator treatment adequately informed by research? A question of questions. *Journal of Aggression, Maltreatment, & Trauma, 5,* 21–44.

Maker, A. H., & Buttenheim, M. (2000). Parenting difficulties in sexual-abuse survivors: A theoretical framework with dual psychodynamic and cognitive-behavioral strategies for intervention. *Psychotherapy, 37,* 159–170.

Malesky, A., & Keim, J. (2001). Mental health professionals' perspectives on sex offender registry web-sites. *Sexual Abuse: Journal of Research and Treatment, 13,* 53–63.

Malik, N. M., Ward, K., & Janczewski, C. (2008). Coordinated community response to family violence: The role of domestic violence service organizations. *Journal of Interpersonal Violence, 23,* 933–955.

Malks, B., Schmidt, C. M., & Austin, M. J. (2002). Elder abuse prevention: A case study of the Santa Clara County Financial Abuse Specialist Team (FAST) Program. *Journal of Gerontological Social Work, 39,* 23–40.

Malmo, C., & Laidlaw, T. S. (2010). Symptoms of trauma and traumatic memory retrieval in adult survivors of childhood sexual abuse. *Journal of Trauma & Dissociation, 11,* 22–43.

Manders, J. E., & Stoneman, Z. (2009). Children with disabilities in the child protective services system: An analog study of investigation and case management. *Child Abuse & Neglect, 33,* 229–237.

Maniglio, R. (2009). The impact of child sexual abuse on health: A systematic review of reviews. *Clinical Psychology Review, 29,* 647–657.

Manly, J. T. (2005). Advances in research definitions of child maltreatment. *Child Abuse & Neglect, 29,* 425–439.

Margolin, G. (2000). Jacobson's domestic violence research: Empirical, social, political contributions. *Prevention & Treatment, 3,* 1–4.

Margolin, G., Gordis, E. B., Oliver, P. H., & Raine, A. (1995). A physiologically based typology of batterers—promising but preliminary: Comment on Gottman et al. (1995). *Journal of Family Psychology, 9,* 253–263.

Marsh, J.C., Ryan, J.P., Choi, S., & Testa, M.F. (2006). Integrated services for families with multiple problems: Obstacles to family reunification. *Children and Youth Services Review, 28,* 1074–1087.

Marshall, L. L., (1992a). Development of the severity of violence against women scale. *Journal of Family Violence, 7,* 103–121.

Marshall, L. L. (1992b). The severity of violence against men scale. *Journal of Family Violence, 7,* 189–203.

Martin, A. J., Berenson, K. R., Griffing, S., Sage, R. E., Madry, L., Bingham, L. E., & Primm, B. J. (2000). The process of leaving an abusive relationship: The role of risk assessments and decision-certainty. *Journal of Family Violence, 15,* 109–122.

Martin, S. L., Macy, R. J, Sullivan, K., & Magee, M. L. (2007). Pregnancy-associated violent deaths: The role of intimate partner violence. *Trauma, Violence, & Abuse, 8,* 135–148.

Martin, S. L., Moracco, K. E., Chang, J. C., Council, C. L., & Dulli, L. S. (2008). Substance abuse issues among women in domestic violence programs: Findings from North Carolina. *Violence Against Women, 14,* 985–997.

Martsolf, D. S., & Draucker, C. B. (2005). Psychotherapy approaches for adult survivors of childhood sexual abuse: An integrative review of outcomes research. *Issues in Mental Health Nursing, 26,* 801–825.

Maslach, C. (1996). *The Maslach Burnout Inventory* (3rd ed.). Palo Alto, CA: Consulting Psychologists Press.

Maslow, A. H. (1954). *Motivation and personality.* New York: Harper.

Matar Curnow, S. A. (1997). The Open Window Phase: Helpseeking and reality behaviors by battered women. *Applied Nursing Research, 10,* 128–135.

Matheny, K. B., Aycock, D. W., Curlette, W. L., & Junker, G. N. (2003). The Coping Resources Inventory for Stress: A measure of perceived resourcefulness. *Journal of Clinical Psychology, 59,* 1261–1277.

Mathews, T., Fawcett, S. B., & Sheldon, J. B. (2009). Effects of a peer engagement program on socially withdrawn children with a history of maltreatment. *Child & Family Behavior Therapy, 31,* 270–291.

Matthews, N. A. (2000). Generic violence prevention and gendered violence: Getting the message to mainstream audiences. *Violence Against Women, 6,* 311–331.

McAlpine, C., Marshall, C. C., & Doran, N. H. (2001). Combining child welfare and substance abuse services: A blended model of intervention. *Child Welfare, 80,* 129–149.

McCann, L., & Pearlman, L. A. (1990). Vicarious traumatization: A framework for understanding the psychological effects of working with victims. *Journal of Traumatic Stress, 3,* 131–149.

McClennen, J. C., Summers, A. B., & Daley, J. G. (2002). The Lesbian Partner Abuse Scale. *Research on Social Work Practice, 12,* 277–292.

McCloskey, K. A., & Fraser, J. S. (1997). Using feminist MRI brief therapy during initial contact with victims of domestic violence. *Psychotherapy, 34,* 433–446.

McCloskey, K. A., Sitaker, M., Grigsby, N., & Malloy, K. A. (2003). Characteristics of male batterers in treatment: An example of a localized program evaluation concerning attrition. *Journal of Aggression, Maltreatment, and Trauma, 8,* 67–95.

McCollum, E. E. (2008). Couples treatment for interpersonal violence: A review of outcome research literature and current clinical practices. *Violence and Victims, 23,* 187–201.

McDaniel, B., & Dillenburger, K. (2007). Can childhood neglect be assessed and prevented through childcare skills training? *Child Abuse Review, 16,* 120–129.

McDonnell, K. A., Gielen, A. C., O'Campo, P., & Burke, J. G. (2005). Abuse, HIV status, and health-related quality of life among a sample of HIV positive and HIV negative low income women. *Quality of Life Research, 14,* 945–957.

McFarlane, J. M., Groff, J. Y., O'Brien, J. A., & Watson, K. (2006). Secondary prevention of intimate partner violence: A randomized controlled trial. *Nursing Research, 55,* 52–61.

McFarlane, J., & Malecha, A. (2005). Sexual assault among intimates: Frequency, consequence, and treatments. Final report submitted to the National Institute of Justice. Retrieved December 1, 2010, from www.ncjrs.gov/pdffiles1/nij/grants/211678.pdf

McFarlane, J., Malecha, A., Gist, J., Watson, K., Batten, E., Hall, I., & Smith, S. (2002). An intervention to increase safety behaviors of abused women. *Nursing Research, 51,* 347–354.

McFarlane, J., Soeken, K., & Wiist, W. (2000). An evaluation of interventions to decrease intimate partner violence to pregnant women. *Public Health Nursing, 17,* 443–451.

McGoldrick, M., Gerson, R., & Petry, S. (2008). *Genograms: Assessment and intervention (3rd ed.).* New York: Norton.

McGregor, K., Thomas, D. R., & Read, J. (2006). Therapy for child sexual abuse: Women talk about helpful and unhelpful therapy experiences. *Journal of Child Sexual Abuse, 15,* 35–59.

McLaughlin, E. M., & Rozee, P. D. (2001). Knowledge about heterosexual versus lesbian battering among lesbians. *Women and Therapy, 23,* 39–58.

McLeod, A. L., Hays, D. G., & Chang, C. Y. (2010). Female intimate partner violence survivors' experiences with accessing resources. *Journal of Counseling and Development, 88,* 303–310.

McMahon, M., & Pence, E. (1996). Replying to Dan O'Leary. *Journal of Interpersonal Violence, 11,* 452–455.

McNary, S. W., & Black, M. M. (2003). Use of the Child Abuse Potential Inventory as a measure of treatment outcome. *Child Abuse & Neglect, 27,* 459–461.

Mears, D. P. & Visher, C. A. (2005). Trends in understanding and addressing domestic violence. *Journal of Interpersonal Violence, 20*(2), 204–211.

Meehan, J. C., & Holtzworth-Munroe, A. (2001). Heart rate reactivity in male batterers: Reply to Gottman (2001) and a second look at the evidence. *Journal of Family Psychology, 15,* 415–424.

Meehan, J. C., Holtzworth-Munroe, A., & Herron, K. (2001). Maritally violent men's heart rate reactivity to martial interactions: A failure to replicate the Gottman et al. (1995) typology. *Journal of Family Psychology, 15,* 394–408.

Meetoo, V., & Mirza, H. S. (2007). "There is nothing 'honourable' about honour killings": Gender, violence, and the limits of multiculturalism. *Women's Studies International Forum, 30,* 187–200.

Melhado, L. (2005). Women who report abuse during pregnancy have an elevated risk of adverse birth outcomes. *International Family Planning Perspectives, 31,* 204.

Merrick, M. T., Litrownik, A. J., Everson, M. D., & Cox, C. E. (2008). Beyond sexual abuse: The impact of other maltreatment experiences on sexualized behaviors. *Child Maltreatment, 13,* 122–132.

Merrill, G. S., & Wolfe, V. A. (2000). Battered gay men: An exploration of abuse, help seeking, and why they stay. *Journal of Homosexuality, 39,* 1–29.

Merritt-Gray, M., & Wuest, J. (1995). Counteracting abuse and breaking free: The process of leaving revealed through women's voices. *Health Care for Women International, 16,* 399–412.

Mersky, J. P., & Topitzes, J. (2010). Comparing early adult outcomes of maltreated and non-maltreated children: A prospective longitudinal investigation. *Children and Youth Services Review, 32,* 1086–1096.

Meyer, H., & Stein, N. (2004). Relationship violence prevention education in schools: What's working, what's getting in the way, and what are some future directions. *American Journal of Health Education, 35,* 198–204.

Migliaccio, T. A. (2002). Abused husbands: A narrative analysis. *Journal of Family Issues, 23,* 26–52.

Milardo, R. M. (1998). Gender asymmetry in common couple violence. *Personal Relationships, 5,* 423–438.

Millar, G. M., & Stermac, L. (2000). Substance abuse and childhood maltreatment: Conceptualizing the recovery process. *Journal of Substance Abuse Treatment, 19,* 175–182.

Miller, B. J., Cardona, J. R. P., & Hardin, M. (2007). The use of narrative therapy and internal family systems with survivors of childhood sexual abuse. *Journal of Feminist Family Therapy, 18,* 1–27.

Miller, E., Decker, M. R., Silverman, J. G., & Raj, A. (2007). Migration, sexual exploitation, and women's health: A case report from a community health center. *Violence Against Women, 13,* 486–497.

Millon, T., Davis, R., & Millon, C. (1997). *Millon Clinical Multiaxial Inventory-III* (2nd ed.). Minneapolis, MN: National Computer Systems.

Mills, L. G., Friend, C., Conroy, K., Fleck-Henderson, A., Krug, S., Magen, R. H., … Trudeau, J. H. (2000). Child protection and domestic violence: Training, practice, and policy issues. *Children and Youth Services Review, 22,* 315–332.

Mills, L. J., & Daniluk, J. C. (2002). Her body speaks: The experience of dance therapy for women survivors of child sexual abuse. *Journal of Counseling and Development, 80,* 77–85.

Milner, J., & Singleton, T. (2008). Domestic violence: Solution-focused practice with men and women who are violent. *Journal of Family Therapy, 30,* 29–53.

Milner, J. S. (1986). *The child abuse potential inventory manual* (2nd ed.). Webster: Psytec Inc.

Miltenburg, R., & Singer, E. (2000). A concept becomes a passion: Moral commitments and the affective development of the survivors of child abuse. *Theory & Psychology, 10,* 503–526.

Mishna, F. (2007). Meeting them "where they're at": Intensive school-based psychotherapy for children who have been maltreated. *Psychoanalytic Social Work, 14,* 15–42.

Mitchell, K. J., Finkelhor, D., & Wolak, J. (2010). Conceptualizing juvenile prostitution as child maltreatment: Findings from the National Juvenile Prostitution Study. *Child Maltreatment, 15,* 18–36.

Mitchell, S. L., & Lacour, M. M. (2001). Reported interpersonal violence and disposition decisions: The impact of client and counselor variables. *Journal of College Counseling, 4,* 142–152.

Mitchell-Clark, K., & Autry, A. (2004). *Preventing family violence: Lessons from the Community Engagement Initiative.* San Francisco: Family Violence Prevention Fund. Retrieved September 29, 2005, from http://endabuse.org/programs/children/files/Preventing2.pdf.

Mize, K. D., & Shackelford, T. K. (2008). Intimate partner homicide methods in heterosexual, gay, and lesbian relationships. *Violence and Victims, 23,* 98–114.

Moffitt, T. E., Caspi, A., Krueger, R. F., Magdol, L., Margolin, G., Silva, P. A., & Sydney, R. (1997). Do partners agree about abuse in their relationship? A psychometric evaluation of interpartner agreement. *Psychological Assessment, 9,* 47–56.

Molina, L. D., & Basinait-Smith, C. (1998). Revisiting the intersection between domestic abuse and HIV risk. *American Journal of Public Health, 88,* 1267–1278.

Moller, A. T., & Steel, H. R. (2002). Clinically significant change after cognitive restructuring for adult survivors of childhood sexual abuse. *Journal of Rational-Emotive & Cognitive-Behavioral Therapy, 20,* 49–64.

Moon, L. T., Wagner, W. G., & Kazelskis, R. (2000). Counseling sexually abused girls: The impact of sex of counselor. *Child Abuse & Neglect, 24,* 753–765.

Moos, R. H. (1995). Development and applications of new measures of life stressors, social resources, and coping responses. *European Journal of Psychological Assessment, 11,* 1–13.

Morey, L. C. (1991). *Personality Assessment Inventory.* Odessa, FL: Psychological Assessment Resources.

Morrison, A., & Ferris, J. (2002). The Satir model with female adult survivors of childhood sexual abuse. *Contemporary Family Therapy, 24,* 161–180.

Mourad, M. R., Levendosky, A. A., Bogat, G. A., & von Eye, A. (2008). Family psychopathology and perceived stress of both domestic violence and negative life events as predictors of women's mental health symptoms. *Journal of Family Violence, 23,* 661–670.

Mouradian, V. E. (2000). Abuse in intimate relationships: Defining the multiple dimensions and terms. National Violence Against Women Prevention Center. Retrieved December 6, 2010, from http://www.musc.edu/vawprevention/research/defining.shtml

Mouradian, V. E., Mechanic, M. B., & Williams, L. M. (2001). *Recommendations for establishing and maintaining successful researcher-practitioner collaborations.* Wellesley, MA: National Violence Against Women Prevention Research Center, Wellesley College. Retrieved August 29, 2008, from http://www.musc.edu/vawprevention/general/recom_report.pdf

Mouton, C. P., Larme, A. C., Alford, C. L., Talamantes, M. A., McCorkle, R. J., & Burge, S. K. (2005). Multiethnic perspectives on elder mistreatment. *Journal of Elder Abuse & Neglect, 17,* 21–44.

Murphy, G., Powell, S., Guzman, A., & Hays, S. (2007). Cognitive-behavioral treatment for men with intellectual disabilities and sexually abusive behavior: A pilot study. *Journal of Intellectual Disability Research, 51,* 902–912.

Murphy, R. A., Rosenheck, R. A., Berkowitz, S. J., & Marans, S. R. (2005). Acute service delivery in a police-mental health program for children exposed to violence and trauma. *Psychiatric Quarterly, 76,* 107–121

Murray, C. E. (2005). Prevention work: A professional responsibility for marriage and family counselors. *The Family Journal, 13,* 27–34.

Murray, C. E. (2006). Controversy, constraints, and context: Understanding family violence through family systems theory. *The Family Journal, 14,* 234–239.

Murray, C. E. (2007). Development of the Couples Resource Map Scales. *Journal of Couple and Relationship Therapy, 6,* 49–70.

Murray, C. E. (2009). Diffusion of innovation theory: A framework for bridging the research-practice gap in counseling. *Journal of Counseling and Development, 87,* 108–116.

Murray, C. E., & Kardatzke, K. N. (2007). Dating violence among college students: Key issues for college counselors. *Journal of College Counseling, 10,* 79–89.

Murray, C. E., Mobley, A. K., Buford, A. P., & Seaman-DeJohn, M. M. (2006/2007). Same-sex intimate partner violence: Dynamics, social context, and counseling implications. *The Journal of GLBT Issues in Counseling, 1*(4), 7–30.

Murray, C. E., & Smith, P. H. (2009). Perceptions of research and practice among domestic violence researchers. *Journal of Aggression, Conflict, and Peace Research, 1,* 4–21.

Murray, C. E., Smith, P. H., & Avent, J. (2010). Solutions to the research-practice gap in domestic violence: A modified Delphi study with domestic violence coalition leaders. *Journal of Aggression, Maltreatment, and Trauma, 19*(4), 424–449.

Murray, C. E., Smith, P. H., Fowler, T. S., White, J. W., & Stamey, M (2009). The Women's Leadership Network for Safe and Healthy Relationships: A case study. *Family Violence Prevention and Health Practice (E-Journal), 8* (Spring). Retrieved April 13, 2009, from http://endabuse.org/health/ejournal/2009/02/womens-leadership-network/

Murray, C. E., & Welch, M. (2010). Preliminary construction of a service provider-informed domestic violence research agenda. *Journal of Interpersonal Violence.* First published on-line on February 2, 2010, as doi:10.1177/0886260509354883.

Murty, S. A., Peek-Asa, C., Zwerling, C., Stromquist, A. M., Burmeister, L. F., & Merchant, J. A. (2003). Physical and emotional partner abuse reported by men and women in a rural community. *American Journal of Public Health, 93,* 1073–1075.

Musser, P. H., Semiatin, J. N., Taft, C. T., & Murphy, C. M. (2008). Motivational interviewing as a pregroup intervention for partner-violent men. *Violence and Victims, 23,* 539–557.

Myers, S., McLaughlin, M., & Warwick, K. (2003). 'The day the touching monster came': Solution-focused and narrative approaches to working with sexually inappropriate behavior. *Educational and Child Psychology, 20,* 76–89.

Nabi, R. L., Southwell, B., & Hornik, R. (2002). Predicting intentions versus predicting behaviors: Domestic violence prevention from a theory of reasoned action perspective. *Health Communication, 14,* 429–449.

Nahmiash, D., & Reis, M. (2000). Most successful intervention strategies for abused older persons. *Journal of Elder Abuse & Neglect, 12,* 53–70.

Nair, P., Schuler, M. E., Black, M. M., Kettinger, L., & Harrington, D. (2003). Cumulative environmental risk in substance abusing women: Early intervention, parenting stress, child abuse potential, and child development. *Child Abuse & Neglect, 27,* 997–1017.

Najavits, L. (2001). *Seeking safety: A treatment manual for PTSD and substance abuse.* New York: Guilford.

Nason-Clark, N. (2009). Christianity and the experience of domestic violence: What does faith have to do with it? *Social Work & Christianity, 36,* 379–393.

National Association of Social Workers (NASW). (2008). *Code of Ethics of the National Association of Social Workers.* Retrieved February 3, 2010, from http://www.naswdc.org/pubs/code/code.asp

National Center for Trauma-Informed Care. (2011). Retrieved on October 20, 2011, from http://www.samhsa.gov/nctic/

National Center on Elder Abuse. (2004). Substance abuse. Retrieved February 21, 2011, from http://www.ncea.aoa.gov/Main_Site/Library/CANE/CANE_Series/CANE_substance abuse.aspx

National Domestic Violence Hotline (NDVH). (n.d.). Domestic violence and the workplace. Retrieved August 24, 2009, from www.ndvh.org/million

National Network to End Domestic Violence. (2008). *WomensLaw.org: Because knowledge is power.* Retrieved May 17, 2012 from http://www.womenslaw.org/

National Violence Against Women Prevention Research Center. (May, 2001). *Fostering collaborations to prevention violence against women: Integrating findings from practitioner and researcher*

focus groups. Charleston, SC: Author. Retrieved August 29, 2008, from http://www.musc.edu/vawprevention/research/Report.pdf
Naughton, A., & Heath, A. (2001). Developing an early intervention programme to prevent child maltreatment. *Child Abuse Review, 10*, 85–96.
Navran, L. (1967). Communication and adjustment in marriage. *Family Process, 6,* 173–184.
Nelson, G., Laurendeau, M., & Chamberland, C. (2001). A review of programs to promote family wellness and prevent the maltreatment of children. *Canadian Journal of Behavioural Science/Revue Canadienne des Sciences du Comportement, 33*, 1–13.
Nelson-Gardell, D., & Harris, D. (2003). Childhood abuse history, secondary traumatic stress, and child welfare workers. *Child Welfare, 82,* 5–26.
Neumann, D. A., & Gamble, S. J. (1995). Issues in the professional development of psychotherapists: Countertransference and vicarious traumatization in the new trauma therapist. *Psychotherapy, 32,* 341–347.
Newcomb, M. D., & Locke, T. F. (2001). Intergenerational cycle of maltreatment: A popular concept obscured by methodological limitations. *Child Abuse & Neglect, 25,* 1219–1240.
Nolan, M., Carr, A., Fitzpartrick, C., O'Flaherty, A., Keary, K., Turner, R., ... Tobin, G.(2002). A comparison of two programmes for victims of child sexual abuse: A treatment outcome study. *Child Abuse Review, 11*, 103–123.
Noland, V. J., Liller, K. D., McDermott, R. J., Coulter, M. L., & Seraphine, A. E. (2004). Is adolescent sibling violence a precursor to college dating violence? *American Journal of Health Behavior, 28 (Supplement 1),* S13–S23.
Noll, J. G. (2005). Does childhood sexual abuse set in motion a cycle of violence against women?: What we know and what we need to learn. *Journal of Interpersonal Violence, 20,* 455–462.
Noonan, R. K., & Charles, D. (2009). Developing teen dating violence prevention strategies. *Violence Against Women, 15,* 1087–1105.
North Carolina Administrative Code. (2004). Title One, Chapter 17, Section .0700: Abuser treatment programs. Retrieved February 6, 2009, from http://www.nccfwdvc.com/documents/abuser/AbuserTreatmentProgramRules.pdf
North Carolina General Statutes. (2005). Chapter 7B, Article 3, § 7B-301: Duty to report abuse, neglect, dependency, or death due to maltreatment. Retrieved February 6, 2009, from http://www.ncga.state.nc.us/gascripts/Statutes/StatutesTOC.pl?Chapter=0007B
Nurcombe, B., Wooding, S., Marrington, P., Bickman, L., & Roberts, G. (2000). Child sexual abuse II: Treatment. *Australian and New Zealand Journal of Psychiatry, 34*, 92–97.
O'Campo, P., Kub, J., Woods, A., Garza, M., Jones, S., Gielen, A. C., ... Campbell, J. (2006). Depression, PTSD, and comorbidity related to intimate partner violence in civilian and military women. *Brief Treatment and Crisis Intervention, 6,* 99–110.
O'Connor, D., Hall, M. I., & Donnelly, M. (2009). Assessing capacity within a context of abuse or neglect. *Journal of Elder Abuse & Neglect, 21,* 156–169.
O'Farrell, T., J., Murphy, C. M., Stephan, S. H., Fals-Stewart, W., & Murphy, M. (2004). Partner violence before and after couples-based alcoholism treatment for male alcoholic patients: The role of treatment involvement and abstinence. *Journal of Consulting and Clinical Psychology, 72,* 202–217.
O'Farrell, T. J., Van Hutton, V., & Murphy, C. M. (1999). Domestic violence before and after alcoholism treatment: A two-year longitudinal study. *Journal of Studies on Alcohol, 60,* 317–321.
Ogle, R. L., & Baer, J. S. (2003). Addressing the service linkage problem: Increasing substance abuse treatment engagement using personalized feedback interventions in heavy-using female domestic violence shelter residents. *Journal of Interpersonal Violence, 18,* 1311–1324.
O'Halloran, T. M., & Linton, J. M. (2000). Stress on the job: Self-care resources for counselors. *Journal of Mental Health Counseling, 22,* 354–364.
O'Leary, K. D. (1996). Physical aggression in intimate relationships can be treated within a marital context under certain circumstances. *Journal of Interpersonal Violence, 11,* 450–452.
O'Leary, K. D. (1999). Psychological abuse: a variable deserving critical attention in domestic violence. *Violence and Victims, 14*, 3–23.

O'Leary, K. D. (2001). Conjoint therapy for partners who engage in physically aggressive behavior: Rationale and research. *Journal of Aggression, Maltreatment, and Trauma, 5,* 145–164.

O'Leary, K. D., Heyman, R. E., & Neidig, P. H. (1999). Treatment of wife abuse: A comparison of gender-specific and conjoint approaches. *Behavior Therapy, 30,* 475–505.

O'Leary, K. D., Malone, J., & Tyree, A. (1994). Physical aggression in early marriage: Prerelationship and relationship effects. *Journal of Consulting and Clinical Psychology, 62,* 594–602.

O'Leary, D., & Murphy, C. (1992). Clinical issues in the assessment of spouse abuse. In R. Ammerman & M. Hersen (Eds.), *Assessment of family violence: A clinical and legal sourcebook* (pp. 26–46). New York: Wiley.

O'Leary, K. D., & Schumacher, J. A. (2003). The association between alcohol use and intimate partner violence: Linear effect, threshold effect, or both? *Addictive Behaviors, 28,* 1575–1585.

O'Leary, K. D., Woodin, E. M., & Fritz, P. A. T. (2006). Can we prevent the hitting? Recommendations for preventing intimate partner violence between young adults. *Journal of Aggression, Maltreatment, & Trauma, 13,* 121–178.

Olson, D. E., & Stalans, L. J. (2001). Violent offenders on probation: Profile, sentence, and outcome differences among domestic violence and other violent probationers. *Violence Against Women, 7,* 1164–1185.

Olson, L. N. (2002). Exploring "common couple violence" in heterosexual romantic relationships. *Western Journal of Communication, 66,* 104–128.

Ondersma, S. J., Chaffin, M. J., Mullins, S. M., & LeBreton, J. M. (2005). A brief form of the Child Abuse Potential Inventory: Development and validation. *Journal of Clinical Child and Adolescent Psychology, 34,* 301–311.

Oosterhoorn, R., & Kendrick, A. (2001). No sign of harm: Issues for disabled children communicating about abuse. *Child Abuse Review, 10,* 243–253.

Orcutt, H. K., Garcia, M., & Pickett, S. M. (2005). Female-perpetrated intimate partner violence and romantic attachment style in a college student sample. *Violence and Victims, 20,* 287–302.

Osofsky, J. D. (2003). Prevalence of children's exposure to domestic violence and child maltreatment: Implications for prevention and intervention. *Clinical Child and Family Psychology Review, 6,* 161–170.

Ostertag, J. (2002). Unspoken stories: Music therapy with abused children. *Canadian Journal of Music Therapy, 9,* 10–29.

Paavilainen, E., & Åstedt-Kurki, P. (2003). Functioning of child maltreating families: Lack of resources for caring within the family. *Scandinavian Journal of Caring Sciences, 17,* 139–147.

Page, C., Conner, T., Prokhorov, A., Fang, Y., & Post, L. (2009). The effect of care setting on elder abuse: Results from a Michigan survey. *Journal of Elder Abuse & Neglect, 21,* 239–252.

Paine, M. L., & Hansen, D. J. (2002). Factors influencing children to self-disclose sexual abuse. *Clinical Psychology Review, 22,* 271–295.

Paivio, S. C., Hall, I. E., Holowaty, K. A. M., Jellis, J. B., & Tran, N. (2001). Imaginal confrontation for resolving child abuse issues. *Psychotherapy Research, 11,* 433–453.

Paivio, S. C., & Laurent, C. (2001). Empathy and emotion regulation: Reprocessing memories of childhood abuse. *In Session: Psychotherapy in Practice, 57,* 213–226.

Pan, A., Daley, S., Rivera, L. M., Williams, K., Lingle, D., & Reznik, V. (2006). Understanding the role of culture in domestic violence: The Ahimsa Project for Safe Families. *Journal of Immigrant and Minority Healht, 8,* 35–43.

Pardeck, J. T. (2004). Treating child abuse and neglect with family therapy intervention. *Family Therapy, 31,* 17–32.

Parks, K. A., Hequembourg, A. L., & Dearing, R. L. (2008). Women's social behavior when meeting new men: The influence of alcohol and childhood sexual abuse. *Psychology of Women Quarterly, 32,* 145–158.

Parra-Cardona, J.R., Meyer, E., Schiamberg, L., Post, L. (2007). Elder abuse and neglect in Latino families: An ecological and culturally relevant theoretical framework for clinical practice. *Family Process, 46*(4), 451–470.

Parrott, D. J., Drobes, D. J., Saladin, M. E., Coffey, S. F., & Dansky, B. S. (2003). Perpetration of partner violence: Effects of cocaine and alcohol dependence and posttraumatic stress disorder. *Addictive Behaviors, 28,* 1587–1602.

Patterson, M., & Malley-Morrison, K. (2006). A cognitive-ecological approach to elder abuse in five cultures: Human rights and education. *Educational Gerontology, 32,* 73–82.

Paulus, D. L. (1991). BIDR reference manual for Version 6. Unpublished manuscript. University of British Columbia.

Paymar, M., & Barnes, G. (n.d.). Countering confusion about the Duluth Model. Retrieved September 20, 2010, from http://www.theduluthmodel.org/research.php

Pearson, Q. M. (1994). Treatment techniques for adult female survivors of childhood sexual abuse. *Journal of Counseling and Development, 73,* 32–37.

Peckham, N. G., Corbett, A., Howlett, S., McKee, A., & Pattison, S. (2007). The delivery of a survivors' group for learning disabled women with significant learning disabilities who have been sexually abused. *British Journal of Learning Disabilities, 35,* 236–244.

Peckham, N. G., Howlett, S., & Corbett, A. (2007). Evaluating a survivors group pilot for women with significant intellectual disabilities who have been sexually abused. *Journal of Applied Research on Intellectual Disabilities, 20,* 308–322.

Peleikis, D. W., & Dahl, A. A. (2005). A systematic review of empirical studies of psychotherapy with women who were sexually abused as children. *Psychotherapy Research, 15,* 304–315.

Pelletier, L. G., Tuson, K. M., & Haddad, N. K. (1997). Client motivation for therapy scale: A measure of intrinsic motivation, extrinsic motivation, and amotivation for therapy. *Journal of Personality Assessment, 68,* 414–435.

Peluso, P. R., & Kern, R. M. (2002). An Adlerian model for assessing and treating the perpetrators of domestic violence. *The Journal of Individual Psychology, 58,* 88–103.

Pence, E. & Paymar, M. (1993). *Education groups for men who batter: The Duluth Model.* New York: Springer.

Pepin, E. N., & Banyard, V. L. (2006). Social support: A mediator between child maltreatment and developmental outcomes. *Journal of Youth and Adolescence, 35,* 617–630.

Perez, P. J., & Rasmussen, K. (1997). An ounce of prevention: A model for working with couples at-risk for battering. *Contemporary Family Therapy, 19,* 229–251.

Perron, B. E., & Hiltz, B. S. (2006). Burnout and secondary trauma among forensic interviewers of abused children. *Child and Adolescent Social Work Journal, 23,* 216–234.

Peters, J. (2008). Measuring myths about domestic violence: Development and initial validation of the Domestic Violence Myth Acceptance Scale. *Journal of Aggression, Maltreatment, and Trauma, 16,* 1–21.

Peters, R., & Barlow, J. (2003). Systematic review of instruments designed to predict child maltreatment during the antenatal and postnatal periods. *Child Abuse Review, 12,* 416–439.

Peterson, L., Tremblay, G., Ewigman, B., & Popkey, C. (2002). The parental daily diary: A sensitive measure of the process of change in a child maltreatment prevention program. *Behavior Modification, 26,* 627–647.

Peterson, L., Tremblay, G., Ewigman, B., & Saldana, L. (2003). Multilevel selected primary prevention of child maltreatment. *Journal of Consulting and Clinical Psychology, 71,* 601–612.

Phelan, M. B. (2007). Screening for intimate partner violence in medical settings, *Trauma, Violence, & Abuse, 8,* 199–213.

Phillips, A., & Daniluk, J. C. (2004). Beyond "survivor": How childhood sexual abuse informs the identity of adult women at the end of the therapeutic process. *Journal of Counseling & Development, 82,* 177–184.

Pifalo, T. (2002). Pulling out the thorns: Art therapy with sexually abuse children and adolescents. *Art Therapy, 19,* 12–22.

Pifalo, T. (2007). Jogging the cogs: Trauma-focused art therapy and cognitive behavioral therapy with sexually abused children. *Art Therapy, 24,* 170–175.

Pitt, E. L. (2000). Domestic violence in gay and lesbian relationships. *Gay and Lesbian Medical Association Journal, 4,* 195–196.

Plichta, S. B. (2004). Intimate partner violence and physical health consequences. *Journal of Interpersonal Violence, 19,* 1296–1323.

Ploeg, J., Fear, J., Hutchison, B., MacMillan, H., & Bolan, G. (2009). A systematic review of interventions for elder abuse. *Journal of Elder Abuse & Neglect, 21,* 187–210.

Podnieks, E., & Wilson, S. (2003). An exploratory study of responses to elder abuse in faith communities. *Journal of Elder Abuse & Neglect, 15,* 137–162.

Poorman, P. B. (2001). Forging community links to address abuse in lesbian relationships. In E. Kaschak (Ed.), *Intimate betrayal: Domestic violence in lesbian relationships* (pp. 7–24). Binghamton, NY: Haworth.

Popescu, M., Drumm, R., Mayer, S., Cooper, L., Foster, T., Seifert, M., ... Dewan, S. (2009). "Because of my beliefs that I had acquired from the church...": Religious belief-based barriers for Adventist women in domestic violence relationships. *Social Work & Christianity, 36,* 394–414.

Potoczniak, M. J., Mourot, J. E., Crosbie-Burnett, M., & Potoczniak, D. J. (2003). Legal and psychological perspectives on same-sex domestic violence: A multisystemic approach. *Journal of Family Psychology, 17,* 252–259.

Potter, H. (2007). Battered Black women's use of religious services and spirituality for assistance in leaving abusive relationships. *Violence Against Women, 13,* 262–284.

Powell, M. E., & Berman, J. (2006). Effects of dependency on compliance rates among elder abuse victims at the New York City Department for the Aging, Elderly Crime Victim's Unit. *Journal of Gerontological Social Work, 46,* 229–247.

Price, D. M. (2004). Rebuilding shattered families: Disclosure, clarification, and reunification of sexual abusers, victims, and their families. *Sexual Addiction and Compulsivity, 11,* 187–221.

Price, J. L., Hilsenroth, M. J., Callahan, K. L., Petretic-Jackson, P. A., & Bonge, D. (2004). A pilot study of psychodynamic psychotherapy for adult survivors of childhood sexual abuse. *Clinical Psychology and Psychotherapy, 11,* 378–391.

Price, J. L., Hilsenroth, M. J., Petretic-Jackson, P. A., & Bonge, D. (2001). A review of individual psychotherapy outcomes for adult survivors of childhood sexual abuse. *Clinical Psychology Review, 21,* 1095–1121.

Price, J. M., Chamberlain, P., Landsverk, J., Reid, J. B., Leve, L. D., & Laurent, H. (2008). Effects of a foster parent training intervention on placement changes of children in foster care. *Child Maltreatment, 13,* 64–75.

Prochaska, J. O., & DiClemente, C. C. (1983). Stages and process of self-change of smoking: Toward an integrative model of change. *Journal of Consulting and Clinical Psychology, 51,* 390–395.

Prochaska, J. O., Velicer, W. F., Rossi, J. S., Goldstein, M. G., Marcus, B. H., Rakowski, W., ... Rossi, S. R. (1994). Stages of change and decisional balance for 12 problem behaviors. *Health Psychology, 13,* 39–46.

Procidano, M. E., & Heller, K. (1983). Measures of perceived social support from friends and from family: Three validation studies. *American Journal of Community Psychology, 11,* 1–24.

Radhakrishna, A., Bou-Saada, I. E., Hunter, W. M., Catellier, D. J., & Kotch, J. B. (2001). Are father surrogates a risk factor for child maltreatment? *Child Maltreatment, 6,* 281–289.

Raj, A., & Silverman, J. G. (2002). Intimate partner violence against South Asian women in Greater Boston. *Journal of the American Medical Women's Association, 57,* 111–114.

Ramachandran, S., Yonas, M. A., Silvestre, A. J., & Burke, J. G. (2010). Intimate partner violence among HIV-positive persons in an urban clinic. *AIDS Care, 22,* 1536–1543.

Ramirez, I. L, & Straus, M. A. (2006). The effect of question order on disclosure of intimate partner violence: An experimental test using the Conflict Tactics Scales. *Journal of Family Violence, 21,* 429–440.

Range, L. M., & Knott, E. C. (1997). Twenty suicide assessment instruments: Evaluation and recommendations. *Death Studies, 21,* 25–58.

Reinert, D., & Edwards, C. (2009). Attachment theory, childhood mistreatment, and religiosity. *Psychology of Religion and Spirituality, 1,* 25–34.

Reinhard, M. J., Wolf, G., & Cozolino, L. (2010). Using the MMPI to assess reported cognitive disturbances and somatization as a core feature of complex PTSD. *Journal of Trauma and Dissociation, 11,* 57–72.

Rentz, E. D., Martin, S. L., Gibbs, D. A., Clinton-Sherrod, M., Hardison, J., & Marshall, S. W. (2006). Family violence in the military: A review of the literature. *Trauma, Violence, and Abuse, 7,* 93–108.

Reyome, N. D. (2010). The effect of childhood emotional maltreatment on the emerging attachment system and later intimate relationships. *Journal of Aggression, Maltreatment, and Trauma, 19,* 1–4.

Rhatigan, D. L., & Axsom, D. K. (2006). Using the Investment Model to understand battered women's commitment to abusive relationships. *Journal of Family Violence, 21,* 153–162.

Rhodes, K. V., & Levinson, W. (2003). Interventions for intimate partner violence against women: Clinical applications. *JAMA: Journal of the American Medical Association, 289,* 601–605.

Ricci, R. J., & Clayton, C. A. (2008). Trauma resolution treatment as an adjunct to standard treatment for child molesters: A qualitative study. *Journal of EMDR Practice and Research, 2,* 41–50.

Riddell, T., Ford-Gilboe, M., & Liepert, B. (2009). Strategies used by rural women to stop, avoid, or escape from intimate partner violence. *Health Care for Women International, 30,* 134–159.

Riger, S. (1999). Guest editor's introduction: Working together: challenges in collaborative research on violence against women. *Violence Against Women, 5,* 1099–1117.

Ringel, S., & Park, J. (2008). Intimate partner violence in the Evangelical community: Faith-based interventions and implications for practice. *Journal of Religion & Spirituality in Social Work: Social Thought, 27,* 341–360.

Rittner, B., & Dozier, C. D. (2000). Effects of court-ordered substance abuse treatment in child protective services cases. *Social Work, 45,* 131–140.

Rivers, M. J. (2005). Navajo women and abuse: The context for their troubled relationships. *Journal of Family Violence, 20,* 83–89.

Rivett, M. (2008). Commentary: Chapters in a book: Putting solution-focused practice into context. *Journal of Family Therapy, 30,* 54–59.

Rivett, M., & Rees, A. (2004). Dancing on a razor's edge: Systemic group work with batterers. *Journal of Family Therapy, 26,* 142–162.

Robarts, J. (2006). Music therapy with sexually abused children. *Clinical Child Psychology and Psychiatry, 11,* 249–269.

Rodenburg, F. A., & Fantuzzo, J. W. (1993). The Measure of Wife Abuse: Steps toward the development of a comprehensive assessment technique. *Journal of Family Violence, 8,* 203–228.

Rodriguez, C. M., & Henderson, R. C. (2010). Who spares the rod? Religious orientation, social conformity, and child abuse potential. *Child Abuse & Neglect, 34,* 84–94.

Roffman, R., Edleson, J., Neighbors, C., Mbilinyi, L., & Walker, D. (2008). The men's domestic abuse check-up: A protocol for reaching the nonadjudicated and untreated man who batters and who abuses substances. *Violence Against Women, 14*(5), 589–605. doi:10.1177/1077801208315526

Rogers, B., McGee, G., Vann, A., Thompson, N., & Williams, O. J. (2003). Substance abuse and domestic violence: Stories of practitioners that address the co-occurrence among battered women. *Violence Against Women, 9,* 590–598.

Rolfe, A., Dalton, S., Krishnan, M., Orford, J., Mehdikhani, M., Cawley, J., & Ferrins-Brown, M. (2006). Alcohol, gender, aggression and violence: Findings from the Birmingham Untreated Heavy Drinkers Project. *Journal of Substance Use, 11,* 343–358.

Romero, V., Donohue, B., & Allen, D. N. (2010). Treatment of concurrent substance dependence, child neglect, and domestic violence: A single case examination involving family behavior therapy. *Journal of Family Violence, 25,* 287–295.

Ronan, G. F., Dreer, L. E., Dollard, K. M., & Ronan, D. W. (2004). Violent couples: Coping and communication skills. *Journal of Family Violence, 19,* 131–137.

Ronel, N., & Claridge, H. (2003). The powerlessness of control: A unifying model for the treatment of male battering and substance addiction. *Journal of Social Work Practice in the Addictions, 3,* 57–76.

Rose, R. C., House, A. A., & Stepleman, L. M. (2010). Intimate partner violence and its effects on the health of African-American HIV-positive women. *Psychological Trauma: Theory, Research, Practice, and Policy, 2,* 311–317.

Rosen, K. H., & Bezold, A. (1996). Dating violence prevention: A didactic support group for young women. *Journal of Counseling and Development, 74,* 521–525.

Rosen, K. H., Matheson, J. L., Stith, S. M., McCollum, E. E., & Locke, L. D. (2003). Negotiated time-out: A de-escalation tool for couples. *Journal of Marital and Family Therapy, 29,* 291–298.

Rosenbaum, A., & Leisring, P. A. (2001). Group intervention programs for batterers. *Journal of Aggression, Maltreatment, and Trauma, 5,* 57–71.

Rosenberg, T. & Pace, M. (2006). Burnout among mental health professionals: Special considerations for the marriage and family therapist, *Journal of Marital and Family Therapy, 32*(1), 87–99.

Ross, G., & O'Carroll, P. (2004). Cognitive behavioural psychotherapy intervention in childhood sexual abuse: Identifying new directions from the literature. *Child Abuse Review, 13,* 51–64.

Rountree, M. A., Pomeroy, E. C., & Marsiglia, F. F. (2008). Domestic violence shelters as prevention agents for HIV/AIDS? *Health & Social Work, 33,* 221–228.

Rowan, A. B., & Foy, D. W. (1993). Post-traumatic stress disorder in child sexual abuse survivors: A literature review. *Journal of Traumatic Stress, 6,* 3–20.

Ruffolo, M. C., Evans, M. E., & Lukens, E. P. (2003). Primary prevention programs for children in the social service system. *Journal of Primary Prevention, 23,* 425–450.

Runyon, M. K., Deblinger, E., Ryan, E. E., & Thakkar-Kolar, R. (2004). An overview of child physical abuse: Developing an integrated parent-child cognitive-behavioral treatment approach. *Trauma, Violence, and Abuse, 5,* 65–85.

Russell, B. S., Britner, P. A., & Woolard, J. L. (2007). The promise of primary prevention home visiting programs: A review of potential outcomes. *Journal of Prevention & Intervention in the Community, 34,* 129–147.

Russo, N. F. (2008). Call to action: Reducing interpersonal violence across the lifespan. *American Journal of Orthopsychiatry, 78,* 383–385.

Rynerson, B. C., & Fishel, A. H. (1993). Domestic violence prevention training: Participant characteristics and treatment outcomes. *Journal of Family Violence, 8,* 253–366.

Saakvitne, K. W. (2000). Commentary on Clinical Protocol. *Psychoanalytic Inquiry, 20,* 1.

Sabatelli, R. M. (1984). The Marital Comparison Level Index: A measure for assessing outcomes relative to expectations. *Journal of Marriage and the Family, 46,* 651–662.

Sabia, J. J. (2004). Alcohol consumption and domestic violence against mothers. *The Journal of Mental Health Policy and Economics, 7,* 191–205.

Sabol, W. J., Coulton, C. J., & Korbin, J. E. (2004). Building community capacity for violence prevention. *Journal of Interpersonal Violence, 19,* 322–340.

Sackett, L. A., & Saunders, D. G. (1999). The impact of different forms of psychological abuse on battered women. *Violence and Victims, 14,* 105–177.

Sacks, J. Y., McKendrick, K., & Banks, S. (2008). The impact of early trauma and abuse on residential substance abuse treatment outcomes for women. *Journal of Substance Abuse Treatment, 34,* 90–100.

Sadowski, C. M., & Friedrich, W. N. (2000). Psychometric properties of the Trauma Symptom Checklist for Children (TSCC) with psychiatrically hospitalized adolescents. *Child Maltreatment, 5,* 364–372.

Sanders, M. R., Cann, W., & Markie-Dadds, C. (2003). Why a universal population-level approach to the prevention of child abuse is essential. *Child Abuse Review, 12,* 145–154.

Sato-DiLorenzo, A., & Sharps, P. W. (2007). Dangerous intimate partner relationships and women's mental health and health behaviors. *Issues in Mental Health Nursing, 28,* 837–848.

Saul, J., Duffy, J., Noonan, R., Lubell, K., Wandersman, A., Flaspohler, P., ... Dunville, R. (2008). Bridging science and practice in violence prevention: Addressing ten key challenges. *American Journal of Community Psychology, 41,* 197–205.

Saul, J., Wandersman, A., Flaspohler, P., Duffy, J., Lubell, K., & Noonan, R. (2008). Research and action for bridging science and practice in prevention. *American Journal of Community Psychology, 41,* 165–170.

Saunders, D. G. (1996). Feminist-cognitive-behavioral and process-psychodynamic treatments for men who batter: Interaction of abuser traits and treatment models. *Violence and Victims, 11,* 393–414.

Saunders, D. G. (2001). Developing guidelines for domestic violence offender programs: What can we learn from related fields and current research? *Journal of Aggression, Maltreatment, and Trauma, 5,* 235–248.

Sawyer, G. K., Tsao, E. H., Hansen, D. J., & Flood, M. F. (2006). Weekly Problems Scales: Instruments for sexually abused youth and their nonoffending parents in treatment. *Child Maltreatment, 11,* 34–48.

Saxe, G. N., Ellis, B., Fogler, J., Hansen, S., & Sorkin, B. (2005). Comprehensive care for traumatized children. *Psychiatric Annals, 35,* 443–448.

Saywitz, K. J., Mannarino, A. P., Berliner, L., & Cohen, J. A. (2000). Treatment for sexually abused children and adolescents. *American Psychologist, 55,* 1040–1049.

Scannapieco, M., & Connell-Carrick, K. (2007). Assessment of families who have substance abuse issues: Those who maltreat their infants and toddlers and those who do not. *Substance Use & Misuse, 42,* 1545–1553.

Schacht, R. L., Dimidjian, S., George, W. H., & Berns, S. B. (2009). Domestic violence assessment procedures among couple therapists. *Journal of Marital and Family Therapy, 35,* 47–59.

Schewe, P. A. (2008). Direct service recommendations for children and caregivers exposed to community and domestic violence. *Best Practices in Mental Health, 4,* 31–47.

Schewe, P. A., & Bennett, L. W. (2002). Evaluating prevention programs: Challenges and benefits of measuring outcomes. In P. A. Schewe (Ed.), *Preventing violence in relationships: Interventions across the life span* (pp. 247–261). Washington, DC: American Psychological Association.

Schmidt, M. C., Kolodinsky, J. M., Carsten, G., Schmidt, F. E., Larson, M., & MacLachlan, C. (2007). Short term change in attitude and motivating factors to change abusive behavior of male batterers after participating in a group intervention program based on the pro-feminist and cognitive-behavioral approach. *Journal of Family Violence, 22,* 91–100.

Schultz, P., Remick-Barlow, G., & Robbins, L. (2007). Equine-assisted psychotherapy: A mental health promotion/intervention modality for children who have experienced intra-family violence. *Health & Social Care in the Community, 15,* 265–271.

Schumacher, J. A., Fals-Stewart, W., & Leonard, K. E. (2003). Domestic violence treatment referrals for men seeking alcohol treatment. *Journal of Substance Abuse Treatment, 24,* 279–283.

Schumacher, J. A., Slep, A. M., & Heyman, R. E. (2001). Risk factors for child neglect. *Aggression and Violent Behavior, 6,* 231–254.

Schumm, J. A., O'Farrell, T. J., Murphy, C. M., & Fals-Stewart, W. (2009). Partner violence before and after couples-based alcoholism treatment for female alcoholic patients. *Journal of Consulting and Clinical Psychology, 77,* 1136–1146.

Schumm, W. R., Paff-Bergen, L. A., Hatch, R. C., Obiorah, F. C., Copeland, J. M., Meens, L. D., & Bugaighis, M. A. (1986). Concurrent and discriminant validity of the Kansas Marital Satisfaction Scale. *Journal of Marriage and the Family, 48,* 381–387.

Schwartz, J. P., Griffin, L. D., Russell, M. M., & Frontaura-Duck, S. (2006). Prevention of dating violence on college campuses: An innovative program. *Journal of College Counseling, 9,* 90–96.

Scott, K. L., & Crooks, C. V. (2004). Effecting change in maltreating fathers: Critical principles for intervention planning. *Clinical Psychology: Science and Practice, 11,* 95–111.

Scott, K. L., & Crooks, C. V. (2007). Preliminary evaluation of an intervention program for maltreating fathers. *Brief Treatment and Crisis Intervention, 7,* 224–238.

Scott, K. L., & Wolfe, D. A. (2003). Readiness to change as a predictor of outcome in batterer treatment. *Journal of Consulting and Clinical Psychology, 71,* 879–889.

Sedlak, A.J., Mettenburg, J., Basena, M., Petta, I., McPherson, K., Greene, A., and Li, S. (2010). *Fourth National Incidence Study of Child Abuse and Neglect (NIS–4): Report to Congress, Executive*

Summary. Washington, DC: U.S. Department of Health and Human Services, Administration for Children and Families

Seeley, S., Perosa, S., & Perosa, L. (2004). A validation study of the Adolescent Dissociative Experiences Scale. *Child Abuse & Neglect, 28*, 755–769.

Self-Brown, S., & Whitaker, D. J. (2008). Introduction to the special issue on using technology to address child maltreatment: Prevention, intervention, and research. *Child Maltreatment, 13,* 319.

Serritella, D. A. (1992). Domestic violence as addiction. In L. L'Abate, J. E. Farrar, & D. A. Serritella (Eds.), *Handbook of differential treatments for addictions* (pp. 113–122). Boston: Allyn and Bacon.

Shamai, M. (1995). Using rituals in couple therapy in cases of wife battering. *Journal of Family Therapy, 17,* 383–395.

Shapiro, F. (1989). Efficacy of the eye movement desensitization procedure in the treatment of traumatic memories. *Journal of Traumatic Stress, 2*, 199–223.

Shapiro, J. P., Burkey, W. M., Dorman, R. L., & Welker, C. J. (1996). Job satisfaction and burnout in child abuse professionals: Measure development, factor analysis, and job characteristics. *Journal of Child Sexual Abuse, 5,* 21–38.

Shapiro, J. P., Dorman, R. L., Burkey, W. M., & Welker, C. J. (1999). Predictors of job satisfaction and burnout in child abuse professionals: Coping, cognition, and victimization history. *Journal of Child Sexual Abuse, 7,* 23–42.

Shavers, C., Levendosky, A., Dubay, S., Basu, A., & Jenei, J. (2005). Domestic iolence research: Methodological issues related to a community-based intervention with a vulnerable population. *Journal of Applied Biobehavioral Research, 10*(1), 27–38.

Shaw, E., Bouris, A., & Pye, S. (1996). The Family Safety Model: A comprehensive strategy for working with domestic violence. *Australian and New Zealand Journal of Family Therapy, 17,* 126–136.

Shepard, M. F., & Campbell, J. A. (1992). The Abusive Behavior Inventory: A measure of psychological and physical abuse. *Journal of Interpersonal Violence, 7,* 291–305.

Sheridan, D. J. (2001). Treating survivors of intimate partner abuse: Forensic identification and documentation. In J. S. Olshaker, M. C., Jackson, & W. S. Smock (Eds.), Forensic emergency medicine (pp. 203–228). Philadelphia: Lippincott, Williams, & Wilkins.

Sherman, M. D., Sautter, F., Jackson, M. H., Lyons, J. A., & Han, X. (2006). Domestic violence in veterans with posttraumatic stress disorder who seek couples therapy. *Journal of Marital and Family Therapy, 32,* 479–490.

Sherr, M. W., & Ellor, J. W. (2009). Elder mistreatment and the church: Potential roles for helping professionals and congregations. *Social Work & Christianity, 36,* 14–35.

Short, L. M., McMahon, P. M., Chervin, D. D., Shelley, G. A., Lezin, N., Sloop, K. S., & Dawkins, N. (2000). Survivors' identification of protective factors and early warning signs for intimate partner violence. *Violence Against Women, 6*, 272–285.

Siegel, P. T., & Fishcher, H. (2001). Munchausen by Proxy Syndrome: Barriers to detection, confirmation, and intervention. *Children's Services: Social Policy, Research, and Practice, 4,* 31–50.

Silberg, J. L. (2004). The treatment of dissociation in sexually abused children from a family/attachment perspective. *Psychotherapy: Theory, Research, Practice, Training, 41,* 487–495.

Silverman, J. G., Pratt, C., Reed, E., Nagy, B. J., Whitaker, D. K., Baker, C., … Pavlos, C. (2004). The Care Communities Project: An academic, practitioner, and federal public health agency collaboration to improve intimate partner violence services for underserved communities. *Public Health Reports, 119,* 590–593.

Simbandumwe, L., Bailey, K., Denetto, S., Migliardi, P., Bacon, B., & Nighswander, M. (2008). Family violence prevention programs in immigrant communities: Perspectives of immigrant men. *Journal of Community Psychology, 36,* 899–914.

Simmons, C. A., Lehmann, P., & Cobb, N. (2008). Women arrested for partner violence and substance use: An exploration of discrepancies in the literature. *Journal of Interpersonal Violence, 23*(6), 707–727.

Simpson, L. E., Atkins, D. C., Gattis, K. S., & Christensen, A. (2008). Low-level relationship aggression and couple therapy outcomes. *Journal of Family Psychology, 22,* 102–111.

Simpson, L. E., Doss, B. D., Wheeler, J., & Christensen, A. (2007). Relationship violence among couples seeking therapy: Common couple violence or battering? *Journal of Marital and Family Therapy, 33,* 270–283.

Simpson, P. E., & Fothergill, A. (2004). Challenging gender stereotypes in the counseling of adult survivors of childhood sexual abuse. *Journal of Psychiatric and Mental Health Nursing, 11,* 589–594.

Sjoberg, R., & Lindholm, T. (2009). Children's autobiographical reports about sexual abuse: A narrative review of the research literature. *Nordic Journal of Psychiatry, 63,* 435–442.

Skinner, H. A. (1983). The Drug Abuse Screening Test. *Journal of Addictive Behaviors, 7,* 363–371.

Skowron, E., & Reinemann, S. (2005). Effectiveness of psychological interventions on child maltreatment: A meta-analysis. *Psychotherapy: Theory, Research, Practice, Training, 42,* 52–71.

Slattery, S. M., & Goodman, L. A. (2009). Secondary traumatic stress among domestic violence advocates: Workplace risk and protective factors. *Violence Against Women, 15,* 1358–1379.

Slep, A. M. S., & Heyman, R. E. (2008). Public health approaches to family maltreatment prevention: Resetting family psychology's sights from the home to the community. *Journal of Family Psychology, 22,* 518–528.

Small, M. A., Lyons, P. r., & Guy, L. S. (2002). Liability issues in child abuse and neglect reporting statutes. *Professional Psychology: Research and Practice, 33,* 13–18.

Smith, C. S. (2005). Domestic violence research: What have we learned and where do we go from here? *Journal of Interpersonal Violence, 20*(4), 448–454.

Smith, C. S. (2007). Coping strategies of female victims of child abuse in treatment for substance abuse relapse: Their advice to other women and healthcare professionals. *Journal of Addictions Nursing, 18,* 75–80.

Smith, D. M., & Donnelly, J. (2001). Adolescent dating violence: A multi-systemic approach of enhancing awareness in educators, parents, and society. *Journal of Prevention and Intervention in the Community, 21,* 53–64.

Smith, D. W., Witte, T. H., & Fricker-Elhai, A. E. (2006). Service outcomes in physical and sexual abuse cases: A comparison of Child Advocacy Center-Based and standard services. *Child Maltreatment, 11,* 354–360.

Smith, M. E., & Randall, E. J. (2007). Batterer intervention program: The victim's hope in ending the abuse and maintaining the relationship. *Issues in Mental Health Nursing, 28,* 1045–1063.

Smith, P. H., Earp, J. L., & De Vellis, R. (1995). Measuring battering: Development of the Women's Experiences with Battering (WEB) Scale. *Women's Health: Research on Gender, Behavior, and Policy, 1,* 273–288.

Smith, P. H., Murray, C. E., & Coker, A. (2010). The Coping Window: A contextual framework for understanding the methods women use to cope with battering. *Violence and Victims, 25,* 18-28.

Smith, P. H., Smith, J. B., & Earp, J. L. (1999). Beyond the measurement trap: A reconstructed conceptualized and measurement of woman battering. *Psychology of Women Quarterly, 23,* 177–193.

Smith, P. H., Thornton, G. E., DeVellis, R., Earp, J., & Coker, A. L. (2002). A population-based study of the prevalence and distinctiveness of battering, physical assault, and sexual assault in intimate relationships. *Violence Against Women, 8,* 1208–1232.

Smith, P. H., White, J. W., & Holland, L. J. (2003). A longitudinal perspective on dating violence among adolescent and college-age women. *American Journal of Public Health, 93,* 1104–1109.

Smullens, S. (2010). The codification and treatment of emotional abuse in structured group therapy. *International Journal of Group Psychotherapy, 60,* 111–130.

Sorenson, S. B. (2003). Funding public health: The public's willingness to pay for domestic violence prevention programming. *American Journal of Public Health, 93,* 1934–1938.

Sotelo, N. (2009). Women hit hardest in bad economy. *National Catholic Reporter, 45*(13), 23.

Southworth, C., Finn, J., Dawson, S., Fraser, C., & Tucker, S. (2007). Intimate partner violence, technology, and stalking. *Violence Against Women, 13,* 842–856.

Spanier, G. (1979). The measurement of marital quality. *Journal of Sex and Marital Therapy, 5,* 288–300.

Spitzer, C., Chevalier, C., Gillner, M., Freyberger, H. J., & Barnow, S. (2006). Complex posttraumatic stress disorder and child maltreatment in forensic inpatients. *The Journal of Forensic Psychiatry & Psychology, 17,* 204–216.

Stalans, L. J., & Ritchie, J. (2008). Relationship of substance use/abuse with psychological and physical intimate partner violence: Variations across living situations. *Journal of Family Violence, 23,* 9–24.

Stamm, B. H. (2002). Measuring compassion satisfaction as well as fatigue: Developmental history of the compassion satisfaction and fatigue test. In C. R. Figley (Ed.), *Treating compassion fatigue* (pp. 107–119). New York: Brunner-Routledge.

Stanley, N., & Appleton, J. V. (2008). International perspectives on child harm. *Child Abuse Review, 17,* 75–78

Staudt, M. M., Scheuler-Whitaker, L., & Hinterlong, J. (2001). The role of family preservation therapists in facilitating use of aftercare services. *Child Abuse & Neglect, 25,* 803–817.

Stebnicki, M. A. (2007). Empathy fatigue: Healing the mind, body, and spirit of professional counselors. *American Journal of Psychiatric Rehabilitation, 10,* 317–338.

Steele, C. T. (2000). Providing clinical treatment to substance abusing trauma survivors. *Alcoholism Treatment Quarterly, 18,* 71–81.

Stevens, M., & Higgins, D. J. (2002). The influence of risk and protective factors on burnout experienced by those who work with maltreated children. *Child Abuse Review, 11,* 313–331.

Stith, S. M. (2006). Future directions in intimate partner violence prevention research. *Journal of Aggression, Maltreatment, & Trauma, 13,* 229–244.

Stith, S. M., Liu, T., Davies, L. C., Boykind, E. L., Alder, M. C., Harris, J. M., ... Dees, J. (2009). Risk factors in child maltreatment: A meta-analytic review of the literature. *Aggression and Violent Behavior, 14,* 13–29.

Stith, S. M., Rosen, K. H., & McCollum, E. E. (2003). Effectiveness of couples treatment for spouse abuse. *Journal of Marital and Family Therapy, 29,* 407–426.

Stith, S. M., Rosen, K. H., McCollum, E. E., & Thomsen, C. J. (2004). Treating intimate partner violence within intact couple relationships: Outcomes of multi-couple versus individual couple therapy. *Journal of Marital and Family Therapy, 30,* 305–318.

Stover, C. S., Meadows, A. L., & Kaufman, J. (2009). Interventions for intimate partner violence: Review and implications for evidence-based practice. *Professional Psychology: Research and Practice, 40*(3), 223–323.

Stowman, S. A., & Donohue, B. (2005). Assessing child neglect: A review of standardized measures. *Aggression and Violent Behaviors, 10,* 491–512.

Straight, E. S., Harper, F. W. K., & Arias, I. (2003). The impact of partner psychological abuse on health behaviors and health status in college women. *Journal of Interpersonal Violence, 18,* 1035–1054.

Strathearn, L. (2009). Child behavior/mental health conditions and abuse: Which causes which? *Child Abuse & Neglect, 33,* 75.

Straus, M. A. (2004). Prevalence of violence against dating partners by male and female university students worldwide. *Violence Against Women, 10,* 790–811.

Straus, M. A. (2006). Future research on gender symmetry in physical assaults on partners. *Violence Against Women, 12,* 1086–1097.

Straus, M. A. (2009). Gender symmetry in partner violence: Evidence and implications for prevention and treatment. In D. J. Whitaker & J. R. Lutzker (Eds.), *Preventing partner violence: Research and evidence-based intervention strategies* (pp. 245–271). Washington, DC: American Psychological Association.

Straus, M. A., & Douglas, E. M. (2004). A short form of the Revised Conflict Tactics Scales, and typologies for severity and mutuality. *Violence and Victims, 19,* 507–520.

Straus, M. A., Hamby, S. L., Boney-McCoy, S., & Sugarman, D. B. (1996). The Revised Conflict Tactics Scale (CTS2): Development and preliminary psychometric data. *Journal of Family Issues, 17,* 283–316.

Straus, M. A., Hamby, S. L., Finkelhor, D., Moore, D. W., & Runyon, D. (1998). Identification of child maltreatment with the Parent-Child Conflict Tactics Scales: Development and psychometric data for a national sample of American parents. *Child Abuse & Neglect, 22,* 249–270.

Straus, M. A., Hamby, S. L., & Warren, W. L. (2003). *The Conflict Tactics Scale handbook.* Los Angeles: Western Psychological Services.

Straus, M. A., & Smith, C. (1995). Family patterns and primary prevention of family violence. In M. A. Straus & R. J. Gelles (Eds.), *Physical violence in American families: Risk factors and adaptations to violence in 8,145 families* (pp. 507–526). New Brunswick, NJ: Transaction Publishers.

Strehlow, G. (2009). The use of music therapy in treating sexually abused children. *Nordic Journal of Music Therapy, 18,* 167–183.

Strube, M. J. (1988). The decision to leave an abusive relationship: Empirical evidence and theoretical issues. *Psychological Bulletin, 104,* 236–250.

Strube, M. J., & Barbour, L. S. (1983). The decision to leave an abusive relationship: Economic dependence and psychological commitment. *Journal of Marriage and the Family, 45,* 785–793.

Stuart, G. L., & Holtzworth-Munroe, A. (2005). Testing a theoretical model of the relationship between impulsivity, mediating variables, and husband violence. *Journal of Family Violence, 20,* 291–303.

Stuart, G. L., Moore, T. M., Gordon, K. C., Ramsey, S. E., & Kahler, C. W. (2006). Psychopathology in women arrested for domestic violence. *Journal of Interpersonal Violence, 21,* 376–389.

Stuart, G. L., Moore, T. M., Ramsey, S. E., & Kahler, C. W. (2003). Relationship aggression and substance use among women court-referred to domestic violence intervention programs. *Addictive Behaviors, 28,* 1603–1610.

Stuart, G. L., Moore, T. M., Ramsey, S. E., & Kahler, C. W. (2004). Hazardous drinking and relationship violence perpetration and victimization in women arrested for domestic violence. *Journal of Studies on Alcohol, 65,* 46–53.

Stuart, G. L., Ramsey, S. E., Moore, T. M., Kahler, C. W., Farrell, L. E., Recupero, P. R., & Brown, R. A. (2002). Marital violence victimization and perpetration among women substance abusers: A descriptive study. *Violence Against Women, 8,* 934–952.

Stuart, G. L., Temple, J. R., Follansbee, K. W., Bucossi, M. M., Hellmuth, J. C., & Moore, T. M. (2008). The role of drug use in a conceptual model of intimate partner violence in men and women arrested for domestic violence. *Psychology of Addictive Behaviors, 22(*1), 12–24.

Substance Abuse and Mental Health Services Administration (SAMHSA). (1997). *Substance abuse treatment and domestic violence.* Rockville, MD: Author.

Substance Abuse and Mental Health Services Administration (SAMHSA). (2000). *Linking substance abuse treatment and domestic violence services: A guide for treatment providers.* Rockville, MD: Author.

Sudderth, L. K. (2003). An uphill climb: The challenge of collaboration in response to family violence in a rural area. *Journal of Aggression, Maltreatment, & Trauma, 8,* 17–39.

Sudderth, L. K. (2006). An uneasy alliance: Law enforcement and domestic violence advocates in a rural area. *Feminist Criminology, 1,* 329–353.

Sullivan, C. M., & Bybee, D. I. (1999). Reducing violence using community-based advocacy for women with abusive partners. *Journal of Consulting and Clinical Psychology, 67,* 43–53.

Sullivan, C. M., Parisian, J. A., & Davidson, W. S. (1991, August). Index of psychological abuse: Development of a measure. Poster presentation at the annual conference of the American Psychological Association, San Francisco.

Sullivan, M. W., Bennett, D. S., Carpenter, K., & Lewis, M. (2008). Emotion knowledge in young neglected children. *Child Maltreatment, 13,* 301–306.

Sullivan, P. M., & Knutson, J. F. (2000). Maltreatment and disabilities: A population-based epidemiological study. *Child Abuse & Neglect, 24,* 1257–1273.

Taban, N., & Lutzker, J. R. (2001). Consumer evaluation of an ecobehavioral program for prevention and intervention of child maltreatment. *Journal of Family Violence, 16,* 323–330.

Taft, C. T., Murphy, C. M., Elliott, J. D., & Morrel, T. M. (2001). Attendance-enhancing procedures in group counseling for domestic abusers. *Journal of Counseling Psychology, 48,* 51–60.

Taylor, C. A., Guterman, N. B., Lee, S. J., & Rathouz, P. J. (2009). Intimate partner violence, maternal stress, nativity, and risk for maternal maltreatment of young children. *American Journal of Public Health, 99,* 175–183.

Taylor, L. R., & Gaskin-Laniyan, N. (2007). Sexual assault in abusive relationships. *NIJ Journal, January.* Retrieved December 1, 2010, from http://nij.ncjrs.gov/App/publications/Pub_Search.aspx?category=99&searchtype=basic&location=top&PSID=29

Teaster, P. B., Roberto, K. A., & Dugar, T. A. (2006). Intimate partner violence of rural aging women. *Family Relations, 55,* 636–648.

Teaster, P. B., Stansbury, K. L., Nerenberg, L., & Stanis, P. (2009). An adult protective services' view of collaboration with mental health services. *Journal of Elder Abuse & Neglect, 21,* 289–306.

Tedeschi, R. G., & Calhoun, L. G. (1996). The Posttraumatic Growth Inventory: Measuring the positive legacy of trauma. *Journal of Traumatic Stress, 9,* 455–471.

Tell, S. J., Pavkov, T., Hecker, L., & Fontaine, K. L. (2006). Adult survivors of child abuse: An application of John Gottman's Sound Marital House theory. *Contemporary Family Therapy, 28,* 225–238.

Testa, M., & Leonard, K. E. (2001). The impact of marital aggression on women's psychological and marital functioning in a newlywed sample. *Journal of Family Violence, 16,* 115–130.

Testa, M., Livingston, J. A., & Leonard, K. E. (2003). Women's substance use and experiences of intimate partner violence: A longitudinal investigation among a community sample. *Addictive Behaviors, 28,* 1649–1664.

Teten, A. L., Ball, B., Valle, L. A., Noonan, R., & Rosenbluth, B. (2009). Considerations for the definition, measurement, consequences, and prevention of dating violence victimization among adolescent girls. *Journal of Women's Health, 18,* 923–927.

Thomas, C. R., Miller, G., & Speck, N. C. (2005). Telepsychiatry program for rural victims of domestic violence. *Telemedicine and e-Health, 11,* 567–573.

Thomas, J. N. (2007). Evidence-based practice can reduce child abuse in low-income communities. *Journal for Specialists in Pediatric Nursing, 12,* 294–296.

Thomas, M. D., & Bennett, L. (2009). The co-occurrence of substance abuse and domestic violence: A comparison of dual-problem men in substance abuse treatment and in a court-ordered batterer program. *Journal of Social Work Practice in the Addictions, 9,* 299–317.

Thomlison, B. (2003). Characteristics of evidence-based child maltreatment interventions. *Child Welfare: Journal of Policy, Practice, and Program, 82,* 541–569.

Thompson, M. P., Basile, K. C., Hertz, M. F., & Sitterle, D. (2006). *Measuring intimate partner violence victimization and perpetration: A compendium of assessment tools.* Atlanta, GA: Centers for Disease Control and Prevention, National Center for Injury Prevention and Control. Retrieved September 14, 2009, from http://www.cdc.gov/ncipc/dvp/Compendium/Measuring_IPV_Victimization_and_Perpetration.htm

Thompson, M. P., Kaslow, N. J., Lane, D. B., & Kingree, J. B. (2000). Childhood maltreatment, PTSD, and suicidal behavior among African American females. *Journal of Interpersonal Violence, 15,* 3–15.

Tigert, L, M. (2001). The power of shame: Lesbian battering as a manifestation of homophobia. *Women & Therapy, 23,* 73–85.

Tilley, D. S., & Brackley, M. (2005). Men who batter intimate partners: A grounded theory study of the development of male violence in intimate partner relationships. *Issues in Mental Health Nursing, 26,* 281–297.

Timmer, S. G., Urquiza, A. J., Herschell, A. D., McGrath, J. M., Zebell, N. M., Porter, A. L., & Vargas, E. C. (2006). Parent-child interaction therapy: Application of an empirically supported treatment to maltreated children in foster care. *Child Welfare: Journal of Policy, Practice, and Program, 85,* 919–939.

Timmer, S. G., Urquiza, A. J., Zebell, N. M., & McGrath, J. M. (2005). Parent-child interaction therapy: Application to maltreating parent-child dyads. *Child Abuse & Neglect, 29,* 825–842.

Tjaden, P., & Thoennes, N. (2000). Extent, nature, and consequences of intimate partner violence: Findings from the National Violence Against Women Survey. Washington, DC: National Institute of Justice. Retrieved December 1, 2010, from http://www.ojp.usdoj.gov/nij/pubs-sum/181867.htm

Todhunter, R. G., & Deaton, J. (2010). The relationship between religious and spiritual factors and the perpetration of intimate partner violence. *Journal of Family Violence, 25,* 745–753.

Tolman, R. M. (1999). The validation of the Psychological Maltreatment of Women Inventory. *Violence and Victims, 14,* 25–37.

Tolman, R. M., & Bhosley, G. (1990). A comparison of two types of pregroup preparation for men who batter. *Journal of Social Service Research, 13,* 33–43.

Topitzes, J., Mersky, J. P., & Reynolds, A. J. (2010). Child maltreatment and adult cigarette smoking: A long-term developmental model. *Journal of Pediatric Psychology, 35,* 484–498.

Tong, D. (2007). The penile plethysmograph, Abel Assessment for Sexual Interest, and the MSI-II: Are they speaking the same language? *The American Journal of Family Therapy, 35,* 187–202.

Topping, K. J., & Barron, I. G. (2009). School-based child sexual abuse prevention programs: A review of effectiveness. *Review of Educational Research, 79,* 431–463.

Toro-Alfonso, J., & Rodriguez-Madera, S. (2004). Sexual coercion in a sample of Puerto Rican gay males. *Journal of Gay & Lesbian Social Services: Issues in Practice, Policy, & Research, 17,* 47–58.

Toro-Alfonso, J., & Rodriguez-Madera, S. (2004). Domestic violence in Puerto Rican gay male couples: Perceived prevalence, intergenerational violence, addictive behaviors, and conflict resolution skills. *Journal of Interpersonal Violence, 19,* 639–654.

Toth, S. L., & Cichetti, D. (2006). Promises and possibilities: The application of research in the area of child maltreatment to policies and practices. *Journal of Social Issues, 62,* 863–880.

Toth, S. L., Maughan, A., Manly, J. T., Spagnola, M., & Cichetti, D. (2002). The relative efficacy of two interventions in altering maltreated preschool children's representational models: Implications for attachment theory. *Development and Psychopathology, 14,* 877–908.

Tracy, E. M., & Johnson, P. J. (2006). The intergenerational transmission of family violence. In N. B. Webb (Ed.), *Working with traumatized youth in child welfare* (pp. 113–134). New York: Guilford.

Trocme, N., & Bala, N. (2005). False allegations of abuse and neglect when parents separate. *Child Abuse & Neglect, 29,* 1333–1345.

Tsui, V., Cheung, M., & Leung, P. (2010). Help-seeking among male victims of partner abuse: Men's hard times. *Journal of Community Psychology, 38,* 769–780.

Turner, R. J., Frankel, B. G., & Levin, D. M. (1983). Social support: Conceptualization, measurement, and implications for mental health. *Research in Community and Mental Health, 3,* 67–111.

Tyagi, S. V. (2006). Female counselors and male perpetrators of violence against women. *Women & Therapy, 29,* 1–22.

Udry, J. R. (1981). Marital Alternatives and Marital Disruption. *Journal of Marriage and the Family, 43,* 889–897.

Ullman, S. E., Najdowski, C. J., & Filipas, H. H. (2009). Child sexual abuse, post-traumatic stress disorder, and substance use: Predictors of revictimization in adult sexual assault survivors. *Journal of Child Sexual Abuse, 18,* 367–385.

U.S. Department of Health and Human Services, Substance Abuse and Mental Health Services Administration (SAMHSA). (2003). *Linking substance abuse treatment and domestic violence services: A guide for treatment providers.* Retrieved from http://store.samhsa.gov/product/SMA00-3390.

U.S. Department of Health and Human Services, Substance Abuse and Mental Health Services Administration (SAMHSA). (2008). *Treatment improvement protocol 25: Substance abuse treatment and domestic violence.* Retrieved from http://www.ncbi.nlm.nih.gov/books/NBK14419/

U.S. Department of Health and Human Services, Administration for Children and Families, Administration on Children, Youth and Families, Children's Bureau. (2010). *Child Maltreatment 2009.* Retrieved from http://www.acf.hhs.gov/programs/cb/stats_research/index.htm#can

Valerio, P., & Lepper, G. (2010). Change and process in short and long-term groups for survivors of sexual abuse. *Group Analysis, 43,* 31–49.

Valle, L., & Silovsky, J. (2002). Attributions and adjustment following child sexual and physical abuse. *Child Maltreatment, 7,* 9–25.

Vandenberg, B., & Marsh, U. (2009). Aggression in youths: Child abuse, gender and SES. *North American Journal of Psychology, 11,* 437–442.

Vaux, A., Philips, J., Holly, L., Thomson, B., Williams, D., & Stewart, D. (1986). The Social Support Appraisals Scale: Studies of reliability and validity. *American Journal of Community Psychology, 14,* 195–219.

Vega, E. M., & O'Leary, K. D. (2007). Test-retest reliability of the Revised Conflict Tactics Scales (CTS2). *Journal of Family Violence, 22,* 703–708.

Veltman, M. W. M., & Browne, K. D. (2001). Identifying childhood abuse through favorite kind of day and kinetic family drawings. *The Arts in Psychotherapy, 28,* 251–259.

Vickerman, K. A., & Margolin, G. (2007). Posttraumatic stress in children and adolescents exposed to family violence: II. Treatment. *Professional Psychology: Research and Practice, 38,* 620–628.

Violence Policy Center. (2006). *When men murder women: An analysis of 2006 homicide data.* Retrieved from http://www.vpc.org/studies/wmmw2008.pdf

Vinton, L. (2003). A model collaborative project toward making domestic violence centers elder ready. *Violence Against Women, 9,* 1504–1513.

Waldman, F. (1999). Violence or discipline? Working with multicultural court-ordered clients. *Journal of Marital and Family Therapy, 25*(4), 503–515.

Waldo, M., Kernet, P. A., & Kerne, V. V. H. (2007). Therapeutic factors in guidance versus counseling sessions of domestic violence groups. *The Journal for Specialists in Group Work, 32,* 346–361.

Walker, C. A., & Davies, J. (2010). A critical review of the psychometric evidence base of the Child Abuse Potential Inventory. *Journal of Family Violence, 25,* 215–227.

Walker, D. F., Reese, J. B., Hughes, J. P., & Troskie, M. J. (2010). Addressing religious and spiritual issues in trauma-focused cognitive behavior therapy for children and adolescents. *Professional Psychology: Research and Practice, 41,* 174–180.

Walker, L. (1984). *The battered woman syndrome.* New York: Springer.

Walker, M. (2004). Supervising practitioners working with survivors of childhood abuse: Countertransference, secondary traumatization, and terror. *Psychodynamic Practice, 10,* 173–193.

Wallace, H. (2008). *Family violence: Legal, medical, and social perspectives (5th ed.).* Boston: Pearson.

Wallach, H. S., & Sela, T. (2008). The importance of male batterers' attributions in understanding and preventing domestic violence. *Journal of Family Violence, 23,* 655–660.

Walsh, C., MacMillan, H. L., & Jamieson, E. (2003). The relationship between parental substance abuse and child maltreatment: Findings from the Ontario Health Supplement. *Child Abuse & Neglect, 27,* 1409–1425.

Walton-Moss, B., Morrison, C., Yeo, T., Woodruff, K., Woods, N., Campbell, J. C., Kub, J., & Dennison, C. (2003). Interrelationships of violence and psychiatric symptoms in women with substance use disorders. *Journal of Addictions Nursing, 14,* 193–200.

Waltz, J., Babcock, J. C., Jacobson, N. S., & Gottman, J. M. (2000). Testing a typology of batterers. *Journal of Consulting and Clinical Psychology, 68,* 658–659.

Wang, M-C., Horne, S. G., Levitt, H. M., & Klesges, L. M. (2009). Christian women in IPV relationships: An exploratory study of religious factors. *Journal of Psychology and Christianity, 28,* 224–235.

Ward, T. (2000). Sexual offenders' cognitive distortions as implicit theories. *Aggression and Violent Behavior, 5,* 491–507.

Way, I., VanDeusen, K., & Cottrell, T. (2007). Vicarious trauma: Predictors of clinicians' disrupted cognitions about self-esteem and self-intimacy. *Journal of Child Sexual Abuse, 15,* 81–98.

Websdale, N. (1999). Making sense of domestic homicide. In N. Websdale (Ed.), *Understanding domestic homicide* (pp. 204-236). Boston, MA: Northeastern University Press.

Weil, J. M., & Lee, H. H. (2004). Cultural considerations in understanding family violence among Asian American Pacific Islander families. *Journal of Community Health Nursing, 21,* 217–227.

Weingarten, K. (2003). *Common shock: Witnessing violence every day.* New York: New American Library.

Weiss, S. J., Ernst, A. A., Cham, E., & Nick, T. G. (2003). Development of a screen for ongoing intimate partner violence. *Violence and Victims, 18,* 131–141.

Weisz, V. (2003). The court-appointed special advocate (CASA) program: Bringing information to child abuse and neglect cases. *Child Maltreatment, 8,* 204–210.

Weitzman, S. (2000). *'Not to people like us': Hidden abuse in upscale marriages.* New York: Basic Books.

Welfel, E. R., Danziger, P. R., & Santoro, S. (2000). Mandated reporting of abuse/maltreatment of older adults: A primer for counselors. *Journal of Counseling & Development, 78,* 284–292.

West, A., & Wandrei, M. L. (2002). Intimate partner violence: A model of predicting interventions by informal helpers. *Journal of Interpersonal Violence, 17,* 972–986.

West, C. M. (2008). "A thin line between love and hate"? Black men as victims and perpetrators of dating violence. *Journal of Aggression, Maltreatment & Trauma, 16*(3), 238–257.

Westby, C. (2007). Child maltreatment: A global issue. *Language, Speech, and Hearing Services in Schools, 38,* 140–148.

Westcott, H. L., & Jones, D. P. H. (1999). Annotation: The abuse of disabled children. *Journal of Child Psychology and Psychiatry, 40,* 497–506.

Westermeyer, J., Wahmanholm, K., & Thuras, P. (2001). Effects of childhood physical abuse on course and severity of substance abuse. *The American Journal on Addictions, 10,* 101–110.

Whitaker, D. J., Morrison, S., Lindquist, C., Hawkins, S. R., O'Neil, J. A., Nesius, A. M., ... Reese, L. (2006). A critical review of interventions for the primary prevention of perpetration of partner violence. *Aggression and Violent Behavior, 11,* 151–166.

Whitchurch, G. G., & Pace, J. L. (1993). Communication skills training and interspousal violence. *Journal of Applied Communication Research, 21,* 96–102.

White, H. R., & Chen, P-H. (2002). Problem drinking and intimate partner violence. *Journal of Studies on Alcohol, 63,* 205–214.

White, J. W., Smith, P. H., Koss, M. P., & Figueredo, A. J. (2000). Intimate partner aggression—what have we learned? Comment on Archer (2000). *Psychological Bulletin, 126,* 690–696.

Whiting, J. B., Simmons, L. A., Havens, J. R., Smith, D. B., & Oka, M. (2009). Intergenerational transmission of violence: The influence of self-appraisals, mental disorders and substance abuse. *Journal of Family Violence, 24,* 639–648.

Whitsett, D., & Kent, S. A. (2003). Cults and families. *Families in Society, 84,* 491–502.

Widom, C. S., Dutton, M. A., Czaja, S. J., & DuMont, K. A. (2005). Development and validation of a new instrument to assess lifetime trauma and victimization history. *Journal of Traumatic Stress, 18,* 519–531.

Widom, C. S., & Hiller-Sturmhofel, S. (2001). Alcohol abuse as a risk factor for and consequence of child abuse. *Alcohol Research & Health, 25,* 52–57.

Wilcoxon, S. A., Remley, T. P., Gladding, S. T., & Huber, C. H. (2007). *Ethical, legal, and professional issues in the practice of marriage and family therapy* (4th ed.). Upper Saddle River, NJ: Pearson.

Williams, J. G., & Smith, J. P. (1994). Drinking patterns and dating violence among college students. *Psychology of Addictive Behaviors, 8,* 51–53.

Williams, L. M. (2004). Researcher-advocate collaborations to end violence against women: toward liberating methodologies for action research. *Journal of Interpersonal Violence, 19,* 1350–1357.

Williams, L. M., & Herrera, V. M. (2007). Child maltreatment and adolescent violence: Understanding complex connections. *Child Maltreatment, 12*, 203-207.

Wilson-Cohn, C., Strauss, S. M., & Falkin, G. P. (2002). The relationship between partner abuse and substance use among women mandated to drug treatment. *Journal of Family Violence, 17,* 91–105.

Winefield, H. R., & Barlow, J. A. (1995). Client and worker satisfaction in a child protection agency. *Child Abuse & Neglect, 19,* 897–905.

Wingfield, D. A., & Blocker, L. S. (1998). Development of a certificate training curriculum for domestic violence counseling. *Journal of Addictions and Offender Counseling, 18,* 86–94.

Winton, M. A. (2005). Treatment paradigms of sex offenders of children: An analysis of professional journals. *Aggression and Violent Behavior, 10,* 569–578.

Wise, E. A., Streiner, D. L., & Walfish, S. (2010). A review and comparison of the reliabilities of the MMPI-2, MCMI-III, and PAI presented in their respective test manuals. *Measurement and Evaluation in Counseling and Development, 42,* 246–254.

Wnuk, D., Chapman, J. E., & Jeglic, E. L. (2006). Development and refinement of a measure of attitudes toward sex offender treatment. *Journal of Offender Rehabilitation, 43,* 35–47.

Wolfe, D., Crooks, C., Chiodo, D., & Jaffe, P. (2009). Child maltreatment, bullying, gender-based harassment, and adolescent dating violence: Making the connections. *Psychology of Women Quarterly, 33,* 21–24.

Wolfe, D. A., & Jaffe, P. G. (1999). Emerging strategies in the prevention of domestic violence. *The Future of Children, 9,* 133–144.

Wolfe, D. A., Wekerle, C., Scott, K., Straatman, A-L., Grasley, C., & Reitzel-Jaffe, D. (2003). Dating violence prevention with at-risk youth: A controlled outcome evaluation. *Journal of Consulting and Clinical Psychology, 71,* 279–291.

Wolfsdorf, B. A., & Zlotnick, C. (2001). Affect management in group therapy for women with posttraumatic stress disorder and histories of childhood sexual abuse. *JCLP/In Session: Psychotherapy in Practice, 57,* 169–181.

Wolfteich, P., & Loggins, B. (2007). Evaluation of the Children's Advocacy Center model: Efficiency, legal, and revictimization outcomes. *Child and Adolescent Social Work Journal, 24,* 333–352.

Wood, J. M., & Garven, S. (2000). How sexual abuse interviews go astray: Implications for prosecutors, police, and child protection services. *Child Maltreatment, 5,* 109–118.

Worcel, S. D., Furrer, C. J., Green, B. L., Burrus, S. W. M., & Finigan, M. W. (2008). Effects of family treatment drug courts on substance abuse and child welfare outcomes. *Child Abuse Review, 17,* 427–443.

Wray, R. J. (2006). Public health communication theory and strategies for interpersonal violence prevention. *Journal of Aggression, Maltreatment, & Trauma, 13,* 41–60.

Wright, M. O., Crawford, E., & Del Castillo, D. (2009). Childhood emotional maltreatment and later psychological distress among college students: The mediating role of maladaptive schemas. *Child Abuse & Neglect, 33,* 59–68.

Wuest, J., & Merritt-Gray, M. (1999). Not going back: Sustaining the separation in the process of leaving abusive relationships. *Violence Against Women, 5,* 110–133.

Wuest, J., & Merritt-Gray, M. (2001). Beyond survival: Reclaiming self after leaving an abusive male partner. *Canadian Journal of Nursing Research, 32,* 79–94.

Wupperman, P., Amble, P., Devine, S., Zonana, H., Fals-Stewart, W., & Easton, C. (2009). Violence and substance use among female partners of men in treatment for intimate-partner violence. *Journal of the American Academy of Psychiatry and Law, 37,* 75–81.

Wurtele, S. K. (2009). Preventing sexual abuse of children in the twenty-first century: Preparing for challenges and opportunities. *Journal of Child Sexual Abuse, 18,* 1–18.

Yampolskaya, S., & Banks, S. M. (2006). An assessment of the extent of child maltreatment using administrative databases. *Assessment, 13,* 342–355.

Yates, T. M., Carlson, E. A., & Egeland, B. (2008). A prospective study of child maltreatment and self-injurious behavior in a community sample. *Development and Psychopathology, 20,* 651–671.

Yoshida, K. K., Odette, F., Hardie, S., Willis, H., & Bunch, M. (2009). Women living with disabilities and their experiences and issues related to the context and complexities of leaving abusive situations. *Disability and Rehabilitation, 31,* 1843–1852.

Yoshioka, M. R., & Choi, D. Y. (2005). Culture and interpersonal violence research: Paradigm shift to create a full continuum of domestic violence services. *Journal of Interpersonal Violence, 20,* 513–519.

Young, H. L., Mancuso, A. F., Faherty, E., Dorman, S. A., & Ubrell, J. R. (2008). Helping child victims of family violence through school personnel: An evaluation of a training program. *Journal of Aggression, Maltreatment & Trauma, 16*(2), 144–163.

Young, M., Read, J., Barker-Collo, S., & Harrison, R. (2001). Evaluating and overcoming barriers to taking abuse histories. *Professional Psychology: Research and Practice, 32,* 407–414.

Young, N. K., Boles, S. M., & Otero, C. (2007). Parental substance use disorders and child maltreatment: Overlap, gaps, and opportunities. *Child Maltreatment, 12,* 137–149.

Zielinski, D. S. (2009). Child maltreatment and adult socioeconomic well-being. *Child Abuse & Neglect, 33,* 666–678.

Zimet, G. D., Dahlem, N. W., Zimet, S. G., & Farley, G. K. (1988). The Multidimensional Scale of Perceived Social Support. *Journal of Personality Assessment, 52,* 30–41.

Zlotnick, C., Johnson, D. M., Stout, R. L., Zywiak, W. H., Johnson, J. E., & Schneider, R. J. (2006). Childhood abuse and intake severity in alcohol disorder patients. *Journal of Traumatic Stress, 19,* 949–959.

Zung, W. K. (1965). A Self-Rating Depression Scale. *Archives of General Psychiatry, 12,* 63–70.

INDEX

Page locators in *italics* indicate figures and tables.